THE LEPCHAS OF SIKKIM

PLATE I

MRS. TAFOOR NURSING HER YOUNGEST DAUGHTER. BEHIND KINCHENJUNGA

THE LEPCHAS OF SIKKIM

GEOFFREY GORER

With an Introduction by
J.H. HUTTON

GYAN PUBLISHING HOUSE
New Delhi-110002

The Lepchas of Sikkim

ISBN: 978-81-212-0125-4

Price: ₹ 1450

Reprinted 2014 in India by
Gyan Publishing House
23, Main Ansari Road, Daryaganj,
New Delhi - 110002
Phones : 23282060, 23261060
Fax : (011) 23285914
E-mail : books@gyanbooks.com
website: gyanbooks.com

Printed at: G. Print Process, Delhi

List of Contents

★

. . . . .

CONCLUSIONS

List of Plates

★

List of the Inhabitants of Lingthem

★

NOTE: This is a list of the inhabitants of Lingthem mentioned in the text and is made to avoid the constant repetition of age, sex, social position and chief relationships in the body of the text. This list is not exhaustive, and only the chief operative relationships are named; further relationships can, if desired, be discovered by inspection of Appendix I, Table 4. Those people most often mentioned in the text have their names printed in capitals. The following social classifications, which are fully elucidated in the text, are used: Muktair, Mandal, *youmi*, *gyapön* are village officials (see Chapter Five); lama and nun are priests of the lamaist religion (see Chapter Seven); *Mun*, *padem*, *Nandjému* are priests of the old Lepcha religion (see Chapter Eight).

The number immediately after the name is the age in years of the person in 1937. Women are designated either by the prefix 'Mrs.' when they are listed immediately under their husband, or by feminine kinship terms. The following abbreviations have been used:

Kinship term in quotes—e.g. 'grandfather'—signifies that the relationship is classificatory and operative.

d.r. signifies 'distantly related to' in those cases where a distant relationship is socially operative.

Ph. pl. followed by a number signifies that there is a photograph of the person mentioned on the plate of that number. Some people appear in several photographs, but only one is given.

Adér, 71. 'Grandfather' of Chano, Chinya, Aga (Ph. pl. 25a).
Aga, 37. Son of Hlatam, 'brother' of Chano, Chinya.
Mrs. Aga I, 37. Mother of three children.
Mrs. Aga II, 43. Sterile widow, should be wife of Zumba.
Agyung, 29. Adopted son of Serving. Married with one son.
Aplung, 29. Brother of Rigya and Gyatso. Son of Ashyok *youmi*.
Mrs. Aplung, 35. Formerly stepmother of Tobgé.
Ashyok *youmi*, 50. Father of Rigya, Gyatso, Aplung (Ph. pl. 11e).
Atyook, 16. Adopted son of Tingkep *youmi*, real son of Ongden, q.v. (Ph. pl. 30).

Bahada, 23, carpenter. Son of Ongden, brother of Chanko, Atyook, Kanchok.

CHALA MANDAL, 59. Head of village (Ph. pl. 7).
Mrs. Mandal I, 28, nun. Sterile. *d.r.* Chélé's wife, Dadool, Kanden (Ph. pl. 19).

Mrs. Mandal II, 36. Has one daughter, formerly wife of Katel's son (Ph. pl. 19).

CHANO, 31, lama. Widower, married to elder brother's wife; 'father' of Mikmar, Pursang; 'brother' of Aga, Chinya (Ph. pl. 31a).

Mrs. Chano, 32, possessed by Mun (Ph. pl. 19b).

Chanko, 29, lama. Eldest son Ongden, brother of Atyook, Kanchok. Married.

CHÉLÉ, 10. Grandson of Kahlyeu. Inherited uncle's wife (Ph. pl. 9a).

Chelim, 46. 'Brother' of Ongden; adopted child. Has adopted Kanchok as his son.

CHIMPET, 14. Eldest son of Tafoor, q.v. (Ph. pl. 12b) training as lama.

Chinya, 37. 'Brother' of Aga, Chano (Ph. pl. 24b).

Mrs. Chinya, 41. Sterile.

CHUDO, 29, lama. Brother of Tafoor. Has three children, eldest boy training as lama (Ph. pl. 12a); Chudo (Ph. pl. 22a).

Mrs. Chudo, 29.

Lharibu (painter), Chujen of Panung (next village), lama. Father-in-law of Tafoor (Ph. pl. 11d).

Dadool, 23. Son of Také, brother of Kanden. Carrying on an intrigue with Mrs. Tobgé (Ph. pl. 26a).

Mrs. Dadool, 23.

DATOOP, 56, lama. Son of first Dorjé Lapoon, father of Pembu, Pichi, Kolok Tyong. d.r. Tafoor, Chudo, Pargeut (Ph. pl. 29).

MRS. DATOOP, 49, nun. d.r. Kurma (Ph. pl. 28b).

First Dorjé Lapoon, 82, lama. Father of Datoop, q.v.

SECOND DORJÉ LAPOON, 69, lama. 'Father' of Tafoor, Chudo, Recently married Pumri (Ph. pl. 11c).

Dunbi, 62. 'Brother' of Muktair, Tafoor's father. Father of Prumtu, Pankek.

MRS. DUNBI (Tafoormu), 54. Formerly married to Muktair. Mother of Tafoor, Chudo, Prumtu, Pankek.

GONGYOP, 47, *Mun*. Brother of Thyak Thimbu, paternal uncle Sangkyar, Satéo (Ph. pl. 14).

Mrs. Gongyop, 41 (Ph. pl. 19b).

Gongyop's son, 18. Betrothed (Ph. pl. 24b).

Gyatso, carpenter, 20. Son of Ashyok *youmi*, brother of Aplung Nariya.

HLATAM, 67, nun. The 'poisoner,' mother of Aga.

Itup, 31. Son of Takneum *youmi*. Married.

JIROONG, 41, lama. Uncle of Tobgé. d.r. Pongring (Ph. pl. 30).

MRS. JIROONG, 28. Sister of Tempa (Ph. pl. 30).

KAHLYEU, 77. Grandfather of Chélé (Ph. pl. 15b).

Kaji, 59. Old man who sees devils.

Mrs. Kaji, 37, *Mun*. Sister of Jiroong, aunt of Tobgé.

Kanchok, 17. Adopted son of Chelim, son of Ongden (q.v.).

KANDEN, 25, defective. Son of Také, brother of Dadool (Ph. pl. 26b).

KATEL, 55, *Mun*. (Ph. pl. 16).

Mrs. Katel I, 56. Mother of three children. d.r. Chala Mandal.
Mrs. Katel II, 18.
Kolok Tyong, 15. Son of Datoop, q.v. (Ph. pl. 29).
KONDÉ, 16. Daughter of Pargeut. d.r. Datoop, Tafoor (Ph. pl. 29).
KURMA, *gyapön, padem*, 37. d.r. Mrs. Datoop (Ph. pl. 27).
Kutt'r, 18, lama. Son of Lumba (Ph. pl. 13b).

Lumba *chithembu*, 51, lama. Father of Kutt'r (Ph. pl. 11a).
Mrs. Lumba I, 47, *Mun*. Daughter of Pumri, sister of Mrs. Tempa.
Mrs. Lumba II, 38. d.r. Mrs. Lumba I, q.v.

Mikmar, 13. Son of Chano, brother of Pursang; betrothed, studying to be a lama (Ph. pl. 24).
MUKTAIR. Dead father of Tafoor, Chudo; first husband of Mrs. Dunbi.

Nahyeun, 41. Bastard son of Dunbi.
Nandjému, 66. Elder grandmother of Patek.
NARIYA, 30. Adoptive brother of Rigya, son of elder brother of Ashyok *youmi*.
Mrs. Nariya, 14.

Ongden, 52, lama. Father of Chanko, Bahada, Kanchok, Atyook; brother of Tinkep; 'brother' of Chelim (Ph. pl. 25a).
Mrs. Ongden, 22. Widow, very recently married to Ongden.

Pankek, 6. Daughter of Dunbi and Mrs. Dunbi (Ph. pl. 21a).
Pargeut, 44. Father of Kondé, Tangvoong, old mother a nun, d.r. Datoop, Tafoor.
Mrs. Pargeut, 38.
PATEK, 17. Head of household of six, including two grandmothers, a *Nandjému* and a *Mun*; brother of Ribu (Ph. pl. 9b).
PEMBU, 29, lama. Son of Datoop, q.v. (Ph. pl. 29), father of Dugoo.
Mrs. Pembu, 23. (Ph. pl. 29).
Pichi, 23. Son of Datoop, brother of Pembu, carpenter (Ph. pl. 28a)
Pongring, 83, lama. Monastery custodian. d.r. Jiroong (Ph. pl. 9b).
PRUMTU, 15. Daughter of Dunbi and Mrs. Dunbi, lives with half-brothers Tafoor and Chudo.
PUMRI, 74, *Mun*. Mother of Mrs. Lumba I, Mrs. Tempa. Recently married second Dorjé Lapoon, being widow of his "uncle" (Ph. pl. 15b).
Pursang, 11. 'Son' of Chano, brother of Mikmar.

Ribu, 12. Brother of Patek, q.v.
RIGYA, 23. 'Brother' of Nariya, whose parents adopted him. Son of Ashyok *youmi*, brother of Aplung, Gyatso (Ph. pl. 26a).
Mrs. Rigya, 26.

Samblyou, 60. Sister of Mrs. Takal and Mrs. Gongyop, a promiscuous woman at present living with Zumba.
SANGKYAR, 36, a cretinous defective. Brother of Satéo, nephew of Gongyop and Thyak Thimbu, with latter of whom he lives.
Satéo, 27, a cripple. Brother of Sangkyar, q.v. lives with Chala Mandal (Ph. pl. 17b).

Seryop Katoo, 17. Bastard son of Itup, q.v., born when his father was only 13.
SERVING, 90. Oldest man of Lingthem, descendant of former village heads. Adopted Agyung, grandson of elder brother (Ph. pl. 8a).
Songpo *youmi*, 67. d.r. Také, Kanden, Dadool.
Mrs. Songpo, 66, nun.

TAFOOR, 35, lama. Father of Chimpet and three daughters, brother of Chudo, 'son' of second Dorjé Lapoon, 'nephew' of Dunbi, 'brother' of Datoop (Ph. pl. 23).
MRS. TAFOOR, 31, nun. Daughter of Lharibu Chujen (Ph.pl. 22b).
Takal. 57, lama.
Mrs. Takal, 58, nun. Sister of Samblyou and Mrs. Gongyop, promiscuous.
Takneum *youmi*, 60. Adopted as a boy by his father's sister, father of Itup. Mother living, 84, nun (Ph. pl. 8b).
Takshyom, 19. Nephew of Kurma.
Tangvoong, 12. Daughter of Pargeut, sister of Kondé.
TEMPA, 44. Stranger to Zongu, married Pumri's daughter (Ph. pl. 7b).
Mrs. Tempa, 44. Daughter of Pumri, sister of Mrs. Lumba I. Three daughters surviving.
Thyak Thimbu, 49, *Mun*. Brother of Gongyop, uncle of Satéo and Sangkyar. Has two wives.
Tingkep *gyapön*, 35. Brother of Ongden, q.v. Adopted Ongden's son. Atyook. His wife bore a child 1934.
TOBGÉ, 22. Son of elder brother of Jiroong with whom he lives (Ph. pl. 6a).
Mrs. Tobgé, 25. d.r. Mrs. Jiroong and Tempa.

Zumba, 48. Living with Samblyou. d.r. Gongyop, Thyak Thimbu.

Introduction

By J. H. Hutton

(William Wyse Professor of Social Anthropology at Cambridge)

★

Early writers on India tell us of a strange people living about the sources of the Ganges, mild and gentle in manners and of blameless life. Some of their other strange attributes are scarcely human, but it is perhaps permissible to recognise in this account of a gentle race living in a remote valley of the Himalayas an echo of some contact with the Lepchas, who differ very remarkably in this quality of mildness from at any rate their more immediate neighbours. No one who has had to deal administratively with the Nepali grazier, for instance, would impute to him an immoderate regard for the property or the predilections of his neighbours, nor is it at all a quality of the Gurkha in general; eastwards, on the other hand, the Bhutanese are not particularly noted for benignity and still less the Daflas and Akas beyond them. To find a cis-Himalayan society in any way comparable to that of the Lepchas in its successful elimination of aggressiveness from its members and the reduction of jealousy to a minimum it would be necessary to go west of Nepal to the districts of Lahaul and Spiti. How far it would be possible to find it there it is not easy to say, for our recorded knowledge of the social and domestic life of the peoples of the Himalayas is scanty. Even the officers of the Assam Government have not yet produced any monograph on any of the tribes on the north bank of the Brahmaputra. Now, however, we are well informed at any rate about the Lepchas, for Mr. Gorer's *Himalayan Village* follows only by two or three months Major C. J. Morris' *Living with Lepchas*, dealing with just the same area and the same individuals as are treated of in this volume.

Mr. Gorer has been at some pains to examine the source of the absence of aggressiveness among Lepchas. He came to the conclusion that 'the Lepchas' failure to develop any pattern of external aggression' is to be put down to 'their isolation, their low material development and the difficulty of wresting a livelihood from their environment'. He considers that although these reasons may be adequate for 'the lack of destructive aggression outside their group, the lack inside it cannot be explained in such general terms'. It is permissible perhaps to doubt whether any distinction can be drawn between the causes of a lack of the aggressive disposition outside and inside the group, but the author makes the interesting and attractive suggestion that an important factor in the latter aspect is the immediate and willing satisfaction of all an infant's expressed physical desires accompanied by a considerable degree of physical restraint, as infants spend most of their time 'firmly tied to the back of their guardian', and a refusal to encourage, but rather the contrary, any efforts of the child to acquire bodily technique, speech and physical independence. 'Young babies get no social approval from their attempts to crawl and walk; on the contrary a mobile baby is more likely to be picked up and replaced on its guardian's back, since there it is easier to control.' When, however, Mr. Gorer goes on to trace a connection between the 'partial extinction of self-assertion in early childhood' and the tendency which he points out in Lepchas to judge their fellows in their rôle of members of the society and not as personalities, and to emphasise this impersonal attitude as 'the chief operative factor for the suppression of competition and aggression in adult life' I must confess to scepticism. Instances of this 'impersonal' attitude, e.g. in the case of Katel, will be found on page 271 of Chapter Ten, and I have several times had just the same experience among Nagas and Kukis, where self-assertion and aggression are a *sine qua non*. It seems to me likely that this impersonal attitude, in which men are regarded as members of a society rather than individuals, is a necessary condition of the very corporate society in which such tribesmen live. Such a society, straitly limited in number and rigidly restricted in area, is in many respects, particularly in such activities as cultivating or house-building, and in Naga or Kuki communities of course warfare, dependent for its immediate existence on the spontaneous mutual co-operation of its members. If this is so, it seems unnecessary to hold that this impersonal attitude has any particular connection either with the attitude to children described, or with the absence of aggression among adults. Probably the same impersonal attitude is traceable in our own society among members of a team, for instance, where the suppression of personal preferences or dislikes is required in the interests of successful combination.

Another aspect of Lepcha life which is almost as striking as the absence of aggression is the apparent obsession of the whole community with sex. I was tempted to suppose that the author of this book had over-emphasised the Lepchas' attitude to sex through an unconscious dramatisation, a journalistic dramatisation, if I may call it so, of a want of reticence on sexual matters of all kinds in a degree quite unfamiliar in his own society. The perusal however of Major Morris' book (and Major Morris is well acquainted with India, so that I can in some measure judge by his standards) shows that I did Mr. Gorer an injustice. At the same time I am rather inclined to feel that the apparent preoccupation of the Lepchas with sex does not necessarily imply that the importance attached to it by them in their lives is proportionately theatrical. One is inclined to wonder whether this consciousness of sex is the cause or the result of the Lepchas' declining population, a decline of which the Lepchas themselves are acutely aware. Probably, if there is any such connection at all, it is by now a vicious circle, but either alternative seems possible. Perhaps the whole complex of want of aggression, sex-obsession and sterility arises from the effects of a long period of undisturbed isolation in an uncoveted terrain where no necessity for self-defence against external enemies was experienced. If this be so it should be possible to find parallels for Lepcha psychology in some island communities in Oceania. In spite of what the author describes as their 'fundamentally optimistic character' a certain lack of belief in their own efforts and future seems indicated among the Lepchas by their cynical attitude to their own beliefs; the way in which a rite should be performed, the occasions on which it is required, the correct precaution to be taken in many events are all known, but if they are not followed with any particularity (and commonly, it seems, they are not) well, *Ket ma-nin*—'It does not really matter.'

A similar attitude is suggested by their apparent proneness to suicide and there is ample evidence that the Lepcha is very conscious of his inferiority to the encroaching Nepali in the struggle for survival and of his dependence not on himself but on state protection for his continued existence as a tribe.

It is not then surprising that the Lepchas are a dwindling race, and it is fortunate that someone has been found to study their society before change and decay have gone further than they have already gone. Mr. Gorer is a new recruit to anthropology. He has indeed published books before this, and an anthropological bias was clearly to be observed in his *Bali and Angkor* and still more perhaps in *Africa Dances*, but *Himalayan Village* is a new departure and a serious and important contribution to anthropological literature. Nor is it so merely in the form of an addition to ethnological material resulting from observation and record in the field, for Mr. Gorer has a definite contribution to offer to anthropological thought in general. This will be apparent to readers of his seventeenth chapter—I have already quoted from it freely above—which would have been hardly less suitable as a prelude than as a conclusion to his volume. It contains both definitions and syllogisms which I do not myself accept, but even such ethnologists as may disagree with his conclusions and find his standpoint distasteful can feel nothing but gratitude for the feast of information which follows and for which it has here been my privilege to say grace.

J. H. HUTTON.

July 12th, 1938.

Foreword and Acknowledgements

★

This study of a primitive tribe suffers from two disadvantages, one inherent in the material, and one personal. The Lepchas are one of a number of mongoloid tribes inhabiting the southern slopes of the Himalayas; since most of the countries in which these tribes live are partially or completely closed to Europeans, there is very little precise information available about this culture area, and consequently many questions of culture contact, which will be inevitably raised in the following account, are at present unanswerable. I myself am not a professional anthropologist, in so far as I have never followed as a student any academic course in anthropology.

As an undergraduate at Cambridge I was much impressed by the work and legend of W. D. H. Rivers, who had died shortly before I became a student, and I followed with very great interest the lectures of Professor Sir William Ridgeway, who died at the end of my second year. But although I found the subject of anthropology an enthralling one, and read all the books I could on the subject, I never at that period of my life considered it feasible that I should myself become an anthropologist. I was at that time more interested in creative writing.

In 1934 I made, almost by chance, a three months' journey in West Africa, a journey undertaken under very favourable conditions; on my return I wrote a book about this journey; and though from the point of view of anthropology it was inevitably so superficial as to be almost worthless, it was indirectly through this book that the present study was made. It was through my book that I made the acquaintance of Major C. J. Morris, late 2nd Bn. 3rd Q.A.O. Gurkha Rifles, and he proposed to me that I should accompany him to India in 1936, after his return from the third Everest expedition; he hoped to make a study of the Gurkhas in their unexplored home in Nepal, but the hoped-for permission to enter that closed land was not forthcoming; so, as an alternative, he got the permission of the Maharajah of Sikkim to study the Lepchas in his country. During the whole of the visit Mr. Morris was my companion, and it was thanks to him that I was able to ignore both the practical and administrative difficulties in a strange land and under strange conditions which would most probably have proved insuperable to me unaided. Through his long-standing friendship with the Maharajah we not only obtained the permission to live indefinitely in Sikkim—a permission not easily obtained—but also his active collaboration in the choice of a site to work in and the co-operation of all the people, official and unofficial, directly or indirectly involved. I find it difficult to express adequately my sense of great indebtedness to Mr. Morris; his knowledge of local customs, both Native and European, were of inestimable help.

It was also through my book *Africa Dances* that I met Dr. Margaret Mead of the American Museum of Natural History, Dr. Ruth Benedict of Columbia University, and Dr. John Dollard, of the Institute of Human Relations, Yale University, New Haven. Under the guidance of Drs. Mead and Benedict I spent the winter of 1935–36 studying the methodology and theoretical background of anthropology, and from Dr. John Dollard I learned to see in focus the interrelated problems of the individual in society. It is quite impossible for me to estimate my intellectual debt to these three inspiring teachers, and I have also to thank them for a very great service; for they undertook the great burden of reading the first draft of this book, commenting on it and advising me on a number of points. The sacrifice of their time by these hard-working people is a gift of inestimable value; my only hope is that this book is, to some slight extent, not altogether unworthy of their pains. If this should happily be so, it is almost entirely owing to their instruction and advice. I must also thank very sincerely Mrs. F. Norman, of the Department of Psychological Medicine, of Guy's Hospital, London, for having read the first draft of this book, advised me upon it, and discussed it with me; her help, particularly in Book Two, has been very great.

I arrived in India at the very end of 1936. Before going into Sikkim I spent two months in Kalimpong studying the Lepcha language with the help of missionised Lepchas. At the end of that period I had an adequate comprehension of the language, but, though I could understand everything that was said with, I think, most of the over-tones, I never spoke it more than very haltingly. Lepcha is a simple language structurally, but the labour of learning by heart several thousand vocables which it was impossible to connect with any language system I knew was a hard one. Fearing my working knowledge of the language might be inadequate I therefore took with me into Sikkim as an interpreter a young Lepcha named Sukra Singh who was being trained as a dispenser. His knowledge of English, though not profound, was adequate, and I was always able to check up on his not infrequent mis-translations. In the event, the presence of this interpreter proved very useful. The Lepchas have a tendency to monologue, for one person to speak continuously while the rest listen. If I can so express it, the Lepchas talk in paragraphs, and not in single sentences; they fall naturally into a long swinging rhythm, and much dislike being interrupted or held up in the middle of a narrative or anecdote. I found I could not possibly keep up my notes and a conversation at the same time; but the Lepchas found it an easy matter to make a long statement and then pause while the statement was repeated. Since none of the Lepchas of Lingthem had had any but the most casual contact with Europeans—indeed most of the men and all the women had never seen one before—they had no set ideas of the way Europeans behave. They have however in their mythology and stories the tradition of nobles (into which group we naturally fell as being under the protection and recommendation of the Maharajah) being accompanied by servants, and doing all business through their intermediary. Without the use of an interpreter who, with his repetitions which I hardly listened to, would slow down the pace of a conversation sufficiently for me to take full notes, I could never have taken down the life-histories and elaborate ritual in anything like such full detail. When he was not present I had to ask people to wait, or to repeat themselves; the Lepchas disliked this, just as much as they disliked questions demanding a direct answer; they were quickly disconcerted and lost the thread of their narrative. Until I knew people well I asked as few questions as possible; as far as possible I checked and counter-checked every statement, but this was mostly done spontaneously by different Lepchas discussing identical subjects, or by their arguing among themselves. The most I would do with strangers was to suggest a subject for discussion; I only cross-examined those people with whom I had already a confidential relationship.

I am aware that the use of interpreters is held to invalidate a great deal of anthropological work; but the Lepchas got used to Sukra Singh—a person of endless patience and constant good temper—as soon or sooner than they did to us, and I question whether his absence would have made for any greater intimacy. I was never really dependent on him, and, without his slowing up the pace of conversation, I could never have got the almost word for word texts that I obtained. When he was not with me I found myself quite incapable of taking sufficiently full notes; and those I made from memory subsequently inevitably lacked the clearness and precision of those I took more normally. Unless I had invented some form of Lepcha shorthand or employed a dictaphone my work among the Lepchas would have been far less detailed; only when talking to children or to big groups was the presence of my interpreter useless or a hindrance.

I have put a few notes on the Lepcha language into an appendix[1] for the benefit of those who are interested in such matters and also a vocabulary of those Lepcha words which I have been forced to employ in the text. I have avoided using Lepcha words as far as possible, and have given no Lepcha texts; I am unable to understand the reasoning of those anthropologists who consider that the inclusion in an English book of sentences in a language which not one reader can understand gives the study greater scientific or objective value. My own feeling is that the value of texts is almost entirely linguistic; and so for the use of philologists I propose to deposit a few selected texts (stories and prayers) with my Lepcha vocabulary with the School of Oriental Languages, London.

I lived in Zongu among the Lepchas during March, April and May 1937. Frequently in this book, in order to avoid clumsiness, I have used the present tense and referred to different periods as 'now', 'three months ago', 'ten years ago.' In all cases the point of reference from which time is measured is the spring of 1937.

In India and Sikkim I received kindness and help from so many people that it is difficult even to enumerate them all. The many people who have experienced the great and unfailing kindness and hospitality of Mr. and Mrs. Norman Odling of Kalimpong will understand that I can find no words to express my gratitude to them; you cannot thank people who have given you a home. I should also like to thank very sincerely His Highness Sir Tashi Namgyal, K.C.I.E., Maharajah of Sikkim, for his kindness and

[1] See Appendix VI.

co-operation; and also Rai Sahib, Tashi Dadul, the Private Secretary to His Highness, Rai Sahib, Sonam Dadul, Rhennock Kazi and official Steward in charge of Palace affairs; the Honourable Mary Scott, D.D., of Gangtok, and the Very Reverend Dr. J. A. Graham, C.I.E., D.D., of Kalimpong, all of whom gave me much help and advice. My thanks are also due to Sukra Singh for his unfailing patience and good temper in situations which would have disconcerted many more sophisticated people.

I have attempted within a single volume to give an adequate description of Lepcha society and in particular of the village of Lingthem; to avoid undue length I have had to suppress a considerable amount of minor detail, but I hope that I have done this without obscuring or falsifying any facts. The religions I have in particular dealt with very summarily, for a full treatment would require a second volume comparable in size to this one, and would heavily overweight the picture I am trying to present. The volume is divided into three books, each of which represents to some extent a different method of description; in Book One I have presented the material and formalised aspects of Lepcha society, in Book Two the mainly unformalised aspects of Lepcha life, and in Book Three the history of certain individuals. I have tried to make a total picture by presenting three view-points: the frame-work of the society, the impact of the culture on the people, and the individuals who are the product of that culture and society. I have employed, to the best of my ability, the various disciplines, anthropological and psychological, functional and Freudian, which seemed apposite to the aim I had in mind; I have used them eclectically, for most of the disciplines seem to me useful and none of them completely adequate alone. My methods of working and my attitude to various aspects of anthropology are described in appropriate places in the text, particularly in Chapters Ten and Seventeen. In Chapter Seventeen I have attempted to answer some of the problems raised by my study of the Lepchas.

It has seemed to me that many sociological works appear to neglect the individuals who compose the societies they are describing; in so far as I claim any novelty in the treatment of the subject-matter of this book, it is in the fact that I have let the Lepchas speak for themselves, that I have tried not to forget that the village of Lingthem is inhabited by one hundred and seventy-six persons, and the reserve of Zongu by about two thousand. I have tried to illustrate every statement from the lives of the people of

Lingthem and this has inevitably forced me to employ personal names a great deal. To make reference easier I am giving a list of the people mentioned in the text, with their ages and chief relationships; this is not quite a complete list of the inhabitants; full lists will be found in Appendix I. Before and after all my thanks are due to those Lepchas of Lingthem who accepted and were kind to an inquisitive and ignorant stranger.

GEOFFREY GORER.

July 1937–*May* 1938.

CHAPTER ONE

THE LEPCHAS AND SIKKIM

i

THE Lepchas[1] are a Mongoloid people living in the Himalayas on the southern and eastern slopes of Mount Kinchenjunga. It seems certain that they were originally the only inhabitants of this large tract of mountainous land, but during the last three centuries, or possibly longer, their land has been taken from them by conquering invaders, the Tibetans, the Nepali, and finally the English. At the time of the 1931 census the 25,780 registered Lepchas were almost evenly divided between the Native State of Sikkim and the Darjeeling district of British India, 13,000 being in Sikkim and the rest in Darjeeling, with the exception of 66 who were employed, chiefly as gardeners, in Calcutta.

There is no generally accepted theory among those anthropologists who believe that every tribe originally came from somewhere else as to the place of origin of the Lepchas. Various parts of Tibet and Mongolia have been suggested and a certain similarity has apparently been found between the Lepcha language and some dialect spoken in Indo-China. The Lepchas themselves have no tradition of migration and place the home of their ancestors—the people of Mayel—in one of the inaccessible valleys of Kinchenjunga.

The Lepchas do not appear ever to have resisted invasion of their own accord. Sikkim was apparently colonised by the Tibetans at some date prior to the beginning of the seventeenth century,[2]

[1] The Lepchas do not call themselves Lepchas ; they call themselves *Rong*. ' Lepcha ' is said to be a derogatory Nepali term—*lap-che*—meaning, though the philology is doubtful, ' nonsense talkers.' A parallel could be found in the Russian name for Germans—*nemetski*, which means ' the dumb ones.' Since all books dealing with the people and district refer to the Lepchas as Lepchas, it would seem merely pedantic and confusing to use the term *Rong*. The word would appear to have no other significance in Lepcha.

[2] I take the suggestion that Sikkim (which at that date included the present Darjeeling district) was colonised or at least dominated by the Tibetans before the beginning of the seventeenth century from *An Account of Tibet* by the

but it would seem as though this original colonisation was little more than a feudal overlordship imposed by a small minority on the Lepcha population. After the internal revolution and Chinese wars in Tibet in the early seventeenth century three 'Red Hat' lamas fled to Sikkim, speedily converted the Lepchas and what other inhabitants there were, and created a Sikkimese Tibetan king; from this king the present Maharajah of Sikkim is indirectly descended. A subsequent legend puts back the conversion of Sikkim to lamaism some centuries earlier; it is said that one of the lamaist saints lived in the country and deposited sacred writings in various caves, where they were subsequently discovered.

From the time of the establishment of a Sikkimese kingdom the Lepchas became an 'inferior' subject race, under the domination of the Sikkimese Tibetans or Bhotias, to which race the Maharajah and the big landowners belonged. For a considerable period the Lepchas were debarred on account of their race from entering the lamaist monasteries, and, though this rule is now relaxed, it is questionable whether a Lepcha could today obtain an important position in the big monasteries outside the Lepcha reserve. During the eighteenth and early nineteenth centuries the Lepchas fought with the Sikkimese against the continued invasions of the Nepali and Bhutanese; the country was then in a very uncertain state, and there was continuous slave-raiding; the memory of this is still kept lively by the threat which older people will make to a crying child that 'If you don't keep quiet a Tibetan (or Bhutanese) will come along with a big bag and take you away.' During the early nineteenth century a number of treaties were made between Sikkim and British India, broken, and re-made; finally in 1835 the Darjeeling district, naturally together with its inhabitants, was ceded by the Maharajah to the British in exchange for an annuity.

It can be seen that the Lepchas have been for a considerable period a subject race, under the domination of the Bhotias and English. They are agriculturists and hunters, but in Sikkim the best land has been taken by the Bhotias, and later by the Nepali who have immigrated into the country in great numbers; in Darjeeling much of the jungle and agricultural land has been turned into tea-estates, and the Lepchas have become workers on the

Jesuit Ippolito Desideri (edited by Filippo de Filippi. London. George Routledge. 1932). Writing in the early eighteenth century Desideri speaks of Sikkim (p. 118 and *passim*) as a province of Tibet, which had to pay tribute to Lhassa, and he makes no mention of its relatively recent conquest. He calls the province Brêe-mê-jong, which means, 'the nice country.'

tea-plantations. In this district too there has been very considerable infiltration of Nepalis, coming from their crowded and relatively infertile country; more industrious and better cultivators than the Lepchas, the Nepali are continuously displacing them everywhere.

The Lepchas also appear to be a dying race; there is a difference of about 5,000 between the 1901 and the 1931 census; but the figures for Sikkim are perhaps not altogether reliable. As a society, with its unique conglomeration of attitudes, the Lepchas are certainly disappearing, for their culture presupposes a homogeneous interlocking community, and this, as well as their almost complete suppression of competition and aggression, causes an inevitable breakdown of their culture in any mixed community. This book would have been impossible if the Maharajah of Sikkim had not made the part of his estate called Zongu into a Lepcha reserve, where he has made a law that only pure-blooded Lepchas may become landowners. It is only in Zongu and in one or two small villages outside the reserve that there is a homogeneous Lepcha society, practically undisturbed by alien influence. These survivals can be considered artificial, as without the indirect pacification of the British government and the benevolence of the Maharajah, these Lepchas would, like their fellows, have been ousted from the little and poor land which remains to them. But beyond the reservation of this piece of land for their exclusive use the society has not been interfered with, nor preserved as a museum piece; it is still, as will be seen later, in a state of constant modification; indeed the economic changes of the last thirty years are likely to be particularly far-reaching.

Of the Lepchas outside Zongu I can say very little, for I only had slight opportunities of observing them. In Sikkim they appear to subsist fairly well in the mixed communities, to a very great extent adopting the habits, culture, and even the language of their neighbours; they share with them the religion of lamaism, which is the official religion of the State. In India they constitute only a tiny minority of the population of the district; they appear to have lost almost all corporate unity; they have practically completely forgotten their own language, and it would appear that none of the children round Kalimpong at any rate can speak anything except Nepali. Lost in the overwhelming mass of alien people, the Lepchas have no social organisation; and since Lepcha life is based on the social group they have been left with little except their appearance and their gentleness which can be called specifically Lepcha. All the Lepchas' ethics and attitudes which go to make a culture are founded on a community of equal citizens; divorced from such a community the Lepcha culture is meaningless. To some extent the Lepchas have adapted themselves to the changed conditions, accepting the way of life and language of their neighbours. But compared with the Nepali and Plains Indians they are wasteful agriculturists and they have a relatively high standard of living; despite some legal protection—the Lepcha cannot be dispossessed of his last five acres of land—it seems as though they must disappear fairly rapidly, either through want or through absorption. In India a certain amount of intermarriage goes on between Lepchas and Nepali; the Lepcha woman is esteemed for her physical appearance and her mild and yielding character.

In the last census nearly all Lepchas are entered as Buddhists; a little over a thousand had been converted to Christianity. Despite the small numbers the Lepchas represent one of the most fruitful fields of missionary endeavour in Northern India; and the conversion of individuals to Christianity seems to have modified the converts' character far more profoundly than the earlier group conversion to Buddhism. The Christians with whom I came in contact exhibited a strong sense of individual sin (an attitude lamaism has been unable to implant) and excessive prudery, with which was coupled a tendency to snigger at excretory functions.

ii

In an endeavour to gain converts the Baptist mission went to the length of translating and printing in the artificial Lepcha script three books of the New Testament. This seems to have been a work of almost complete supererogation, for the Lepcha script, never widely known, has now completely fallen into disuse; in order to read the scriptures Lepchas have to learn a new, and otherwise completely useless, alphabet; most of them are far more familiar with Nepali.

The Lepcha alphabet was invented at the end of the seventeenth or the beginning of the eighteenth century by King Cha-dor of Sikkim. According to Albert Grünwedel the Lepcha alphabet is derived from a form of the Tibetan U-med alphabet.[3] Some sort

[3] This resemblance is not very obvious to the lay eye; out of the 56 Lepcha characters 18 have no parallel in the U-med alphabet, and, of the 38 signs common to both, over half have very different forms.

of literacy is absolutely essential for the practising lama, and until the Lepchas could be taught Tibetan it was necessary that translations of the scriptures should be available in their own tongue. All the existing Lepcha manuscripts of which I have heard are translations of the Tibetan lamaist scriptures; it is said that some specifically Lepcha compilations of mythology and anecdote have been made and possibly some may have escaped the destructive zeal of fanatical lamas. In Lingthem only one very old lama possessed or could read a Lepcha book.

Nowadays religious instruction is given in Tibetan. In Zongu literacy is exclusively confined to the reading of Tibetan scriptures and has no sort of influence or use in everyday life; lamas who can read religious books and write religious formulas are quite incapable of reading or writing a letter in any language. As will be seen later this factual illiteracy puts the Lepchas at a considerable disadvantage in their commercial transactions. Some of the lamas of Lingthem read the Tibetan scriptures with ease and even fluency; others appeared to me to have learned portions of the scriptures by heart and to know when to turn over the pages; but I was never able to prove this. Tibetan books are printed from wooden blocks in long narrow rectangular pages; to learn to read the pupil gets by heart the contents of one page at a time, only passing on to the next when he has completely mastered and is able to recite the first.

During the second half of the last century one Colonel (later General) G. G. Mainwaring took the Lepchas and their language under his special protection. General Mainwaring was, judging by his literary remains,[4] so perfect a type of the eccentric Indian officer who supports freak religions and fantastic prophecies derived from the pyramids that he seems almost to be an invented caricature. After profound thought General Mainwaring came to the conclusion that not only were the Lepchas the descendants of our first parents, but that—as could be simply shown by a device of the General's called the Power of Letters—Lepcha was the language spoken in the Garden of Eden. Of the people and the language he writes:

'It is impossible that a people with language so comprehensive; with manners, though primitive, so superior, as to entitle

[4] *A Lepcha Grammar*, by Col. G. G. Mainwaring. Calcutta 1876.
Dictionary of the Lepcha Language, compiled by the late General G. Mainwaring, revised and completed by Albert Grünwedel, Berlin, printed and published by order of Her Majesty's Secretary of State for India in Council. Berlin 1898.

them to rank high among civilised nations, could be engendered amidst the wilds and fastnesses of the Himalayas. They retain, in so marked a degree, all the simple ways of the patriarchs of old, as to lead to the conclusion that they must have remained isolated ever since such customs were in vogue. The type of features indicates that before settling in the Himalayas, they had probably resided in Mongolia and Manchuria and in, or near one of these countries, the body of the people might still be found. The language is a monosyllabic one (though not altogether an isolating one, as it possesses in a degree—as all languages however primitive do—an agglutinative structure) and is unquestionably far anterior to the Hebrew or Sanskrit. It is pre-eminently an *Ursprache*, being probably, and I think, I may without fear of misrepresentations, state it to be, the oldest language extent. It is a most comprehensive and beautiful one; and regarded alone, as a prolific source of the derivations and etyma of words, it is invaluable to the philological world. It however recommends itself to us on higher grounds; it possesses and plainly evinces the principle and motive on which all language is constructed.[5] But like everything really good in this world it has been despised and rejected. To allow the Lepcha race, and the language itself to die out would indeed be most barbarous, and inexpressibly sad.'

Although, or perhaps because, the good General was so conscious of the invaluable qualities of the Lepcha language, he was inclined to be severe with the Lepchas who spoke, to his mind, incorrectly. He constructed a huge grammar on Indo-Germanic principles (Lepcha is an uninflected language with no grammar at all) in which he administers severe reproofs to casual speakers; thus

'The Lepchas are apt to pronounce o as u, and hence when writing to confound it with u; this error should be avoided and corrected in the Lepchas.'

'Different local pronunciations, however, and often ignorance, etc., render the change, in the first syllable of dissyllabic words, very common, and sometimes, very irregular; this disorganising tendency should be, altogether, discouraged; and the proper

[5] *Note by Gen. Mainwaring*: In the structure of the Lepcha language I have discovered the system on which, I consider, all language is based. By an exegesis which I have, in part, prepared (combined with a diagram showing the rudimental power of letters), the root and true signification of all words in all languages, are, at once, apparent.

prefixed syllable, when decided upon, should be adhered to. The principle should be laid down as a canon, and systematically impressed on the Lepchas.'

The General was so occupied with his teaching—he founded a sort of college for Lepchas near Darjeeling—that he died before he had time to publish The Power of Letters, and the Lepcha dictionary which was to illustrate his points. After his death his manuscript was edited and published by a German Tibetan scholar who knew no Lepcha and not too much English; all the General's fantastic etymological derivations were cut out and the Lepcha script abandoned in favour of an almost incomprehensible system of phonetic transliteration. The government official in charge wrote to Herr Grünwedel 'The so-called Lepcha alphabet used by General Mainwaring is a pure fiction. The language has properly speaking no written character, though it is possible that on a few occasions a debased variety of the Tibetan character may have been resorted to. There is however no necessity whatever and no real justification for incurring the expense of starting Lepcha type, nor as a matter of fact can a complete fount of such type be constructed.' Considering that there were then numerous Lepcha books in manuscript in existence, and that the Baptists had already founded a complete Lepcha type, the instructions are, in a small way, a fine example of Imperial diplomacy. The dictionary is almost entirely Lepcha-English, and is chiefly useful for its indication of Tibetan loan-words; the identifications of plants and animals are in many cases questionable.

As far as I know the only other person who has paid more than passing attention to the Lepchas is Miss C. de Beauvoir Stocks, who made two tours in Sikkim in 1925 to collect folktales; she spent three days in Lingthem. I came across a number of the stories Miss Stocks had printed[6] and though many of them had been bowdlerised almost out of recognition (probably through the prudery of her interpreter) the almost word-for-word similarity of passages of no particular dramatic interest was striking. Miss Stocks also added some notes on Lepcha customs which correspond in practically no particular with my observations; many are the same as those made about the Sikkimese in the *Gazeteer of Sikkim.*

[6] 'Folklore and Customs of the Lap-chas of Sikkim.' By C. de Beauvoir Stocks. From the Journal and Proceedings of the Asiatic Society of Bengal (New Series), Vol. XXI, 1925, No. 4.

iii

Sikkim is today an independent Native State ruled by an hereditary Maharajah; in his work he is assisted by a number of large land-owners and hereditary ministers called *Kazi*, and also by the advice of a resident British Political Officer. The state, which is less than the size of Wales, lies between 27 and 28 degrees north and 88 and 89 degrees east; its population at the last census was 109,808 persons. It has no railways and no organised transport, but a motor road leads from the capital Gangtok into British India and there is a regular postal service. British India coinage is used.[7]

It is unnecessary for me to discuss in any detail the major policies of the State of Sikkim. The Maharajah is a fervent Buddhist and gives active encouragement to the lamas; and with a couple of exceptions[8] there are no Christian missionaries in the state. There are only half-a-dozen resident Europeans in Sikkim; and for Europeans to enter the state it is necessary to get permission from the political authorities of Gangtok or Darjeeling. Permission for a short visit of a fortnight or so is usually easily given, and Sikkim is a favourite spot for camping holidays among the inhabitants of the plains of India. There are a number of well-appointed *dak*-bungalows along the main routes and it is very seldom that travellers leave these routes. The chief reason for the partial closing of the State is that Sikkim acts as an, as it were, buffer state to Nepal, Tibet and Bhutan. The frontiers to these completely closed States are relatively unguarded and much embarrassment and annoyance has been caused by adventurers or notoriety seekers entering those countries without permission. Consequently nowadays all applicants for passes to Sikkim have to make a written

[7] The basis of British India coinage is the rupee, a large silver coin worth a little over 1/4, or about 32 American cents. The rupee is divided into sixteen annas, worth about a penny or two cents each; there are coins of one, two, four and eight annas, of nickel. The anna is again subdivided into pice and pies, represented by small copper coins. Sums larger than one rupee are paper banknotes, worth Rs. 5, 10, 50, 100, etc. The silver content of the rupee is said to equal its purchasing power. The usual method of denoting sums in rupees is to place first the sign Rs. then the number of rupees, and a bar with on the right side the annas. Thus two rupees, eight annas is printed *Rs.* 2/8. As this method is already customary in works dealing with India, I am employing it in this book.

[8] For a great number of years the Hon. Mary Scott, D.D., has represented the Church of Scotland in Gangtok; and I am told that there are a couple of women missionaries of the Finnish Churches in Lachung.

declaration that they will not pass the frontiers of Tibet, Bhutan or Nepal; those who break this obligation are liable to imprisonment and punishment if caught.

As far as I can see the State of Sikkim is well and paternally administered; the extremely precipitous nature of the whole country has rendered road-building extremely difficult; but the main mule roads into Tibet are kept up in a good state, and solid bridges have been built on these roads. Sikkim has few natural resources except for some small copper mines in the south and (as far as I could tell, undeveloped) large quantities of mica-bearing stone in the north. Sikkim is strategically important as being on the main road between Tibet and India, and nearly all the trade between the two countries passes through it. The Political Officer, assisted by trade agents inside the Tibetan frontier, overlooks this traffic; he also advises the Maharajah on questions of policy.

Since the middle of the last century Sikkim has been free from war and the fear of war, and its history has been as uneventful and as happy as the poorness of the country allows. The only diversion of a military nature in which Sikkim has been involved was the Younghusband expedition to Lhassa in 1905–06 in which several Sikkimese and Lepchas took part. In recent years there has been so great an immigration of Nepalis into Sikkim that it is probable that in the southern part of the country these invaders outnumber the original inhabitants; laws have been passed prohibiting their settling to the north of certain fixed points, but it is not certain to what extent these laws are enforced.

The pacification of the whole country through the British protectorate has given the Lepchas general security; besides abolishing slave-raiding it has also put an end to the mild peonage which formerly existed among the Lepchas themselves. One day in Lingthem the lama Jiroong, when he was rather drunk, embarked on a widely applauded panegyric of the beneficial influence of the British, and of their confirmation in power of the Maharajah. Before the English came, he said, we Lepchas were harried by Tibetans and Nepali and could not settle anywhere for fear we should be sold as slaves; now we have our homes and can cultivate our crops.

Jiroong himself is the descendant of former slaves. Some generations ago his ancestor, then a small boy, was kidnapped by Bhutanese; but the boy was rescued by the then head of the village

—Serving's father—and brought up as his peon. Such Lepcha slaves were either the children of slaves, orphans, or the children of very poor parents. A man would bring up such children and they in turn had to serve him all their lives. If the owner got a child on a female slave the child would be treated as his own, and, if a boy, would inherit, though a smaller portion than the legitimate sons. Slaves could only marry slaves, but otherwise were not distinguished by any special treatment; they received religious attention like ordinary people, and could not be sold or transferred. As in all other cases of emotional relationship among the Lepchas, there was no fixed or expected attitude between masters and slaves; if the master was kind, he was loved like a father. There was a fixed limit to the number of slaves one person could own.

A modification of this situation continues today. If there are children with nobody to look after them, as occasionally occurs, the head of the village, the Mandal, will take them into his household. When they are young they work for the Mandal like a servant, but when they grow up the Mandal arranges a marriage for them and they are then independent; there is at no time any coercion.

iv

In some respects the Lepchas are in a different state to most groups hitherto described by anthropologists. A few studies have been made of tribes who have only had contact with other tribes in a similar state of development, but far and away the greater number had already been more or less seriously influenced by Occidental culture, either through colonisation, missionaries, or traders. Sometimes this external modification is taken into account, sometimes practically ignored; in either case the extent and direction of European influence is easily calculable and understandable. The Lepchas on the other hand have not been in any way directly exposed to European colonisation or missionary influence. Except for an occasional tourist to Talung monastery, and the passage of a couple of mountaineering expeditions attempting to climb Kinchenjunga, Europeans have not entered Zongu. A few of the men had seen Europeans prior to our arrival through trading expeditions to Gangtok and Darjeeling, but practically none of the women; they considered us 'amazing,' particularly on account of the colour of our skins and the shape of our noses.

Although they have not been influenced by Europeans the Lepchas have been very greatly influenced and their ways of life much modified by the contact and pressure of their more highly developed neighbours, the Sikkimese, the Nepali, and above all the Tibetans. The extent of this modification is almost incalculable, owing to the fact that there is no precise information available about these neighbouring societies. Tibet is, I suppose, the most written-about country in the world, but none of the literature that I know of is sufficiently detailed to allow comparisons between the Lepchas and any equivalent Tibetan group. Although there are many books on lamaism I have found none which describes the Lhatsun-pa subsect of the Nyingma-pa sect—the variation followed in Lingthem monastery—so that it is impossible to state definitely whether the Lepchas have ignored or considerably modified any aspect or aspects of the religion to which they have been converted. It is as though an investigator were trying to find out about Baptists and could only get information about Christianity in general, with some of the more obvious distinctions between Roman Catholicism and Protestantism noted.

With regard to the Sikkimese and non-Gurkha Nepali the situation is in some respects simpler; there is practically no information of any sort available about them. The *Gazeteer of Sikkim* published over forty years ago, contains some generalised statements about the habits of the Sikkimese; and the writings[9] and conversation of Major C. J. Morris who had studied the Gurkha soldiers under his command have given me information on certain points. Despite this slight help it is impossible in nearly every instance to state with any sort of certainty whether a given custom, belief or story is confined to the Lepchas, is shared by them with some other tribe, or has been relatively recently introduced from without. On the whole the only available source of information has been Lepcha tradition. Until other tribes in the same area have been studied (and the fact that Nepal, Bhutan and Tibet are practically closed to Europeans makes such studies in the near future problematical) precise questions of culture contact must remain unanswered.

The Lepchas are a mongoloid people, with, it would seem, slightly more pronounced Mongolian features, fairer complexions and greater stature than their present neighbours. Many of the children have carroty or auburn hair, but the hair of adults is always

[9] *Handbooks for the Indian Army: Gurkhas.* By Major C. J. Morris. Delhi 1937.

dark brown or black. I took no measurements, for such behaviour would have been too disconcerting, but I calculate that the mean height for men is about 68 inches, the women being three or four inches shorter. The people are solidly and rather squarely built, with, like most mountain races, very strongly developed calves and leg muscles. The men, with the exception of the lamas, wear their hair in a long plait reaching down to the waist; the women also plait or braid their hair. Although the dresses of the two sexes differ in detail both wear skirt-like garments down to the knees with the legs and feet bare, and it is often extremely difficult to guess a person's sex when seen from behind. Very few Lepcha men have any facial hair, and when I have shown my photographs to friends there have usually been a great number of mistakes in the sex of the subjects.

V

The first two stages of the road from Gangtok to Tibet are Dikchu and Singhik. The mule-road follows the left bank of the Teesta river; a little before Dikchu on the right bank starts the reserve of Zongu. About a mile before Singhik there is a tiny settlement called Mangan; it is situated about a thousand feet above the river. Mangan is a halting-place for muleteers going to and from Tibet; it is a small bazaar and contains the only stores within a radius of about twenty miles. There are half-a-dozen stores with a cheap stock of mixed goods; they are owned by members of the Indian Mahawari caste; their dealings with the Lepchas will be described later. There is also there a government-trained dispenser, a postmaster (the post from Gangtok is brought out twice weekly, on which days the post-office is open), an elementary schoolmaster, all these three government officials, a couple of Tibetan prostitutes for the use of the muleteers, and some liquor shops where the native commercial spirit, *arak*, can be bought. There are perhaps thirty houses.

Branching off from the main mule road on the left is a narrow and extremely precipitous path which descends to the Teesta; at this place the river is crossed by a plank bridge with steel supports; this has recently replaced the fragile and giddy-looking Lepcha bridge made entirely of bamboo, and represents the only permanent link between Zongu and the rest of Sikkim. For a little while the path on the other side skirts the river, passing on its way a substantial wooden shed which has been erected to receive the cardamum fruit[10] at the time of harvest, and which some Lepchas hope will be converted into an elementary school. A little after this the track shoots sharply upwards, barely indicated by the presence of rocks and felled trees, running through poor and ragged stony ground sparsely sown with maize. The path leads directly to the crest of the hill which is surmounted by a small stone cairn or *choten*, perhaps three thousand feet above the river and five thousand above the sea-level. This cairn is almost opposite the junction of the Teesta and Talung rivers, and from it paths wander west and south, to the different villages of Zongu.

Proceeding westward from the cairn you reach in a couple of miles the small village of Panung; a couple more miles and you come to the village of Lingthem. Without our knowledge—we were only making for Zongu, and until the last hours believed that was the name of a village—it had been arranged that we were to stop there, and the first storey of the monastery had been placed at our disposal, in such a manner that it was almost impossible to refuse. As a place to live in the monastery suffered from several disadvantages; it was extremely cold and draughty, and fires were forbidden because the smoke would defile the images of the Gods; smoking was forbidden, except on the balcony which for my special benefit was temporarily considered outside holy precincts; the place was overrun with rats, which it would have been the greatest possible sin to kill in the monastery, and which could not be driven away supernaturally because none of the lamas knew the correct ritual, which involves the use of sand, ashes, and paper charms; there was never any privacy for at any time people might feel impelled to come to worship the images which were housed in this upper chamber, and regularly at dawn and sunset a young lama came to arrange the altars; and during big monastery feasts sleep was often impossible for two or three nights. But some of these disadvantages had compensating advantages; and as the focal centre of Lingthem, and to a lesser degree of the whole Talung side of Zongu, our living quarters were ideally situated for constant observation.

[10] Cardamum is the money crop of the Lepchas. Cardamum is a spice consisting of the seed-capsules of the perennial plants of a species of *Amomum* and is much used as a stomachic and condiment.

BOOK ONE

Lepcha Life

CHAPTER TWO

THE HOMES OF THE LEPCHAS

i

Zongu is a roughly triangular portion of very mountainous land, approximately forty miles on each side, bounded on the south-east by the river Teesta, on the north-east by the river Talung and on the third side by the mountains south of Kinchenjunga. The land is excessively precipitous; the rivers are at about 2,000 feet above sea-level and the average height of the hills is about 12,000 feet; but the peaks rise to more than double that height, Kinchenjunga at the head of the Talung valley, which dominates the western horizon, being over 28,000 feet. Except for a few artificially levelled places there is probably not a hundred square yards of flat ground in the whole district; and the tracks are too steep and too uneven for it to be possible to employ mules, let alone horses; all travelling has to be done on foot, and all goods transported by human porterage.

The river valleys are hot, steamy and somewhat malarious, and consequently there are no houses right on the river, though the ground is used for raising subtropical plants; there are however occasional houses about 500 feet higher up. Most of the houses and cultivated land are between 3,500 feet and 7,500 feet above sea-level, a relatively narrow band above the two rivers, though occasionally fields are made at even higher altitudes. Above the cultivated land is the forest in which wild produce is gathered, a decreasing amount of hunting done, and to which the cattle are sent up to pasture in the winter months. Above the forest level comes first the rhododendron forest, and then the snows, rarely visited except by hunters searching either for ibex and musk-deer or for the wild aconite which forms the basis of their arrow poison.

The climate of the Talung valley is excessively wet, even for the Himalayas; it is only in the autumn months—from the end of September to the end of November—that there is no rain.

During the rest of the year it falls intermittently, and in the full monsoon period, June to September, almost continuously. Owing to the precipitous nature of the land water does not lie, and the ground will be dry within six hours of a heavy downpour. In Zongu there are a great number of mountain streams running down from the snows to the rivers.

The temperature varies very considerably at the different heights. Only once in this century has snow fallen down by the river; that was in 1906. Above about 8,000 feet snow lies regularly every year, and there are often powderings of snow down to about 4,000 feet, the level of most of the houses; but the presence of oranges and peaches suggests that at this level snow and frost are neither severe nor continuous. Except for the warm and clammy monsoon period, when dysentery epidemics are liable to break out, the weather is generally cool on the habitation level, and there is considerable difference between day and night temperatures. Judging from the weather I did experience and the comparisons made I should say that the mean temperature varies between about 40 degrees Fahrenheit in winter to about 86 in summer. It follows that clothes are very necessary for warmth.

Both men and women wear thin knee-length drawers, and on the upper body a shirt; men's shirts are slightly shorter. Over this women also wear a sort of bodice made out of a thin material, formerly obtained from Assam through Bhutan. The original Lepcha outside dress was a thick piece of home-woven striped material, fastened over one shoulder with a brooch, belted at the waist with a sash and reaching to the knees. The colouring of this sash has a certain significance, those of lamas[1] usually being yellow and of laymen red or purple, though other colours are sometimes used. Within the last generation women have completely given up this indigenous type of dress in favour of the Tibetan costume, which consists of a coloured long-sleeved under-bodice, and a dark sleeveless overdress, reaching half-way down the calves and fastened with buttons. Women often tie up their hair with a head-cloth, generally resembling a dirty table napkin. Quite a number

[1] Lama is not a Lepcha word. The Lepchas call lamas either *yook-mun*—this means honoured Mun, that is ' honoured priest of the Lepcha Mun religion ' —or more generally *cho-bu* which means ' book man ' since the essential part of the lamaist education is reading, a talent not enjoyed by the layman. I have thought it better however to use the word ' lama ' as it is already familiar to western readers in its meaning of priest of the Tibetan lamaist religion.

Above : LINGTHEM MONASTERY FROM BELOW
Below : LINGTHEM MONASTERY FROM ABOVE
Note the prayer flags.

of men still wear the Lepcha dress, though the original Lepcha head-dress—a small sugar-loaf of woven bamboo surmounted by a feather—has been almost completely abandoned in favour of the biretta-like Tibetan hat decorated with coral beads. Hats are only worn on fairly ceremonious occasions. Lamas, and a few of the richer and older laymen, wear the outer dress of the Tibetan lama—a thick red, purple or dark-blue sleeved garment, joined from the waist to below the knees, and buttoning from the waist to the throat.

Until the beginning of this century Lepchas used to weave all their own cloth, but nowadays only a couple of women bother to weave; people wear instead ready-made and fairly shoddy clothes. These bought clothes have had one rather serious effect, to my mind; children are usually dressed in the adapted cast-offs of their elders, and the poor and thin material in the cold winter renders young children even more susceptible to colds and bronchial trouble and has probably increased the infantile mortality. Very few people over the age of ten were troubled by colds and coughs—it would seem as though they acquired, if they survived, some sort of immunity—but there was hardly one child who was not, and the most frequent request which was made to me was for medicine to relieve these complaints. Three young children in Lingthem or the neighbourhood died of bronchial trouble during my stay there. Adults take reasonable precautions against chills, changing their clothes and taking a hot drink as soon as possible after a wetting; children who are not with older people often neglect to do so.

There would appear to be a considerable difference in humidity and temperature between the portion of Zongu which faces the Teesta and that which faces the Talung river; the former is considerably warmer, as the cultivation of sugar-cane, manioc, and other subtropical plants shows, and it would appear that the rainfall is less. The inhabitants of the Teesta side are geographically nearer the main mule-road between Tibet and India; but it does not appear and is not believed that this propinquity with the outside world has modified the character or habits of these people in any way; they are considered to be essentially similar to the people of the Talung valley and there is constant intermarriage all through the district.

On the far side of the Talung valley the ground is excessively rough and precipitous and is to a great extent not amenable to cultivation. Although geographically outside Zongu the few settlements are administratively part of it, being attached to the bigger villages on the Zongu bank. Excluding the Talung monastery, which is a couple of days' journey from most of the villages, and which, save for a guardian, is empty except during certain festivals, there are no lamaist monasteries and very few lamas on this bank. The inhabitants of this portion are considered by the people of Zongu to be uncivilised and rude, keeping much more to the habits of their forefathers. For a great deal of their food they rely on hunting and forest produce; their religion is still almost entirely that of the Mun, the lamaist propaganda having reached them very slightly. Owing to the excessively precipitous nature of the ground I never went over to this side of the river; on a few occasions however I saw some of the inhabitants.

There are in Zongu itself twenty-two settlements with distinctive names, and across the river eight more; some of these named settlements only consist of two or three houses and they are administratively and emotionally divided into twelve districts. Although it is convenient to speak of villages these settlements have no sort of geographical unity; the houses are either isolated in the fields and forests, or gathered in small groups of three or four; I never saw more than four houses which were close neighbours. Except for the three villages—Lingthem, Gyatong and Tangvoong—which possess a monastery, there is no sort of focal centre to the village, and it would be possible for a casual traveller to pass through quite a large village without being aware of its existence. Lingthem, where I lived, consisted of 33 houses; it is the biggest village on the Talung side of Zongu, and the second biggest in the reserve; the biggest of all is Gyatong, which, with its neighbour Hi, contains 60 houses. From the spur of one hill in Lingthem it is possible to see eight houses at once; I should reckon that there were quite three miles and three thousand feet between the lowest house to the east and the highest house to the west in the village.

When three or four houses are grouped together they are usually given a distinctive name. This grouping does not necessarily correspond to any emotional or kinship ties among near neighbours; people living in adjoining houses may be closely related, or they may be complete strangers, and full brothers may live separated by the full distance of the village.[2] The metaphysical desiderata, described later in this chapter, for the choice of a house site and

[2] For the plan of the houses of Lingthem and their inhabitants, see Appendix I, b.

the hazards of inheritance account sufficiently for the meaningless grouping of neighbours.

The names of the villages on either side of the river Talung are accounted for by the following oft-repeated etymological myth:

'On any clear day there is visible from Lingthem a large gendarme of black rock rising from the mountain Siniolchi, or, as it is called in Lepcha, Sanyol-koong. On that gendarme there lived once upon a time a devil called Lassoo-fo *moong* (the Lassoo bird devil). This devil was a man-eater; he used to capture people all through the neighbourhood and take them away to Tibet where he would kill and eat them. Therefore the Gods Kansi *thing* (lord), Kom-yo *thing* and Saktsum *thing* consulted together as to how they could kill this demon. They tried to find a man who was capable, but they could not do so. They then went to the caterpillar *pi-sik-bu* who gnaws trees so that they become hollow and fall down, and they told him to go and cut down the tree in that place.[3] The caterpillar agreed and hollowed the tree so that it fell down, after which the demon had no place to live and went wandering about. Then the three gods sent for Rum-nam (a mythological hero) to kill the demon, and wherever the demon went Rum-nam followed.

'The demon went down the Talung valley and came to Sakyong (so called because Tag-kyong-ka was killed there), Pantoong, Thong-to, Lavén, Tangvoong, Lungdeum (where he killed children), A-dong, Ling-them (*tem-la tem-la taa*: he ate each in turn): the village opposite is called Liklyang, the place of crying, because people cried out from there.[4] Rum-nam chased him and eventually overtook him at Lasso-tsong-nyong, in the Teesta valley to the west, and there killed him and scattered his flesh over the land. From this scattered flesh arose leeches and mosquitoes, and the small predatory bird *kar-hu-fo*. His bones turned into stone, and at the place where he was slain there is a huge stone which can be seen to this day.'

Except for questions of the size of the population and the fertility of the land and some minor details of internal administration,

[3] There is a verbal confusion here between the various meanings of the word *koong*—(1) mountain peak, and (2) tree, worked wood, and finally house-pillar. There are obviously no trees on the gendarme which is well above the snow level. However I heard this story repeated several times in identical terms.

[4] All the other village names have etymological derivations from the same legend, but it seems unnecessary to give them all.

there is not considered to be any sort of difference in customs or character between the various villages of Zongu, with a single exception. This exception is the village of Pantoong, on the far side of the Talung valley and the nearest settlement of all to the foot of Kinchenjunga; this village was until a generation ago the home of a group of serpent-eaters. These serpent-eaters all belonged to one *ptso* or patrilineal group, the Salong *ptso*. This *ptso*, though dying out, is not yet extinct, but its living representatives no longer eat snakes. Old Lepchas of Zongu have however seen these people eat the snakes; they would stone the reptile, cut off its head, and devour the body. The origin of this habit is the following story:

'One day the ancestor of the *ptso* was going through the forest when he came on what he thought was a dead bear; but really this bear was an incarnation of Pong *rum*, the king of all animals and the patron God of hunters, who was at the moment taking a rest outside his incarnation's body. The ancestor cut up the animal and ate part of it; whereupon Pong *rum* appeared to him and said "You have eaten part of my body; henceforward you and your children must serve me and worship me and make offerings to me. Henceforward also you and your children may eat all animals, even snakes, with impunity." This is the reason why the people of Pantoong could eat and enjoy snakes, whereas the rest of us would die if we ate them.'

When I was studying the language in Kalimpong, my teacher, a missionised Lepcha, told me that the story of eating snakes was a cruel libel spread about the Lepchas by the Nepali; there was not, he insisted, an atom of truth in it, and he obviously felt that it was deeply insulting and even shameful. For the Lepchas of Zongu however the story was without unpleasant affect; it is frequently repeated as a curious and amusing anecdote, and a certain respect is felt for those people who can boast of actually having seen snakes eaten. It seems improbable that these Lepchas would feel any repulsion to eating serpents if they thought they could do so with impunity; their disgust reactions are very limited; they will eat dead domestic animals and even carrion found in the forest; and they prefer their meat to be as high as possible, provided it is not maggoty. Except during the training of the Mun priests there are no food prohibitions of any sort, except the ban on horse and dog flesh ('He who could eat the flesh of horse or dog could eat the flesh of man, for all three are similar ') and such animals and vegetables as are considered poisonous.

Snakes are regarded with a certain amount of affect, though on the whole with less than might be expected. To see a snake, particularly the *pamol-beu* (a black non-poisonous snake) approaching you is a bad omen, and should it enter a house it foretells a death in that house within the year. All dreams are meaningful, and snakes in dreams have an ominous significance. Snakes do represent a considerable danger, for they are fairly common, particularly in the lower valley and in the forest, and cultivated land is always surrounded by low scrub and secondary growth in which snakes can and do hide. I was frequently asked for medicine against snake-bite, particularly by hunters, but always as a preventative, for there were no serious cases of snake-bite while I was there, nor did I hear of any fatal ones. The Lepchas know of a dioeceous plant which is believed to cure these bites, but apparently they have not much faith in it. Snakes occur very little in mythology and fable, and have no overt phallic significance ; the most common phallic symbol is the maize cob, which is almost a rude word.

ii

Lingthem monastery is a two-storied rectangular building standing on an artificially levelled terrace about 5,500 feet above sea-level, with its principal façade facing north. The first building on the site was erected in 1855 but it has since been rebuilt three times. The first building was made by Panloak, the grandfather of old Serving, the last of his line to be head of the village ; the first and second renovations and enlargements were made under the direction of learned lamas who had travelled from Tibet ; the third and greatest alteration was made fifteen years ago under the direction of, and to a great extent at the expense of, the Muktair, the dead father of Tafoor and Chudo. The rebuilding was done entirely by local labour in the three winter months, with help from neighbouring villages. The material was paid for chiefly by local subscription helped by donations from the State and the British Political Officer and the structure when completed was free from debt. The monastery however still owes Rs. 600 to Lhassa for the copies of the sacred books, and the heirs of the Muktair still owe money to the money lenders for the sums the Muktair undertook personally for the materials which had to be bought and for the big metal images which he bought from Bhutan to replace the small existing ones. The monasteries are the only occasions in Lepcha life for conspicuous display and ornament and there is a constant feeling of emulation and friendly rivalry between the different villages as to who shall have the largest, most beautiful and best equipped monastery. Until recently that of Lingthem was easily the finest in every way, but in 1937 the people of Gyatong decided to build an even bigger one (in the building of which the people of Lingthem will aid). Although the people of Lingthem hope in time that they will be able to rebuild their monastery so as to be even bigger than the new one at Gyatong they cannot consider doing so yet; but to counterbalance the effort of their neighbours the people of Lingthem are collecting money to replace the present thatched roof with one of corrugated iron. From the aesthetic point of view the change will be an unmitigated disaster, but the present thatch, though pleasant to look at, is inadequate to keep out the almost continuous rain, as the condition of the painted woodwork and hanging pictures on silk (*tang-ku*) shows.

The monastery is made of stone, wood and plaster; the walls are coloured white with a broad band of red (the dye is a clay brought from a considerable distance) and picked out with blue; the windows, doors and porch are made out of wood and are quite pleasantly carved in stylised geometrical patterns. The main place of worship is on the ground floor with the entrance in the middle of the north wall, consisting of a pair of wooden doors. These doors are protected by a built-out porch, on the top of which is a balcony which runs the whole length of the first storey; this porch is enclosed except for a fairly narrow entrance in the centre and on three sides there are inserted prayer wheels[5] about four feet from the ground. These prayer wheels are filled with written prayers or *mantra* inside a wooden drum which is set on spikes so as to revolve freely; the outside of the drum is covered with paper inscribed with a prayer in Len-za script. When the pious approach the monastery they circumambulate it three times, always keeping the

[5] One of the tenets of lamaism is that a prayer repeated mechanically is as valid as one said orally. The two chief mechanisms for mechanical praying are (1) prayer drums filled with written prayers or *mantra*: turning the wheel is equivalent to uttering all the contained prayers, and (2) prayer flags. These are strips of linen stamped with printed prayers; each time the flag flutters in the breeze it is as though the setter-up had said all the prayers printed on it. These devices are described more fully in Chapter Seven, pp. 190–191.

wall on their right side (as must be done for all lamaist holy places or objects) turning the prayer wheels as they come up to them.

The chief holy place is a large bare room, occupying almost the whole of the ground floor of the building. The interior of the room is empty except for four supporting pillars in the middle of the floor, and two slightly raised seats running in parallel lines from the altar to the door on which the lamas sit during ceremonies. In the centre of the back wall is the altar, inset in a carved wooden frame; on it are three large images, Sangyi Youbami in the centre, flanked by Gamyang Kanché Rimbuché and Chérézi; in front of these larger images are four smaller gods. On either side of the altar are worked wooden pigeon-holes, in which are kept the hundred and eight volumes of the Kangyour, one of the two Tibetan scriptures. These volumes consist of loose leaves bound up in a cloth and fastened between two plain pieces of wood as bindings. Scattered about the room are the various musical instruments which are not in use—drums, gongs and cymbals; the metal instruments similar to trumpets and clarionets, the conch shells and the flutes made out of a human femur are kept either on or before the altar. Every morning at dawn a *kané* (sacristan) places on the altar before the images seven bowls of water for the gods to drink and wash in; every evening at sunset these bowls are emptied and replaced by *chimi*—altar lights, consisting of a small metal container with a wick of bamboo or cloth, filled with melted butter or oil. There also stands on the altar a copper jug containing blessed water (*tyü*) and usually a pair of vases filled with flowers. There are also occasional offerings of cones of ground grain. During important festivals the front of the altar is completely hidden by elaborate constructions, chiefly made out of dough and butter which represent those gods who are being specially worshipped. Anybody approaching this or any other lamaist altar for the first time is meant to prostrate himself three times, standing with joined hands, falling to the knees and then touching the ground with the forehead. After these prostrations no special attention is paid to the altar, and it is quite permissible to turn one's back on it.

To the west of the main room, with a separate entrance also on the north wall, is the *lha-gong*. This is a high and narrow chamber almost entirely filled with four huge prayer wheels, reaching up to the ceiling; indeed the first and biggest of the wheels, which is called Betsa Guru, pierces the ceiling and its top, a cone surmounted with drapery of many colours, stands in the middle of the floor of the storey above. The four prayer-wheels practically touch each other; there is about a yard of free ground between the wheels and the side walls, and a larger space between the doorway and the first wheel. The *lha-gong* is primarily the place of worship of the nuns—*in-é-bu*—and they are meant to be responsible for the services and good order of this place. The big wheels are turned by people sitting down, and there are wooden handles attached to the base which make this operation easier. Each time one of the big wheels completes a revolution a small bell is rung. The wheels are covered with paper of a vaguely Chinese design, representing fantastic flowers and goddesses.

The first storey is approached by an external wooden staircase on the east side. It leads first of all into a corridor with an unused cooking place; at the back of that is a small and completely dark chamber called *tyang-gong* which is employed for mystic fasting and contemplation and also for the weekly ceremony of *kong-so klon* which is performed, at considerable risks, it is believed, to the officiant, to cleanse the monastery and neighbourhood of those devils which are infesting it.

The main first-storey room is very similar to the one below, except that the books and images on the altar are different. This first-floor altar is flanked by a pair of thunder-birds—*sa-dher*—resembling Chinese dragons in silhouette cut out of cardboard. A couple of books are also kept permanently on the altar. To the right of the altar is a cupboard containing the sacred book Rin-chet; this book is treated with great reverence and the cupboard which holds it receives bowls of water and *chimi* as though it were an altar. But none of the lamas of Lingthem can read this book, nor do they know the proper ceremonials which should accompany the reading. On the four supporting columns hang wooden masks such as are worn when 'devil dances' are performed; but these actual masks, though representing named supernaturals, are not made for wearing, nor are dances performed in the monastery. Suspended from the cross-beams—for there is no ceiling and the reed thatch can be seen between the beams—are a number of sacred scroll pictures (*tang-ku*) but they have suffered so much from the weather that they are practically indecipherable.

To the west of the main room, above the *lha-gong* is a lumber room containing paper-presses and other paraphernalia not in constant use. The Lepchas make paper out of the pounded underbark

Above : A LEPCHA HOUSE

Below : A *MOONG LI :* A HOUSE FOR THE 'HOUSE-GOBLIN' *THYAK-DUM*, SITUATED IN A CARDAMUM FIELD: BEHIND ANOTHER HOUSE

of two species of daphne (*ri-kan-too* and *dé-nok*) cooked to a pulp and then spread over coarse canvas on stretchers under flowing water. Paper can be made by anyone, either for monastery use or for sale; but since there are no printing blocks in Zongu books have to be sent away to be stamped. For ordinary writing an ink is made out of black earth.

To the front of the monastery is a piece of artificially raised level ground of perhaps fifteen yards depth. It is covered with fairly rough short grass; and at the far edge against the low stone wall are set up a number of prayer flags in memory of the dead, and a few for the benefit of the living. There are one or two small outcrops of rock. All round the building, except in front of the porch, is a narrow flower border in which are grown European flowers, of which seeds or cuttings have been brought from Gangtok—hollyhocks, petunias, sweet william, geraniums, dahlias, and flowering cactuses. In the grass near the wall are several large bushes of small-flowered pink and red roses and some large clumps of hydrangeas. The flowers from these plants are used to decorate the lamaist altar, in preference to the numerous orchids which can be found in the neighbourhood.

Below the monastery wall is a small wood chiefly composed of juniper and *ficus*; about fifty yards from the monastery inside the wood are four *choten* walls—long rectangular stone barrows with stones inscribed with prayers let into the side. The most considerable of these is surmounted by a terra-cotta decoration of a half-moon and three diminishing circles. These *choten* are not funeral piles, nor even cenotaphs; their intention is apotropaic.[6] Some religious ceremonies are performed by the *choten*, particularly those in which both lamas and Mun (the priests of the old Lepcha religion) take part, for the latter are not allowed to officiate within the monastery precincts. The wood is also used as a public latrine during festivals, and animals, particularly pigs and cows, come to pasture there.

To the right of the monastery is an ordinary Lepcha house (except that the entrance is on the west instead of the east side) which is normally the home of the monastery custodian who looks after the garden and ground. He has a small garden (*sing*) in front of the house and also one or two little enclosures with

[6] I am employing the term *apotropaic* for all religious actions whose aim is preventative rather than curative. The *choten* are to keep devils away, not to expel those already present.

tree tomato bushes, chilli bushes, onions, etc. inside the monastery precincts; but for the greater part of his food he is dependent on gifts from the villagers. The holder of this office was a very old man called Pong-ring, born in 1852; he was very feeble, half blind, suffered from polyps which made him almost incomprehensible even to the Lepchas, and his body was covered with the most revolting open sores. To accommodate our staff he had been turned out of his house and was taken as a boarder by the next nearest house, the owner of which, Jiroong, could trace a very distant relationship with him. In his very old age he was abnormally pious, hardly moving without his personal prayer wheel. He had never received proper religious instruction and could not read (or go through the motions of reading); his devotions were limited to those of the uninstructed and usually illiterate nuns and a number of rather unkind jokes, considering his age and feebleness, were made about his position as head of the female congregation. As an old man past his work, unable to support himself and without children, he was not respected by the other Lepchas, most of whom felt, as I did, that he would be better dead; and some of the rather heartless children used to call out to him 'Why don't you die now while the Europeans are here, so that they can see your funeral?'. He was constantly having attacks of illness, but always recovered, to my, I hope, disguised distress; he was a very unpleasant spectacle and neighbour, and I should have liked to have seen the funeral of a lama, which I was not able to do.

At the back of the monastery the wooded hill goes up steeply to some cultivated land and a small group of houses. To the west is a small open alp with a few fruit trees in it, and beyond that slightly rising ground, this year not cultivated, and then about half a mile or more away another group of four houses.

iii

The monastery is almost exactly in the middle of Lingthem. Of the 33 houses 14 are above the monastery and the rest below, 14 to the east and the rest to the west. There are five groups of four houses each, one of three, and the rest either isolated or in pairs.

Lepcha houses are rectangular buildings raised about four feet off the ground on stone piles which go round three sides of the building; the east side is left open, and the space underneath serves as a shelter at night for domestic animals. The building itself is made of wood, plaster, bamboo and thatch. All buildings have their entrance to the east and face north; the north-south sides are the longest. The first portions of the building to be erected are the five upright supports, one in the centre and one at each corner; they consist of roughly shaped tree-trunks. For the erection of these supports and for the building of the stone wall an overseer is necessary; for the rest of the building no director is used. The floor is usually woven bamboo, but some of the richer people cover the bamboo with smoothed planks; the walls are always of bamboo covered with plaster, occasionally with wooden supports. Except in the Mandal's house, where there are a couple of window frames, the south and west walls are blind; the entrance, which is reached by a pair of notched logs or rough steps, is always on the east; and round the east and north side runs a balcony of plaited bamboo. The north wall is mostly open to the balcony but there are usually wooden shutters which can be closed when the nights are cold. The balcony is used a great deal; for gossiping in the daytime or during warm evenings, for a great variety of household tasks, since there is seldom much light inside the house, as a place where fowls can roost, and as a latrine for infants, invalids, the drunk or the lazy. The roof is made of reeds hung over bamboo and supported on a wooden frame; the north and south sides of the roof cover the whole space between the roof-tree and the top of the wall, but the east and west sides are somewhat inserted at a slightly lower angle, so that there is a triangle (either empty or filled with widely-woven bamboo) on the east and west sides under the roof-tree which is meant to provide ventilation and an escape for the smoke; the device is not very successful and often of an evening I was half-blinded by smoke so that I could not see across a room and the tears streamed down my face. The Lepchas are completely inured to this atmosphere and could not understand why I coughed and choked.

The great majority of Lepcha houses consist of two rooms and an attic; a few of the poorest have only one room, and a couple of the biggest houses have a third small store-room beyond the *dé-ong*. The first room on entering from the east is the *thop-song*, or, as I shall refer to it in future, the kitchen. Round the side are either slightly raised shelves or a bar set into the wooden floor, which marks the sleeping places of the members of the household. During the day the bedding and pillows are rolled up and put away in boxes and are only brought out just before retiring to sleep. Except for the sleeping places of grandparents or parents-in-law, which are avoided out of respect, these sleeping places serve as seats in the daytime. In the centre of the dividing wall is the cooking place; this is a built-up square of pounded earth and clay, perhaps five feet in each direction and raised about a foot off the ground; into this while it is still soft are inserted four upright stones to support the cooking pots over the logs of wood. Above the fire-place is a drying ledge of woven bamboo hanging from the rafters. There is a very fragile ceiling of bamboo which serves as a store-house; it is entered through a trap-door which is placed nearly directly above the cooking-place so as to allow the smoke to escape and which is reached by a notched log.

The dividing wall which separates the two rooms is usually a wooden partition (occasionally bamboo) with a door, or at least a door-frame, in the side nearest the balcony. This second room is called *dé-ong*. In the houses of lamas and of the more pious laymen there is an altar against the south wall. This altar varies enormously with the wealth and inclinations of the individual; some of the most elaborate are miniature reproductions of the altars in the monastery, with large metal images and musical instruments and other decorations; and in one or two houses there are pigeon-holes on either side containing the sixteen volumes of the Boom, the shortened version of the Kangyour. In other houses the altar is no more than a wooden box set up on end, with one small metal image inside, and sometimes not even that.

The *dé-ong*, whether it is fitted up as a private lamaist temple or not, is always more or less of a ceremonial room, for in it are performed the numerous ceremonies which occur in the life of everyone, for feared or actual illness or death, or for marriage. Ordinarily the room is little used and is only slept in by lamas, and not always by them. The attitude to the *dé-ong* is similar to that held towards the parlour in lower-middle-class English homes. It is the place where distinguished visitors are received, where emotionally important events of a slightly ceremonious nature take place; it is not a room which is used by the family in ordinary everyday life. In one or two houses there is a small and narrow store-room beyond the *dé-ong*; in other houses the *dé-ong* is used for this purpose also. Heads of maize and millet are suspended from the bamboo ceiling to dry, and sacks of grain and flour are kept under the altar. People fetching stores from this place are meant to prostrate themselves three times at each visit, but usually these reverences are merely sketched out. In the *dé-ong* too will be kept the chests containing spare clothes and jewels.

With the exception of the altar, and of a couple of the biggest houses (those of Tafoor and Chala Mandal) which have rough coloured frescoes on the external plaster and slightly carved doorways and windows, Lepcha houses are entirely unornamented within and without. As a generalisation it may be said that the Lepchas possess neither arts nor crafts, though they show considerable dexterity in adapting natural materials to domestic uses. Lepchas are capable of becoming very efficient craftsmen; the locally done carpentry work in the monastery is as good as could be desired; but such useless decoration is for them entirely pointless, an alien craft to be learned from aliens at the command and expense of the state. Datoop, a master carpenter, who had studied the craft for nine years and who had done the fine work in most of the monasteries of the neighbourhood, had not a single piece of carved wood in his house.

Painting is an even more alien art, confined exclusively to specially trained lamas. The only painter in the neighbourhood was the Lharibu (painter) Chujen of Panung, the father-in-law of Tafoor, and he had had to give up the practice of the craft with increasing years and failing eyesight. He started with a natural propensity for drawing, which was noted by his lamaist instructor, who advised him to learn to become a painter. He studied for nine years at the monastery of Pensong. The method of instruction was the following. The pupils were provided with a piece of oiled wood covered with black earth, on which was placed a thin layer of white powder; when this was scratched with a pointed stick a black outline drawing resulted, which could be wiped out so that the board could be used again. The teacher would draw a model and the pupils would copy that for some days, only going on to the next model when the first was copied perfectly. Thus the first five or six days were occupied with the head of the God Chum-den-dé; then nine or ten days were occupied in learning to draw this God's body naked; then the body draped; and finally the whole figure coloured. In this mechanical way a whole repertoire of sacred pictures were learned during the nine years' teaching, and the Lharibu later learned others by copying existing models.

According to the Lharibu's view of art, all pictures are approximations to a divine original, varying in merit chiefly by their nearness to this ideal, but also partly through the fineness and detail of the work. He disapproves of the habit which some painters have of adding novelties or original motives to the work. His view of his art is entirely mechanical and he knows little of a painter's technique. He practically only uses bought colours, and though he knows that a paint can be lightened by the addition of chalk, he does not know how to darken colours or how to mix his own colours. It is worth noting that before he started to learn to paint he occasionally drew people and birds for his own amusement, but that after he had been taught he never drew a line for the pleasure of it, but only when required to do so. His own house is completely undecorated.

All lamas acquire considerable dexterity in the fashioning of impermanent sacrificial objects for different ceremonies; these are made at great speed, with astounding agility and deftness. The most complicated objects are the *deu*, or house of supernaturals, which consist of varied and elaborate geometrical designs in various coloured thread twisted round bamboo splinters, and fastened on to a single bamboo upright. Models of different supernaturals, of a more or less life-like appearance, are made out of the flour of different grains mixed with water to form a paste, or out of mud, and are decorated with butter, plain or dyed to different colours, various coloured wools and pieces of thread and cloth. The Mun decorate their sacrifical objects far less, but they occasionally use containers of green bamboo, on the outside of which elaborate geometrical designs are quickly and accurately scratched with the point of a knife.

The knife is practically the Lepcha's only instrument. The knives are of iron with a wooden handle and a blade about eighteen inches long and three inches wide; the whole of one side is a cutting edge and the tip is square, not pointed. These knives are now bought from traders in Mangan or Gangtok; formerly they were got from Tibetans in exchange for produce. As soon as a boy achieves physical independence he is given a small knife of his own, and, except in the case of lamas when they are officiating, you can never see a Lepcha outside his house without his knife in a one-sided bamboo scabbard slung by his side. This knife is used for every conceivable purpose, from lopping trees on land about to be cultivated, to cutting up meat or wood for any domestic or agricultural task. Except for a couple of hatchets, which are loaned about the village when big trees have to be cut down, and short hoes for terracing, these knives are the universal instrument for every purpose. Girls and women wear a curved sickle, thrust without a sheath into the sash round their waist at the back; but this instrument is of less general use than the men's knives, and women are frequently forced to borrow knives from men who are near them.

Far and away the most important single material for the Lepchas is the bamboo, or rather the numerous varieties of different bamboos that they grow and recognise. In the house bamboo is used for the floor, ceiling, walls and balcony; out of it water-carriers, and on occasion water conduits are made. The drinking vessels—*patyoot*—are made from ten-inch sections of old and hollow bamboo; each *patyoot* is cut off just below a joint, where the natural growth forms a bottom for the vessel. The principal beverage drunk from these *patyoot* is *chi*, a sort of beer which is formed by pouring boiling water on fermented grain; this is drunk through a 'straw'—*pa-hip*—which consists of a section of a small-growing bamboo with the pith at the end loosened so as to form a rude filter. Pins and brooches are made from bamboo; bows and arrows, the Lepcha's only hunting weapons, quivers and scabbards, all are made of different sorts of bamboo; and the catalogue could be continued almost endlessly. Finally the young bamboo shoots are good to eat, and the leaves are fed to temporarily restrained domestic animals, such as oxen when they are needed for ploughing.

The Lepchas of Zongu do not know how to make pottery. Plates are usually replaced by big leaves, but there are a certain number of rudely carved wooden plates which are used on ceremonious occasions, and a few metal and china dishes and containers which have been got by trading from Tibetans or bought in exchange for cardamum.

The Lepchas weave strong and regular mats and baskets out of the bark of bamboo and various reeds, which they employ for a variety of purposes. This weaving is ideally men's work, as the weaving of thread is women's, but a certain number of women are as good mat-makers as any of the men, and there is felt to be no disgrace in employing articles made by women. During the summer months a mat called *tuk* is worn over the head as a protection against sun and rain; it is made of a double layer of finely woven bamboo filled with big leaves and has a rope in the centre to fasten it round the neck; it measures about three feet by four. Although the making of this article is considered to be specifically man's work, the best *tuk* in the village were said to be made by a woman, the mother of Gongyop.

The weaving of cloth is, as has already been said, now almost extinct in Zongu; in Lingthem only a couple of women—the wives of Datoop and Jiroong—weave at all regularly. Lepcha cloths are extremely finely woven; nearly all are in striped patterns, sometimes over a plain, and sometimes over a patterned background. I have been shown such cloths further ornamented with needlework embroidery, but I did not see any so enhanced in Zongu. Although weaving is now almost a lost art, the spindle is considered the typical feminine symbol, as the arrow is the masculine one; and in stories the heavy bar of the loom is the woman's chief weapon.

Although no attempt is made to add 'beauty' to the ordinary objects and surroundings of life, both men and women wear a certain amount of jewellery. The men wear turquoise ear-rings and rings, the women heavy and elaborate necklaces of big and usually unworked semi-precious stones, often with a charm-box of fretted gold or silver inlaid with turquoise and coral suspended from them, and also occasionally brooches and bracelets; but all these jewels are bought ready-made. They are considered to enhance the beauty of the wearer; they are also a display of wealth and the only possible form of investment. Young people occasionally display a certain amount of coquetry in their dress, but the effect is usually unfortunately marred for the stranger owing to the Lepchas' habit of not washing their bodies.

iv

Nowadays new houses are built very rarely. According to Chala Mandal—the head of the village of Lingthem, and also of the smaller village of Panung to the east with ten houses, and Lik-lyang (five houses) Salim and Safo (three houses each) on the other side of the Talung river—only four new houses have been built in the present century. Ordinarily the members of a Lepcha household do not separate, but if the family gets too numerous, or if brothers, either real or classificatory, do not agree, the household will split and the land be divided and the younger brother will build a house of his own. Three of the four new houses—those of Ongden, Kurma and Nahyeun—were built for this reason. In the case of the fourth house—that of Katel—the situation was more complicated and irregular. Katel, a man from a village on the far side of Zongu, married a woman of Lingthem, an orphan who had been brought up in the Mandal's house, and took her home to his village. But

EVERYBODY HELPS WITH THE THATCHING OF PEMBU'S ROOF

Mrs. Katel[7] was both unhappy and unpopular in her husband's community, and ran away for refuge to the Mandal who had brought her up. Her husband Katel followed her, and asked the Mandal's permission to settle in Lingthem; this was given and he was provided with land on which to build a house and which he could clear for cultivation. During the period when these four houses were built an equal number fell into decay either through family lines dying out, or through households amalgamating. Thus Tobgé, a young married man, all of whose family had died, had abandoned his house to go and live with Jiroong, who was his father's youngest brother.

According to the oldest inhabitants the number of houses increased very greatly in the second half of the nineteenth century. Ninety-year-old Serving, who was almost in his dotage, said that when he was a child there were only four houses in Lingthem; and Kahlyeu, born in 1860, says that in his childhood there were about twelve households. Kahlyeu ascribes the increase to the fact that in those days families were larger and split up as the sons grew older; but it seems probable that the indirect pacification after 1860 made possible a considerable increase in the number of permanently settled inhabitants.

According to Kahlyeu—and the tradition is supported by others—until about the beginning of the seventeenth century the Lepchas were entirely nomadic, only building temporary mud huts, and travelling about the forests, living on such animals they could kill, and the wild plants, of which the Lepchas have considerable knowledge, for they know the edible (but not, as European tradition believes, the medicinal) properties of nearly every tree and plant. Iron for knives, Kahlyeu says, was introduced in the time of his father's grandfather, that is to say in the first half of the eighteenth

[7] Some objection may be taken to my referring to married women as Mrs. X. Among the Lepchas married women are never named, and there are three different methods of referring to them: mother of A, wife of B, or woman from C, that order representing the frequency of usage. Thus Mrs. Tafoor is usually called Chimpet-mu (mother of Chimpet, her eldest son), less often Tafoor-veu (wife of Tafoor), or Panung-mu (woman from Panung). 'Mother of A' seems to me unnecessarily confusing, and since, in nine cases out of ten, a married woman owes her presence in the community to the fact that she is married to her husband, I have found it most convenient consistently to refer to married women as 'wife of X', or, in the English form 'Mrs. X', since this term seems to me to approach nearest to the cultural reality.

century; about a generation later the Lepchas started living in permanent houses and were able to hold or increase their stock of domestic animals. Private property in land must have developed somewhat later; according to native tradition the land below the monastery—that is to say the more protected valley ground—has been divided into private property from time immemorial, but the higher ground was common property and was acquired and cleared as was wanted. At the time of Kahlyeu's father—that is to say about 1840—this ground too was divided up, and today all cultivatable ground is privately owned. Kahlyeu also said that until about 120 years ago only millet was cultivated, and not dry rice; but this seems to me improbable in view of the fact that the religious observances[8] are much more concerned with dry rice, than with millet or any other crop.

When new houses are made they are always built in the late autumn months, after the gathering of the harvest. This date is dictated by two reasons; at no other period would people have sufficient leisure and other dates would be ill-omened. The intending builder gathers materials for some months beforehand. The site of a new house is decided by a number of metaphysical considerations.

First of all there is a lamaist book called Sachet Zai Putta which contains general rules of a very minute nature, indicating what sites are lucky, and what unlucky. This book is said to have been composed by four Gods who gathered together at Gyakar (perhaps Benares) to compile rules so that people should know which sites are good and which bad, which fruitful and which barren, where children can be born, and where they cannot. The following is a small selection of these very detailed regulations.

'A good site is, if there is a mountain to the south and below a slope. It is good if there is a stream on either side of the slope and trees in front. It is good if there is an outcrop of rock to the east and a flat plain to the west and a water fall opposite. Roads from east and north are good, but those from south and west should be avoided as they are used by Deut *moong* (fever devil). If there is a tree to the north directly below the house it should never be cut down; if, however, there is one to the south directly above it, it should be cut, or, if it be too big to cut down, a knife or some other piece of iron should be stuck into it. If the earth on which the

[8] See Chapter Nine. It is probable that millet was historically the earlier crop: what I question is the date of the introduction of dry rice.

house is built is soft the house-mother will die. It is bad if there is not a hill between the north and the east because you will get the wind.

'*Choten* and *Mani* ('Mani walls' and prayer flags) should never be placed to the east or the inhabitants of the house will die, they should be on the north and west. It is good if the hill behind be covered with trees. It is bad to have a red cliff behind to the south; people born in the year of the Horse or the year of the Snake will be particularly troubled. (This can be averted by elaborate ceremonies.)

'It is bad if there is standing water below the house which will reflect the light; if there is, gold, silver and copper should be put in the water. It is bad if water seeps through the ground below the house, above it does not matter. It is bad if there is a cave to the north or west; for that would be the home of Mamoo *moong* (a malevolent female devil). It is bad to be below a pass between two hills, with a land slip below you, this is a devil's road. It is bad if there is a juniper tree (*sanden koong*) to the west, . . . etc.'

When an intending builder has chosen a site which fulfils these general desiderata, he has still to find out whether that site will be propitious for him personally. To do this he digs up a small piece of earth from the intended site, concentrating fixedly all the time on the question of whether the ground is good-omened or not, and takes it to a competent lama[9] who will then consult the book *Tong-yoop* and cast a horoscope to see if the site is suitable in relation to the intending builder's horoscope, reckoned by the various year-cycles.[10] If the first site chosen is not propitious others must be looked for until a suitable one is found. It consequently follows that all other considerations are secondary; it is better to be near a stream (for water for domestic use and also in case of fire) and to have suitable ground near for a field-garden, and, if possible, to be near friends and relations; but the verdict of the lamas comes first.

When the site is finally determined upon the lama carefully replaces the sample of earth, and then offers *cherkem*—that is mixed grains floating in strained *chi*—which is thrown on to the ground

[9] In Lingthem only Tafoor and the two Dorjé Lapoon knew how to cast this horoscope; the Lharibu Chujen of Panung was the only lama in the neighbourhood to possess or be able to read Sachet Zai Putta.

[10] See Chapter Seven, pp. 209–212) and Appendix III.

so as to gratify the devils which have taken up their abode in the neighbourhood so that they shall not trouble the work in progress. Then the four corner-posts and the centre post are set up, and the low stone walls, on which the house will rest, are built. The building should always start from the east. After the pillars and stone walls have been set up straight by an overseer the building proceeds without direction, the walls, flooring, ceiling, rafters and finally the thatch being built. When people know that a house is being built or repaired they come to help spontaneously; they are given no pay or wages of any sort except a meal at the end of the day; but they know that they in their turn will receive help when they need it. Men, women and children all lend a hand at the various tasks; but women are considered incapable of handling the biggest pieces of timber.

Some time after its completion the house must be consecrated by lamas and Mun with the ceremony of *Tashi chéné*; ideally this should be performed as soon as the house is completed and repeated twice in subsequent years; but it is often not done immediately for the owner may not possess the ox and other necessary materials. When the first meal is eaten in the completed house some old and experienced man (not the house-owner himself, but it does not matter who else) must make a small hole in the roof immediately above the fireplace and throw out a live ember and some water; this is done so that the smoke may go out properly and not fill the house.

The ceremony of *Tashi chéné* is as follows. First of all incense leaves are burned to pacify the demons who live in the earth below the house and who may have inhabited the trees of which the house is built. Then a live ox is dedicated by a Mun to all the gods, slaughtered and cut up; the head, right foreleg and left hind-leg (these portions are called *ga-zook*) are given to the carpenters who have worked on the house as their fee. After this a lamaist ceremony, with music and readings from the appropriate books, is performed, at the end of which the chief lama present (if possible one of the Dorjé Lapoon)[11] will anoint the house-pillars with blood, *chi*, liquor and butter, starting with the western pillar and proceeding to

[11] Dorjé Lapoon is the title given to the oldest, wisest, and most revered lamas; it is not strictly translatable: dorjé is the sacred 'thunderbolt' which is part of the lama's sacred paraphernalia; lapoon means teacher. In works dealing with Tibet the title is usually translated as 'abbot', but this term seems to me inappropriate for non-resident dignitaries.

the northern, eastern, southern and central. After the anointings the pillars are stamped with a large cone made out of ground rice, called *Gett'r tho-mu.* Finally all present throw rice mixed with flour at the pillars, shouting in as loud a voice as possible *Ta-shi shu.* This ceremony is meant to avert illness from the inhabitants of the house.

Tashi chéné is occasionally performed after major repairs. Thus while we were there Katel had the ceremony performed after a new floor had been put into his house (but he had omitted to have the ceremony done when the house was first built); and Jiroong, whose house had been gutted by fire, intended to perform the ceremony when he should have completed his repairs.

Minor repairs and alterations can be performed at any convenient time, and without any ceremony. The most frequent of such repairs is re-thatching, which needs doing at least once every seven years. The reeds used for thatching are collected about three months beforehand, bent while still green, and left to dry. The necessary bamboo supports are also collected and cut to the required length and creepers whose bark will be used for fastening the bamboos are fetched from the forest. (It is technically an offence to take these creepers without paying for them; and when Pembu's roof was being re-thatched the old man who was stripping the creepers sat isolated from the other workers so that they should not be cognisant of the crime being committed. The gesture was entirely symbolical, for the old man had chosen as a hiding place a piece of ground on the side of the main path leading to the house, so that he was the first thing seen by most people arriving to work.) When all the material has been collected the house-owner decides on a day for the re-thatching and informs all his friends and neighbours.

First of all the thatch and rotten bamboo are stripped off three sides of the house and burnt; the thatch on the east side is left till the rest is completed to serve as a shelter in case of rain. Then the bamboo cross-pieces are lashed into position and the reeds slung across them; the distance of the cross-pieces is so calculated that there is a triple layer of thatch. Finally the thatch may be kept in place by bamboos fastened above it, but this is not done in all houses.

For such a piece of work as this helpers arrive all through the day and set about doing whatever job they consider necessary at the moment, without consultation or instruction, and often without much relation to what the other workers are doing. Men, women and children all work together, and the task proceeds in a rather haphazard fashion, to the accompaniment of a constant fire of jokes, most of them obscene. When the work is finished all those who have helped are given a feast.

Attached to some households and fields is an ambivalent supernatural called *Thyak-dum* (white head). If this supernatural is good-tempered and contented he will bring health and prosperity to the home, and possibly, though people are not so sure about this, punish marauders in the family's fields; if he is angry he will bring disease and loss to the people who neglect him. Consequently when people live in a new house they must find out if *Thyak-dum* lives there, and if so, if they can control him. His whereabouts are discovered by a Mun going into meditation and seeing his presence mystically. If the house-owners can control *Thyak-dum* they will burn butter and incense leaves on some embers, and then sprinkle these embers with water and tell the supernatural to go away. If this fails they will make the *lafét* sacrifice (this sacrifice recurs constantly in the ceremonies of the Mun). On a wicker winnowing tray are placed banana leaves, and on top of them three rows of ground corn, and pieces of ginger, wild bird and dried fish; this offering is dedicated by a Mun who also offers *chi* in a cup ceremonially buttered; after which the sacrifice is taken to the top of some high place and left there, uneaten.

In some houses however it is divined that though *Thyak-dum* is present the house-owner cannot control him. In such cases a little house has to be built for him, standing in the fields near the house. This 'devil's house' consists of a miniature Lepcha house about two feet wide, thatched and made of bamboo, raised about four feet off the ground on four bamboos. Nobody except the sacrificer (preferably a Mun, but any man who knows how and is not a lama will do) must touch, or even go too near this 'devil's house'; were anyone to do so they would become seriously ill. Twice a year, when the barley and when the rice is ripe, sacrifices must be placed inside this devil's house; the sacrifice consists of the fresh grain, together with meat, fish and silver money. When the new sacrifice is made the old one is removed and thrown away; the money however can be taken back into use. Besides these sacrifices a special pig must be kept penned for *Thyak-dum*; this pig is always called the pig of *Thyak-dum*. When it gets old it must be replaced by a young piglet; the old one is killed, and its cooked intestines—the heart, liver and lungs, the *shafot*—are cooked with rice and offered to *Thyak-dum* together with three *patyoot* of fresh *chi*. *Thyak-dum* is partially attached to the house, and partially to the inhabitants thereof; that is to say that people coming into a new house would have to exorcise him were they able to do so; but if the old inhabitants had moved to another dwelling *Thyak-dum* would accompany them, spending most of his time with them, but occasionally returning to his and their old home. This last point is almost purely theoretical, for it very very seldom happens that Lepchas change their homes. If a house proved consistently unlucky, with many people dying and nothing prospering, and if it were divined that the house was the cause of these disasters, the survivors might move; but although some houses in Lingthem had had far more than their share of death and misfortune the inhabitants still stayed in them. The only reason for which houses were actually abandoned was loneliness, because the few survivors preferred to live with relations rather than cope with the work alone.

V

In front of each Lepcha house is a field fenced in with bamboo; it is called the garden (*sing*), and in it are raised those vegetables and roots which are used for flavouring food. These however are only grown in small quantities on the edge, and the greater part of the field is sown with grain crops; first of all barley and spring wheat mixed, which ripens in April, and subsequently maize. This garden is the only portion of Lepcha land which receives animal manure; it is against the house, under which domestic animals shelter at night; their dung is collected and thrown over the fence. At the bottom of nearly every garden is a plantation of bamboos, cultivated so as to have an easily available supply of this invaluable material. Near the house too are usually a small number of fruit trees—oranges, peaches, apples, pears, plums, tree-tomatoes—and occasionally one or two shrubs, usually roses, are grown for their flowers.

The rest of the land of the household is scattered all over the surrounding district, and it is seldom that people own the land near their house. All possess some strips of land—often more than a dozen for a single household—on the warmer lower slopes of the valley, where the climate is suitable for the cultivation of wet rice, cardamum, and some of the earlier millets or eleusines.

The big fields, which are cleared by burning once every eight years, where the main crops of dry rice, buckwheat and millet are raised, are mostly above the level of the houses; so that it is by no means unusual for people to have fields three or more miles away from their houses, and three thousand feet higher up or lower down the mountain side. Consequently field-houses are built for those periods when there is heavy work to be done in the fields—either weeding, or chasing away predatory birds and beasts from the ripening crops, or harvesting. In the permanent cultivations down in the valley these field-houses are solidly built structures, consisting only of a single room but otherwise in all respects similar to the ordinary Lepcha house. In some cases they are permanently inhabited by one or two members of a household either for reasons of health or because they do not agree too well with the other members. These field-houses however are built at any time without any ceremony for the selection of the site or at any time in the course of construction; and they are not included in the house-tax. The field-houses in the temporary cultivations are very flimsy affairs chiefly made out of matting.

The extremely precipitous nature of the ground renders travelling extremely difficult for Europeans who are accustomed to levelled paths and who walk shod. The Lepchas, owing to long habit, are magnificent walkers and climbers, and can cover enormous distances without apparent fatigue or breathlessness. I found the descent to the river which I made one day to witness the repairing of the bamboo bridge—a descent of about three thousand feet in a mile and a half—and the return therefrom, almost exhausting; the Lepchas will make the same journey without discomfort two or three times a day. Their physical strength and agility is amazing; over paths, or rather tracks, where experienced mountaineers need to use both hands, the Lepchas will carry heavy loads on their backs. Indeed one day Chala Mandal, the head of the village, after he had been recounting semi-legendary, semi-historical stories of the past exploits of the Lepchas, said with a deprecating smile 'Nowadays all the Lepchas are good for is carrying loads.'

vi

Writers about Sikkim and Tibet who incidentally mention the Lepchas refer to them with surprising unanimity as 'animists'; and the references to devils' habitations in the desiderata for a house-

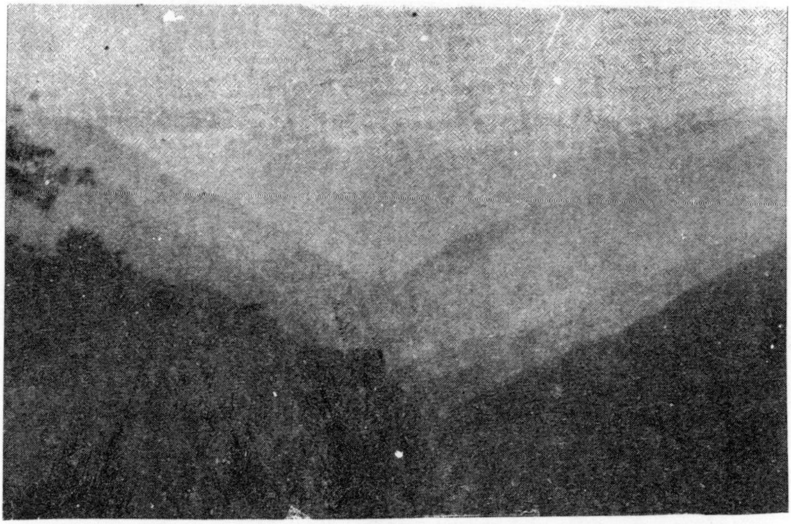

Above : TALUNG VALLEY LOOKING TOWARDS KINCHENJUNGA

Below : TALUNG VALLEY LOOKING EASTWARDS TOWARDS TIBET

site given above might suggest that such a term was justified. To my mind however such a conclusion would be completely erroneous, if animism is understood to mean the worship or reverence of natural objects for the forces implicit in them. The very complicated beliefs of the Lepchas' two (I should perhaps write three) religions will be dealt with fully later, but the religious attitude towards natural objects can be briefly summarised. All supernaturals, good and bad, though eternally living outside the world, have innumerable manifestations with which this world is filled. These manifestations, or replicas, of the supernaturals, choose various natural phenomena for semi-permanent habitation, agreeable phenomena—lakes, or fruit-trees or fruitful land—if the supernaturals are generally benevolent; disagreeable places—useless trees, water-falls, rocks or barren ground—if the supernaturals are generally malevolent. Each type of supernatural has a preference for a particular kind of habitation; thus all the deut *moong*—fever devils—live in big isolated trees, sabdok *moong*—skin-disease devils—in outcrops of rock.

According to lamaist beliefs everything in the world (with the exception of the earth itself and some big mountains) possesses a soul; for the soul is the animating principle of all life, without whose intermediary nothing could move or grow. But the souls of objects and animals below the vertebrates are very weak and transient things; they are easily killed and never reincarnate. For the lamaists the soul is the verbal equivalent of life; and the 'soul' of a rock or tree is only the essential quality of the rock or tree with no powers beyond making the rock hold together or the tree grow in due season. The soul of a rock or tree or river is not altered if a supernatural takes up his abode therein.

The word with which Lepchas invariably refer to the habitations of supernaturals is *li*, the word which they use for their own houses. The houses of supernaturals—particularly malevolent supernaturals—are avoided, because the devil might be annoyed at the intrusion on his privacy and would show his resentment by inflicting illness on the intruders. Similarly the supernatural would resent any injury done to his house, such as cutting down his tree or chipping off parts of his stone, and would punish the rash man by paining him in that portion of his body which corresponded to that portion of the house which had been destroyed; thus cutting from the top of a tree or a rock would result in head pains, from a branch or an outcrop in arm ache, and so on. Consequently the recognised habitations of devils are paid the respect of avoidance; and should a man be forced to go near to one of an evening he would perhaps burn a little incense—either juniper leaves or rice mixed with butter—so that the devil shall be gratified and not pursue him.

Except for being avoided and pointed out as local curiosities these devils' habitations are not distinguished in any way. Sacrifices are generally not made to or near them; if it were divined that illness was caused by a manifestation of a devil whose exact habitation was known, offerings might be made at that place; but I neither came across nor heard of one specific instance of this. All the numerous ceremonies that I witnessed and heard about took place in or just outside the house of the actual or potential sufferer; and though the offerings were often carried away after, they were never taken to the devil's habitation, but either to uncultivated ground, or to a place where two paths crossed. Only in one case did I hear of a devil's habitation being paid attention to. In the 'garden' of Jiroong are two outcrops of rock, which are the homes of Sabdok *moong* and his wife Loo *moong*. This female devil causes a specific skin disease, and if a person living in the neighbourhood should suffer from this, her stone (the lower of the two) will be anointed with holy water by a lama, and with milk by a Mun. It had been discovered by divination that this was the only home of Loo *moong* in the immediate neighbourhood, and the somewhat rare skin-disease, which is her speciality, could only arise from the anger of that particular manifestation.

The three big stones called *Kali lyang* in different parts of Lingthem fall into a different category. They are the places where laymen make sacrifices to keep away predatory animals. These sacrifices of different sorts of food are made once in the hot weather and once in the cold, and at other times if predatory animals are causing anxiety or annoyance. The stones themselves have no supernatural value at all; they are just the places where the sacrifices are always made.

There is however one big exception to the general rule. Nearly every family line—*ptso*—originated from the union of a particular lake and a particular mountain, the lake being the mother.[12] To these maternal lakes either annual or triennial (depending on the customs of the *ptso* in question) offerings must be made by all the descendants, or the inhabiting supernatural will withdraw her

[12] The Salong *ptso*, to which the serpent eaters of Pantoong belonged, is peculiar in tracing its original ancestor to the union of a woman with a monkey.

favour and the people will not prosper and may suffer from sore eyes. It is not necessary that everyone should visit the lake in person; gifts can be given by proxy by another member of the same *ptso*.

There is another lake, *Luksom partam*, high up in Zongu, from whence birth is meant to have originated. Sterile couples who wish for children should visit this lake, spend the night on its bank copulating, and then in the morning throw into the waters a silver rupee and a *chimi* (altar light) to please the gods. If necessary this may be repeated annually for three years. The old widow, a nun, who told me about this had performed the complete rite with her husband, but unsuccessfully.

The connection between water and birth runs all through the Mun mythology. In the divine world where the two gods Tak-bo-*thing* and Narzong-*nyou* live there is a stream called Lungfung which represents the birth of male children, and a well called Rung-zel *oong-lap* which represents the birth of female children. This well is guarded by a supernatural boy called Sathim *ong*, and on occasion a family which has many girls and no boys will get a Mun to make sacrifices to the boy and the two gods to make the two pieces of water change place.

It will be noted that even in the case of these sacred lakes an explicit distinction is made between the lakes themselves and the supernaturals who inhabit them.

Devils have been occasionally seen by some people, sometimes looking like fierce animals, sometimes more or less like human beings (though generally covered with hair), sometimes as misty and gigantic shapes. They are far more frequently heard, whistling and crying, sometimes wailing like a banshee; and the god of hunters, Pong *rum*, persecutes those who displease him with poltergeist-like performances, throwing stones at the people or their houses and so on. To see or hear a devil is alarming, but not excessively so; there is nothing to be done except to run away or to turn aside one's eyes; though some bold people throw stones at devils and shoo them away as though they were marauding dogs. In the case of poltergeist performances the sufferer will burn incense, or perhaps just smoke a cigarette at the devil. To guard against the accidental meeting of devils the lamas prepare amulets, composed of charms written on paper and sewn into a piece of cloth which is worn on the dress; and Mun give the specially prepared roots of *s'lek* (a dioeceous plant which grows above the snow level) to be rubbed over the body. Some men also carry a little arrow poison in a bag fastened inside their clothes over the heart. The greater number of people however do not take any of these precautions.

For the Lepchas devils are rather similar to the witches in European folklore; they are malevolent but not necessarily particularly intelligent; and there are numerous stories of devils being fooled by fairly simple devices, just as the witch was fooled in the story of *Hansel and Gretel.* There is no belief at all in ghosts or *revenants*; should the simulacrum of a dead person be seen it would be a devil in disguise. But although many people told me of having heard or seen devils, I did not hear a single story of any one seeing the dead or absent.

vii

This then is the landscape in which the rest of the book is set. To the south the hills rise steeply to an invisible crest; to the north the ground descends precipitously to the hidden Talung river, and then rises opposite even more steeply; behind the fairly barren hills are the peaks of Siniolchi and its eastern neighbours, jagged black rock topped with gleaming snow. At the western end of the Talung valley rises the stupendous mass of Kinchenjunga and its neighbouring peaks, Gods and the home of Gods. To the east are the green hills of Sikkim, and beyond the ragged snow-mountains which mark the frontier of Tibet.

For the European the landscape is one of overwhelming beauty, spoilt only by the very considerable difficulty of travelling about, so rocky and precipitous is the land. The picture I should like to convey is of a very steep and broken series of hillsides, except in small clefts nearly bare of big trees, but almost entirely covered with low growths of shrubs and saplings of various tints of green, flecked with patches of colour at some seasons; the yellow sweet-smelling daphne *edgeworthiana*, the blue hydrangea-like flower of *dichroa febrifuga*, the rich purple of the Sikkim rose. Here and there, scattered over the hillsides, are pieces of cleared and burned land, with the larger tree-trunks standing up lopped and charred; pieces of land placed in seemingly quite arbitrary positions, with large stretches of green between them. Down in the valley the ground appears slightly more cultivated; there are roughly terraced fields fenced with bamboo hurdles, and occasional small rectangles of a deeper yellow-green where the cardamum grows. Scattered here and there among the prevailing greens may be seen the glow of a fruit-tree in flower, and nearby the low thatched roof of a house, barely distinguishable until you are close upon it. The paths are the faintest tracks, invisible until you come upon them; there is no main road, nothing to guide your way; except that there are usually more stones—for the bigger stones will have been removed from the neighbouring fields and piled on the path to make drier walking in the wet weather—there is little to indicate what is path and what merely rough ground. Overtowering and dwarfing all the works of man are the enormous ramparts of the gleaming snows, cutting short a quarter of the horizon in almost every direction. You can see that the land is in part cultivated and inhabited, but the part seems insignificant; in the battle between man and nature, nature seems everywhere the winner.

That is the landscape for the European; for the Lepcha not a single feature is the same. Except when they refer to them as the habitations of the high Gods, the Lepchas do not remember the mountains; they do not lift up their eyes, they look down on the ground. Every piece of land is meaningful for them, for every piece, unless it be the home of a supernatural, is, has been, or will be cultivated. They think and speak of their country as a poor country, demanding disproportionate labour for the food they require for themselves and their families. For them the land is not a friend; it is a material; and when they look at it they see therein the work and sweat they have fed it with all their lives. Every piece of land, every step they take, reminds them of the past and the present, of their own work and struggles, and those of their neighbours; the houses and fences they have helped to build, the land they have helped to clear and weed and harvest, the places where they have played as children, or, later, met for amorous encounter. They see too the cliffs and rocks and lonely trees where dwell the devils who menace and destroy their otherwise peaceful and happy existence; these visible signs remind them of those evil forces—disease and death, blight and famine, childlessness and enmity and quarrelling—that mar a life which, though hard enough, would otherwise be easy and friendly, full of health and happiness. The Lepchas do not see the landscape; they see the records of their lives, and of the lives of their ancestors, and of the lives to come of their children.

CHAPTER THREE

GETTING FOOD

i

For the Lepchas, as for almost all primitive peoples, by far the most important subject in their lives is food. Far and away the greatest part of their lives is centred round food-getting; it is impossible to over-stress its importance. But because food-getting is so constant a preoccupation, and because it is fairly featureless and uneventful, it nearly always, it seems to me, receives far less attention than it deserves. The features chiefly dealt with by ethnologists, including of course the greater part of this book, are those which take place during the primitive's leisure. Some peoples, I am aware, centre their social and religious life about food; but this is not the case with the Lepchas. Food-products play a considerable rôle in the objects of sacrifice, but with the lamas this aspect is not stressed; most ceremonial objects are made out of grain-flour and butter, but this is because they are the most convenient and easily accessible materials; by the time they have been fashioned the edible qualities of these objects are not apparent. A minor sacrifice is made when a new field is taken into cultivation for the first time, and prayers are said, usually by a layman, after each sowing; and the Mun make elaborate ceremonies, to be described later, yearly at the flowering of the cardamum, and at the sowing and gathering of dry rice. In the annual cycle of lamaist ceremonies there are a certain number which are devoted to the protection of crops from hail and predatory beasts, and, before the sowing starts, some seed is collected from each household and given a communal blessing at a monastery service; but these rites take an insignificant place in the yearly sum of religious ceremonies. Lepcha religion is above all occupied with health.

Food does however play a very important rôle in the Lepchas' emotional lives. Love, whether between spouses, friends, or parents and children, is considered to be the result of mutual benefits, and foremost among these mutual benefits is the gathering and preparation of food. For Lepchas love is never automatic; if they say they love a person they will always explain why they do so. Even with young children this attitude is firmly implanted; if you ask one if he loves his parents he will almost certainly reply 'I love my father and mother because they give me my food.' If you ask about their feelings towards other people they have visited the answer again is always in terms of what they were given to eat. Rigya, a young man of twenty-two, said of his parents 'I love them both very much, but especially my mother; when I was young they gave me food and clothes and looked after me; now in my turn I must look after them.' He has been fairly recently married and at first he and his wife did not get on at all well together: 'At first we could not even look at one another, but now we are good friends; when I go out to work and come back tired my wife has food ready for me and looks after me; then I love her and think to myself "this is my wife", and I am pleased in my belly.' It may be noted that the bellv is considered to be the seat of the emotions.

All ceremonial occasions among the Lepchas—birth, marriage, and death, religious ceremonies, exorcisms, and civil consultations—are marked by the consumption of extra large quantities of food and drink. Even the most solemn religious ceremonies are turned into picnics. Important past events are often remembered in terms of what the participants had to eat on such occasions. When I tried to get some of the best-adjusted Lepchas to talk about their own early lives they replied by giving me lists of menus.

The Lepchas are practically omnivorous; the only animals that they do not eat which some other races do are cats and dogs, rats and mice, horses and snakes. They eat all wild animals that they can kill or find dead, and keep and eat oxen, goats, pigs and hens; they also eat a great variety of wild forest produce, chiefly tubers of different wild yams, and various leaves which are used as seasoning; both meat and vegetables are supplementary dishes which add a relish to the cultivated cereals.

As has already been said, in former times and still today in the less fertile regions, the Lepchas relied on hunting for a great deal of their food; but in Lingthem and most of the other villages of Zongu game is hunted less and less. There are a number of reasons for this which interact on one another; the stigma which the Lepcha interpretation of lamaism places on the killing of animals excludes some of the community entirely from this pursuit, and even those who are not lamas feel a certain disclination to killing animals. The settled houses and the greater amount of ground under cultivation and increasing domestic herds make the necessity for wild animals less urgent, and the growing commitments of agricultural life give less time for hunting. Indeed nowadays if a young man wants to go hunting (and some of the more adventurous ones do) he usually has to sneak away when his elders are not looking, and is liable to get a good scolding when he does return for withdrawing his labour from the fields; of course if the father is a hunter the son would be encouraged, but in Lingthem the only consistent hunter was Ashyok *youmi*, the most conservative man of the village who still wore the Lepcha dress and the little straw hat with a feather in it, which was once the typical Lepcha headgear, and now practically only survives as an archaic and picturesque article of dress among the servants of the Maharajah. Moreover the presence in the neighbourhood of shops where grain can be bought considerably mitigates the stress of the hungry season just before the harvest, when formerly people used to be driven into the forest for food.

When a youth, usually about the age of fifteen, wants to start hunting, it is necessary for him to acquire a bow and arrows and also to learn the requisite ritual. In most cases he cannot get either the weapons or the instruction from his father, who would be angry at the boy withdrawing his labour from the fields; the weapons he will most probably get from an elder brother or uncle or a friend, the instruction from some learned old man, probably quite unrelated. The first few times he will go on a hunting-party without weapons, but from the moment he has been on one even though he has not killed he must make the requisite sacrifices. No ceremony is connected with his first kill but he himself must not eat a piece of this kill, nor of the first hundred animals he kills with his bow (animals killed with a gun do not count; they can always be eaten). Were he to eat the first hundred animals he would develop sores and leprosy; but after he has killed this number a hollow will develop in his shoulder blade and after that he can eat with safety. The earlier animals he takes home to his family who eat them, giving him some domestic food instead. The commonest game animals are various sorts of deer; when bears are trapped their flesh is eaten, but they are seldom caught nowadays; one reason is that sexual abstinence for three months after setting a trap is imposed on bear hunters (there is no similar abstinence for the hunting of any other animal); if this rule is not observed the bears will escape from their trap unharmed. Bear skins and also their gall bladders which are much sought after by the Chinese as aphrodisiacs (they fetch Rs. 5 apiece in Kalimpong) were an inducement to catch these animals when money was not plentiful or non-existent; nowadays with money from cardamum there is less economic justification for taking the risks involved. Catching small birds in snares does not count as hunting; it is one of the commonest pursuits of boys after the age of about eight, who take their catches home as presents for their mother.

ii

The agricultural land in Zongu can be divided into two categories: the land under permanent cultivation, and the land which is cleared for crops once in every eight years. The permanent cultivation is of three types; there is the *sing* or field-garden against the house, cardamum fields and rice terraces. The two latter types of cultivation, which are now of very great importance in Lepcha life, are both very modern: cardamum was introduced at the beginning of the century, rice terraces for wet paddy less than twenty years ago. Potentially this permanent cultivation has introduced a new note into Lepcha life, though so far the effect is not noticeable. Both cardamum fields and rice terraces demand a certain amount of hard initial labour, after which they acquire, as it were, a capital value; this is less true of cardamum, which needs replanting every ten years, than of the rice terraces; to build these a considerable amount of work is needed, but once they are made a heavy crop can be raised from them with relatively little labour.

Until the beginning of this century the wealth of a Lepcha household depended on the energy of its members and on the proportion of able-bodied adults to dependants—children and the old and invalid—; if there was more than one dependent to one able-bodied adult life was liable to be rather hard. Nowadays it is theoretically possible that a lazy heir of industrious ancestors might be in a better position in the community than his own industry warranted. Formerly the inevitable rule of Lepcha economy was 'from each according to his ability; to each according to his work', tempered by the co-operation and willing help which was and is freely given to those afflicted by temporary or permanent misfortune. Today this is not quite so true; the creation of permanent fields requires the renunciation of immediate good for future benefits, for the household which builds these fields will not be able to get as large a harvest as would otherwise be possible. The consequence is that the difference between the richest and the poorest in the community has somewhat increased, and that households which have a proportionately larger number of working adults to dependents are in a temporarily favoured position. So of course is the Mandal,[1] who can use the free labour to which he is entitled to have terraces made for him.

Up to the present as far as I can tell this new state of affairs has made no important difference to the Lepcha community; their habits of co-operation nullify the differences in wealth. One man even went so far as to say that he would not like to be the richest person in the community, unless everybody else was equally prosperous, as he would have to give all his superfluity to help others. Extra wealth carries with it extra duties; and in point of fact the richest people in Lingthem were also the most heavily indebted. At the same time it must be emphasised that it is the desire of every Lepcha to be rich; when I asked children what they would most like to be, a clever man, or a learned and respected lama, or a great hunter, or a rich man, they would one and all plump for being rich. Chimpet, the son of Tafoor, a member of the most devout lamaist family in Lingthem, and who was himself starting his religious instruction said 'I should like to go and study religion in a Tibetan monastery, but I don't want to go to the State school at Gangtok; the things they teach you there are quite useless, while a lama always gets good presents and feasts. Why, when a rich man dies even the *kané*, the accolyte attending the officiating lama, is given a fine plate and cup and clothes!'[2]

Unless the whole orientation of Lepcha life is changed even greater differences in actual wealth will not fundamentally alter the situation, for there is no possibility of any Lepcha, however rich, exploiting his neighbour, however poor. Help in the work of house or field is always repaid by equivalent help; the most

[1] See Chapter Five, p. 128.

[2] Chimpet's view of the value of secular education is not shared by his father or the other more serious adult members of the community. They have petitioned the State to establish a boarding school in Zongu, for they consider that the extra work entailed by the older children's absence would be counterbalanced by the value of the education received.

feckless or unlucky who have not the ground to use the help which is their due are given grain for their labour. Only with cardamum, which is a money-producing, and not a food-producing crop, is help paid for with money. The care of orphans, cripples, idiots and other helpless people in exchange for the labour they can give cannot be considered as exploitation.

Although riches and prosperity are so desirable they are fraught with supernatural dangers; there is a devil called Ginoo *moong* which attacks the over-prosperous; it is in a way Nemesis, and in a way the incarnation of other people's envious thoughts. The origin of Ginoo *moong* is told in the following story:

'Once upon a time there was a family called Ginoo, which consisted of seven brothers and one sister. The seven brothers had a house in Lingthem up above the monastery; they had seven wives and seven sons and seven daughters and seven sons-in-law and seven daughters-in-law; they were so numerous that they could do all the field-work between here and Mangan in one day and would eat between them a whole goat at one meal. However these people had no oxen, no jewels, and no permanent cultivation.[3] When they went out to work two people had to stop at home to do the cooking and one to gather leaves for the fire. Their sister lived lower in the valley; she was a widow and had a single daughter, but she had sixty heads of oxen and many necklaces and jewels, so heavy that they weighed six seers. This woman was a Mun; she lived in the house, while her daughter slept in a shed.

'Now the brothers grumbled and spoke among themselves saying "We have nothing, no jewels and no cattle, and we could use them; our sister is a widow and excessively rich; if we were to kill her we should possess all her wealth." So they made a plan and they went up to her house at dead of night and cut her to pieces with their knives and crept back unobserved. When this occurred the daughter who was sleeping in the shed woke up with a start thinking "What is the matter with my mother?" And she was frightened and ran to her mother's house. When she arrived there she found the verandah spattered with blood, and inside her mother sat trembling. The brothers had hacked her body to pieces but she was a very powerful Mun and all the pieces had joined together. The mother said to her daughter "Why have you come? Your maternal uncles have killed me. Now you are here go and gathe

[3] It is interesting to note the manner in which these very recent signs of wealth have been incorporated into the old story.

the tips of the *shang-no* tree, but of that tree only." The daughter went and gathered the twigs and put them into her mother's lap. Then the mother said " If I can cover the sun with these twigs I can go all over the world. Watch what I do." Then she went out on to the verandah and threw up the twigs, so that the sun was covered and she would be able to go all over the world. Then she returned to the house and said to her daughter " You had better go soon, for your maternal uncles will be coming to look for my body. They will take away three bags of jewels and only leave you three tiny necklaces; but wear those and look after them. They will take all the cattle and only leave you one baby calf; look after that. Do not be sad, for in seven days a man will come and marry you, and your children will be *Jem-mi* (that is Mandal) of this place. Now go away." The daughter did as she was told.

'When morning broke the brothers came to fetch the corpse, but they could see nothing; only there was a trail of blood leading to a lake situated above a big tree, and behind that a cliff with a door in it. The mother entered that cliff and there she *munthen* (performed the religious contemplation of the Mun) for seven days.

'Meanwhile the brothers had divided the property just as had been prophesied; and the girl stayed with her calf and her three small necklaces in the shed; and in seven days a hunter arrived and lived with her and married her. This hunter was named Tsel-telim, and from him the Tsel-telim *ptso* sprang.[4]

'For seven days the mother *munthen* and at last she summoned the devils from their home; she vowed vengeance on all who had great wealth or many children and she sent out the devils. These devils are called Ginoo *moong pan-di* (' Queen devil Ginoo ') after the name of the murderers, and Lingthem *anyou* (' Lady Lingthem ') after the place of the murder.

'Within one year all the huge family had died and the door of their house was closed. Lower down in the valley was another family which had ten married sons and ten married daughters. These too Ginoo *moong* attacked and killed, all except two women called Safi and Sakyon who were weeding the distant fields. But as they were weeding they heard a voice saying " I want Safi." " I want Sakyon." The next morning when they woke up in the field house they both had elephantiasis and quickly died.

[4] See Chapter Five, p. 127. Serving is the last survivor of this *ptso* in the neighbourhood.

'From that time Ginoo *moong pandi* and Linthem *anyou* destroy all those who are too prosperous or have too many children. That is the reason why you should never remark on a person's prosperity; for if Ginoo *moong* hears you they will lose everything.'

Ginoo *moong* still claims victims today. One of the latest was the wife of Ongden, one of the richest members of the community, unique in having six healthy sons. She was always grumbling, saying how poor she was and how little ground they had been able to sow; to which the neighbours would reply 'How greedy you are; you are really very prosperous.' Ginoo *moong* heard this talk, and so she died, while still young. It is also perhaps the fear of Ginoo *moong* which makes Lepchas so reluctant to say what their property is; it was practically the only subject on which people were secretive and unwilling to talk; most of the information I obtained on the subject I got from neighbours. The majority of the households are all on nearly the same economic level; four or five are somewhat above, and three below the average.

iii

The chief crops raised by the Lepchas on the Talung side of Zongu are wet rice, dry rice, buckwheat, maize, cardamum, and different varieties of millet or eleusine. On the warmer Teesta side a certain amount of sugar cane and manioc is also raised. The wet rice is naturally exclusively cultivated on the terraced fields, which are capable of being flooded. Seven different types of wet rice are recognised—two of them being suitable for cultivation on the higher terraces, while the other five need the warmer climate of the valley. Some of the richer people grow these five varieties in rotation, as this is believed to rest the soil, the variety sown depending on individual choice; in these cases the seed is not saved, but is bought each year, generally from Gangtok. The majority however only grow one variety and save their own seed.

In Lingthem wet rice has been introduced for less than twenty years, and in other villages even more recently; some places, especially on the far side of the Talung, where the natural water is less plentiful, do not grow it yet. When the Mandal first learned about this crop he had experimental terraces made for three years; it was then gradually adopted by the other villagers, as they became convinced of the superior yield of this crop, and the amount of terraced ground is increased annually. Almost every household has at least a couple of terraces and some considerably more. These terraces are scattered all over the valley, and it is rare for two contiguous strips to belong to the same owner. It is theoretically permissible to exchange plots so that they shall be better grouped, but nobody considers doing so.

The rice terraces are turned with a rough single-pointed wooden plough drawn by a pair of oxen, as is the *sing* or field-garden near the house. Except on these artificially levelled places the ground is too precipitous for the use of a plough to be possible. Two main crops are raised in the field-garden annually; first a mixture of barley and wheat, and subsequently maize. These grains are chiefly raised as stop-gap crops, and for fermenting; maize is thought little of, and to eat much of it is the surest sign of poverty. A number of fruits and vegetables are also raised on the edge of the field-garden to give a variety of flavourings to the main rice dish; the greater number of these are importations from India, such as various varieties of pulse, tomatoes and chilli; some of them however are wild plants found locally and domesticated; such are various lavatera, arums and alliums. The collection of some of these wild plants have some ritual attached to them; the allium *safyou* for example, which is only found in one place, must be dug up with sharpened sticks; if knives are used the supernatural Jamfi *moong* will be angry and throw sticks at the collectors and cause hail and thunder. Even more unpleasant is the mountain plant *chok-li bi* (probably a sort of rhubarb) which is said to be delicious; however you gather that plant hail will fall as the stems are picked.

Cardamum is grown in small clearings all over the lower slopes of the valley. It is a perennial plant propagated by cuttings which are taken in the early spring; the plant reaches its full bearing period within three years; at the end of ten years it starts to decline and new plantings have to be made; this can however be done on the same ground as the plant does not exhaust the soil. The plants need a good deal of care, and have to be hand-weeded at least three times a year, for the buds and fruit form close to the ground. When the fruit is gathered the old growth is cut down and burned. Cardamum plants are a favourite hiding-place for snakes. For the Lepchas cardamum is a foreign importation from Nepal; they always refer to it by its Nepali name—*elaiji*—and with the cultivation of the plant has come a whole complex of alien beliefs and ritual. Nothing is done when the cardamum is planted, but every year at the flowering time a sacrifice is performed in honour of the supernatural Elaiji-*nyou*, whom the Lepchas equate with Maknyam *moong*, the devil of death. When they first planted cardamum they did no ceremonies, but they got ill; then a Lepcha from outside Zongu learned the proper ritual from a Nepali Jhankri (these priests are somewhat similar to the Mun) and taught it to the Lepchas of Zongu. The rather elaborate ritual has two surprising features; it is only permitted for male Mun to officiate, and the chickens, one of which is given by each household, are hung by their feet while still living during the ceremony and only afterwards killed by a small boy who hits them on the head. Both of these features are unusual in Lepcha ritual; only for the sacrifices to *Thyak-dum* and in the hunting ritual, and a couple of new exorcisms divined in the last ten years are women Mun excluded; and in no other sacrifice at all that I know of are the sacrificial animals ill-treated or made uncomfortable before they are killed. It was also from this foreign source that the Lepchas learned that the presence of menstruating women would blight the plant in flower; this is a completely alien idea, for otherwise menstruating women are paid no attention to. The Lepchas have modified this notion by saying that the plant dislikes any strong smell; soap or excreta would have just the same effect; they will not accept the prevalent Hindu idea of women being essentially unclean.

The main crops of dry rice, millet and buckwheat are grown in the temporary fields. These consist of clearings made in the forest, or rather secondary growth, for one year, and then allowed to lie fallow for seven years before being cultivated again. Nowadays all suitable land is divided up into private holdings, the landmarks consisting of big trees or streams or stones set up at irregular intervals. On the whole these clearings are not isolated; three or more households have all their portions next to one another and travel round together every year. Related households do not usually have adjacent grounds; when the land was originally distributed care was taken, it would seem, that nobody should be especially favoured; and since then the hazards of death and inheritance and split families have assigned the present neighbours.

The clearing of the land is started in the early spring; the women cut down the lower growths with their sickles, while the men climb and lop the bigger trees and saplings. Until recently the trees used to be cut down if possible, but now there is a Court order forbidding the destruction of trees. When all the debris has been collected the straight sticks are sorted out and the rest is put into heaps and set fire to, the ashes acting as a loosener and fertiliser of the soil. After burning, the ground is cleared of charred wood and the remaining weeds by hand and is then sown with the main crop. This is done in the simplest manner possible; holes are made in the ground with a pointed stick and the seed dropped into and round them.

The principal crops of these temporary fields are dry rice and millet. Twelve varieties of dry rice are named and recognised by small differences in their height, colour of seed and earlier or later ripening. Wild rice is found in the neighbourhood and most of their varieties come from seed selected from these wild plants. One of their most esteemed sorts, the 'black' rice, comes from a small amount of seed collected in the jungle by the elder brother of the Muktair, Tafoor's father; it was grown exclusively for seed for some years and now all the villagers have a good stock of it. The seed of all crops except wet rice is saved from year to year; it is the special business of the 'house-mother' at harvest time to select and put aside the grain which will be needed for the next year's seed. The sowing and harvesting of dry rice is surrounded with an elaborate ritual which will be described later.

A great number of different millets and eleusines are cultivated. Small fields of the earlier ripening varieties are made in the valley and a big field for the main crop is grown higher up. Only one field of dry rice and one of main-crop millet are made every year. Sometimes other grains or plants are grown among these crops, a certain amount of maize or different vegetables if the field-garden cannot take enough. In the autumn, after the rice or millet is gathered, the fields are sown with buckwheat which ripens in about five months; when that is harvested the ground is allowed to lie fallow for seven years. Two sowings of buckwheat are made annually; a big one in the autumn for food, and a smaller one in the spring for seed.

Lepcha agriculture is extremely inefficient by the standard of yield per acre. It is also absolutely inefficient. I was shocked at the carelessness of the sowing, with perhaps a third of the grain lying on the bare ground and the seed in the holes inadequately covered. When I remonstrated I was told 'It doesn't matter; if all the rice were to come up it would be too thick; so that if the birds eat some it will be just right.' To prevent the birds taking too much a prayer is said (usually by an experienced layman) after each sowing. It is arguable that more intensive cultivation would not result in a bigger yield per hour of work; and the continuous change of ground, only possible with a light population, prevents erosion and soil exhaustion. The accompanying table shows schematically the work of the Lepcha agricultural year.

LEPCHA AGRICULTURAL CALENDAR
(for the Talung valley)

(*Note*: The Tibetan year begins in February, and the first of the Tibetan month falls on about the tenth of the English. Consequently 'February', e.g. should be interpreted as 'February 10th to March 10th.')

TANGBU (February).	Clear the ground and finish sowing buckwheat. This and the two preceding months are the period of intense cold when poor old people may die for lack of warmth.
NIBU (March)	Finish clearing ground and sow dry paddy in temporary fields; sow maize and early millet in valley. Weed cardamum in flower and strike new plants. This and the following month is the time of rain and hail-storms.
SUMGU (April)	Harvest barley and wheat. Clear ground for main-crop millet. Weed cardamum again round new-formed fruit.
ZIBU (May)	Harvest buckwheat. Sow maincrop millet. Sow maize in 'garden' burning the wheat straw for fertilising. This and the three following months are the period of constant rain and heat. Head-coverings are necessary.
NAPU (June)	Plant wet rice. Weed dry rice. This is the leanest month when people may go hungry. In this and the following month is the greatest infantile mortality, through diarrhoea and dysentery.
TIKPU (July)	Harvest earliest millets in valley. Weed maincrop millet.
DENGBU (August)	Harvest earliest variety of wet rice. Make a shed to dry cardamum fruit. Make a small sowing of buckwheat for seed.
GEBU (September)	Harvest dry rice. The women start harvesting the millet, the men the cardamum. This and the two following months are relatively dry.
GOOBU (October)	Cardamum picking continues. Wet rice is harvested. Barley, wheat and onions are sown in the 'garden'.
CHOOPU (November)	The seed-buckwheat is harvested. Cardamum is sold. This and the next two months are the prosperous period, the time of little work and much feasting, of shopping and trading expeditions. Most marriages are celebrated now.
CHUCHIKPU (December)	Taxes are paid. The harvested temporary fields must be made ready for buckwheat.
CHUNIPU (January).	The big sowing of buckwheat.

Work in the fields, whether sowing, weeding or harvesting, is nearly always done in large parties. These parties are made up partly of relations by blood or marriage, and partly by friends. Since the Lepchas trace relationship back nine generations on the father's side and at least four on the mother's there is a tendency for most villagers to have some relationship; I should guess that out of a dozen Lepchas of Lingthem taken by chance, a relationship chain could be established between eight of them. But this relationship is not necessary for field-helpers; in nearly all the lists I made there were a few people quite unrelated.

Help in the fields is always repaid with a similar amount of labour; for sowing and weeding the helpers are also always given a meal with meat. At harvesting a meal need not be given to people who volunteer their services, but must be given to those who are asked to help. At harvest payment is given in kind: forty to fifty pounds of rice to an adult worker, a big basket of millet or maize, thirty to forty pounds of buckwheat. Children are given proportionately less. The first person to harvest his dry rice, and the last to harvest the wet, must make a small present of the grain to all the other householders. Because cardamum is a money-producing and not a food-producing crop help with it is paid for in money; a rupee a head is given for work in the fields and Rs. 3/– for carrying a maund[5] to market.

iv

The most general food of the Lepchas is rice. This is prepared in four main ways; boiled whole after husking in water and eaten with meat or vegetables or other seasoning; boiled whole in milk; 'puffed', or ground fine and made into a pudding. This ground-rice pudding is often given to children. Wheat and maize may be eaten in the same way if there is no rice, but they are not liked. Buckwheat is ground and mixed with water and baked on the

[5] The *maund*, which is divided into 40 *seers* is the current measure of weight in India. A maund is meant to represent the load one man can lift, and its equivalent in European measure depends partly on *what* is measured, and partly on *where* it is measured. (Similar confusion can be found in various English measures of agricultural produce such as a bushel, or a truss.) On the Indian railways a maund is equated to 80 lbs., which makes the seer 2 lbs. The Lepchas have their own measures according to the size of the basket used. Since all these measures are very rough I have generally given an approximate equivalent in lbs. avoirdupois.

cooking stones; it makes a greenish cake, or 'bread' as the Lepchas call it, of an astonishingly leathery consistency. On ordinary days, besides snacks, the Lepchas eat two meals; the bigger one in the morning, drunk with tea, Tibetan fashion, before going to work; and a second meal in the evenings with *chi* to accompany it.

Millet is grown exclusively for fermenting for *chi* and is never eaten by human beings; if there is no millet any other grain will be fermented in the same way; if there is no grain bootleg liquor is made out of the pith of different tree-ferns, which is pounded and buried. The making of this alcohol from forest produce is formally forbidden but is done almost continuously; it is very strong and potentially poisonous, and has a strong purgative effect. This alcohol is under the protection of a supernatural called Manoong *moong* and when the fermented pith is pounded on a piece of wood offerings of sticks placed on the press are made to the supernatural, who will make the drink stronger or weaker according to the size of his offerings.

Chi can be prepared in about nine days, but it is stronger and more appreciated if it is left to ferment longer. Specially strong *chi* is always prepared against a woman's lying-in and is given to her as a strengthening food for a month after delivery. To prepare *chi* the grain is first trodden to separate it from the husks and then put in a basket and well washed in a stream. A copper vessel is also well washed and the grain put in it; it is then covered with cold water and boiled until all the water is absorbed, being stirred all the time with a wooden spoon. To make sure that all the water is absorbed the wooden spoon is stuck down to the bottom of the pot; if it comes up dripping further cooking is necessary. When it has cooked sufficiently the pot is upset on to a bamboo mat; after an hour it is removed and the cooked grain is spread all over the mat. Then a big wicker basket is well lined with bracken; the grain is mixed with powdered yeast and put into the basket which is covered with more bracken and a tightly tied cloth. The basket is then set in a corner, well away from the fire, for two or three days, at the end of which time the smell of fermentation becomes noticeable. Then special big leaves are fetched from the forest and a new basket is lined with them and the grain is transferred to the new basket, which is well tied up and set over the fire on the drying ledge. It is fit to drink after three days but it is better kept longer; it becomes undrinkable after four months.

Above : CLEARING THE GROUND OF WEEDS AND TWIGS; TOBGÉ TALKS TO CHÉLÉ

Below : PLANTING DRY RICE WITH PLANTING STICKS

N.B.—The camera was not tilted for these pictures.

Nowadays nearly everybody buys yeast cakes in the bazaars, where they are sold very cheaply, but the old method of making the yeast is still known and employed by some of the older women. For five days before making the yeast the maker must not eat high meat or drink sour *chi* or the yeast will go bad; and it is thought that these prohibitions are the chief cause for people now buying it. The native yeast had six ingredients: the roots of two trees which I could not identify, and the leaves of a gaultheria ground to powder mixed with powdered chilli and ginger and powdered millet and water. The whole is made into a cake and left to dry for three days.

All *chi* is not uniformly good; its goodness depends on the proportion of yeast and its proper distribution and the care taken in the arrangement of the basket. Some houses are noted for their consistently good or bad *chi*, the best being obtained from the Mandal's and Tafoor's and the worst at Jiroong's and, surprisingly enough, Datoop's. This is peculiar because both Mr. and Mrs. Datoop are very fond of *chi* and Mrs. Datoop is in all other respects the most obviously competent woman in the village. To prepare *chi* for drinking all that is necessary is to put the fermented grain into a bamboo container, *patyoot*, and upset boiling, or nearly boiling, water on to it; the liquid is drunk through a specially narrow bamboo called *pahip*, which has one end cut so as to make a sort of filter to prevent the grains being sucked in at the same time as the liquid. The drink is quite pleasant, somewhat sweet and insidious; at a guess I should place the alcohol content at about the same as a strong beer or a light red wine. The *patyoot* is refilled with water at least three times and consequently the drink gets weaker as more is drunk. Until the water is poured on the *chi* it is perfectly easy to handle and transport, and the presents of *chi* which take place on almost all formal occasions consist of a packet of the fermented grain wrapped in a cloth or held in a basket. Strained *chi*, which is the fermented grain given a single sousing of water and then drained in a wicker bag, is a delicacy and is very considerably stronger than the *chi* drunk through the straw. The Lepchas are also fond of *arak*, commercially distilled liquor, and usually buy it when they go to a place where it is obtainable.

Except in the poorest households, or on those occasions when one lot of *chi* has been exhausted and the next is not yet ready, adult Lepchas drink at least one *patyoot* of *chi* daily: if they did not, they say, what would the poor pigs have to eat? Pigs are normally fed on the used grain, unless it is rice *chi*, when the soused grain is eaten by humans. The Lepchas believe that *chi* has medicinal qualities, and especially that it is a protection against chills; it is always given to invalids. They start drinking it from the moment that they can walk and continue all their lives. It does not seem to me to be strong enough to have any deleterious effect; except for very young children and a few unstable adults, *chi* does not produce any of the usual stigmata of drunkenness. Lepchas are very conscious of the risk of drink producing quarrelling; in the myth which tells of the origin of *chi*[6] the original yeast was stolen from an old woman who put the curse of quarrelsomeness on it. In point of fact I heard practically no quarrelling at feasts, though people became loud-mouthed, and more shameless in speech than ever, and a couple of men, Dumbi and Katel, used to get maudlin and say how miserable they were and threaten suicide. Unconsciousness induced by drink is unheard of, and so is physical incapacity; but at a feast people usually sleep where they are and only go home in the morning. Drink is mellowing, soothing and pleasant, rather than stimulating and exciting.

Fish is occasionally caught and eaten boiled, as a relish, but not very often. Meat is somewhat of a luxury, and on the whole people do not kill animals except as a sacrifice or when giving a big feast. There are, however, some exceptions to this; Tempa, who had a number of oxen and not very much grain, killed a couple of his cattle and exchanged the meat for the grain he needed. Fowls, wild birds and goat meat are eaten fresh; but beef and pork are preferred high; according to the weather the meat is kept from four days in the hottest season to a fortnight or longer in the coldest weather, before it is considered to be at its most tasty. Only if meat is maggoty will it be thrown away unused. Dead domestic animals and carrion found in the jungle will be eaten unless putrid. Meat is nearly always boiled; and sausages are made from the intestines of bigger animals which are cleaned and stuffed with the edible internal organs chopped fine together with flavouring herbs. These sausages are always made immediately after an animal has been killed. Another favourite form of relish is bullock skin which has been exposed to the sun and then boiled for a very long time until the inside fat is tender; it is eaten cold. There is a certain amount of variety in the manner

[6] See Appendix IV: The Sacred story of the origin of marriage.

of cooking dishes and compounding the various ingredients ; but on the whole the material provided is of more importance than the cooking. Except that a meal with meat is universally preferred to one without there does not seem to be any particularly favourite food ; Tafoor voiced the general opinion when he said his favourite dish was *chi*. I did not get enough detailed menus to be able to state with certainty how often meat is usually eaten inside the household ; from such information as I have got I should say richer people eat it three or four times a week, poor people once or twice. When it is available it is eaten in the morning and evening.

Lepcha diet is relatively monotonous, notably less highly spiced than the food of the Nepali or Indians ; there are no devices for tempting jaded palates ; food is to satisfy hunger, and enough is as bad as a meal. A feast definitely implies over-eating, and it is quite a common subject among old people to deplore that their powers of over-eating are failing ; that once upon a time they could eat fourteen pounds of meat in a day, and now they cannot manage four with comfort ! These actual figures were used by Adér, who is well over seventy and has lost half his teeth.

As can be seen, the Lepchas have, for a primitive people, a remarkably high standard of living, as far as food and drink is concerned ; it is certainly far higher than that of the Lepchas outside Zongu or any of the neighbouring peoples that I know of. Levelling out the answers I have received and my own observations, I should say that the average consumption of grain annually by an adult Lepcha is about 400 lbs. ; besides that about another 300 lbs. is consumed for *chi*. These quantities naturally do not allow for entertainment or gifts. There are three households who perhaps do not quite reach this standard, those of Dunbi, Nahyeun and Pargeut. Dunbi is said to be the poorest man in the village, but this is chiefly his own fault, for he sits about drinking and gossiping instead of working. Nahyeun is a young man fairly recently married ; he is reputed to be Dunbi's bastard and is himself not over energetic. He recently married Tobgé's sister and they have set up house on their own because his wife did not agree with the two wives of Asang, with whom he formerly lived ; they consequently have no reserves and few permanent fields. The third poor man, Pargeut, is really unfortunate ; he has six small children of which only the two eldest are of an age to help him, and they are girls betrothed outside the village ; he has also a very old mother to support, and he suffers himself from some sort of recurrent fever.

These households, and a few others, may get short of grain in the early summer and be driven to look for food in the forest to supplement the gifts they get; most households have usually a a small surplus at the end of the year which they use for extra feasting and presents. From the point of view of crops, though not necessarily of money, the richest householders are the Mandal, Tafoor, Takneum *youmi*, Tingkèp and Chelim. The first two are considered to be the best hosts, at whose house the finest food and drink is obtained.

V

Although of secondary importance as far as diet is concerned, domestic animals play a considerable rôle in the life of the Lepchas. Nearly all the ceremonies of the Mun demand animal sacrifices; animals are essential for the socio-religious celebrations of birth, marriage and death; and consequently people with few or no animals who get ill or have children or marry or die are at a considerable disadvantage and have to borrow animals for these ceremonies. Much of the indebtedness incurred with money lenders has been for the purchase of animals. Though the Lepcha can, and often does, borrow animals from his neighbours, he appears to feel a discomfort in being indebted to a friend which he does not feel towards the money lenders.

By far the most important animal is oxen;[7] they are still the chief sign of wealth and a person with twenty head of cattle is considered a rich man. Their meat is the most esteemed and at important feasts, or if a person wants to make a display, it is always an ox which is killed. They are never used as beasts of burden (no animals are so used) but occasionally for ploughing; a certain amount of milk and butter is got from milch-cows. Only the most savage bulls are castrated. Cows are not mated and no pedigrees are kept.

Except for young calves, milch cows, and bullocks temporarily in use for ploughing, the animals are never tethered or herded; they wander all over the common land round the village where pasturage and wood-gathering are free; every evening they

[7] The Lepcha cattle have no hump; they resemble small European rather than Indian cattle. They have small horns and every variety and combination of colouring.

return by themselves to their owners' houses, where they are given a feed of salt and powdered grain. Tethered animals are also fed with gathered leaves. Each animal has its name, which it knows; unless they wander into enclosed fields they are never beaten nor spoken to roughly. As you walk about Lingthem you come upon untended cattle in every direction; and one of the strangest sights is to watch the animals returning home of an evening. A herd of cattle, perhaps a score or more, will arrive in the centre of a group of houses, and will then each turn away to their own homes; as soon as they have settled under their houses they are given their evening feed. Stranger still is the fact that during the cold months—roughly from February to April—all the cattle, except the milch-cows, are sent in an untended group into the forest up the hill behind the village. When people want their cattle back they go up the hill to the place where they are liable to congregate, or, as the Lepchas put it 'where the cattle live in the forest', usually under some noticeably big tree. Within twenty-four hours cattle which have been completely untended for four months can be collected and brought back. While the cattle are in the forest a State tax of two annas a head a month is charged.

The taming of animals so completely is a remarkable feat in itself, and is also a good symbol of the Lepchas' chief attitudes; I think it has also an important bearing on their psychological development. In neighbouring tribes herding cattle is one of the major occupations of growing boys; in this way they achieve a certain self-reliance and learn to exercise their judgement. This discipline is almost completely absent for Lepcha boys; only when predatory animals are known or suspected to be in the neighbourhood are they set to watch animals. All through his childhood and adolescence the Lepcha boy is under the supervision of, and usually in company with his elders; and I feel sure that the lack of self-reliance, the inability to stand alone, which is one of the most obvious characteristics of the young Lepcha man, is enhanced by the lack of any work specially given over to children.

The size of the herds varies very considerably. The average is about six or seven head; a few households have considerably more and some people have only one or two, or even none at all.

Goats are raised exclusively for food and sacrifice and are never milked; they are not highly esteemed and people usually only have a few pairs. All goats are fed on salt, and billy goats are also given maize. Kids, and other young animals, are never killed for food.

Pigs also are raised for eating and sacrifice, but their meat is more popular and a large number are kept. They are the only animals which are generally killed for domestic eating. They are fed on the remains of *chi* after the grain has been three times soused. It is not rare for pigs and piglets to get quite drunk on this diet; there is quite a heavy mortality among them, and also occasionally among goats, who take the food by mistake, through their falling down dead drunk. The pig would appear to be a variety of the Himalayan wild pig; it is a relatively thin black animal, covered with bristles. All boars are castrated at the age of three or four months, by which time, it is said, they will have been old enough to cover the sow once. There are two reasons for thus castrating the boars; if it is not done it is said they would become savage and wander away into the forest. But there is a greater danger than this; if a man should happen to eat the flesh of an uncastrated pig he would thereupon commit sodomy. This is an example of the notion of *tamtoom*, an extremely important major Lepcha idea; if two events are believed to be inevitably connected, though the actual causation of the second by the first is not obvious, the second event is said to be the *tamtoom* of the first. With our logical attitude to the external world we have no proper parallel to this notion; the nearest approach would be if our common superstitions were believed to be specific and ineluctable. If for example walking under a ladder were believed to produce, say, a financial loss, this loss would be the *tamtoom* of walking under a ladder. The two acts need not necessarily be performed by or happen to the same person; when pre-natal precautions and body-marks are discussed, it will be seen that the child often suffers the *tamtoom* of his parents' actions.

Sodomy is strongly anti-social—it is called *nam-toak*, an act producing a year of disaster, the term which is also applied to incest—and an extremely embarrassing subject, one of the very few people don't like discussing. There is one man in the village, Takneum *youmi*, who has twice sodomised people when he was drunk and the victim asleep. In the second case, which occurred recently, the victim was old Lharibu Chujen, himself a grandfather; he was not angry at the indignity offered and did not claim the recompense of a pig and five rupees and ceremonial cleansing by a

Mun to which he was entitled. No neighbouring village is renowned for sodomy which is usually called by the periphrasis *mon-bo taa tyoul*—the effect of eating uncastrated boar. It is a typically Lepcha attitude to view such unethical acts as being out of the control of the aggressor; nobody would willingly or knowingly eat uncastrated pig, and therefore a sodomite who brings, or risks bringing a 'year of disaster' on the community is not responsible for his acts. No disgust is shown for Takneum *youmi*: but people avoid sleeping near him when he is drunk. The Lepchas state specifically that this *tamtoom* does not apply to other races, but only to themselves; other people can eat uncastrated pig without evil results; and if they commit sodomy it is because their habits are different. The eating of wild boars does not carry any such dangers.

Pigs, together with dogs and hens, are scavengers of human excrement; indeed it is necessary to be armed with a stick to drive them away, as these animals will follow people out into the forest; and they are so aggressive that young children are always accompanied by an elder in order to keep the animals away. There is a story of the dog, the pig, and the hen quarrelling over a piece of excrement, the things they say being given in words like their cries. The dog arrives first and says 'I am going to eat this, I am going to eat this.' 'Eu you might share it, eu eu' says the pig. 'Shant, shant' barks the dog. 'All right keep it, all right keep it' clucks the hen and goes away. Afterwards people usually clean themselves with sticks or stones or grass.

Dogs are kept and loved. Hunters will have three or four; other people just one or two. The lamas say that they give away superfluous puppies; other people kill theirs. All the dogs are watch-dogs and keep away wild animals and thieves. They are always fed by their owners. They are not supposed to come into the house; in point of fact they frequently do and are turned out again.

Cats are kept to keep down mice and rats. Whenever chicken is killed the cat is given some of the *cooked* meat. In this way, it is said, they will not kill live chickens. Occasionally if hungry they will kill and eat wild birds.

Fowls are kept both for food and for their eggs. Each hen has its own nest made for it, usually on the balcony. Two or three eggs are always left in the nests and therefore the hens do not go and hide clutches away from the house. Hen's wings are never clipped nor are they enclosed, and they seem, like the other animals, remarkably tame. Our diet was, alas, almost entirely confined to chicken, and we ate so many that we exhausted the supply of the immediate neighbourhood and fowls had to be brought in to us from distant villages. When they arrived carried in open-work baskets they would just be thrown out in front of the house; they would wander about the neighbourhood picking at the plants and occasionally flapping over the fences which shut in the fields; but they never tried to get away and every evening would come under the house for the grain they were given and would roost quite happily in the strange building. They very seldom run away and children can quite easily pick them up in their hands.[8] In the late evening the sight under the house where a number of animals are gathered together is very strange; cattle, pigs, goats, hens, dogs and cats are all tangled up in a heap sleeping on top of one another. Children have absolutely no fear of domestic animals, and one of the favourite games of little boys of five and six is to play at butting matches with young goats.

Animals must never on any account be killed by a woman; this is the only complete and absolute prohibition of any form of activity for either sex. There are some acts which are more commonly or indeed exclusively practised by men or by women only, but there is no sort of prohibition for members of the other sex doing them if they feel so inclined. For example only women spin and only men weave baskets; but there is no reason why a man should not spin if he wanted to and knew how, and in point of fact some women do weave baskets and mats. There are some things which women's relative lack of strength prevents them doing, particularly dealing with the big blocks of wood necessary for house building; that is considered a natural limitation and is not a cultural law. Men are expected to be better tree climbers than women, but there are quite a few cases of women being more efficient at this than their husbands; the husband feels no humiliation at this superiority on the part of his wife nor is he laughed at by other members of the community; if anything he is rather lucky in having an exceptionally able partner. But for the killing of animals the prohibition is absolute. It would be a sin to eat, even unknowingly, an animal killed by a woman, though in that case the lamas can cleanse the unwitting offender by ceremonies and offerings

[8] There is an odd variety of fowl with almost black flesh and skin and a great number of rudimentary feathers. Although the colouring does not alter the taste this type is despised and is only used as a cure for orchitis.

to the monastery. But to eat an animal so killed wittingly is a sin without remedy and which will be heavily visited in the next reincarnation.

Lamas naturally cannot kill animals nor should they eat them on the same day that they have been killed; these prohibitions, however, do not extend to the lay members of the lama's family. In a house where there are no laymen lamas will call one in to act as a butcher for them; the butcher will get as fee twelve to fourteen lbs. of meat from the crutch of an ox, smaller but similar amounts from a goat or pig, and a drink of *chi* for a chicken. Cattle are usually killed with a bow and arrow, shooting from very near; sometimes they are stoned or killed with a pointed knife. Pigs and goats are killed with a pointed knife if there is one, otherwise with a piece of sharpened bamboo. Chickens are usually knocked on the head. Boys above the age of ten can kill chickens and goats, and pigs after fifteen; but only a completely potent person will have the courage to kill an ox.

vi

With small exceptions the land and animals are considered to be the property of the householder, in whose name the house is registered and who is responsible for the payment of taxes. This householder is usually the oldest man in the prime of life in the family; a grandfather who has living sons usually gives the control in his life time over to his eldest son. In theory the property descends from elder to younger brother, and then, when all of the first generation are dead or too old, to the sons of the elder brother. In point of fact it is seldom that there is more than one family of each generation in one household; if the group becomes over-large the sons usually set up house on their own. If a son wishes to set up on his own during his father's life time, the father assigns to him, with the consent and co-operation of the Mandal and *youmi*[9] his proportionate share of the land. If when the father is dead the sons wish to separate the property is divided by the Mandal, *youmi*, and *gyapön*. The house is given to the eldest son, the animals and movable property divided up equally; the land is also divided up equally, the eldest son having the first choice and, if there is difference in the size of the fields, the biggest fields. In the event of the number of fields not being exactly divisible by the number

[9] *Youmi* and *gyapön* are village officials: for further explanation see Chapter Five, p. 131.

of sons the biggest fields will be split in two. Should two or more brothers wish to continue to live together they will be given adjoining fields. In recent years there has only been one such division; Ongden and his two brothers separated during their father's life-time.

An example of the working of the joint family can be given from Tafoor's household. This, the biggest in the village, consists of fifteen people: the second Dorjé Lapoon, the elder brother of the Muktair, Tafoor's dead father, and his newly-married wife Pumri who was formerly his aunt: Tafoor, his wife and four children; Chudo, Tafoor's younger brother, with his wife and three children; Prumtu, a fifteen-year-old half-sister of Tafoor; and a distantly related celibate lama. The whole household work together on the temporary fields, of which only one of each sort is cleared each year. Beyond a few animals, the second Dorjé Lapoon and his wife own no property; it would not be seemly for him to do so as a revered Dorjé Lapoon. Tafoor and Chudo have separate rice and cardamum fields and animals; but the produce, though kept separate, is taken in approximately equal quantities for household consumption. They share in the payment of the taxes and the liquidation of the debt left by their dead father; the rest of the cardamum money each spends as he thinks fit. Though there is only six years difference in their age they act and appear as if they were of different generations; Tafoor is notably serious and responsible, Chudo rather childish and always joking. The second Dorjé Lapoon and his wife are treated as honoured guests and have no responsibilities; Mrs. Tafoor fills the rôle of 'house-mother', saving the sowing seed and giving out the stores to be cooked, Mrs. Chudo that of 'youngest daughter-in-law', doing the cooking and making herself useful.

Land can only be owned by men; in the event of a woman or group of women being left sole possessors of a property they must acquire, either by marriage or adoption, a male who can inherit the property. Some childless couples adopt a son (*kup-tṣop*—literally a substitute child) to look after them in their old age and to be their heir. In nearly all cases such adopted sons are the children of near relations.[10] Should a person die without heirs or should the heirs be too young to work the property a *ké-tsop* (a word formed on the analogy of *kup-tsop*, a substitute tax-payer) will

[10] Further details about adoption will be found in Chapter VI, p. 177.

be appointed by the Mandal; for the purpose he will choose the younger son of a large family. If there are no direct heirs the *ké-tsop* will keep the property permanently; if the heirs are infants he will hand over the property when the boy is big enough to work the land himself. In such a case during his guardianship the *ké-tsop* will be responsible for the payment of the taxes; he works the land and supports the ward, but can keep for himself any profit he can make. He receives no other fee for his services. To give an example, Ongden's eldest son was acting as *ké-tsop* to Kahlyeu; Kahlyeu, who is getting on to eighty, is too old to work the land, and his only surviving grandson Chélé is too young. I asked if there was any possibility in such a case of a *ké-tsop* trying to claim the land permanently and was told that such behaviour was absolutely unthinkable. Indeed the idea was so grotesque that it was treated as a good joke.

In the case of a childless couple the *ké-tsop* keeps the property permanently. When a rich and childless couple grow old there is occasionally a certain amount of intrigue by parents to get their child adopted by them; but this is always done indirectly and through intermediaries; it would be shameless for parents to offer their own children for adoption. A year ago an old couple died in Lingthem whose only children were two daughters who were married in other villages; during their lifetime the old people did not want to adopt a boy and struggled alone to pay their taxes and work their fields; after they died the Mandal and *youmi* decided that Pichi, the second son of Datoop, should be made *ké-tsop*. The married daughters took all the movable property and animals between them; Pichi only got the house and land, and his father had to pay for the funeral expenses of the old couple. This property now belongs to Pichi and his descendants for perpetuity; he and his younger brother and his parents have moved into this house, leaving the old house and property to Datoop's eldest married son Pembu. The houses and fields are at some distance from one another.

If the household consists of more than a single married couple and one child, the dependent members of the household usually have a little private property of their own, in the form of a few animals and small portions of rice terraces and cardamum fields. When children achieve physical independence they are given their own clothes and knife or sickle and usually a wooden cup; and usually at about the same time a baby chicken or kid or piglet.

The children look after and feed these animals a little, and will cry if they are sold. The parents however are at perfect liberty to sell them, if they wish to, without consulting the owner; the money is said to be set against the expenses incurred for the child's clothes. If on the other hand the parents kill the animals for sacrifice or food, they have to replace them, and any young the animals bear belong to the owner. Also when they are still very young children are given a tiny piece of land as their own field; at first the parents help them with their work, but by about the age of twelve the children are expected to be able to look after them by themselves. As the children grow older the size of their field is increased. The grain from the children's fields is harvested separately and kept in a special container, but the house-mother can use it for household purposes without consulting the child. The produce is stated to be set against the children's clothes and knife, and, in the case of young girls, jewels. In general the privately-owned animals and grain are not set apart from the others in any way; only when girls go to their husband's village they take with them their private animals and the last year's harvested grain as a sort of dowry. When a wife settles into her husband's home she is generally given small portions of rice terrace and cardamum field, from the proceeds of which she can buy jewels. In this manner everybody, even the youngest children, is given the appearance of being self-supporting, of feeding and clothing themselves by their own work.

It seems as though nearly everybody except the very poorest have a few private animals. Mrs. Datoop, one of the richer women in Lingthem, says that at her marriage she brought with her six or seven cattle and other animals. She now owns ten head of cattle, three rice terraces, and two cardamum fields which yield about sixteen maunds; she bought her very fine jewels with the proceeds. When her two daughters were married each took with her a pair of each sort of animal, a big copper pot, and jewels which had been bought from the proceeds of their grain and animals. Her daughter-in-law Mrs. Pembu, brought with her when she was married oxen, goats, chickens and crops; but most of these have been used for the household, and now she only claims as her own two pigs and three chickens. Her jewels are all presents from relatives. Since she and her husband are the sole owners of their property she has no private land.

Chimpet, Tafoor's oldest son, aged fourteen, owns a pig given to him by his father, a black heifer called Katikmu, a present from his 'grandfather '[11] the second Dorjé Lapoon, and a tiny cardamum patch yielding half a maund, which was given to him by his mother's father, Lharibu Chujen. His twelve-year-old sister only possesses a single hen. Tempa's five-year-old daughter owns three chicks and a piglet. Only children, and the wives and children of the poorest people are the only ones not to possess any property. Land which is given as a gift can be given again as a gift provided it does not pass into the possession of people living under another Mandal; it cannot be sold without the permission of the Mandal and of the original owner.

All the land of Zongu belongs to the Maharajah and cannot be owned by anybody not of Lepcha blood. Transactions of land between residents inside Zongu need the consent of the Mandal, and if necessary the confirmation of the Court. In the event of a Lepcha from outside Zongu wishing to settle therein, he will apply to the Mandal in whose village he wishes to live, who will forward the request to Court. If the request is granted the Mandal will summon all his 'tenants' and instruct each of them to give the newcomer a strip of land; he himself will give a piece of uncleared forest. These pieces of land are really gifts; the immigrant only pays for them with a drink of *chi*. The Mandal, it is believed, will always be glad to get a new 'tenant'; the householders may dislike giving up their land, but there is nothing they can do about it. It is extremely rare for immigrants to arrive in this fashion; in the last thirty years only one such has come to Lingthem, and that was Katel, who followed home his runaway wife. Such strange men as do come to Zongu usually do so either through marriage or adoption.

vii

It is perhaps permissible to speculate a little on the historical development of the Lepchas of Zongu in regard to their food-getting habits. Primitive economies are usually divided into three

[11] Throughout this book I have put into quotation marks kinship terms when they are employed by the Lepchas in their extended meaning, in cases where they do not correspond to our classification. Thus the second Dorjé Lapoon is by our classification Chimpet's paternal grand-uncle; this actually has no corresponding term in Lepcha; and since both the two themselves and anybody else referring to them would call them 'grandfather' and 'grandson' I have consistently employed the Lepcha terminology.

categories—food-gatherers, cultivators, and herders.[12] In a way the Lepchas today straddle all three types, though domestic animals play a relatively small part in their economy.

Lepcha tradition, as has already been stated, places the transition from food-gathering to cultivating about two centuries ago. But I question whether this statement can be taken at its face value. It is extremely difficult to count on the age of tradition or mythology, but it seems to me *ipso facto* improbable that the Mun mythology would have been completely changed and re-made after the Lepchas' conversion to lamaism. Now in the Mun ritual and validating mythology domestic animals play a very important part for they are the only acceptable articles of sacrifice; wild animals can only be used by hunters. Also the most constant and important of the Mun's calendrical ceremonies are connected with crops, and in particular with dry rice and millet. These are ceremonies which affect the whole population. There is also the tradition that, while the upper slopes of the valley were common ground until quite recent times, the land down by the river has been privately owned from time immemorial. The private ownership of uncultivated land which would never be particularly rich in game seems quite pointless.

It seems to me probable that up to about three centuries ago the Lepchas—presuming they were already living in the same country, and there seems no reason to question it—cultivated a certain amount of rice and millet on the lower slopes of the valley, probably selecting the wild varieties which grow in the Himalayan forests, and kept some domestic animals, probably oxen. They very likely did not cultivate enough for all their needs, and eked out the cultivated food with hunting and wild forest produce. When the tribes of Tibet, and later of Nepal, amalgamated into single states with expansionist policies, the Lepchas found themselves confronted with war-like enemies against whom they were practically defenceless, for in their lonely Himalayan valleys they can have seen few strangers. There is no account of their resisting the Tibetan colonisation, but they fled from the invading Nepali and Bhutanese. These foreigners represented for them death and slavery, at the least loss of their possessions; and so to save themselves they abandoned their cultivation and took to a nomadic life in the forests. Throughout the eighteenth and early nineteenth

[12] See for example C. Daryll Forde's *Habitat, Economy and Society* (London 1934).

century Sikkim was, we know, the seat of constant wars; and it is not surprising that old Serving claims that about 1850 there were only four houses in Lingthem. As the country became peaceful the Lepchas settled down again to a mainly agricultural life, only to find, outside Zongu, that they were unable to compete with the more industrious and competent Nepali and Sikkimese. They had developed a way of life suitable for isolation; neither in war nor in competition could they stand up to other people. In the reserve of Zongu the introduction this century of cardamum and terraced fields bound them more securely to the land. They had neither time nor reason for hunting. The money-producing cardamum crop did away with the necessity, which existed in earlier times, of travelling to trade forest produce against cloth and salt and metal. From partial or complete nomadism the Lepchas have become almost completely attached to their fields; they have less reasons for dealing with strangers than at any time in the last three centuries. It is probable that this growing isolation will increase even more the Lepcha's great natural timidity in the face of an unknown person; even today 'unknown' has almost the same connotations as 'dangerous'.

CHAPTER FOUR

MONEY LENDERS AND TRADING FRIENDS

i

At Mangan, on the main mule road between Tibet and Gangtok, above the only solid bridge which connects Zongu with the mainland, are a group of half-a-dozen mixed stores. These stores are owned by Indians, members of the Mahawari caste, a caste of hereditary money lenders and misers. They have been settled in the neighbourhood about thirty years; before Mangan was developed they lived at Singthem. Ostensibly they are only shopkeepers; in point of fact their chief profit is made by advancing cash and goods to the neighbouring peasants against their produce. Formerly they used to deal with every sort of crop, but since the introduction of cardamum they have concentrated exclusively on that. The State has given these traders, or, as they are locally called, kanya, the monopoly of the cardamum trade, and they are therefore able to impose a uniform price.

The presence of these kanya in the neighbourhood has been an almost unmitigated disaster for the Lepchas. Were they honest it would still be bad, for their proximity has to a considerable extent sapped the Lepchas' energy. It is easier to buy ready-made clothes than to go long journeys to obtain thread and then spin and make up the cloth; and so they buy cheap and shoddy cloth and ready-made clothes; they are colder, dirtier and more ragged than they used to be and their children die of bronchial complaints. In the lean summer months it is easier to get grain on credit than to search for food in the forest; and so, through the line of least resistance they get more and more heavily into debt.

The Lepchas are at a complete disadvantage in dealing with the kanya. Neither they nor anybody outside the caste can read the peculiar script of the Mahawari; but the Lepchas cannot deal with figures and are unable to calculate the prices they should receive or the debts they owe; when they get receipts they cannot read them nor tell if they are correct. Though they have a strong conviction that they are badly cheated by the kanya they can do nothing about it; intentional dishonesty in any form is so alien to them that they cannot comprehend or deal with it; they puzzle about the sums that the kanya say they owe; they are convinced that they are too high, but they cannot dispute them and have to pay. Since the kanya have the cardamum monopoly and collect the selling tax the Lepchas cannot take their produce elsewhere; and it is questionable if it would pay them to do so, for against the higher prices obtainable in Gangtok and Kalimpong must be set the cost of porterage. As with many such crops the price is often higher at the end of the season than at the beginning, but the kanya will not let them wait on the market; at the beginning of the season they send representatives to their debtors claiming immediate payment, and threatening Court proceedings if the cardamum is not forthwith handed over. If the kanya would give cash for the surplus crop the Lepchas would be better off; but it is extremely difficult to get ready money, beyond what is needed for tax-paying, out of them. When the cardamum is brought in the kanya claim that they have no money to hand and force goods, either metal ware, or china, or cloth, on to the sellers. And if during the rest of the year people come in to buy goods, rice seed, or cloth, or salt, they refuse to take cash except for quite small sums (say under Rs. 10). They bully and force and persuade the Lepchas to take goods on credit whether they want them or not.

Their rates of interest are extortionate. For a maund of rice or Rs. 10 worth of shop goods they demand a maund of cardamum. The cash price of rice at Mangan is Rs. 5/12; the present price of cardamum is Rs. 12 and it has been considerably higher. If there is not sufficient cardamum to pay the debt at harvest time the arrear is carried forward at a maund-and-a-half for a maund, or Rs. –/6 for Rs. 1. The rate of interest charged on loans comes to 25% per year at the lowest. According to a reliable informant outside Zongu I was told that according to the laws of Sikkim State no interest is allowed to be charged on goods sold on credit and a maximum of 12½% on cash loans.

Some years ago, it is said, a complaint was made to the Central Court that the kanya were using false measure, taking off 5 seers in the maund (10 lbs. in 80); the kanya were fined Rs. 3,000 and they told the Lepchas that they would take it out of them; it is the opinion of the most intelligent of them that they are doing so. The Court has made various rules to try and control the devices of the kanya. Nowadays they are not allowed to make out the bills themselves and if the Lepchas were literate this would be a great help; as it is it is usually the postmaster who makes out the bill and the debtor puts his thumb mark on it. Nowadays too during the buying season there is an official checker—a Nepali. An application was made to Court in the spring of 1937 to have the kanya removed because their proximity was the chief reason for the indebtedness and distress. Some years ago the Court sent out an order that people were not to borrow so much and the kanya were not to cheat so much; but with the shops there on the spot and with cunning and insinuating salesmen, the Lepchas are unable to resist.

With the exception of, I think, only one household (Nariya and Rigya) everybody in Lingthem is indebted to the kanya; the average debt is between Rs. 20 and Rs. 100, but some people are much more heavily indebted. The biggest single debt is that left by Tafoor's father the Muktair; this amounted to Rs. 1,200 and was chiefly contracted through the expense he incurred in rebuilding and re-furnishing the monastery, though a certain amount went to the improvement of his own house and the entertainment of distinguished guests and of the workers from distant villages who helped in the monastery building. Before his death the Mandal organised a village feast for him at which everybody gave cash gifts according to their ability; but the sum was too great for the neighbourhood to liquidate. His heirs, Tafoor and Chudo, have commuted the debt, arranging to pay off both principal and interest at the rate of six maunds of cardamum each every year for ten years. Their personal debts are quite small, and are regulated at the end of each year. Of living people probably the most indebted is the Mandal, who owes about Rs. 500, also chiefly borrowed for entertainment. After him comes Katel; the principal of his debt nobody knows, not even he himself; but out of the sixty maunds of cardamum he harvests (this is almost the biggest crop of anybody in the village) forty have to go in debt.

To illustrate the way the indebtedness works I propose giving the complete history of two debts. In 1933 Datoop incurred considerable expense on account of the funeral of his father's fifth wife, who was a nun, and of his eldest son's marriage. He therefore borrowed Rs. 100. Since 1933 he has made the following payments :—

1934	2 maunds of cardamum	at Rs. 8 –	Rs. 16
1935	3 " "	at Rs. 10 –	Rs. 30
1936	5 " "	at Rs. 12 –	Rs. 60
			Rs. 106
	Less tax at Rs. –/12		Rs. 7/8
			Rs. 98/8

He is told that he still owes Rs. 40, but he hopes this year if the price and harvest is good, to clear off the debt. He does not know what interest is charged : 'nobody can work it out, and you have to pay what the kanya claim. You *can* get cash from them, but it is very hard to do so ; they push goods on to you and try to force you to take them.'

Thirteen years ago, when his step-father died, Kurma *gyapön* borrowed Rs. 100 for the funeral expenses. Cardamum was fetching a high price then ; the next year he gave four maunds and asked the kanya to tear up the bill. Apparently he just tore up a piece of paper, for the next year he reclaimed the money, and as Kurma had no receipt he could not dispute the bill. For a couple of years he did nothing about it and then the kanya sent a policeman to bring him to Court ; Kurma protested that as he had already paid the bill he would go directly to the Maharajah and present the case to him ; and with that intention he took with him a hurricane lantern and an umbrella. The policeman left him at Mangan and Kurma went to buy oil for his lantern ; the kanya saw him and asked what he was doing ; to which Kurma replied that he was setting out for Gangtok to present his case to the Maharajah. The kanya suggested that this was a little drastic, and suggested that he go and fetch Balyoop of Panung to act as an intermediary. Finally a compromise was arranged whereby the debt—both principal and interest—was set at a fixed sum to be paid off at the rate of one maund a year ; Kurma believes that the full value of the maund is being written off. Today he still owes Rs. 40.

Until very recent years the kanya were able to send the police of their own accord to distrain animals and jewels against long-standing debts ; nowadays they are only allowed to do so after an award from the Chief Court at Gangtok. About ten years ago the kanya sent their servants to seize Songpo *youmi*'s cattle and his wife's jewels; but the Mandal stood security for the cattle with his own cardamum and neighbours clubbed together to redeem the jewels. About the same time Patek's father had two bullocks and a milch-cow distrained; fifteen householders banded together to stand security and returned the animals to their owner. Only three years ago the kanya attempted to sell by auction three orange trees, a rice terrace and a cardamum field belonging to Tempa, who had an outstanding debt of Rs. 100. This however was a complete failure for nobody bid at the auction except Tempa himself; he bought back his property at Rs. 60 which cleared his debt. In 1937 a man of Panung had a cardamum field sold by auction, but this was after judgement had been given against him at Court; he and the kanya had both been found guilty of buying and selling cardamum without paying the sales tax. In this case the field was bought by a man of Lik across the river, who paid off the debt and now uses the field as his own.

It is only the internal co-operation of the Lepchas and the paternalistic rulings of the Court which have prevented the Mahawari getting a stranglehold on the lives of the Lepchas of Zongu such as they hold over nearly every Indian peasant and piece of ground. They are such a powerful caste and so incalculably rich that they appear to be able to defy all governments, whether British or Native; they together with the Kabuli and the other leeches are far and away the greatest cause of misery, distress and poverty in the whole Indian sub-continent.

There are also debts inside the village, but they are of a very different nature. If a person is short of crops he will borrow from a neighbour. If he returns the loan within a year he has no interest to pay, if over a year he must repay three measures for every two borrowed, for it is considered that the seed will have produced a harvest. If an animal is borrowed it will simply be replaced or its equivalent in cash given in due course. If the repayment is long postponed a chicken and a load of *chi* will be given when the debt is repaid. There is no interest on cash loans for the first year; after that there is an interest of Rs. –/3 on the rupee and a feast should be given by the debtor to the creditor every year. If after, say, three years the debtor finds that he can only repay the principal he will bring the money, together with a dead fowl and a load of *chi* to the creditor and ask for the interest to be remitted; this is always done. Inside the village the hire of a pair of bullocks is 8 lbs. of grain for one day or 12 lbs. for two.

ii

Before the beginning of this century when money was introduced and shops set up in the neighbourhood, Lepchas had to travel abroad to obtain cloth and thread, salt and metal goods. They used to collect in the forest the red dye-wood called *vyim* (the Nepali call it *majita*) and take that and whatever surplus crops they had up to the Tibetan border, where they would exchange it for salt and wool. Some of the salt they would then take to Darjeeling to exchange for thread and cloth. In order to be able to trade continuously and to receive hospitality and protection in foreign countries a formal relationship with religious sanctions was instituted. This relationship, and the two parties who entered into it, were called *ingzong*,[1] which means literally 'like a younger brother'. For the formal establishment of an *ingzong* relationship a pig must be killed and the intestines (*shafot*) offered to the Gods, in particular Komsi*thing*, the Lepcha supernatural who invented the relationship and who is, as it were, its patron saint; then a feast is held and the pig eaten, and the two contracting parties swear solemn oaths always to love and help one another, and never to do or think evil; after this an old and experienced man (not a lama, but it matters not who else) prepares the rite of *sakyou-faat*, the sacrifice of butter, which recurs in almost all Mun ceremonies; a cup is filled with strained *chi* and four dabs of butter are smeared round the sides; holding this the old man addresses the two who wish to become *ingzong*, impressing on them the seriousness of the occasion, and the sanctions which would follow the breaking of their vows. Each of the *ingzong* then drinks out of the cup and eats two of the dabs of butter. This solemnises the situation, and should either thereafter speak evil of or harm the other the god Komsi*thing* will send the devil Sankyor *moong* to punish him. It is said that Komsi*thing* first thought of the institution in the early days of creation when he was drunk; he then made *ingzong* with all the foreigners who had goods which he did not possess: with the Nepali for their pigs, with the Plains Indians for their copper vessels, with the Bhutanese for their fine cloth, with the Tibetans for their rugs, and with the Sikkimese for their oxen.

[1] Lepchas tell me that the Tibetan term is *re-koo*, the Bhutanese *pre-koo*, the Nepali *mit*.

Once the full ceremony has been performed the two *ingzong* are regarded as being in truth sons of one father, and intermarriage between their descendants is forbidden as incestuous for nine generations. The relationship between one *ingzong* and his *ingzong*'s wife is a respectful one, and to mark his respect he will usually address her as 'mother'. It would be almost incestuous to sleep with your *ingzong*'s wife, but a woman does not have to hide from her husband's *ingzong* as is the case with the *mit* of Nepal.[2] As a general rule the *ingzong* relationship is hereditary, the sons of *ingzong* being themselves *ingzong*; but there is no compulsion about this and if a son does not get on with his father's *ingzong* and his sons he can set up new relationships. Even with hereditary *ingzong* the full ceremonial must be performed in each generation.

Nowadays the Lepchas only set up the relationship with Sikkimese and Tibetans, for the exchange of crops and dye-wood for salt, carpets and metal vessels; they are, they say, no longer friendly with the Nepali and will have no relationships with them. *Ingzong* is not an exclusive relationship. At the end of March a Sikkimese-Tibetan husband and wife from Lachen arrived in Lingthem with rugs which they wished to exchange for crops, dye-wood and cash. In the whole Talung valley they had eleven *ingzong*, three of whom were in Lingthem; they spent one night in the house of each. When an *ingzong* arrives on a visit efforts are made to feast him as well as possible; and when Lepchas go to visit their *ingzong* they take with them presents of grain, and, if possible, meat. Most of the men of Lingthem have at least three Sikkimese or Tibetan *ingzong*.

Properly speaking the term *ingzong* is only applicable to the ceremonial trading-relationship set up between Lepchas and foreigners; but the word is very frequently used between Lepchas with the meaning 'my special friend.' It sometimes happens that two men will drink *chi* together ceremoniously to give some formality to their relationship; but they do not perform the full ceremony for that would entail the nine-generation marriage ban, and in the small community of Zongu, where the choice of wives is already limited, this would speedily produce an impossible state of affairs. It took me a considerable time to straighten out the different implications of the term *ingzong*, for the word is in constant use,

[2] For this fact and for other details in this book concerning the Nepali I am indebted to information derived from Mr. C. J. Morris, either in conversation or from his book '*Gurkhas*' *Handbooks for the Indian Army* (Delhi 1936).

chiefly with its derivative meaning; nowadays the necessity of trading is so slight and the country relatively so peaceful that the earlier implications are being forgotten by most of the Lepchas.

In Lingthem and the neighbouring villages there are eight pairs of men who call themselves *ingzong*; they give one another an elaborate feast every year, and always make rather special efforts to entertain their friends when they visit. Two reasons are advanced for setting up this inter- and intra-village relationship: either because the two men love one another, or because one or both lack anybody they can call 'brother' and wish for somebody they can look to for help in emergencies and who will care for their dependants in the event of untimely death. There is no ban on the children of such '*ingzong*' marrying; the children call one another *ingzong-bo* which is an abbreviation for 'child of father's *ingzong*'. A wife and her husband's *ingzong* will usually call one another mutually *ingzong* if they are not otherwise related; if the husband's friend is markedly older than the woman she will call him 'father'. These Lepcha relationships are not very stable and are often allowed to lapse; this is of no importance as the relationship has no religious sanctions. I was told that two women could set up such a relationship but I neither found nor heard of any instances of this.

Sometimes the term is used even more loosely, without any sort of ceremony having taken place; two boys or young men, not nearly related, who spend much time together working or hunting, or even who are close neighbours, will call and speak of one another as *ingzong*. Used this way the term is almost meaningless, though it has a trifle more warmth than *tyol*, the ordinary word for friend. There is no sort of overt homosexuality or even physical intimacy in the relationship. The Lepchas have almost completely separated the notions of love and sex; they use the same word to say they 'love' their friends, their parents and their wives; sexual activity is always referred to in direct and unambiguous terms. Homosexuality is a meaningless concept for them.

iii

There is an obligation on the part of the Lepchas of Zongu to supply boys to act as servants for the Maharajah in his palace at Gangtok, and young men to be trained as State carpenters. When people are wanted to fill either of these posts an order is to the Mandal, who then makes up his mind as to which boys the most suitable and then goes through the formality of ulting the parents. This is really only a formality, for the dal will choose the most suitable boys, and there is usually a limited choice.

Datoop's eldest son, Pembu, spent nearly eleven years in gtok in the Maharajah's palace, first going there when he was a little boy; he lived with a distant 'aunt'. He rose to be a man and received quite good wages; he finally left owing to spute with his 'aunt' and 'uncle'. Chudo, Tafoor's younger ther, when he was about fifteen, spent a year as scullion in the harajah's kitchen; at the end of that time he ran away because was forced to kill chickens almost every day, and for one coming m such a pious family of lamas this sinful act was intolerably nful. He apparently showed some aptitude, for the cook tried persuade him to stay so that he could take his place. When he t returned home Chudo exhibited a certain fussiness about cleanli-ss and such like follies, but he soon grew out of them. He made attempt to introduce 'European style' cooking which he nsidered a complete waste of time. Both he and Pembu were arried shortly after their return home and they have settled ck completely into their society.

Such is not the case with Pichi, Datoop's second son, and hada, Ongden's second son, both of whom spent three years in e State carpentry school at Gangtok. They received their training d free board and lodging; in repayment they have to hold emselves and their skill at the disposition of the State, and to go herever they are needed. In the spring of 1937 these two were nly lately returned home and both seemed rather disgruntled at e change. Pichi, who was taken ill and had elaborate exorcisms erformed over him, privately expressed considerable scepticism. Most disquieting of all, they refused to accept the marriages which had been arranged for them; when they wanted to get married, hey said, they would choose their wives for themselves. In the ace of their obstinacy their elders were powerless; but it was elt and said that this modern self-reliance would come to no good. It is possible that in a few years' time they, like their elders who underwent similar experiences, will settle down comfortably into their native society; at the moment both of them are rather seriously maladjusted.

Except for such State servants, and for the Mandal and those who accompany him to Gangtok to take in the taxes, the Lepchas of Zongu have little call to travel ; they occasionally go to shop in Gangtok or to visit their *ingzong* on the Tibetan border ; but it would seem as if such journeys are undertaken for the love of change, rather than for any real necessity.

Twelve years ago a party of six men and two women, including Tafoor, his father the Muktair, and his uncle the second Dorjé Lapoon went on a pilgrimage to the valley of Kathmandhu in Nepal. They were away for two months, spending twenty-three days on the journey each way ; in India they travelled by train, which surprised but did not frighten them. As far as I know Tafoor is the only young Lepcha of Lingthem who has been outside Sikkim ; a number of the older men visited Darjeeling and Tibet in their youth.

CHAPTER FIVE

LAW AND ORDER

i

Zongu, as part of the Maharajah of Sikkim's private estate, is administered for him by one of the Kazi, or hereditary ministers and landowners. It is at present under the Rhennock Kazi, who has succeeded the Mali Kazi. Except on very rare occasions the Kazi does not visit the reserve; the Mandals and Muktair pay relatively frequent visits to Gangtok to pay over the taxes to him and to consult him on any problems of internal administration.

Administratively Zongu is divided into twelve villages, each with a Mandal[1] at its head. Until the beginning of this century there were no intermediaries between the Mandals and the Kazi in charge; but some thirty years ago, at the instance of the Maharani, the aunt of the present Maharajah, the office of Muktair[2] was instituted. The Muktair is superior to the Mandals; he can deal with misdemeanours carrying a fine of not more than Rs. 60, while the Mandals can only deal with fines of Rs. 30 or less; he has to supervise all tax-accounts, and visits each village twice yearly to inspect the fields and see that grain has not been planted in excess of the amount on which tax has been paid; he has also to make a register of births and deaths. At first he was also responsible for the collection of taxes, but Tafoor's father, when he held the office, made a muddle of this job, and the actual collection and payment of the monies reverted to the Mandals. I was told that the Muktair receives as salary 4 per cent of the money collected and 4 annas on each house, but the sum seems to me excessive.

The history of this office of Muktair gives a good illustration of

[1] The term *Mandal* is not a Lepcha nor even a Sikkimese word. It is the common word for the head of the village throughout Northern India. It is however in universal use among the Lepchas, having completely displaced the Sikkimese-Tibetan *La-chen* and the Lepcha *Jem-mi*.

[2] The Sikkimese-Tibetan term is *Tong-yoop*.

the workings of Lepcha democracy. The original appointee of the Maharani was a Tibetan (or Sikkimese; the Lepchas do not distinguish the two races) who lived at Hi; but the Lepchas did not like having a stranger set over them and asked for the office to be given to Lepchas; the Court, which is always sensitive to such petitions, acquiesced, and the office was split into two: the seven villages on the Teesta side were put in charge of a man of Hi, and the five on the Talung side in charge of Tafoor's father. The man at Hi fulfilled the office satisfactorily, and his son is now the Muktair of the whole of Zongu; he is a youngish man and has so far no male children; he gives general satisfaction in his performance of the office.

When Tafoor's father died in 1935 Tafoor should normally have succeeded him. There were however some objections to his taking the office; he could not read or write Nepali or Sikkimese, in which all official business is transacted, but only ecclesiastical Tibetan. Even more important was the fact that he was the only relatively young lama who was sufficiently learned to be able to direct the monastery when the present old Dorjé Lapoon died; and he was the only lama in the whole neighbourhood who had the requisite knowledge and who had gone through the mystic training necessary for the stopping of rain and hail. This power is firmly believed in by the lamaists of Tibet and Sikkim, and in the extremely rainy Talung valley is a most useful and necessary accomplishment. If Tafoor had become Muktair he would not have had the necessary time for these religious pursuits, and therefore, somewhat against Tafoor's private desires, the householders requested that he might be allowed to continue his ecclesiastical work.

While the matter was still undecided the Rhennock Kazi and the Political Officer came to stop at the *dak*-bungalow at Singhik. An individual called Tempa from Lingthem went and offered his services to them, and with his fluent Nepali and Tibetan made himself very useful. At the end of their visit he asked the Rhennock Kazi to appoint him Muktair of the five Talung villages, and the request was granted.

Tempa is a man of forty-four who was born in Savong near Gangtok, well outside Zongu. He claims to be a pure Lepcha, but both his character and appearance are different to the Lepchas of Zongu. He was the only man in Lingthem to have any facial hair; he had a straggling fringe of coarse black beard round his face. When he was about fifteen he became a coolie of the present

Maharajah's father, doing menial out-door work. He was subsequently transferred to the service of the present Maharajah's maternal uncle and accompanied him to Lhassa where he spent three years in his service. At the end of that period his master was killed fighting against the Chinese, and in the same year the then reigning Maharajah died. Tempa returned to Gangtok and resumed service with the reigning Maharajah. Part of his service consisted in carrying letters and offerings to Talung monastery and bringing things back from thence. On his way to and from Talung he used to stop at Lingthem, in the house of Pumri, his present mother-in-law. Pumri and her husband had no surviving sons but only daughters, one of whom Tempa married; as is permissive in such cases Tempa did not take his wife home, but stayed in her house as *komok myok*, or resident son-in-law; thereby he became the heir of his wife's parents.

In character Tempa combines obsequiousness with domineering. Alone among the Lepchas of Lingthem he adopted a special voice, low and wheedling, when speaking to us Europeans; he despised us and thought we could be fooled by flattery, he tried to exploit us and to exploit others through our presence. If we went to the house of a third party when Tempa was present, he would assume all the rights and duties of host, elbowing the real host out of the way; he would offer the host's presents as if he were the giver, would fuss about and scold as if he had been appointed to look after our comfort, and would hand us over stones and ladders as if we were blind and infirm. He used to salaam and put his hands to his head whenever he met us, an action which has no place in Lepcha life; for very important personages Lepchas will unbraid their hair, but bowings and prostrations are uniquely reserved for the images of the lamaist gods. Tempa had a monomania about orphans, or else he thought it was a point to touch European compassion; nearly everybody he referred to, no matter what their age, was tearfully described as having no father and no mother; all other dead relations were also always named. Like Kurma, Tempa was always inclined to show himself as more influential than he was in fact, and insist that people had done certain things or followed certain courses at his advice or through his intervention. These claims were not always true.

When he was appointed Muktair the authority that he gained made him overweening and boastful and he used to threaten everybody who annoyed him, even, it is said, animals and inanimate objects. He is one of the very rare people in Lingthem who habitually hits animals. Finally, after he had been Muktair for about six months he assaulted with his stick old Takneum *youmi*, beating him after an argument about a matter of no importance. Immediately after this an agitation was started to get rid of him. The first person to make the discontent vocal was an old man of Tasso, in no way directly connected with either of the parties of the dispute. The Mandals of the five villages consulted together, and then each Mandal held meetings of all the adults where the matter was discussed in the greatest detail; these meetings were held in Lingthem monastery and at the houses of the different Mandals.

While these discussions were taking place, Tempa, though officially the superior of the Mandals, was forbidden by them to be present at any feasts or public gatherings either in the monastery or in private houses. Finally it was decided that so violent and irresponsible a man was unsuitable in a position of authority. A petition signed by all the householders of the district demanded that Tempa be removed from his office; they explained that he was using unjustifiable violence; they said that he was a stranger and did not know their ways; and they requested that the second office of Muktair be abolished and that the Muktair of Gyatong should in future administer their territory also. The Court granted their request, after which Tempa, reduced from all authority to the position of a private householder, was readmitted to the communal feasts and gatherings. No lasting animosity was displayed against Tempa but everybody knows the history and draws the moral; Tempa was angry, but being faced with complete unanimity he could do nothing. Today he is still angry with Takneum *youmi* and the two never visit each other on any occasion; they will, however, eat together in neutral places without quarrelling. This possibility of exclusion is the major Lepcha sanction; the person who is not allowed to feasts and who is not visited, who is in fact 'sent to Coventry' leads a very dull and lonely life; but more than that, if he is not allowed to help other people other people will not help him and it is hard to get through the agricultural and domestic work without help. Similar pressure, it is said, is brought to bear whenever anybody in authority, whether that authority be hereditary or through Court appointment, shows any tendency to abuse his position. It is a most effective control.

ii

The office of Mandal is hereditary, within the Lepcha meaning of the term; that is to say that the title resides in the extended family, and when the holder dies or becomes feeble through old age, it is given to the next most suitable male in the family; it often is the holder's eldest son, but may equally well be a younger brother or nephew of the holder. The position is probably older than the Tibetan colonisation of Sikkim, for some of the Mandals of Zongu are the eleventh or twelth of the family line to hold the position. In Lingthem Chala Mandal, the present holder of the title, is the third of his line to hold office; he has been Mandal for twenty years, succeeding his father's younger brother Tasso Nungyen, who in his turn had succeeded his own eldest brother Ogen. Before Ogen the office had been in old Serving's family; but Serving's father Pépo was exceedingly stupid and the only other suitable member of the family was already a lama attached to Talung monastery; therefore the title was taken from his line (the Tsel-telim *ptso*) and transferred to Chala Mandal's (Jam-yong *ptso*). The Tsel-telim *ptso* was originally by far the most powerful in the neighbourhood, but is now almost extinct, owing, it is said, to the *tamtoom* resulting from one ancestor who sold Lepchas as slaves to the Bhutanese.

The Mandal is normally spoken of as the 'landlord' of the village, and the other householders are called his 'tenants.' The Mandal holds the land under the Maharajah, who is the ultimate owner; the householders have the usufruct of the land but cannot transfer it outside their family without the Mandal's consent; for land to be transferred to a stranger from outside the village the permission of the Court is also necessary. The Mandal is responsible to the Court for the maintenance of good order in the village and for the collection of taxes; if there is a deficit he is liable to have to make it up. In relation to the other villagers he stands in the position of an elder relative—father or uncle or elder brother; he arranges the marriages of most of the young people, he looks after everybody's welfare and happiness, giving advice on personal or agricultural matters where they appear needed, and acting as intermediary between the villagers and the Court. It is necessary for the Mandal to be slightly richer than his 'tenants'; he has to entertain all distinguished visitors; he has to look after the orphaned and homeless (Chala Mandal had permanently living in his house lame orphaned Satéo and an invalid childless widower from Liklyang); he has to give more feasts than anybody else, and these feasts are expected to be better than those of ordinary people. The office carries with it certain privileges; the remission of house and seed tax, and the right to free labour, or *béti*. The Mandal has the right to three days' work a year from each household, but I do not think a careful tally is kept in Lingthem; Chala Mandal is not unreasonable in his demands and has I think free workers whenever he needs them.

Chala Mandal is a rather fat, benign-looking man of 59 with a mobile and expressive face and rather sardonically amused, twinkling little eyes; he has a small wen which, he explained, was the *tamtoom* of one of his parents while he was in the womb having killed a namprek-*fo* (a bird which developed a dewlap because it stole rice from the God Komsi*thing*). Compared with the other Lepchas of his age he is rather fat and short of breath; he suffers from lumbago, and is much distressed at his failure to produce a son. He has had in all four wives but only the last one, a widow, has been fertile; she bore him two daughters but of these the elder died and the surviving child is a baby.

Except that he had rather better food and clothes than his neighbours Chala was in no way distinguished as a child, or given preferential treatment; but as he grew up his parents and elders taught him how to talk to people politely and avoid evil words. When he was about fifteen he was taken by his 'grandfather' (actually his father's elder brother) to the then reigning Maharajah, and told how to address him. For three years he worked at the Court as a sort of groom, and then the reigning Maharajah died and was succeeded by the present Maharajah's elder brother. A month after his death Chala returned home. A little later an order came from the Court that he was to accompany the Maharajah on a long voyage; but together with his father, his 'grandfather,' and an old white-haired lama from Talung monastery he went on a deputation to the Court, taking with him as a gift a ceremonial scarf and a rupee.[3] His 'grandfather' begged the Maharajah to excuse

[3] In Tibet and the neighbouring countries which have been influenced by its customs all formal occasions and gift-giving are accompanied by the present or exchange of a ceremonial scarf; this is a long piece of cloth, varying, according to the means and disposition of the giver, between butter muslin and the finest silk. In gifts from an inferior to a superior, or between equals if the giver wishes to flatter the recipient, one or more coins are given with the scarf. In the strictly graded society of Tibet there are infinite nuances in the

CHALA MANDAL, THE HEAD OF THE VILLAGE

TEMPA, THE DEPOSED MUKTAIR

Chala from accompanying him abroad, explaining that the young man was to be his heir and that he, the 'grandfather,' was getting old and past his work and wanted Chala to help him. The Maharajah granted the request; he put a scarf round Chala's neck and presented him with a coat and length of cloth and gave him a certificate confirming him in the office of Mandal.

Chala Mandal is completely illiterate; he has never learned to read or write; he has, he says, to carry everything, all the accounts and the personal relationships and the long stories he knows and tells 'in his heart and belly.' He must not drink too much *chi* or his memory would go. In a very real way the Mandal has acted as uncle for almost all his tenants, for, in the last twenty years, he has arranged every marriage except two in the neighbourhood. He does not plan in advance; when he thinks a boy or girl ripe for marriage he looks round for a suitable partner and then makes the suggestion to the child's uncles; if the arrangement is satisfactory to both parties the lamas consult the horoscopes to see if the projected marriage will turn out well and the arrangements are proceeded with. Even today when he is growing old he still has to arrange every marriage, in spite of the long marches which the rôle of *bek-bu*, or marriage arranger, entails. Chala Mandal also regulates most of the private affairs of his villagers, scolding and helping if they are extravagant or quarrelsome, or unco-operative; he is called into consultation and consults others on any affair of moderate importance.

With me he pretended to be extremely diffident but was obviously pleased with the respect I paid him; all the visits which we paid one another started out somewhat ceremoniously, though after a few minutes he would settle down and gossip and tell stories happily. He was an extremely good story teller with an astonishing memory; as well as the more serious mythology he would tell comic fables and anecdotes extremely well, mimicking the various voices and actions with most humorous precision; one of my most vivid memories is of him representing a rather foolish female devil consulting the oracle of her pubic hair which waved about in

manner of giving and receiving scarves to indicate the social distance between the two parties.

This giving of a scarf and coin, either alone, or with other gifts, has been completely accepted by the Lepchas, and will be found as a constantly recurring theme in sociological payments, such as marriage, and also often in sacrifices to the supernatural.

answer to questions and which gave an answer which seemed so foolish to the devil that she tore the oracle up by the roots.[4] He is perhaps a trifle too easy-going and a few people appear to take advantage of his good nature; the village, as opposed to some of its less prosperous neighbours, has considerable arrears of taxes; the Mandal himself is considerably in debt. When animals are slaughtered for sacrifice he is in great demand as butcher to distribute the different portions; everybody knows him to be fair and nobody questions his decisions on this or other matters of greater importance. He is very explicit about the main orientations of the culture; for example, he explained that the help that will be given by everybody to poor or indebted men was a special Lepcha custom; 'and I think it is a very good one because it makes everybody realise that they are part of one group and the happiness of one is the happiness of all.'

In some respects Chala Mandal exaggerated the casualness with which all Lepchas, except lamas, treat the minor details of religious rites or the performance of ordinary actions. A constantly recurring phrase, which almost turns into a catchword, in Lepcha conversation is *ket ma-nin*—'it doesn't matter'. The grain isn't covered and the birds will get it—*ket ma-nin*. There is no dried fish and the offering ought to have it—*ket ma-nin*. Chala Mandal was completely sceptical about new-fangled notions, such as the danger to people or plants from menstruating women, which have been imported from outside.

In the event of the Mandal dying without a suitable heir the *youmi* (see below) will act as substitute until the householders have chosen one of their number to become Mandal; preference would probably be given to a member of the same *ptso* but there is no obligation to do so. When a unanimous choice has been decided upon the name will be submitted in a petition to the Rhennock Kazi. For two years the candidate will be on approval, and only after he has shown himself to be thoroughly satisfactory will his tenure of office be officially confirmed. Even when the new Mandal is closely related to the old one he must be formally elected by the householders and confirmed in office by the Maharajah and Kazi. The chief qualifications demanded of a Mandal are wisdom, character, popularity, and adequate wealth.

The offices of Muktair and Mandal can be held by lamas; the other two offices, *youmi* and *gyapön* can not, as these offices may

[4] See Appendix V. b.

entail directly or indirectly the slaughter of animals. In some villages the two offices are combined in a single holder, but in Lingthem they are kept quite distinct. The office of *youmi* is undoubtedly the older, as the linguistic evidence shows; for *youmi* is a Lepcha word and *gyapön* Sikkimese-Tibetan; nor is there a Lepcha equivalent, the only other term used being the general north-Indian *karbari.* I have no evidence as to the time when the specific work of *gyapön* was distinguished; in Lingthem the office has existed at least three generations.

In Lingthem the *youmi* are selected from those who have already held the office of *gyapön*; they consist of old and experienced men who assist the Mandal with their advice and efforts in his various works; they also with the *gyapön* try to compose quarrels or minor misdemeanours without bringing them to the official notice of the Mandal. *Youmi* are selected by the Mandal in consultation with all the responsible householders; as one *youmi* gets too old, or wishes to give up work, or dies, the Mandal nominates another from the ex-*gyapön* to replace him. In Lingthem itself there are three *youmi*; Takneum, Songpo and Ashyok. There is also a separate *youmi* in Panung and a fifth at Liklyang across the river. The *youmi* have no privileges of any sort beyond such prestige as the title gives, but they also have comparatively little work.

The chief work on the administrative side of the village falls on the *gyapön.* Each householder in turn has to hold the office for three years; a sort of rota is established, and people know for some time beforehand when their turn of office falls due. The work is distinctly arduous; it entails the actual collection of the taxes, the summoning of all citizens for ceremonies or when collective work for a village (for example bridge- or road-repairing, or carrying loads) is required, the collection of grain from each house for communal ceremonies and the prevention of crime and quarrelling. A great deal of the *gyapön's* time is taken up in communal business, and consequently their own work and cultivation may have to be somewhat neglected; except for such rare characters as enjoy the power of commanding their neighbours the office holds no advantages. It is clearly stated that it is part of the duty of a householder to undertake this arduous and unrewarding work for his fellows; on that condition will his fellows in their turn look after him. The present *gyapöns* in Lingthem are Kurma and Tinkep. Their term of office finishes in the early autumn of 1937 and they will be replaced by Agyung, the adopted son of Serving, and Itup the son of Takneum *youmi.* There is also a *gyapön* in Panung and one in Liklyang.

iii

The objects of the four above-named offices are twofold; the regulation of intra-village affairs and the collection of taxes for the State. Within the village crime has to be prevented and possibly punished, quarrels stopped, and the poor and needy helped.

There is a fixed tax of Rs. 5 a year on each house, a small tax on certain grain seeds which are sown for crops and a sales tax on the cardamum fruit, which is regulated according to the price fetched and automatically deducted at selling.[5] The total tax payable by the fifty houses under Chala Mandal's jurisdiction is Rs. 3500, averaging Rs. 70[6] per household. The money is collected by the *gyapön* and taken by the Mandal to Gangtok. Although the payment of the taxes is somewhat resented, especially by the older men, it does not seem to me to bear hardly on the Lepchas. Both money and the cash-producing crop of cardamum were introduced together at the beginning of this century—formerly taxes were paid in kind —and everybody grows more than sufficient cardamum to pay their taxes. There are nevertheless some arrears of taxes in Lingthem; indeed a couple of households are seven years in arrear, and that not through poverty but through fecklessness. So feckless are they that the Mandal has threatened that if they do not pay by the next year he will refuse to be responsible for them, in which case they will be summoned to the chief Court in Gangtok. Generally

[5] The actual taxes on seed are as follows :—

Wet rice	Rs. –/8 on 8 lbs.
Millet and maize	Rs. –/12 on 8 lbs.
Dry rice	Rs. 1/– on 32 lbs.

Other crops are not taxed. The tax on cardamum is graduated according to the selling price per maund of 80 lbs.

If the maund fetches	Rs. 10/–	the tax is	Rs. –/14
” ” ”	Rs. 20/–	”	Rs. 1/8
” ” ”	Rs. 40/–	”	Rs. 2/8.

This tax has recently been reduced. Formerly it was at Rs. 2/8 at under Rs. 20, and Rs. 5/– over that sum. The 1936 price of cardamum was Rs. 12/– a maund. There is also a small tax, not very efficiently collected, on animals pastured in, or produce gathered from the forest.

[6] About £5 7 0 or 26 dollars.

the Mandal makes up outstanding debts as far as he can out of his own property.

If through misfortune or poverty a man falls behind with his taxes the Mandal will advise him to collect materials for a feast. At this feast, called *hloang-zok*, the guests will contribute presents of money according to their ability, the money contributed being considered as an absolute gift, and not as a loan. In the last three years three people have thus been cleared of debt by voluntary contributions.

Actual crime takes up very little time. The only generally authenticated murder in the neighbourhood took place two centuries ago; but there are fairly constant rumours and suspicions of poisoning, and at least one instance of suspected foul play[7] which have to be cleared up.

In Lingthem an old widowed nun, Hlatam, the mother of Aga, is generally believed to possess a mysterious slow-acting 'poison,' which either she, or one of her ancestors, is said to have obtained from the Plains people. So strong was this suspicion that twenty years ago the Mandal had her seized while she was working in the fields; she was brought to the monastery where she was given a complete body search by some women, while the *youmi* and *gyapön* ransacked her house: no trace of any poison was found, and after the accusation she prayed in the monastery, calling on the Gods to kill her if she possessed any poison.

Nevertheless the majority of the people of Lingthem still believe that she possesses poison. Chala Mandal says it is both a folly and a sin to call her a poisoner; there is no evidence of her murderous activities, there would be no advantage in her pursuing them and anyhow, where could she obtain the poison? Jiroong and one or two others agree with the Mandal, but the great majority take up the attitude that there is no smoke without fire, and some implicitly believe in her poisoning and are too frightened to take food or drink from her hands. Thus the lama Tafoor says that when he has to go to her house for a ceremony he makes it quite clear that he has come as a priest, and tells her that if he is ill subsequently everybody will know who to blame. Kurma believed that his second wife and her father were both killed by Hlatam; both died of stomach trouble which started almost immediately after receiving food from her, though death did not ensue till some months later.

This poison is considered to have partially natural and partially

[7] See Book Three. Chapter Fifteen pp. 402–403.

supernatural qualities. The poison is meant to be a solid substance, but it does not act unless Hlatam has evil intentions towards the person to whom she gives it. Neither poison nor ill-will are sufficient by themselves; the combination of the two is necessary. The possession of this poison carries certain disadvantages; it cannot be got rid of, for then the supernatural attached to it would destroy the person who threw it away; and it is also necessary to employ it once ever so often or the supernatural will attack the possessor; if no external enemy is the victim it must be given to somebody in the owner's household.

Those who believe in the poison think that before she dies Hlatam will give the poison to her son Aga. If he were to proclaim her guilt during her life-time, people might trust him after her death; if however he says nothing they will fear him, even though he go through the gesture of throwing the poison into the water. Aga is almost the nastiest person in Lingthem; he has a squint and a ullen and leering expression, and is one of the few people on whom .epchas are willing to pronounce moral judgements; two said of im vehemently that he was evil-minded. I considered him below verage intelligence and somewhat malicious; it is possible that e universal fear and suspicion of his mother has rendered him rly and malevolent. Hlatam herself seemed a cheerful and rather wdy-minded old lady, ever ready to joke; outside her own house ople did not distinguish her in any way, but the majority said ey were frightened to visit her and would not take food from her nds unless she tasted it first.

I personally do not believe in Hlatam's 'poisoning'; it reminds of the accusation of Mary Baker Eddy that her third husband s killed by 'arsenical poison mentally administered'.[8] At the ne time it has seemed worth while to treat the subject fully for it almost the only instance of suspected (and possibly repressed and nsferred) aggression among the Lepchas. As will be seen later, misfortunes, whatever their nature, are generally ascribed to the ion of supernaturals, and even personal aggression is usually presented as being outside the aggressor's control. Hlatam has en converted into a sort of scape-goat; among Lepchas even otivated aggression is socially disapproved of; Hlatam is believed exercise almost motiveless malevolence. In general theory her oison' is said to be useful for acquiring property and securing venge; but in the case of her actual named victims there was no

[8] See *Mrs. Eddy* by E. F. Dakin. (London Scribner's 1929.) pp. 166–, 227.

property gain and no feud; at most somebody in the victim's family had at some time said something derogatory about Hlatam. Quarrelling is socially so strongly disapproved of that people of naturally aggressive temperament probably suffer from considerable psychological discomfort and get some relief from the thought of unrestrained aggression practised by somebody else. I have statements by nine people about Hlatam and her poison, for the subject was rather an uncomfortable one and could only be broached to people I knew well; the three most emphatic about her guilt were potentially aggressive in other ways; those who protested her innocence were themselves gentle. The motive of poison obtained from strangers—plainsmen or Nepali or Tibetans—crops up fairly often in anecdote and legend; but I never heard of the strong aconite arrow-poison, which nearly every man possesses, being employed for illegitimate purposes, though when men commit suicide they usually do so by taking it.

Theft is unusual; it practically never occurs from houses, which, if there is nobody at home, are usually padlocked; but this padlock is in point of fact more a social sign that the house is momentarily unoccupied, than a protection against possible entry. Sometimes indeed the padlock is fastened on to a thin loop of bamboo fibre which could be torn to pieces in the hand; and it would never be difficult to make an entry into a Lepcha house through the bamboo floor or walls. A few cases occurred about four years ago of cardamum fruit being stolen off the plants in the field, but there have been no instances of this in the last three years. If a theft is witnessed the robbed person goes and informs the Mandal who then consults with the *youmi*; then the Mandal and *youmi* go to the thief and try their utmost to persuade him to restore the stolen property; if he does so he is given a severe talking to and the incident is considered closed. Should he refuse, however, and should there be clear evidence against him, the matter would be reported to Gangtok; such a course is to be deplored and in fact has not occurred within recent years. If a child commits a theft the father has to insist on restitution and to give the child a severe beating as punishment.

To take even the smallest quantities of fruit or grain from other people's gardens or fields without obtaining permission is regarded as theft, and people would be ashamed of acting in this way, however hungry they might feel. A child who picked a fruit off a neighbour's tree would be severely punished.

There is no supernatural protection against thieves in the house or fields, though there is a feeling (not very strong) that *Thyak-dum*[9] will protect the houses to which he is attached. Lepcha economy is founded on the supposition that people do not steal and that no precautions are necessary against theft; consequently when thefts do occur they are particularly disquieting. There is no social apparatus for discovering the unwitnessed thief, or for forcing a confession; in such cases recourse may be had to supernatural powers, in the form of malicious sorcery. Malicious sorcery can in theory be directed against a personal enemy, but all the instances that I heard of were directed against unknown thieves.

Both lamas and Mun have traditions of malicious sorcery, of getting devils to plague a man or devour his soul; but Mun are considered to be less expert in the matter, taking a month while a lama should only take three days. The Mun are said to work by feeding a particular devil until it is contented and grateful, whereupon it will do whatever is asked. Lamas have two methods; the most learned can summon the victim's soul in the form of an insect and destroy it ritually, whereupon the victim dies at once, or they can summon a devil and hand over the victim to him. To kill a particular person by sorcery it is necessary to have some of their 'dirt'[10]—that is hair clippings, finger nails, or clothes that have been long worn; in the case of an unknown thief a portion of the stolen object, or of some other object which had been in long association with it is desirable, though not essential.

To kill the soul of a person an altar should be erected in the home in front of which is placed a plate covered with rice flour or very fine ashes; around this is arranged a fence of twelve pieces of wood inscribed with the victim's name arranged in pairs meeting at the top: inside the fence is the man's 'dirt' wrapped up in a piece of paper inscribed with his name. The lama then waves a stick with a piece of cloth on it and summons the victim's soul, which will presently arrive in the form of some winged insect; if the man is innocent the insect will not pass the fence but will go straight to the altar and worship there; if it settles on the plate it can be killed, whereupon the victim will immediately die.

To give a person over to a devil the proceeding is somewhat different. The victim's dirt is wrapped up in a piece of paper which

[9] See Chapter Two, pp. 74–75.

[10] The collective noun, used by Lepchas to indicate the exuviae, the portions of a victim's body or clothing which can be used for malicious sorcery, is *mari* which means literally 'body dirt.'

NINETY - YEAR - OLD SERVING, THE OLDEST MAN IN LINGTHEM

TAKNEUM *YOUMI*, WHO ATE BOAR-PIG

has been smeared with blood and arrow-poison, and inscribed with the victim's name and a spell written in Tibetan characters (the spell itself is believed to be in Burmese). This is put into a bamboo *patyoot* and is then offered to a man-eating devil, together with *cherkem*, consisting of grain floating in *chi* and blood, and other offerings. When the sorcerer is apprised of the arrival of the devil, either by a dream or by seeing him in reality he says to it 'So and so is my enemy, and I give his flesh to you to eat'; after that the bamboo is buried near one of the devil's houses. To make a person ill a quite simple ceremony is performed inside the monastery.

Tafoor, who told me about these rituals, is one of the three lamas of the neighbourhood who know how to perform them; the other two are the two Dorjé Lapoon, who received the knowledge from learned Tibetan lamas. Tafoor has never practised himself, and is not sure if the first Dorjé Lapoon ever did, but his uncle, the second Dorjé Lapoon, who taught him, has killed two people by sorcery. The first was when he was a student; a man came to his teacher and asked him to sorcerise somebody for him, and the teacher told his pupil to try his hand. The second instance was many years later, when his knife was stolen at a monastery feast; the thief, though he did not know it at the time, was one of the second Dorjé Lapoon's young pupils; the pupil did not know that the sorcery had been started against him or he could have averted it by returning the knife; only after his death, three months later, was his identity known and the lost knife recovered.

Nowadays the second Dorjé Lapoon refuses to perform sorcery any longer. The Maharajah has issued stringent orders forbidding the practice, and he himself, when on pilgrimage to Kathmandhu, made a vow not to indulge further in such wicked acts. Some time ago both Tafoor and Takneum *youmi* had cardamum fruit stolen and asked the second Dorjé Lapoon to sorcerise the thieves; but he replied that it was wicked to kill a man and that thieves should be dealt with by the police. According to lamaist ethics, it is a sin to kill a man by sorcery, but not a grievous sin if the lama afterwards helps his victim's soul to heaven. To kill a man with weapons is a far greater sin; for every person's body is the home of a hundred small gods called Tamba Rigya, and they are destroyed with the body.

About eighteen years ago the husband of Pumri—now the wife of the second Dorjé Lapoon, but at that time his uncle's wife—had a goat stolen; he found some of the stolen meat and brought t to the second Dorjé Lapoon and requested him to sorcerise the unknown thieves. Since the aggrieved party was his uncle, he agreed and started the necessary preparations. But while he was making the *cherkem* his elder brother, also a lama, arrived, saw what he was doing, and dissuaded him. Thereupon Pumri's husband took the meat to a Mun who has since died; he performed the sorcery and all the members of the thief's family (it is the family to which Kurma's second wife belonged) died one after the other; eight or nine are now dead and the family is almost extinct.

This is the last recorded case of sorcery being exercised in the district. The tradition is generally known about, and a certain awe of the three lamas who have this special knowledge is felt. But in Zongu there is no fear of one's 'dirt' being taken and used maliciously, and cut hair or nails are let lie where they fall; when they are in foreign parts however Lepchas say that they take care to burn or bury their 'dirt'. The Lepchas have also added an uncanonical rider to the Tibetan tradition of sorcery to the effect that the sorcery when it is directed against a particular person will only hurt that person if he or she is actually guilty; if he is not, the devil will return and destroy the sender. As opposed to the fear of poisoning the fear of sorcery is non-existent, and the subject is practically never mentioned in casual conversation.

Adultery, as will be seen later, is practically never taken any notice of; but if the instance should be particularly flagrant the aggrieved husband has two ways of punishing the lover; he can either beat the lover, thereby shaming him, or he can go and inform the Mandal. If he does this the Mandal will summon a meeting of the elders of the village and will then go to the house of the lover and summon him to confess; if he does so he has to pay to the husband either one chicken and a pig, or Rs. 5/–. If neither lover will confess the matter is abandoned. Discovered adultery is not a cause of enmity either between husband and wife or between husband and lover; only in the case of persistent adultery, and of the woman showing a really marked preference for the lover, would the marriage be broken up.

The only other cause of dispute inside the village is the suspicion of boundary marks to fields having been moved. The only case recorded of this occurred fifteen years ago between an old man, since dead, and the father of Aga; this dispute, however, was patched up without calling in the Mandal, *youmi* and *gyapön* who would normally settle such disputes, if the first representations were ineffectual. In such cases the person who thinks he is wronged may curse his suspected aggressor by calling on *Rum Adum*, the Just God, to punish him by making him halt, maimed and blind. If the aggressor should be guilty he or his relations will die.

In the case of disputes between individuals a solemn oath may be made with religious ceremony, and also in the case of people who are suspected of evil doing without having any definite accusers; for instance, it would be open to Hlatam to make a solemn oath that she was not a poisoner; she has not done so. About twenty years ago, however, a man in a neighbouring village who was suspected of poisoning made the requisite ceremonies to swear that he was innocent of the victim's death;[11] his guilt is now believed to be firmly established, for he and all his kin subsequently died the same painful and lingering death. False swearing is for the Lepchas one of the most important and unsocial crimes; the false swearer and his family would be shunned. But there is more to it than that; a perjurer among one's ancestors constitutes an hereditary taint; all the descendants of such a one will die young; and therefore in arranging marriages care must be taken to see that the intended spouse does not come of such a family.[12]

Personal quarrels are felt to be the concern of everybody, and every effort is made to prevent them, or to stop them once they have broken out. Annually in the autumn an elaborate ceremony is held in the monastery to destroy the trinity of devils (enmity of speech, thought and deed) who cause quarrelling; and the first action in any public or private lamaist ceremony is to invoke and destroy Gett'r *moong*, the quarrel demon, to prevent disputes among the celebrants, and especially the noisy abuse which may occur when people have drunk too much. In the unhappy event of a quarrel taking place despite these precautions a mutual friend of the two disputants will give a feast for them to try and make up the trouble. Should the quarrel continue for no apparent reason

[11] See Chapter Fifteen, pp. 392–393.

[12] The heredities which render a person undesirable as a marriage partner are the following:—

(1) *Sanaar Tsuk git* an ancestor has been killed by a bear.
(2) *Doam git* an ancestor has died of leprosy.
(3) *Rumdong git* an ancestor has died of a violent jaundice.
(4) *Ryak mat git* an ancestor has committed perjury.
(5) *Arot moong git* an ancestor has died by violence.

All these disabilities are believed to be hereditary.

it will be presumed that this is owing to the malevolent action of a supernatural, and exorcism will be resorted to.

It may happen, however, that the quarrel is of a more serious nature and consists of accusations and counter-accusations. Should such a quarrel break out there is a whole apparatus for patching it up without official notice being taken of it; should the Mandal hear of it in his official capacity, worse still should it go to the Court, it would be a terrible thing; there would be strict punishment and bad blood and that would be a slur on the community.

When a quarrel does break out the *gyapön* will in the first instance go to both houses to find out the cause of the quarrel, and, if possible, to a third neutral person as witness. He talks diplomatically to both parties, softening each other's version of the incident; if he can make peace in this way all three will drink *chi* together and that is the end of the matter. If, however, the two parties persist in quarrelling (owing to a sense of injury) the *gyapön* will instruct both parties to prepare *chi* and to have a certain sum of money ready—always considerably larger than what would actually be needed—in order to make the people realise the seriousness of their offence.

Chi takes about eight or nine days to be ready, and while it is brewing the *gyapön* consults with the *youmi*; they then make another effort to compose the quarrel without calling in the Mandal. The three adjudicators take a statement from each party and then, unless the blame is obviously on one side, they call them together and threaten them that if they do not make peace, they will be very heavily fined (say Rs. 25 from each of them). The sum demanded is calculated to be beyond their reach, so that they beg the *youmi* and *gyapön* not to proceed further; whereupon the *gyapön* agrees to be contented with a much lesser sum, say Rs. 2/8 from each, or if they have no money, with a copper vessel or plate or anything of equivalent value. After that the two quarrellers and the three adjudicators eat and drink *chi* together; at the end of the feast the two quarrellers are given a wordy and imposing sermon on the duty of living amicably at peace one with another; at the end of the sermon the fines are returned and the whole matter is at an end.

In the last three years in Lingthem there have been two serious quarrels. Both of them centred round Mrs. Jiroong; she is Tempa's sister, like him a foreigner to Zongu; she is far more aggressive and has a far more active ego-feeling than the other local-born Lepcha women. The first quarrel was with the wife of the lama

Datoop whom she accused of seducing her husband; they had two noisy and public quarrels in the guardian's house by the monastery, so that the Mandal was forced to interfere. Mrs. Datoop easily proved her innocence; as a punishment Mrs. Jiroong has been permanently forbidden to enter the monastery compound when feasts are in progress. This effectively cuts her off from the major community relaxations, and incidentally gives her hen-pecked husband, who is a lama and therefore has to be present, an opportunity to escape from her constant scoldings.

The second quarrel was of a more complicated nature; like the first, it represents an attitude towards sex which is completely alien to the Lepchas of Zongu. The facts are briefly as follows. Jiroong, the youngest son of a very poor family, was married by the Mandal to an old and childless widow (his first wife, since dead) so that he could inherit her property. His eldest brother had a son Tobgé who, on his father's death, gave up his old home, and went with his wife to go and live with his uncle and aunt. Mrs. Jiroong never liked Tobgé, whom she considered treated her without sufficient respect; so, to revenge herself, she persuaded Mrs. Tobgé to run away with a young married neighbour named Dadool. To forward the elopement she accompanied Mrs. Tobgé and Dadool on a visit to Mrs. Tobgé's parents who live on the far side of the Teesta beyond Zongu. After they had been absent three days the matter was reported to the *gyapön*. Before they could take any action however it was learned that Jiroong and Tempa had already gone in pursuit. On their arrival they asked what was the meaning of the escapade, to which the women replied that they had come to see Mrs. Tobgé's family. Tempa and Jiroong were furious at this reply, and, they said subsequently, felt that they could have killed Mrs. Tobgé, whom they considered irresponsible and of a bad character; but the girl had many 'brothers', and they undertook to be responsible for her and to send her home. Dadool returned separately. On their return the Mandal lectured the two young people and told them that they were to live quietly with their own spouses and to behave in future.

Since then Tobgé and Dadool have kept the peace and appear friendly enough; but the enmity between Tobgé and Mrs. Jiroong is stronger than ever, and there is no certainty that the affair will not flair up again. It is known that Dadool and Mrs. Tobgé are still sleeping together for they have been surprised in a field-house, but there is no way of telling if Tobgé himself knows of this.

For a few days Dadool worked for us, fetching fire-wood and water. Jiroong's house is one of the nearest to the monastery. One night, it was believed, Dadool did not return home, and in the morning his wife was not in the home either. Towards midday a a very serious deputation, headed by Mrs. Datoop and Kurma *gyapön* came and asked us to dismiss Dadool; the proximity of Jiroong's house, it was felt, put temptation in his way. The situation was discussed very seriously in low and distressed voices; it was not, as similar circumstances would probably be with us, a rather spicy piece of scandal—for the people involved were in no way directly related—but the threat of impending general unpleasantness. If Mrs. Dadool had gone to complain to her 'brothers' there would be a considerable upset; they would send their *bek-bu* (marriage go-between) to the Mandal, who had been Dadool's *bek-bu*, to say 'You persuaded us to consent to this marriage, and now see what has happened.' If this occurred the Mandal would have to inflict two fines of Rs. 5/– each on Mrs. Tobgé which she would have to pay to Mrs. Dadool, and Dadool would have to pay Rs. 5/– to Tobgé. Fortunately on this occasion their apprehensions were not realised; Dadool turned up in the afternoon with a reasonable account of how he had spent the previous evening; and later in the day his wife returned from Mangan, whither she had gone to buy cigarettes.

The whole situation is a good illustration of Lepcha attitudes. Normally sexual intercourse would not be the subject of serious conversation at all, though it might be joked about; and it seems probable that without Mrs. Jiroong's continual encouragement the affaire would have lapsed long ago, for Dadool appears fond of his wife and contented. But a quarrel or dispute is a menace to everybody's happiness; half the pleasure is lost from a feast if there is a feeling of discomfort in the air. For the Lepchas quarrelling is not natural or inevitable, but a deplorable accident which it is everybody's business to stop.

CHAPTER SIX

THE RULES OF KINSHIP AND MARRIAGE

i

When a Lepcha speaks of 'we' he generally means all the people of his village. But besides these geographical divisions Lepchas are divided up into other groups by birth and marriage; these groups are the patrilineal clan, or *ptso*, and the immediate and extended family. Unlike their neighbours, the Nepali, the Lepchas have a very small number of kinship terms;[1] fewer even than we have, for they exclude all the category of cousins, and, except for the mother's brothers, make no distinction between the paternal and maternal lines. For people younger than the speaker, too, they do not make any distinction of sex; the same word is used for a younger brother or a younger sister, for a son or a daughter, for a nephew or a niece. Only in the case of children's spouses are different words used for son-in-law and daughter-in-law.

Old age is considered by the Lepchas to be a desirable quality; the polite term of address to anybody you are not related to is 'old man'; and there is a tendency to push anybody older than the speaker into a higher generation. Thus, when a man has had a child he calls his wife's parents 'grandfather' and 'grandmother', and the parents call their own elder brothers and sisters 'father' and 'mother'; the wife's elder brother, or her elder sister's husband (and conversely) are equated with her father. The opposite tendency is also manifested towards the wives of younger brothers (the elder brother calls them 'daughters-in-law') and the husbands of younger sisters (the elder sister calls them 'sons-in-law'). In the joint family which dwells under a single roof only nine terms are normally used: 'grandfather', 'grandmother,' 'father',

[1] A complete list of Lepcha kinship terms and other common forms of address are given in Appendix II.

'mother', 'elder brother', 'elder sister', 'younger brother-or-sister,' 'child' and 'grandchild'. It does not matter how many brothers and their wives live together; all the brothers are called 'father', all their wives 'mother' by all the children; if it is necessary to distinguish which 'mother' or 'father' is meant, the child will say 'big mother', 'little mother', and if necessary 'middle mother'; his own mother he will call his 'real mother'. If the married brothers live in different houses the children of the younger brother will still call the elder brother and his wife 'father' and 'mother'; but the sons of the elder brother will call the younger brother 'uncle', and his wife 'potential spouse' (*azong*), for, as will be seen later, they may under certain circumstances inherit her.

The Lepchas count descent nine generations back on the father's side, and at least four on the mother's; a person with whom you share a common ancestor on the paternal side nine generations back is addressed in the same way as your real brothers and sisters, and their parents as though they were the brother and sister-in-law of your father. In theory a person should always be given the correct title reckoning back to this common ancestor, without regard to the relative age of the two people, but when the situation becomes too ridiculous the terms are modified. For example the co-wives of Lumba *chithembu* were 'grandmother' and 'grandchild' (the first wife was the grandchild of a younger brother, the second wife the great-great-grandchild of an elder sister) though there was only nine years difference in their ages; but the younger wife called the elder 'mother', because calling her 'grandmother' made her appear too old. Similarly Tafoor had a half-sister Pankek who was younger than his own children: he therefore told his children to call her by her name until she grew up, as the proper term for an aunt, *a-nyou*, is a very respectful one, and would be brought into ridicule if given to a little girl of six.

Except in the case of very young children people are almost always referred to by the proper kinship terms, or by their ecclesiastical or lay titles. Women are practically never named after marriage; they are referred to firstly as their husband's wife, and, as soon as they have borne a child, as their child's mother. Occasionally they are referred to as the inhabitants of the village they were born in. Only occasionally do childless widows start using personal names again. I know the names of very few women in Lingthem, and that is not because of bashfulness on my part or on the part of the people I talked to; men may remember the names of their wives, and do know those of their daughters, but practically never those of any other married women.

Personal names are of practically no importance to the Lepchas of Zongu and they have no sort of permanence. On the third day after birth, when the lama casts the infant's horoscope, he will discover his 'sacred name'; but this is never spoken by anyone, merely inscribed on the horoscope; it is never used subsequently; and nobody knows their own sacred name. On the third-day birth feast one of the people present (usually an 'aunt' or the officiating Mun) will give the child some name; it may refer to some physical peculiarity (e.g. *Thyak Thimbu*—Big Head), to some incident which took place while the mother was carrying the child, or may just be the day of the week on which it was born. In the case of a child born after several previous children had died young, he or she is often given a deprecating name such as Peut, which means a wandering Tibetan beggar-monk, or Tafong, which means a manger. But these names are equally impermanent. As the child grows older anybody may give him a nickname; thus Kurma *gyapön* as an infant was named by an aunt Tayout; his mother called him Kurma because as a suckling he was bad tempered (people say *kur kur* to a cross child). As children grow up their nicknames increase; and a person's name is simply that which is used most often. Many people have two or three names of equal validity, a state of affairs which at the beginning caused me enormous confusion. Thus Peut, Chano's 'brother', was also called Chinya, Nariya Kochet, Serving Aving and so forth. Except for outsiders names are of very little importance; the householder in whose name the property is registered must keep that name in use; otherwise names are almost non-functional.

It occasionally happens that as part of the cure of an illness the lamas will order their patient to change his or her name for a year; in such cases a new nickname is provided. If the banned name is meaningful the word is not avoided in ordinary conversation. The names of dead siblings are never given to new-born children, and those of the recently dead very seldom. It occasionally happens that the lama finds from his horoscope that the new-born child is the reincarnation of a dead ancestor; even in such cases, though the situation is considered mildly auspicious, the child is not given the name it bore in the earlier incarnation.

Names have a certain negative effect; a person should never

mention the names of his parents or parents-in-law; a man should never mention the name of those women he calls daughter-in-law (that is the wives of his sons, of his younger brothers, and of his brother's sons), nor a woman the names of those men she calls 'son-in-law' (that is her daughter's husbands, her younger sisters' husbands, and the husbands of her sisters' daughters). These prohibitions hold good even after a person is dead; but here likewise there is no avoidance of the same or similar-sounding words in ordinary conversation. To call a person by name, rather than by their title or a kinship term is considered to be somewhat ill-mannered; it has the same effect as though one were treating him as a child or inferior. In Europe a parallel situation is created when a stranger is immediately addressed by his or her Christian name; it is classing that person as a child or a servant.

It is difficult to gauge the emotional weight which is carried by terms primarily employed in the immediate family when they are applied to more distant connections. My impression is that the use of such terms as 'mother' and 'father' does carry, and is intended to carry, some of the emotional attitudes derived from the original application of the terms. No child who was able to talk had any doubt as to who were his real father and mother, but many would say 'I have two mothers; my real mother is little mother.'

Among the Lepchas the crucial situation arises when a young man lives in the same house as the wife of his father's younger brother. If these two lived in different houses the woman would be a potential spouse for the boy; he would call her *aẓong* and would have the right to sleep with her. But if they live in the same house he will call her 'mother' and, on account of the emotions of respect and incest surrounding the term, is meant to respect her. In Lingthem there were five or six young men in this situation, and I was not, in any of the cases, able to decide to my own satisfaction whether they did or did not sleep with their 'little mothers'. In the presence of other people they would always deny doing so, for they would be ashamed to say otherwise; three or four confessed privately to having done so, but all on later occasions tried to withdraw or modify their statement, saying for example that though they had slept together they had not done anything. Third parties would never speculate on such private behaviour; to direct questions they would reply with the catch-phrase 'Who can read what is in the heart of another?' Such behaviour, though considered rather shameless, is not stigmatised as incestuous or even immoral, and there are no sanctions against it. The boy is meant to respect the name of 'mother', but whether he does or not, 'depends entirely on the hearts of the two people concerned.'

A Lepcha is expected to respect his parents and grand-parents, his parents-in-law, and his sons- and daughters-in-law. Of these 'respect-full' situations by far the most important is that between a Lepcha and his parents-in-law. A person is more respectful to his spouse's parents than to his own; he uses more honorific words to them and is careful never to use directly obscene language in front of them. A person must never witness his parents-in-law copulating nor must he be seen doing so by them. Should either of these situations arise the elders will be ashamed and angry.

The tensest of all situations, and one which lasts during the whole life-time of both parties is the relation between a man and his wife's mother, and a woman and her husband's father. These relationships are always rather strained and uncomfortable. If for instance a man's mother-in-law says something immodest, the man himself will feel uncomfortable, and may get up and go away. For a man the situation is most uncomfortable in the period between his betrothal and his bringing his wife home. During that period he has to spend about half his time in his father-in-law's home, helping him in his work; he is almost treated as a servant, under the orders of his father-in-law, and has to be modest and circumspect in his speech and behaviour; the male relations of his wife on the other hand have complete licence to tease him as much as they will and to use every sort of obscene term; if he is provoked into answering back he is humiliated. A woman when she first comes to her husband's house is also delicately situated; but after the actual marriage feast there is no licenced teasing of the bride and, if she is living continually in the same house as her father-in-law, the strain, though it never quite wears off, is considerably lessened. Once he has brought his wife home a man still has to avoid the crudest sexual phrases in front of his parents-in-law; but it is considered a rather amusing and risky game to sail as near the wind as possible.

In theory equal modesty of speech and behaviour should be shown in front of one's own parents and siblings of the opposite sex, but in point of fact in Zongu it is not; one of the things that most shocked our Lepcha servants, who came from the mixed community of Gangtok, was that parent and child, brother and sister, would joke and act without the least restraint in one another's presence. In fact the Gangtok Lepchas dubbed their brothers of Zongu shameless and uncivilised. Obscene remarks, gestures and actions are never directed towards people nearly related; but the presence of such people is no restraint. Adult brothers and sisters should not, and on the whole do not, touch one another except in cases of actual necessity, such as helping a person at work or if they are ill. This prohibition does not extend to dressing the hair, which can be performed by anybody for anybody else, with the exception of a son- or daughter-in-law and parent-in-law of the opposite sex.

ii

Every Lepcha belongs to a patrilineal clan or *ptso*, which is believed to have originated from some supernatural or legendary ancestor. Nowadays the chief function of the *ptso* is the regulation of marriage and the prevention of incest; it is, to all intents and purposes, an exogamic unit. In theory people of the same *ptso* are allowed to marry if they are separated by nine generations from a common ancestor, and to indicate that a person of the same *ptso* is very far removed a Lepcha will always say 'we can marry'; but in point of fact I did not come upon nor hear of a single instance of two people of the same *ptso* marrying. It was generally stated that though such a marriage was permissive, people would feel shame in it.

It is allowable to marry back into a mother's *ptso* after four generations; but so near a connection is considered somewhat shameless. Datoop's father, the first Dorjé Lapoon, took as his second wife a woman he called 'aunt' (*a-nyou*); his grandmother was a sister of her mother. This marriage was considered quite shameless, and even nearly sixty years later was a subject for embarrassment; but it demanded no sanctions against it, such as would have been invoked if the connection had been on the father's side.

It seems to me possible that in former times the *ptso* represented a geographical unit; in the very small villages there is a tendency for all, or at any rate the majority, of the men to be members of the same *ptso*. But nowadays this has broken down (if indeed it was ever institutionalised) completely; in Lingthem there are male representatives of twelve *ptso*. Of these the most populous and powerful is the Jamyong *ptso* to which Chala Mandal belongs. Eleven of the thirty-two households belong to this *ptso* representing in all sixty-two individuals, or nearly a third of the population of the village (176); but from this number must be subtracted the twenty-one married women from other *ptso*; I have not reckoned the daughters who have married into other *ptso*. Zumchyung *ptso*, to which Tafoor and his family belong, is the next most populous; it represents five households and thirty-one people, less the ten married women. At the other end of the scale are the Demik and Lubdong Rabji *ptso*, with only a single representative of each—Katel and Pargeut—in the neighbourhood. As far as I can tell from questioning visitors to Lingthem, the situation is similar in the other bigger villages; one or two large and numerous *ptso*, of which the Mandal is nearly always a member, and several other smaller ones.[2]

There is a slight advantage in belonging to a numerous *ptso* because you have more people you can call ' brothers ' on whose help you can count automatically; but it is not an overwhelming advantage, on account of the Lepcha habits of co-operation, and some of the richest and most successful people of Lingthem were members of small *ptso*. In the choice of a son- or daughter-in-law the size of the *ptso* is sometimes taken into consideration; it is better for a child-in-law to come from a numerous *ptso*, for then there will be greater possibility of obtaining a second spouse, in the event of the first one's sterility or death. A stranger such as Tempa who marries into a populous *ptso* (his wife's father was Jamyong *ptso*) has the same advantages as if he were himself a member of it and his wife's relations behave to him exactly as if they were his own.

Each *ptso* is under the guardianship of certain supernaturals, who are worshipped by all the male members of the *ptso*; every third year all the men of one locality gather together and make a sacrifice of an ox and certain jewels and valuables (these latter are only symbolically offered and are subsequently retaken into use) followed by a feast; these feasts are held in rotation in the houses of the members of the *ptso* who live in the neighbourhood. This sacrifice is entirely under the direction of the Mun, with no admixture of lamaism at all, and a few of the more pious lamas refuse to participate in them, claiming that the lamas have in Chukyoong *rum* a ' guild ' supernatural more powerful and more worthy of worship than the

[2] The distribution of *ptso* in Lingthem is tabulated in Appendix I, b.

gods of the *ptso*; but the greater number of lamas feel no metaphysical qualms and bear their full share in this Mun ceremony. The *ptso* supernaturals are always invoked by the Mun when they perform a ceremony for the benefit of a particular individual. In the Mun theogony all the *ptso* supernaturals are friendly and there is no rivalry between the groups; it is thought that the more populous the *ptso* the stronger the guardian supernaturals.

The *ptso* supernaturals descend, as it were, from father to son; women have other different supernaturals which descend from mother to daughter; with the consequence that brothers and sisters have different guardian supernaturals, although all children are counted as members of their father's *ptso*. (An exception must be made in the case of unacknowledged bastards, who are considered to be members of the *ptso* of their mother's father.) These women's supernaturals are invoked, along with numberless others, at the Mun ceremonies after sowing and harvesting, and special sacrifices are made in their intention in the case of illness. Special sacrifices are also made to them at the time of the marriage feast, and the questioning of the bride about her special supernaturals is one of the most formalised incidents in the marriage ceremonies. There are certain other supernaturals which are common to all women; these include Ami *rum*, the god of riches, and Katong Fi who visits women in their dreams and copulates with them at the time of their menses; this dream-copulation is meant to continue throughout life, and should a month pass without this dream it means that the woman is shortly going to die. Parallel to these exclusively female supernaturals are Pong *rum*, and his wife Shing *rum*, the patrons of hunting, who are worshipped exclusively by men. There are also other supernaturals who are as it were patrons of each sex respectively, and yet others who belong to the family, as distinct from the *ptso*. Among the countless supernaturals with which the world is filled these personal and private ones have no great significance; along with numberless others—the enumeration of gods in a Mun sacrifice may take two or three hours—they are prayed to for the blessings of long life, many children, and prosperity, but their power is not considered to be great.

Except as an exogamic classification the *ptso* is now functionless. Although members of the different *ptso* are scattered, not only throughout Zongu, but wherever Lepchas live, the triennial unions only gather those members who live near one another; to the best of my knowledge there has never been, nor has there ever been a reason for, a general gathering of all the members of the *ptso*. A traveller among strange people has no claim on the hospitality of unknown members of his *ptso*, though it would still be shameful for two members of the same *ptso* to have sexual connection. More than anything else, the *ptso* is a device for the prevention of incest.

iii

Incest for the Lepchas is horrifying; they do not call it a sin but *nam-toak*, an act which produces a year of disaster for the community. Sin is a lamaist conception and is on the whole only applied to acts like the killing of animals; *nam-toak* is the phrase used for personal acts which are felt to be strongly anti-social. Any sexual connection with blood relations for nine generations on the father's side and four on the mother's is considered incestuous; but children under the age of puberty, or, as the Lepchas say 'who are not old enough to know shame', are not considered capable of committing incest and no watch is kept on children's play. Besides blood relations sexual connection with the following relations-by-marriage is considered as incestuous: for a man to sleep with any of the women he calls 'mother-in-law' or 'daughter-in-law' (that is his wife's mother, his wife's elder sister, the wife of his wife's elder brother, and his sons' wives, the wives of his *younger* brothers, and the wives of his brothers' and sisters' sons); for a woman, to sleep with any of the men she calls 'father-in-law' or 'son-in-law' (that is her husband's father, her husband's *elder* brothers, the husband of her husband's elder sister, and her daughter's husbands, the husbands of her younger sisters, and the husbands of her brothers' and sisters' daughters). Such relationships, besides causing a year of disaster to the community, would call down a devil on to the guilty couple who would cover them with sores. Should children result from such a union they would be allowed to live, but they would either be of an evil mind or idiots. and would be short-lived.

No cases of mother-son or father-daughter incest are known of; nor does the situation occur in any mythological story. Brother-sister incest on the other hand is a motive in a great deal of Mun mythology, inevitably so, for the world and all that therein is are the children of Itpomu the Creative Mother. The origin of devils and noxious animals arises from the incest of her first two 'human' children (if I can so express it) Komsi*thing* and Narzong-*nyou*. I only heard of one case of true brother-sister incest, and that occurred in another village some generations ago. There are however two contemporary incestuous couples from Zongu whom the Lepchas classify as 'brother' and 'sister'; in both cases they were two generations removed from a common ancestor, or in our classification second cousins. These couples were shunned as irremediably unclean and contagious; they were exiled from their villages and neighbourhood; neither neighbour nor relative would visit them nor help them; when they die nobody would see to the disposal of their body, nor conduct their soul to paradise. One of the couples died after their guilty association had lasted ten years; the other couple, who came from the village of Parfok eleven years ago, are still living at a village three days' walk from Zongu; people from Zongu have seen them on their travels and recently one or two have spoken to them; so far no Lepcha has entered their house nor taken food from them.

It is considered very wicked, though the act will only affect the actual performers, for a man and his son to sleep with the same woman, or a mother and her daughter with the same man; if this is done the line will die out. This situation does however occur occasionally; there is a recent case from Pantong of a man living with mother and daughter; the trio died after three years. Another recent instance occurred at Liklyang on the other side of the river, where a woman was living with her married daughter and son-in-law; a stranger came and married the mother and subsequently slept with the daughter. Although such behaviour is very disgraceful instances of it are recounted with considerable relish, and not with the shocked embarrassment with which stories of true incest are recounted; it is a bad thing to do, but there is something rather attractive and dare-devil about it. The man who told with enormous gusto the story of one man living with mother and daughter seemed shocked and disgusted when recounting the incident of Takal's wife sleeping with Satéo and his father. The emotion which these stories of one man possessing both mother and daughter evoke seems to me to indicate that the rivalry between father and son, or father and son-in-law, so successfully muted by the Lepchas' cultural arrangements, is not entirely suppressed, and finds some gratification in dwelling on these wicked people who have displaced a potential rival.[3]

[3] It should be noted that in both these cases the man first married the mother and then afterwards slept with the step-daughter. Had he acted in the reverse order—marrying the daughter and then sleeping with her mother—the situation would have counted as fully incestuous.

A child should know who are his *num-neu-zong*, that is those people with whom all sexual contact is prohibited, by the time he is nine or ten. By the time he is twelve or thirteen a boy should also know those women whom he is permitted to sleep with—usually a very much smaller number than those who are forbidden. In the case of those relations of a generation above his own—that is to say, the wives of his father's 'elder brothers', he also has to know which of these women his father has slept with beforehand, for in that case the potential partner becomes permanently forbidden. Thus for example, Chimpet can never sleep with nor inherit his 'aunt' Mrs. Datoop (Tafoor calls Datoop 'elder brother' although they are actually three generations away from a common ancestor) because several years ago his father slept with her. Since sexual relationships outside the prohibited degrees are not considered embarrassing or important, no unpleasant or guilt-ridden situation arises through the father having to inform his son about his earlier sexual life. Such subjects are rather a matter for joking, but it would be a disaster if, through ignorance, the son cut short the family line.

iv.

Owing to the wide application of the incest ban it often happens that a boy or girl has not a single potential spouse or unmarried love-partner in the same village; and consequently in the far greater number of cases a boy's wife has to be sought from a distant village, and a girl has to leave her home far behind when she goes to her husband. Of the sixty married women in Lingthem all but thirteen were from outside; and of these thirteen four had married newcomers to the village.[4] The remaining nine were either representatives of small *ptso*, or else their husbands were.

Lepchas make their first marriage extremely young. In Lingthem there was only one girl over fourteen unbetrothed, and that was Prumtu, who had a bad squint, was reputed to be lazy, and had a rough and unpleasing character. Eight boys over sixteen were unbetrothed; they were the two carpenters,[5] three mental defectives who will never be married, and three orphans. These orphans were Satéo, who was very badly lame and without property

[4] For a full list of married women and their place of origin see Appendix I, a, Table II.

[5] See Chapter Four, p. 121.

whom the Mandal was looking after, Takshyom, Kurma's nineteen-year-old nephew, and Kanchok, the seventeen-year-old adopted son of Chelim. Of these three it is possible that Satéo will never be married; if he were hale and able to do his work properly his poverty would not stand in his way; but nobody would want to give their daughter to a poor cripple. In Lingthem there is no suitable unrelated girl; if there were one the Mandal would probably arrange the match. The other two wards are expected to be betrothed shortly, as soon as a suitable partner with a fitting horoscope can be found. Mental defectives are never married, and people with incapacitating physical defects practically never.

There are two stages in Lepcha marriage: *asék*, or betrothal, and *bri* or bringing home the bride. *Asék* is actually the validating ceremony at which the formal gifts from the family of the groom to that of the bride are presented; these gifts are called 'the price of the bride' and once they are accepted the groom has full access to his bride and all children born after *asék* are considered as legitimate. But until the large and expensive marriage feast or *bri* has been performed, the wife and, possibly, her children, stay at her father's house save possibly for short visits; and during this period the son-in-law is, as it were, his father-in-law's servant, and has to go and work for him whenever he is summoned and cannot leave without obtaining his permission; he is in a subordinate position, and, though he may be taunted, must never answer back.

Marriages are always arranged through the offices of two *bek-bu*, or between-men, one representing each party. In theory any old and experienced man who knows how to make the formal and flowery speeches in *tang-bor* or allusive periphrases[6] can fill this rôle and in other villages there are a number of *bek-bu*; but in Lingthem in the last twenty years in all but two of the sixty marriages which have taken place the Mandal has filled this rôle. In theory the biological parents should have nothing at all to do with their children's marriages; were they to do so either the children would die young or the marriage would break up. All the negotiations concerning a marriage are carried on by the paternal or maternal uncles of the children, preferably a paternal-uncle-older-than-father, or people standing in this relation; but in point of fact the parents are always surreptitiously, and sometimes fairly openly consulted. The demand for marriage is always made in

[6] For further explanations of *tang-bor* and examples see Chapter Ten, p. 265.

the first place by the boy's *bek-bu*, acting under the uncle's instructions; he visits the girl's village, going to some strange house, and inquires who is the man who will act as the girl's *bek-bu*. The girl's *bek-bu* then acts as intermediary between the boy's *bek-bu* and the girl's 'uncle'.

When a son-in-law is proposed some representative of the girl is always sent to the boy's village to inquire about his character, whether he is peaceful and a good worker; formerly tests of felling wood used to be imposed. Some parents take into account the prospective property of the boy, but personal appearance and the relative age of the two parties are not generally considered. The more pious lamas will only consider lamas as suitable sons-in-law. Care has to be taken that neither party suffers under any hereditary taint.[7]

It usually happens that the boy and girl do not know one another at all before the betrothal; occasionally however a boy and girl who know one another wish to marry; in such cases the boy approaches either his uncle or his *bek-bu* and ask him to enter into negotiations. When widowers with property remarry this is always the case; and usually the man will have already impregnated his wife before the first overtures are made.

There is a distinct tendency for several members of two families or neighbourhoods to marry each other; once one woman from a strange community is brought into a village, she is liable to establish further contacts between members of her old community and those of her new one; and, provided the rules of a descent are not infringed, there is a tendency for a woman's daughters to marry back into their mother's old village. It is quite common for two siblings of one family to marry two siblings of another, whether it be two brothers marrying two sisters, or an exchange of sisters, each brother marrying the sister of the other. The marriage of two people does not affect the subsequent marriages of their families in the same generation in any way, but it is considered preferable for, say, the elder brother of the groom to marry the elder sister of the bride, and the younger, the younger; contrary arrangements are not forbidden, but they involve a readjustment of relationships which is felt to be awkward and uncomfortable, and I never came across nor heard of such an arrangement. In the case of the exchange of daughters the full marriage presents are meant to be given on both sides, and this is nearly always done, though in

[7] See Chapter Five, note 12, p. 139.

point of fact it comes to an exchange of identical goods. The formal marriage gifts are always meant to be new and unused; and it is a point of honour for all those who can afford to give them to do so.

The length of the period between *asék* and marriage varies between a few weeks and a few years according to the wealth of the people providing the marriage feast. In the case of young people this is entirely provided by their families and does not entail any feeling of indebtedness nor does the expense have to be repaid; it is an absolute gift, a further link in the chain of mutual benefits which bind Lepchas together. This is not the case if men of property wish to marry or re-marry; they have to provide the expense themselves and if they borrow from others they have to repay what they borrow. In the case of poor people who wish to marry there are two possible solutions; from a suitable groom the girl's parents may consent to receive the symbolical gift of a piece of roast meat (*akut*) instead of the proper *asék* presents, which represent a cash value of about Rs. 60; or the Mandal may advise and help the prospective groom to give a feast, at which all the neighbours will contribute in money or kind to pay for the marriage feast. In Lingthem this has been done twice in recent years. The cash value of the gifts, animals and grain demanded by the complete *asék* and marriage ceremonies is computed to be about Rs. 300. By far the greater part of this is involved in the food consumed at the marriage feast.

There is one other potential arrangement by which men without much property or a large family can obtain a wife. In a family where there are no sons it is possible, if the parents so wish, that the groom, instead of taking the daughter away to his home, shall live permanently in the home of his parents-in-law, acting as their son, and eventually inheriting their property; in such cases only small *asék* presents are given and the expense of the lesser marriage feast is borne by the girl's family. But this arrangement is not very popular or very common; people do not much like the idea of having a stranger permanently in the home, and prefer either to adopt a young child, or else to let the property pass at their death to a *ké-tsop*;[8] and for most men the probable permanent separation from their families and friends is undesirable. This resident son-in-law is called *komok myok*. There are two men so situated in Lingthem, Tempa and Kurma *gyapön*, both somewhat maladjusted. Kurma is not a real stranger, for he was

[8] See Chapter Three, p. 106.

born in the neighbouring village of Panung; the wife to whose house he went is now dead, though her mother is still living there; Kurma is *asék*'d to another woman whom he hopes to bring home in 1938. Besides these two men there are two other men living in Lingthem who were not born there; these are Katel, whose story has already been told, and Takneum *youmi*, who was adopted as a boy by his father's married sister.

V

It sometimes happens that after *asék* has been performed the boy and girl feel a really strong repulsion for one another. In many cases a girl will simulate repulsion and will refuse to let her groom sleep with her; but this is thought to be chiefly due to shame and to dislike of having to leave her parents' home; and therefore the young people are cajoled and bribed and threatened and even sometimes beaten to make them like one another. If however the repulsion felt is really strong and there seems no possibility of breaking it down, two solutions are open; either the whole arrangement is called off and the gifts or their equivalents in money returned, or else an alternative spouse, usually a younger brother of the groom and occasionally a younger sister of the bride, is offered instead. The best example of these arrangements can be shown in the history of Rigya. Rigya, who is twenty-two years old, was *asék*'d when he was about fifteen to one girl, but they did not get on at all well together and after a time the Mandal arranged for the marriage payments to be given back. His eldest brother, Aplung, was also *asék*'d to a girl he disliked; he therefore gave her to his youngest brother, Gyatso, who did not want her and ran away to Gangtok to work as a carpenter; thereupon the girl was given to Rigya, who was the middle brother. This is a somewhat irregular arrangement because Gyatso was younger than Rigya; but since Aplung was older she was looked on as being originally the wife of the elder brother and therefore marriageable. Aplung subsequently married a widow, a woman considerably older than himself.

Most consummated marriages are stable and divorce or separation is very rare. The chief cause of divorce is usually for incompatibility of character or refusal to work properly on the part of the wife. If a man sends his wife away he has to pay a fine of Rs. 88 to the girl's father and has to divide with the wife all the movable property, animals and children. If there is only one daughter the parents will divide her marriage price; she can live with either. If there is only one son the spouse keeping him must pay to the other Rs. 40, a cow and a pig and if the father keeps him a length of cloth to the wife, if the wife keeps him a copper vessel[9] to the husband. The last formal divorce in Lingthem was that of the first Dorjé Lapoon from his third and fourth wives (see Chapter Sixteen); a distant 'aunt' of the Mandal's was also divorced in this way in Sakhyong but there were no children.

If a woman runs away the husband's relatives will come for her and ask for her back or else claim the marriage price; but if the wife is unsatisfactory the husband will merely claim and get compensation in the form of the head and two legs of an ox and a scarf and rupee. Should such a girl re-marry a representative of the husband goes to the marriage; if the representative is the maternal uncle he is given Rs. 3 and half a leg of an ox; if the paternal uncle, Rs. 5 and the rump. By a recent decision of the twelve Mandals of Zongu in council it has been decided that these small recompenses shall be generally accepted for a runaway wife, instead of the large sums demanded earlier.

In the event of a woman showing a marked and continued preference for some man not her husband, the husband will almost always let her go to the lover. If the man cannot be classified as a 'younger brother' he must pay to the injured husband all the marriage expenses which he himself had paid earlier; or alternatively the girl's family will provide another girl as a substitute without further payment, but in that case the payments which the husband would have recovered from the lover will go to the girl's parents. If the lover is classifiable as a 'younger brother' the wife will probably be given to him for a small symbolical payment without any formalities; but it is understood that the younger brother will give special help if the elder brother remarries. Adultery, without really marked preference, is not a reason for divorce; and no anxiety is felt or expressed about the paternity of a man's children.

vi

In Lepcha theory marriage is not only a contract between two individuals, but also a contract between two groups; and they have

[9] A copper pot is the most conspicuous Lepcha valuable: it is used in a great number of sociological transactions.

a set of rules by which the union can be continued despite the death of one of the partners. These rules are not uncommon in non-European societies and have been given the technical terms of levirate, by which a man marries his deceased elder brother's wife, and sororate, by which a woman marries her deceased elder sister's husband. The Lepchas employ both of these devices, but their application is very different, and the levirate claims are much more strongly pressed.

In Lepcha theory the husband's group purchases the wife, as is explicitly recognised in the term 'price of the bride', *nyom-sa afaar*, which is used for the *asék* presents; therefore if the husband dies the wife is still the property of his group, and can be married to another member of the same group without further reference to her parents, though on such occasions the wife's parents are actually given small courtesy presents. In theory too the wife has no right to refuse the man offered in the place of her dead husband, or, if she feels an unconquerable repulsion, her group should supply a second woman to replace her. Similarly if the husband wishes to refuse the wife he has inherited he should supply another man in place of himself. In practice these regulations are not always carried out, and relatively seldom if the woman is childless; if the heritable spouse really dislikes her inheritor no compulsion is used to force her to marry him, nor are there any sanctions for this; three women formerly married to inhabitants of Lingthem have in recent years returned to their own homes on the death of their husbands because they did not like their inheritors, or because their inheritors did not like them. In such cases, if the women remarry, the marriage payments are made, not to their family group, but to the family groups of their dead husbands.

The sororate claims are enforced rather differently. On the forty-ninth day after the death of his wife the widower must visit his parents-in-law, taking with him as presents a load of *chi* and a pig; on the receipt of which the parents-in-law consult with all their male relatives and offer him as wife another girl, preferably a real or classificatory younger sister of the first wife. If the man does not wish to accept the offered girl (and if there is nobody else suitable sometimes babies are offered) on the following day he must present his wife's parents with an ox, or, failing that, a pig, a load of *chi*, a big basket of rice and Rs. 5, and ask their permission to refuse the girl and to marry, if he feels so inclined, into another *ptso*. After the presents this permission is always given automatically.

If the man accepts the girl offered the *asék* is performed one year after the death of the first wife, and the marriage usually shortly after. For second marriages the ceremonies are similar to first marriages but on a rather smaller scale; both the presents and the feasts are only about two-thirds as expensive as for first marriages. When widows remarry the ceremony is slightly altered, and the bride enters her husband's house on the first, instead of the second, day of the marriage feast. Except for sororate spouses it is considered rather difficult for a widower to get an unmarried girl for his second wife, especially if his first wife died young, for this is believed to be a sign that he is unlucky; consequently it is fairly usual for widowers to marry widows. The situation is naturally altered if a widower makes an unmarried woman pregnant.

Among the Lepchas a man can inherit the wives of all his *elder* brothers, real or classificatory, the wives of all his paternal and maternal uncles real or classificatory, provided these 'uncles' are younger than his parents but not younger than himself, and all the *younger* sisters of his wife, real or classificatory. Conversely a woman can be inherited by all her husband's younger brothers, all the sons of her husband's uncles, and all the husbands of her elder sisters, real or classificatory. With all these potentially hereditable spouses the Lepcha has the right to copulate during the lifetime of their husbands (or wives) and in nearly all cases these rights are taken full advantage of, as opportunity offers; opportunity is naturally greater with people who live in the same district, and distance often prevents men taking advantage of the right to sleep with the younger sisters of their wife, and women with the husbands of their older sisters, since they most often live in different parts of the country.

With the wives of their real elder brothers Lepchas have in theory a right to use force, if they will not copulate willingly; the younger brothers are considered to have contributed to the marriage price of the bride and therefore to have, as it were, a legal right. In point of fact such a use of force never arises; Lepcha women know that their husbands' younger brothers have the right of access; and casual sexual relationships are so unimportant emotionally for Lepchas that few women would think it worth while making a fuss. If the women have a real repulsion for their husband's younger brothers nothing can be done about it, for,

CHÉLÉ, WHO DOES NOT WANT TO MARRY HIS AUNT

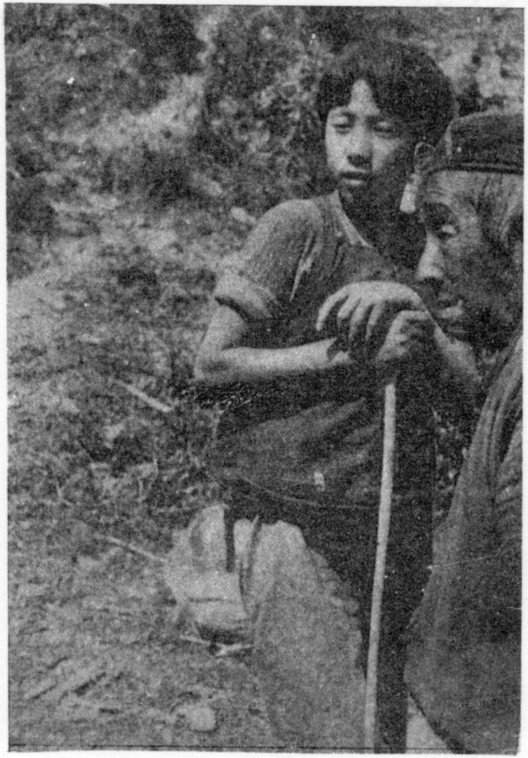

PATEK, THE HEAD OF A HOUSEHOLD OF SIX AT 17. WITH HIM PONGRING, THE MONASTERY GUARDIAN

as several Lepchas said when the point was raised 'Who can force a grown woman against her will?' More distantly related women, such as 'aunts', may put up a certain amount of semi-playful resistance, but no rancour is felt if it is overborne.

It is considered to be an act of excessively bad taste to copulate with a heritable wife in her husband's presence, or in such situations that there is a possibility of his witnessing it. These legalised adulteries usually take place during the husband's temporary absence, or else outside the house, in the forests or fields or field-houses; these outdoor encounters are usually very brief, and have a slightly romantic flavour. Copulation inside the house has the advantage of giving longer time, but it also exposes the couple to questionable remarks and a good deal of teasing.

One of the results of this situation is that almost all boys and young men get their first real sexual experience and training from an older married woman. Elder brothers usually explicitly instruct their younger brothers in their rights. In Lepcha theory a woman should never make direct sexual advances—the common Lepcha words for sexual activity are, like the English ones, transitive and one-directioned—but in point of fact I found that in nearly every case men had had their first real sexual experience with the wife of an 'elder brother' or 'uncle' at the woman's direct invitation and solicitation. This is considered altogether desirable; although sexual activity is thought to be as natural and as necessary as eating, it is necessary that boys should be taught to do it properly. Thus Chudo said one day 'If I caught Chimpet (the son of his elder brother Tafoor) sleeping with my wife I shouldn't be cross at all; on the contrary I should be very pleased, for she would be teaching him how to do it properly and I would know that he was in the hands of a good teacher! On the other hand, if I caught a married man, who had a right to sleep with my wife, doing so I should reproach them for their lack of shame in doing in my presence what might better be done in my absence; if I was really angry I should tell other people about it, so that everybody might know how shameless the man had been.'

I have already suggested that the *ptso* was possibly earlier a geographical unit; if this were the case, it seems to me possible that these permissive regulations were evolved to meet the special circumstances. For, with the *ptso* as the geographical unit, the young men would have had no possible sexual partners except through adultery or incest; and, as numerous examples show, such situations inevitably lead to jealousy, fighting, and the splitting of the group. By their regulations the Lepchas have reduced intra-group aggression to the minimum. The potential rivalry between father and son is mitigated by taking the arrangements for the child's marriage entirely out of the parents' hands; the potential rivalry between brothers is mitigated by allowing the younger brother access to his more favoured and stronger elder brother's wife, while making the relationship between an elder brother and his younger sister-in-law strongly incestuous. In this connection it is worth while noting that in the very large and elaborate Lepcha folklore and mythology I did not come upon a single instance of the otherwise almost universal compensatory story of the conflict between brothers, in which the despised, or ill-used younger brother or sister makes good after the elders have failed.

There is no specific word for 'jealousy' in Lepcha. When I presented hypothetical jealous situations to Lepchas and asked them what their feelings would be, the greater number say they would be angry; but this word, *sak-lyak*, does not carry very strong emotional connotations; it is the word used by parents if their children are naughty, or by workmen if they come across an unexpected difficulty in their work. It is also the most general euphemism for a sexual erection; I cannot untangle the associations which have produced this metaphor, but there is no question that the word is used in both senses; more than once I have heard a workman say when, for example, cords have got tangled 'I am as angry as a standing penis.' Despite the one-directioned sex-words, sexual activity is never openly equated with aggression; it is generally believed that both sexes enjoy it equally, though a few people maintained that women enjoy it more; almost all were agreed that women enjoy it later in life than men do. On the other hand point may be given to the metaphor by the fact that during copulation only the man is active; the woman lies completely passive and relaxed.

The Lepchas of Zongu have dissipated nearly all the highly-charged emotional feelings which in many other societies are centred around sex, and on the whole neither sexual activity nor jealousy are strong motivating factors in their lives. There are a few exceptions to this generalisation; the quarrels fostered by the outsider, Mrs. Jiroong, have already been described in Chapter Three; and married women who show marked preference even for perfectly hereditable spouses, and married men who show preference for women other than their wives produce and have produced many disquieting situations, sometimes leading to open disputes and even suicide.[10] Such disturbances can however be put down to uncontrollable personal temperaments, which go strongly against the Lepcha ideal of behaviour; the regulations of the Lepchas have been devised to reduce to a minimum the conflict and aggression within the group. This has not however been followed by added aggression to people outside the group; William Sumner's generalisation[11] does not hold good here, possibly because through the greater part of their history Lepchas have only had slight and intermittent contact with other groups. Practically all the aggression manifested by the Lepchas is directed against and is supposed to originate from hostile supernaturals. Historically Lepchas have nearly always answered outside aggression by retreating and hiding in the forest; and in the semi-historical stories which they recount about the invading Tibetans or Nepali or Bhutanese, the Lepchas get the better of their enemies, not by violence but by cunning—through cutting off the water supply, shooting fire into the fortress, blocking up mountain paths, and similar devices.

It is worth noting that the Lepchas who live in mixed communities, though they generally know of the theoretical right of access to potential spouses, all deny with great apparent sincerity that these rights are ever taken advantage of; many who have imbued the views of their neighbours the Tibetans or Nepali, regard them with horror. The Lepchas of Zongu themselves are culturally tolerant and know that their neighbours have different rules of conduct; for example the Tibetans forbid the marriage of aunt and nephew, but both they and the Nepali permit the marriage of first cousins which for the Lepchas is the most horrifying form of incest. The habits of other races, particularly the Tibetans, are a fairly constant subject of conversation; many of these habits are viewed with disgust, but disgust tempered by considerable amusement.

In the case of two or more marriages taking place within the same generation of two groups, the levirate and sororate claims are readjusted to meet the situation; for example if two brothers marry two sisters, the younger brother will not have the right of access to or be able to inherit his elder brother's wife, because she

[10] Instances of these disruptive situations are given further on in this chapter and in Chapter Fifteen.

[11] 'The relation of comradeship and peace in the we-group and that of hostility and war towards others-groups are correlative of each other.' W. Sumner: *Folkways* (Boston 1906), p. 12.

will also be his wife's elder sister and equated with his mother-in-law; similarly the elder brother will not have access to or be able to marry his wife's younger sister, because she is equated with his daughter-in-law. If there was an interval between the first and second marriages both parties would have the right of access until the second *asék*; to avoid such complication it is desirable that the marriages of pairs of brothers and sisters take place as nearly simultaneously as is possible.

The semi-diagrammatic complementary relations which are set up when two brothers marry and have sons are worth tabulating. The elder brother has to respect his younger brother's wife as his 'daughter-in-law', but his son need not as he can sleep with and inherit her; the younger brother need not respect his elder brother's wife as he can sleep with and inherit her, but his son must respect her as his 'big mother'.

In the event of a widow being left with young children it is essential that a husband be supplied from her husband's group, and this is usually done without any sort of friction. Thus Chano, himself a childless widower, recently inherited the wife and three young children of his dead elder brother. This is the one situation in which the provision of a levirate spouse is imperative; if the widow is sterile or the children all grown up and married there is no compulsion and such women often return to their own home. Not always however; at the age of 68 the second Dorjé Lapoon married *en secondes noces* his widowed 'aunt' (actually the wife of his grandmother's brother's son) Pumri, who was then aged 73. The two had however carried on a fairly constant concubinage in the last forty years of Pumri's husband's lifetime.

The chief disadvantage of the sororate and levirate claims is that it quite occasionally happens that there is considerable disparity between the ages of the spouses, and in particular that the woman will be considerably older than the man. A relatively poor family is liable to hand on a satisfactory woman even to a boy of nine or ten; the converse seldom occurs as a man will not accept a very young girl as a second wife. During my stay in Lingthem such a case was causing considerable dispute. Kahlyeu's grandson, Chélé, at the age of ten had inherited the wife of a dead younger uncle. This girl had only been married a year before the death of her husband, and was at the time only fifteen, but the psychological difference in their ages was far greater than the real difference. Chélé was a very bright and intelligent little boy, but nervous and physically thin and rather undersized. He was remarkable for having an almost complete memory of all that had happened to him after the age of eighteen months. Unlike the vast majority of Lepcha children he showed a marked disinclination to grow up, and appeared happiest playing in the company of children younger than himself. His mother died about three years ago, and when he was about six his father committed suicide by eating arrow poison and attempted drowning, after he had been publicly reprimanded by his wife's family for neglecting her while she was ill. After the death of his parents Chélé lived alone with his grandfather and a middle-aged distantly related 'aunt'.

As opposed to Chélé's psychological backwardness his wife, a younger sister of the Mandal's first wife, was somewhat advanced for her age and appeared a fully-developed self-possessed young woman. After the death of her first husband she had gone home to her family for a year, but in May 1937 she returned to take up life with her husband, staying for the time being with her elder sister. Chélé did not want to get married at all, and would run away from his wife whenever he saw her. Old Kahlyeu used to run after him and gave him extremely severe beatings to bring him to his senses; but Chélé was obstinate, and when he was scolded, used to threaten to drown himself in the river. A few children occasionally make such suicide threats when they are publicly reproached or consider themselves ill-used (most of the children I know of who make or have made such threats have exceptional early histories, usually orphans or adopted children) but these threats are never taken seriously and there is no instance of a child putting such threats into action. But with Chélé people are a trifle anxious; he is an abnormal child, with his exceptional intelligence and babyish behaviour.

The situation did not advance in any way while I was observing it. Chélé continued obstinate; his wife seemed fairly placid and non-attached about the whole affair, but even presuming the two do live together the situation is naturally somewhat unstable. A few years ago Takneum *youmi*'s son Itup inherited a wife under rather similar circumstances; when he was twelve his wife became pregnant with an obvious bastard. This wife died young and Itup married again; the bastard, Seryop Katoo, was brought up as a younger brother of Itup. It also occasionally happens, as in the case of Kurma's stepfather, that a man is childless because he has inherited a wife near the menopause.

vii

If, after a number of years of marriage, a man's wife is sterile, he has a right to apply to his wife's family for a second wife, providing his first wife agrees. The formalities entailed in this request are the same as those which have to be performed after the death of a first wife;[12] an extra preliminary present has to be given, but the subsequent expenses for the marriage are slightly less. In theory it is only permissible to take a second wife from the first wife's *ptso*, and ideally this second wife should be the first wife's real or classificatory younger sister. This is recognised in the terms with which co-wives are always referred to; the Nepali words *jethi* and *kanchi*, meaning 'eldest sister' and 'youngest sister' are always used; Lepcha has no equivalent terms to indicate the position of a child in the order of birth. In the great majority of cases the ideal conditions are observed, and the two wives, if not actual sisters, are of the same *ptso* and use kinship terms. In cultural theory the co-wives have already an established habit of cooperation and cohabitation which only needs to be renewed, and the situation of co-wife is meant to be an agreeable one. This expectation is not always justified; occasionally co-wives quarrel; but the majority are glad for the companionship of a close relative, and the lessened work which their presence means. The husband is meant to spend alternate nights with each of them.

In Lingthem there are seven men with two wives each; but only in three cases was the second wife taken because the first wife was sterile. In two of the cases the second wife is indeed only a co-wife by courtesy; Asang gave a home to the middle-aged widow of his elder brother, because she had nowhere else to go; and for the same reason Gongyop took in his wife's sister. In this second case the hospitality was not long accepted; though nearly sixty years old, this woman, Samblyou, with her elder sister Mrs. Takal, is the most promiscuous woman in the village, and after distributing her favours in nearly every direction, including the seduction of a number of the younger boys, she is now cohabiting with Zumba, a widower twelve years younger than herself.

Chala Mandal has had in all four wives in two pairs; the first wife he gave to a 'younger brother', who lived with him; after her death he also gave him her equally sterile sister; this second wife returned to her family after the death of the

[12] See p. 159.

'younger brother'. Chala Mandal then married two more wives, 'sisters', and nieces of the first two wives; the last wife of all was the widow of Katel's dead son to whom she had already borne two daughters who stayed with their grandfather; after her marriage to the Mandal she bore two more daughters, one of whom still survives.

Thyak Thimbu has also had four wives in two pairs. The first two died childless; the second two, though not related to the first wives, are themselves aunt and niece. Almost after hope of Thyak Thimbu—he is Gongyop's elder brother—producing a child had been abandoned his youngest wife bore a son in May 1937. Lumba *chithembu* has also had two wives, 'grandmother' and 'granddaughter'; the second wife has borne him three children. Lumba *jethi* is a rather independent old body; though she gets on well enough with her co-wife she dislikes what she calls 'living in a crowd' and consequently has made a permanent home for herself in a field-house, which she shares with her younger stepson; it is a rule that, if for any reason co-wives separate, the children shall be equally divided. The two wives cooperate in all the field-work. Lumba is meant to divide his time equally between the two of them, but well-authenticated rumour says that he spends much more time with *jethi*; she is a jolly and extremely bawdy old party. She is a Mun and is nearly always the singer on those occasions when singing is ceremonially called for.

By his first wife Katel had one son and three daughters; but the daughters married away, and the son, a thief and a ne'er-do-well, died a violent death in foreign parts. Therefore ostensibly in the hope of begetting another son Katel married a second wife, of a different *ptso* to his first one (who is still living) a woman twenty-seven years younger than himself; she is only eighteen now. Very exceptionally for a Lepcha, he is deeply in love with this young wife of his; she on the other hand cannot stick Katel, and the marriage is extremely stormy, with threats of and occasional attempts at suicide on both sides. For a number of years this young wife refused to go to live with Katel; finally two years ago the Mandal threatened her parents that if they permitted their daughter to live with or return to them, they must refund the marriage price. So for two years she has been living with Katel, but she still refuses to sleep with him, despite the jewels and presents with which he has smothered her; it is rumoured that she finds pleasanter bed-fellows elsewhere. Katel though rich and fairly industrious, is so stupid as to be almost defective, and has a very unpleasant look of low cunning. He is one of the most unpopular people in the village: I personally found him quite repulsive.

Finally there is the case of Aga, the son of Hlatam the 'poisoner', which represents one of the most disruptive situations possible in Lepcha life. Aga has been married a number of years; his wife has borne him three children, and was in the spring of 1937 pregnant with a fourth. During the greater part of his married life Aga slept, quite legitimately, with the sterile wife of one of his paternal uncles. When this uncle died in 1935 the aunt returned home to her blood-relations in the neighbouring village of Lungdeum, as there was no suitable man in her husband's family to inherit her. At the end of the year of mourning she was *asék*'d by Zumba of Lingthem; but six months after this *asék* she came and settled permanently in Aga's house, with whom she had continued her intercourse uninterruptedly. Aga's first wife was naturally very angry and reproachful, as there is no possible excuse for bringing home a second wife when the first wife is fertile; and, as marriage is the concern of the whole group, all her family are angry with Aga and his aunt. This aunt has been argued with for days on end; people have pointed out to her how desirable Zumba, with his fine house and many fields, is as a husband; but she remains obdurate and refuses to go and live with him. The situation is naturally extremely unpleasant and disturbing, and is under constant discussion by the Mandals of Lingthem and Lungdeum. There is a constant fear that the first wife's family will come and demand elaborate reparation from Aga, or alternatively that she may return home with her children to them. This behaviour is loudly condemned by the other Lepchas; it is chiefly for this that Aga is called 'evil-minded'.

Some years ago there was another similar but more pathetic situation. After the Muktair was married and his wife, Tafoor-mu, had borne him two children, he went to Gangtok for five years to study in one of the big monasteries. During this long absence he fell in love with another girl, and on his return he asked Tafoor-mu to let him bring a second wife home. She at first naturally objected; she had borne him two sons; what was the justification for bringing home a second wife? But the Muktair promised that he would love both wives equally, and she finally allowed herself to be persuaded; the Muktair then *asék*'d the girl from Gangtok and brought her home two years later: their only child, a daughter, was born in this interval. When she came home this second wife proved to be jealous and possessive, and refused to allow her husband to sleep with Tafoor-mu.

Dunbi was the 'younger brother' (actually the son of a younger paternal uncle) of the Muktair; at the period when the second wife was brought home he was completely alone, for his parents, wife, and children had all died in a dysentery epidemic. The Muktair took him into his house, and there he so well consoled Tafoor-mu that she became pregnant. The Muktair thereupon offered her to Dunbi; he *asék*'d her with the symbolical gift of one pig, and the families separated. One year later the second wife died.

The position of Tafoor-mu is one of the saddest in Lingthem; formerly the wife of the most prosperous man in the neighbourhood, and with two prosperous sons, she is now married to the poorest and most feckless man in the village. She has borne him three daughters; the eldest is married away, the second lives with her half-brother, Tafoor—she is unbetrothed Prumtu, the girl with the squint—and the youngest is a child of six. Although Tafoor and Chudo give her occasional presents she lives and dresses poorly, and has to work hard to compensate for her husband's sloth. As far as I could observe, Tafoor and Chudo feel little love or respect for their unfortunate mother.

We in Europe make passionate and personal love one of the chief pivots round which our society moves; the Lepchas of Zongu have completely excluded it, and it is liable to be extremely disruptive when it does flare up. The normal emotional situation is one of reasonable affection founded on mutual rights and benefits; people love one another for statable and stated reasons. No love is considered automatic; it is not considered inevitable that parents should love their children nor brothers their brothers and sisters; it is merely considered probable, because their situations entail the mutual obligations on which love is supposed to rest. Unless people are strongly deviant Lepchas are chary of pronouncing judgement on their neighbours' characters; most people, they say, are much of a muchness. Consequently it is to be expected that arranged marriages will turn out well, unless one of the partners has a really bad character; since love is founded on mutual obligations and benefits, these mutual obligations can be set up between any two people. It is worth noting that all three men whose love stories are recounted above fall well outside the Lepcha norm. The Muktair was, it would appear, an exceptionally strong-willed and ambitious man, and his love affair started when he was living in foreign surroundings; also his second wife came from a mixed community. Katel and Aga on the other hand are both subnormal; they are foolish, suspicious and disliked.

For the Lepchas of Zongu sexual activity is practically divorced from emotion; it is a pleasant and amusing experience, and as much a necessity as food and drink; and like food and drink it does not matter from whom you receive it, as long as you get it; though you are naturally grateful to the people who provide you with either regularly. One of the most difficult of all concepts for the European to take into consideration is the non-European attitude to sexual activity; with us, explicitly on the part of men, sexual desirability is most intimately bound up with aesthetic considerations. Although there may be individual disagreement as to who are included in the terms, potential sexual partners are divided into the categories of 'attractive' and 'unattractive'; and we believe that only perverts or prostitutes will have anything to do with the second category. Primitive people, I believe, do not make this distinction; there is social kudos to be acquired from being the known possessor of a beautiful wife or mistress; but for temporary sexual gratification any willing partner is equally acceptable. I found it extremely difficult to accept the notion that most of the men with young and pretty wives at one time or another slept with the two sixty-year-old haridans who were the promiscuous women of Lingthem; but as far as I can make out their invitations were never refused.[13] Fourteen-year-old Chimpet gave a good illus-

[13] Professor Malinowski records a similar situation in the Trobriands in *The Sexual Life of Savages* (Routledge: London, 1929) page 247–8: 'The (medical officer) was once baffled by finding all the boys in a community afflicted with a very virulent and obviously recent gonorrhea, while all the women to be considered in this connection were as yet quite healthy. Finally he obtained a confession from one of his patients that he and his companions had copulated among others with a woman, so old, decrepit, and ugly, that the medical officer had thankfully and unhesitatingly omitted her in his several inspections. . . .' 'I was able to ascertain that the ugliest and most repulsive people have, not only sporadic but regular intercourse.' Professor Malinowski finds this notion so repulsive that he accounts for it 'by their manner of carrying out this physiological activity', which in the Trobriands may entail very slight physical contact. This explanation does not however hold good for the Lepchas; see Chapter Twelve, p. 330. I think primitives dissociate, in a way we cannot, the public attitudes of parading a desirable partner, and the private ones of physiological gratification. In this connection it is perhaps worth noting that in the Somerset village where I live potentially jealous situations arise in the case of people whom I personally would consider, either through age or ugliness, to be almost sexless.

tration of the cultural attitude to sex when he said that he had twice slept with a girl at Parfok, at her request, when he accompanied his father there to help perform religious ceremonies; he enjoyed the experience and would willingly repeat it; but he does not want to marry the girl because he does not like her.

It is permissible for a man who feels himself unable to cope with his field-work, either on account of physical weakness or because he has other work which takes him a great deal from the neighbourhood, to invite an unmarried younger brother to live with him and to share his fields and wife. The co-husband is co-opted without any sort of ceremony, but thereafter he is no longer free in the choice of a wife of his own, if he desires one; he must make the request for a wife of the same *ptso* as the shared wife, exactly as if he was taking a second wife in the normal course of events. The co-husbands sleep with their common wife on alternate nights, but all the children are presumed to be begotten by the first husband, and he alone has to observe the pre-natal precautions; an exception is only made to this rule if the first husband's prolonged absence makes his paternity a physiological impossibility.

In the recent past there have only been two cases of such polyandry in Lingthem; one is that of Chala Mandal, described above, who first shared and then gave his first two wives to a 'younger brother'; the second is that of the second Dorjé Lapoon, who shared his wife with his real elder brother; this brother was a lama attached to another village who was almost always away, so that the second Dorjé Lapoon had almost the exclusive use of his shared wife. It is not allowable for two unrelated men to share a wife, but two who call themselves 'brothers' may do so; unless the two men are closely related this is considered undesirable, as it is liable to lead to quarrelling. There are some obvious advantages for a first husband in co-opting a second husband; it is an easy way to get rid of a wife of whom you are tired; it gives an extra adult worker and a care-taker for your property and wife when you have to be absent. The position of second co-husband on the other hand seems to offer few attractions except to the poor and unambitious, under-sexed man, and it is understandable that there are very few examples of such polyandry. In the event of polyandry or polygyny the incest prohibition against sleeping with your husband's younger brother, or your wife's elder sister, are obviously suspended.

viii

It occasionally happens that a woman becomes pregnant befor[e] she is *asék*'d, or when either the youth or the absence of her husban[d] renders legitimate paternity impossible. These accidents are considered deplorable, but the effect is very different according t[o] whether the woman is married or not; if she is married the bastard[y] is a private affair; if she is not it threatens the whole communit[y] with a storm of hail which will destroy the harvest. The dange[r] of these illegitimate pregnancies apparently only arise in the late[r] stages;[14] grown men, especially widowers, often impregnate thei[r] future wives and only perform *asék* in the third month of pregnanc[y] (under these circumstances parents will usually give their daughters to widowers) and they do not have to perform the ceremony of *thip-song* which is required for bastards. It also happens very occasionally that a boy and girl will present their elders with a *fait accompli* through the girl's pregnancy; this also does not involve the ceremony.

The *thip-song* ceremony which has to be performed for illegally pregnant women is costly and elaborate. An ox, or, failing that, two pigs have to be sacrificed by a Mun, and a long and involved ceremony performed by the lamas. This ceremony should properly last two days, and all the village should be feasted, to recompense them for their harvest which the hail would spoil. If the father of the child is unmarried, and wishes to marry the girl, he pays for this ceremony, after which the *asék* is performed in the normal manner. If for any reason he cannot or will not marry the girl his group should offer a substitute husband. Should the father be a married man this paternity is a cause of considerable scandal; all his family group, as well as his wife's, will turn against him and upbraid him publicly; they may even shame him by paying for the *thip-song* ceremony to be performed. It is possible however that his first wife may be agreeable to his *asék*-ing the girl and taking her as his second wife.

If a man acknowledges his paternity but refuses to marry the girl or provide an alternative husband for her the girl's family will pay for the *thip-song* ceremony, in which case the father will have no claim on the child; he will be obliged however to present the

[14] There is, as far as I know, no formulated rule on the subject; but it seems probable that, on the analogy of the pre-natal precautions which only have to be observed in the second five moons of pregnancy, it is only when the bastard is fully formed, at the end of five moons, that it becomes socially dangerous.

girl's parents with Rs. 15 and a pig as 'soup money'; these gifts represent the price of the soup given as special food to nursing mothers. Should he want the child and not its mother he must pay for both the *thip-song* and the 'soup money'. If the father is unknown or refuses to acknowledge his responsibility the girl's family performs the ceremony; at the end of the ceremony a tree is designated as the child's father; a wooden phallus is stuck into the trunk and it is then spat on and otherwise insulted by all present. The tree is meant to wither after the child's birth.

It is a very great disgrace for a girl to produce a bastard, and it is believed that possibly some girls somewhere bear their bastards in field-houses or the forest and kill them rather than confess to the act. I could get no concrete instances of this and the idea of infanticide is so appalling to Lepchas that they will not even willingly entertain the idea of its being practised by strangers. There is no known method of avoiding conception and the only abortifacient believed in, and that very half-heartedly, is the bathing in hot sulphurous streams which are found some distance away in Zongu.

When a bastard is born there is no gathering of friends and relations for the birth feast on the third day and a lama will not come to the house to cast the child's horoscope; instead either the child's or the girl's father must visit him. Apart from this the child is treated normally. Should the girl marry later the child will stay with its maternal grandparents and will be brought up as their child; it will be considered as a member of their *ptso*, and, if a boy, will have the same share in the heritable property as his maternal uncles. Although bearing a bastard is an act of the greatest shame, once it is over and done with no attempt is made to hide the matter or to hush it up. People will announce quite openly that they or their relations are bastards, or have born or begotten bastards; the shame situation has been successfully passed and is therefore no longer a cause for unpleasant feelings. Bastards are believed to suffer from one of three inherent weaknesses; either their mothers will die young, or their health will be bad, or they will suffer from goitre (three of the six supposed bastards of Lingthem have this complaint). Goitres are of two sorts; one of them is extremely lucky and productive of wealth and prosperity;[15]

[15] The seven men of Mayel (see Chapter Nine) who are the patrons of grain harvests are all said to have enormous goitres and as people sow the grain they murmur in prayer to them '*Ta-yoot thimbu : sambo thimbu*'—'May we have big goitres; may we have big harvests.'

the other is the *tamtoom* of bastardy. It is possible to diagnose bastardy goitres because these will ache in the presence of corpses or in the houses where bastards have been born.

There are six reputed bastards in Lingthem, but only two of these were born from unmarried mothers, and for only one of them, the old mother of Pargeut, did the father perform *thip-song*. The first Dorjé Lapoon is said to be the son of a travelling Sikkimese; he was born during his father's prolonged absence. Lumba *chithembu* is believed to be the bastard of a lama of Talung on the ground that they look exactly like one another, and Dunbi, for the same reason, is said to be the son of his father's 'younger brother'. In the face of strong physical resemblance with a possible father, it is generally believed that this man, rather than the husband, was the begettor. Nahyeun is generally believed to be Dunbi's bastard; he was born of an unmarried girl when his father was already married. Little Seryop Katoo who was born when his mother's husband was twelve has already been mentioned; his begettor is said to be Jiroong's elder brother. In her time Kurma's mother bore two bastards, one before her marriage, and one when she was a widow. There are cases in which a man believes himself to be the father of another man's child; but these suspicions are always kept very quiet.

The production of a bastard is no draw-back on the girl's subsequent marriage; on the contrary, the fact that she has shown herself fertile makes her if anything more desirable. The Lepchas have a great and justifiable fear of sterility; they do not on the other hand manifest or express any fear of impotence, and no aphrodisiacs are employed. One or two extremely peculiar and incongruous ones are known of, for they are hawked about in Gangtok and other towns where there is a ready market for them among the Hindus, and, somewhat less, among the Nepali. For the Lepchas these are extremely funny; they cannot conceive of the loss of potency, any more than the loss of appetite, except through illness or old age.

There is an altogether surprising amount of sterility among the Lepcha women of Zongu.[16] Of the fifty-six married women over twenty, eighteen were completely sterile and one had only produced a still-born daughter. Of these seven had reached or passed the menopause without producing any children; four are between

[16] For the complete fertility tables of the women of Lingthem, and also for complete life tables see Appendix I, a.

the ages of fifty and thirty; the remaining seven are between twenty and thirty and for them there is still some chance of producing a child, for though copulation normally starts at or before puberty the average age for bearing the first child (worked out from the women of Lingthem) is over twenty-two; there are only three instances of a woman bearing a child before she was twenty. Most exceptionally for a primitive community it was possible in Zongu to get the exact age of every individual for the following reason. It is absolutely essential for participation in all lamaist ceremonies for every Lepcha to know in which year of the twelve-year 'animal' cycle[17] they were born, for this affects birth and marriage, the diagnosis of disease, the suitability or otherwise of individual exorcists, and many other occasions in ordinary life. Also after he has completed his third (or exceptionally his fourth) cycle—that is to say when he is 36 or 48—it is obligatory for a Lepcha to make prophetic consultation as to the hazards and misfortunes which await him in the next twelve years. Although no Lepcha can state his age in years, everybody knows their 'animal' year, and with few exceptions, which can be checked by cross-reference, the number of cycles they have completed.

I have not been able to make up my mind as to the reason for the great sterility of the Lepchas. It would seem as though it were the women rather than the men who were sterile, for in the greater number of cases of a man remarrying on account of his first wife's sterility the second wife has borne him children. A suggestion put forward by some Lepchas with whom I discussed the matter, though others considered it absolutely ludicrous, is that sterility may be due to premature copulation. The Lepchas do not recognise and have no word for physical puberty, and most of them believe that the signs of female puberty (swelling of the breasts and beginning of menses) are the result of copulation and that therefore girls have to be copulated with in order that they may develop. A number of people admitted (if they were women) copulating with men when they were only ten or eleven, or (if they were men) more or less raping young girls. A number of the sterile women however emphatically deny such premature experience, and I have no reason to suppose they were lying; and anyhow on the medical evidence it seems doubtful whether such premature experience would cause subsequent sterility, though it might render childbirth more difficult.

17 This will be more fully explained in the next chapter; see also Appendix III.

Another possible cause might be the epidemics of some sort of genito-urinary disease which occasionally breaks out. The Lepchas call this disease *tanji*, which is the term used by mission-trained dispensers for gonorrhœa; although some of the symptoms, notably great pain in micturition, a discharge of pus, and occasionally orchitis, are similar, it seems to me more than doubtful if the diagnosis is correct. For one thing the disease comes in epidemics, and seems to attack people indiscriminately, old people and infants as well as adults; on one occasion it is said that the animals also suffered. Again trustworthy people have told me that though they or their spouse had the disease, and though they continued marital copulation, the other spouse was not affected. The discharge lasts for about three weeks, and then clears up automatically, without, as far as is known, leaving any after-effects, nor necessarily recurring. The final argument against its being gonorrhœa is that there was not a single blind baby in the neighbourhood. Whatever the disease may be, it does not inevitably cause sterility for some of the parents of the larger and still growing families had suffered from it. It is possible however that it is a complicating cause. Unlike their neighbours the Nepali, the Lepchas of Zongu do not suffer much from mumps.

Since their principal food is grain in one form or another it seems to me that the question of vitamin-E deficiency can be excluded. I think it is worth considering the suggestion that the sterility and very low fertility are due to genetic factors. The Lepchas are a 'pure' race within the meaning of the act, for at any rate in Zongu intermarriage is excessively rare; in Lingthem besides the two supposed bastards there was only one other person not of pure Lepcha blood, and that is Mrs. Tinkep who is three-quarters Sikkimese. Despite their stringent exogamic laws the Lepchas are a relatively inbred community, and if, as seems possible, fertility is genetically determined, it may be that the low reproduction rate of the Lepchas is a genetic characteristic.

Compared with any of the neighbouring tribes the fertility of those Lepchas who have children is extremely low. Of the thirty-seven women in Zongu who have children still living, only one has produced seven and two six; the average is just over two per fertile woman. Infantile mortality is naturally high, but not, according to the figures I could get, excessively high; most mothers of families seem to have lost one child, but only in three cases have all or most of the children died young. It is possible however that my figures may be incomplete on this subject; young children have little emotional importance for Lepchas and dead ones, other than the recently dead, may easily be forgotten.

On the figures available it seems doubtful if the Lepchas of Zongu will be able to maintain their numbers in the future. Out of a total population of 176 in Lingthem, there are twenty girls (who will probably marry outside the village) and ten boys under the age of ten and eighteen boys and eleven girls between the ages of eleven and twenty. At the other end of the scale there are thirty-seven people (or a fifth of the total population) aged fifty or over, including three men and one woman of over eighty.

The Lepchas account for the presence or absence of children chiefly as a matter of luck and the results of former incarnations; there is however a myth accounting for the relatively small size of the Lepcha family as compared with the Nepali; the Lepchas they say have only seven ancestral supernaturals,[18] the Nepalis twelve. I have no complete figures for any of the other villages in Zongu but such information as I received, and such observations as I was able to make, seem to indicate a similar situation throughout the whole reserve. I think the psychological reasons given by Rivers for the breakdown in fertility among the Melanesians, supposing them to be an adequate explanation of the situation there, are inapplicable in Zongu.

ix

Of the forty-one married couples in Lingthem (the other nineteen married women are either co-wives or widows) fifteen were childless in the spring of 1937. Eight of these couples were young people recently married, who still had hopes of bearing children; four of them were old people living alone who had no longer any hope of children; the remaining three had adopted boys. There are also six adult men in Lingthem who were adopted as children.

The arrangements for adopting a child[19] vary according to whether the child is the son of a near relation, of an unrelated person, or an orphan. With a nearly related person the adoption is conducted with little formality; the adopting parents present the real parents with a milch-cow and a new dress for the mother: these

[18] The people of Mayel: see Chapter Nine.

[19] The adopted child is called *kup-tsop*—substitute child—and the adopting parents are called *jiut-bo* and *jiut-mu*; the adopted child addresses them as *abo* and *amu*—father and mother.

presents are called 'the price of milk'. For the child of a stranger besides these presents must be given a big pig, a load of *chi* and two big baskets of rice and pop-corn; the giving of these presents is equated with the giving of betrothal presents and both are called by the same word, *asék*: in the adopting *asék* however no *bek-bu* is required; the adopting father takes the presents himself and brings the child away with him. In the case of a destitute orphan no ceremonial presents are given; the child is merely fed and housed in exchange for his labour; if there are no other direct heirs and if the child does not quarrel with his adopting parents he will normally inherit the property. Formally adopted children are treated in every way as the real heirs of their parents. It is permissible to adopt a child at any age between weaning and marriage; the most usual age is between three and seven.

Two reasons are given for adopting a child: to have the benefit of the child's labour, and to have an heir and a support in old age. The first reason is much stressed; almost as soon as children acquire physical independence they do a number of chores about the house, which increase with their age and strength; for example, fetching wood and water and helping their elders by fetching tools and preparing simple implements for work. On the whole people only adopt children after many years of marriage.

The health of the child is the only consideration when adoption is considered; up till marriage good or bad looks are not regarded. The child will be allowed to return to its real parents from time to time; if the adopting parents and the adopted child get on really badly the child may be returned with a present of a big copper pot; but if the child runs away because it is unhappy it will be sent back by its parents. There is no supposed emotional relationship between the adopting parents and adopted child; if they are treated well the children will love them; if not, not. For example, Atyook says that he loves his adopting parents better than his real ones; Kurma detested his and though he has now left them for twenty years he still bears a grudge against them. For the adults concerned adoption is generally a matter of convenience; a man with a large family (a son will only be given away if there are at least two others at home) places a son without expense to himself and assures his future; the adopters get a general servant and a support in their old age. Adopting parents naturally pay all the marriage expenses of their adopted son.

Very occasionally a girl is adopted; there was one case of this in the village. Chelim, who was himself adopted and who has in turn adopted a young boy, has also adopted the daughter of his younger brother (this brother who lives in another village has six daughters and no sons). This is done to get the services of a child; the adopting parents also get the marriage payments.

It is generally considered that the parents of large families do well by their children in giving them to childless relations to bring up as their heirs; it is considered though rather deplorable to give one's child to complete strangers or to people quite unrelated. For the adopted children however the situation appears to be unpleasant and emotionally complicated; children are seldom given away before the age of about four, by which time the patterns of affection within the biological family have been firmly established; consequently there is a considerable emotional struggle, and in nearly all the histories of adopted children that I obtained there are frequent stories of running home to the real parents, and of being beaten and sent back. An adopted child is lonely; adults do not normally talk to or play with children once they have achieved physical independence; and the isolation of Lepcha houses renders contact with neighbouring children, if there are any, slight and intermittent. It seems also (though with so few cases it is difficult to generalise) that the adopting parents have a tendency to make the child work harder than the real parents would do. Adopting parents are generally considerably older than the biological parents—adoption before the age of forty is uncommon—and more set in their ways; and the child has no companions to share his labours with him and lessen them with play. Adopted children appeared rather silent and awkward; they were more sullen than those children who lived with a group of siblings, and, unlike only children, neither demanded nor received attention from adults. After weaning normal Lepcha children habitually depend more on their elder siblings than on their parents; there seems to me to be a tendency to identify with elder siblings rather than with parents (owing to the extension of family terms and groupings a couple's first child is still likely to have 'elder siblings') and to participate, through this identification, in their emotional and sexual life. This phase of development is lost for adopted children; also they usually have not witnessed childbirth—children are normally always present at subsequent births in the household—and they appear to develop a complex of emotions around facts which are very simply accepted by the vast majority of children. Of the six adults who were adopted as children five show very considerable deviance from the Lepcha norm; Takneum *youmi* is bad-tempered, especially with children (it will be remembered that he was the man who twice committed sodomy); Kurma has a desire for power, is boastful, and shows decided sadistic traits; Rigya is a horder who gloats over his hidden wealth; Agyung is surly and very rude and heartless towards his elders, and especially to his adopting father Serving, who is ninety and nearly blind; and Gongyop is extremely nervous. The sixth adopted adult, Chelim, appeared to me to be a normal and well-adjusted Lepcha; I did not have much contact with him and was unable to get his life-story.

The Lepcha manner of life is arranged on the supposition that birth and death will take place regularly and at the proper times; and when these suppositions are falsified by fact, readjustments, which often result in maladjustments, have to be made. The Lepchas plan for big households of four generations with the chief authority in the third generation; a man is thought to be in the prime of life and to be capable of exercising authority chiefly in his fourth and fifth cycles—that is between the ages of thirty-six and sixty. Before the age of about thirty-six Lepcha men are extremely un-self-reliant and diffident; they act as though they were unused to making decisions for themselves, almost as though they were not fully grown-up. Among the Lepchas I nearly always considerably under-estimated people's ages. After the age of sixty a man should be able to retire somewhat from the harder labours of life to be supported by his children and grandchildren.

Such is the ideal; but sterility and a very unevenly distributed death-rate destroy these expectations; old men find they have to work either because they have no sons, or else their sons are dead; children who should be living in a large family find themselves isolated. The ideal Lepcha household would consist of about sixteen people; in Lingthem the average is a little over five to a house. Only six households are relatively complete, and of these only two, the households of Tafoor and Ongden, are considered by other Lepchas to approach the ideal arrangement

CHAPTER SEVEN

RELIGION I: LAMAISM

[*Lamaism, or, as it is sometimes called, Mahayana Buddhism, is a subject of the greatest complexity, to the study of which scholars of world-wide repute have devoted their whole lives. Its organisation is as elaborate as that of the medieval Catholic church, its hagiology, demonology and ritual are infinitely more complicated, and it is split into nearly as many sub-sects as contemporary Christianity. My ignorance of Tibetan prevents me discussing it in any great detail. Among the Lepchas of Zongu the practices of lamaism present more variety of detail than any other single facet of their lives; my notes on lamaist ritual far exceed those on any other subject. I had at one moment considered comparing the lamaism as I saw it practised in Lingthem with the accounts given by other people of more orthodox practices in unmixed lamaist communities, but even confining myself to those rites at which I was present, I soon discovered that the bulk of the material involved would be out of all proportion to its place in the social and religious life of the Lepchas. I have therefore limited myself to a generalised account of the impact of lamaism on the life of the Lepchas of Zongu; in practically no instances have I given the details of ritual or of the fabrication of ritual objects, not because I do not know them, but because they would overweight what is from my point of view a subsidiary subject. To a lesser degree these remarks also apply to the rituals of the Mun and to the extremely elaborate mythology and folklore derived from both religions. Possibly in the future (I hope with the collaboration of Mr. C. J. Morris) I may publish the full details of the ritual and belief of both religions in a different work.*]

i

The discussion of the Lepchas' religion is rendered extremely complicated by the fact that they practise simultaneously, and without any feeling of theoretical discomfort, two (or possibly three) mutually contradictory religions: of these the older Lepcha religion is nameless but, on the analogy of lamaism, I propose calling it the Mun religion (after the title of the priests); the worship of the people of Mayel, which was possibly originally separate, forms nowadays a part of the Mun religion; and this religion is in all its major beliefs opposed to lamaism. For the Mun priesthood goes by the possession of a manifestation of a supernatural spirit which is attached to a family line, so that there can never be more than one simultaneously in each group (there may be two in one biological family, one spirit descending from the father's group, and one from the mother's). The chief function of the Mun is to ward off the misfortunes and illnesses caused by devils, which is done, partly by sacrifices, especially animal sacrifices, and partly by direct communing with the supernaturals. On certain occasions the Mun become possessed by their guardian spirit and prophesy; at death ceremonies they summon the soul of the dead man to speak his last wishes through their mouth, and then conduct it into the *rum lyang*—the place of the Gods—where it is reborn as an infant, and grows up to an eternal life similar to the life here on earth.

In lamaism on the contrary priesthood and sanctity are acquired by learning and not by inspiration; the sacrifice of animals is a heinous sin; the future can be learned by calculations from the holy books and not by inspiration; the soul of the dead wanders for a short time in a sort of purgatory, before being reincarnated either in another form on this earth, or going to some heaven or hell, as different as imagination can make them from anything experienced on earth. Most important of all, lamaist ethics are founded on a belief in individual destiny and a sense of sin; lamaism contains a long, explicit and detailed list of sins which can be performed by human beings, and which are visited on the evil-doer, first by feelings of remorse and secondly by punishment either in this life or in future reincarnations. Lepchas have a word for sin, because they have borrowed the Tibetan word, but they have, I think, no idea of sin; and the only act to which the word is commonly applied is to the killing of animals; by a few who have accepted lamaism it is also applied to envy or slander, expressed in thought, word or deed. With these exceptions they do not use the word 'sin,' *la-yo*, in connection with individual behaviour; the supernatural sanctions which punish disapproved-of actions are expressed as *nam-toak*, a year of disaster which affects the whole community. Even for acts less violently disapproved of, which incur supernatural dangers, it is not the wrong-doer alone who is involved, but the whole of his family group; punishment is seen if members of a person's family die or suffer, even though the evil-doer survives himself. Indeed according to Lepcha ethics it could be said that anti-social acts are graded according to the number of people they may affect; only for acts of minor importance is there personal and individual punishment which falls on the evil-doer.

On some subjects there is agreement between the two religions, notably on the ambivalent nature of supernatural beings; in both religions the supernaturals are divided into three categories, mostly benevolent, neutral, and mostly malevolent. The supernaturals which are mostly benevolent are called gods, *rum*, those mostly malevolent devils, *moong*; but both agree that if the gods are displeased they take on a terrifying and threatening aspect, and that the best way to deal with devils is to flatter them temporarily by treating them as gods; and whether gods or devils are prayed to the ceremony always ends by begging them vehemently to *go away*. Whatever their chief aspects the supernaturals are potentially dangerous. The ambivalent supernaturals, such as *Thyak-dum*, or Hlamen Djémé (a lamaist supernatural equated with the Mun spirit), are called either *moong* or *rum* according to the personal dealings of the speaker with them at that moment.

Lamas and Mun are also agreed on the meaningful and prophetic character of dreams. The dreams of everybody are significant for those who have the knowledge to interpret them; the significance lies, not in the actions of the dream (as a rule), but in the seeing of certain objects which have a symbolical meaning. The causation of dreams is however different for the two religions, as is to some extent their interpretation; for the Mun dreams are sent by supernaturals, for the lamas they are the experiences of the soul released from the body by sleep; unbound by space or time the soul has experiences with the souls of other people, supernaturals and objects, and, on its return, informs the body it inhabits. For the Mun the soul is a very vague concept, practically only having an independent existence after the death of the body; the lamas however know all about souls.

The content of dreams can be divided into two classes; those that foretell some future 'natural' event, and those that foretell the presence of some, usually dangerous, supernatural. For the latter some apotropaic ceremony is usually available and in some cases essential; according to the supernatural indicated the ceremony will be performed by a lama or Mun.

The following objects seen in dreams are lucky: gathering sand, collecting wood, seeing a woman with a big goitre: they foretell a good harvest; to put on new clothes or gather firewood or to have stones thrown at you mean the acquisition of property. Solid excreta indicate a good buckwheat harvest, liquid ones that the harvest will be destroyed by storms. To be covered with filth indicates coming wealth. To dream of climbing or going up hill is propitious. If you dream you are cut or are given silver it means that you will the next day be given a present of *chi*. The following objects are unlucky: a sick person lying down indicates a bad harvest: a tooth coming out means a relation will die, if from the right side of the mouth a paternal relation, if from the left a maternal; hair coming out or even combing hair also foretells death. A neighbour pounding rice foretells a death in his house. To dream of drinking foretells rain. A lake, swimming, or falling into water all foretell illness. A river foretells a message from the State authorities, agreeable if the water is clear, disagreeable if muddy. To dream that you are excreting in public means that your relations are slandering you. Being naked in a crowd foretells illness, as do dirty or ugly people. The setting sun foretells the death of kings. To dream of the dead foretells illness, to dream of a landslide, death, and also to dream of picking fungus. A dream of a red cloth or red flower means you will cut yourself, to dream of chicken's droppings means that some one is going to poison you. The list could be continued almost indefinitely.

Specially ominous dreams are: to dream of a kite or of men flying (this indicates the presence of Shook-sor *moong* and demands a ceremony by a Mun): to dream of fire (this indicates illness and also demands a ceremony by a Mun): to dream of a storm blowing into your house and lifting off the roof (this indicates that you are the object of malicious sorcery and lamas must perform ceremonies): to dream of going down hill carrying a load (this foretells illness; lamas and Mun can both avert it): to dream of a snake (this foretells danger and needs elaborate lamaist ceremonies); and so on. These specially ominous dreams are fortunately rare, for it would be considered dangerously rash to neglect the proper ceremonies. For less strongly ill-omened dreams it is permissible to make a hole in a leaf of a special species of wild arum and spit through it; this will avert the danger.

Above : THE MONASTERY ALTAR DECORATED FOR THE CEREMONY IN HONOUR OF KINCHENJUNGA

Below : THE LAMAS PRAY. OPPOSITE SITS CHIMPET TO BEAT THE GONG

Note the *patyoot* of *chi* by each lama.

The interpretations of certain dreams are emotionally neutral: other dreams are said to be meaningless. Thus to dream that a living person is lying dead merely means that the person dreamt of is lying sleeping with a full belly. To dream that you yourself are flying means that you have inadvertently eaten birds' droppings. Meaningless dreams are dreams of running, of local landscapes, of naked people, and so on. Everybody with whom I discussed the subject denied the existence of dreams with a manifestly sexual content, whether permissive or incestuous, or of committing crimes; the only sexual dream allowed for is the woman's monthly dream of copulation with a supernatural. If a man's wife is sleeping with an unpermitted partner the man will be apprised of the fact by dreaming of the big wooden ladle which is used for pouring the water on to the *chi*; if the partner is a permitted one the man will not have this dream, but he may suffer from diarrhoea; in that case he will ask his wife to procure a portion of the 'younger brother's' clothing which he will wear; this will clear up the symptoms.

Everybody dreams to a certain extent, but this varies with the individual; it is believed that much dreaming foretells a long life, and little dreaming a short one. There is no necessity to try to recollect dreams if they are dim or forgotten on waking. According to lamaist theory the child in the womb dreams continuously about its previous incarnation; it thinks it is going to be born and makes up its mind to inform its parents of its future plans; but when the cord is cut most of this knowledge goes; just a little remains in the infant's dreams, but that too disappears before he has learned to talk.

As an illustration of the interpretation of dreams I can give two prophetic dreams which were made about me on an occasion when I was slightly unwell with a stomach upset, followed by a head-ache. Both the dreams were told to me by the dreamers as soon as I saw them, and before I had said that I had been unwell; Tafoor indeed came to see me because of the dream. He had dreamed that while we were living in the monastery he and the other lamas came up to practise their musical instruments for the reception of some great lady. The doors opened outwards instead of inwards, and beside them was some dried buckwheat. These were sure signs that there was illness in the monastery.[1]

[1] It may be of interest to record that the last three times that he saw me Tafoor said on each occasion that his heart was heavy about me and that he feared that when I left I should have some misfortune or illness. At the time

Kurma foretold my headache with the following dream: he saw me walking along the riverbank with his mother-in-law, came to salute me, and I gave him a silver rupee. Later in the day I asked him to repeat the dream which he did as follows:—' The Sahib[2] dressed in his usual clothes went to the valley with my mother-in-law. I was coming from the forest along the river and I saluted the Sahib with joined hands[3] whereupon he presented me with a silver rupee. I then said to my mother-in-law " The sahib has come to see us: what can we set before him as a present?" My mother-in-law replied " The sahib has come to walk and to fish in the river; we have nothing suitable for him—no chickens, no eggs. What can we give?" After that I woke up.'

The interpretation of the dream was fulfilled; to dream that you are given silver means that you will get a good drink of *chi*, and this was fulfilled when Kurma called on the Mandal earlier in the day to discuss village affairs with him. The mother-in-law in my company showed that I was the victim of a female devil Langteun *a-nyou* who brings head-ache and eye-ache and thirst. Any ugly or dirty or badly-dressed woman represents this devil; the fact that it was his mother-in-law was without significance.(!) Had the head-ache persisted I should have hired a Mun to drive the devil away with offerings of *chi* and incense.

The demonology and, to a lesser extent, the hagiology of lamaism and the Mun religion are unified by a system of cross-identification in the two mythologies. Devils, and to a lesser extent gods, in one mythology are equated with differently-named supernaturals with similar attributes in the other. It thus happens that supernaturals have nearly all two names at least; but for Lepchas, as has been said, names are impermanent and without significance and no discomfort is felt from this. Some extraordinary tangles result from these identifications: the most popular lamaist god, called alterna-

I put these remarks down to courtesy. In fact, however, I was taken ill within a week of leaving Lingthem and had to go into hospital almost immediately on returning home. I did not recollect Tafoor's repeated prophecies till some months later, when going over my notes.

[2] The polite Lepcha term for a European is *Sé-pano*, which I believe to be a corruption of Sahib. *Pano* means a king, but the first syllable is apparently meaningless. The less polite word is *mik-dum*—white eyes. Europeans or fair people in dreams are good-omened, dirty people ill-omened.

[3] The two hands cupped together and held in front of the breast is a respectful attitude and gifts must always be received with joined hands, to indicate that the gift, whatever its nature, is overpoweringly large.

tively Sakya Muni, Guru Rimpuché (beloved teacher), or Tashey-*thing* has been equated with Tak-bo-*thing*, in Mun theology the first man and the first hero, the grandson of Itpomu, the Creative Mother, and the two change places in mythology, according to the preference of the speaker, even in stories quite unsuitable to lamaist ethics (for example in the stories of the origin of eating fish and pork, where the hero kills the original fish- or pig-devil). And the confusion does not end there; after Tak-bo-*thing* and Tashey-*thing* have been telescoped into one person they are again separated into two with two simultaneous births in different places: the Mun hero is said to have been born underground at the same moment as the lamaist saint was born in heaven.

These confusions however are more obvious to the analytical European than to the practising Lepcha. With the exception of the crucial point of killing animals the Lepchas do not appear to be conscious of the implied contradictions; and the lamas through their education in the scriptures and through the casting of horoscopes have already such a training in sophistry that they almost automatically reconcile any implicit contraditions. In by far the greater number of ceremonies for private individuals Mun and lamas perform simultaneously contradictory rites for identical ends, with the Mun usually in the 'kitchen' and the lamas in the 'parlour.' Inside the monastery precincts Mun are never allowed to practise; but in a number of the calendrical festivals on 'neutral' ground the two perform side by side. Only for one private ceremony are the Mun entirely excluded; they can take no part at all in the funeral ceremonies of a lama. On the other hand the Mun have the speciality of most of the ceremonies connected with crops and hunting and some apotropaic rites.

Theoretically there is no quarrel between the two religions, but there is a certain veiled rivalry between their priests. The lamas accuse the Mun of using their supernatural powers for unworthy private ends, for instance killing magically the spouses of people they desire so as to be able to enjoy them without interruption, and the Mun accuse the lamas of being more sensual than the average man, more dependent on constant sexual intercourse and drink; abstention is possible for the layman, intolerable for the lama. As far as drink is concerned I think the charge is justified; the amount of *chi* consumed by lamas is incalculable. As soon as they settle down for a ceremony a *patyoot* is placed beside them, and constantly refilled and renewed; the chanting—and lamaist ceremonies may last anything from six hours to as many days—is thirsty work; and in the latter half of the services the officiants are seldom quite sober. These charges are never made openly or by one priest to another; in public they are quite amicable, though they usually affect to ignore the other's presence and performance.

The mythological justification for this amity between the two religions is that the patron spirits are husband and wife: the lamaist Tashey-*thing* is the husband, and the Mun (always a female spirit) the wife. For this reason, it is said, the lamas are stronger, and especially have more influence with the gods; the Mun on the other hand are perhaps more competent to deal with devils.

This attitude towards husband and wife, in which the husband is considered automatically the more powerful, is in itself probably a Tibetan import. For the Mun spirit has also another husband in the Padem (or Bum-*thing*); this latter resembles the Mun save that only men are possessed by it; a Padem is far less powerful than a Mun, and for many men this possession is the first step towards becoming a Mun. In the case of this supernatural husband and wife it is explained that the Mun is the more powerful because she is the wife; and this is far more congruent with the specific Mun mythology in which the female supernaturals are almost always the most important.

It would require far more knowledge than is at present available to be able to state definitely of the Lepcha folk-lore what elements are indigenous, what borrowed from Tibet, and what from other neighbouring tribes. My impression is that by far the greater number of stories told in Zongu, though many have foreign accretions, are of domestic origin. I only heard specifically Tibetan-lamaist stories from pious lamas, and by no means always from them.

ii

It is said that lamaism was introduced into Sikkim in or near 1641, the date of accession of the first lamaist king Penchoo Namgyé. He is said to have been made king by three lamas of the Nyingma-pa or 'Red Hat' sect, the unreformed branch of lamaism; these three lamas were fugitives from Tibet, following the violent struggles between the Yellow Hats and Red Hats and possibly Chinese or Mongolian intervention.

I have not been able to find any conclusive evidence as to the date of the conversion of the Lepchas to lamaism, or of their admission into the lamaseries. The fact that in the beginning of the eighteenth century King Chador invented an alphabet for them so that they could read the scriptures suggests that by that date the majority were already converted; but for a long time—and even today in some of the monasteries of Sikkim—Lepchas and other foreigners are not accepted for training as lamas, this privilege being exclusive to pure-born and healthy Tibetans and Sikkimese (Bhotiyas). But in lamaism the layman has practically no rôle at all; he cannot pray to, address or influence the supernaturals save through the intermediary of a lama; and therefore conversion to lamaism without admission to instruction could mean little more than a sort of voluntary tax. The first monastery in Sikkim, that of Sanga Chelling, was founded in 1697, the Talung monastery in 1789, Lingthem monastery in 1855, and Gyatong in 1860.[4] The Lepcha monasteries are said to be under the jurisdiction of Pemiongchi monastery—the largest in Sikkim—which belongs to the Lhatsun-pa sub-sect of the Nyingma-pa.

Like all other religions lamaism is a compound of a number of heterogeneous elements. The chief component is Mahayana Buddhism, or 'the greater vehicle' (itself an elaboration of Hinayana or primitive Buddhism—'the lesser vehicle'), to which has accreted a good deal of tantric Hinduism, some Chinese and Mongolian elements, and possibly the original Tibetan Bön-po religion.[5] Like other religions too, lamaism presents three aspects: a justifying mythology and scriptures, an ethic, and a social organisation.

The foundation and justification of lamaism is contained in the scriptures, above all in the two enormous collections of holy writings, the Kangyour or commandments (the Bible) and the Tangyour or commentaries (the Talmud). In these, together with other minor works, are to be found all knowledge and all necessary instruction for the conduct of life. The books have by themselves a talismanic virtue, and the reading of them is the essential preliminary to acquiring merit. These books apparently contain a

[4] I have taken these dates, and one or two other general statements from *The Gazetteer of Sikkim*, vol. 1 (Calcutta 1894), particularly from the section *Lamaism in Sikkim* (pp. 241–391) by L. A. Waddell. Here, as in his book *The Buddhism of Tibet* (2nd. edition Heffer's, 1934), Dr. Waddell is exclusively concerned with the Tibetans and Sikkimese, and only mentions the Lepchas incidentally.

[5] Some modern critics suggest that this Bön-po religion may be the remnants of an historically earlier and unrecorded conversion of Tibet to Buddhism.

very great variety of matter. Hinayana Buddhism was an atheist religion, and lamaism, though it deals with and reveres countless hosts of supernaturals, is in a way also atheist; it contains no major God or father-figure, and also no mother-surrogate. In many ways, as the early missionaries especially noted, lamaism in its organisation and ritual corresponds very closely with Roman Catholicism; but in their hagiology there is no equivalent to God the Father, or to the Virgin Mary; their gods, with their countless incarnations, correspond rather to the saints. Sakya Muni, Guru Rimpuché, is an object of special love and reverence, and might be likened emotionally to Jesus Christ. In the iconography and legends Guru Rimpuché is almost always a young man, an 'elder brother', rather than a 'father'. The demonology is as elaborate as the hagiology, but here also there is no principal figure.

The lamaist ethic is founded on the belief of the immortality of the soul, the principle of reincarnation, and on an automatic justice which rewards individual virtue and punishes individual sin in this and future incarnations; and, as a derivative, that an individual's condition in this life is the result of his actions in previous incarnations. This determinism is modified by behaviour during each life; and the object of the lamaist is by the active practice of virtue and the negative abstention from sin so to improve the soul that it can eventually escape from 'the wheel of cause and effect' and enter into the bliss of Nirvana or non-existence. The long list of sins of which a person is capable derive from three main causes—lust, ill-will and stupidity; virtue is acquired partly from abstention from acts deriving from such sources, partly by practising their opposites (love instead of hate, freeing captive animals instead of slaying them), and chiefly by the practice of religious ritual, including mystic contemplation. These last methods of acquiring perfection are only open to lamas; all that it is possible for laymen to do is to abstain from sin and support the lamas, in the hope that they will be rewarded by being themselves lamas in their next incarnations. Lamas and laymen alike can gain merit by repeating, or causing to be repeated, various prayers or *mantra*; the most famous of these is the six-syllabled *Om! mani pudme hum!* which is believed to be of great efficacy. It is not necessary to say these prayers with the lips; if they are inscribed on anything and this inscribed prayer is moved it is the equivalent to the actual uttering of the prayer. There are a number of devices for this automatic praying, the chief of which is the prayer wheel; prayer-wheels are made in every size, from the smallest to be held and turned in the hand, to enormous ones several times bigger than a man, all stuffed with repetitions of the *mantra*; every turn of these wheels is an acquisition of merit and a remission of sin. It is not even necessary that the pray-er should go to the effort of turning these wheels; wheels driven by mechanical power are just as efficient. Tafoor has four water-turned prayer-wheels set over a small stream by his house. The next most conspicuous method of automatic praying is the prayer-flag; this consists of a piece of cloth stamped with various *mantra* and attached to a pole; each time the wind makes the cloth flutter it is as if the prayer were uttered. There are a variety of these flags, some being for the benefit of the dead and others for that of the living. Finally the inscription of a *mantra* on stone (either in Tibetan or preferably Lenza characters) and set into a monument or building, acts as though this inscribed prayer was being said continuously.

The metaphysical beliefs of the lamas concerning the soul are various and self-contradictory. The soul of man can die, but the soul is immortal. The soul can be devoured by demons or destroyed by sorcery and will nevertheless be reincarnated. With the exception of the earth itself and certain mountains, which are the homes of supernaturals, everything possesses a soul; but the souls of rocks and plants are very weak and only survive as long as their owner survives. With plants every seed, as soon as it is formed, possesses a potential soul of its own, as does a cutting, as soon as it is separated from the parent plant and stuck in the ground. It is a meritorious act to increase vegetable souls but no punishable sin is committed by destroying them.

The souls of animals (with the exception of leeches and mosquitoes, which are believed to be emanations of devils and soul-less) are far more important; it is a major sin to destroy an animal for it is possible that its soul may be that of an ex-human being; and pious people will erect prayer-flags for animals killed through accident or in the normal course of human life. Partly by divination, and partly by the observation of footprints near the place where the body was disposed of, it is possible to tell if the soul of a recently dead relative has been reincarnated as an animal; if this does occur it is said that the near relations should abstain from eating this species of animal. I never came across nor heard of such an instance of ritual prohibition, for dead people are never discovered to have migrated into any animal which was fit to eat.

The reincarnated soul of a human being arises at the moment of conception and is all through life as it were the mirror image of the body it inhabits. Thus a baby's soul is as weak and feeble as its body; and it is for this reason that Lepchas always attach a snail-shell round their baby's necks or wrists; it may be that the soul will be pursued by demons and will not have time enough to get back to the midriff under the heart—the normal home of the soul in waking life; the pursued soul can then creep into the snail-shell where it can hide in safety. The souls of very old people are equally feeble; but no hiding place is necessary for them as they are too tough for devils to eat. Anything which happens to the body also happens to the soul, which is aware of it a split second earlier; if the body is cut or maimed or feels any sensation, the same thing occurs to the soul; if this were not so how could we feel anything? In normal waking life a man's body and soul are only separated in the case of violent accident; if for example a man should fall from a tree the soul would make a tremendous effort to separate itself from the body, get down safely and then return to its body afterwards. If the soul falls with the body the soul will be killed and the body die; but if the soul escapes the man will fall unconscious and be later revived when the soul re-enters its house.[6] Only in sleep or through mystic practices can the soul be separated from the body during life. Madness is believed to be the possession of a demon which imprisons the soul inside the body.

Finally lamaism is a social organisation. The lamas (to a lesser extent the nuns) are arranged in a disciplined hierarchy. They are a section of society which performs for the whole society its religious functions; in return the rest of society should give material support to the lamas. In Tibet this social aspect is extremely important; the lamas possess the greater part of the temporal power and are also as a group an exploiting class; the monasteries own land and the peasants attached to the land are practically monastery serfs. The lower-ranking lamas also work for the benefit of those of higher rank and are possibly as much exploited as the peasants; but they have, at least in theory, the possibility of rising to the higher ranks, which possibilities are completely shut out from the laymen. In Sikkim, as far as I can learn, the social influence of the lamas is considerably less; in Lingthem the monastery as a 'legal person' owns no land; the villagers help to pay for its building and upkeep,

[6] The Lepchas only recognise fainting or unconsciousness through pain; they do not consider fainting through fear or disgust or grief possible.

(a) LUMBA *CHITHEMBU*
(b) JIROONG *CHÉNÉ* IN TIBETAN HAT
(c) SECOND DORJÉ LAPOON WITH THE HAT OF HIS RANK

(d) THE PAINTER MONK, LHARIBU CHUJEN OF PANUNG
(e) ASHYOK *YOUMI*, WEARING THE OLD-FASHIONED WOVEN LEPCHA HAT

and they are expected to support, at any rate in part, the Dorjé Lapoon and the monastery custodian; they also have to give fixed contributions to the feasts which validate the rise in grade of the higher ecclesiastics.

The Lepchas have been converts to lamaism at least one, and probably two centuries, but they have, if I may so express it, sterilised and ignored those aspects of the alien religion which were sharply opposed to their major existing attitudes. They have as it were, swallowed lamaism whole, but excreted the irritating portions. The mythology presented no difficulties; their pantheon was always large and expanding, through the divination of new supernaturals, and further numbers of similar supernaturals were easily accepted; it was understandable that foreigners should know of large numbers of new ones, almost as worthy of worship as the older established ones. The idea of a priesthood in which the priests need training by older priests was also one they already possessed; and that priests should be designated by divination (the horoscope) or by heredity, rather than by the possession of a hereditary spirit was an easy modification of existing attitudes. So too was the idea that the future could be learned by calculation, as well as by dreams and inspiration; the Lepchas have a complete belief in horoscopes and have incorporated them into their lives. Similarly the idea that an essential part of the efficacy of ritual lies in word-for-word repetition was one they already possessed; that, instead of learning by rote, these rituals could be found through the alien art of reading, was to their mind a distinct advantage for lamaism, and the books and those that read them are respected and revered. Similarly mystic contemplation, to expel devils or acquire supernatural powers, had its parallel in the *mun-then*, the mystic communion, of the Mun.

The social organisation was a more alien concept; to a certain, though not completely formulated, extent, they have equated the organisation of lamas with that of the family; for a lama to sleep with the wife of an inferior lama is likened to the incest of an elder brother sleeping with his younger brother's wife, though there are no sanctions against such acts; the Dorjé Lapoon are equated with the grandfathers who withdraw from work at the end of their lives to be supported by their sons and grandsons. Nevertheless this parallel does not hold good altogether, and, in so far as they have accepted the social organisation of lamaism the Lepchas have incorporated a new and alien element into their lives. This new element is however not of major importance; although religious titles are used in civil life no other distinction is made between layman and lamas; the social organisation is confined to the monastery. There is a difference in appearance between laymen and lamas; laymen wear their hair in a long plait whereas lamas have their heads shaved or at least close cropped; and though lamas often wear ordinary clothes for field work, on social occasions they always wear Tibetan, and not Lepcha dress. But lamas do not form a group within the society; the fact that a man is a lama is only one of the aspects of his personality, less important than his wealth or poverty, his industry or laziness, his relations by kin and marriage and friendship with other people. Only in their death are lamas given distinguishing treatment; they are usually cremated and never buried, whereas laymen are usually buried and never cremated; both laymen and lamas may, if the horoscope indicates it, be thrown into the river.

As a generalisation it may be said that the Lepchas have accepted the ritual, the validating mythology, and the organisation of lamaism; what they have completely refused to accept is the ethic. Like the other 'higher religions' lamaism is individualist; it holds that a person's chief concern should be with his own spiritual welfare. This, the key-concept of lamaism, was and is an alien attitude to the Lepchas. As has already been said, the Lepcha attitude to disapproved-of acts is social, and not individual; it is the society, and not the evil-doer, which bears the brunt of wicked acts. The Lepchas admit feelings of shame—feelings so strong that they can lead to suicide—following exteriorised social disapproval; they do not admit guilt-feelings. The more pious lamas and some laymen accept intellectually the idea of reincarnation, but they do not accept emotionally the idea of reincarnation being the result of personal acts. The form of reincarnation is discovered from horoscopes, and those depend on the time of birth or death, that is to say on chance, and not on individual behaviour. Sin is practically equated with the killing of animals; this is felt to be a dangerous act and is thoroughly congruent with the Lepchas' inhibition of aggression in other spheres of life. But the idea of asceticism, for example, being meritorious is so alien to the Lepchas, that even pious lamas have confided their private belief that the *gé-long* (as the monks who have taken their vows of asceticism are called) get their satisfactions on the sly.

I should like to suggest that this selective conversion to a new religion, with the rejection of those elements which are alien to the major cultural attitudes, is probable when the converted culture is fully integrated; I think parallels might be found in the conversion to Hinduism of the Nepali, and some of the native Christian and Mahomedan sects in Africa, and, possibly, among the American negroes. When the society is more or less disrupted and the convert feels himself to be alone in an alien world, individual conversion is likely to be much more complete; the Christian Lepchas with whom I came in contact in India and Gangtok had accepted the individualised Christian ethic, with its sense of sin, completely; their whole character-formation and major attitudes appeared to be modified by this conversion; and I very much regret that I was unable to study this character alteration in any detail. I should like to suggest the axiom that *Fully integrated cultures will only accept in an imported complex those elements which are congruent to the existing major attitudes, or which are felt to fill a want; those elements which are violently opposed to existing attitudes will either be excluded or so modified as to bring them into congruence with existing attitudes.* If this axiom is correct it would appear that we can learn from the observation of primitive societies much about the probable results of imposing violent social changes on simple or more complex societies.

iii

The vocation to become a lama is determined by the horoscope which is cast on the third day after birth. All the children of lamas should themselves become lamas, but in practice usually only the eldest son follows the whole career; the younger ones receive sufficient preliminary instruction to enable them to read one or two sacred manuals. The children of laymen are also occasionally predestined to become lamas, usually because they are reincarnations of dead lamas; should a child so predestined not follow his vocation as a lama he will become a half-wit. It occasionally happens that people who are not predestined to become lamas wish to study; they may do so, but 'their destiny will overcome them'.

If it is seen that the infant is going to become a lama he is presented with a yellow sash, and from a very early age his father will bring him to monastery ceremonies to allow him to get accustomed to the special atmosphere. Between the ages of ten and fifteen a teacher is chosen for the child. The choice of a teacher is supposed to be determined by his knowledge exclusively; under no circumstances can the biological father teach his own son; any other relative who is properly qualified may do so. Thus Chimpet was being taught by his 'grandfather' the second Dorjé Lapoon. If the teacher resides in the same house no formalities occur, but this is very rare; nearly always teachers are strangers, and often live in a different village to the pupil's parents. When the teacher has been selected the parents present him with a big pig, a load of *chi*, a ceremonial scarf and a rupee and the child goes to live with his teacher for three years, usually working for his teacher in the day-time, and receiving instruction in the evening. The child is allowed to visit his parents from time to time, but if he runs away he will be beaten and sent back. According to Tafoor, when he was a student one teacher might have six or seven pupils, and in consequence emulation increased the general level of knowledge; nowadays in Zongu most teachers have only a single pupil at a time, so that there are no spurs to overcome native indolence.

The preliminary instruction is almost entirely confined to the teaching of reading; there are small excerpts from the scriptures specially prepared for this purpose; the pupil learns by heart one page at a time. He is also taught to a certain extent methods of prayer and the playing of musical instruments, but these branches are pursued more fully when the teacher has given his pupil his ceremonial qualification or *loong*. I cannot find out to what extent this notion of *loong* is Tibetan, and to what extent specifically Lepcha; it recurs in all stages of Lepcha life whenever there is a teacher-pupil situation. When the pupil has learned whatever he is being taught—the ritual of the Mun, a sacred story, the correct method of sacrificing after hunting, the offering of *sakyou faat*—his teacher gives him a scarf and usually a ceremonial meal or drink, after which the pupil does whatever he has been taught in front of and for his teacher. When the teacher has given his pupil *loong* the boy is formally presented at the monastery with the ceremony of *di-tset*. This ceremony is a very small affair; the pupil and his teacher drink tea with two lamas and then the novice is presented with some *chi*, a scarf and a rupee in the name of the monastery. A novice so received is called *chapti-bu*. Even before this reception a pupil will often accompany his teacher or father to all ceremonies, making himself useful by helping in the fashioning of ceremonial objects, by holding the big metal instruments, and possibly by beating the gongs or drums.

Above *chapti-bu* there are six grades of lamas; to pass from one grade to another demands firstly increasing knowledge and secondly validating feasts—*chaptok klon*. There must be an interval of at least three years between each rise in grade. It is expected that the expenses of the first two validating feasts will be borne by the young lama's family, the subsequent ones by himself. In the validating feasts for the higher grades everybody in the neighbourhood has to make fixed contributions. All the feasts are accompanied by prayers and readings from the scriptures.

The grade above *chapti-bu* is *tongpeun-bu*. These are the players of the musical instruments—the conch shells, the *galing* (a metal instrument between a clarionet and a trumpet), the long telescopic trumpet (*pak-doong*) and the flute made from a human femur (*kong-ling*). People learn how to play these instruments by watching experts; for the *galing* which has a reed mouthpiece and is capable of a variety of notes, the learner holds a grass between his teeth and copies the fingering of the player; he may also be privately taught by friends. To my Occidental ears all the music sounded like the cacophony of a zoo in a thunderstorm, but the lamas recognise and teach tunes, or, as they say, 'numbers.' The validating feast which demands a pig, two maunds of grain and four pounds of oil, only lasts one day. *Tongpeun-bu* cannot perform any offices on their own, and practically occupy the position of choristers.

Next in grade comes the *kané* whose one day feast calls for an ox, three maunds of grain and a maund of *chi*. The chief business of the *kané* is looking after the monastery and assisting the Dorjé Lapoon in their ceremonies; he also plays musical instruments. The *kané* are the only people who have to visit the monastery daily, to place the bowls of water on the altars at dawn, the *chimi* at sunset, and to burn incense. In the absence of superiors the *kané* is permitted to perform all offices of which he is capable; usually however his knowledge is slight and he has to ask his superiors for help; this help must be paid for with *chi*. The *kané* roughly corresponds to a deacon.

Kané and the ranks below barely qualify as lamas; they are in a way still students. Between the *kané* and the next grade *chéné* there is a very great gap. A *chéné* can perform all offices and in the absence of superiors can overlook monastery ceremonies; if he is old and experienced enough he can take pupils. The *chéné* is really a qualified priest. His validating feast is the most expensive of all: he has to give an ox, a pig, six maunds of grain, and ten maunds of *chi*. Each household has to contribute twenty pounds of *chi* and eight pounds of grain. The feasting lasts for three days at the end of which period the *chéné* by himself constructs an elaborate altar and dos eworship.

After the *chéné* comes the *chithembu.* His one-day feast calls for a pig, two maunds of grain, and ten pounds of oil. Each household must contribute twenty pounds of *chi* and eight pounds of grain. The *chithembu* overlooks the good order of monastery gatherings and can take disciplinary action against quarrelsome, riotous or impious people; he also has the right to beat any lama, including his superiors, who may arrive late for a service or make mistakes in the reading. There is a special thonged stick called *pankar* which is kept for this purpose in the monastery. The *chithembu* are also meant to prevent the monastery or its precincts being used for improper purposes on the days when no services are held.

Only one man at a time can hold the office of *chithembu. Omzet,* the grade above *chithembu* demands considerable knowledge, and there are many not over ambitious or intelligent lamas who have risen to the grade of *chithembu* but are unable to go beyond. For these people, and for such as have not completed the six years since they were *chéné* there has been created the title of *chichembu. Chichembu* take their part in the monastery festivals; they are allowed to, but usually do not, perform ceremonies outside. The *chichembu* roughly resemble canons. No validating feast is required for assuming this title.

The validating feast for *omzet* lasts two or three days and calls for an ox, seven loads of *chi,* two loads of grain and 20 lbs. of oil. Each household must contribute 20 lbs. of *chi* and 16 lbs. of grain. The *omzet* and Dorjé Lapoon are the two highest ranks in the lamaist organisation, the Dorjé Lapoon being selected rather for their age than for any other qualification; they are the oldest and most respected of the learned lamas. The *omzet* is the instructor *par excellence*: he is in charge of all monastery ceremonies and is expected to be most learned and competent. The one-day validating feast of the Dorjé Lapoon only demands a pig, two maunds of grain, and ten pounds of butter; everybody else must contribute twenty pounds of *chi* and eight pounds of grain and must present the new Dorjé Lapoon with a scarf and a rupee. The Dorjé Lapoon do no organisational work beyond examining candidates before each rise in grade; they particularly go in for mystic practices and contemplation and they alone are capable of conducting the dead man's soul on its journey through the other worlds after death. The Dorjé Lapoon are supposed to have renounced the things of this world; they are meant to be without property and to renounce such as they do possess; their nourishment is meant to be looked after by the other villagers; and, since they are meant to be fairly ascetic, it is expected that the Dorjé Lapoon will feast the other lamas yearly on their superfluity. Both *omzet* and Dorjé Lapoon can perform the mystic ceremony of *kong-so klon*: this ceremony, performed fasting in a dark room to make up for arrears of duties left undone and to appease the devils in the neighbourhood, is believed to be fraught with considerable danger which would result in the death of anybody not properly qualified who tried to perform it. The rank of *omzet* corresponds fairly closely to that of bishop; but as far as I know there is no equivalent in the Christian hierarchy to the rank of Dorjé Lapoon.

There are about twenty lamas attached to the monastery of Lingthem; eleven live permanently in the village, two others more or less permanently; the rest live in neighbouring villages. The two Dorjé Lapoon are the father of Datoop and the 'big father' of Tafoor; they are always addressed and referred to by their title. Tafoor and Ongden are *omzet*, Tafoor being by far the more learned; Datoop is *chichembu*, Lumba *chithembu*, Jiroong *chéné*, Chudo and Pembu *kané*, Chanko (Ongden's eldest son), Chano and Takal *chapti-bu*. All the *tongpeun-bu* live in the neighbouring villages. Chano and Takal are both full-grown men—Chano is thirty and Takal fifty-seven—but they are both too stupid to rise above the lowest rank. There are four boys studying to become lamas: they are Lumba's eldest son Kutt'r, aged eighteen, Tafoor's eldest son Chimpet, aged fourteen, Chano's eldest 'son' Mikmar, aged thirteen, and Chudo's eldest son aged four. The last named has not yet started to learn to read, but he is dressed in lama's clothes, and he plays on the floor at conducting services; this is considered to be a most auspicious omen, and when he does start studying he should learn quickly and easily.

Corresponding with the hierarchy of lamas there is a hierarchy of nuns (*in-é-bu*). Each rise in grade carries the same validating feast of a load of *chi*, 40 lbs. of grain and ten lbs. of oil or butter. The titles are similar, but they are completely pointless. Nuns cannot conduct ceremonies or perform exorcisms; in a very few of the lama's services, chiefly those connected with death, they have a subordinate role. There is no sort of compulsion or prophetic horoscope which forces a woman to become a nun; the duties are undertaken through individual piety, though it would seem as though the influence of father or husband was preponderating; of the nine nuns in Lingthem six were the wives or daughters of lamas: the other three were the wives of laymen who came from distant villages and I did not find out the positions of their fathers. A nun can start to study at any time between marriage and old age, taking as a teacher either a lama or the Dorjé Lapoon or *omzet* nun. Literacy is not insisted on for nuns and by far the greater number are in fact illiterate; the worship of nuns consists in the turning of prayer-wheels and the chanting of *mantra*. From such information as I can obtain nuns play a very small rôle in other Sikkim monasteries; and I suspect that the organisation prevailing in Lingthem is a Lepcha elaboration designed to give equal opportunity to men and women, since the Lepchas have a tendency not to disqualify anybody from any pursuit on account of sex.

Owing to the personality of the holder one exception must be made to the generalisation that the nuns' grades are meaningless. Mrs. Datoop was *inébu chithembu* and she showed that she would be well able to wield the *pankar* if necessary. Men say that they would be ashamed to be beaten by a woman, but they would not be able to protest.

The nuns are meant to spend three days every month at the monastery, worshipping by circumambulating the monastery turning their hand prayer-wheels and chanting *Om! mani pudme hum!* and sitting in the *lha-gong* turning the big wheels to the accompaniment of the same chant. These visits take place on the 9th of the Tibetan month in honour of Chérézé, on the 14th in honour of Zobu Sangé Chumdendé, and on the 31st in honour of Guru Rimpuché. Little attention is paid to these festivals and often only two or three nuns turn up. Unlike the lamas, whose conduct is not so controlled, the nuns have to observe certain prohibitions; on the eve of a monastery visit they must not eat an evening meal nor copulate with their husbands; and on the day of the visit they must avoid eating meat and drinking *chi*. Most of the nuns, and all the more pious ones, were old women.

iv

The duties and devotions of lamas can be divided into three categories: personal and individual devotions, set monthly and

PLATE 12

APPRENTICE LAMAS

The four-year old son of Chudo.

Chimpet in lama's dress, with his hands joined in prayer; taken inside the monastery porch.

calendrical services, and ministering to the sick or threatened as individual necessity arises.

Lamas are meant to perform various private devotions when they wake in the night, early in the morning and in the evening. Tafoor and the second Dorjé Lapoon were aware of these duties, but I naturally have no evidence as to whether they or any other lamas did in fact perform these devotions. Also during the day when a lama is alone and unoccupied he is meant to tell his beads, repeating *mantra* hundreds and even thousands of times. Lamas always wear a rosary of one hundred and eight beads with a couple of attached smaller objects; during ceremonies these rosaries are worn round the neck; during work they are often twisted round the wrists. They are used for devotion in exactly the same way as a Roman Catholic rosary, as a memento of the number of prayers which have been said. Rosaries are also used for divining; the rosary is thrown on to the ground and picked up at the place where it has fallen into a coil; the beads are counted from this place to one of the attachments by twos or threes; the presence or absence of a remainder gives the answer to the question divined. In the case of illness a twig is brought from the invalid to the diviner; the twig is placed on the ground and the diviner holds the rosary to his forehead, concentrating on the devil which he thinks may be disturbing the sufferer; the beads are then thrown on to the twig, and those between the bead touching the twig and one of the attachments counted; if the answer is negative the procedure will be repeated with the diviner concentrating on another devil. Rosary-divining is not confined to lamas; Mun and Padem also have divining rosaries but they are made somewhat differently, with red beads interspersed among the black and with different attachments; knowledgeable laymen also are able to divine by rosaries, if they have received *loong* from a qualified teacher. The rosary is considered in a way more personal than the other sacred implements—bell, skull-drum, sacred dagger, 'thunderbolt'—which the higher lamas have to possess and employ in different rituals; those of old lamas possess a certain talismanic virtue.

The lamas have to visit the monastery twice every Tibetan month; on the 10th. a festival is held in honour of Guru Rimpuché and on the 15th. in honour of Kinchenjunga. The feasts which accompany these festivals are meant to be given by a pair of householders in turn, so that from the villages of Lingthem and Panung each householder is responsible for half a communal feast every year. There are actually only forty-two householders for twenty-four feasts, but some of the richer households or those which consist of more than one working family give the feasts by themselves. The feasts for Guru Rimpuché are provided by lamas, those for Kinchenjunga by laymen. The duration of the ceremony depends upon the amount of food and drink provided; if the feast is plentiful, it may last thirty-six hours, starting at sunset on the preceding evening and continuing till the following dawn; if the feast is a poor one it will only last during the daylight hours of the day of ceremony.

In essentials the ceremonies are all similar. An altar-piece—its elaboration depending on the size of the festival—is fabricated by the competent lamas out of a variety of materials, of which the chief are flour mixed to a paste, butter either white or coloured and occasionally coloured threads. The ground-work of the altar pieces are blocks of wood, usually flat for Guru Rimpuché and raised in five mounds (thrones) for Kinchenjunga. On these are placed more-or-less life-like dough images of the chief gods, surrounded by innumerable and almost shapeless cones to represent the minor gods and attendants and satellites. Round the image of Kinchenjunga are represented the hundred gods which inhabit the body of the donor of the feast. Those dough images are decorated with white and coloured butter to represent their clothes and jewels. Sometimes a 'halo' shaped like an arum leaf is placed behind the chief gods; the halo consists of elaborate and very pretty flower decorations made in coloured butter on tin shields. Occasionally the altar-piece is surmounted by small dough birds fixed on thin splinters of bamboo; or alternatively there is added to the monastery altars materials which are practically always used in private and personal ceremonies: a *deu* or 'palace of supernaturals' consisting of elaborate geometrical shapes in coloured thread fastened round a central bamboo; and splinters with tufts of wool stuck at odd intervals down their length which are called *pong* and which are considered to represent the clouds which surround the homes of the supernaturals. Always before the commencement of the preparation of the altar-piece a small cone is made to represent Gett'r *moong*, the demon of quarrels. The quarrel demon is first invoked and then destroyed in order to prevent quarrelling or evil words taking place during the ensuing ceremony and feast.

When the altar is prepared the musicians start playing in twos and threes and big groups. If the altar has been made the night before the ceremony the musicians will continue playing at intervals all night, but the laymen do not start arriving till the next morning. In the morning all those who have been invited by the givers of the feast, which, except in the case of very poor people or very unpopular ones, means practically the whole village, start arriving at the monastery, each bringing with them some contribution in the form of food or *chi*, which will be of assistance to the giver of the feast. During the whole day the lamas sit in their seats in two parallel rows from the altar to the door, except when they go out for a slight rest and change of air. Their food and drink is brought to them at their seats in the monastery and they have permanently a *patyoot* of *chi* in front of them. The worship consists of special readings and chantings from the sacred scriptures interspersed with music.

Owing to the fact that the feasts in honour of Kinchenjunga are given by laymen certain precautions are taken and certain opportunities are given for acquiring merit which are not considered necessary for the feasts given by lamas. The precautions consist of the offering of *cherkem*—grain floating in *chi*—which is thrown out to the devils by a layman with cries of *Lo chi-do*—'take this' —and the burning of a bonfire of aromatic herbs and leaves to gratify the supernaturals. The lay-giver may, if he wishes, acquire merit by performing the ceremonial dance called *da-floh* before the altar, prancing and chanting in front of a folded cloth on the top of which his hat is laid, with the knife to the right and the scabbard to the left. In the evening the altar-piece is perambulated three times round the monastery and is then broken up; the dough is eaten (lamas however may not eat it) and the butter smeared on the heads of those standing round; this butter is regarded as a sort of sacrament which conveys blessings on those whose head is smeared with it. The Dorjé Lapoon in person anoints the heads of the lay-givers of the feasts and their families. Although this ends the religious part of the ceremony, gossiping and drinking may continue all night if sufficient *chi* has been provided.

Calendrical festivals take place frequently, at relatively fixed dates throughout the year. The greater number are apotropaic, intended to ward away those evils inherent in the season: illness in the winter and summer, hail and predatory animals when the crops are growing, quarrelling when the harvests are gathered, misfortunes in the new year, and so on. These ceremonies vary very considerably in elaboration. Some, such as the ceremony to appease Débrong *pa-no*, the king of hail, will be performed semi-privately in the house of the officiating lama, a little grain for the sacrifice having been collected by the *gyapön* from every household in the village so that the ceremony is felt to be for the benefit of the whole community, though practically none may be present at it. Others are extremely elaborate; Boom koor lasts for three days. This ceremony is somewhat similar to beating the bounds; the sixteen volumes of the Boom are carried in procession with all the musical instruments by the lamas in their finest dresses, all round the village; the procession follows a fixed route with points where it stops for prayers and feasting, the feast taking place in the biggest house in the neighbourhood and being provided by all the dwellers in that district; the procession itself takes forty-eight hours and the night is spent at some house half-way distant on the route, in the procession I saw, at the Mandal's house. The evening before the procession starts an elaborate ceremony is held to ward off all the predatory animals and thieves and destructive demons who would harm the growing crops; and when the procession has returned to the monastery and the sacred books have been replaced an all night service and picnic follows. This ceremony is held after the sowing of crops is completed to protect the crops and ward off all evil from the community; everybody except infants in arms, invalids, and the old and infirm join in it.

To describe in detail all the calendrical ceremonies which I have witnessed, let alone those that I have been told about, would be beyond the scope of this book. The ceremonies occur at almost weekly intervals, and though each differs considerably in detail from all the others, the general effect and intention of all are very similar. An extremely elaborate and detailed effigy of the supernatural whom it is intended to appease is made; the supernatural is invoked with prayer, music, readings from the scripture and gifts; is adored as a god; and then, whether it be in general benevolent or malevolent, is prayed to go away, and its image is taken some way away and abandoned or destroyed. Some of the ceremonies which take place outside the monastery are accompanied by parallel ceremonies performed by Mun.

I only propose to describe in detail a single calendrical ceremony, the destruction of the quarrel demon, which takes place in the autumn. This ceremony is more vivid and dramatised than the greater number of lamaist exorcisms; its details however resemble most of the other exorcisms.

Quarrelling is caused by a trinity of three devils Soo-*moong* (enmity of speech), Gé-*moong* (enmity of thought) and Thor-*moong* (enmity of action). To prevent quarrelling this trinity Soo-gé-thor is symbolically destroyed once a year in the monastery in the month of November; the ceremony is called *Thorsu*; every person of the village should be present; those who are unable to come should send gifts and crops instead.

First of all a very large image of the supernatural Thorgyop *rum* is made and at the four corners are placed containers, one filled with blood mixed with poison, one with milk, and two with *chi*. Somewhat in front of this is made a smaller image of Soo-gé-thor and in front of that is an unshaped heap of earth (the other images are also made of mud) with an egg on top so arranged that the egg is opposite the demon's heart. The demon is three-sided with images made of butter impressed with a wooden printing block[7] on each side. By the egg stands an archer with a bow and arrow ready. First of all the god is invoked and when he is considered to be present the lama says in Tibetan 'we are giving your life into the hands of a cruel man'. After this the devil is invoked and when it is thought to be present in the image the archer will shoot an arrow in such a way that it pierces simultaneously the egg and the heart. This is repeated three times with different eggs.

Another image is made of Soo-gé-thor, this time recumbent and with open mouth and arms. He is summoned from wherever he may be, whether he is in the skies or on the earth or under the earth; when the devil has entered the image it is hacked into small pieces and offered to the god mixed with poison and blood; then these pieces together with pieces of paper inscribed with the devil's name are rammed into a hollow bamboo which is covered with a thick cloth and put among the firewood under an iron griddle and set fire to. After this the lamas again read from the scriptures.

Finally a third image called Sor-so-mu is made; this is a three-sided pointed lump of mud smeared with blood and stamped on each side in butter with the name of the devils and their effigy. The lama after long prayers holds this pyramid above his head and throws it forward; the direction that the pointed end turns to

[7] A number of engraved blocks with representations of different supernaturals are kept in the monastery for use as circumstances require. The most generally employed is the *lo-kor*, the representations of the patron supernaturals of the twelve year 'animal' cycle.

is the direction in which the devil has gone. Should the pointed end turn backwards, that is towards the thrower, it is a very bad omen; it means that quarrelling will take place in the succeeding year.

V

The exorcisms and apotropaic rites performed by lamas for the benefit of individuals are even more numerous and varied than the calendrical rites. There is scarcely an ill which man is heir to which has not its individual and appropriate ceremonial remedy. Like the calendrical ceremonies by far the greater number consist of making an image of the possessing devil, invoking it, worshipping it, and then destroying it.[8] Besides the image of the central devil there are always a number of minor ritual objects, the most important of which is a twisted piece of dough called *chongbu-tipkü*. At the end of the ceremony the sufferer, or, in some cases all present, have this piece of dough ceremonially waved over them (*pék*) by the officiating lama as a ritual cleansing. In the greater number of ceremonies this is the only rôle which the sufferer plays. He is often not even in the same room as the lamas. At the beginning of the service the devil is always erected facing the lamaist altar; when the ceremony is finished the model with its stand is turned round to face the house-door; a double line of flour is traced from the devil to the door as the route it must take to go out, and the image on its board is then carried away either into the forest or to the place where four roads meet. For some exorcisms those who carry the devil have to go through some ritual or be ceremonially purified before they are readmitted into the house.

In some of the exorcisms a dough image of the sufferer is made and offered to the devil in lieu of the body of the sufferer; and in others, especially when it is divined that the devil has been sent through human agency (usually unwittingly: evil or envious thoughts can unleash a devil without the responsibility of the thinker) the devil, in the form of a winged insect, is ritually killed by the lamas with their sacred dagger. Finally, in some apotropaic ceremonies the threatened person himself plays a rôle; thus, for the ceremony *doak-po doat* the sufferer has to progress through the smaller squares of a big magic square, gradually having all his appearance changed: he starts off dressed in black, carrying a stick,

[8] Outlines and descriptions of some lamaist ceremonies will be found in Chapter Thirteen and especially in Appendix III.

and ends up dressed in white with a bow and arrow. This is believed to fool the devil, as is the device of taking a new name for a year.

Some of the sacrificial objects are elaborate and expensive and demand several hours and a great deal of material to make. All the rituals are described in various sacred books, and when making the sacrificial objects these books are always consulted.

I think the nearest parallel to the attitude of the Lepchas towards lamaist and Mun ceremonies can be found in that of an ignorant and somewhat hypochondriac European towards germs (the devils) and vitamins (the gods). There are a number of precautionary antiseptic measures to be taken against germs: salad is washed in disinfectant, food wrapped up in cellophane, children not kissed for fear of infection, the nose held when there is a bad smell from a drain, inoculations made against the fear of various diseases at regular intervals. Psychologically these precautions correspond almost exactly to the general and regular apotropaic services, either those held for the whole community or the obligatory consultations which have to take place at the beginning of each twelve-year cycle after the third. Once a germ has got a hold the disease has to be diagnosed and various remedies applied, for some of which you call in a doctor while others are traditional. These remedies correspond to the special services held in the case of illness or misfortune, the lama being rather regarded in the light of the consultant specialist and the Mun as the purveyor of old-world and traditional remedies. To keep in good health one has to follow certain rules about ventilation and sunlight and a correctly balanced diet. For the Lepchas these precepts are replaced by the worship of the gods. It is important to worship the gods and to have plenty of vitamins but to drive away devils and to get rid of germs is emotionally far more urgent and important. Though the other-worldly aims of lamaism are on the lips of some lamas they do not seem to me to be of great emotional importance; people say 'there are fewer devils here now that we have the lamas and their books' rather as they might say 'there is less diphtheria here now that we have got the new drainage system'. Though the lamas are considered to have driven away a number of the older devils an almost equally great number of new devils have been brought in following the arrival of Sikkimese and Nepali, as new diseases have arisen from new occupations and conditions of life to replace those which have been destroyed by a stricter application of hygiene.

To a certain extent the employment of lamas or Mun to drive away devils depends on the wishes and wealth of the sufferer or his near relatives; as with us some people are hypochondriac, some people refuse to take even necessary precautions when they are badly ill and some say and feel that they cannot afford the time or money. Some illnesses everybody can diagnose and tell which is the causing demon and what is the necessary curative ceremony, just as many people can recognise and know the treatment of the commoner illnesses. Others are more obscure and consultation has to be made. For the lama there are two possible forms of consultation; he can divine with his rosary, as has already been described, or he can consult the astrological books employed in horoscopes which will tell infallibly what devil on that day would be troubling the person born on the date of the sufferer's birth. In nearly every case a Mun and a lama are consulted simultaneously; should their diagnoses differ a third opinion will be sought and even a fourth and fifth until the Mun and the lama are in agreement as to the cause of the illness and therefore as to its cure. The Mun divines partly by his rosary and partly by *munthen*-ing, that is, communicating with his or her possessing spirit. Very often before consultation with a Mun consultation will be made with a layman who possesses a rosary and knows how to use it to discover which Mun—or rather the Mun born in which year—will be most suitable to deal with this particular patient.

The fear of illness and the ceremonies against it form by far the largest impact of religion on the life of the average Lepcha; a lama is far more a doctor than he is a priest in his function. Medicine in our sense of the word plays no rôle in the lama's cures; the patient is given no drugs of any sort to take; the cause of all illnesses and misfortunes is considered to be supernatural and therefore only supernatural methods are suitable for dealing with them. The Lepchas' knowledge of drugs is anyhow very slight but those who do know medicinal herbs can employ them without any form of ceremony. Religious consultation is very seldom held in the case of the illness of infants or young children; if a child is badly ill the most usual form of cure is to try a change of air, to take the child on a visit to the house of some relative—usually a relative by marriage, either the wife's parents or the wife's brothers. Children until they achieve complete physical independence are barely considered as fully human; they are not given any burial ceremony nor are they the subject of other ceremonies. Children

LAMAS PLAY MUSICAL INSTRUMENTS IN THE MONASTERY COURTYARD

Above : The son of Lharibu Chujen and Tafoor play ' clarionets '.

Below : Kutt'r, Lumba's son, and Chudo play telescopic trumpets.

dying before the age of about ten are usually said to be reincarnations of dead people whose life was cut short before it had attained its full span (for the Lepcha the normal human span of life is four score years) and have therefore returned to the world as a human being to finish their term of life before proceeding to their next incarnation. Although live children are so insignificant, dead ones turn into num-een *moong*, almost the most malevolent and dangerous of all devils. As a generalisation it may be said that in so far as human beings remain attached to this world after death, it is as devils, and, the younger the dead person, the more dangerous the devil he may leave behind. Even seeing dead people in dreams (unless they are climbing snow mountains, which indicates that their souls are entering heaven) is dangerous; for the simulacra of the dead are in reality the devils which caused the death.

In the case of minor physical injuries no religious cure is employed; but more serious accidents, such as falling from a tree or a high rock, are considered to be due to malevolent supernaturals and exorcisms have to be performed to avert the repetition of such injuries for the sufferer or other members of his household. If one member of a household dies a violent death the survivors should repeat annually and at the birth of each new member of the family certain apotropaic rites. It will be remembered that a propensity to violent death, like a propensity to being chased by a bear, is an hereditary taint which must be guarded against in selecting a marriage partner.

Horoscopes differ somewhat in their emotional affect from the other lamaist ceremonies. They are obligatory and implicitly believed in and have very considerable influence on the life of the person for whom the horoscope is cast. The first horoscope is cast on the third day after a child's birth; in this is determined the child's character, future employment and span of life, and also those illnesses and dangers with which he is threatened and the ceremonies that the parents must perform to avert these dangers. The second horoscope is cast at the instance of the parents and uncles before a marriage is arranged to see that the conjunction of the joint horoscopes is not endangered by unfavourable omens. This is the least compulsive horoscope of all; there are at least twelve signs in it which can be positive or negative and in by far the greater number of horoscopes the signs are mixed; only if the sign for children is entirely negative will the marriage almost always be abandoned. The third horoscope is cast when a person has completed his third, or occasionally fourth, twelve-year cycle to discover what is foretold for the next twelve years, and, in the event of illnesses or misfortunes being threatened, to perform the indicated apotropaic ceremonies. These consultations are repeated every twelve years. The final horoscope is cast immediately after death; this shows the cause of death, the future state of the man's soul and his next reincarnation, the most propitious mode of disposing of the body, the direction in which the body should be carried and the people who should handle it, and also what ceremonies should be performed to prevent the death-causing devil from attacking further members of the household, or, if the devil has gone elsewhere, into whose house the devil has entered.[9]

Though entirely mechanical the casting of horoscopes is an elaborate and difficult business which entails the collating and interpreting of a great number of cross-references. In Lingthem the only lamas who know how to do so are the two Dorjé Lapoon and Tafoor, and in nearly all cases it is Tafoor who is consulted.

Years are reckoned by four different and independent cycles: the most important, and the only one laymen know of is the twelve-year 'animal cycle'; next in importance comes the ten-year 'element' cycle; the importance of these two reside in the fact that a person is considered to possess the qualities of the animal and element of his year, and in horoscope conjunctions these qualities are of the greatest importance.[10] There are also two independent nine-year cycles founded on different magic squares (*mariwã and parrko*) so that, calculating by the year alone there are 9,720 different combinations. Besides the year calculations there are also calculations for the hour (of birth or death), the time (morning, midday, evening, etc.), the day, the month, the stars, the birth number, and so on. Altogether there are between ten and sixteen cross-references, depending on the elaboration of the horoscope, which can be made to check, counter-check and modify one another. Any apparent contradictions arising from the various modes of calculation are resolved by being explained as contingent.

[9] Complete horoscopes for birth, marriage and death will be found in Appendix III.

[10] The animal cycle is Rat, Ox, Tiger, Eagle, 'Thunder-bird', Snake, Horse, Sheep, Monkey, Fowl, Dog, Pig. The element cycle (each element lasts two solar years) is Fire, Earth, Iron, Water, Wood. 1937 was Ox year and the second Fire year; 1938 Tiger year and the first Earth year.

Lamaist horoscopes, like European ones, are automatic in their application, and, in the event of two or more people being born or dying in the same hour the horoscopes will be identical. The Lepchas thoroughly believe in the validity of the horoscopes and almost always carry out their instructions implicitly. It is believed that the defectives are abnormal because they or their parents neglected the indicated precautions.

It is only with the ceremonies prescribed by horoscopes that the possibility arises of a Lepcha failing to perform indicated ceremonies. Lamas come spontaneously to assist the soul of a dead man, and their presence, though usual, is not essential on any other occasion; in the case of present or threatened illness or danger the sufferer summons the lama to perform the requisite ceremonies; if for any reason he did not wish to perform the ceremonies he would not send for the priest.

On the whole the extent of employment of lamas by laymen depends on the personal inclination and beliefs of the layman in question. The greater number of lamaist ceremonies demand less expenditure than equivalent ones by Mun, since they do not involve the killing of animals. This generalisation must however be modified in one particular. Apart from jewels the only possible method of conspicuous expenditure for the ambitious is the erection of a lamaist altar in the *dé-ong* of his house and the purchase of the Boom or some other anthology of the lamaist scriptures. Once these are installed the visits of lamas at fairly constantly recurring intervals are essential for the reading of the scriptures and the performance of the necessary rites. Scriptures have to be read four times a year and since no layman can read, lamas have to be hired, feasts given to them and fees paid to them. This expense can only be stopped by selling or giving away the sacred books or objects.

Belief in horoscopes does not induce a feeling of fatalism, for every misfortune foretold carries with it its appropriate remedy. Unless a layman's child is predestined to become a lama people usually know nothing at all of their own first horoscopes, nor do parents usually remember for long the horoscope cast for their children. I never heard of an instance of an angry parent or elder sibling reproach a child because of the expense it had necessitated, nor throw in their face their unfavourable forecast. Even when people were trying to convince me of the validity of horoscopes they never quoted the realisation of past horoscopes, but only the negative results which occurred through not following their instructions. Not even Tafoor had any knowledge of his first horoscope, though he could have re-cast it if he had been curious.

vi

The higher lamas, the *omzet* and Dorjé Lapoon, perform mystic exercises for the good of their soul and to acquire supernatural powers. These exercises consist firstly in acquiring the requisite instruction and then being immured in a specially prepared and completely dark room called *tyang-gong* for a certain period. While they are immured they naturally see no light at all; for periods up to a fortnight they fast completely; for longer periods food is handed through a series of doors so arranged that no light and no possible contact with the external world reaches the mystic. During the whole period the lamas naturally cannot wash; a hole is especially prepared in the floor through which they can excrete.

As has already been explained this discipline is used for short periods for the ceremony of *kong-so klon*; it is also used for some other similar rituals. It was employed by Tafoor in order to obtain his supernatural power of stopping (or rather moving on) rain. Tafoor received his preliminary instruction from his 'big father', the second Dorjé Lapoon, who had been taught by a third lama who had learned the art in Tibet. When his instruction was complete a *tyang-gong* was constructed inside his house (there is a permanent one on the upper floor of the monastery) and Tafoor was immured. For ten days he did without food, drink or sleep, concentrating his mind on the special words and 'thoughts' that he had been taught, and counting his rosary. During the whole time the other people in the house had to take every precaution against his hearing human sounds or voices. At the end of the tenth day the second Dorjé Lapoon read the proper holy books, offered *cherkem* to the devils, opened the *tyang-gong* gradually, and fed Tafoor on boiled and powdered rice and milk. For two days Tafoor could not eat solid food; he was very weak and thin when he came out of the retreat.

Tafoor is now the only lama in the whole neighbourhood who practises the sending-away of rain; his uncle naturally knows how, but nowadays he concentrates exclusively on stopping hail. While Tafoor is keeping away the rain he must stop indoors concentrating; nobody must speak to him while he is doing this, nor may any member of the household go near a big stream nor pour water on the ashes in the house. Tafoor also must refrain from sexual activity, for at the time of the orgasm the gods would look down and be angry.[11] Control of rain can be as localised as is wished; it can extend over a single field or the whole of Zongu, and can be held off as long as the officiant prays. I suggested to Tafoor that he could ruin an enemy by concentrating all the time and preventing any rain falling on the enemy's fields; he agreed that this was so, but the idea seemed to him so ridiculous that he burst out laughing, although he treats this power of his otherwise very seriously and does not jest about it. The control of hail does not require the same precautions but necessitates the presence of some magical objects including a ram's horn.

There is no question but that not only Tafoor but all the people of the neighbourhood believe completely in this power of stopping rain; people from some way away will come with big presents to get Tafoor to stop rain when they want to work their fields and will work for him also as recompense. I unfortunately only found out about this claim to power of Tafoor's in the last month of my stay in Lingthem. Lingthem is very rainy and there were very few days in which no rain fell. In the last month of my stay there were six occasions when Tafoor announced beforehand that he was stopping rain and on those days no rain did in fact fall. The most extraordinary were the three days of the Boom koor ceremony whose date was fixed after some argument about a fortnight before it took place; when the date was finally decided upon Tafoor said immediately that no rain would fall during those three days, and in point of fact those were the only three days during my whole stay in Lingthem during which no rain fell. There were two other fine days during this period without rain for which I asked Tafoor if he was responsible; he said that on those days he had done nothing. In the event of rain falling while he was meant to be stopping it he has the alibi that some more powerful lama has been sending the rain away from his village to Lingthem or the neighbourhood, for the power consists only in shifting the rain and not in destroying it.

It would naturally need far longer observation than I was able to make to pronounce any judgement on this claimed power. It is worth noting that there is no sort of compulsion for the Lepchas to hire Tafoor; many people do not, because they say they cannot afford to, but everybody I questioned was certain that this

[11] Semen is called *tik-oong*—penis water.

rain-control worked, and cited numerous examples from their past experience to prove it.

This is the only instance of powers which the Lepchas themselves deem supernatural being used in ordinary life. The tradition of sorcery has already been referred to ; its use is so rare that it plays no part in the life of most people. There is a tradition of love magic in which the hairs of the two people meant to love one another are plaited and concentrated upon. Although they know the ritual, lamas themselves say that nobody living has performed it. It is said that Mun are requested to do this by one spouse if the other is unfriendly or by parents if their child and his or her spouse disagree : I never heard of an actual instance of this and it would seem as though it were only a tradition.

CHAPTER EIGHT

RELIGION II: THE MUN

i

As opposed to lamaism the Mun religion carries with it no social organisation; the Mun and their parallel priests are simply individuals who, through their possession by a spirit, have certain gifts and duties; unlike the lamas and the civil officers their position carries with it no sort of title in ordinary life. Besides the Mun three other types of priesthood by possession are recognised; these are the Padem, the Yaba, and the Pau. The Mun spirit is a female spirit, the other three are male. They are attached to family lines and are roughly hereditary; they often descend from grandfather to grandson or from grandmother to granddaughter; but there is no regularity about this and a man may inherit a possessing spirit from a woman, and *vice versa*; once the vehicle dies the spirit may not choose another body immediately and large groups may be without the possessing spirit for a number of years. The manifestation of the spirit (for the spirits themselves live immortal beyond Kinchenjunga) may choose anybody for its vehicle, with one exception; none of the spirits will enter a lama or his own children, though they may enter his family.

Both men and women can be Mun, but only men can be Padem (or Bum-*thing* as they are called outside Zongu); these are both pure Lepcha spirits and are essentially similar, save that the Padem are far less powerful, and that instruction by an already qualified Padem is optional, whereas for Mun a three year course of instruction is obligatory. Padem are weaker than Mun and capable of exorcising far fewer devils; they cannot prophesy nor perform the death ceremony. For many men Padem is the first step to becoming Mun; in Lingthem there are altogether eight Mun[1] of which four

[1] They are (men) Katel, Gongyop, Thyak Thimbu (Gongyop's elder brother) and Agyung (the adopted son of Serving): of these Gongyop practises regularly, Katel occasionally, the other two hardly at all. (women)

are men ; of these three were first of all Padem. Kurma is Padem only ; he can diagnose but can only perform a few sacrifices and exorcisms.

The other two groups of possessed priests resemble one another and differ from Mun and Padem in so far as neither can make sacrifices nor perform exorcisms, but can merely get possessed by supernaturals ; they dance until the supernatural speaks through them and discloses its wants and whereabouts. Both wear special clothes for their performances : the Yaba (women are called Yama) wear bandoliers of tinkling bells and have their clothes fringed with bells ; they hold a metal plate and beat it as they dance. Pau (women are called Nandjému) wear elaborate wool head-dresses and dance with a skull-drum in one hand and a bell in the other. Both Yaba and Pau are and have been very rare because the possessing spirits are not Lepcha but have been introduced through inter-marriage with foreign women, the Yaba spirit comes from Limbu women (the Limbu are a Nepali tribe) and the Pau from Sikkimese-Tibetans. There is a tradition that there is a similar spirit called Jhankri belonging to the Chetri,[2] but this spirit has never manifested itself among the Lepchas as there has been no inter-marriage between the two groups.

There is only one representative of this group in Lingthem : the 'elder grandmother' of Patek, an old woman over seventy, is a Nandjému. The service of these diviners is only called in when lama and Mun fail to agree on a diagnosis, or when there is reason to suppose that a new devil has taken up its abode in the neighbourhood. In such cases a Pau or Yaba, usually from another village, will be called in to discover its home and its needs.

It is believed that there are two sorts of Mun, a good group called Tang-li Mun and a bad group called Mun-mook Mun ; the difference is similar to the traditional difference between white and black magicians. 'Mun-mook Mun are like thieves : they think and do evil and are possessed by devils which they employ for their own selfish ends ; they alone can send devils (the term used for sorcery).' They are believed to have an influence like the evil

Pumri (wife of the second Dorjé Lapoon), the elder wife of Lumba *chithembu* (she is the daughter of Pumri and has the paternal spirit) the 'younger grandmother' of Patek, and the sister of Jiroong (the wife of Kaji). All four women practise.

[2] This Lepcha tradition is incorrect : the Chetri are a fairly pure Hindu tribe ; the Jhankri occur among the Gurung.

THE MUN GONGYOP

eye. On the other hand 'When Tang-li Mun sacrifice they do so with benevolence in their heart towards the people and houses to which they are summoned.' It is thought that none of the Mun now inhabiting Lingthem are evil, though one lived there about a score of years ago; there are however some in other villages. The type of Mun a person becomes depends on his or her teacher, and not on the possessing spirit.

I think the best way of describing the possession and functions of a Mun is to repeat the description of his spiritual life given by Gongyop. For the greater part I was not able to take down his exact words, for he speaks extremely quickly and very easily falls into the sing-song rhythm of a Mun's invocation, often saying the same thing twice or four times in different words, rather after the fashion of the Hebrew psalmist. He uses onomatopoeic words a great deal, many of his own invention. He has a prodigious memory and once started goes on like a clock-work machine; but if he is interrupted his train of thought breaks down and he cannot extract one point out of a sequence for elaboration.

Gongyop is far more in demand than any other Mun in the village; he officiates in nearly all the ceremonies except those which are performed in families of which a member is a Mun. When sacrificing he falls into what is almost a very light trance; his eyes become glazed and unfocussed as he intones his rhythmic chants. He is a man of forty-six, with a rather whimsical and wild-eyed expression and very small and expressive hands. He is easily amused and laughs freely. He is very nervous and jumps perceptibly at any sudden sound, a thing no other Lepcha does; he is aware of his peculiarity and ascribes it to a fall he had from a bamboo when he was thirteen. After that fall blood spurted from his ears and he couldn't see and for a time lay like one dead. Three years later he had another fall, but was not hurt much and climbed the tree again. Nowadays he says he can't climb big trees; if he were to do so he would feel giddy. Even in normal life he suffers from giddiness; 'his eyes turn' and he can't see properly. He can't walk along a cliff; the ground feels as though it were moving up and down, nor can he walk among big trees for he feels that they are going to fall on him. He has frequent unpleasant dreams of falling down or flying down. I did not come across similar nervousness or anxiety among any of the other Lepchas whether Mun or laymen, and such instability is in no way essential for a Mun.

Even for a Lepcha Gongyop is preternaturally shy and I had to woo him very assiduously before he would talk to me. But I found with him as I did with others that once his confidence was gained he was willing to talk absolutely without reserve. Indeed one day I had to run away from him because I had asked him a question about his divining necklace; he explained in great distress that if he told anybody the full details about it he would loose all the power of divining through it, so please would I not ask him. I changed the subject, but naturally curious, kept glancing at the necklace, and after a little he started to tell me about it. A similar dilemma arose three or four times with Lepchas; it would seem as though once they had accepted you they can neither lie nor prevaricate, and will tell secrets which they will bitterly regret mentioning later. Towards the end of our relationship Gongyop asked me very shyly (for it was, in a way, a confession of failure for a Mun) for medicine for sores: and then he showed me on his shoulder a growth which to my unpractised eye looked like cancer.

Gongyop was the youngest of four children; almost as soon as he was weaned he was adopted by the younger brother of his paternal grandmother in whose house he spent the greater part of his life; recently however he has returned to look after his blind old father. His eldest brother, who was a lama, died with his wife and two of his children in a dysentery epidemic; his two surviving children are Sangkyar, a cretinous defective, and Satéo, who is lame and rather silly. The next brother is Thyak Thimbu; he too is a Mun (he has the paternal spirit, Gongyop the maternal); after him came a sister, now dead, who was married, first to a 'brother' of Dunbi, and then to Kurma. Gongyop became a Padem twenty years ago, the spirit descending to him from his father's maternal uncle who died five years before the possession; he became a Mun five years ago, the spirit descending from his mother's elder sister who died ten years before the possession.

'At the time of the onset of the illness which showed the possession of Padem I had been married for five years and my wife was pregnant; she was later delivered of a still-born daughter. Subsequently we had a son who is still living. I was taken very ill, so ill that I could not eat or drink *chi* or move or even go out of the house to relieve myself; I felt as though I was bound with ropes. After another Mun had recognised the spirit which was possessing me I recovered quickly and was then able to perform all the rituals of which Padem are capable. There is no need of a teacher for the work of Padem; the spirit will instruct before each ceremony as to what is needed in the way of sacrifices by means of dreams in which the spirit will be represented by Europeans or Kings of Sikkim and other States. This divination by dream never failed, before each ceremony I would dream the requisite ritual.

'After I had been a Padem for some years I was taken ill again as before, so ill that I lay like one paralysed and all my hair fell out. My senses were confused and I could neither see nor hear properly. By night I used to dream of huge bridges and roads and of myself walking and riding over them to all the countries of the world, Tibet and Bhutan and Nepal and India and Europe. There I would meet people and talk with them in their own language; in the neighbouring countries I would meet and talk to the Kings: in Europe I stayed in people's houses and there were so many houses you could not see the ground. I lay almost like one dead.

'Before I got really ill like this I was acting almost like a madman wandering into the forest and other people's houses; I did not know what I was doing and I did not recognise people. I used to travel about very quickly and not know how I had got to where I was; the neighbours called in the Mun and Padem but it was no use.

'When I lay ill the Mun and lamas exorcised unavailingly; but finally a lama recognised that I was troubled by the Mun god and he told me that I must make her my private god. The lamas then divined who was the most fitting person to perform the ceremony of *Rum keuk* (recognising the god) and decided upon an old female Mun who lived some way away. She came and a sacrifice was prepared consisting of a tray covered with offerings of dried fish and dried bird and ginger and pop corn and rice and other crops and various sorts of *chi*; this she offered to the gods saying in *tang-bor* (circumlocutions) that she was making these offerings for the invalid and would the gods please accept both them and him. An ox was then killed and she took away the intestines and the head and two legs; she was also given Rs. 5 but she gave them back and only took them for herself when I was fully instructed. When the Mun had made her sacrifice she fed me with *chi* by hand and she put a silver rupee in my hand and a ceremonial scarf round my neck and said to me "From today the *rum* will be with you and you must learn all the work of the Mun". She stayed three nights and then returned home. From that day I started recovering;

two days later I was able to go outside the house and within a month I was strong enough to go and visit the Mun. On my first visit I took with me a load of *chi*; I used to pay her visits of varying length—five, ten, or fifteen days, according to the amount of time necessary to learn completely one sort of ritual or story—and I would return home to meditate upon it before proceeding further. I studied in all three years before I could be given *loong*.[3] I had to know the history of every devil and how to exorcise it as well as the story of creation and the birth of Tak-bo-*thing* and many things more. During my training I was not allowed to eat pork or goat or chicken or hen's eggs for if I had there would have been devils I could not have controlled. At the end of my three years' training when I had got my *loong* my teacher had all the forbidden foods boiled and put in a basket; then after she had given me *chi* and butter to drink and a ceremonial scarf she told me that now I had power over all the devils and could eat all forbidden foods, after which with her own hands she gave me three mouthfuls of each sort of food. When I was given my *loong* a second ox was sacrificed; the first time I was so weak that I had to stop indoors while the sacrifice was made.

'Until I got my *loong* I could not officiate as Mun but I could continue to do so as Padem; there is no quarrel between the Padem *rum* and Mun *rum* as they are husband and wife respectively and are pleased to inhabit the same body. They do so however comparatively rarely as no woman can be Padem though she may be Mun and a man can be Padem without being Mun, and *vice versa*. A person like myself can call down Padem *rum* or Mun *rum* at will; before possession the Padem *rum* does not call down the Mun *rum* to visit him though he is pleased when she comes. The spirits are not permanently present in their dwelling;[4] they come down from their home, which is reached from a passage beyond Kinchenjunga, when they are summoned. When they do come down the vessel which receives them feels as though bowed down by a heavy weight.

" The Mun only takes full possession of this vessel twice a year, once in the hot season and once in the wet season. This is a big ceremony and elaborate sacrifices are made. The day before the sacrifices I start feeling ill; I feel heavy and pressed down and cannot bear any noise; I tremble constantly and am covered with

[3] See Chapter Seven, p. 196.

[4] Gongyop constantly referred to his body as the *li*—the house of the spirits.

THE CHERIM CEREMONY I

Above : The Mandal and Gongyop (arm only) fill the containers of the *rum* offered to the devils with milk and tea.

Below : Pumri offers strained *chi* in a cup to the gods of Kinchenjunga. Old Kahlyeu, on her left, offers grain.

sweat. I pray to the gods to let me off and I offer them *chi* and incense in preparation for them to wait for the true sacrifices. The next day the ceremony is held inside a house and many people are present. I sit down cross-legged in front of the offerings. Besides the ordinary offerings there is a wreath of flowers and a flower-bedecked stick. When I sit opposite these I feel as though a heavy burden were pressing over my shoulders and as if my flesh were being poked with sticks—zinga—zinga—zinga—zinga—; suddenly a sort of darkness comes over my eyes, it is as if I was in a dream so that I know, see and remember nothing. But from what other people have told me and from what I have seen when other Mun have prophesied I know what takes place; I put on the flower necklace and take up the stick and go and walk outside in the courtyard. (Were anybody else to put the necklace on me the gods would be angry and the rash man would receive the burden of the gods.) When I return everybody is hushed, even the children. I blow into each person's face and on the offerings; then I scatter *chi* and prophesy in a loud and audible voice the things which are going to take place in the following half-year. After the prophecy I recover consciousness but not till cock-crow the next day do I feel all right again.[5]

'When I am called in in the case of illness the god does not fully enter me but I see the devil which is attacking the sick person either in the form of some animal or insect or person, depending on which devil it is; thus Lum dong *moong* appears as a pig, Sor *moong* as a dirty ragged old woman, Arot *moong* as a red butterfly. I see these visions out of the corner of my eye; if I look directly there is nothing there. But I watch these devils carefully out of the corner of my eye; if they go away without eating anything the patient will recover quickly; but if they take food the patient will probably die though I only tell him that the illness is very serious.

'A Mun must on no account touch a human corpse; should he do so the god will depart and he will be very ill for two months and lamas have to perform ceremonies to cure him. This is the only occasion on which the spirit will leave a Mun. A dead Mun is buried in the ordinary way and his soul has to be conducted to the *rum lyang* (place of the gods) in the normal manner; the gods

[5] All Mun do this ceremony twice a year (no more and no less) but on different days; informants agree that their prophecies are never mutually contradictory; they are always fairly generalized.

which have inhabited the live body have no concern with the soul after death.'

Gongyop said on another occasion that he thinks it an unhappy thing to be a Mun. He would have preferred not to have been one himself and he prays that his son will escape the visitation. 'May Tangen *moong* spare my son.' The perquisites do not make up for the illness and the work.

Among laymen it is a very general feeling that it is a misfortune to be a Mun; as well as the psychological and physical distress there is the added fact that Mun are responsible for the killing of many animals; but the Mun themselves say that this sin is not borne by them but by the devils who make the sacrifices necessary.

The onset of possession is described in much the same way by other Mun and Padem also. Kurma who was possessed by the Padem spirit when he was ten said he felt ill and almost mad for three months; he ached so much that he could not move, his body felt as though it were going to burst. He neither saw nor heard properly; he ate little and drank nothing. At times he felt as though he were flying or sitting on trees; at other times his body felt as big as the monastery whereas other people seemed as small as twigs. The symptoms disappeared after diagnosis and acceptance of the Padem god.

I was unfortunately not able to see anybody during these initial phases of possession. During my stay Mrs. Chano was diagnosed as being possessed by the Mun spirit but the sense delusions and wanderings had passed and she merely stopped at home very listless and apathetic. Gongyop performed the ceremony of dedication and was going to become her teacher.[6]

It is worth noting that except for the bi-annual prophecies[7] the Mun do not possess supernatural powers as the Lepchas understand them, and they differ in degree rather than in kind from the laymen; they can always see devils, whereas only some laymen can see them and that only on some occasions; they can always communicate with supernaturals, whereas only certain old and experienced laymen can do so. A great deal of the Mun ritual, as opposed to the divination, can be performed by laymen.

[6] This is described in Appendix III.

[7] And calling up the soul of a dead man and making him speak; but only very few Mun possess this art, and none in Lingthem. See Chapter Thirteen.

ii

The Mun religion has a very copious validating mythology and theology. The origin of everything in the world, visible and invisible, animate and inanimate, and the changes they have undergone to bring them to their present state are told in a great number of stories of varying emotional importance. Some of the simplest of the 'origin' stories are known and told by everyone; the more important ones require *loong* before they can be told; and the most important of all, the story of creation, is only known in its full details by the Mun; one of the chief parts of their training is the learning of this story, which it is said takes seven whole days in its telling, by heart. By far the greater part of it consists of lists of pairs of supernaturals who produce the phenomena which greet our eyes today.

'Under this world is an ocean; under that ocean is another earth of twelve super-imposed stories, and under that there lives Itpomu, the Creative Mother, and her husband Débu. Their first children were Tak-seu and Tak-from, who are also called Narzong-*nyou* and Komsi*thing*. After them were born Mlum Mukyam, Sakyeun-faat-it, Saba-faat-chaum, Suk-dum-lung-ming and Chi-lel, all of whom are the present earth; Palyou and Pakyam who are gladness and joy; then Ta-lyang, Ta-kook and Ta-kok who are the blue sky without ornament: then Bru-nong, and Jil-vong, Long-mu and Tso-kor who are the forest in the sky where the stars live: then Tak-bru-num and Jit-it who are the stars. The ocean between the two worlds is called lyang-tak-yoor *oong*, tagum-lyang-shin-mu *oong* and is the home of Tal-i-nau and her husband San-go. Under the second earth are two huge copper vessels beside Itpomu, full of water, and under them is a fire; this is the reason why the earth becomes warm and wet. Then was born Panjer-roong and Pantsong-roong which is the Rungit river; then Kum-zer roong which is the origin of hot streams which cure all ills . . . then were born Num-ri and Num-ra who begat the thunder-bird, *sadher*. . . .' The greater part of the story continues in this vein.

Later on in the same story the origin of devils and the creation of the Mun spirit is recounted. This is also a very long story but is far better known than the Genesis. I only propose to give an outline of it.

'The first children of Itpomu and Débu were Komsi*thing* and Narzong-*nyou*; although they were brother and sister they married, and as a consequence all their children were devils and snakes and lizards. As soon as they were born their mother cast them aside without giving them milk. Finally she produced a normal child called Rilbu Shingbu whom she nursed; but when the devils saw this child getting the milk that had been denied them they were jealous and they took counsel and killed the child. Their incest was betrayed by the dog who guarded the door. When the parents were shamed and the child killed they buried the child in the black rock on the right of the Talung valley, which can be seen to this day, and thereafter in disgust they divided their property and separated. Komsi*thing* went to Tibet and he took with him all the riches and jewels and animals which the Tibetans have till this day. Narzong-*nyou* turned towards our country but she was careless and that is why our country is so poor.

'After that Komsi*thing* summoned all the devils to him and all came except Doam *moong* who is the devil of leprosy, and he counselled the devils and said to them "You are devils and you must act according to your nature; but you must take an oath that when men are born you will accept them if they give you pigs and oxen and rice and other things to eat; if you are looked after you must go away, you must obey the Mun and Padem and the sacrificer". They all took this oath except Doam *moong* who was not present and that is the reason why you can never drive him away and leprosy cannot be cured.

'But still there was no Mun; Itpomu had placed all the devils in the big plain Azum Patham; but there they had nothing to eat. So then Itpomu created the Mun spirit and sent her to feed them. When the Mun arrived at Azum Patham she said to the devils "You are older than I am and I am helpless; I will return to Itpomu". But the devils begged her to stay, saying that if she went away they would always be hungry; if she stayed they would promise to obey her. They swore this by three great oaths; first they cut their finger nails and swore on them: then they spat on the Kashou tree and the tree withered, finally they spat in the sea and the sea dried up. Since that time the Mun must find out what sacrifices are needed and give them to the devils and the devils will always obey them.'

The other important story for which *loong* has to be obtained before it can be publicly repeated is the story of the *Origin of Marriage*. With its internal repetitions and lists of names it takes between two and three hours to repeat; it is always repeated

THE CHERIM CEREMONY II

The model of Mamoo *moòng* with the '*deu*'—the nine-storeyed devil's palace made out of coloured threads—in position down by the *choten* just before the worship begins. In the foreground are Katel and Jiroong. Behind, Chala Mandal and Lumba.

verbatim, though not necessarily to an audience, by the Sacrificer on the second day of the marriage feast. I am giving a somewhat shortened version of it in an Appendix,[8] but there are one or two points to which I should like to draw attention. Tarbong-bo, the inventor of marriage, was Itpomu's youngest son, and was still drinking her milk when he saw, desired and tried to rape Na-rip-nom; when he failed in this because he had not given the proper presents his mother sent him to his elder brother Komsi*thing* for advice and help. It will be noticed that there is no sort of transition or *rite de passage* between the child and the boy of marrying age; and that the elder brother, and not the father or paternal or maternal uncle is the natural person for a young man to turn to for help and advice. In the Mun mythology the father is never important; Débu, the husband of Itpomu, is merely a name, without personality or independent existence; it seems possible that he is a relatively modern importation. I think the same is possibly true of Tak-bo-*thing*, the grandchild of Itpomu and the child of Narzong-*nyou* (sometimes his father is Komsi*thing*, sometimes some other male supernatural); Tak-bo-*thing* is simultaneously a supernatural and the first human being and a great number of stories are told about him, chiefly to explain the origin of different human customs; but he is inextricably confused with Tashey-*thing* or Guru Rimpuché, and it seems to me probable that he is to a very great extent a Tibetan import, though probably anterior to the Lepcha's conversion to lamaism.

The chief supernaturals of the Mun are the two feminine deities Itpomu and Narzong-*nyou*. Itpomu herself is never directly invoked; it is always her creations who are sacrificed and prayed to. Narzong-*nyou* is really the chief Lepcha goddess; she is as it were the local God of Sikkim, of the Lepchas' country; she lived in the country and is responsible for its geography, flora, and, especially fauna. She is also responsible for a great number of institutions. Her elder brother and husband Komsi*thing* is also responsible for a number of habits and institutions, but he is in a way a foreigner; after he and his wife separated he took himself to Tibet. Except in the harvest rites the two of them are always mentioned in prayers and sacrifices, together with all the other supernaturals involved. The invocation usually takes hours, for all the relevant gods in all their manifestations, with their wives and their children must be mentioned by name; in private sacrifices

[8] See Appendix IV.

all the personal and *ptso* gods of the sufferer and his family must also be included.

Apart from the two long 'scriptural' stories there are a vast number of shorter stories which are known by most of the older people and recounted on a variety of occasions. Nearly all of these the Lepchas call *lung-then.*[9] In its general meaning *lung-then* is the word applied to any traditional custom which cannot be neglected, such as the giving of feasts; applied to stories it means roughly 'tales of origin'. All *lung-then* end with the words 'And that is why today . . .' expressed or implied.

Lung-then can be divided into two groups: those dealing with supernaturals and human beings, and those dealing exclusively with animals. The most peculiar feature of the stories dealing with anthropomorphic characters is the preponderating rôle played by the genitalia, which are almost endowed with independent life; various semi-heroic humans and supernaturals possess genitalia of peculiar formation and characteristics, and the adventures of these organs together with the bodies to which they are attached are told in a number of tales. One of these stories I think worth repeating, for it is, as far as I know, unparalleled in any other mythology; it is the story of the Origin of Menstruation. The story is universally known and is repeated whenever the subject is brought up. The story would appear to be capable of two interpretations, both of them congruent with the Lepcha attitude to the similarity and difference between men and women. On the one hand it indicates an extraordinary conception of the equality of men and women, for menstruation is considered almost everywhere as one of women's greatest disabilities. But it can equally well be interpreted as male envy of women and their more conspicuous physiological functions, a deeply hidden envy which can be supported by the Lepcha belief[10] that male intervention is necessary to start the physical signs of female puberty. The story is as follows:

'Originally women had their vulvas on the top of their heads. Then the menstrual blood used to flow all over their faces and it looked so unpleasant that the gods transferred the blood to men's knees; but then, when they went hunting and travelled about the country the blood used to drip everywhere, and Narzong-*nyou* saw this and was displeased thereat. Moreover the gods still did not like the vulvas on the top of the heads, so they called for volunteers

[9] Examples of these and other Lepcha stories are given in Appendix V.

[10] See Chapter Twelve, p. 315.

to move this unpleasant thing. First one bird was asked to undertake this task and tried, but failed; then the *nambok* bird tried for a year and failed; and then the *mong-klyok* bird (? a sort of bul-bul) said that, given a suitable reward, he would change its position. What reward? asked the gods. The bird asked that when the crops were ripe if it were to eat the grain it should not be driven away but should be let feed freely. This was agreed upon and then uttering its cry " *tabék—tabék* " (*abék* means between) it pecked and pecked and eventually moved the vulva to the forehead; there it stuck and then after a time moved slowly to the nose, the upper lip and the chin; at the chin it stuck a year, then travelled slowly down sticking five years at the navel; eventually it got to its proper place where it now is and where it is hidden. Seeing this hidden place Narzong-*nyou* who had invented menstruation so that people could tell when babies were going to be born retransferred the blood thither. As the *tamtoom* (that is the inevitable result) of this deed the Mongklyok bird has a red spot on its tail to this day as can be seen on all birds belonging to this race.'

As opposed to the stories about gods and humans, the stories about animals do not contain any sexual element at all. On the other hand excretion as a humorous situation or a sign of defiance recurs with great regularity. Outside these stories the Lepchas of Zongu do not consider 'natural functions' funny, and there is a complete absence of the cloacal jokes which form the main part of the repertoire of the puritanical missionised Lepchas. The greater number of the animal stories explain the cause of enmity between two species: they usually start by the statement that 'once upon a time the spider and the wasp (for example) set up an *ingzong* relationship,' but then one broke the pact, 'and that is why today wasps and spiders are enemies.' These stories show a great deal of observation, and many of them are extremely elaborated with a variety of comic situations.

iii

The overwhelmingly greater number of Mun ceremonies are performed for the benefit of individuals, households, or geographical groups of households. Even the prophetic possessions, described earlier, are only for the benefit of the household of the Mun and the Mun-less houses near his; and the calendrical harvest rituals, described in the next chapter, have to be performed separately for each household. There are however a few ceremonies when a Mun sacrifices and prophesies for the whole community; but all that I have seen or heard of are adjuncts to lamaist ceremonies.

In the Cherim ceremony which is held twice yearly, once at the beginning of the rains, and again at the beginning of winter, to keep off illness from the community, three separate rituals are performed, two by Mun, and the third by lamas. The communal nature of these sacrifices is emphasized and at least one individual from each household has to be present, and each household contributes a little of the grain. So that the Mun can participate the ceremony is held on neutral ground, when I saw it on March 28th., by the *choten* below the monastery and just outside the sacred precincts.

The first part of the ceremony consists of an offering to the devils: this ceremony is called *rum* after the name given to the chief article of sacrifice. This is a large basket filled with earth and covered with a banana leaf into which are inserted a number of varied articles with eight[11] of each sort of article: 'devil's walking-sticks' consisting of decorated bamboos with flowers inserted in holes, containers of water, milk, tea and *chi*, pieces of mica, stems of wormwood decorated with threads, fresh eggs, heaps of grain, and dried bird, dried fish and ginger. There are also offered two *ta-ming* which consist of long sticks to which are attached wrapped in leaves samples of every sort of food and drink. When the offerings have been made the Mun, sitting opposite them, intones a long chant to invoke the gods, and then takes the eggs and holds them to his forehead while he shuts his eyes and concentrates; the line which he envisages inside the eggs foretells the future health of the community. In the spring of 1937 Gongyop saw 'a fairly straight path' which signifies that there will be a mild epidemic of stomach trouble. Four years ago, when there was a bad epidemic of dysentery he saw 'a curved, almost spiral path, with a knot at the end of it.'

The second ceremony, also performed by Mun, consists of offerings to the Gods of Kinchenjunga and the Plains, and is called Tsandong. The offerings consist of rice, butter, *chimi*, a rupee and eggs. The sacrifice is in two parts; first grain and strained *chi* are thrown out by the Mun and her assistant (in March 1937 Pumri was assisted by old Kahlyeu) and later a goat is dedicated and then killed.

[11] It may be noted that for Mun and lama odd numbers are lucky, even unlucky.

THE CHERIM CEREMONY III

Above : Mamoo *moong* in detail ; she is made of buckwheat flour decorated with butter. Note small kite-shaped *deu*, inscribed labels, *nahleut* at the base.

Below : The lamas invoke Mamoo *moong*. Right on the left is a *chazé* table with bowls of water and rice for the gods' refreshment ; seated on the left is the second Dorjé Lapoon fingering his rosary ; on a cloth in front of him his sacred bell and brass *dorjé* or thunderbolt. Tafoor, who made the nine-storey palace is playing the cymbals. On the right, half out of the picture is lame Satéo, ready to strike the gong. Note the *patyoot* of *chi*.

These two ceremonies together took about four hours. None of the people present took any notice of either of them. The few who weren't cooking, eating, gossiping or braiding one another's hair, watched the lamas preparing their very elaborate ceremonial objects. The chief of these was the *deu*, the 'nine-storeyed palace' consisting of elaborate regular polyhedra in different coloured threads supported on bamboo splinters through a central bamboo. This 'palace', which took over four hours to complete, is made to mollify the ghost-devil of an old king of Tibet called Dayom; in his lifetime his palace and monasteries were destroyed so that he had nowhere to live; in revenge his spirit roams about harming people. The palace is offered to beg his pardon and to persuade him to return home without hurting the people in the neighbourhood.

This palace however only formed the background of the whole object. The foreground was occupied by an elaborate representation of the female devil Mamoo *moong*, portrayed as a snake-haired female riding on a tiger, and surrounded by hundreds of lesser objects. The devil was made out of buckwheat powder, and it was impressed on the onlookers that any laughter while the buckwheat was being handled would automatically result in a thunderstorm with thunderbolts. When the whole object had been made with frequent consultations of the sacred book the invocation and readings from the scriptures with musical accompaniment began; then an offering of boiled rice and fresh buckwheat bread was offered to all the gods and devils; then the ground was cleared and *cherkem* offered to the devils; then Mamoo *moong* herself was summoned and gratified with the offerings of copper pots and cloths (these are only offered symbolically and are later retaken into use); and when Mamoo was presumed to be in a good temper the *chongbu-tipkü* round her image were handed out for all to wave over themselves; then the image was taken off the temporarily erected altar. It was getting dark by the time the ceremony had reached this point, and therefore there was no time to carry the image in procession across three streams, accompanied by musical instruments, as should be done; instead it was only carried across one stream that day, and the following two the next morning. If animals have not devoured the image within three days it is a sign that there will be sickness in the coming season; if however they have devoured it in one it is a sign of prosperity. Before the image was taken away the procession was held up while a Mun (in this case Lumba *jethi*) sang an unaccompanied song thanking the gods for their kindness in coming when they were invited, and begging them now to go away. On those occasions when singing is called for it is nearly always the Mun who sing, and they possess a considerable repertoire of more or less sacred songs. All these songs are in the minor key, more or less rhythmic, with a great stressing of the last syllable of each line, which is prolonged for several notes, usually in a descending scale. The tunes are not set, and allow of easy improvisation. Songs are often sung at feasts, and always at marriages; they are always unaccompanied. The bamboo flutes which some young men make and play are used entirely as a solitary diversion.

iv

The services of the Mun are continuously necessary in the life of every Lepcha. They must always be present at birth, at marriage they are the only essential priests, and at the death of laymen their rôle is of more emotional importance than the lamas. Throughout life they are necessary for cleansing from supernatural danger, for blessing and solemnising different undertakings, and, above all, for expelling devils.

Ceremonial cleansing is performed by *pék*-ing, by the Mun waving certain objects over the actual or potential sufferer. The objects waved differ with the circumstances; thus in the fifth month of pregnancy both parents are *pék* with a bunch of elephant grass to insure an easy delivery: if labour is difficult the mother in childbirth is *pék* with a live chicken, and, if she or her husband have neglected a pre-natal precaution, with the object which has been wrongly handled or finished. Similarly after an abortion or still-born child has been thrown into the river, a Mun will *pék* the carriers with a bunch of stinging and thorny plants and the parents will be *pék* with a live animal which will later be sacrificed, in order to prevent the devil which has caused one death causing more. *Pék*-ing is employed in a number of circumstances, sometimes alone, and sometimes as part of an exorcism. It is the nearest approach in Lepcha life to ritual cleansing.

Blessings are invoked and pacts solemnised by the ritual of *sakyou faat*, the pouring or drinking of strained *chi* from a cup on the sides of which dabs of butter have been placed. It is not absolutely essential that Mun perform this ritual; any old and experienced man who has received *loong* may do so. *Sakyou faat* cannot be offered by women, except by women Mun inside their own homes, by lamas, or by people in mourning. The ceremony is performed to solemnise a marriage, to set up the *ingzong* relationship, to mark the formal swearing of an oath or before starting any unusual undertaking. It is used in all ceremonies for which a blessing is invoked (as opposed to exorcisms), sometimes alone, sometimes with the *lafét*[12] sacrifice. It is always made privately in each household after the sowing of a field. It is the most solemn sacrament in Lepcha life.

When a Mun is called in to exorcise a devil the most usual situation is as follows. After the specific devil has been divined the Mun spends a night in his own home *munthen*-ing—that is summoning and communing with his possessing spirit—to discover the reason for that particular devil having attacked that particular person, and to learn what sacrifices or ritual are necessary to exorcise it. The question of causation is bound up with the conception of *tamtoom*—the necessary consequence of an earlier act; often this act was not committed by the sufferer, but by fairly remote ancestors. Thus the Mandal suffered from lumbago as the *tamtoom* of one of his ancestors having abandoned a baby in a field-house, where it was burnt to death. A complicating cause, which also accounted for his failure to produce a son, was that the spirit of his first dead wife was plaguing him because, although herself a Mun, she had been cremated and conducted to heaven by lamas (as though she were a nun) instead of being buried and led to a heaven by a Mun. Angered at this treatment her spirit had been transformed into Sabdok *moong* and in this guise came from the *rumlyang* from time to time to plague her husband and to prevent his having any sons. In this task she was assisted by the Hit *rum*, the Mun god who looks after the new-born dead.[13]

Such a *tamtoom* as this is almost impossible to lift but the Mandal did all in his power to persuade Sabdok *moong* and Hit *rum* to lift the curse, making many sacrifices, and even summoning with many presents an old and widely famed Mun[14] from a village two days journey away. Before Gongyop started performing the

[12] See Chapter Two, p. 74.

[13] The Mun worship two supernaturals, Hit *rum* and Dé *rum*, who are considered to be ancestral gods who look after all dead Lepchas. Their positions and functions in the Mun eschatology will be more fully described in Chapter Thirteen.

[14] This man, besides being a Mun, was also a Pau and Yaba. Gongyop, who assisted in the sacrifice, said that he had heard he was a 'black' Mun—Mun-mook Mun—, but he was not able to form any opinion from the prayers he heard him say.

more customary part of the invocation he told me this story of the reasons of the dead wife's anger with, for him, considerable gusto; it is possibly rather comforting to know that the neglect of the religion of which you are the priest is the cause for such elaborate ceremonies.

When the Mun has discovered as much as possible about the supernatural and immediate causes of the illness he indicates the necessary objects of sacrifice. These are almost always animals, but on occasion other objects are needed as well or instead. Sometimes these objects are valuables, which are just displayed to gratify the supernatural; sometimes other edibles—crops, *chi*, dried bird, dried fish, ginger. According to the ceremony these are either abandoned to be eaten by wild animals, or consumed, as part of the ritual, by all present except the Mun himself.

When animals are sacrificed they are first offered alive to all the supernaturals, including those specially involved; then they are slaughtered by some layman and divided up. Parts of the intestines —the lungs, liver and heart—called the *sha-fot* are singed or cooked with rice and chopped up and thrown to the devils, and the head, one fore-leg, and one hind-leg (these portions are called *gazook*) are laid out and dedicated to the devil specially involved. After the dedication the meat is eaten; it is often the Mun's fee but he does not always take it all. The Mun intones prayers both before and after the animal is killed; the praying may take four hours, and is usually not attended to by the other people present. In daylight ceremonies, when the weather is fine, the Mun often withdraws a little distance from the house in order to pray without disturbing or disturbance.

This relatively simple sacrifice is usually performed when there is a parallel exorcism being performed at the same time by lamas; for some other devils, particularly those with which lamas cannot deal in any way, much more elaborate ceremonies are necessary. It is impossible to generalise about these exorcisms as one can about the lamaist ones, for they have no apparent common principle. I have therefore selected three 'prescriptions' out of the considerable number I have witnessed or heard about, as samples; in their different aspects they embody the greater number of motives in elaborate Mun ritual.

(1) *To get rid of Sor moong (violent death) or Apang moong (genito-urinary diseases).* A goat is tethered by a long rope which has three knots tied in its length; first of all, all the members of the

afflicted household must touch the knots and then the Mun; then the Mun will call on all the devils to be contented with the blood of the sacrifice and not to take the patient, after which he throws the rope into the air; if the rope falls end outwards (i.e. the end away from the goat falls towards the door) it means the devils will be satisfied; if it falls towards the house the prognosis is bad. After this the animal is killed and the *gazook* and *sha-fot* offered to the devil with a plate and a pot filled with rice, a rupee and a ceremonial scarf, together with some of the invalid's ornaments and clothing (these last are only offered symbolically) and also a cup of *chi* with different grains in it. Then the Mun constructs a phallus out of wood, which is called in its guardian function *moong long tik*; this is set up between two stones leaning slightly forward, somewhere in the forest, and anointed with the blood of the slain animal and *chi*; this will keep the devil away, for no devil can pass this guardian.

(2) *To drive away the ghost of a dead child, called Num-een moong, which kills young children by infantile diarrhoea.* After an animal has been sacrificed the person who is troubled by the *moong* goes down to a narrow stream; the troubled person stands on the right of the stream and the Mun on the left of it. Then a 'gateway' is made over the stream of two bundles of elephant grass and brambles; and the Mun holds in each hand a bundle made out of wild raspberries, nettles and all other thorny and prickly plants. These bundles are dipped in water and *pék* over the sufferer several times; then a bamboo *chi* holder filled with blood and *chi* and shut up at both ends, and a leaf filled with fried rice and meat and blood are *pék* over the patient and thrown through the gateway for the devil; then the bunches of thorny plants are thrown through the gateway and finally the gateway is filled up with thorny plants 'so that it looks like a tree'. The Mun does this at two other places some way apart on the stream; he must do these second two—one above and one below the original one—alone, and after completing them he must return straight to his own house without meeting anybody; should he meet people Num-een *moong* will start haunting them.

Num-een *moong* is the devil released by the death of young children under the age of about ten; this devil pursues living people and especially other children; older people who die do not let loose a devil. The Num-een *moong* persists for about three years after the child's death; when there are bad storms the devil can be heard hooting 'Oo-oo-oo.' Children are particularly frightened of this devil and a great number of Lepchas claim to have heard it cry.

(3) *To get rid of Chyom moong (that is the devil who causes people to die by falling from a tree or cliff) or Rot moong (that is the devil who causes people to commit suicide).* This ceremony is called Moong Sot, killing the devil, and should be performed by the surviving members of the family in which one member has either died violently or committed suicide.. It *should* be performed every three years, but it is sufficient if the ceremony is done after the violent death and at the birth of each new member of the household. If the ceremony is not performed the devil will return and claim another victim.

A dead goat is skinned except for its legs below the joint and is lain on its back with its hind quarters towards the bowman. Beside it is a hole already dug and above it is made a small shelter of bamboos thatched with reeds. Beyond that is set up a red head of banana flower stuck into the ground and against it a post on top of which is attached the goat's heart, in such a way that the blood drips on the banana flower. In a line with this stands a bowman with an arrow in his bow ready to shoot. The Mun is at one side not looking at the post. The other men who are present are all armed with knives.

After a time the Mun starts shivering uncontrollably and summons the devil in a loud voice. As he calls some insect or other will climb up the pole towards the heart, and the bowman must shoot it with his arrow before it reaches it. As soon as he has shot he must call to the Mun to say whether he has hit or missed the insect; if he has missed the Mun must recall it. When the insect is killed it and the goat are chopped to pieces by the bystanders with their knives and buried in the prepared hole; stones and earth are rammed on top of the sacrifice to fill up the hole, and then a second time to make a little mound.

Padem can offer *sakyou faat* and can generally perform some of the simpler exorcisms; there is no general limitation of their power to deal with different devils; it depends entirely on their individual knowledge and capacity. On the whole Padem cannot deal with the more dangerous devils, nor sacrifice animals more important than a chicken or, in a few instances, a goat. The most general form of offering for Padem is the *rum*—the basket filled with various containers. Yaba and Pau, as has been said, can make no sacrifices but can only indicate what sacrifices other priests should make.

CHAPTER NINE

RELIGION III: THE PEOPLE OF MAYEL

i

I stated earlier that the Lepchas have two or perhaps three religions. My reason for this statement is that the ritual connected with harvesting and hunting, though performed by Mun, have a number of features which do not occur elsewhere. It seems to me possible that the worship of the people of Mayel, and perhaps of Pong *rum* the god of hunters, is of a different origin to the other Mun ceremonies; unfortunately too little is known about the ritual of neighbouring tribes to enable profitable speculation to be made as to whether either or both ceremonies are relatively modern importations from outside, or whether they are on the contrary the oldest Lepcha customs. The most outstanding differences with other Mun ritual, and indeed with ordinary Lepcha life, is, first, a discrimination against women, secondly, an insistance on virginity for some of the celebrants, and thirdly a suggestion of the danger of menstruating women. Women may perform the sacrifice to the people of Mayel, but if they do so the ceremony is curtailed and fewer objects employed; they not only cannot sacrifice to Pong *rum* but must not even be aware when the sacrifice takes place; and the popped corn and *chi* which are employed in it, if not made by a man, which is preferable, must be made by a virgin girl. The chief offerings to the people of Mayel are the *lafét* sacrifice and *sakyou faat*; the small bird for the *lafét* must be killed by a virgin boy, and the strained *chi* poured into the buttered cup by a virgin girl.

This insistance upon virginity is unparalleled in Lepcha life;[1]

[1] The only other instance is in the sacrifice to a pair of demons who cause a coughing disease (? tuberculosis) and whose presence and ritual were divined and by a Nandjému less than ten years ago. For this ceremony the popped corn must be made by a virgin girl, and the Mun must fast for twenty-four hours before the sacrifice. Only two people know how to perform this very modern importation.

indeed Lepchas have no word for 'virgin' and either have to say 'clean' or else directly 'a person who has not copulated.' They claim that this insistence on virginity in connection with the objects of sacrifice for the people of Mayel is a custom derived from their father's fathers; if the special bird were not killed and if the killer and the *chi*-pourer were not virgins the gods would be angry and the harvest spoiled. But, as so often in Lepcha life, theory and practice do not necessarily coincide; young children are chosen to fill the rôles who it is hoped are virgin; if not—*ket ma-nin*: it doesn't matter.

The people of Mayel consist of seven brothers each with their own name and each patron of some sort of grain. These seven brothers are the progenitors and ancestors and guardians of the Lepchas. They were created by Itpomu who placed rice and millet and maize in their charge when she made these crops. The people of Mayel live in seven huts; they are immortal; each morning they are infants, at midday they are grown men and in the evening they are old. They all have huge goitres and it is from them that people know that big goitres are a sign of prosperity and a large harvest. They wear the traditional Lepcha costume of clothes made of nettle cloth and small basket-work hats. They are somewhere between the gods and ordinary human beings; they are not gods because they live on earth but they are not human because they do not die. The land of Mayel is far up the Talung valley, somewhere behind Kinchenjunga; at one time in the past the road thither was open but now it has been closed and is as unpassable as the cutting edge of a knife. On the road to Mayel are three guardian spirits called Sok-po, who are brothers; the eldest is called Mayel Yook *rum*; he is also called Pong *rum* when hunters sacrifice to him; his younger brothers Mi-tik and Tom-tik are cruel deities who kill and eat men and animals; Tom-tik is like a bear. They are the special guardians of the ibex and musk deer which come from Mayel, which is the reason why these animals are so difficult to kill.

In the country of Mayel crops grow a hundred times as big as here and it is from that country that the seeds of our present crops originate. These crops are always ripe for harvesting. The migratory birds are called Mayel *fo*, birds of Mayel, and they are sent out by the people of Mayel to the Lepchas to indicate the seasons and the times when the various agricultural acts should be performed. When the time comes for the migratory birds to return to Mayel the parent birds die on the way and only the newly hatched ones survive the arduous journey to Mayel from whence they are sent the next year to act as indicators for the Lepchas. The people of Mayel have no wives living with them but the two oldest of the people, Adoo Yook and Alau Yook, have in a way as wives the two sisters called Talyeu Nimu and Sangvo Nimu, who are the spirits of the earth; these two women lie on their backs under the earth and on their bellies are the cultivatable lands; into this Adoo Yook and Alau Yook send rice and millet and maize, just as if it were human seed from a husband, and the women are fertilised and fruitful.

In the old days the path to Mayel was open and sometimes the people of Mayel used to come into the other parts of the world and occasionally adventurous hunters found their way into the Mayel country. Thus the people of Mayel helped to build the palace of Fyung Di near Pemionchi where the Kings of Sikkim lived before the war against the Nepali. While they were building the palace they ate and talked like ordinary people; but when, after its completion, people were accompanying them home, the people of Mayel walked and talked with them as far as a certain mountain and then disappeared in a clap of thunder. Old people also say that in the spring the people of Mayel go into Tibet, either to Lhassa, or to Yambo Zikchu, where they sell pumpkins and cucumbers and egg-plants and chillies. When the Maharajah was living at Chumbi some old Lepchas accompanied him there and saw the people of Mayel selling these plants; the rest of the suite being Sikkimese and Tibetans did not recognise them but the Lepchas naturally did so immediately; as soon as they were recognised the people of Mayel disappeared; as it was nobody knew whence they came or whither they were going.

About six generations ago two people found their way into the Mayel country. One of these was Jiroong's ancestor who was hunting and went past Sakhyong and over two distant peaks; there he saw floating in a stream a branch of a certain sort of tree which he realised must have been thrown there by the people of Mayel and he followed the stream up. He reached a path as narrow as a razor edge on which were the feathers of the Mayel birds which had died on the return journey. After passing this ridge the hunter followed the road for three days round the mountain and came to the village of Mayel and there saw seven houses and asked for shelter for the night. They had big pigs lying down and they killed a pig and gave him pork to eat and rice and *chi*. The hunter stayed there seven days and when he went away the people of Mayel asked him not to talk about them when he returned; and they gave him as gifts rice seed which he sowed and the fruit of pumpkin and cucumber which turned into stone.

Another hunter from Sakhyong also found his way there but he was not so fortunate. When he came to the village he found a child and asked him 'Who are your father and mother?' The child said 'We are our own fathers and mothers, we are babies and young people and old people'. The man then picked and cooked some rice. When the people came near he threatened them with his knife. At this they said to him 'Do not do that; cook and eat your rice and go away. If you do not we will drive you away with our dogs'. When they said that he looked round and saw huge dogs like bears with enormous eyes. Then he was very frightened and ran away at once with some of the cooked rice in his hand. As he ran home there was a terrific thunderstorm, and he was pelted with snow and hail. Since the time of these adventurous travellers the road has been closed with an enormous rock.

ii

The people of Mayel are worshipped exclusively in connection with the crops of dry rice, millet and maize; on all other occasions they are markedly excluded from the long lists of supernaturals who are called on to partake of the sacrifices and give their blessings. Everybody must worship them on two occasions, after the completion of sowing and at the harvesting of the dry rice; in those houses where there is a Mun or a knowledgeable old man they are also prayed to in the winter to keep away snow and hail, in the spring to protect young crops, and, after the sowing of each of their grains, they are offered *sakyou faat* to ensure a good harvest. Only the three crops are connected with the people of Mayel; the others come from different supernaturals. Barley, wheat, buckwheat and wet rice come from Kongsen-bu, the God of Kinchenjunga, a Sikkimese deity; no important ceremonies are connected with these crops. Cardamum, as has already been said[2] comes from Nepal and is under the patronage of the foreign Elaiji-*nyou*, who dislikes women, in particular menstruating women. The people of Mayel are said to share this dislike, and should a menstruating woman visit them there would be the terrible result that all the

[2] See Chapter Three, p. 92.

people of Mayel would fall asleep and would not send the migratory birds. There is a fairly vague tradition that menstruating women should not approach the flowering plants which bear the fruit that the people of Mayel sell—pumpkins, cucumbers, egg-plants and chillies—or the plants will rot.[3] Opinion about this prohibition was very mixed; some people, especially those who have had much contact with other races, think there may be some truth in the matter, while the more conservative, such as the Mandal, think the statement ridiculous.

The preliminary ceremonies, in those houses where they are held, are small repetitions of the big ceremony after the sowing of all the grains which must be held in each house. It is considered desirable that the same people should officiate in each ceremony, and also that the woman who sings in the spring should take the rôle of Talyeu-mu at the harvesting, and, if possible that the sacrificer should take the rôle of Mayel-mu. If the sacrificer is a woman this of course cannot be done.

The spring offerings consist of the *lafét* sacrifice and *sakyou faat*. The food on the *lafét* is divided into three lines of three heaps each; the centre line is for the people of Mayel, that on the right for all men's patron gods, and especially those of the house-father, that on the left for all women's patron gods, and especially those of the house-mother. The dried bird's flesh in the *lafét* must be a special very small bird which has been killed by a virgin boy; if bigger birds are used or if the boy is not a virgin the gods will be displeased and will not eat and there will be a bad harvest. If the sacrificer is a man there is also offered a *taming* which consists of a long stick to which are attached tiny parcels containing every sort of crop and also tiny *patyoot* of *chi*; this is suspended from the roof above the officiant's head. Before the ceremony begins a song is sung in honour of the people of Mayel and then the Mun offers to them *sakyou faat* and powdered portions of the objects on the *lafét*, calling on the people of Mayel to accept the offerings and throwing them before him or her on to the floor. The cup is constantly re-filled with *chi* with a wooden ladle by a young virgin girl who is sitting beside the Mun. After that everybody except the Mun officiating has to drink some strained *chi* from the buttered cup and eat a part of the offerings and sing songs in honour of the people of Mayel; those people who do not or cannot sing them-

[3] I am told that this is a formal rule among the Nepali, who also consider that these fruit should never be pointed at with the finger.

selves will give a small present to the Mun who will sing for all of them. The grain which is used in this sacrifice has to be specially ripened in the sun in the same way as the grain for seed is ripened. This completes the ceremony of sowing and it is always followed by a feast in which meat is eaten.

The ceremony of harvesting is far more complicated. It is only employed for the dry rice. When the dry rice is ripe a little is picked to be prepared for *chi* and when the *chi* is ready the owner of the field summons all his friends and they go together to pick rice. Until the ceremony is completed nobody, not even children, may pick any grain or he would get ill; if anybody gets stomach-ache at that period people will say that he has picked rice before it was harvested.

It is necessary to have ready beforehand the smoke-dried *tafoot* of a pig. The *tafoot* would seem to be the gall-bladder or spleen; it is round and has a white smelly liquid inside and is found near the bladder, but in pigs and musk deer it is said to be found near the penis at the end. On the day of reaping this *tafoot* is taken up to the field of dry rice together with two burning brands from the house-fire and also a *patyoot* of *chi* made from the new rice. When the party arrives, a place in the centre of the field is chosen as the *zo-lam* (the place where the crops are heaped); some rice-plants in the centre of the *zo-lam* are tied together into a sheaf and then the two burning brands will be held above them and on these a piece of the *tafoot* will be put. Then an old and experienced man—not the owner of the field but any one of his workers—will be chosen to represent a man of Mayel (called for the ceremony Mayel-mu) and he will blow on the *tafoot* and speak; while this is done a special measuring basket is held upside down over the brand. The old man will summon the gods and the ancestors and will say 'Come and see the smoke; burr—burr—burr—burr'. Then all the people present will repeat, 'burr—burr—burr'. By this invocation it is hoped that the gods will come and bring back all the grain eaten by wild birds and animals.

Standing by the speaker is a woman not directly connected with the field owner, who has been chosen for the day to represent Talyeu-mu, one of the earth sisters. When Mayel-mu has finished his invocation the measuring basket is put on his back and Talyeu-mu cuts the tied grain and puts it in the basket. Then Talyeu-mu and Mayel-mu, who acts as her load carrier, go round the *zo-lam* cutting a basket of rice for Talyeu-mu; at the same time the others cut two baskets of rice for the people of Mayel. When the three baskets have been cut four or five reed mats are put down on the flattened ground and all dance on the rice to separate the grain from the chaff. All the dances are round dances and semi-acrobatic, consisting chiefly of hopping and jumping; nine different types are recognised and three rounds of each type are danced in turn. After the dancing Talyeu-mu goes round the edge of the field cutting another basket while all the other reapers work in a row to fill two more baskets which are heaped up like the first; after these have been put on the *zo-lam* the *nam-toak* (potential curse) is lifted and all can cut as they like; but during the whole day Talyeu-mu and Mayel-mu cut apart from the others. When the second heap of rice has been poured on to the *zo-lam* a fence is erected to the south of it consisting of three leafy saplings joined by a bamboo; on it a mat is hung and then from the three posts are fastened three bundles of rice-plants, ears downwards, hanging over the mat. After this fence is set up the *patyoot* of new *chi* is placed against it and Mayel-mu offers it with an invocation. Then at the four corners of the *zo-lam* are erected four posts of a sort of reed or bamboo; the top part is split into three and the two side pieces are bent down to make loops.

When the *zo-lam* has been completed all do as they like; some gather rice, some dance, some drink *chi* and so on. The harvesting must be completed before the sun has touched the hills; if all is not cut by then the work must go on the next day and the people must spend the night on the harvest field, as will be explained lower down. Right at the end must be gathered another three baskets of rice which must be completed at the same time; these three baskets are all emptied at the same time to the east of the heap and all present cry 'burr, burr, burr'. The rice is now put in eight heaps; that of the morning is put in the centre where the house-mother works; that of Talyeu-mu to the east and the other six heaps in a semi-circle to the north; these six heaps are named after six big mountains in the neighbourhood. Then the rice is separated from the chaff and straw partially by hand and partially by dancing; all work together at the different heaps except the house-mother and Talyeu-mu who work theirs by themselves. When all the rice is sifted the house-mother and Talyeu-mu push the heap of Talyeu-mu to the centre heap saying 'May the heap support us firmly and be as the sea'. After that all the other heaps are pushed into the centre, one after the other in due order. Then a wreath of rice straw is placed on top of the big heap and on that three pieces of charcoal and then the *tafoot* is put on top. Then all except Mayel-mu withdraw and look on from afar and Mayel-mu makes a fixed invocation starting 'To—burr, burr, burr; you different gods, we summoned you this morning to bring the rice which grows like a tree and the maize which grows like a tree from Mayel. If storms have destroyed and wasted our crops bring that grain back, if birds or rats have destroyed or wasted our crops bring that grain back, burr, burr, burr.' After this all present say, 'burr, burr, burr', and he too will withdraw and watch to see if the grains of rice roll down off the heap; if they do it is a good sign; if not it means that the harvest will not last long. Then the charcoal and *tafoot* are taken away and the big basket of Talyeu-mu is used as a measure for the grain. If all this has been done while the sun is still high each helper is given his wage of about 30 lbs. of rice and goes back to the owner's house. There they drink *chi* and sing, Talyeu-mu competing against the rest; she will sing summoning the people of Mayel and the others will reply impersonating the gods, saying 'No, we won't come', and mocking her. As much *chi* as people can drink is given and everybody sleeps the night at the house.

If, however, the sun touches the hills before the rice is reaped another procedure is followed; the cut grain is covered with mats, a fireplace is set up and food cooked and the night is spent on the straw. On that night anybody may sleep with anyone else provided the rules of incest are not broken; and if a man should see his wife sleeping with another he must never refer to it, not even to his friends. There may only be two or three copulating couples, but it is better if there are more, for then Talyeu-Nimu and Sangvo-Nimu will be pleased at seeing so many people copulating and will send them a good harvest. If boys are too young to copulate they will just sleep with their friends. This ritual copulation is called *zo-tsom-thap* (pressing the rice; this is an elegant periphrasis for copulation). The rest of the rice is cut in the morning.

As soon as chi has been prepared the *lafét* is offered with the new *chi* to the people of Mayel and all the people pray, saying 'May these crops feed us long'. After the sacrifice all must eat the new rice together; should any one person eat before the others he would be ill.

Until everybody in the neighbourhood has performed the sacrifice grain must not be dried in the sun, nor may people even look at grain drying in the sun. Until that time grain must be dried over the fire; for if the gods of Mayel saw grain drying in the sun before they had been offered any they would be angry and would not come the next year and there would be a bad harvest. Until everybody has made the sacrifice people who go where they may see rice drying in the sun—across the river or to Mangan or Gangtok—must cover their face with a cloth. If a man who has not made his sacrifice were ordered by the Mandal to go abroad where he might see rice being dried, he would have a valid excuse for not going and a substitute would have to be found for him. Should a man by any chance see crops drying he would be considered to have *amik-her*, which is almost the evil eye; if a man with *amik-her* were to look on a field the people of Mayel would be terrified as if by an enemy and would run away and would not return next year. Therefore a man who has accidentally seen drying crops would live in the jungle or in a field-house or cardamum field until the rice of the neighbourhood was gathered; if he should be a person who would normally sacrifice he would not do so that year. To avoid this danger Lepchas who have to go to Mangan at the harvesting season only go at night so that they will see no drying crops. For a man with *amik-her* to look at the harvest would be *nam-toak*—a year of disaster—as bad as if incest had been committed. When people have performed their sacrifices they send and tell the Mandal who then sends the *gyapön* round with the message that now all have sacrificed and crops can be dried in the sun. All the inhabitants of Lingthem, Panung, Liklyang and Salim have to wait till they get the message before they can expose crops. Should anybody expose his crops before all were ready the Mandal would fine him Rs. 15; but such a case has not occurred in the last twenty years, though some are known of earlier. Besides dry rice, maize and three varieties of millet cannot be exposed to the sun. This prohibition does not apply to the other sorts of millets nor to barley, buckwheat, and wet rice. Grains must also not be exposed until a sort of wild grass which grows on the far side of the Talung river has turned yellow.

The Lepchas of Zongu are very serious about this prohibition on seeing drying crops in the sun; it is a custom which has descended from the ancestors of our ancestors. 'The people outside Zongu say they don't care; "the grain is in the sun when it is on the stalk; what is the difference when it is cut?" they say; but we people in Zongu have always acted in this way.' For Lepchas living outside the closed community the prohibition is impossible to observe; the Lepchas of Zongu are well aware that there are good harvests where this prohibition is disregarded; but they consider that were *they* to neglect it their harvests would be bad as they live nearer the people of Mayel.

The people who represent Mayel-mu and Talyeu-mu when reaping are not paid any special honours; they represent the gods but they are not considered to have anything divine about them during this representation. For other crops there are not any elaborate ceremonies. When buckwheat is ripe a little of it is offered in the householder's house to Konchen, with an offering of buckwheat *chi*. 'The people of Sandong make a buckwheat cake and offer it but we don't.' At the time of planting the wet rice a general ceremony is performed in which a chicken or a goat is offered and also a plate with *chimi*, etc., on it; 'terraced rice comes from Nepal so it isn't really necessary to give thanks, but here we live near Mayel and it is better to be careful.' When a field is cleared in the forest for the first time a chicken is offered for each member of the household and also a plate with *chimi*, etc., to keep away illness and predatory animals. This ceremony can be performed by anybody who knows how to do so.

iii

For the annual sacrifice to Moot *rum* Tseu, who is also called Pong *rum*, the popped corn and *chi*, if not prepared by a man, which is more desirable, must be prepared by a virgin girl. Pong *rum* together with his wife Shing *rum*, is the lord of all wild animals and the patron saint of hunters. Every year in October a joint sacrifice has to be made to him by all the hunters of the neighbourhood; the sacrifice consists of popped corn, *chi*, dried fish and bird, ginger, arum root, some other tuber, sugar cane, banana and wormwood flowers. If possible all the prepared ingredients should be made by a man and no woman must witness the sacrifice or even know when it has been performed. Pong *rum*, it will be remembered, is the guardian of the road to Mayel.

In the forest as soon as an animal has been killed and cut up a sacrifice must be made to Pong *rum*. Big leaves are cut and put on the ground and then the animal is divided up and the head is put in the front with a foreleg and hind leg on either side and singed intestines in the middle. This is all 'offered' to Pong *rum*, and the hunter crouching behind and speaking very slowly and softly, gently throws the burnt intestines bit by bit over the animal's head. On his return to the village great care must be taken that no woman sees the animal's head; if she did the hunter would have no success in future.

To know how to sacrifice to Pong *rum* it is necessary to learn how to, and to receive *loong*; for this purpose the novice goes to anybody who knows—maybe his father or some other relation or a friend—taking with him *chi* and a ceremonial scarf and a rupee. Great care must be taken that no woman is present at this time. When the older man sees the gifts he enquires what they are for and is told it is to learn how to sacrifice. The older man then arranges the sacrifice and tells the neophyte to sit with his back to him: he must not look but must listen most attentively. After that the neophyte on the next suitable occasion will make the sacrifice; the instructor will be near him and if he makes a mistake will nudge him, whereat the sacrifice must be stopped short. Subsequently the neophyte will take another lesson, continuing until he is word perfect and has received his *loong* and can sacrifice on his own.

A person who has once been to the communal sacrifice to Pong *rum* should continue to do so all his life; he may, however, give it up, in which case he is liable to be troubled with poltergeist manifestations by Pong *rum*, who anyhow if he is displeased with a hunter will pursue him whistling, and the thump of heavy stones falling will be heard, though no stones are seen to fall. It is even preferable for hunters' children to continue the ritual.

Kurma used to hunt but does so no longer and has given up going to the sacrifice to Pong *rum*; for he is afraid that should he go and then not hunt he would become mad. As things are he is somewhat persecuted by Pong *rum*; he describes these persecutions with the greatest detail and indifference. He says quite freely that he does not care a bit.

Near his house is an orange tree and some time ago on a moonlight night he heard distinctly the sound of big stones being thrown under this tree; but there was nothing to be seen so he knew it was Pong *rum*; he therefore returned to the house, lit some incense leaves and butter and came out and offered it to the god saying 'Please forgive us; we have no intention of hunting'.

'Only a month ago when some friends were in my house with me drinking *chi* I heard my dog which was tethered some way from the house barking furiously; I went outside expecting that somebody was passing but I could see no-one. When I returned to the house we heard the dog whimper and then stop; we went outside and found its dead body in front of the house. Of course Pong *rum* had killed it, but I do not care: I just offered the gods some incense.'

Kurma's younger brother used to hunt but never learnt how to make the sacrifice properly; Kurma used to do it for him. But on one occasion when he was away, his maternal uncle sacrificed and instead of making the offering to Pong *rum* made it to his own god. This is one of the reasons given for this young man's subsequent violent death in the forest.[4]

Kurma's family are now very unlucky hunters and the reason is as follows. Three generations ago their forefather was a very lucky hunter who worshipped Shing *rum* (the wife of Pong *rum*). At that time the Mandal of the village was an unlucky hunter; he worshipped Pong *rum*. Now these two agreed to change gods. To do this they killed an ox and then drank three cups of *chi* mixed with the blood, with dabs of butter on the side, for this constitutes the most binding oath. From that day the descendants of the Mandal were always successful hunters while the descendants of the other man were always unlucky. Pong *rum* and Shing *rum* are naturally exclusively male gods.

Before drinking *chi* (in the case of lamas also before drinking tea) or eating food a little is offered to the gods. If the food is domestic in origin it is thrown away from the eater, if of wild origin towards the eater, that is backwards. These offerings are tiny and quite automatic; the 'straw' is lifted from the *chi* and flicked outwards; a few crumbs are dropped from the first handful. No form of prayer accompanies these offerings.

[4] See Chapter Fifteen, pp. 402–403.

BOOK TWO

Life of the Lepchas

CHAPTER TEN

THE RHYTHM OF LEPCHA LIFE

i

Those travellers who mention the Lepchas in their accounts of their journeys in Sikkim and Tibet refer to them with startling unanimity as 'fairies' or 'elves' or 'woodland folk', according to the fantasy and self-consciousness of the different writers. The Europeans in British India who have had more prolonged contact with them stress as their chief qualities their mildness and truthfulness.

If one accepts Dr. Margaret Murray's account of the Fairies[1] as the original inhabitants of England who after the invasions of various conquering races lived in very hidden places and who were extremely timid in their contacts with the conquerors, the comparison of the Lepchas with the Fairies is extremely apt. The Lepchas who still retain a more or less integrated culture do live in relatively hidden and inaccessible places; they are remarkable climbers and walkers, they know the forest and its produce far better than any of their neighbours, and it is quite possible that they may appear in places where there is no visible path. They are pathologically shy of strangers; a foreigner passing through their villages, were he to notice the scattered and inconspicuous houses, might well think them deserted. The first few days in Lingthem we scarcely saw a soul; walking about the village we saw only shut and smokeless houses, with a very occasional dodderer or infant. The majority of the inhabitants had simply taken to the forest.

After a time this timidity wore off. I insisted that all goods bought locally should be paid for without bargaining, so that they should not fear requisitions; if too high a price was asked the goods were to be refused. I stated that I had got medicines and could cure certain sores and diseases, and after a couple of bold people

[1] *The God of the Witches*, by Dr. Margaret A. Murray. London Sampson Low n.d.

had been successfully treated a great number of people came for medicines and stayed to talk. People who came for their own reasons were given betel nut, cigarettes and sweet tea; those who came at my request and who stayed a long time were paid at the same rate as they would have been for a day's coolie work (eight annas); when I found their information particularly interesting I gave something extra as well. As far as possible I avoided the system of direct question and answer; nearly always some topic would arise naturally and I would let the speaker develop it as he wished; at other times I would suggest a topic. Only when a certain rapport was established did I start cross-questioning. The greater part of the conversations took place in the monastery enclosure, where there were a number of convenient outcrops of rock for sitting on; but some of the most valuable information was obtained casually on walks or through over-hearing conversations.

Once they got used to the shock of my arrival my presence did not, as far as I am able to judge, affect their actions or behaviour in any way, except possibly for an occasional affectation of modesty on the part of the women. At first nursing mothers used to cover their breasts in my presence, but after a few weeks they no longer bothered to do so. In so far as Lepchas divide humanity into 'inside our group' and 'outside our group' they placed me after trial in the former category. This is not to claim that they accepted me 'as one of themselves'; they certainly never did so; but they did not regard me as a dangerous stranger. I think they regarded me in three lights: as a dispenser of good medicine and other useful or pleasant articles; as an eccentric who asked questions to which everybody knew the answer, who paid for conversation, who made silly jokes in bad Lepcha, and—most peculiar of all—talked to and played with children; and finally, owing to the colour of my skin and the messages sent from Gangtok, as an honoured guest and, in a way, as a representative of the Maharajah. In this last aspect I was a slight nuisance; if we visited a house a special seat in the *dé-ong* was always prepared and *chi* served in the best container; a certain amount of deference and formality always marked the beginning of such visits. But although they were deferential they were never servile; nothing was done, as far as I could tell, with the intention of ingratiating themselves with me. If I wanted to speak to a person and that person was busy a message would be sent to that effect; if I wanted to be present at anything at which it was the custom that strangers should not be present (that is at a birth, certain moments in the marriage feast or at death) or in a house at which I was not welcome I would be told politely but firmly that I was not wanted.

My relationship with the Lepchas was, I thought, more intellectual than emotional; they quite liked and respected me, but did not feel about me at all. Consequently I was very surprised and moved when on my departure three of the people whom I had got to know best actually said goodbye to me with tears in their eyes and appeared genuinely sorry that I was leaving; this surprised me the more as Lepchas are not at all in the habit of dramatising emotions or situations; the only time I saw any of them cry was when two sisters broke into tears when a prayer-flag was set up in memory of a third sister who had recently died.

I do not think that my colour or appearance was the chief bar to emotional contact with the Lepchas; my habits were a more formidable obstacle, for I ate somewhat different foods, lived in a different way, and, above all was absurdly fussy about cleanliness, a completely meaningless concept to the Lepchas. But most important of all was the fact that I was alone, without wife or family or kin (it was generally believed that C. J. Morris was my father but for some obscure reason—probably because I was a bastard—we refused to acknowledge the relationship) and had no shared experiences with them; also, although present-giving on both sides was fairly constant, I naturally could not build up in the time a system of mutual benefits and obligations on which their own emotional relationships rest.

Present-giving forms a continual motive in Lepcha life. If you go as a guest to a feast you take a present with you, and you are given a present—usually some uncooked meat—to take away with you; if you go on a visit you take a present, and you are given a present on leave-taking. Casual visitors to another's house are always offered food and drink. Except for the formal gifts of *asék* and marriage these presents are really presents and not exchanges, except symbolically; it is a point of honour and gives a feeling of self-satisfaction to be able to give as good a gift as possible; and consequently when there is disproportion between the means of two people there is an equal disproportion between the gifts they give and receive.

I often found these gifts a subject of embarrassment, for the Lepchas would constantly try to overdo me in generosity, giving more than they could afford or I could want; particularly as practically the only present I could give was money, which is not of very great use to them. I had frequent tussles with them on the subject of payment for medical services; I insisted that medicine should not be paid for; they considered that it was shameful to take something for nothing and I frequently had to bully people with bad sores, which I knew I could cure easily, to come up for treatment; they were unwilling to do so because they thought they had nothing suitable to give as presents, and they were ashamed to take something for nothing. An interesting sidelight on their attitude towards gift-giving and strangers is shown by the behaviour of two of the bigger households who on my first arrival refused to sell to the servants either eggs or milk; and later when they got to know us used to come with presents of these commodities for which they refused to accept any return payment except after long argument.

When the Lepchas got to know me well they were not at all shy of asking for things; but except for cigarettes, betel nut and iodine or dressings for small cuts they always offered something in return for whatever they asked for and were in no way offended if their requests were refused. They were particularly attracted by illustrated papers and asked frequently to be given them; to a certain extent they recognised very clearly the objects portrayed in drawings and photographs, though their explanations to one another of the situations depicted were, as might well be imagined, very peculiar. I got far more amusement out of hearing three Lepchas explaining to one another what the pictures in *Punch* were about than I ever got out of reading that paper. One or two people asked for pictures of special subjects; Rigya kept on asking for pictures of war because 'he was amazed at them and had never seen or thought of anything like it'; Chudo liked pictures of cars and fashionable life, for he had spent nearly a year in Gangtok as scullion in the Maharajah's kitchens and knew about the lives of Europeans and was able to explain them to his less fortunate compatriots. For him European life consisted chiefly in extremely formal and uncomfortable meals at which there was never enough to eat, interspersed with quarrels of an extremely dramatic nature. In one of the numbers of the *Illustrated London News* there were several reproductions of Chinese Buddhist frescoes and there was quite a competition to possess these among the older and more pious lamas. After I had had some photos enlarged and had shown people their photos I was bombarded with requests for photos of individuals and groups; people used to come up dressed in their best clothes and stand very firmly at attention as if they were expecting to be shot any minute. A never failing source of amusement was looking through the view-finder of the camera, or, better still, field glasses; people would return again and again with their friends with demands to look through these wonderful appliances.

I had brought with me several packets of Japanese water flowers to amuse the children, and also in the hope of getting a lead as to whether they would interpret the sudden changes in these flowers in an animist fashion or not. The children quite liked looking at them but were not nearly as interested as their elders, who pointed out the changes taking place in the flowers in hushed and enthralled voices to the children and to each other. The children stared at them and said they were very pretty; when I asked 'who made them grow' they said 'the water makes the flowers grow', or else just 'the flowers bloom'. One child even corrected me when I said 'who makes the flowers grow', telling me I should say 'what makes the flowers grow'; and when I put leading questions asking whether gods or devils made the flowers grow they always replied in an emphatic negative. The children know about devils and are frightened of them and some of them have heard them; but the devils' and gods' spheres of action are rigorously defined and nothing which falls outside those spheres should be ascribed to them. What the children liked best about the flowers were the brightly coloured envelopes and the white paper they were contained in. They would treasure these most carefully and in the case of the paper would fold it up extremely neatly and tidily into small squares.

Lepcha children and Lepcha adults are extraordinarily unselfish; after a little experience I never bothered to divide collective gifts among them; I would give a packet of cigarettes or a handful of barley sugar to the person nearest to me, certain that it would be divided completely fairly among all present. Even with the Japanese flowers I would open a packet, show one child how to put the flowers in water and would then leave the open packet by the glass; one of the children would be sure to divide up the dry flowers equally among all present and if another child arrived later those who still had some flowers or paper would at once give a share to the new arrival. Except in the case of youngest or only children I never heard or saw children quarrel about the ownership of anything or the sharing of it. With little tots of three or four the gift-giving habit was already established; very often after I had given them some Japanese flowers a small child would come tottering up to me with either a live flower or a few bright coloured seeds tightly clutched in its hand. Almost the only positive lesson in good manners the children are taught is that when elders give them a present they must receive it with joined hands; and one day Pembu's four-year-old son scolded me severely because I took his gift of a cactus blossom in one hand only.

ii

My type-picture of the Lepchas is of a crowd gathered for some feast or ceremony. In point of fact this only represents a very small portion of their lives; but on work-days they are so widely scattered as to be invisible and almost unfindable in the open country; often for days at a time they are absent from home, working in distant fields, and sleeping in the field-house; when they do return home in the evening they are usually tired and go to sleep fairly shortly after the evening meal.

The Lepcha working-day starts at cock-crow when everybody gets up; a substantial cold meal, usually consisting of grain, with perhaps some milk and any meat or flavourings which may be available is eaten; it is usually accompanied by tea. Then everybody goes to their work in the fields or forests, taking with them some popped corn or cold cooked rice in their haversack to nibble if they feel hungry during the day's work. In the evening towards sundown they come home for the second meal of the day. The youngest daughter-in-law is meant to do the cooking, under the direction of the house-mother, or, if she be too old, of the eldest daughter-in-law, who gives out the supplies; but in practice all the women present lend a hand. If there are no women free, men will do the cooking; but it is considered slightly degrading for a house-father to have to prepare his own meal. Each evening enough is cooked to serve for that evening and also for the following morning.

While the food is being prepared the men may weave mats or baskets, or do other odd jobs about the house, or they may sit and drink *chi*. Everybody eats the main meal together; the house-mother hands out the food, serving the oldest members first; if there are young children the fathers will feed the daughters and the mothers the sons. After the evening meal there may be a visit either to be paid or received; one or two friends may come in to drink *chi* and everybody will sit around and gossip, or perhaps one will tell one of the long stories which take several evenings to repeat. The younger children can listen to the conversation if they wish to; if not they can go and amuse themselves; very little notice is taken of them, and, except possibly for malicious gossip, no subject is avoided because of their presence. A few people own oil lamps, but for the majority the only illumination is the wood-fire. A couple of hours after the evening meal the bedding is brought out of the boxes where it is stored during the day and laid out with the more or less padded wooden pillows at the appropriate places round the walls. People sleep on a cloth, generally quilted, and have another blanket as covering; Lepchas never sleep with their heads under the bedclothes as they think they would then suffocate.

When the bedding is laid out the fire is damped down with ashes and darkness is presumed to reign; people undress more or less, according to their personal habits (most adults remove their outer clothes and sleep in their drawers, but some, especially poorer people who have not sufficient coverings, retain the formerly general habit of sleeping naked near the fire) and settle down in their proper sleeping places for the night. Everybody has his own mattress, but married couples share pillows and blankets. The smallest infants sleep in their mother's arms; but as soon as they are big enough they are given their own bedding, for fear they should wet their parents'. Occasionally a child is placed between husband and wife, but more usually on the far side of the wife. An only or youngest child may sleep beside its parents until it is ten or eleven, but if a younger sibling is born it is placed to sleep either with an elder sibling or some older relation, often a widowed aunt or grandmother. A child usually sleeps in an elder person's arms till about the age of eight, after which, except in the very poorest familes, it usually gets its own bedding; but until marriage unmarried siblings of the same sex usually have their beds laid side by side. Children must always respect their grandparents' bedding, and in the day-time the place where it is laid; and adults must respect the bedding and sleeping-places of their parents-in-law.

Once the fire is damped down and the bedding laid out people are presumed to be invisible and inaudible; but this is merely a social convention, and people can and do tell in the greatest detail just what goes on in the night. Occasionally a young man may wait till everybody else is asleep, and then creep out on hands and knees to visit a girl with whom he has made an appointment, to return home before dawn; but most people sleep heavily after the day's work.

Nine days out of ten this represents the normal Lepcha life, for the Lepchas are extremely hard-working and industrious; though they do not work fast they work steadily and for very long hours. But the monotony of working life is continually broken up by feasts and ceremonies; there are the regular bi-monthly monastery feasts, and in most months there are one or more calendrical lamaist festivals; people are born, or marry, or die, or fall ill, and these are all occasions for feasts for the friends and neighbours of the people affected. There is also a continual current of visits; married women return to their native village, taking with them their children or some relative of their husband's; young men go to visit their *asék*'d bride, accompanied by a friend or relation to help carry the gift; trading partners come on a visit or are visited. All these visits are also occasions for feasts, not so elaborate as the big ceremonial feasts, but a pleasant interruption of everyday routine. The occurrence of feasts varies somewhat with the calendar; they are most frequent in the autumn after the harvests have been gathered and the cardamum sold, and least common in the early summer before the harvest is ripe, when supplies may be running short.

The most regular of all are the bi-monthly monastery feasts, and since, owing to the fact that I was living in the monastery, I was inevitably in the centre of them, it is these gatherings which represent for me the typical Lepcha crowd. At an ordinary feast about eighty or ninety people will be present; occasionally the feast-givers are poor or unpopular and then there are only thirty or forty; and once, when Tafoor was responsible for a bumper feast, there were well over a hundred. About a dozen lamas are seated in the prayer room; six or seven nuns and a considerable number of other women and old men and young children are crowded together on the floor of the small prayer-drum room, the *lha-gong*. Inside the porch, on the right-hand side, is seated the Mandal; next to him is probably Gongyop, as these two are great friends, and the givers of the feast if they are laymen, and strangers and visitors to the village. Outside are probably two cooking places; one to the front of the monastery is fairly small and on it is probably cooking the vegetable 'curry' (*bi*) which is served as a relish to the staple cereal. On the east side there are probably two or three big pots cooking, one

PLATE 18

MONASTERY FEAST

with boiling water for *chi* or tea, one with cereal and one with meat, if there is meat. Overlooking these pots to the east of the monastery will be old Dunbi, who has got a sort of honorary post as monastery cook; he does not do very much and the position is more or less of a sinecure invented to give this lazy and incompetent man a feeling of importance and to provide food, which will be given as payment for his services, for his wife and children. Usually the wives of the givers of the feast supervise the cooking, giving out the materials and so on; but everybody lends a hand as he feels disposed. Sitting about on the grass and stones outside are a number of the younger men and women and elder boys; they chat and joke and pass indecent remarks and occasionally lend a hand at fetching firewood or water, or bamboos to be cut up into *patyoot*. The younger boys from about the age of eight to fourteen hang about with these elders when they are not doing chores for their parents or the feast-givers; they mostly sit fairly quietly, but occasionally they go on to the hill outside the monastery precincts and run about playing catch with flowers of daphne or chasing the hens or imitating bird calls. They are used as messengers a great deal if the parents have left anything behind; they are in the feast but are on the fringe of it. The girls are more inclined to tag along with their parents, or with an elder sister; many of them are carrying younger siblings, though they often hand over these burdens to their brothers. Almost all the time everybody is eating and drinking.

The lamas and possibly the feast-givers arrive the evening before; the lamas to make the decorations for the altar and the feast-givers to stack the provisions in the porch. Most of the night and almost continuously from dawn the lamas have been reading their books and playing their musical instruments; from the moment they arrive they start drinking *chi* and eating and the *patyoot* in front of them are continually filled. The crowd starts arriving in driblets at about eight o'clock, each person bringing some contribution to the feast; some people arrive later and the full concourse will not be present till nearly midday. Some of the more pious people on their arrival circumambulate the monastery three times, always keeping the wall on the right, and turn the prayer wheels; they may go into the monastery room and prostrate themselves three times before the images. As soon as they are settled each person is provided with a *patyoot* of *chi* which they take and sit down and drink; a small *patyoot* with several 'straws' in it will be provided for the toddlers of three or four, and set firmly on its base into the ground some way away from the grown-ups. It is quite a common sight to see little children who can hardly walk solemnly drinking their *chi* sitting in a circle round the communal cup. These babies quite often get rather drunk and flushed and hiccupy and unsteady on their legs and loud spoken; but this is usually followed very quickly by sleep and after a couple of hours they seem to wake up no whit the worse for their experience.

From about midday food is being served almost continuously; there seems practically no limit to what a Lepcha can eat and drink on a feast day. This is a typical menu of the food consumed per head between say, 11 o'clock in the morning and 9 o'clock at night at a good feast: 3 lbs. of rice served in two helpings; 3 *patyoot* of *chi* which were constantly replenished, and 3 cups of strained *chi* which is very much stronger and resembles a mild spirit; 2 double fistfuls of popped corn; about 2 lbs. of meat, one to eat and one raw piece to take home;[2] four helpings of tea; plenty of curry and vegetables with the rice and as much soup made from vegetables and stock as people cared to consume. For this feast every guest brought some contribution, but if the hosts had had to buy all the materials they provided the cost would have been at least Rs. 60 (about £5). This was considered a good party, but nothing extraordinary or out of the way.

All the time the feasting is going on the service continues intermittently; but there are intervals when the lamas come outside the monastery for a rest and to relieve themselves. Early in the day they wander down into the wood below the monastery, but later on, as they have eaten and drunk more, they just go to the edge of the built-up wall at the end of the monastery compound and squat down with their backs to the people. During these intervals also they shave one another's heads. Also from time to time they put their heads under a running stream to take away the fumes of the *chi*.

The rest of the people also get somewhat mellowed, though usually not noticeably drunk; I have never seen an adult Lepcha lose control of his movements through drink, though one or two of the older people get somewhat fogged in their speech. The younger women move about more than the others carrying the big ladles of boiling water to replenish the *chi* and handing out the food; they

[2] It is always the custom when the last dish is served at a Lepcha feast to put on top a portion of raw meat or sausage for the guest to take home and eat at leisure.

seem, however, to drink quite as much as the others, for as a mark of affection they will take a drink out of the *patyoot* of anybody they like or anybody who invites them. As the drinking continues voices get louder and gestures more vehement and there is a great deal of laughter; most of this laughter arises from obscene remarks which may be *double entente* or may consist merely of the Lepcha monosyllables (they are actually bi-syllables). Occasionally some rather crude and childish practical joke may be played; big leaves or some other incongruous object may be tied on to a man's pigtail while he is not looking, or the skirt of his coat hitched up behind, but these jokes are comparatively rare; the one thing which seems to the Lepchas continually and inexhaustibly funny is sex. There is a certain amount of rough sexual by-play; a young man, or occasionally a young woman, will make a gesture of grabbing at another young man's private parts; this is considered extremely funny. The bolder young men will also try to fondle the breasts of the younger married women but they are usually repulsed extremely roughly; on the whole Lepcha women have rougher and brusquer gestures than the men and it is not uncommon for a woman who is being teased to give her teaser a resounding smack on the face; this is always taken in good part. It is also quite common for a youth to hang on to the back of an older man he is fond of, putting his hands over the older man's shoulder and touching his breasts; with this gesture the youths resume the position of a child being carried on its father's back. I do not think there is any conscious homosexual intention in this behaviour; it is noticeable that it is always the younger man who clings to the back of the older and never the reverse. A somewhat parallel type of behaviour is for oldish boys round about the age of ten or twelve to put their arms round a seated older woman whom they are fond of and apply their face to her dress over the breasts; this is the type of behaviour which is abandoned 'when boys are old enough to learn shame'.

The poorer Lepcha feasts finish at nightfall; if all the provisions are finished then people go home to sleep. But the better feasts continue far into the night, and some go on into the subsequent day; a really good feast, such as the Boom Koor, lasts for three days and three nights. People doze intermittently, wherever they happen to be, but on the whole little sleep is had; under such conditions the Lepchas seem to manage with very little rest, and I have seen people after forty-eight hours almost continuous eating and drinking go off, apparently quite fresh, to work in the fields. When feasts go on into the night, and especially at marriage feasts, couples may go away into the forest or to a neighbouring shed; this depends entirely on individual wish and opportunity, and sexual activity is not a necessary or even a particularly common concomitant to a feast; on the other hand sexual conversation and jokes are inevitable and continuous, and in some of the longer feasts practical jokes with a sexual tinge are played: young women set on an old man, strip him naked and chase him round the monastery, and so on; it is nearly always the older men who are made the butts of such pleasantries.

iii

One of the things which most surprised me about the Lepchas was this constant verbal preoccupation with sex. Whenever a group of men and women were gathered together for any purpose, however solemn or important, every possible remark was given sexual significance. On the whole when there were only members of one sex present, except sometimes among the younger men, or when there were only three or four people present, the conversation was not so indecent, but in mixed groups it was practically continuously so, and each sally was greeted with as hearty laughter as if an entirely novel joke had been made. A certain amount of ingenuity was shown in giving apparently ordinary phrases a sexual meaning (almost any transitive verb could be twisted into a periphrasis for copulation) but apart from this the theme was not embroidered in any way; simply every possible opportunity was seized for mentioning the primary sexual characteristics and copulation.

It is difficult, especially with the English taboos on the anglo-saxon monosyllables, to give any illustrations of these jokes. But the following verbal transcription of an extremely solemn occasion may give some idea of the sort of pleasantries which are the constant accompaniment to Lepcha work and feasts. As has already been described[3] Chala Mandal went to a great deal of expense and trouble to summon from a distant village an old and widely-famed Mun in order to appease the spirit of his first dead wife, so that his lumbago might be cured and he might beget a son. This occasion was for the Mandal, for his two wives, and for the dozen or more other people present one of very great importance. This is the conversation which took place when the Mun was already in the position

[3] See Chapter Eight, p. 231.

where he was going to pray: the table with the cup filled with strained *chi* and the incense burner already lit was in front of him; the Mandal was seated beside him, with his wives opposite; everything was ready for the ceremony to begin. Before praying the Mun made an, as it were, introductory speech, addressed partly to the Mandal, and partly to the other people present.

The Mun: I'm a very old man, and I found the journey very trying indeed; I was tired and felt I'd like to rest, and —— a girl. I'm really a very old man now; but since you're the Mandal, and this is your house I shall do what I can. When you first sent a messenger with a load of *chi* I said 'No, I cannot go'. But you sent twice and three times and I couldn't resist you. It is true that in rank as Mandal you are above me; but in age you could be my grandson. Just as a small girl is frightened when she sees a big penis and runs away, or as a little boy is frightened when he sees a big vulva, so am I frightened of you. Nevertheless I shall do what I can. I am very sorry for you because although you have had four wives you have got no son. I think this is a source of great worry to you, but what can be done? It is not your fault; you have treated your wives well. It is not a bad deed but misfortune which makes you childless. Were I to say I could do nothing for you, you would be disappointed; shall I do this ceremony and nothing result I shall be ashamed. Nevertheless I will do what I can. You—his wives—you are my sisters and daughters: tell me, my daughters, does this husband of yours treat you badly?

The Mandal: My parents-in-law are very strict with me, and were I to do so they would punish me.

Tafoor: And then you'd take it out of your wives—or put it in —very roughly. (*General laughter*)

The Mandal (while the Mun smears butter on the cup): When I was ill it was discovered that Sabdok *moong* was troubling me, and Hit *rum* was angry, so I sent for you, because you are an old and experienced man. So please be so kind as to sacrifice properly, so that I may be troubled no longer. Please do so, whether my body is cured thereby or not.

The Mun: Were you to die, what would happen to your wives and daughter—women who are all alone?

The Mandal: Don't worry about that; in that case they can go home.

The Mun: I have already said that I am old and weak; if my sacrifice is unsuccessful, don't blame me. I take all you here to witness what I have said. (To Ashyok who had fetched him): If I fail in this I'll never dare look at you again. The Mun then began to pray in a loud and clear voice, and the rest listened quietly and almost reverently—an unparalleled situation in my experience of Lepchas. The Mun first mentioned the Mandal's year of birth and *ptso* and then summoned Sabdok *moong* and Hit *rum* to deliver him, and then called on the gods collectively to give the Mandal a son. 'Why is it,' he asked the gods, 'when he has two wives, and there are lots of other girls going about with gaping vulvas, that he has no son?' (*General laughter*) He then sprinkled the *chi* and said to the supernaturals 'Now I am only doing this small ceremony; when I return to my own home the day after to-morrow I shall repeat the ceremony better.' He then announced in his normal voice that he had done all he could and called on Gongyop to take over from him and finish the ceremony.

This ceremony was, I repeat, the most solemn that I witnessed in Lingthem, and the sexual jokes were therefore comparatively rare; also there were no direct invitations or solicitations, such as would occur in more convivial circumstances.

I found this continual harping on the humorous aspects of sexual physiology puzzling, since most Lepchas have a full and adequate sex life, and face sex extremely simply, without guilt or secrecy; but the town Lepchas found it extremely shocking, for the Lepchas of Zongu would make such remarks before their parents or children; a man would not direct such remarks to his mother-in-law or daughter-in-law, or *vice versa*, but he is not very careful as to whether these people are in ear-shot or not. On the grounds of this openness of speech the town Lepchas called the Lepchas of Zongu uncivilised and shameless. I think it is legitimate to call such remarks obscene, since they are avoided in front of relations-in-law and would cause shame if for example they were uttered by a third person in the presence of a son-in-law and mother-in-law, and since the three operative words are always referred to in circumlocutions before a superior. They are certainly relished as obscenities.

I think one of the reasons for this constant verbal preoccupation with the comic aspects of sex is the fact that at any village gathering or feast the great majority of the people present are, owing to the stringent incest laws, forbidden sexual partners; there is a release from tension in thus jesting about these dangerous subjects, although even in jest direct invitations are not made to people who would count as incestuous. Another reason is the cultural concept that there is no temperamental difference between men and women; except that men are usually stronger physically identical standards of behaviour are expected from both sexes; the standards of beauty are identical; except that they may not kill animals nor perform lamaist ceremonies nor own land women suffer under no disability because they are women. With this general conception of the similarity of the two sexes the differences of appearance and function of the primary sexual characteristics becomes even more striking and worthy of comment; and it is worth noting again in this context the extraordinary amount of fantasy about the independent life of the genitalia which occurs in the Lepcha stories. It is also possible that in removing all intense emotion from sexual activity the Lepchas have also destroyed some of the emotional release and psychological satisfaction.

Some of the young men were particularly given to obscenity, particularly Tobgé, a ne'er-do-well whose wife, it will be remembered, was carrying on with Dadool, and Chudo, Tafoor's younger brother. Chudo was twenty-nine, the father of three children, and very fond of his wife. He always gave the impression of being very much younger than his years; he was particularly sweet-tempered, even for a Lepcha, and very industrious, but he was extremely childish, perhaps because his elder brother, Tafoor, was so very learned and responsible. He had rather a grotesque sense of humour and was very fond of imitating lamaist dances, almost parodying them, and of making surprising jokes and unexpected little presents. When he learned I was fond of flowers he used to bring me nearly every day some orchid or other odd flower that he had found in his work travelling about the country-side. If the younger men were more inclined to obscenity so were the elder women, particularly Lumba's first wife, a Mun aged forty-seven, who was completely outrageous and shameless in her speech and behaviour; she was a jolly bawdy old creature, rather in the tradition of Marie Lloyd. As far as my information goes, and on such matters it is very extensive, she was relatively chaste in her private life; nobody repeated any scandal about her. When I talked to women about sex and childbirth and similar subjects the older ones used always to answer quite freely; but occasionally if there was a young woman in the group, she would ask why I talked about such things which made her feel ashamed; if this happened the older women would usually stop the conversation, giving the impression that they had been caught out in a breach of formal manners to which sensible people did not pay any attention.

Young unmarried girls did not on the whole join in these jokes, though they might laugh at them; boys started making them at about the age of fourteen. Girls and young women were very careful about exposing their bodies and often a great deal of fuss went on if a father or husband brought up a girl to have sores on her leg dressed; I think some of the women did feel genuinely distressed at having a stranger touch their legs before witnesses. Grown men were also fairly modest before me, but the younger men and boys were not; if they had torn pants or no pants, and thereby exposed themselves, this was a cause for laughter rather than confusion. On occasion, especially when we first arrived, women would reproach young children for showing their nakedness; this was always done very quietly and in a calm voice without emotion; the warning was often observed for quite two minutes after the woman had spoken. Excessive modesty of speech or action is a great part of the pattern of respectful behaviour, and is enjoined towards parents-in-law and social superiors; except in these situations it is considered a juvenile trait which people grow out of; it is usually given as the chief reason for the difficulty of establishing the marriage of young people on a firm basis. It is a legitimate subject for teasing; and one of the permanent jokes of the younger men was to push the more modest women into my arms, or to tell them that if they wanted really good medicine they should come and visit me late in the evening. A few of the girls seemed really distressed at this behaviour and all attempted to appear bashful; but with many the pretence was not successful.

iv

Speech has very great importance for the Lepchas. Indeed, apart from such knowledge as is necessary for the priests of the different religions, it may be said to represent their art, their science, and their intellectual entertainment. To be able to speak well is after being able to work well the highest social commendation. A good speaker is always in demand, and is essential on formal occasions, such as the entertainment of a stranger, or as *bek-bu* in marriage transactions.

There are two kinds of excellency in speech; first there is the person with an elegant vocabulary, and second the person with a

WOMEN PREPARE FOOD

Chlaa Mandal's two wives winnow rice on the balcony of their house.

Mrs. Gongyop and Mrs. Chano join together to pound rice in the courtyard. Behind, a dog has got on to the balcony, where it has no right to be.

large repertoire of stories. In Lepcha speech there are two kinds of variation to the everyday vocabulary for added richness and elegance; there is the honorific vocabulary, and allusive periphrasis, or *tang-bor*. The honorific vocabulary consists, I am informed, entirely of loan words from Tibetan or Sikkimese; it is meant always to be used to social superiors, but in Zongu only a few of these honorific words are current, and then only in connection with religion. The honorific terms for the parts of the body are used in describing supernaturals, and the honorific terms for 'presents' and 'to offer' are used for religious gifts and sacrifices. Those who can manage this honorific vocabulary would use it in talking to representatives of the State.

The *tang-bor* on the other hand are used a great deal. The nearest parallel to a *tang-bor* is an analogy or comparison which is used in the place of the idea which is intended to be conveyed. To give a somewhat over-simplified illustration, it is as though an Englishman were to say 'I am a horse' or 'I am a lord', instead of 'I am as hungry as a horse' 'I am as drunk as a lord'. A great number of these *tang-bor* are traditional; a good speaker however will make up his own. Quite a number are now incomprehensible, either because the references are forgotten, because they retain archaic terms, or because they have been borrowed from another district. A great number of the allusions are local, and a stranger will often be unable to understand the local *tang-bor*. Some are used for toning down disagreeable or shocking expressions, such as 'he has closed his eyes' for 'he is dead', 'the maize harvest is ripe' for 'has a sexual erection'. Others are humorous: a monkey is called 'pretty-face', a he-goat 'daddy-talk-too-much'; Lepchas are referred to as 'the drinkers', Nepali as 'the contradictory ones'. Others again are descriptive; the bear is 'he who leans forward', the fish 'he who throws away water', stolen goods 'prison comes after'. *Tang-bor* can be used as a secret language, but it is chiefly employed for elegance and humour. In stories, especially the semi-historical stories, the principal characters always speak to one another in *tang-bor*.

Story-telling is the major Lepcha art and distraction. The favourite of all situations for story-telling is round the fire after work in the evenings; on these occasions the long stories will be told, stories which may take five or six evenings in their telling, one person doing the talking and the others listening. But this is not the only time when stories are told; in long tedious work, such as weeding, one person will tell (usually short) stories while the others work; sometimes there is one person appointed as story-teller for the day; that person will get special tit-bits at the evening meal. Only short stories are told at feasts, because there is too much noise and distraction for the necessary prolonged attention. Stories are also told on completely unformalised occasions; the sight of an uncommon bird or insect usually calls forth from somebody the story connected with this animal.

Lepcha stories are characterised by their vividness and by the number of internal repetitions. The Lepchas visualise extremely precisely and concretely; there are no half-tones in their stories; a thing or a person either is or is not present, and no attempt is made to fill the gap with guesses or conjectures. Although their stories are told extremely vividly, there is little tendency towards dramatisation for its own sake; changing of voice and mimicry of characters only occur in the humorous tales. Apart from the two sacred Mun stories there is no insistence on verbatim accuracy, provided all the points of the story are remembered.

Most of the older people have one or two long stories which are, as it were, their speciality; but there is no feeling of ownership in them and if another person can remember them he is at liberty to tell them. It is considered that to be able to recount a long story accurately it is necessary to listen to it attentively three times. Except for one or two of the animal fables the stories are never told to children; when they begin to learn sense and can sit quietly—that is when they are about ten—they are allowed to listen provided they don't interrupt. Some of the young boys know one or two short stories, and were very pleased to tell them to me, as unmarried youths do not easily get an audience.

It is not considered permissible to invent new fables or *lung-then* as they have a semi-scriptural value; the most that is allowed is a little individual embroidery or emphasis. Indeed I question whether stories are ever consciously invented; new ones are added to the repertoire through guests or visiting strangers.

Besides stories Lepchas are very fond of recounting anecdotes and events of their own past life or of their neighbours'; some of these anecdotes, such as the ordeal of the poisoners at Lungdeum[4] are half-way towards turning into stories, since they are told by people who were not themselves present. These anecdotes are told extremely precisely and concretely; when Lepchas describe

[4] See Book Three, Chapter Fifteen, pp. 392–393.

a scene from their own past they describe it minutely and statically, as though they were looking at a picture. They frequently like to make their descriptions clearer by employing twigs or pebbles to represent the people and things described.

It is probable that the value which is placed on story-telling has greatly influenced the Lepcha tendency to monologue, to talk as it were in paragraphs, to which I have already referred ; this tendency is noticeable even in the speeches put into the mouths of the characters of their stories. Stichomythia is only applied to jokes.

V

Besides being the greatest social diversion, speech is also the greatest social sanction. For through speech is produced the strongest unpleasant psychological sensation that the Lepchas recognise—shame ; and shame is on occasion so unbearable that it leads to suicide.

The training and education of Lepchas from their earliest childhood stresses social approval and disapproval as the motive for adopting or abstaining from certain types of behaviour. A child is told that if he does certain acts—takes other people's property for example, or refuses to work—other people won't like him and won't help him. The emphasis is always on the disapproval of the community in general and not, as with us, on the losing the love of the parents, or the gods, or on the punishment by people in authority. It would seem (though without further evidence this is only a speculation) that this emphasis on anonymous social approval together with the fact that the extended family is a psychologically operative group, and that positive training takes place relatively late in the life of the child, has the result of producing a much weaker internalised control (or super-ego) than is the case when the approving and punishing mechanism is introjected in the image of the parents and parent-surrogates. It is also noteworthy that the Lepcha social organisation only renders possible identification with the community as a whole, and, though to a lesser extent, with the extended family ; the Lepchas have not, as most European children and adults have, smaller groups in the community with whom they can identify, and whose approval will support them against the condemnation of another part of the community.

If this is an accurate representation of the case it would follow that the ego, though normally less disturbed, is also more vulnerable to attacks from without. The mechanisms of self-justification and self-criticism have been brought into play much less. When feelings of guilt are continuously evoked the ego acquires a capacity to deal with them more or less satisfactorily, and is able to balance the support of friendly objects against the actual or believed punishing tendencies of the hostile objects; but when the evocation of guilt feelings depends on exteriorised social disapproval, and when the community which expresses this disapproval is relatively tolerant without over-exacting standards, the occasions when the individual has to deal with such situations are very rare—indeed may never arise after childhood. Consequently the strength of the negative feelings is enhanced by the fact that they are more or less novel; and if the extended family join the community in exteriorising their disapproval the shamed person has no moral support left; in psychoanalytical terminology the whole of the super-ego has turned against the ego and this will produce suicide.

The Lepchas describe shame as producing a very unpleasant physical sensation, chiefly located in the belly. When I was trying to discover the Lepcha attitude to sin in the lamaist sense of the word, several people told me that the difference between sin and shame was that, although sin may possibly have some effect on your body or on your after-life, it does not affect you mentally nor do you feel anything in your belly when you commit a sin comparable to that which you would feel if you were reproached for doing your work badly. At one of the big monastery feasts a man from a neighbouring village informed me that turning one of the big prayer-wheels would remove a thousand sins. 'What are sins?' I asked him. 'Killing animals, thinking evil thoughts, doing evil deeds.' 'Do you mind killing animals?' 'No.' I then turned to the people standing around and asked them what sins were? The Mandal, speaking for the community said 'You had better ask a lama; we laymen don't know.' The majority agreed to this; but twelve-year-old Ribu standing by said that sin was killing animals; but it was no sin if the animals were, had been, or might have been eating your crops.

It is extremely easy to shame a person. For example one morning fourteen-year-old Chimpet arrived with an extremely dirty face, after I had made him a present of a cake of soap. I made fun of him in front of his father who joined in; whereupon he turned down his mouth, refused to speak and went and fidgeted with the monastery window with his back to us for a few minutes, before he went away looking quite different to his usual boisterous self. He did not return home till the evening. On another occasion Lumba's eldest son Kutt'r, aged nineteen, came up to have a wound on his hand dressed, after which he went to the kitchen to have a cup of tea. A little later I sent and asked him to come and talk to me and he sent back a reply that he didn't want to. A couple of days later he returned to have his hand dressed again, and I then asked him why he thought I would give him medicine when he would not come and talk to me? He was almost dumb with embarrassed shame and tried to slink away; I had to employ a good deal of tact before I could get him to accept the medicine. Had I made such a remark in front of witnesses it is quite possible that he would have tried to take poison.

Considering the size of the community suicide is fairly frequent among the Lepchas. There have been six suicides in Lingthem and the neighbouring smaller villages in the last twenty years, and in every case the suicide has been immediately subsequent to a public reproof. In five out of the six cases the suicides were relatively young men; the sixth case was that of a young girl of Panung who drowned herself because her uncle and parents reproved her for her laziness and promiscuity. Chélé's father killed himself because his wife and her family publicly blamed him for neglecting her and his work while she was ill. Kurma's uncle killed himself because he was blamed for not keeping his wife in order, and Kurma's brother because he was blamed for his uncle's suicide.[5] The possibility of suicide from grief is admitted, but the only case I heard of was of a woman in the neighbouring village of Lungdeum who killed herself shortly after the death of her husband, and the details of this case were not properly known. Women kill themselves by drowning, men usually with the aconite poison they use on their arrows.

Besides the successful suicides there have been a number of suicide attempts which have been thwarted. It seems to me probable that a Lepcha can establish his innocence on a specific charge by going through the gestures of committing suicide in such situations that he is bound to be saved; some stories of attempted suicide which I heard seemed to me not to have been intended seriously; they were theatrical performances arranged in such a manner as to convince everybody of the sincerity of the libelled person without

[5] See Part Three for fuller details, Chapter Fifteen, p. 396–397.

actually endangering his life.[6] One of the reasons for believing in the guilt of Hlatam the 'poisoner' was that both she and her son Aga must have been aware of what was said about them and neither had demonstrated their innocence by attempting to kill themselves.

Verbal threats of suicide are occasionally made, but they are taken little notice of. When they are drunk Dunbi, because he is poor, and Katel, because his second wife won't sleep with him, threaten to kill themselves. Children also occasionally threaten to kill themselves if they think they are unjustly scolded or ill-treated; when he was young Pembu, an exceptionally nervous man, used to make such threats, and Chano's younger son, who was brought up by an 'aunt' also does so occasionally; to such threats the parents retort that nobody wants such a naughty child.[7]

With this ever-present possibility of provoking shame and even suicide it can be seen that malicious gossip and scandal assume very considerable emotional importance. People are worried as to what their neighbours are saying about them behind their backs; one or two even said that the reason for having '*ingzong*' (special friends) in one's own village was so that if people spoke ill of you you would have somebody whom you can completely trust to tell you what is being said. My impression is that very little scandal is spoken, and that when people did discuss potentially scandalous or disagreeable situations they did so very seriously and with hushed voices, taking care that no children or ignorant neighbours should listen to what they were saying.

The potential influence of hostile talk has I think further results; it is a very strong sanction to encourage Lepchas to conform to the approved methods of behaviour; and it also makes people chary of expressing judgements about their neighbours. If you ask a Lepcha who in his village has any outstanding quality, whether good or bad, he will almost certainly reply that everybody is much of a muchness. In many ways I think this does represent the real Lepcha attitude; affection is based on mutual services, not on emotion, and consequently difference in character is of much less importance than difference of treatment. Only character traits strongly opposed to Lepcha ideals were spontaneously commented on, and those seldom; cruelty, avarice, untruthfulness,

[6] For an example of this see the story of the attempted suicide of Jiroong's sister in Chapter Sixteen, p. 428.

[7] See also the history of Chélé's threats of suicide; Chapter Six, pp. 164–165.

quarrelsomeness were on the whole justly ascribed to those people who manifested these qualities; but I could never get people to allot differences in socially valuable qualities, to say for example that A. was a better or worse worker than B. or more or less generous.

I think that I was more conscious in the difference in the characters of the various Lepchas of Lingthem than the Lepchas themselves were; as a member of my culture I naturally judged people emotionally and liked or disliked them for differences of character rather than for their behaviour towards me. Towards the end of my stay I found that I had taken a really firm dislike to some people, particularly to Aga and Katel, whom I considered mean and sly and altogether unpleasant. Aga was fairly generally disliked, but when I told the people I was intimate with that I disliked Katel they obviously could not understand my reasons: he had not treated me badly in any way. When I tried to explain more fully my reasons for disliking him they would explain that he was foolish and did not know how to behave properly. For them this was a sufficient explanation; it wasn't his fault he was a fool and this was no reason for disliking him, provided he fulfilled his obligations. In the same way although lame orphaned Satéo through his clumsiness and incompetence always botched whatever work he was doing, nobody thought of reproving him or preventing him joining in the communal work—he was a liability on any job—because he was patently doing his best and couldn't help his clumsiness. If on the other hand he had been an able-bodied man who through laziness or spite was doing bad work he would undoubtedly be reprimanded and publicly shamed.

Lepchas are very unwilling to speculate on the motives of another's behaviour, whether in the past or present; they always turned aside such questions with the catch phrase 'Who can see into the heart of another?'

vi

Although it is difficult and of questionable value to try to describe the intellectual and temperamental characteristics of the average Lepcha it is perhaps worth while to point out some of their more pronounced group attitudes. The Lepchas possess remarkably vivid and exact verbal and visual memories. They do not prize intellectual quickness and it is on the whole not one of their characteristics. Numbers are practically meaningless to them and numerical concepts play a very small rôle; in any question demanding numbers they will nearly always give in answer three or four alternatives. In some situations this is almost ludicrous; except for one or two lamas nobody knows his own age or even that of his youngest children in years; they all know the year they were born and what year they are now in, but if a child was born in Dog year they would be quite unable to work out its age today (1937 was Ox year and the child would be four) and they might just as well say that the child was two or eight. More than that, if you asked a person how many people were living in his house he would almost certainly get the number wrong; he could naturally recite immediately the names or rather the kinship terms of the people in his house; but it does not cross his mind to tot up the number and it is a mental operation of which nearly all Lepchas are incapable. The Lepchas count by twenties and use their fingers for all calculations; they count with the thumb against the fingers, putting the thumb on the base of the little finger for one, the first joint for two, the second joint for three, the tip for four and then going down to the base of the next finger for five and so on. There used to be long consultations to try and work out in how many days a fixed date for a calendrical feast would arrive; and on one occasion everybody except one lama arrived a day late, and the Muns frequently made a mistake of a day or more for their special festivals. They are quite incapable of working out what money they should receive for their cardamum; they may know that they have ten maunds and that each maund is worth Rs. 12; but unless they use sticks or some other memory guide they have absolutely no idea of what the total should be. The Mandal has to keep in his head the taxes due from each household but he does this by remembering the words and not the figures.

The Lepchas do not dramatise; and they do not alter their pace of thought or action except in emergencies which for the reason that they demand such alteration are considered particularly unpleasant. My impression is that the Lepchas think much more slowly than either the Nepali or the Indians, but since my knowledge of both these races is slight this impression is of little value; they certainly think quicker than the ordinary Somerset farm labourer, though infinitely slower than a European town dweller. I got the impression that they talked quickly, but that I think was due to the fact that the language was an unfamiliar one, and that I was straining to catch every shade of meaning.

THE POT OF *CHI* FOR THE TODDLERS IS SET INTO THE GROUND WELL AWAY FROM THE GROWN-UPS

The Lepchas are remarkably tolerant. They are perfectly ready to admit the validity for other peoples of habits and customs which for them would be shocking or disgusting. For example the marriage arrangements of the Nepali, and some of the sexual habits of the Tibetans would be horrifying and disastrous if committed by Lepchas; the Lepchas know of these habits, and are inclined to laugh at them; but they do not reproach the Nepali or Tibetans for them, do not try and convince them that they are wrong, and do not fear moral contamination through contact with them. This tolerance is not accompanied however by any feelings of inferiority; the very strong sentiment of fundamental equality among individuals is carried over to a sentiment of fundamental equality between groups. Some people are richer, more industrious or cleverer than their neighbours; similarly the Tibetans are more learned and the Europeans richer than the Lepchas; but since the Lepchas are as learned and as rich as they can be, they do not, I think, feel any fundamental inferiority in comparison with more favoured groups, any more than they do in comparison with more favoured individuals. It is worth remembering in this connection how Gongyop in his prophetic dreams under the possession of Padem *rum* would visit the rulers of neighbouring states and Europeans and would be treated by them as an equal. It is noteworthy that the richer households and the learned lamas who can read do not, except when the lamas are performing their special functions, demand or obtain any special preferential treatment.

This tolerance of the Lepchas can be ascribed I think partly to contentment, and partly to indifference. Straightforward consumption—food, drink and sex—fills the forefront of their desires and aims in life; provided these physical needs are satisfied—and for the majority they are continuously satisfied—the other aspects of life are emotionally of less importance. In their dealings with the supernatural they are particularly tolerant and receptive; it is important to be able to deal with the devils but they have not any deep-set preference for one special method of dealing with them. Completely alien methods will be tried, and, if they prove satisfactory, adopted, however little they may be integrated into their general outlook; thus they have accepted the taboo on menstruating women in the treatment of cardamum, and retained the insistence on virginity in the sacrifices to the people of Mayel, though except in these instances virginity is a meaningless concept and menstruating women suffer under no disabilities. This capacity of accepting and isolating irrelevant and unintegrated attitudes comes I think from indifference and not from scepticism. A comparison might be found in the way Occidentals under the orders of doctors will accept temporary but profound modifications of their habits or diet without considering that their former habits were wrong or that others should follow them; they give up meat for example because the doctor says that for the moment it will disagree with them, not because they have become convinced vegetarians. The Lepchas are not sceptical about various methods of dealing with the supernatural, but their belief has no intensity or rigidity. It is possible that before their conversion to lamaism the Lepchas felt more strongly that they possessed the only correct way of dealing with the supernatural; but now that they have accepted the idea that there are two alternative methods for dealing with nearly every devil they can accept without difficulty further alien methods founded on similar hypotheses. It is worth remembering also that religious rituals are only performed by a very small part of the population—by the lamas and Mun; the lay population merely summon them when they think they need their services and provide the raw materials from which the lamas will fashion the religious objects. The vast majority of Lepchas never perform any religious rites (beyond perhaps turning a prayer wheel and prostrating themselves before the lamaist images); religion with the Lepchas is the occupation of a minority of specialists.

Within limits the Lepchas are also extremely tolerant of individual variations in temperament. They are adamant in resisting any encroachment on their individual and group independence, and they will not permit overt aggression or ambition, or the sidestepping of communal duties; but provided a person fulfils his private and public obligations, keeps the peace, and does not seek to impose on or exploit others, or to go counter to the rules of the society, he is permitted considerable latitude. The Lepchas insist on very considerable social conformity; but if an individual carries out his social obligations adequately and does not seek to interfere with or destroy the privacy and independence of others, others will also respect his privacy and independence. The Lepchas so dislike being ordered about, that even on construction jobs which could be quicker and more efficiently performed with a director of operations, they insist on working independently, and appear to ignore anybody who tries to give orders.

This antithetic emphasis on social conformity and individualism produces the result that most Lepchas have two types of behaviour; they are far more restrained in public and with strangers than they are in the privacy of their own homes. I was naturally never able to observe this, but in people's stories of their own lives there was a constant undercurrent of grumbling and scolding, particularly on the part of the women.[8] Sometimes these undercurrents came fairly near the surface in public in the guise of playful teasing. Public quarrelling of any sort is so violently disapproved of that even minor irritations and annoyances have to be repressed in public; in the home there is not the same social restraint and I have the impression that the majority of wives are given to nagging on occasion. It must be remembered that most wives are strangers to their husband's community and therefore lack the moral and emotional support of their families which is always available for the majority of the men.

The pace of Lepcha life is very leisurely; the Lepchas are never in a hurry. When they are doing something, be it work or pleasure, they like to do it thoroughly. With work as with pleasure there is no hurry or greed; everything gets done eventually, but it gets done slowly, with intervals of rest in between. The Lepchas never seem to mind waiting; often after everybody has gathered for a religious ceremony there will be a delay of several hours, while the lamas prepare the ritual objects; nobody objects to this or thinks to hurry another up; they are content to sit and wait until everything is ready. When a piece of communal work such as the repairing of a house or the building of a bridge is in progress only about half the people present are likely to be working at any one time; the others will be taking a rest, or joking, or helping to prepare the evening meal. The Lepchas work very long hours and do not grudge their labour; but they detest being ordered about and see no sense in hurry; work is a disagreeable necessity which should be made as pleasant as possible. A few state that they feel happiest after a good day's work; but for the majority the reason for work is to provide for the sensual pleasures which form the chief object of life.

Although Lepchas do not allow for quarrelling they admit bad temper to be natural, particularly if a person is hungry or if he is finding difficulties in his work. The expression of bad temper is stylised; it is called *shadong ding* and is externalised by the annoyed person breaking any of his own property which comes to hand, or

[8] Numerous examples of this occur in Book Three.

by his hacking at a piece of wood with his knife, or by throwing stones. Even in this state nobody would destroy another's property, and only a savage foreigner like Tempa would hit or throw stones at people; but on occasion people might hit animals, or throw things at them. Normally people only beat animals if they stray into cultivated land; to hit them on any other occasion is considered cruel. *Shadong ding* is considered to be a natural and almost automatic state, like hunger; it is not caused by a supernatural and no notice is paid to a person in a temper.

Except for shame, hunger and sexual desire the Lepchas do not equate physical sensations and emotional states. Neither blushing nor fainting for emotional reasons are recognised. Squeamishness varies considerably with the individual. Some people are frightened of corpses; the Mandal was unwilling to approach the dead bodies of his first wife and of his parents. A few, such as Pembu, cannot even bear to watch a wound being dressed. Such squeamishness is considered rather stupid; and a certain admiration is expressed for those people who have the courage to rip open the corpse of a pregnant woman, and take out the foetus, which has to be done before the body is disposed of. A queasy person is not made fun of nor considered disgraced by his sensitiveness; but some admiration is felt for those people who do not manifest it, rather similar to the European admiration for a person with 'plenty of guts'.

The disgust reactions of the Lepchas are remarkably low. They will not avoid walking in human or animal excrement and will merely rub their feet on the grass if they should do so. People will clean babies often with their bare hands; and I have seen women collect the mucus from a baby with whooping cough in their hands and just rub them on the ground. They have no disgust for menstruation though they have some fear of it: if the menstrual blood falls into food or water it would be fatal to humans or animals though it nourishes fishes; a menstruating woman is not debarred from any action. After menstruation a woman will always wash both her body and her clothes, a thing which Tibetans neglect to do; the Lepchas consider, and correctly, that the Tibetans are far dirtier than they, and a number of anecdotes are told about the Tibetan lack of attention to their bodies and their various filthy, but to the Lepchas amusing, personal habits. The Lepchas themselves are extremely dirty on the whole and particularly the laymen; lamas shave and wash their heads and also their hands before making the ceremonial objects and women usually have a good wash at least once a month; grown men on the other hand wash exceedingly seldom. But even though they are so dirty they are in comparison with the Tibetans relatively clean; it is true that they have a much more clement climate and an abundance of water, so that there is no external reason for their being as dirty as they are.

vii

The chief attention that a full-grown Lepcha pays to his person is the care of his hair. Until about puberty children of both sexes have their hair cut short, and lamas always have their heads shaved or close-cropped; but the hair of a woman or layman must never be cut after *asék*. Indeed were a woman after betrothal to cut her hair it would be *nam-toak* and would produce the death of a member of her family. Men wear their hair in a single long plait hanging down their back, often with a thread ending in a tassel braided into it; women nearly always have their hair in two plaits, taken from either side of the nape of the neck; sometimes these two plaits are bound separately round the head; others wear them with the two ends joined together with a piece of braid. Men nearly always have longer hair than women; many men had plaits reaching down to the waist; the women's hair rarely fell below their shoulders. Men with long pigtails often twist them round their heads when working, as the swinging queue gets in the way. In the presence of a superior men and women always let their hair hang down as a mark of respect; and the first act of a nun on coming to worship at the monastery is to remove her head-cloth and let her hair fall on her shoulders.

Once a week if possible the hair is unplaited, if necessary deloused, washed, oiled, and then replaited. With the exception of a spouse and the parent-in-law of the opposite sex anybody may perform this service for anybody else; even adult brothers and sisters may dress each other's hair. Hair-dressing is considered an impersonal and unintimate act; at feasts and large gatherings there is often a long line of people seated with each arranging the hair of the person in front of him.

Long and lustrous hair is one of the points of beauty for members of both sexes; other points which are considered desirable are a straight nose, a flat face, a fair rosy complexion, a round head and a straight body without prominent curves. Big eyes, small eyes, pop-eyes or folded eyelids are ugly; so are dimples, too big or too small a mouth, a protuberant bottom or big breasts. Particularly disliked is too big a head or a 'curved face', that is a face which in silhouette does not fall into one plane. White and even teeth and a pleasant smile are also desirable. Men and women are considered equal in beauty but a woman is considered to be at her most beautiful at the age of twelve, a man at the age of twenty. It is considered that on the whole a beautiful man will marry a beautiful woman and an ugly man an ugly woman, but this does not happen invariably; and the ugliness of a person is not considered to be a valid reason for refusing a marriage. A woman's beauty is considered to be somewhat spoilt by childbearing.

The differences in beauty of children are remarked but little importance is paid to childish beauty as it is considered essentially impermanent. A girl with a big head and eyes and body and feet is considered somewhat man-like and it is thought that she will work slowly in everything. A man with small features and particularly long eyelashes is considered to look like a woman; such a person will be a swift runner and a clever climber of trees and rocks, able to go where others cannot. Apart from these qualities the idea of temperament is not linked at all with physical appearance.

Freckles are considered disfiguring; they are the *tamtoom* of children who are not orphans eating bamboo shoots when the rice is ripe. 'Just as children have parents above them so rice has bamboo above it; consequently children who have no parents are not affected by this.' Black marks on the skin are caused by young people eating pig's stomach. There is no remedy for either of these disfigurements. On the whole beauty is not of much positive emotional importance; it is only when people are markedly unbeautiful that they are liable to be shunned. Beauty adds to the desirability of strangers as sexual partners; I do not think it is remarked at all in people with whom one is familiar. At the big monastery feasts I often asked people whom they considered to be the best-looking person present; when they did not produce an obscene joke as an answer they would usually refuse to pronounce judgement unless there was a stranger present, in which case the stranger was nearly always chosen. Good-quality and clean clothes and jewels add to the self-confidence of the wearer and to a certain extent enhance the wearer's beauty; but clothes and jewels could never be a substitute for beauty. Nobody would think of borrowing other people's clothes or jewels in order to appear finer and richer than they really are; they would be frightened of spoiling or losing them, though girls might try on the clothes and jewels of a friend for a moment just to see how they look. The only occasion on which clothes are borrowed is in the case of emergencies, for example if a person gets very wet far from his own home. Sometimes, it is said, a girl will dress up in men's clothes as a joke, but it would be considered rather shameful for a grown man to dress up as a woman, though young boys occasionally do so in play. One or two lamas told me that men were essentially superior to women, but I never heard similar opinions from a layman. Various details suggest that there is a sentiment of sex-rivalry, but it only seems to be openly formulated through contact with Nepali or Tibetans. In specifically Lepcha contexts this rivalry is unformulated and unstressed.

viii

The ideal life of a Lepcha could be schematically represented by a slightly undulating curve, at first rising steeply, and then gradually flattening out, but still rising somewhat till the very end, when there is a tendency to drop again. The first years of life are a period of relative obscurity; a young child consumes more than he gives, and is therefore a weight on his parents and the community. Children are not on the whole harshly treated, but once they have achieved physical independence very little attention is paid to them. Grown-ups do not talk to or play with children; except when they are by themselves children are in the background to do simple chores and to be taught to equip themselves for adult life; they are a responsibility, not companions. There are no organised games for children, and no instruments which are intended to be children's toys; nor for that matter are there any games for adults. A few Lepchas know of the Nepali game of 'Cows and Tigers' (an elaborate form of the game of which the European 'Fox and Geese' is another representative) but they do not play it and do not understand why other people should do so.

After about the age of ten a boy takes an increasing share in the productive work of the community and, as he grows up, is co-opted more and more into the communal life. There is no abrupt transition for the male between childhood and manhood; a youth takes on additional responsibility and work, and mingles more in the pastimes and discussions of his elders, according to his ability and private inclinations. Sexual experiment and adventure, marriage and children follow in due course, but the Lepcha man is still growing up till about the age of thirty-six. At that period his responsibilities are liable to be heaviest; his parents will be retiring from the management of affairs, and he will have, if he is lucky, a number of young children to look after. As his sons grow up and become capable adults in their turn he is able to withdraw somewhat from work; if he is intelligent he is a *yeum-bu*—a man who knows—and as such will be often asked for his advice by the Mandal and by his juniors. If he retains his health and prosperity as he grows older, and if his children and grand-children are still alive he acquires a sort of talismanic virtue; younger men will take valuable presents to so fortunate an old man in order to get in return either his drinking cup or his rosary and to share a meal of rice with him, in order to acquire the desirable qualities of this prosperous great-grandfather. But if an old man survives his children and loses his capacity to work his position is an unenviable one; he too, like the young child, consumes more than he produces; he is a nuisance, not respected or listened to, treated at best with casual deference. For the Lepchas the normal span of life is four score years; until that age a man or woman should be capable of doing sufficient work to keep himself; those that survive longer are a misery to themselves and everybody else.

With one extremely important exception the curve of a woman's life follows that of the man's. Except for the accident of death there are no breaks or sudden transitions in a man's life; for the majority of women there is the geographical transfer to her husband's home; although the marriage customs soften this as much as possible it represents a psychological change for a woman which has no parallel in the life of a man. It is probably for this reason that young married women appear so much more self-possessed and grown-up than their husbands. A man who stays in his own community is perpetually classified as weaker, or younger, or stupider than his elders or contemporaries; a woman in a new village is free from such comparisons and takes her place according to her own merits and abilities. A woman of twenty takes her full rôle in the group of adult women; a man of thirty is still somewhat bashful and is inclined to hide behind the knowledge and experience of his elders.

The undulations on the curve of Lepcha life are the alternations of plenty and scarcity, of feasting and everyday life. There is no absolute contrast between plenty and scarcity, between a feast and an ordinary meal; it is a question of quantity rather than quality.

There is no seeking for ecstasy, for experiences contrasting sharply with the normal, no desire for sudden and dramatised pleasure or grief which will stand out sharply against the background of life. Unexpected death is inevitably dramatic, and is therefore particularly disliked and feared. The only dramatic situation welcomed in normal life is a short and illicit sexual encounter. The Lepcha ideal is a constant state of euphory without sharply contrasing situations.

Since the Lepchas do not divide life up into different periods it is understandable that they should have no formulated notions as to what is the best time of life. The greater number whom I questioned said that they considered that the happiest time was when people were *fleng* or *num-leng* ; this term (the second is the female of the first) has no exact equivalent in English ; it means a full-grown person or animal who has not yet borne young and can only be translated by the blanket term of 'youth and early married life'. Not all, however, agreed that this period was the happiest ; Jiroong, for example, considered the happiest period to be old age, provided a person had children and was not infirm. Perhaps the best illustration of the general attitude is given by Tafoor when he said: 'The happiest time of all is *fleng*. If a married couple have no children they have no anxieties or cares ; they can eat their fill of the best and need only think of themselves. But when they get old life will be very bad indeed ; they will have no one to look after them, they will be lonely and live badly.

'If, on the other hand, they are like me with lots of children, life will be very hard. They will have to work a great deal to feed and clothe them, and they themselves will only have coarse food to eat. Like me they will be torn with anxiety because they have to work in the fields while a child is ill at home. (His three-year old daughter had a bad attack of chicken-pox.) Like me they will pass sleepless nights ; last night I did not shut my eyes. But when they are old and their children are grown up, then life will be easy for them ; they will have the best of everything and will not have to work hard ; their children will look after them, and the end of their life will be good.'

CHAPTER ELEVEN

BIRTH AND CHILDHOOD

According to Lepcha theory a child's life starts at the moment of conception. When the two secretions mingle[1] the soul arrives from heaven or the place of the gods (the first being the lamaist, the second the Mun, repository of unborn people); the father's semen provides the bones and brain, the mother's vaginal secretions the flesh and blood. The first portion of the foetus to be formed is the eyes, which are completed at the end of the first month; then from round the eyes the head develops and then the rest of the body downwards. The foetus is completely human with all its organs, and even its hair, at the end of the fifth month.

Within the womb is something resembling a nipple through which the child draws nourishment; this nourishment is something like butter, and is the transmuted food of the mother, just as milk is after birth. Consequently the mother is not permanently depleted by child-bearing; none of her body has gone to feed the child.

Conception is shown by the cessation of the menses, which were instituted for that purpose. The child does not feed on the menstrual blood; menstruation is exclusively a calendar.

At the fifth month when the baby is considered fully formed the expectant parents must start observing the numerous pre-natal precautions which have to be followed if the child is not to be born malformed, or if the mother is not to have a difficult delivery. The entering into this period of pre-natal precautions is established by a Mun *pék*-ing both parents with a bunch of elephant grass in one hand and a live fowl in the other. Both parents are equally capable of influencing the child within the womb, and in point of fact the greater number of the precautions to be observed are concerned with work which is liable to fall to a man rather than a woman. Copulation after conception has no influence on the foetus, except incestuously, which would produce a miscarriage, and may

[1] The Lepchas consider semen and the vaginal secretions to be parallel substances; they are called penis-water and vagina-water.

be continued right up to birth; in the last weeks it is generally performed *a retro* lying on the side.

It would be tedious to give a complete list of the pre-natal precautions to be observed, but the following are some typical examples. If either of the parents are engaged in making a fence he or she must do the whole work by himself; otherwise the baby cannot be born properly. The father must not take any fish out of a trap in the river or the child will be born with its nose stopped up. Neither parent must lock up anything except their own box or the child will not be able to be born until what is closed is opened; even the house door must not be fastened. Neither parent may eat animals which have met their death by accident or by being killed by a wild beast; the father must never look at a recently killed animal; he can kill animals but must run away at once. The father must not touch the iron or rope of a horse's bridle; should he do so the mother and child are liable to die, but this can be prevented if a bridle is kept in the house which can be *pék* over the woman during delivery. If either parent should be weaving a mat or cloth he or she must never quite finish it but must leave a little bit over. The mother must not eat any joined fruit such as a double banana or the child's toes will be webbed. Neither parent must stick poles into the ground or tie knots or drive in nails or put small stones into the cracks between bigger stones when building a wall; all of these prevent proper delivery. Expectant parents must not look at a solar or lunar eclipse or the child will be born dead; in the case of a solar eclipse both parents must stop in the house all day. If a child has recently died the paths it used to walk in and its house must be avoided; and as a general precaution it is better to avoid the paths and houses of all recently dead people. Expectant parents must not watch a dog being born; if they do so the child will have one eye smaller than the other. If expectant parents move a sacred image the child will be born dumb. Should either parent look at or kill a field-mouse or should they eat rice which has stuck to the bottom of the cooking-pot the placenta will not descend. There are a very great number of prohibitions similar to those listed above; the second half of pregnancy is a period of constant watchfulness for both parents.

There is a disease called *tamdit* which afflicts expectant parents; one loses all appetite while the other eats voraciously. This does not affect all people and may strike either sex.

The sex of a child is fixed after five months; and one can tell whether the infant is a boy or a girl by the fact that a boy is always higher in the womb. The sex can also be diagnosed by a Mun at about eight months when the Mun *péks* the body of an expectant mother.

The sex of a child is, however, not really fixed; its sex can be changed for that of another child in the womb either with the consent of the parents or surreptitiously. This is done very simply by a pair of expectant fathers or mothers exchanging any article. Tafoor's two middle daughters should really have been boys; when his wife was carrying the eldest daughter who was then a son, a lama from some way away asked him to change; Tafoor refused, whereupon the lama surreptitiously exchanged tassels on his rosary. The result was that a daughter was born, but with a boy's character which will continue until she has slept with a man; she climbs trees, kills birds, makes bows and arrows and has a large frame more like a boy than a girl; she is indeed considerably taller than her brother Chimpet, who is two years older. The second boy-in-the-womb Tafoor exchanged voluntarily with his younger brother Chudo, who had already had one daughter and whose wife was pregnant with another daughter; the exchange was successful for both parties. This exchange, however, cannot be performed if the two pregnant mothers are blood relations. This belief, which is universally held, is, I think, another excellent illustration of the Lepcha attitude towards the correlation of sex and temperament; sex is a question entirely of the primary sexual characteristics and nothing more.

Quickening of the foetus is merely diagnosed as a sign of life; but if a child moves a great deal inside the womb the forecast is that when it is grown up he or she will be excessively lascivious.

Miscarrying is caused by a devil Sor *moong* and is an hereditary sex-linked disability (as indeed is difficult delivery). As soon as a woman has miscarried she, unless she is seriously ill, and at all events her husband, must carry the foetus down to the river accompanied by a Mun who will there *pék* the couple with a bunch of elephant grass to which coloured threads, two rings, a rupee and a turquoise have been attached. On returning home an animal must be sacrificed and the Mun will *pék* the couple again. The wife is considered 'unclean' after a miscarriage and must be well washed and fed on chicken soup and butter. Ordinarily after the sixth month of pregnancy the mother will be *pék* by a Mun to avoid miscarriage as a routine precaution. If a woman who has miscarried is not *pék* other miscarriages will follow. A miscarriage is merely a dead child and has no sort of moral significance. It is possible that if a woman were pregnant by a bastard she would try to hide the miscarriage; this is *nam-toak* and she and her village will be punished with storms and hail which will destroy the crops. Except in the theoretical case of a girl being delivered of a bastard in the forest and there killing it, infanticide is not permitted for any reason whatsoever; neither monsters nor deformed infants nor even incestuously begotten children will be killed.

To procure easy delivery a Mun will offer two chickens to Sor *moong* in the seventh or eighth month of pregnancy. Easy or difficult labour is considered to be a hereditary quality; a woman who after easy deliveries suddenly has a difficult one is considered either to have helped a woman in child-birth who had difficult labour, or to have eaten some of the food of such a woman. If labour is difficult a Mun and lama will be called in to find out the cause of this, which is almost certain to be the breaking of some pre-natal taboo, probably by the father. If this is discovered by divination the appropriate steps will be taken to remove the *tamtoom* by the undoing or unlocking that which had been incorrectly completed or locked. It may be noted that it is impossible to procure an abortion or still-birth by the intentional breaking of pre-natal precautions; any such act which can kill the child will also kill the mother.

About a month before delivery is expected some specially strong *chi* is prepared and put aside; this must on no account be touched by anybody until the third day after delivery, when it is served at the birth feast; and, for a month after, it is given as a specially strengthening food to the newly delivered mother. Apart from this no special preparations are made for birth, which takes place in the husband's house; all the members of the household are present at the birth, but no strangers unless a Mun or lama has to be called in to give his services to help a difficult delivery. The mother is delivered in the kitchen; a rope is suspended from the ceiling to which she clings, squatting; she may be helped by the father or parents-in-law or anybody who knows how, who will squat behind and press on the woman's breasts and belly. As soon as the baby has appeared the cord is cut and the part attached to the baby tied up; then the baby is washed in luke warm water, wrapped in a cloth, and given the breast. Anybody who knows how can cut the navel-cord—th[illegible] or father or anybody else who has experience and a small knife. Babies are not slapped to make them cry or take in air; they do so, it is said, automatically. Nothing is done to the mother's breasts to induce lactation. Considerable anxiety is felt, especially by the father, if the afterbirth is long in descending; if there is a delay the severed and tied navel-cord is attached to the mother's toe and she is then *pék* by a Mun. As soon as the afterbirth has appeared it and the cord are rammed into a bamboo container which is carefully covered with a cloth. Somebody not too nearly connected with the delivered parents will take this and either throw it into the river or fasten it high up on a tree out of the way of insects and animals; for should it be eaten the child will suffer from skin eruptions. Formerly the afterbirth used to be buried but now this is no longer done; for if it is buried in wet ground the child will get eye disease, if in cultivated ground the crops will be spoilt. One or two people said that in certain family lines the afterbirth is still buried, but I could not get any concrete examples of this practice.

If after the birth the blood does not flow freely a blood clot will be formed; to remove the clot the mother is given hot soup and drinks, and fish boiled in butter; if the clot does not come down she will die.

If labour is difficult a fowl and a goat should be sacrificed; the mother must eat the fowl by herself. The goat's heart, lungs, and liver must be boiled and hashed and mixed with rice and offered to the gods and devils; the rest of the meat belongs to the officiants.

It is believed that with breach presentation it is impossible for the baby to be born alive and it is rare that the mother should survive this; it is due to one of the parents having tied up a packet at one end to carry food and then, instead of taking the food out of the mouth, to have taken it out of the tied end. It is good if a new-born baby has hair, but should a child be born with a tooth in its head (a thing unheard of) that baby will be an incarnate devil. It will be reared, but when it grows up its thoughts and curses will be able to kill people. No cases are known of a child born in a caul; if it did occur it would be lucky. A child is unaffected by being born with a strangulating cord; it is the *tamtoom* of one of its parents having twisted a rope or string round their neck in the later stages of pregnancy. Birth-marks vary in their significance according to their place and colour. Big splodgy birth-marks show that in its former incarnation the child was a cow; red marks on the hands and arms that the child was formerly a killer of men—a soldier or murderer. Marks with no definite significance show that the expectant parents had daubed their bodies or faces with paint.

Multiple births are excessively rare. There is one case of girl triplets being born in the neighbourhood, but none of them survived the age of three months. Twins are also very uncommon; twins of the same sex are considered lucky; if they are disparate it is lucky if the girl is born first; should the boy be born first it is bad and the children will die young. It is a cultural axiom that it is desirable for the first child to be a girl as she will be more help to the mother with subsequent children. But this axiom presupposes large families which are now uncommon; and many people have said to me that, though most people would prefer their first child to be a girl, they personally would prefer a boy, so as to be certain of having an heir, and somebody to live with them and look after them in their old age. It is also a cultural axiom that a father is more pleased at the birth of a daughter, and the mother at the birth of a son, and it is expected that parents will prefer their children of the opposite sex, but this is by no means always borne out in practice.

A still-born infant will be immediately taken down to the river by two or three friends of the parents; a Mun will prepare a bunch of stinging and prickly plants and will wait for the carriers to return, so that he can *pék* them some way away from the house. In such a case the mother's milk will be expelled on to a hot stone to dry up the flow; she cannot nurse other babies as her milk would be harmful for them.

Still-born babies and infants reincarnate immediately as the devil Ing-bong *moong*, and in this guise try to kill other children by giving them infantile diarrhoea. Ing-bong *moong* takes the form of a 'small wind' (probably a dust devil) and makes a noise first like a bird and then like a child. If two people together come across one they can dispose of it in the following way; one will chase the 'small wind' towards the other who will hack it with his knife when it arrives. If on the morrow a dead insect is found at the spot where the wind was it is a sign that the devil is dead.

Should the mother die in child-birth, there is considered to be little hope of saving the child, unless there happens to be a nearly related woman willing and able to nurse the baby. If the baby is three weeks old or over when its mother dies it may be reared on cows' milk; this is given in a cup through the stem of a plant which, when the outer bark is removed, resembles an indiarubber teat.

CHILDREN

Six-year-old girl, Pankek, with her sickle.

Four-year-old girl with her necklace with the snail-shells on, so that her soul can escape from devils. On the right the little packet with her sloughed navel-string.

Milk may also be given to such orphans by the feeder taking it into his or her mouth and squirting it into the baby's. Two boys in Lingthem were artificially reared in this way. If the mother and child both die the child is placed in the mother's lap before the body is disposed of; similarly if the mother dies in the last months of pregnancy the foetus is ripped out and placed on her lap before burning or burial.

Children normally witness the birth of subsequent siblings and of other children born in the house. Except for one nervous adult, Jiroong, who said he was frightened when his younger sister was born, children do not seem to regard child-birth with any deep emotion. Twelve-year-old Ribu voiced the general sentiment when he said that during birth he was not frightened, though he was anxious for his mother. Children take birth in a very matter-of-fact way; 'first of all a woman becomes pregnant and then she puts out a child'. Only adopted children or only children who have not had occasion to witness child-birth surround the situation with any emotion or curiosity.[2]

ii

For the first three days of life the baby is considered to be still in the womb and all the pre-natal precautions have to be observed. It is not even referred to as a human child; it is called a rat-child. During those three days the mother must on no account touch the ground; were she to do so the blood clot would not descend. The father may go out but must not do heavy work such as lifting stones or cutting trees; such actions would cause the woman pain in her belly. Also nobody except those who live in the house must enter the house or see the child; should they do so the mother will have terrible pains. If the mother has recovered she can do ordinary household work. After the birth feast on the third day the mother may go outside as soon as she feels that she is strong enough to do so; no ceremony marks the first going out of a newly delivered mother, though for the first month she is fed on a special strengthening diet of chicken soup and extra strong *chi*.

On the third day the baby is officially born and a special birth feast is held for it. Before strangers enter the house the floors are scrubbed with wormwood plants, and incense burnt, and every member of the house washes his body, first in hot water indoors, and then in a stream, and also his clothes, to remove the uncleanness

[2] See Chapter Fifteen, p. 390.

of birth. The mother is also washed on the third day and should be dressed in a new cloth, or if the family is especially poor, in a properly cleaned and good one. After this the mother is washed every three days for a month. The baby is washed in luke-warm water morning and evening. For the third-day feast the mother sits in a corner of the kitchen with the baby wrapped in a piece of white cloth on her lap.

The first person to arrive at the house must be a Mun; if a Mun has been employed to assist in delivery the same one must officiate at the birth feast. A chicken is killed and boiled and cut in half and placed on a *lafét* with other offerings. When the *lafét* is ready the guests arrive. If the child is a first child or a first son many people come; but for subsequent children, especially if a good number have been born, only perfunctory ceremonial visits are paid. If the child is a boy each guest will bring a scarf and Rs. 1, if a girl Rs. –/6.[3] Nearer relations of the parents may also bring presents of chickens or eggs or rice for the mother; the money will be spent on things for the child. After the presents are given, the Mun offers the sacrifice with a prayer to the Birth god (*gek rum*); he then waves an incense burner over all who are present, starting with the parents. Then the offerings on the *lafét* are eaten by all except the Mun. It is believed that the baby will only start to sleep properly after the ceremony has been performed.

For a male child an ox, or, failing that a pig or a goat, is killed for the feast; for a girl no animal is killed but bought meat is often added to the vegetables and rice provided for the guests. Only on one occasion is an ox killed for a girl; if the parents very much desire that the next child shall be a boy, and have the means, they dedicate an ox to Narzong-*nyou*, after which the Mun goes into deep meditation at his home to persuade the goddess to make the next child a son. During the feast every guest is given three *paṭyoot* of the special 'lying-in' *chi* and as much strained rice *chi* as they can drink. There are no formalities in the presentation of a new-born child to its relations and neighbours and no fixed remarks or attitudes. It is bad mannered to speak ill of a child but its resemblance to relations may be commented on. There are no preconceived theories of resemblance of siblings to each other or to their parents; but if a child looks strikingly like a man who is not

[3] No equivalents in kind were told to me for these cash presents, which suggests that the discrimination in favour of male children is of very recent origin.

its father it is a strong presumption that the begettor of the child is the person to whom it bears so striking a resemblance.

Some time during the day and usually fairly early the child's horoscope is cast by a lama. For this the lama may be summoned to the house or the father may go to visit the lama with 14 lbs. of *chi*. The approximate hour of birth must be noted for the proper casting of the horoscope. A lama may cast the horoscope of his own child. In this horoscope will be found the child's 'sacred name', what ceremonies are necessary to be performed by the parents to avert any threatened evils and also the future career of the child. The colour of the sash given to the child depends upon the forecast of the lama; thus a baby who is going to be a lama will be given a yellow cloth, a hunter a red cloth, and so on.

A woman whom the baby will call 'aunt' ties on its wrists three threads, one black, one white, and one red to which a snail shell is attached. When the child gets a bit older and stronger the snail shell is put on its necklace. This snail shell is a refuge for the baby's soul when the baby is sleeping; for like its owner the soul cannot move quickly and if it is frightened or pursued by demons it may not be able to get back into the body in time; therefore the shell is provided for the soul to crawl into; the demon cannot pursue it there. This snail shell is worn until the baby throws it away of its own accord. The bracelets of coloured thread will be left on till they drop off; if they get too tight they will be enlarged. At the same time the child is given a little necklace; if it is a boy the necklace will have three small beads of turquoise, if a girl three small beads of coral. To this necklace is attached the child's navel-string when it sloughs off; if it sloughs off before three days have passed it means that the child will die young; but if it stays on longer than a week it is a bad omen and means that the child will probably be foolish. The sloughed navel-string is tied up into a piece of cloth and attached as a tiny packet to the necklace. It is very bad indeed if the child should lose this sloughed navel-string before it throws it voluntarily away; if it does so as soon as it is able to crawl it will go looking for it everywhere, scratching about in the ashes and upsetting the cooking stones, and will always have its eyes on the ground and be unobservant. On the third day also the child's occiput is smeared with butter and soot scraped from the bottom of a cooking-pot to make the fontanella close; this precaution is absolutely essential. I was told that the mixture is only put on once, but it was clearly visible on a child over a year old.

Some time during the ceremony the child is given its first name. This may be given by the officiating Mun, or suggested by anyone else present. Usually the father invites suggestions. Unless the child has some physical peculiarity or some peculiar circumstance connected with its birth the first (temporary) name is usually the day of the week on which it was born, in Tibetan.

Either three, seven, or twenty-one days after delivery the husband copulates with his wife ritually, on the side and *a retro*, moving very slowly and gently, so that the semen may take away the pains of child-birth. If this is done after three days, it is called *sak-non mon-lok*, if after seven *tang-bong zaam*. It is only put off after seven days at the request of the wife, and there is no name for a later performance. Copulation *a retro* is fairly usual, though some people dislike it; it is considered more discreet than the normal position and is used when quietness is desired, and to avoid being noticed.

iii

For the first two days the baby is fed exclusively on its mother's milk; on the third day, at its birth feast, it is given a tiny pellet of pounded rice mixed with butter; and thereafter it is given a small bit of this mixture three times a day. At about the age of eight months it is given a little cooked and pounded rice, and after that the solid part of its diet is gradually increased. Babies are not usually weaned until the birth of the next sibling, and there is usually an interval of three to four years between births; consequently the greater number of children are on a completely solid diet before they are weaned. It sometimes happens that the mother becomes pregnant again fairly quickly; in such cases the babies are fed on cows' milk and rice, a diet which produces pot-belly. This is exceptional, and only a couple of babies are thus malformed.

In the greater number of cases children are old enough to understand talk before they are weaned, and they are told that they cannot suckle any more because the new baby wants the milk; if the child will not accept this the mother smears her breasts with the new baby's excreta to disgust the older child. Children are always told that the new-born baby is Sang-rong *moong*, who is a bogey the size of a small child specially invented to frighten children; this is done to prevent young children handling the new-born infant, and also to scare them into renouncing the rivalry for the mother's breast.

On occasion weaning is accompanied by physical separation.

Jiroong, who has extraordinarily precise memories of his infancy said that 'he was three when his sister was born. He was taking his mother's breast till the birth, which he witnessed and which frightened him very much. He was told that the new baby was Sang-rong *moong*. He was weaned in two ways; his mother's breasts were smeared with excrement, and a sister of his father took him away to her home and told him he must not cry because "San-rong *moong* was with his mother and would eat him". He remembers vividly that for a week he cried every night for his mother's breast, and then resigned himself to doing without. For some time his aunt looked after him, sometimes keeping him with her at her house, and sometimes going to his home and sleeping with him.' In the same way Tobgé's wife had sent her son, aged a little over two, to live with her parents in their village a day's journey away. Since she was not pregnant again this conduct was disapproved of; it was considered to be a further illustration of Tobgé's irresponsibility and her immorality.

Normally a child is only suckled by its mother, but if the mother dies, or for any other reason becomes incapable of suckling the child, it may be suckled by another woman whom the child will call 'mother', or occasionally by the grandmother. A child does not have more than one nurse at a time, and would not be given a feed by a lactating woman during the mother's temporary absence. The reason given for this is that in taking another woman's milk the child would contract a debt which it would never be able to repay; and this debt would be a burden to it after its own death.

It is a general Lepcha belief that any woman who has once borne a child can produce milk spontaneously when a baby sucks; and this seems to be borne out by the fact that on occasion if the mother dies the grandmother will suckle the grandchild. I myself saw Kurma's mother-in-law suckling her granddaughter, though it was over twenty years since she herself had borne her last child. Some women too can produce milk without having borne a child; at first this milk is indigestible for the infant, but it is subsequently perfectly all right. If the mother dies the husband's breasts will very often swell; but they only produce a sort of lymph and not proper milk. As far as my observations and inquiries go it seems clear that Lepcha women lactate with far more facility than European women.

A youngest child will continue sucking until the mother's milk dries up, or until the child 'becomes ashamed'; this may continue up to puberty. Gongyop's only surviving son took the breast until he was ten; and Pursang, Chano's second 'son', was suckled by a childless aunt[4] until her death, which occurred when he was eleven.

Babies are nursed continuously whenever they cry. Very young children are held in the mother's arms and she nurses them standing; but when the babies get a certain control of movement the favourite nursing position is for the mother to sit cross-legged while the baby lies freely on its back in the mother's lap. The mother leans forward slightly so as to bring the breast within reach, and supports the baby slightly with one arm. The suckling situation is pleasant and comfortable, but save perhaps for patting the baby's bottom gently with one hand the mother does not pet or play with the child and will usually talk to people standing by while the baby is drinking. I never saw a mother withdraw the breast until the baby had quite finished. At night the baby's bedding is so placed as always to be within reach of the mother's breast.

After the age of about ten months a baby does not cry for food if it is in its mother's arms but claws at the front of her dress in an attempt to undo it; only if the desired food is then withheld does it start whimpering. If it is being held by other people, whether men or women, it will also claw at the front of its carrier's clothes; if the mother is absent the baby can often be quieted by letting it lay its head against the warm body of its carrier.

Nursing mothers should not eat bones or other hard things or else they will lose their teeth; apart from this there are no diet restrictions unless the baby falls seriously ill (accidents, infantile diarrhoea or teething trouble are not considered serious illnesses). In such cases the mother must avoid salt, meat, and *chi*; divination will discover whether wet or dry rice is more suitable for her, and she will live on that together with buckwheat, a *lavatera* leaf, and butter. Besides this she has to avoid sitting in the sun or in damp places. None of these restrictions apply to the father.

During the first year of their lives young children are washed in warm water morning and evening; after that they are washed once

[4] I was told that this woman had never borne a child, but the people who told me about her were not near relations, and it is possible that she had borne a still-born infant or one who had died very young. The death of very young children is not taken much notice of, and often not remembered except by the parents. The three people I discussed the matter with however all declared that this aunt had never borne a child.

a day until they can walk and look after themselves. Except at these washings the baby's body is not cleaned. Children do not usually have any fitted clothes until they can walk, but are instead wrapped in loose cloths.

The teaching of sphincter control is meant to start at the age of three months when the children are taken out on to the balcony at regular intervals; they should learn to cry when they want to be taken out and by the time they can crawl should be able to crawl there by themselves. This is, however, an ideal rather than a real statement; sphincter control and bodily cleanliness are not regarded as of emotional importance, and some quite big children refuse to accept the discipline and excrete inside the house, especially if the house has bamboo flooring. Children aged three or over who cannot or will not learn sphincter control are considered to show a bad prognosis; when they grow up they 'will show forth a bad heart (disposition)'. If big children are dirty they may be given a smack or other slight punishment; but as often as not no notice will be taken and the dirt just cleared away by some older person. Only if the child spoils or dirties somebody else's property will he be severely punished. When a child can move about by itself it is taught to go outside to relieve itself; it is always accompanied by an older person till it is quite big to keep away the scavenging dogs and pigs. It is cleaned, and taught to clean itself with sticks and leaves.

Lepchas say that children should start noticing things at two months, start crawling at six months, stand when they are a year old, and walk three months later. This time-table seems to me to be in point of fact over-quick and none of the children under eighteen months that I saw could walk. The child is helped to stand and walk a little by its elder siblings. If a baby learns to walk early it is a sign that the next child is coming soon. Children are not expected to talk until they are two years old, and certainly not before they can walk; but they understand certain baby sounds, such as *ka-ka*—don't—*aah-dji*—take care—and *bam-bam*—keep quiet—in their second year.

The baby's first tooth should appear at the age of eight months and it should have all its milk teeth within the year unless by any misfortune a pregnant woman has looked at the baby, in which case the baby will not teeth until the woman is delivered and her child also teeths. It is most important that with a boy the teeth should come through the lower jaw first and with a girl through the upper. Should the contrary occur it will indicate that the child is a victim of the evil supernatural Sumoo Thor. When such people grow up all their domestic animals will fail; if the child is a girl her husband will die young and she will be left an early widow; if a boy all his children will die in infancy. There is no unanimity as to whether parents would inform their children when they grow older of such evil prognosis; the general opinion is that though parents themselves would not tell the children the elder siblings are liable to know of the fact and to mention it in the course of family squabbles. Tobgé's sister is believed to have Sumoo Thor as she has pointed teeth in the front of her lower jaw. People have teased her about this but she has replied that she 'doesn't care, and anyhow her odd teeth are the result of a *tamtoom* and have nothing to do with Sumoo Thor.' There is nothing to do to avert the misfortunes from teeth arising in the wrong place; it is the destiny following a child from its previous incarnation. Similarly moles above the level of the eyes in boys and below them in girls portray the presence of Sumoo Thor; moles in the contrary positions are lucky.

A baby should not be given either bear or frog to eat or it will be late in speaking. You can tell from the way a child cries when it is six months old if it is going to be dumb or not.

Until children start walking they do not usually have clothes at all; in the house they are wrapped up in warm folded cloths, not so tightly as to restrict their movements, and usually lie on their back on the floor or raised bed-partition. For the first month or six weeks and occasionally longer they are carried in the arms; after that they are carried on the back of a parent or elder sibling. There are two positions in which the child is held on the back; the most usual is a semi-foetal one with the enveloping cloth catching the child under the knees which are folded up to the body so that the child only touches its carrier from the knees to the feet and with the upper part of the body. Occasionally, however, children, especially when they have passed one year, are fastened with their legs spread on the hips of the carrier. The baby is completely enveloped in a big cloth folded three or four times, which goes round the baby's body and is fastened round the front of the carrier. It always needs the help of a second person to place a baby on the carrier's back; the carrier supports the baby from behind with his or her hands and the helper folds the cloth round and supports the baby while the carrier ties it. The enveloping cloth usually comes up to the neck and the baby's head lolls com-

PARENTS AND CHILDREN

Above : Chudo with his youngest daughter in the monastery porch.
Below : Tafoor, his wife, Chimpet, the eldest and youngest daughter.

pletely freely; sometimes, however, if it is sunny and the baby is sleeping the cloth will be pulled out over the baby's head so as to support the head more firmly against the body of the carrier.

For the first eighteen months or two years at the smallest reckoning the baby is continually carried when out of doors and is only put on the floor inside its own house. Unless the baby is a first or only child it should be able to walk slightly by about two years and should not need carrying after thirty months, if it is in good health. Of course if the children are ill they will be carried much later; and the youngest child, or an only child, is liable to be carried very much longer. When babies start to crawl they are usually laid somewhere near the mother while she is working, or near somebody else who can keep an eye on them. It occasionally happens that babies will crawl to the fire and burn or scald themselves; Aga's son was scalded and Chelim has a permanent scar from burning. It is, however, very seldom that crawlers get wounded in this way among the Lepchas; among the Nepali Major Morris says that there is scarcely a grown-up who does not carry scars from childhood burns.

It is considered that the use of a cradle would be fatal to Lepcha children, and they are normally never used. There is, however, one exception to this rule; the family line of Mrs. Datoop have the custom of employing Nepali cradles (these are small cradles on rockers which can be carried); she herself was reared in one and reared all her children in them. She is the most independent, self-willed, and competent woman in Lingthem; of her three sons the eldest, Pembu, is exceptionally nervous, and the other two notably independent. The daughters, who have married back into their mother's community, I saw too little of to judge. Since there is only this one family, and since Mrs. Datoop is herself such a strong personality, it is quite impossible to decide whether the use of the cradle, with its somewhat greater freedom of movement and its slight restriction of contact with other bodies, had any influence on the formation of the characters of these rather exceptional people.

Except in the first few weeks of its life a child who is not an eldest or only child does not receive exclusive attention from its mother; the mother is the only woman who feeds it, but a great part of its time is usually spent in the company of elder siblings. Children are more often carried by women than men; in a mixed family the elder daughters spend much more time looking after their younger siblings than their brothers do. If, however, the first child is a boy a great deal of the care of the next child will fall on him; Chimpet's parents accounted for his rather small stature by the fact that he had to carry his sister, two years younger than himself. This sister in her turn shared with her mother the care of the two baby girls; only when one was ill with chicken-pox, or when her mother wanted her help, did Chimpet have to act as nurse. Fathers often carry their children on their backs, especially if they are going a long journey; men nurse children, holding them in their arms or on their laps; but I never saw a baby tied on to the back of any man except their father, grandfather, or elder brother. Women on the other hand always appear willing to carry any baby, even if they are completely unrelated.

During the first few weeks the baby sleeps in its mother's arms; afterwards it is given its own mattress beside its mother, with the mother's breast always within reach. There has apparently never been a case of a mother overlaying her baby. During the first few weeks of a baby's life the parents copulate on the side and *a retro* but return fairly soon to the preferred prone position. It sometimes happens that when the baby becomes capable of movement it feels its parents' bodies and pats them while they are copulating. I have no leads as to what psychological effect, if any, this has on the children; even those older children and adults who remember lactating do not appear to remember feeling their parents copulating; I only heard about such behaviour from the parents of young children.

Children should not cry. If a child starts whimpering some attempt is usually made to find out why; if it is hungry or sleepy or uncomfortable an effort is made to gratify the desire it expresses. Should this be impossible somebody tries to distract the child's attention by waving something bright—a flower or a piece of paper—in front of it, and then giving it to the child to hold. Should this fail the baby is usually walked up and down, while the carrier gently taps its bottom; this treatment appears to be very soothing to Lepcha babies. If bigger babies cry they may be threatened that 'a Tibetan will come with his big bag to take you away, or with his dagger to kill you', and even if they do not understand the words, the tone of voice will frighten and hush it. Grown-ups and older children are quite unscrupulous in using bogies, in which they themselves do not believe, to quiet younger children. Only babies believe in the kidnapping or murdering foreigner, in the big bear round the corner, in the tiny Sang-rong *moong*.

Lepcha babies are in fact extremely quiet and I practically never heard one cry; often during the day-long ceremonies there would be five or six children under three present, and one would really not be conscious of their presence. Even when children can move about they are remarkably quiet; and the complete absence of fidgeting is one of the most noticeable characteristics of Lepcha children.

The mental reactions of Lepcha babies seemed to me very slow. Often a baby under a year old would catch hold of my finger; after about half a minute it would recognise that I was a stranger and start whimpering; but quite a little more time would pass before it would let go of me. Babies have far more confidence when they are tied on to the back of an elder person than when they are held on the lap or are on the ground. I frequently dressed small wounds and washed the eyes of babies fastened on a back without their showing the slightest fear or making any noise, whereas when they were held in the arms or seated in the lap they were much more nervous; indeed when parents brought up their babies for medical attention I found it was much easier to treat them if the babies were first put on their backs.

It is practically only after nightfall and on the rare occasions when its guardian has work to do inside the house that babies are laid on the ground. Unless its guardian can keep a constant eye on it babies under the age of three are all the time strapped on somebody's back, irrespective of the work the guardian may be doing; neither grown-ups nor elder children appear to be impeded by the burden of a baby. Lepcha babies spend a great deal of their time in the first three years of their life learning to abandon themselves completely passively to the movements of their active carriers. It is a common sight to see a woman pounding rice—a very violent exercise which necessitates alternately straining the body and raising the arms and then bending sharply almost double—with her baby strapped on her back and possibly sleeping; the baby's head lolls in every direction with each movement.

Youngest or only children are usually carried much longer than other babies and consequently have an even longer training in complete passivity. In a mixed gathering I always found it easy to spot youngest or only children, partly by their timidity and their fear of leaving their elders, and partly by their insistent demands for attention and the bad-tempered crying in which they indulged if this attention was not given—types of behaviour ordinary

Lepcha children do not manifest. The extra timidity and lack of self-reliance seems to persist amongst such children until they are themselves parents. Amongst adults I did not notice any consistent type of behaviour which would indicate an only child, but the youngest, if there were elder siblings living, seemed to carry a great deal of their attitude of reliance on their parents over to their elder siblings until relatively late in life. The Lepchas agree that a youngest child is generally the best loved and most spoilt and given the best food, but they did not consider that there was any consistent difference in character between the youngest and other children ; some might be cleverer than their elders, others duller.

Babies are very little talked to, and when they are it is usually in baby language. They are patted and kissed quite a lot. Kissing—the pressing of the lips on to another's cheek—is exclusively a pattern of behaviour between adults and young children. It forms no part of adult sexual behaviour. Adults who have been in the relationship of parent and child click their tongues at one another when they meet after a prolonged absence. Occasionally a woman will play with a baby's lips and tongue with her own tongue—a pastime both parties appear to enjoy ; but by far the most common stimulation of children is patting their bottoms while they are being carried on a person's back ; both men and women do this almost automatically when they are walking about or standing talking while carrying a baby ; the patting is gentle and rhythmic.

Until a child is fairly well developed its parents do not encourage it to acquire physical independence and body techniques, chiefly I think on account of the long distances people have to go to reach their fields ; a toddling and stumbling baby is far more of a handicap than a carried one. Elder siblings are more likely to encourage a baby in walking and balance, as the baby is a far greater burden and drawback to a child of six or seven than to an adult. The Lepchas consider that the backwardness of only children is due to the fact that they have no elder siblings to encourage and teach them.

While a baby is still at the breast its chief diet is pounded grain cooked in water or milk. When they have all their teeth they are given little pieces of meat, but only as titbits and not as the main part of the meal. They are given fruits as they ripen. After about the age of two they are given popped corn and cooked grain to nibble while they are hungry, and from about that age they start getting a sip of *chi*.

By the time a Lepcha baby is three it is already a recognisable member of its society, and the vast majority have the warm, sensuous, and fundamentally optimistic character which is typical of the Lepchas in later life. The child has an almost complete reliance on all the older members of its group ; it has been trained physically and mentally to yield to its elders, who in their turn will gratify as quickly as possible all its expressed wishes. It has come to expect from the rest of the society a rather negligent and impersonal but consistent kindness ; unpleasant sensations, and especially hunger, have been reduced to a minimum. Except under extraordinary circumstances a child is never alone nor is it allowed to cry without receiving attention. The training in cleanliness is not given any strong emotional importance, nor are any bodily functions in any way a subject for embarrassment or shocked shame ; the impetus to restraint is chiefly social approval. The child receives very early a notion of fear from the voices and expressions of those around him ; these fears are soon centred round certain words—devils, bears, tigers, snakes, Tibetans, strangers. But except for the accident of death, an unweaned child is unlikely to have undergone any obviously traumatic experience ; the usually delayed weaning and birth of a younger sibling is likely to be the first really frightening experience. To my mind the chief formative influences in the earliest years of the life of a Lepcha child are firstly continuous physical satisfaction, secondly the learning of passivity, thirdly the impersonal attitude of the majority of parents, and finally the looking to elder siblings as much as, and even more than, to the parents for attention and help. The relying on elder siblings as though they were parents is certainly a major force in adult life. It is, I think, the habits and memories of this prolonged and satisfactory infancy which support the children through the less pleasant educative years of later childhood.

iv

In Lepcha an infant in arms is called *ing-ha*, a child that can walk *a-kup*. The word *ing-ha* is only used in this connection, but the word *a-kup* can be used as a suffix to any noun to indicate that the thing referred to is smaller than usual ; a *ban kup* is a little knife, a *li kup* a little house. I think this linguistic point is of importance, as an indication of the attitude held by Lepchas towards children: they are *little adults*, and as such bound by adult rules ; they are not, as with us, almost a different species with their special 'childish' rules of conduct and ways of thought. It follows that—save perhaps individually in the immediate post-infancy period—childishness is not considered an excuse either for anti-social behaviour or for stupidity; a child is capable of committing crimes as much as an adult is, and may be punished as severely, though in different ways; and, judged by adult standards, their conversation is stupid and largely meaningless.

But although in one way adults regard children as potentially small adults, they have a somewhat ambivalent attitude towards them. Children are not quite human. If they survive they will turn into proper members of society; but if they die they will turn into particularly malevolent devils—num-een *moong*. There is no assurance of survival, either realistically or supernaturally; the horoscopes always hedge on this point: 'Should he survive his tenth day, his tenth month and his ninth year . . . he will live to be seventy-one.' A child who dies before about his tenth year is treated very differently to an adult; no funeral ceremonies are held for it and the body is thrown unceremoniously into the river; but elaborate apotropaic ceremonies are performed[5] to ward away its ghost-devil; and even should a child die at a distance these apotropaic ceremonies are performed, whereas for dead adults who die abroad no sort of funeral service is performed. The more attached a child was to his home and family, the more vigorously will his num-een *moong* attempt to reduce the other members to the same state as itself. Consequently a child represents potential supernatural danger. A dead infant turns into ing-bong *moong*, which is far less dangerous and much easier to get rid of.

The attitude of parents towards a child between the ages of about four and ten are therefore twofold: the child is a potential adult, but one in need of training and education to make him a socially valuable adult; at the same time the child is a potential source of supernatural danger, and as such it would be uneconomical to lavish too much affection on it. Should the child live it will be a great source of comfort and help; should it die it would be a source of great danger; the two contingencies must be taken into account. Finally, in the present a young child is often a nuisance and always an expense.

Some time between the child's third and fifth year—usually about the age of four—a child's achievement of physical indepen-

[5] See Chapter Thirteen, p. 352–353, also Chapter Eight, p. 233.

dence will be formally recognised by its parents in a number of ways. In their earlier years children are fed from their parents' plates, the son usually eating from the mother's and the daughter from the father's. At about the age of four the child is given a plate and cup of its own, or, if it is not given a plate, will be given its food on a separate leaf to eat by itself. At the same time a child is also given its clothes and a piece of cloth; the mother gives it a small haversack which she has woven out of nettle cloth and the father gives a boy a small knife, a girl a small sickle. These articles are the absolute property of the child and he can, if he wishes, give them away. The young child is not censured if it breaks or loses the property, for it is very young, but if it persistently spoils or loses it the property is not replaced until it is older and wiser. The actual age on which the knife and sickle are given varies very considerably with the character of the child and the disposition of the parents; some children in their fourth year had already got these implements while others in their sixth year had not. Parents manifest no sort of anxiety lest their children should hurt themselves with these instruments; and I frequently saw adults lend children of five or six their own knives, which are nearly as long as a child's leg and are quite capable of killing a man. This confidence seems to be justified, for I never saw a child badly cut by a knife, though a couple of adults came to have their feet dressed after they had wounded themselves with a hatchet. The haversack plays an important part in the child's development; every morning the mother gives it some grain which it can nibble whenever it feels hungry; actual hunger seems to play very little part in the life of the Lepcha child. By the time it has got its haversack the Lepcha child has fully developed the habit of sharing and will always give some of its grain to anybody who asks for it, and indeed if it is eating will offer it without being asked. If I was talking to or playing with children of five or six they nearly always gave me a handful of popped corn or cold rice.

With this achievement of the signs of physical independence a child's conscious education begins. As far as manners are concerned the only consciously inculcated habit is that of receiving gifts with joined hands. Children have to learn to respect the bedding and sleeping places of their grandparents, but otherwise respect for older people is not verbally inculcated; children do not usually alter their behaviour in any way on account of the presence of elder people or people of importance; when they grow older young people copy their elders in showing reverence where reverence is considered to be due.

The child's moral education or moulding is performed in two ways—by precept and by punishment. Moral axioms stressing the desirability of social approval are frequently repeated to children: 'As long as you help others, others will help you'; 'Nobody will help a thief', and so on.

If a child is naughty or tiresome—if it gets in the way, or makes a nuisance of itself, or if it excretes inside the house when it can walk out by itself—the annoyed adult will probably hit it in some way; it may be rapped over the head with the knuckles or have its ear tweaked, flicked with the fingers or cut with a switch; a man may catch it on the calves with the thin strap of his knife scabbard, a woman hit it with a stick such as is used for stirring food. These punishments for being a nuisance are given in a very impersonal way, almost as an automatic reaction to a disagreeable stimulus; a single movement is made, usually without the adult interrupting more than temporarily the work he or she is engaged on and without any verbal remonstrances or scoldings beyond that which may accompany the blow. The emphasis is on the annoyance or work caused to the adult, not on the naughtiness of the child. The punishments are always given immediately after the offence and in anger; they are given capriciously without any emphasis that they are for the child's good; children mustn't be a nuisance and mustn't cause unnecessary work. Occasionally when they are really cross people will hit a child harder than is necessary; Chimpet still carries the scar on his forehead from a blow he received from his mother when he was three or four years old; he kept on getting in her way while she was busy cooking, until she picked up a piece of firewood and hit him with it, unfortunately catching his forehead with a pointed edge. It is considered that usually one parent will punish a child more than the other, and it is generally the mother who does the most punishment. Often if one parent is cross with a child, the other will defend it: 'If both parents are angry together with a child at the same time they might kill it; if both spoil it the child will grow up naughty.'

But besides being an occasional nuisance, a child is also capable of committing crimes, and in such cases the punishment is severe and even drastic.[6] If a child steals (even fruit from the garden of a neighbour) or spoils anybody's property, or insults people or

[6] Many examples of these punishments are given in Chapter Fifteen.

METHODS OF CARRYING CHILDREN

Tafoor and his youngest daughter: Jiroong behind.

Tafoor's two middle daughters.

draws its knife in anger, if it tells lies or quarrels, it will be given a really severe thrashing, or otherwise hurt or frightened. The punishments are often proportionately more severe than they would be for a similar crime performed by an adult in order to act as a deterrent; badness is an inbred characteristic—the child is born 'with a bad heart'—and unless this badness is eradicated by education, especially from the parents, the child will become a socially undesirable adult. It is exceptional for children to be so drastically punished, and the great majority grow up without having any experience of such treatment.

At the same time as its moral education a child's technical education starts. Children are taught work techniques by being instructed to copy their elders, by verbal admonition, or by having their arms held while they are put through the appropriate gestures. Boys are especially taught agricultural work and mat weaving, girls spinning, the pounding and winnowing of grain and cooking. On occasion boys prefer to spin and do their mothers' work, and girls to copy their fathers; little attention is paid to this; as the children grow older they learn to do their proper work. There are no 'occupational inverts' in Lingthem.

From about the age of six children should be able to assist and accompany their elders in all forms of work. Boys are thought to be a little slower in learning than girls. A six-year-old girl should be an active help to her mother; boys at that age are still learning and aren't a real help to their fathers till a year or so later. When a child has acquired complete physical independence any signs of precociousness or adaptability which will make it more quickly a useful member of the household are looked for and encouraged. There are a number of household chores—particularly the fetching of water and firewood—which are considered specifically children's work; adults who have to do such jobs for themselves feel that they are slightly ill-used; it will be remembered that one of the reasons for childless people adopting a boy was to get somebody to do such work.[7] Children also do light work in the fields; a child can collect twigs and drop seeds as well as an adult.

As soon as children can talk properly adults stop using baby language to them; indeed young children are talked to very little, for it is not considered that they will be able to talk reasonably until they have lost their milk-teeth. At about the age of five children —especially the children of lamas—are taught and encouraged to

[7] See Chapter Six, p. 178.

copy their elders in prostrating themselves in front of the images of the lamaist gods, whether these gods are in the monastery or private houses.

The Lepchas are very explicit about their aims in the education of their children. Children fall into two categories—*ko-chet*, or good, and *ta-né*, or naughty. These terms are only applied to children and are clearly defined. 'A good child (*ko-chet*) will help its parents in the fields and in the house; will tell the truth and own up if it is charged with wrong-doing; will listen carefully to its elders and learn what they teach him; will help old people and will be peaceable. A bad child (*tané*) will tell lies and quarrel and insult people; if it is reproved it will draw its knife in anger and won't own up; it will take other people's property, and not do its proper share of the work.'

A child is not placed into one of these two categories early, for they are final and not temporary qualifications. The character of a young child is considered malleable, and the early years are used to evoke the *ko-chet* qualities and destroy the *tané* ones; a child is only called *tané* when it appears that education has failed. There is considerable variation of opinion as to when judgement can be finally made; some consider that a child's character is fixed at the age of eight, others that it will not completely manifest itself till the child is married; the general consensus of opinion is, however, that a child will fall into one of the two categories by the age of ten. Whatever age is chosen, it is believed that at that time, the child's character, previously vague and undetermined, is finally fixed and will not later be modified.

A child which may, if great care is not taken, later become *tané* is indicated in its earlier childhood by several characteristic traits; if it hacks at the house and door when it is given its knife, if it cries because it is scolded or because something is taken away from it which might be harmful or which does not belong to it, if it uses abusive language, these are all signs that the parents must be especially watchful. It is the parents' duty to eradicate such inborn naughtiness. A child's companions are also considered to be of great importance: 'Good companions will make a good child, bad companions a naughty one.' It is believed that excessive spoiling and indulgence by both parents may warp a child's character, but not irremediably.

If a child is not good by about the age of ten there is very little hope for it. The experiment may be tried of sending it away to be reared by strangers, but this is seldom successful. This course was tried with a boy from Lungdeum and also with Katel's eldest son; but both boys ran away and wandered all over the place, Katel's son finally dying young in foreign parts. The only person in Lingthem who was really *tané*—a quarreller and a thief—was Sangkyar, who is a cretinous defective.

V

When a child stops being a baby and becomes a young Lepcha the world becomes a more difficult place for him. Instead of being treated with a rather impersonal kindness, he is now treated with a rather impersonal neglect. He has the compensation of adult equipment—the knife and haversack which are the outward sign of physical independence—but he is also judged by adult standards; he is capable of committing adult crimes, and has to show that he possesses the adult virtues. By negative standards the children form a group; the younger ones leave the baby group to become trained to be adults; the elder ones are by their increased knowledge and initiative more and more accepted into the group of full-grown adults, as they become more self-supporting—it is considered that at the age of twelve boys and girls should be capable of doing the full work of a man or woman—and marriage arrangements are made for them. The children are not in opposition to the adults; they are not as a group ill-treated, though possibly individuals may be, except for the occasional blows they may get if they are a nuisance; they are provided with plenty of food as before; and, except for only children, or children of the very poorest parents, they have an animal or so and a little piece of ground as their private property.[8] Full adult status is a goal they have to work towards; they see this goal and the greater number of children are very anxious to grow up. This is particularly true of the boys, who have to wait longer before they can be considered fully adult; the girls attain psychological maturity much earlier, for by the age of twelve they are considered to be at their most beautiful and are usually *asék*'d; and even earlier they may become sexually conscious and realise that because of their sex they have a quality which makes them important and desirable to adults. It is only temperamentally or socially maladjusted children who appear to be oppressed by the neglect and occasional harsh treatment which is part of their

[8] See Chapter Three, p. 108.

education, and who do not see the desirable goal of full status approaching constantly nearer.

Very often shortly after their emancipation—that is round about the age of five or six—children go through a stage of excessive bashfulness and timidity. Adult Lepchas think this silly and rather funny, and, with their habitual insensitiveness to differences of character, are liable to tease such shy children—to imitate them or make remarks about them in front of their faces. This bashfulness passes off gradually; boys generally get rid of it earlier; with girls it may last till marriage.

Between about the ages of five and twelve little girls spend much more time with their parents than little boys. Both boys and girls are with their elders nearly all the time that there is work to be done in the fields, but in the evenings and on holidays the boys are usually freer; the girls are wanted to help their mothers with the cooking and especially to mind and hold the younger siblings. The boys, especially if they have no sisters, may be wanted for the same work, but most of them have more liberty. A few of the girls—the tomboys—like to get away to play with the other children, but adults try to discourage this as a reputation for neglecting her work to go and play would tell against the girl's chances of marriage. The same holds good, but within somewhat wider limits, for boys; a boy who spent too much time amusing himself instead of working for the household would get a reputation for laziness, which would make him an undesirable groom.

The choice of companionship for playmates is usually extremely limited; companionship is chiefly based on approximately equal age, though, if there is a choice, relations or near neighbours are usually preferred. Boys usually work and play in groups of two or three; but these groups do not appear to be constant and depend more than anything on the children being at leisure, or engaged in the same work, simultaneously.

Lepcha children have no toys, nor is there any sort of organised game. To a great extent children play by themselves; in the house they will make piles of corn cobs or amuse themselves by arranging grains in patterns (a characteristic trait of Lepcha children is a great feeling for tidiness and neatness, and a predilection for straight lines; anything which can be folded straight or arranged in lines is so done with remarkable trueness; curves do not come into childish patterns, nor, for that matter into adult construction or weaving); out of doors they will play catch with suitable flowers or fruits, or kick them about, or perhaps improvise syphons out of bamboo. Very often at feasts and large gatherings half a dozen children will play simultaneously at the same thing, but each playing by himself. At the numerous feasts and ceremonies I was present at over three months I only once saw children playing together; and this was a tug-of-war which lasted two or three minutes.

One of the chief pursuits of the older boys is the imitating of bird calls and the catching of small birds, usually in bamboo and thread snares. Nearly every boy over the age of nine could imitate bird calls accurately through whistling, and some of them were extraordinarily good at it; Chimpet in particular was so exact that unless I looked I could never tell whether it was a boy or a bird calling. Besides this direct imitation of bird calls, which is often used to lure birds to snares, the Lepchas have nonsense-syllable equivalents (similar to our *tu-wit to-whoo*), most of them extremely unlike the calls they represented, though the Lepchas maintained they were accurate. If the boys catch edible birds in their snares they take them home as presents to their mothers. A few of the older boys also learn to make and play bamboo flutes, receiving instruction from some older brother or friend.

When children do play together it is always an imitation of adult life (the one rare exception is the imitation of fighting animals). The courtyard outside the house is the favourite scene for these plays; using small sticks or bamboos which they cut with their little knives they play at building houses or making bridges or at fencing fields; at other times they may intimate a marriage or the performance of some religious ceremony. These plays are relatively rare, for they demand the simultaneous liberty of four or five children, which does not occur very often. They hold very little place in the childhood memories of adults. The chief things adults seem to remember from their childhood are physical mishaps, usually from falling, and being punished; nearly all adults remember being carried by their elders before they could walk properly.

Children between the ages of five and ten have a special almost private vocabulary which they use in talking to one another and which is much employed in their plays. Part of this vocabulary is baby words—deformations of ordinary Lepcha speech and onomatopoeic words; the rest is made up of rather violent terms of abuse—*pahoo zo*, may you be a feast for devils!, *kan-tit*, heap of dirt !—and so on. As a child grows up he will completely abandon this language, and older people seem quite honestly to forget it. Rather like English preparatory school slang, these words only have currency during a few years of the life of the individual ; they are taught to the young recruits of the childhood-group, and dropped as the child takes his place amongst the grown-ups : they are always in currency but unused and ignored by three-quarters of the population.

A certain number of these plays are sexual ; thus the play of marriage always ends in simulated copulation ; if the 'bride' is another boy, the children tie their penises together. From about the age of ten children at marriage feasts and similar gatherings are likely to sort themselves into pairs and attempt copulation ; there is also a certain amount of mutual masturbation among boys. (Everybody, young and old alike, denied the practice of adolescent masturbation, and since they were perfectly frank on all other questions I have no reason to suppose that they were not telling the truth.) Adult Lepchas consider such sex-play extremely funny, though very childish ; far from disapproving of the children, they are more likely to egg them on.

A ten-year-old child should know perfectly well the permissible and forbidden sexual partners in the neighbourhood ; there is the general prohibition against sleeping with *num-neu*, and usually also a catalogue of permissible partners. In point of fact there is considerable variation of the age at which the incest barriers are recognised concretely ; some nine-year-old children knew their relationship to everybody in the village, while twelve-year-old Ribu, for example, though he knew that he must not sleep with his *num-neu* was quite vague as to what people were actually included in that term. Ribu's ignorance may possibly be explained by the fact that his father was dead ; it is essentially the rôle of the father to instruct his son in the rules of incest, and possibly Patek, his seventeen-year-old brother, had not done so.

Although adults never play with children, the children showed great pleasure when I used to play with them, and after I had been in Lingthem about six weeks used to manifest obvious excitement at my arrival, and if I was engaged in something else would do all they could to provoke me to play with them. The chief game that I used to play was to pretend to chase them ; I would make one or two menacing steps in their direction, whereupon they would run about a quarter of a mile away, shrieking with laughter, and then come back from another direction, often beating a home-made drum or singing some Lepcha equivalent to 'Who's afraid of the big bad wolf?' It may be remarked that a show of violence or a threatening gesture is always greeted with laughter by Lepcha children, whether made by an adult or another child; a cross voice on the other hand will quieten them at once and make them stop whatever they are engaged in.

There were some rather curious sidelights on these chasing situations. Chudo's four-year-old son was sadly torn between expectant pleasure and fear; he could see that his elders enjoyed being chased and rather felt he would like to be himself; he used to peep round obstacles at me and would invent errands for himself which would make him run quickly round me in a semicircle; but if I took any notice of his overtures and made a menacing gesture he would start to cry. Although he never got quite courageous enough to let himself be chased by me, he ended by having considerable confidence in me; and one day when he fell down and grazed himself he stopped crying as soon as I picked him up.

At the other end of the childhood range boys of fifteen and sixteen looked as though they would like to join in the game, but felt that their dignity should prevent them doing so. Patek, Ribu's elder brother, was particularly torn; he was seventeen, married, and, owing to the recent death of his father, the head of the household of six people, including two grandmothers; at the same time the desire to play was very evident and once or twice when there were no witnesses he joined in. Datoop's youngest son, aged sixteen and engaged, was in a similar state, but he yielded more often. On the whole the girls did not play much; the greater number of them were usually looking after a younger sibling and the girls tagged along with their mothers much more than the boys did. One girl, however, very much wanted to play. This was Prumtu, the fifteen-year-old daughter of Dunbi, and Tafoor's stepsister, who was afflicted with a very bad squint. This girl was the one really unhappy child in the village. Nobody liked her and she did not live at home but with her stepbrother, Tafoor, where she was a very unimportant portion of the large household. She had not yet been *asék*, partly because of her deformity and partly because she had the reputation of being lazy—*bla-bla-bla* as Chimpet said of her—and disobedient. She was a girl of singularly ungraceful and violent movement and was very rough; in play she would pinch people really hard and did not seem to distinguish between mock violence and real violence

The only times she appeared happy were when somebody would give her a baby to nurse. She was always begging mothers to let her hold their children; the request was comparatively seldom granted; when it was she was completely happy for a few minutes. The adults thought my playing with children, or indeed taking any notice of them, extremely eccentric; they were, however, quite amiable about it.

Even before they attain to physical independence Lepcha children know about devils, and nearly all their fears are centred round them. They are quite unscrupulously threatened with devils whenever they are naughty. The bogies which particularly frighten children depend partly on individual choice and partly on the emphasis given by elders. The childish ghost-devil num-een *moong* is feared by all children, and a great number claim to have heard it moaning; other favourite bogies are Tong-ryong *moong*, who looks like a tiger and runs after and kills people, Mi-toor, the unkillable dog, and other theriomorphic devils. As far as I can make out these fears are not obsessive; for one thing they are shared by every member of the community, and hand-in-hand with the idea of devils is learnt the capacity of the priests of the two religions to deal with them. The idea of devils is most frightening if a child is alone in the forest by day, or alone in the house by night; everybody is rather frightened of devils in the forest after nightfall. It very rarely happens that a child is left alone at night; and children are not frightened of the dark in their own homes (except sometimes very young ones) for they always sleep in practically complete darkness. If a child alone in the forest thinks he sees or hears a devil his only course is to run home as soon as possible.

Open fear of devils is considered a childish trait, and a person claiming to be considered as an adult will deny fearing them any more. The chief sign of a child overcoming what is considered to be its excessive fear of devils is when it voluntarily throws away its necklace with the attached snail-shells and sloughed navel-string which acts as a sort of amulet. No pressure is put upon children either to make them retain the necklace or to throw it away. Chudo's eldest daughter, aged seven, who had had her sickle several years, still wore her necklace, while her four-year-old younger brother had already thrown his away.

When I asked fourteen-year-old Chimpet if he was frightened of devils he shouted 'No' in a very loud voice; if he saw one, he said, he would throw stones at it and drive it away. He admitted that when he was younger he had been a little frightened ; nowadays if his baby sisters cry he tells them that a devil will come and take them, and they stop at once. By the house of his lamaist instructor at Purfong there was a big tree which was the home of Jamfi *moong*. One evening this devil leant over the roof of the house, black and high as the sky ; his teacher burnt a bunch of herbs and smoked a cigarette at it, whereupon it took itself off to the forest, whistling as it went. The visit of this devil did not produce any untoward results, but Chimpet admitted that at the time he was a little frightened.

Besides devils most children are frightened of houses in which there has been a recent death and of burial- or burning-places, and will usually run past them as quickly as they can. This fear persists as a motive for panic longer than the fear of meeting incarnated devils ; thus twenty-two-year-old Rigya, after saying that as a child he used to run away from such places, later admitted that it was only in the last year that he was able to walk by them at an ordinary pace. Nearly all adults have a certain fear of devils when alone in the deep forest or on high mountains ; and alone in the forest everybody is frightened of snakes and wild beasts ; but these fears are perfectly rational ; people are still occasionally poisoned by snakes and mauled by bears.

It sometimes happens that smaller children will be bullied by older ones ; but this is rare, and if it does occur the children will be rescued either by their parents or elder brothers or by any adults present and the bullies will be well punished. As with other Lepcha relationships, love between siblings is not considered automatic ; it is usual however, and there is a cultural expectation that elder brothers and sisters will instruct, help and protect their younger siblings who out of gratitude will love them in return.

Those children who are going to become lamas usually start to learn to read about the age of twelve ; but here too there is no definite rule, and instruction may start three or four years earlier or later. Lepchas under instruction appear to regard their lessons as an unpleasant piece of extra work, only made tolerable by the hope of easy gain in the future. Except for future lamas or carpenters Lepchas appear to have finished most of their formal education by about the age of twelve. Children of that age could usually identify for me as many plants and trees as their elders ; children under ten usually knew very few.

Very few children have an alternative home to go to if they feel unhappy in their own; near paternal relations usually live in the same house, and maternal relations generally live far away. If, however, there is living in the neighbourhood a maternal grandfather or married aunt children can always go and pay them short visits. Thus Chimpet, who was not very happy at home and who was rather neglected in favour of the numerous younger children, used to go fairly frequently to visit his maternal grandfather, the Lharibu Chujen at the next village of Panung; sometimes he would go by invitation, either alone or with other members of his family, and at other times he would run away there of his own accord for a few days; no comment was raised if he did so. There are, however, very few children who have such an alternative home.

Only and adopted children are often very lonely, but except for these it is I think extremely rare for a child to be actively unhappy at home. The girl Prumtu was the only really unhappy child in Lingthem; after her perhaps came Chélé, who has been discussed earlier;[9] he lived alone with his old grandfather and a distantly related middle-aged woman. Besides Chélé, Pursang, Chano's second son who was for so long suckled by his aunt, occasionally threatens suicide; he has no obvious reasons for being unhappy but he is a rather difficult character, and shows some signs of turning into a bad boy, a *tané*.

For the majority of Lepchas childhood is not an actively unhappy time, but a time of obscurity, of being unimportant; children are not taken much notice of and their tastes are little consulted. But most of the children realise, though perhaps they would not enunciate it so clearly as their parents, that the obscurity and occasional harshness of these earlier years are a necessary preliminary and training for the wholly desirable goal of full adult status.

[9] See Chapter Six, p. 164–165.

CHAPTER TWELVE

SEX, MARRIAGE AND MATURITY

i

On the question of attaining sexual maturity the Lepchas differentiate between men and women far more overtly than they do in any other phase of the life cycle. Theoretically they ignore physical puberty, have no word or words to express it, and pay no sort of formal attention to its arrival. With males the achievement of full sexual potency is considered to be a slow maturing process, taking place automatically over a period of years, with actual puberty marking, as it were, a half-way stage ; though most boys produce emissions from about the age of fifteen, they are not considered to have achieved full potency till from three to five years later. With women, on the other hand, the physical signs of puberty—the beginning of menses and the swelling of the breasts—are believed only to occur through the external influence either of a man or of a supernatural named Kandoo *moong*. It is thought that normally a virgin girl will not menstruate nor will her breasts swell ; these physical alterations only take place after copulation. It does, however, occasionally—though, it is thought, rarely—happen that a virgin starts menstruating ; this indicates a visit of the supernatural Kandoo *moong*, and is considered to be a sign of good luck ; some of the older women boasted that they had thus been signalled by this supernatural. The majority of women, however, depend on the intervention of a man ; the physical signs will start whenever a girl experiences copulation, and there is therefore no stigma attached to grown men forcing little girls of nine or ten, and this does occur occasionally. It is possible that this cultural explanation of physiological processes masks a deep-seated male envy of the more conspicuous and dramatic life-giving functions of women and an attempt to make them appear dependent on male intervention. It would seem that this notion is at the base of the initiatory rites in many tribes of New Guinea and Australia, where through ritual and symbolism men attempt to arrogate to themselves women's physiological functions; perhaps the most striking of these rites is the urethral sub-incision practised by some Australian tribes. Since, unfortunately, nothing is known of the other Mongolian peoples of the Himalayas, it is impossible to state whether this notion is peculiar to the Lepchas, or whether it is shared by their Northern neighbours. The Hindus and the Nepali converts to Hinduism stress overtly the rivalry between the sexes, and adduce the inferiority of women through their magically dangerous and infectious functions of menstruation and child-birth.

Just as there is no formally marked beginning of sexual life, so there is no formally marked end of it. The menopause is ignored; the dream of copulation with a supernatural, which marks the menses, is meant to continue after it; and sexual pleasure is considered to be equally strong at any period of life. There appears to be no fear of impotence; sexual appetite and an appetite for food are openly equated, and it is considered that, except through illness or old age, the loss of one is as unlikely as the loss of the other.

Some men make a distinction between pre-puberty and post-puberty sexual activity, but this distinction is personal and not cultural. Most men, when talking of their past lives, emphasise what was their first 'real' sexual experience; but some place this first experience very early, at the age of eleven or twelve. I think the operative distinction in the mind of the Lepcha is whether the sexual adventure formed part of a play, or was undertaken seriously for its own sake.

Lepcha society gives the children a sexual rôle very early; girls are betrothed and occasionally married from the age of eight onwards, and boys from the age of twelve. In Lingthem it seems as though this very early age for betrothal has been somewhat raised in recent years; Mrs. Datoop and one or two other of the elder women in the community were betrothed at the age of eight and married shortly after; but in 1937 there was no betrothed girl aged less than twelve, nor was any young man betrothed to a girl under that age. It is quite probable that this change in the age of betrothal is local and temporary; the Lepchas did not consider that the situation had altered in any way. Even today most young people are betrothed before or at any rate as soon as they arrive at physical puberty, and consequently enter that state with an already selected sexual partner. In 1937 the only unbetrothed girl over thirteen was Prumtu; there were eight boys over sixteen unbetrothed, but of these three were mental defectives, one was a cripple, and two were carpenters just returned from the state school at Gangtok;[1] the remaining two were adopted children, and in both cases the adopting fathers said they were searching for suitable spouses.

Some of the boys and girls may have had a little sporadic sexual experience before betrothal, especially if their elder siblings of the same sex are married; but it is by no means unusual for both parties to be complete virgins at the time of betrothal. The period between betrothal and marriage is usually the time of greatest sexual adventure and promiscuity; but this naturally depends on the affection the two betrothed feel for one another and, to a lesser extent, on the distance between their two villages; a betrothed pair who are fond of one another may quite probably be sexually exclusive; where they do not get on, and particularly if there is overt hostility, they are likely to look elsewhere.

A marriage is never arranged by the parents of the child concerned; were the parents to do so either the parties would die young or the marriage would break up. In Lingthem the marriages are usually proposed by the Mandal and negotiated through the intermediary of the child's uncles and grandparents on both sides, and especially the father's elder brother, or if such a man does not exist, anyone who stands in a similar relationship. Thus, in the marriage of Datoop's children, Tafoor acted as the 'father's elder brother'; actually Tafoor is nineteen years younger than Datoop and they are four generations removed from a common ancestor (their respective paternal grandmothers were biological sisters); Datoop was an only child and Tafoor the most responsible related man of the same generation; since they are connected by females they are obviously of different *ptso*.

All the real marriage negotiations are carried on between two *bek-bu* (between-men) representing each side. Any experienced and tactful man with the exception of the spouse's father, who knows the correct things to say and the correct way to say them and has a sufficient vocabulary of *tang-bor* may take this rôle; in Lingthem the Mandal has performed this office for nearly every couple in the last twenty years, but in other villages a variety of people perform this rôle and the choice of *bek-bu* is a personal one dictated by the friendliness of the betrothed person and his family. In by far the greater number of cases the two children to be betrothed do not

[1] See Chapter Four, p. 121, and Chapter Six, p. 153.

know one another at all before betrothal. In a relatively few cases they are near neighbours, in which case the betrothal is more likely to have been arranged at the request of the boy, or the children may have met casually on visits. This is particularly liable to happen when a woman's daughters marry back into their mother's village. Before the actual betrothal visit is made an 'uncle' of the boy may take him on a visit to inspect his future spouse; the boy may be asked if he fancies the girl, but the question is really a formality, for if he says 'No' this reply is usually put down to shame, and the betrothal is proceeded with regularly.

The first preliminary to arranging a marriage is a visit of the *bek-bu* by himself to the girl's village; on this visit he will take with him a load of *chi*. He will go to some neighbouring house—never the house where the girl herself lives—and will discover what man of the village is acting as the girl's *bek-bu*; to this man he will give the load of *chi* and start negotiations for the marriage. The girl's *bek-bu* will discuss the proposition with the girl's family—particularly her uncles—but the father and mother are also unofficially consulted. As a matter of form the girl's family will belittle the match on the first conversation, saying that they do not wish yet to get rid of their daughter, that the proposed match is not good enough, and so on. If they do not know the boy proposed they will send to make enquiries about his character, as to whether he is a good and industrious worker, peaceable and generous. The girl's family will always refuse at the first discussion and usually at the second; if they have not agreed when the subject is broached for the third time the negotiations are called off. If they do agree the *bek-bu* will present them with a ceremonial scarf and a rupee and a date will be set for the formal *asék*, dependent on the lama's horoscope not being completely unfavourable. This preliminary is called *kachyoong*.

For *asék* considerable gifts are demanded, and these are called the price of the bride'. These gifts do not actually represent the chief expense of the marriage—that is involved in the marriage feast—but they are articles which are not consumed in common but which are given over to the family of the girl. After these gifts have been accepted the marriage is considered to be legitimatised, even though the groom has not brought his bride home; children born after *asék* are fully legitimate, and if the betrothal is broken, either the gifts or their equivalent in money must be returned, or another girl provided as substitute. The *asék* gifts consist of two pigs, a large copper pot, or in lieu of it Rs. 20 for the girl's father, a length of fine cloth, or in lieu Rs. 13 (formerly Rs. 20) for the mother, Rs. 3 for the bride, and a ceremonial scarf and a rupee for the girl's *bek-bu*.

When these gifts have been collected, they are consecrated by a special Mun ritual in the groom's house before being taken to the girl's family. If the house contains a lamaist altar this is decorated and *chimi* are lit, and the offerings placed before it, the disembowelled pigs in front, and behind the copper pot with the other gifts on top of it. An officiant is needed to consecrate the gifts; it is preferable that the 'sacrificer', the *rum-faat-bu*, should be a Mun, but it can also be performed by any old and experienced layman with the necessary qualification. Incense is burned, *chi* from a buttered cup and rice offered, and a long invocation is made to the gods to bless the marriage and make it fruitful; besides the personal and *ptso* supernaturals of the groom special emphasis is placed on the appeal to Komsi*thing* and Tarbong-bo, who are involved in the original institution of marriage.[2] After the consecration a ceremonial meal of rice and sausages made from the pig's intestines is eaten, and the groom then sets off with his *bek-bu* and three men to carry the presents. The carriers should be ideally a paternal uncle, a maternal uncle and an elder brother; failing them, people standing in a similar position are employed.

At this visit the groom and his party usually stop three or four days at the girl's house. The two betrothed are meant to keep together, sitting by one another and feeding one another, and to sleep side by side. At this initial meeting the attention of all the elders is concentrated on noticing the way the two young people behave towards one another; because of this attention, and on account of the general situation, the young couple are usually in an agony of self-conscious shame and can hardly bear to look at or speak to one another.

After this initial visit the *asék* party returns home, but a few days later the groom makes a second visit, taking with him a gift of meat and usually accompanied by an uncle. At this visit the young couple, if they are of a suitable age, are meant to copulate together, and their uncles are meant to supervise this operation to make sure it takes place; if they do not, the one who refuses to do so—and it is considered equally likely that the refuser will be the boy or the girl—will be severely admonished and may be thrashed by

[2] See Appendix IV. The Sacred Story of the Origin of Marriage.

his or her uncle to make him like his partner. For if the two do not sleep together the girl will not be able to 'lighten her mothers' shoulder' (that is, help her mother-in-law), and the boy will shame his parents and all the expense that the parents have been put to will be wasted. Moreover, should the couple separate, the girl's family will be blamed for not seeing that they made love.

This is another situation in which the Lepchas' formulation of ideal behaviour differs very considerably from their practice. Betrothal is very often a period of great emotional stress, especially for the girl who will energetically refuse to have anything to do with her proposed husband. In all the cases that came to my notice of betrothed couples getting on badly together the pair had never achieved copulation and the older Lepchas in referring to these situations always stated that the difficulties would be got over if the pair slept together—a statement which seems to be borne out by experience. But just because the girls also hold this belief they repulse their husbands with even greater energy; I am almost certain that this repulsion is actuated not by physical or emotional distaste for the husband but by a deep-seated fear of leaving their family and their surroundings. In such situations the Lepcha theory calls for physical punishment of the recalcitrant party, but Lepcha practice makes such behaviour very unpleasant. The result is a good deal of threatenings and grumblings and no actions at all. In such situations those adults not directly responsible for the behaviour of the children are full of loud talk as to the energetic steps which should be taken; the responsible adults are full of excuses for putting off the crisis until another occasion.

In Lingthem in 1937 there were five boys or young men who were *asék*'d and three who had only had their wives home a few weeks or months. Of these, three had had very stormy betrothals in which the hostility had lasted for several years. In one case, that of Nariya, who was thirty years old (he had been married earlier but the marriage had broken down because of the girl's promiscuity followed by her running away with all the available valuables and cash), this hostility continued even after the performance of the marriage feast and a peaceful settlement only approached during the last days of my stay there. Nariya's wife was fourteen, a large overgrown girl. After three years' betrothal the marriage feast was celebrated in the late autumn of 1936. Immediately after the marriage the girl returned home and refused to have anything to do with her husband, saying: 'I do not want to see your face,' and

MIKMAR AND CHIMPET PLAYING

MIKMAR GOES OFF WITH THE *ASÉK* GIFTS TO SEE HIS NEWLY AFFIANCED BRIDE, WHOM HE DOESN'T KNOW

He is wearing his best clothes. With him are on the left Gongyop's son, with the pig on his back, and Kurma's nephew Takshyom holding a lantern, and with the copper bowl on his back; on the right Chinya, Mikmar's " paternal uncle " (really his second cousin once removed) and Chala Mandal, who is *bek-bu*. The wife lives two days' journey away. On the fence are reeds which have been bent when green drying for thatch.

exclaiming: 'May that man die!' Whenever Nariya went to visit her she used to throw stones at him to drive him away. It was said that she was carrying on a love affair with a Nepali in her distant village. On one occasion the girl's parents came to Lingthem, but Nariya was too shy to say anything. At the end of April Tempa said that he threatened the parents that if they did not send the girl he would apply to the police station. He explained that he spoke after consultation with the Mandal because Nariya's uncle Ashyok had not enough sense.

On May 11th, 1937, Nariya went to fetch his wife home; on May 17th she returned with him but bringing with her a younger brother aged twelve to sleep with her as a chaperone. On May 18th she went away again to Mangan to see her father, but she returned still accompanied by the younger brother on May 20th. On this day took place one of the bi-monthly monastery feasts and Nariya's wife took this opportunity to become formally introduced into the village community. Although she still did not sleep with her husband she seemed to be settling down and was helping in the preparations for the big annual feast of Boom koor which was to take place three days later, helping with the cooking and so on. She did not talk much but sat about quite comfortably in the groups where people made rather a fuss of her. All the time she kept some small child by her, either her own younger brother or Pankek, a little girl of six. She seemed to find comfort in the presence of young children. Tobgé was familiar with her, hugging her and feeling her breasts, but she showed no resentment. She had on a clean new green blouse but a filthy dirty skirt. The general belief was that in a day or so Nariya would succeed in sleeping with her and that then the marriage would settle down completely and happily.

Nariya it is true was not a very attractive character. He had an extraordinarily high-pitched almost eunochoid voice and a slightly sly expression. He was an orphan; his father, when he lived, was the richest man in Lingthem and a great deal of the wealth in cattle had been expended on the funeral feasts for him and many other relations of his generation who had died very close to one another. Nariya wished to regain his father's wealth and was therefore, most exceptionally for a Lepcha, engaged in strenuous economies, spending as little as he could, except when he had to give feasts, on clothes or food; he was rather secretive.

Of the other recently married men Rigya, Nariya's cousin and adopted brother, and Kutt'r were now getting on all right with their wives after a preliminary period of conflict in each case lasting about four years. Kutt'r who was eighteen years old was married at the age of fourteen to a wife one month after *asék*, before which he had never met her. She had only come to live with him in the last few months. First of all they disliked one another thoroughly; then by the pressure of their families they were brought to sleep together but did not do anything. Only in the last two or three months have they copulated together; now they like one another.

Gongyop's son was born in 1919; he is a very girlish-looking and under-developed boy and preternaturally shy; it will be remembered that he was drinking his mother's milk up to the age of ten. Before *asék* he did not know his wife; *asék* took place about six months ago. The girl is older and bigger than he and at first he was frightened of her, though she spoke nicely to him. On May 19th he returned from his third visit to her at which they had slept together. He came home with a look on his face like a cat which had just been fed on cream and seemed rather proud of himself; he said that now he likes his wife. Datoop's younger son was *asék* by proxy for his elder brother Pichi; but Pichi at the beginning of May definitely refused the marriage and instead the youngest son was going to marry the girl. On May 9th he went off with his father to pay a visit to his bride. I asked the boy what present he was taking to his parents-in-law, at which his father replied 'His present is between his legs'. He was, however, also taking a leg of meat with him. Datoop hoped that, if the harvest was good, the girl would be brought home in the autumn.

On March 19th Mikmar, Chano's eldest son, aged thirteen, was *asék*'d to an unknown girl three or four years older than himself. By May 9th he had paid the girl three visits. They are patently unable to sleep together for Mikmar is still very childish, but they get on well enough together and give each other food.

In Lingthem there were only four unmarried girls over the age of twelve; of these Prumtu, the girl with the squint, is likely to wait some time before marrying and Tafoor's eldest daughter has only just passed twelve and has not yet been asked for. The other two girls are the two eldest daughters of Pargetu, aged sixteen and twelve respectively; they have been *asék*'d to two brothers. The younger girl, Tangvoong, gets on well enough with her young husband, but the older one, Kondé, does not; the two both fight like cat and dog. This girl had a very unpleasant eruption of boils all over her face and I saw a great deal of her because she used to come up every third day to have her boils dressed; they were cured before I left. According to Tafoor, who is a very distant sort of uncle, the girl got her boils from a devil which was brought by her husband with the *asék* presents. She does not like her husband, and has so far refused to sleep with him (or, Tafoor thinks, anybody else). Tafoor considers that the fault really lies with the husband, who should have forced her to sleep with him when she came to his house; he did not, probably because he was ashamed. If she persists in not liking him she will be spoken to and given a beating to make her; it is simply naughtiness on her part.

During my stay in Lingthem Kondé was taken to visit her prospective husband once and the husband came also twice to her house to help her parents work. The situation did not develop in any way. Kondé had got set into an attitude of rebellious mutism in which she refused to do anything or to speak to anybody unless it was absolutely necessary. The only person who seemed to have any influence with her was Mrs. Datoop, who was a distant 'aunt by marriage'. Her attitude was completely mulish; so to speak, she dug in her feet and put back her ears and refused to budge. She showed no preference for anybody other than her betrothed; her attitude was entirely negative, she did not want to marry and especially not to marry the man provided for her. When she addressed him she used to use the childish abusive phrases, which have normally been abandoned and forgotten by people of her age. Kondé was a good and industrious girl and a considerable help to her parents, but she did not and would not get married. It was, I think, much more the fear of separation from her parents and home, even though she would be accompanied by a younger sister, which motivated her refusal, rather than actual dislike of her husband, who chiefly personified exile.

These examples will show that in about half the cases of betrothal there is considerable hostility on the part of the girl. For the girl marriage means nearly always geographical separation from her family—almost a second weaning—and many of them do not face this prospect cheerfully. This psychological disturbance cannot by any means be equated with puberty for betrothal may take place at any age from eight upwards. It is an intellectual and not a physical disturbance. It seems to me very probable that it is the successful overcoming of this second weaning which gives to young women so much more self-assurance than young men of similar age possess.

Occasionally the hostility to the marriage comes from the young man, but except in the rare cases where a boy is betrothed to a woman—the Lepchas do not regard disparity of age and in several marriages the wife is four or five years older than her husband—opposition is personal and not emotional. It is that particular girl which the boy dislikes, very often because he has already chosen somebody else whom he prefers. Aplung refused his wife (who was subsequently married to Rigya) because he wanted to marry Tobgé's stepmother, a woman considerably older than himself. When young men do choose wives for themselves they seem almost always to chose mature women. In the case of young boys who are *asék* to older women or who inherit them as levirate spouses the hostility is to marriage and sex as such. They simply have no desire for marriage yet. Thus, Chélé refused, or tried to refuse, to have anything to do with the wife he inherited from an uncle, and Itup, Takneum's son, refused to have anything to do with the wife he inherited when he was ten.

Although all the boys that I talked to very much wanted to be grown up, they displayed an almost uniform lack of interest in marriage. The only boy who said that he wanted to get married was Ribu, aged twelve ; and he said he wanted to get married so as to have somebody to help him in the fields. In his particular case extra help was welcome and necessary ; the household consisted of two old widowed grandmothers, a widowed mother, and an elder brother Patek, aged seventeen, and his wife ; the proportion of dependents to adult workers was particularly adverse. With the exception of Chélé all the boys over ten wanted very much to grow up, and especially to achieve complete sexual potency 'so as to be able to —— the girls properly', but marriage as such was considered as an inevitable but not particularly desirable condition of full adulthood. Chimpet based the adolescent attitude of marriage neatly in the antithesis that (*a*) marriage is a great waste of money and animals and (*b*) if you don't get married and sleep with other men's wives you will be fined.

For boys betrothal is a much more actively disagreeable time than for girls. Between *asék* and the marriage feast the groom is in a more openly dependent and humiliating position than at any other period of his life. His parents-in-law have powers of compulsion and shame over him which his own parents do not possess ; he has to visit his parents-in-law and help them with their work whenever he is summoned; incapacitating illness is the only acceptable excuse for refusing a father-in-law's order; neither personal nor family interests may stand in the way. When he is in his father-in-law's house the groom is under considerable restraint; he must be modest and circumspect in his language and behaviour and must be consistently respectful to his bride's parents and elder siblings. His wife's brothers have considerable licence to tease him and to use obscene language to him; he must on no account retort in kind; if he were to do so he would be shamed. Though his bedding is placed beside that of his bride he can only copulate with her in semi-secrecy; he has to wait until he is certain that everybody else is sound asleep, or otherwise he would be considered shameless. Even if he is on friendly terms with his bride his visits to her home are periods of constraint and humiliation; if, as so often happens, they disagree, these visits are likely to be the most positively unpleasant circumstances in his whole life. A groom can only leave his wife's family at the express permission of his father-in-law.

This period of semi-servitude is felt to be extremely disagreeable; but it is also considered inevitable, and no attempt is made to side-step it. For the parents of the groom this service with the father-in-law is to a great extent considered as the continuance and finishing of the process of education which started when the child achieved physical independence. Their attitude could, I think, be paralleled with that of English middle-class parents who send their sons away to boarding school; they realise that the boys will be less happy than they would be at home but they consider it an inevitable stage in the attainment of full adulthood.

During the period of *asék* the groom spends about half his time with his parents-in-law. The length of each individual stay depends on the distance between the two villages; if the two houses are not more than a day's journey apart about a week will be spent alternatively in each; if they are farther away, about a month. The period of *asék* varies considerably, according to the wealth and inclination of the groom's parents; marriage may be performed one month after *asék* or there may be an interval of several years; the average period is about eighteen months. It is also necessary that the lamas find an auspicious day for the marriage from their horoscope books, but that does not usually entail a delay of more than a few weeks.

ii

Betrothal does not by any means necessarily imply sexual connection between the betrothed. It does, however, usually indicate the commencement of sexual activity for both parties, and almost always for the boys. The majority of Lepcha men receive their sexual initiation and education from a potential levirate spouse—the wife of an 'elder brother' or 'uncle'—and very often at the woman's direct invitation. It is a Lepcha axiom that women never make the first advances and most people repeat this statement; but a number of men when recounting their own early sex experiences tell of direct invitation and solicitation from these potential spouses; timid Jiroong indeed was at the age of fifteen as nearly raped as it is possible for a man to be by his elder brother's wife. Fathers instruct their sons as to the women they have a right to sleep with, and the women whom, though potentially heritable, they must avoid because their fathers have already slept with them.[3] Elder brothers, too, on their marriage give their younger brothers formal permission to sleep with their wives. These legitimate copulations must be practised discreetly and nearly always take place during the temporary absence of the real spouse. It is considered desirable that a boy should first sleep with a woman older than himself so as to be taught how to do it properly. For the Lepchas there is nothing incongruous in a man sleeping with a woman twice his age, and it would seem indeed that young men find older women more attractive; in the few cases where a young man has been able to choose his own bride they have always chosen elder women. It has already been remarked that fully grown younger brothers transfer many of their attitudes towards their fathers to their elder brothers; I find it, however, impossible to gauge to what extent if any the elder brothers' wives are equated with the mothers.

Although the great majority of men receive their sexual initiation from an elder sister-in-law, a few have their first experience with contemporaries. Thus Chimpet has twice slept with a girl of his own age at Parfok at her invitation; he enjoyed the experience and would like to repeat it, but does not want to marry the girl because he does not like her. Similarly Rigya was seduced at the age of fifteen by a girl of the same age in a neighbouring village;

[3] See Chapter Six, p. 153.

it was not her first experience, though it was his. Subsequently his parents tried to betroth him to her, but she was already bespoke.

I unfortunately was not able to obtain as much or as precise detail on the early sexual life of women as I was of men;[4] from such information and reports as I was able to gather it would seem that potential sororate spouses play a much smaller rôle in the initiation of young girls, chiefly no doubt because they generally live some way away. When they are not deflowered by their spouse (this happens sometimes) girls would seem to start their sexual life with unrelated men, often it would appear with visitors to their village. Among the Lepchas the difficulty of talking to women on such subjects was not, as more usually happens, the jealousy of the husbands, but the fact that almost every woman from eight to eighty interpreted any sort of special attention as an attempt at seduction, an attempt which—no matter what their youth or age—they had no intention of repelling.

Until the husband brings his wife home, and indeed till the birth of the first child, Lepcha men and women have complete sexual freedom at every point where this freedom does not endanger the social fabric; that is to say that all potential partners outside the stringent incest categories are permissible, provided that adultery, as the Lepchas understand the term, is not flagrant, continuous or emotionally important. After the birth of the first child adultery—that is to say connection with a woman who is not a potential wife—on the part of the father is thought to endanger the life of the child or children. Except for casual encounters at the forest or at feasts my impression is that adultery is uncommon, and that copulation with permitted partners only takes place intermittently in the absence of the actual spouses.

Lepcha sexual experience can be divided into four categories: legitimate copulation with one's spouse, which almost always takes place in the house; semi-legitimate copulation with potential sororate and levirate spouses, which usually takes place either in the house during the husband's temporary absence or in casual encounters in the forest or field-houses, since it is considered tactless to allow the husband to witness such copulations; thirdly, intrigues with unmarried girls which entail clandestine visits by the young man by night; and, lastly, sudden and clandestine encounters

[4] I was told the precise details of the early sex experience of at least half the men of Lingthem, but only three or four of the women. It was one of the most popular subjects of conversation among the men at the monastery feasts.

which may or may not be adulterous, in the fields or forests or at big feasts. The last-named are always excessively hurried and rather romantic; hurried because there is the fear of being surprised and romantic because they are unforeseen and unprepared. Occasionally to seduce an unmarried girl men will promise to give them presents of money and clothes and they will do so if the woman consents; she will either tell her parents that she has bought the new clothes, or, if this is too improbable, that she has borrowed them. If the woman refuses, men do not insist. It quite often happens that a girl will give her lover small presents—straps she has woven herself or food smuggled out of the house in her dress. It is said that presents are not given to seduce married women.

If unmarried and unrelated men and women wish to sleep together, the man will find out from the girl her exact sleeping position in her house; then at his own home he will wait till he can hear everybody sleeping, creep out on hands and knees, run to her home, which may be a couple of villages away, and creep in beside her. He must return to his own home before cockcrow. Normally if a man is surprised he will run away and not come back again; but it occasionally happens that these originally clandestine intrigues become socially recognised and the lover goes to live, either temporarily or permanently, with his mistress, particularly if the latter is past the age of childbearing. Thus Patek's 'elder grandmother', the sixty-six-year-old Nandjému, has as paramour a lover of the same age, a lama who travels round the country making prayer wheels; whenever he is in the neighbourhood of Lingthem he lives with the old woman as her husband. Similarly Kurma lived with his first wife, Gongyop's sister, for some years before he married her.[5] If the wife is of childbearing age she will more often go to live with her lover, especially if he is a householder in his own right; thus Tobgé's sister lived with Nahyeun, Tempa's sister with Jiroong, and Ongden's second wife with her husband for considerable periods before their marriages were legitimised.

Sex does not form part of the Lepcha pattern of hospitality, but if a visitor can make his own arrangements this is agreeable to all parties. In such cases once the visitor has got the girl's consent to sleep with him he learns from her the exact position of her sleeping place, and visits her as quietly as possible as soon as the rest of the company are apparently asleep.

[5] See Chapter Fifteen, pp. 398–399.

The Lepchas have not elaborated seduction in any way, and the verbal intricacies which are employed on formal occasions are not used for it. In most cases the man usually asks the girl in so many words if he may sleep with her; if she refuses at first there may be a little pleading and persuasion; but, except when they are very young, girls do not appear usually to refuse. Courtship barely exists among the Lepchas and no preliminary stimulations in the way of kisses or embraces are employed, though a man may fondle a woman's breasts immediately before copulation; fondling of the breasts in public is considered slightly shameless but rather funny; it is the equivalent to a direct invitation. Sexual desire is not believed to need any provocation; nakedness is not considered in any way exciting or stimulating; one or two men said they were excited at the sight of a woman's naked thighs; but for the majority immediate anticipation is the only stimulant. Neither sex indulges in any obvious exhibitionism when sober (men, especially older men, sometimes uncover their genitals when drunk) nor in any special coquetry.

There is no overt jealousy on the part of fathers or brothers towards the lovers of their sisters or daughters; and it is considered that men have no call to interfere in the sexual life of their female blood-relations unless an unmarried girl produces a bastard. Fathers will generally warn their daughters to be circumspect on this account when they think they have reached an age when this becomes possible; but it was agreed that unless a girl were pregnant a father would have no justification in being angry with her or the man if he discovered his daughter with a lover.

Except in the case of recent adultery sexual success is not made a secret of and a successful lover will almost certainly inform his friends. Adultery which is past and finished and pre-nuptial copulation with married people is a subject for open jest and teasing. One day Chudo explained in great detail how and when he had slept with Mrs. Jiroong when they were both unmarried, in the presence of Mrs. Jiroong and a number of other Lepchas. She showed her resentment by throwing a bunch of leaves at him, but forgot even to appear embarrassed.

The casual encounter in the field or forest has a somewhat more romantic aura; but it is considered altogether preferable that love-making should take place indoors because of the greater time it allows the pair. In their youth and young manhood (the period Lepchas call *fleng*) Lepcha men would appear to be remarkably potent ; trustworthy people said that when they were first married they would copulate with their wives five or six, and even eight or nine times in the course of the night, though they would then be tired the next day. I have got no comparable information from women but such statements were often made in mixed company without the women present making any comment or in any way expressing incredulity. This potency diminishes around the age of thirty, but copulation once nightly is still the general rule for married couples. Tafoor claimed that in his youth he was almost indefatigable, but says that now he only sleeps with his wife once every three or four nights ; this is the reason why he is relatively fat, for chastity induces fatness. It is believed that people accustomed to regular copulation will feel extremely uncomfortable for the first few days if for any reason their partner is removed ; but it is considered that people over thirty should be able to support long periods of chastity (with the exception, some laymen say, of the lamas, who cannot do without sex even for a week).

The normal position for Lepchas copulating is for the woman to lie absolutely prone and relaxed, while the man kneels in front of her between her legs. In situations where discretion is necessary both parties lie on their sides, copulation taking place *a retro ;* and in some sudden and quick encounters both parties remain standing, the woman leaning against a tree or wall. During copulation the woman lies completely motionless and relaxed, but this passivity is not equated with non-participation, and the orgasms of both sexes are considered identical in nature. The Lepcha attitude to semen is practically the same as that commonly held in Europe ; it is thought to be a secretion which is constantly produced and stored against use, so that a husband who has been for some while separated from his wife will have particularly large reserves. The testicles are regarded as the reservoirs of semen ; they are not paid much attention to in conversation and have little rôle in the constant flow of sexual jokes. It is believed that if a man's testicles hang lower than his penis he is more likely to be fertile than if the contrary is the case. Semen is considered to be a rather unpleasant and soiling substance, and these characteristics are advanced as one of the major reasons against masturbation. Lepcha men consider that copulation is most enjoyable either with a very young girl or with a woman who has borne more than one child ; in the latter case there is the added advantage that copulation is thought to be much less exhausting. Men with large penises are considered to give women more immediate satisfaction, but to be on the whole less fertile; there are, however, some anecdotes told of mothers procuring large-penised lovers to impregnate their daughters when their husbands have been unable to do so. The size and shape of the genitals of the men in the neighbourhood is a common subject for conversation; and such exact anatomical details are known and described that it would seem as though the privacy and secrecy enjoyed after the fire is damped down were by no means absolute.

A couple of Tibetan prostitutes live at Mangan on the other side of the Teesta River to cater for the transitory Tibetan muleteers. A couple of the Lepchas of Lingthem have made use of their services for the fee of one rupee. Kurma said he preferred these women because, in contrast to Lepcha women, they were energetic during the act. The hiring of these women constitutes a display of superfluous wealth and an act of dare-devilry; the Lepchas consider their presence as one of the comic curiosities of the neighbourhood, but think it rather absurd for anybody to pay for sexual intercourse.

It is considered by most Lepchas extremely dangerous to sleep with a menstruating woman; Chala Mandal said that he personally would not be afraid, but the general belief is that the man who does so will be unwell and doltish afterwards for a period that some men put at a week and others at three years. It is a general belief that women are particularly desirous directly after menstruation and a few consider that impregnation is most likely to take place at that time. Old Hlatam the 'poisoner' has even gone so far as to warn her daughters to be particularly careful of that period so as to avoid bastards; but this belief is by no means generally held, and it would seem to be an importation from the Nepali, who, Major Morris says, have turned this belief into a cultural act of faith. During their actual periods girls will tell their lovers that they are unwell, but the great majority pay no attention to the subsequent days. There is also a vague belief that it is possible to foretell conception if the man is especially tired and the woman especially passionate.

Although sexual enjoyment is believed to continue for both sexes up to an advanced old age, the sexual activities of old people are considered rather ludicrous. One of Chudo's most successful and appreciated jokes was his vivid description of the noises he heard nightly coming from the sleeping place of his sixty-nine-year-old 'grandfather' the second Dorjé Lapoon and his seventy-four-year-old bride Pumri; and the first Dorjé Lapoon's attempts at eighty-two to *asék* a woman of forty were also considered funny. These two old stalwarts were, however, somewhat exceptional; most Lepchas after the age of seventy abandon all such thoughts and actions. I question whether the generally expressed fear of surviving one's strength into extreme old age is in any way consciously connected with the fear of losing potency.

The Lepchas' attitude towards sex is extremely forth-right and unemotional. They openly equate sexual activity with eating, saying that the one is as natural and as necessary as the other; and they tend to treat both activities as of about equal emotional importance. Sexual activity, unless it forms part of a larger pattern of give-and-take, sets up no social obligations between the two parties; neither is considered to be indebted or especially benefited, and copulation entails no further duties. The Lepcha attitude to a transitory sexual partner is summed up in the Edwardian smoking-room joke: 'Since when does sleeping together constitute a social introduction?' The Lepchas are much occupied with sex; it is the subject of much of their conversation and nearly all their humour; it is regarded as almost as essential as food. Sex is intended to be exclusively sensual and almost impersonal; the culture makes no allowance for deep personal relationships passionately adhered to between sexual partners. If sex becomes emotionally serious it is always a nuisance and, if either of the partners are betrothed or married, it may be disastrous.

iii

The majority of marriages take place in the autumn months after the harvest is gathered; a few, however, take place at other periods, particularly second marriages, which are usually celebrated an exact calendar year after the death of the first spouse. It is necessary to find an auspicious day for the marriage, taking into consideration the birth years of the two contracting parties. Should a relation on either side die on the marriage day it is a bad omen, and signifies either the sterility or early death of the wife.

The groom's family usually spend several months before the date fixed in collecting the necessary food and animals. Just before the marriage date (the number of days before depends on the journey necessary) the groom goes with his *bek-bu* to his bride's house taking with him the hind leg of a pig, a scarf and a rupee as a present for his mother-in-law. On his arrival the sisters and other girl friends of the bride will lie in wait for the groom armed with nettles and other thorny plants and will pretend to drive him away; to be allowed to go on the groom must give them all a present of at least six annas. As soon as the groom has given his presents he returns to his own home, and almost immediately after the bridal procession sets out.

The bridal procession consists of twelve people besides the bride; they are (1) her *bek-bu*, (2) an old and experienced man, usually the Mandal of her village, (3) a 'sacrificer', preferably a Mun, (4) a paternal uncle, (5) a maternal uncle, (6) an elder brother, (7) an elder sister or aunt, who is called the bride's friend, (8) a younger sister, (9) a younger brother, and finally three men to carry the presents from the bride which consist of a load of *chi*, a load of popped corn, and a pig. The girl's parents stay behind and play no rôle in their daughter's marriage; for them it is considered to be a sad time, for it marks the formal loss of their child. In the bridal procession the six named relations may always be classificatory ones if there are no 'real' ones available.

Three times on the way to the groom's house the bridal party stops for ceremonial food and drink, which is provided by the groom. The first stop is called *chang yook*, when food and *chi* are provided; the paternal uncle and the sacrificer must drink two *patyoot* of *chi* at this place; the rest may do as they please. The second halt is called *long-so* and there three big bamboo holders of strained *chi* are provided for the party. The final halt is called *Gorshoon*; this is very near the groom's house and here a shed is erected to accommodate the bridal party. As soon as they arrive at this shed another container of strained *chi* is provided.

When the bridal party has entered the temporary shed the girl's *bek-bu* goes into the house with a ceremonial scarf which he offers to the groom's family; if there is a lamaist altar in the house the scarf is put on this. Then the bridal party is regaled on ground rice and *chi* and this is followed by a ceremonial meal called 'wiping away the sweat of the bride' and consisting of eight big handfuls of rice and eight fowls, which are boiled and given to the bride's party and also to the older men and lamas present. Following this the girl's *bek-bu* ceremoniously offers the presents which have been brought in the name of the bride's family to the elders of the groom's family. These presents are received by the old men of the groom's family with a show of great surprise and some indignation: 'Why do you bring these?' they say, 'we only want the bride and no presents.' The *bek-bu* answers: 'We have brought these to make a sacrifice.' These gifts are then dedicated by a Mun or experienced man; the day after the marriage this dedicated pig and grain will be carefully divided up and all the girl's relations-in-law and the other inhabitants of her new village must eat a small portion; in this way the new wife is formally accepted into the community. Everybody has eaten food of her providing.

Since the bride and her party have usually come from some way away this ceremony generally takes place towards evening and it is followed by a feast after which people go to sleep. Unless the bride is a widow or already the mother of her husband's children she will not enter the groom's house that night but will pass it in the shed which has been specially erected for that purpose.

There may have been some guests present on the first day, but it is the second day which is the really big feast, at which almost everybody in the village will be present.

The lamas arrive about nine o'clock with their books and musical instruments and will take up their position at the right-hand wall of the *dé-ong* against the altar, with one of the Dorjé Lapoon at the end nearest the altar. Intermittently during the whole day they will burn incense and read their books and play on the musical instruments. Except for the ceremony of 'receiving the bride' described lower down, they will only leave their position for a very few minutes at a time to go out and ease themselves. They eat and drink where they pray and from the moment they arrive a *patyoot* of *chi* is placed in front of them, which is constantly replenished and renewed.

Early in the morning the first ox—'the ox for eating'—will be killed and cut up; its ribs are boiled for the feast and sausages are made out of the intestines; the head, right foreleg, left hindleg, and half the sausages are preserved for the bride's family. Then a second ox—the 'ox of the groom'—is tethered fairly near the house but somewhere in the forest—that is not on cultivated land. By this ox is erected by the Mun or sacrificer a sort of altar on which is placed a scarf and a rupee and a big container of strained *chi* and also a bowl with butter at the side from which the strained *chi* will be drunk. Then the Mun dedicates the live ox to all the gods and repeats the long sacred story which tells of the origin of marriage.[6] This prayer and rehearsal of the story takes upwards of three hours; unless somebody wishes to be able to tell the story in his turn, the

[6] See Appendix IV.

officiating sacrificer will probably be completely neglected. The rest of the company will be talking and eating and drinking. The bride and her party will probably remain fairly isolated in their shed. When the sacred story is finished the bride and groom and the bride's party and the groom's party are all summoned to the Mun's altar. Then the Mun calls on all the gods of the neighbourhood and prays to them not to be angry but to let everybody enjoy the ox which is going to be killed and to bless the married couple and give them many children. He then turns to the bride and groom and preaches a sermon to them, telling them to love one another and not to quarrel; if they separate may the ox they are going to eat burn and poison them. After that he hands to the bride the buttered bowl filled with strained *chi*; she sips it three times and after each sip the bowl is refilled as each sip is a symbolic emptying of the bowl. After the bride the groom drinks, and then the members of the bride's party and the groom's party in turn take three ceremonial sips from a smaller buttered bowl. This drinking of the buttered *chi* is really the sacramental consecration of the marriage and represents a pact of friendship between the bride and her new family and village.

When the ceremony has been completed the ox of the groom is killed with a bow and arrow. It is absolutely necessary that the wife's younger brother, or if she has not got one the nearest possible classificatory younger brother, should kill this ox; if anybody else were to do it the bride's family have to pay a fine of Rs. 5 to the groom's family. The ox is shot twice from a very short distance and an attempt is made to pierce the heart behind the left foreleg. It is a very messy way of killing an ox, which takes about a quarter of an hour to die. When the ox is finally dead the bride's younger brother pours water over its muzzle after which this ox is also cut up. The meat from this ox is not consumed at the feast; the head and one of the hind legs will be taken back to the wife's family as well as half the intestines turned into sausages; the rest of the meat will be cut up and divided and given away as parting presents to all the guests.

After this ceremony the bride and her party are conducted by the two *bek-bu* into the *dé-ong*, where they take up their special positions against the left-hand wall facing the lamas. These positions are, starting from the altar, the old and experienced man, the sacrificer, the paternal uncle, the maternal uncle, the elder brother, the 'bride's friend', the bride, the younger sister and the younger brother; on the opposite side with the lamas are, starting from the same direction, the Mandal, a *youmi*, a paternal uncle and the groom. Standing between the two parties are the *bek-bu* of the bride and the groom.

When the two parties are settled the two *bek-bu* make a collection of money from every guest; each guest should give at the very least a ceremonial scarf and a rupee; those who can will give more. The husband's *bek-bu* makes a list of all the gifts given and the return presents of meat are apportioned roughly in proportion to the money given. When the money is collected it is divided up by the two *bek-bu*, the greater part going to the bride's party who have to receive Rs. 3 each, with the exception of the paternal uncle who gets Rs. 4 and the bride's friend who gets Rs. 6. The *bek-bu* receive Rs. 5 each. If there is any excess of the money it goes to the married couple, but if there is a deficiency the husband has to make up the required sum out of his own pocket. After this the *dé-ong* is cleared except for the parties of the bride and groom. In the kitchen a Mun of the husband's village will be calling on the gods. Just before the ceremony starts a ceremonial meal of a boiled pig's head and chickens is partaken of by both parties.

Then is performed the ceremony of 'receiving the bride'; in this ceremony the man's *bek-bu* plays no rôle. The conversation chiefly takes place between the girl's *bek-bu*, her uncles, and the bridegroom's party. The girl's *bek-bu* takes a scarf in one hand and a rupee in the other and addresses the girl as follows: 'You have been married into —— *ptso*; now you are bound to them and if you had any other lovers you must leave them; now you have no connection with people other than this *ptso*. In the beginning Tarbong-bo and Naripnom and Komsi*thing* originated marriage and so we perform it today. Now you are bound.' With these words the girl's *bek-bu* puts a scarf round her bowed neck and the rupee into her joined hands and then the girl's *bek-bu* sits down.

After this the Mandal will ask the bride who are her special *moong* and *rum* (devils and gods) and what sacrifices are necessary. Should she say there are none, or keep silent, the *youmi* will say, 'Don't tell a lie; we know there must be at least one *rum* and one *moong* and if you have children and they get ill a Mun or a lama will find out what supernaturals you have brought here; so speak up and tell the truth.' After that someone on the girl's side, most probably her paternal or maternal uncle, will tell who are her private supernaturals and what are the sacrifices necessary for them.

ONGDEN'S WEDDING

Above : Ongden in a clean dress. Behind him old Adér.

Below : The feast.

Somebody of the groom's party will convey this information to the Mun in the other room, who will then perform the necessary sacrifices with *chi*, incense, rice, and the chest of an ox.

When this business is dealt with the girl's paternal uncle will say to the representatives of the groom: 'We are giving this girl to the —— *ptso*; if you are not good to her we will take her back and punish you.' The groom's party give elaborate thanks and promise that the bride will be well treated and happy.

After this there is a considerable hazing of the bride by the two parties, the girl's paternal uncle referring to her in complimentary *tang-bor*, to which the groom's side will retort, if possible making the remarks obscene and derogatory to the bride, who will be sitting with her head hidden in her head-cloth so that it cannot be seen if she is or is not confused. For example, if the girl is older than the groom the girl's uncle may say: 'We are giving you the yolk of this egg which we have peeled for you.' One of the groom's party may reply: 'It is very kind of you, but it seems to us as if this egg has been considerably nibbled at! And we would not be surprised if her pubic hair were not as long as that of Sor *moong*, or in appearance rather like a field of ripe corn!' 'We assure you that the egg has been freshly peeled—just so as to make it easy for you to eat.' 'Well it seems to us the shell has been off a very considerable time!' 'And what does it matter if her pubic hair *is* like a tangled bush? A clever goat can find its way through any bramble. . . .' Pleasantries in this metaphorical vein continue for some time. If the bride is a young girl the *doubles ententes* will be altered to suit the circumstances; thus, if the *tang-bor* about the egg is made an apt reply would be: 'Thank you so much for the new-laid egg; we will eat it very carefully, just a little bit at a time; in that way it will get used to it and like it.'

When the teasing of the bride is finished the lamas return; the bride and groom present the Dorjé Lapoon with a plate of rice and then the lamas chant a formal prayer over the couple called *ong-shu-shet*—a prayer for future children.

After this the rest of the day and all the night is given over to feasting and drinking and singing and dancing. Five young women of the groom's family are appointed to carry round the ladles of boiling water to fill the *chi patyoot*, and five older women to refil the *patyoot* with fresh *chi* and give out the food. The songs are mostly improvised, but there are some traditional comic ones; the girl's *bek-bu* almost always sings in a feigned falsetto voice the song beginning, 'Father, help me! Mother, help me!' The dancing is completely unorganised, and merely consists of individuals hopping or stamping more or less rhythmically as they feel disposed. Unlimited food and drink are provided, and it is considered desirable and almost inevitable that everybody should get as drunk as possible. There is a strong sexual overtone to the atmosphere and towards evening many couples separate and go off into the forest for a short spell; they mostly return to the house where the feast is being held before night has completely fallen.

At the only marriage feast that I witnessed—that of Ongden with his second wife—I noted 'About seven o'clock the noise was exactly like a very crowded English pub at closing time: the atmosphere was unbelievable. Nearly a hundred very dirty people in two small rooms which had been shut up as much as possible with the balconies closed by wooden partitions and so on; there was a huge fire of wet wood smoking hard so that one could only just see across the room. In the kitchen some people were sleeping round the fire while others were still cooking; at one side there was a very bloody mess where sausages were being made from the entrails by three young men; others were asleep in the muck. In the *dé-ong* the ground was so crowded with sitters and sleepers that there was only just room for the female relations of the husband to circulate with their wooden ladles of boiling water with which they constantly replenished the bowls of *chi*; they appeared to be the only relatively sober people present. The bride and her party sat as if they had never moved, in their long line against the wall of the *dé-ong*; the groom wandered about rather disconsolately, talking very little to anyone. Old Adér, who had previously pulled up his dress and exposed himself during the sacrifice, started singing in a minor key dragging over the syllables; whereupon Lumba's *jethi* (that is his first wife), who is renowned as a singer, got up and asked for some meat to be given her as a fee for the song she was going to sing; she was given some and started singing, but nobody took much notice though everybody said "hush"; the singers walked about as if they were cabaret artists. The pace of the evening got slower and slower and sleepier and sleepier; the children sat about or slept. It would have been very rude for anybody to go home before sunrise the next day.'

This marriage of Ongden with a widow was slightly irregular and abbreviated, first because it was for both parties a second marriage, and secondly because the bride had been living with her husband for some months before he had assembled enough food for the ceremony. The ceremony only took place for one day instead of for two and the bride and her party went straight away on arrival into the house. The day before the marriage the bride withdrew to a village one day's walk away instead of to her own home which was three days away, where she met her bridal party. After the ceremony the post-nuptial visits were curtailed, but it was considered improper for the newly married couple to start living at home at once and so they spent a few days at the house of his 'nephew' Tingkep.

Early in the morning after the marriage feast the bride and groom, together with the bride's party and two friends of the groom to carry the heads and legs of the oxen, set out on a return visit to the bride's house. When they have arrived the groom stops as little time as possible; overnight if the bride's home is some way away, otherwise not even that. On that day all the guests who were present at the marriage feast return with gifts of crops or *chi*, which they give according to their wish and ability as a help towards the very considerable expense of the marriage feast.

Two weeks later the groom goes to fetch his bride again. Either at this visit or at the subsequent one the girl's father provides a feast for the newly married couple. When the bride and groom leave the girl's house her father sends back as a present to the man's father a load of *chi* and a load of rice. The couple then stop a week in the husband's house; at the end of that time they go back to the girl's house, taking with them as presents to the girl's parents from the groom's parents exactly the same presents as the girl herself had brought. The couple then spend a few days at the bride's home and then finally return to the groom's. At this final removal the girl brings with her such private property as she may possess in the shape of animals or harvested grain as well as her clothes and jewels.

Some time during the first year of marriage the bride may go to visit her parents with a present of a pig and they will in return give her a milch cow or a heifer. This does not always take place, usually only if the bride's parents are relatively rich.

If the horoscopes of the married pair are unfavourable or if ill-luck is foretold, this ill-luck can be temporarily averted in the following way: two lamas will make small millet images of the husband and wife called *parr-ko* and into these the lamas will transfer all the ill-luck which is foreseen in the sacred books. When this is done the husband and wife must each carry away their own image and throw it into the forest. The cost of this service is either Rs. 3 a head or enough grain for two months. This ceremony, however, only postpones the ill-luck for two or three years, after which it must be repeated.

As can be seen, these spaced visits are carefully arranged to make the bride's severance from her family as gentle as possible. It is only very exceptionally, as in the case of Nariya described above, that after the marriage ceremony the bride will refuse to return to her husband's house. It is also worth noting that until well after the ceremony the parents of the children being married play no rôle whatsoever.

The marriage feast represents very considerable expense—if everything had to be bought somewhere between Rs. 200 and Rs. 300; for most people this entails saving up for a couple of years. Nearly everybody who can provides this feast; in the case of very poor people general contributions will be made such as were outlined in Chapter Six.[7] In the case of a *komok myok*—that is a man living with his wife's family and taking the place of the non-existent son—the feast is very much smaller and is chiefly provided by the girl's family.

iv

The newly married girl is likely to find herself in a somewhat subservient position; it is her task to do the cooking and most of the household chores under the direction of the 'house mother', who is almost always her mother-in-law. She also has to maintain constantly respectful behaviour towards her father-in-law and the other men—her husband's elder brothers and her husband's father's brothers if they live in the house—who are so classified. If her husband is not the youngest brother she will only have this subservient position until the younger brothers marry; then their wives in their turn will occupy the position of youngest daughter-in-law and have to do the greater part of the household work. There is usually considerable friendliness between the mother-in-law and daughter-in-law; the daughter-in-law is taking a lot of work off her mother-in-law's shoulders and in return the mother-in-law instructs her and cajoles her to keep her happy.

There is no bar on the girl paying relatively frequent visits to her parents; she need not necessarily be accompanied by her

[7] See Chapter Six, p. 156.

husband, but can take as companion any other member of her husband's family except her father-in-law; very often these visits are the means of producing further marriages between the groups.

The husband practically does not change status at all through marriage. Unless there have been premature deaths in the family he is still a very minor member of the household; he has a wife to work with him, but he has if anything to work harder now that he is a more responsible person. There are no outward signs of any sort which will show if a person is married or not. Marriages take place, as has been said, when the parties are still very young, and there is usually a considerable lapse of time between marriage and the birth of the first child. Only two women in Lingthem bore children before they were eighteen and the greater number usually had their first child somewhere around the age of twenty. These preliminary years are passed in the married couple getting accustomed to one another and setting up the pattern of mutual rights and duties on which Lepcha affection is founded. It is extremely uncommon and is considered very disreputable for a husband and wife who have children to separate, or even to show marked preference for anybody other than their own spouse. Such behaviour is stigmatised as shameless.

At the wife's first pregnancy the young couple acquire greater importance and responsibility and the second half of the pregnancy is, as has been described, a period of great care and watchfulness for both parties. With the birth of the child the couple become more important; now they are really part of the village and are carrying on the family line, and as a sign of this their names are changed and also their mode of address to their nearer kinsmen. The father and mother are called after their child—father of X and mother of X—and all the members of the generation above them are called grandfather and grandmother out of compliment to the child, and members of the same generation, especially if older, may be addressed as father or mother, though this latter is optional. But unless death has intervened they are still a minor part of the household; they continue working harder than ever now they have children to bring up, and it is only when their own family is growing up that they in their turn become the head of the household or one of the more important members of it. As the man's father gets older he gives over more and more responsibility to his eldest son, even possibly having the property registered in this son's name;

then the son is responsible for the taxes and the management of the household and his father and mother almost assume the rôles of honoured and leisured guests. At this period his sons in their turn will probably be getting married and he has to make the necessary economies for their marriage expenses; then his wife too will become a 'house mother' and will have the work taken off her by her younger sisters-in-law and daughters-in-law. Some younger brothers never achieve the position of house father; all their life until they are too old the position will be held by their elder brother and then when the elder brother wishes to retire it is probable that the younger brother will be about the same age and will prefer to hand over the work and responsibility to his nephew. If, however, there is considerable discrepancy in the ages of the two brothers the elder brother will hand over the management of the property to his younger brother, who will then in his turn re-transfer it to his elder brother's eldest son. Theoretically there are some advantages in being house father as the house father has control of the crops and their proceeds; but in point of fact there are more duties than advantages; the house father has to look ahead for future expenses and to make provision against them; he has to take what few decisions need to be taken; he has responsibilities but relatively very few rights, for if he started abusing his position, say taking all the money and grain for himself and his family and neglecting his dependants, either there would be a public scandal or the family would break up. The younger brothers would demand and get their share of all land and property so that the house father would be left alone with very diminished resources and would probably find considerable difficulty in getting the necessary help for the work in his fields and so on.

Such a gradual evolution and development is the ideal pattern of Lepcha life, but owing to the high incidence of sterility and a very uneven death-rate few people attain even a near approximation to it. As has already been explained[8] if the first wife is sterile it is permissible to take a second wife from the same family group as the first, but not every man has the money or inclination to do this, and there is no guarantee that the second wife will be fertile. It is said that in the majority of cases the first wife welcomes the arrival of a 'younger sister' as this will considerably lessen her work; it is not, however, unknown for co-wives to quarrel.

Perhaps the least disruptive death is that of the wife; after a year's

[8] See Chapter Six, pp. 166–169.

obligatory mourning the husband can re-marry. But a dead man is irreplaceable, and it is the death of men which destroys the expectations of the Lepchas. Thus Patek by the deaths of his father and grandfather was left the head of a household of six at the age of seventeen, and Tobgé was left alone with a wife and a young child at the age of twenty. Tobgé's case, however, was less desperate, for he was able to abandon his lonely home and go to live with Jiroong, his father's younger brother, who had previously been a *komok myok* and had therefore a separate establishment of his own.

At the other end of the scale there is old Kahlyeu who had two wives and twelve children; but all his sons died young and his daughters married away; and so at the age of seventy-seven, instead of living a life of ease, supported by his children and grandchildren, he has to work hard and lives alone with his grandson Chélé and the middle-aged widow of one of his brother's sons. His brother's family is settled in a distant village some way away. Kahlyeu is a rather melancholy, unhappy old man, but one of the shrewdest in the village. 'Times have changed', he complained once to me when I was asking about earlier conditions, 'since I was a boy; nowadays the youngsters know more than I do, and if I start telling them about the old times they rebuke me saying: "Why talk about that? It is all over and done with."' Similarly ninety-year-old Serving, almost completely in his dotage, without teeth and half-blind, has survived all his descendants and nearly all the members of his *ptso*, a century ago the most important in Lingthem; now he lives with the grandson of his elder brother, a rude and ungracious man, with his wife and baby son. Death, which has been so unmerciful in taking the young men has been equally unmerciful in letting these old lonely and unhappy men survive.

CHAPTER THIRTEEN

DEATH

i

Death is the real enemy of Lepcha life. Disease and hail and failure of crops occupy the Lepchas more emotionally, for these are possibly preventable accidents and against them precautions can be taken. But death is absolute and final and cannot be fought against; some precautions can be taken against a death which has struck one member finding other victims in the community, but against death itself there is nothing to do. Death is too terrible to envisage clearly or discuss often; death, and, to a lesser extent, the dead who have suffered death are hated and feared and not talked about.

Once a person is dead there are two things to do; the danger of the devil that has caused his death finding another victim in the community must be averted and the dead man must be got rid of as thoroughly and completely as possible. People who have left this world never return to it benevolently; if they do have any contact with the living it is as malevolent supernaturals, as devils. The older a person grows the less likely is he to hanker after the world he has left and therefore the less he is to be feared; children and young people suddenly torn from their life will surely turn into malevolent devils.

The infection and danger of death is strictly local and therefore if a person dies away from home no sort of ceremony is held for him; the body is just unceremoniously thrown into the river. Why should strangers be at the expense of a funeral? No relics will be returned. When the survivors hear of the distant death of a relative they will simply set up prayer flags. They will not hold a *sanglion* (death ceremony), for if the soul has turned into a *moong* it will haunt the place where it died and will not trouble *them*. That the soul of the dear departed will not be able to find its way to the *rumlyang* (paradise) does not matter. The ceremonies to be described later are more for a protection for the living than as a help for the dead. Only if a young child were to die away from its home would the ceremony of Dek Flee[1] be held to keep away its haunting demon.

It is at death and the ceremonies which surround death that the beliefs and ritual of the Mun and lamas most obviously clash and contradict one another. Both creeds hold that the soul outside the body is lost in some dangerous region through which it must be conducted; and therefore representatives of both creeds help to conduct the soul away. But the soul's destination on these wanderings is completely different; for the lama the soul wanders for forty-nine days in a sort of purgatory, after which it is judged and rewarded and sent on to its next incarnation, whether it be on the earth as another human being or as an animal or to heaven for a period of blessedness or to hell for a period of torment. For the Mun the soul is conducted to the *rumlyang*, where it is born again as a tiny child, very often of a different sex to its former life; in the *rumlyang* the child grows up to maturity and leads a happy and immortal life among all the other dead, a life similar to that here on earth except that there is no death or disease or want.

The implicit contradictions in these beliefs are realised in the case of lamas and nuns, for whom the Mun perform no ceremonies; the souls of lamas and nuns are not led to the *rúmlyang* but conducted through the *bardo* or purgatory. But for laymen ceremonies of both religions are held simultaneously; the lamas perform inside the house while the Mun does his ceremonies outside.

There are three alternative methods of disposing of a corpse; it may be burnt, buried, or thrown into the river. Which method is adopted depends partly on the condition of the deceased and partly on the lama's horoscopes. The lamas and nuns are never buried; they are almost always burnt unless they die in the wet season, in which case their bodies are thrown into the river. Laymen are never burnt; whether they are buried or thrown into the river depends on the lama's horoscope; the greater number are buried. Young children should always be thrown into the river, but occasionally an exception is made; thus Patek's mother when she lost in rapid succession four children in infancy burnt the body of the last one in anger and as a protest at the way the supernaturals were treating her; but such behaviour is extremely uncommon.

As soon as a person dies the position in which he has expired

[1] Vide sub, p. 352–353.

and the hour thereof is noted and told to a competent lama, who then consults the book, *Detseu*, in which are specially drawn diagrams for each calendrical division and body position. These diagrams show in which direction the corpse should be removed for disposal; this is never on any account through the door, but may be through either the walls or the floor; a hole is made especially for this purpose which will be filled up immediately after the body has been taken away. The lama also casts the dead man's horoscope[2] from which is learnt the supernatural causes of his death and the ceremonies which must be performed by his survivors to help the dead man and ward off his fate from the living. The horoscope also indicates what sort of people—that is people born in what year—should attend to and carry the corpse and whither the devil which has caused this man's death has gone and whom it menaces next. Also if this devil has been brought by some object this object is designated so that it can receive ritual cleansing. On the day of the death of an adult and also on the day of the disposal of the body and the disposal of the ashes from the burnt paper face nobody in the village should work.

Lamas are summoned immediately after death to help the soul of the man to find heaven by giving him advice and showing to the corpse pictures of the devils and perils which he is likely to encounter. If the dead man is a lama the corpse is tied to a pole along the back; the knees are bent up to the body and held by a length of cloth; the head is propped up with a stick and the hands are joined with the palms together as in prayer. After the first day the corpse is placed in a big copper pot (after the cremation this pot is returned to its normal use after being given a thorough wash). In front of the corpse is placed a small table on which are arranged three water-containers, two dishes of rice and a *chimi*; beyond this is placed another table on which all the sorts of food which the dead man used to eat in his lifetime are placed; the food is changed at every meal and the old food is taken away and can be eaten by anyone. This preliminary ceremony lasts for one, three or seven days, according to the wealth of the deceased's family; however long the ceremony continues the lamas who are watching and instructing the dead man must not sleep at all. The others can and do sleep, often in the same room as the corpse; the corpse soon starts to stink even though it is anointed with butter mixed with cloves, nutmeg and camphor and dressed in clean clothes.

[2] See Appendix III, c.

While the corpse is in the house the people of that household must not eat salt or butter.

The corpse of a layman is also doubled up in the same way, but the hands are crossed on the breast and the head is allowed to flop. The body is put in a big openwork basket. Usually for a layman there is only one day's wait between death and burial, but occasionally people will wait three days. A layman also is instructed and advised by lamas, but at the same time the Mun who will perform the *sanglion* and any other benevolent people who know how to are helping the corpse on the road to the *rumlyang* by meditation—*munthen.*

ii

Before the body of a lama or nun is carried out of the house a pyre must be prepared; this consists of a square pile about seven feet high, with eight layers of wood if the deceased is a man and nine if a woman. The pyre must be made of the wood of one of two designated trees and must not be composed of more than three trees; the first tree of all must be cut down by the nearest available male relation of the deceased. The place where the pyre is made and its direction in relation to the house of the dead man will have been indicated by the lamas' horoscope; there are about half a dozen burning and burial places around Lingthem in more or less every direction; they are all removed some way away from any habitation and are placed on uncultivable spurs of land. The hour at which the corpse should be removed and also the year of birth of the people carrying the corpse are designated by the horoscope.

The journey from the house to the pyre must be made without a break. The body is put on the pyre seated to face west—that is towards Kinchenjunga. If the dead person is a woman in an advanced state of pregnancy, just before the corpse is placed on the pyre or in the grave the body is ripped open so that the navel-cord is torn and the foetus is placed on the mother's lap. This can be done by anybody who has sufficient courage. Then all the male relations of the deceased stand at all four sides of the pyre and set fire to it simultaneously. If the corpse has left a widow or widower a portion of that person's hair is cut off and burnt at the same time as the body. It is essential that every piece of wood and bone should be burnt to ashes; if necessary the corpse will be broken up to this end. About 8 lbs. of butter, a big basket of rice and all sorts of other grain are burnt with the corpse; a sort of long-handled shovel is used to make these offerings and they are thrown on to the pyre a little at a time, the officiating lama counting out loud and finishing up with a shout. The lama counts up to five ten times, up to seven five times and up to eight ten times. A pig, or very occasionally an ox, is killed at the house and this is put on to the pyre as food for the corpse after the corpse has been consumed. This animal is not usually consumed completely but merely cooked; the people who gathered the wood for the pyre are given this meat as their fee; if there is no meat they are given money. The relations of the dead man must stay by the pyre until the ashes are quite extinct.

All the unrelated people who have accompanied the family to the burning place are given a meal of rice, and a small gift of money —usually one or two annas—is given to a representative of each household present. Similar presents are also given to those who attend a burial if the mourners can afford it. On the way back from the disposal of a corpse a small bonfire is built for the mourners to jump over, and a knife or some other piece of iron is put in the doorway of the house for people to step over; both these precautions are taken to disinfect the mourners from the possible magical contagion of death.

Except that the corpse is not dressed and anointed in the house, but only when it is brought to the place designated for burial, the preliminaries for burial are exactly the same as those for burning. The corpse is carried in the basket to the burial place by one man, a near relation if possible; a husband must always carry his wife and a son his mother. As well as the friends and relations of the deceased a Mun accompanies the buriers. When the party arrive at the chosen site the corpse is placed on the ground and is washed and anointed with the mixture of butter, cloves, nutmeg and camphor, and wrapped in a new cloth which is arranged so as to cover the face. Then a circular grave about the height of a man is dug; a big stone is put at the bottom and the sides are lined with stones and four ropes are placed against the four corners. While these preparations are being made the surviving spouse or eldest son will stay by the corpse and talk to it saying: 'We are preparing this new house for you.' The body is put into the grave still sitting in the basket, orientated to face Kinchenjunga; then on the top of the grave and corpse is put a big flat stone and on the top of that four cooking stones supporting another flat stone. On the top of this is placed a little white stone which serves as an indication that the place is a grave and should not be touched. When all is in place the four ropes are pulled away simultaneously. The Mun then ceremoniously cleanses the hands of the buriers with a pot of strained *chi* and a bristle brush.

For disposal by water all the early preparations are the same except that a lama goes with the burial party and before the body is put into the river offers *cherkem*—that is strained *chi* with grain floating in it—to the supernaturals of the water. The basket is put into the water first and then the body, head downwards; it is pushed out with a forked stick under the arm-pits and floats away. In the case of a small child the body and the basket are thrown away without any sort of ceremony. No gifts are put in the grave or thrown into the river; the corpse has merely its new cloth and the basket. In all forms of disposal of the body the knees are fastened to the body by a cloth.

iii

After the disposal of the corpse there are still two actions which must be performed: the getting rid of the devil which has caused the death and the safe conducting of the dead man's soul well out of the world. The order in which these are performed depends on whether the horoscope has divined that the death is caused by Sandé *moong*, or by Shidook *moong* or by Arot *moong* (death by violence). If the death has been caused by Sandé *moong* the disinfecting ceremony is performed immediately after the removal of the corpse and before the *sanglion*—that is to say the speeding of the dead man's soul; the other ceremonies are performed about two months after death.

To remove Sandé *moong* the presence of two lamas is necessary, one to read the sacred books and one to perform the necessary actions. On a rectangular board they construct out of powdered grain and water a life-sized Cat with a very long tail with a horse's saddle on its back and a relatively smaller rider on it; in front are two more men, behind two more. Three triple strands of coloured thread are put round the Cat's neck, one of which is held by the rider and the others by the two men in front. These images are decorated with various sacred and symbolical devices made out of wood and thread and there are offerings of crops. Besides this object, one big and two smaller torches are prepared and also some heaps of small pebbles and dried buckwheat powder, mixed with rotted bamboo (here called 'dust').

When all is prepared the lama reads the book Sandé Kangyour; while this is being read a layman offers *cherkem*. When the reading is finished the Cat is turned round towards the door and a path of powdered 'dust' made for it. Then the real expulsion starts. The lama throws 'dust' on to the torches to make them flare; pebbles are thrown into the corners of the room. Then all the neighbours and friends who are present take the weapons they have provided themselves with—axes, knives, hammers, or for women the heavy weaving shuttles or sickles—and start beating in every corner of the house. Others armed with the torches go round the village, or at any rate to the neighbouring houses, and some with their weapons go and beat in corners of adjoining houses. Still others accompany the Cat, which is carried a little way along a path and then upset. Should its head turn towards the house there will be another death in the village. Those who accompany the Cat whistle and shout 'Ya-Ho-o-o' and throw stones and beat around with their weapons.

If it has been found from the horoscope that the death infection was brought in some object in the house, this object is taken away with the Cat and left on the path. A couple of days later it is taken back, thoroughly cleaned and re-taken into use.

When all taking part in the devil-chasing have gone out of the house those who remain shut the door. By the door is a big copper vessel full of water from a stream with a woman beside it. After the Cat has been upset the carriers return shouting '*Hla-gélo : dé pam*' (God has conquered and the devil been defeated'). The woman will sprinkle with the water all who have gone outside; only then will the door be reopened and the people given strained *chi* which has been prepared for them by those who stayed inside.

If the death is discovered to have been caused by Shidook *moong*, the ceremony of *shidook kyop* is performed about two months after the death. For this ceremony it is necessary to kill an animal, either an ox or a goat, and the offering is made on the skin of this animal, of which the head and forelegs are left unskinned and attached. In the centre of this skin is made a 'throne' of a mound of earth in tiers, on which is placed a black 'devil's palace' or *deu* of thread; in the four corners are four small images of dough stamped with butter and decorated; below them are thirteen smaller images on stands, to which are given thirteen bamboo bows-and-arrows, thirteen knives, thirteen sickles and thirteen black 'devil's palaces'.[3] In front of all these is placed a special plate of pottery made with nine handles; this is left empty. The ceremonial is the same as for Sandé *moong*.

If the deceased ha met his death by violence, that is through Arot *moong*, the ceremony of Tikar Sangyour has to be performed. After a death by violence has occurred in a family the descendants should keep up the ceremony yearly for ever, for violent death is infectious and hereditary; it can also be performed apotropaically. The path by which a corpse, who has died violently, has been carried should be avoided; and at the *sanglion* of such people no raw meat is given, but only cooked meat, as raw meat will carry the infection. Tafoor performs this ceremony because his grandfather fell from a height and was drowned; so do Ongden, Nariya, the Mandal (although in his case this is precautionary) and many others.

On a block of wood one large and four small images of a horse with a rider are made of millet powder coloured red. In front of this is a black image of the female supernatural Mamoo *moong*, and in front of her an inflated animal's bladder. In front of this again is a *chimi* and at the four corners are four pots containing respectively scrapings of iron, tree tips, poison, and water from five rivers. There are also small offerings of grain and various decorations. While the special sacred book is being read *cherkem* is offered. When the offering is carried out a torch is laid down on top of it facing in the same direction; on top of this are placed leaves of wormwood and a stone on top of that.

In the case of a child dying before the age of about ten none of the ceremonies described above are performed nor is a *sanglion* made for it. Instead of these the ceremony of Dek Flee is performed by a Mun three days after death. For this ceremony a goat is required and also a tray covered with a black cloth on which is put samples of every sort of grain and a bundle of seven pieces of wood tied up with reed; besides that a bundle of elephant grass and other prickly plants are needed. The ceremony is performed inside the house.

The goat is tethered to a pole and a second rope made out of reed with three knots in it is tied round the goat's neck. This the Mun and all the members of the household in turn touch, and then the Mun throws the rope forward out of the house door three times. If by any chance the knot should point inwards there will be another

[3] Thirteen, being an odd number, is lucky.

death in the same household. After this a young boy takes some firebrands from the hearth some way away from the house; then the goat is led to the same place, stabbed to death and singed. After this the crops on the tray are *pék* over the inhabitants of the house and set down by the goat. Then the Mun takes the bundles of leaves already prepared in his right hand and a live hen in his left and *péks* the members of the household. The hen is then given to some neighbour to kill and eat; for neither the Mun nor any members of the household may eat anything used in this sacrifice. Then the intestines of the goat are cooked and mixed with rice; the Mun throws *chi* from a buttered cup to the devils, his assistant the chopped meat and rice.

When this is finished a wooden phallus (*tiklyong-kup*) is set up between two stones on the way to the house; it is given hundreds of small cuts, each cut representing one year that the devil cannot pass. It is anointed with blood and *chi*. All that night the Mun communes—*munthen*—but he does not go into a trance. No food is given to the soul of a child. If the child was young he did not eat in real life and even if he did eat solid food, he was fed in his life time.

iv

As has been said earlier, except for the expulsion of Sandé *moong* all these ceremonies are performed several days, or weeks, after the removal of the corpse. If it is possible, however, immediately after the corpse has been disposed of the *sanglion*—the speeding of the soul—is performed. Occasionally it is necessary to wait a few days while the requisite animals and food and materials which are involved are collected, for the *sanglion* is a very expensive ceremony. At this ceremony the mourners should not eat any of the meat provided, but should give it all away. The same term, *sanglion*, is used both for the lama's and the Mun's ceremonies and if both are performed they take place simultaneously; for lamas and nuns the Mun ceremony is not performed and for laymen the lama ceremony is much abbreviated. Another controlling detail as to the date when the *sanglion* is performed is the time necessary to prepare a sufficiency of *chi*.

The lama ceremony is as follows. First of all an image of the dead person is constructed in the following way: on a mat is drawn a circle of about ten inches across of powdered grain, with nine loops on the circumference[4] and NI in Tibetan script inscribed in the middle. On this is set a bamboo *patyoot* about a cubit high and a little broader than that usually employed for *chi* drinking, with a rupee in the bottom and filled with grain; into this is stuck an upright bamboo of the height of the corpse when sitting and at shoulder height is an inserted cross-piece the width of the dead person's shoulders. On top of this is placed a piece of paper supported on a square stretcher: this is stamped with a die representing a divine face; it is the same for all ages and conditions, but different for each sex; it is inscribed with the name of the dead person. Then this dummy is clothed with the clothes of the dead person so arranged as to look as if it was sitting with the legs crossed and feet hidden and hands folded. A big scarf which has to be borrowed or bought for the occasion is draped from the image's behind up the back and over the face, so that the paper mask is hidden.

This image is placed in the *dé-ong* facing the lamas, who sit on the right of the altar; in front of the image are three tables. On the first table are seven small cones of rice, seven *chimi*, two pots of water and two pots of rice; on the second table is a plate and cup and all sorts of food; on the third are the dead person's jewels, if it was a woman, or the knife and bow-and-arrows if a man. A little to the left before the first table is a *patyoot* of *chi*; behind and also to the left must sit the Mourner—the surviving spouse if there is one, or failing that any near relation. The Mourner only has to be present when the image is given food or talked to. Except right at the end other ordinary people do not come into the *dé-ong*.

If the dead man was a lama all the lamas of the neighbourhood will come automatically; if he was a layman only two are necessary, a Dorjé Lapoon and a *kané*. Old and experienced men are allowed to sit with the lamas. A certain number of nuns with their prayer-wheels are necessary; they sit against the wall opposite the altar.

The length of the ceremony depends on the wealth of the deceased. If he was a poor man it will only last twenty-four hours; if he was rich, up to seven days. The *chi* offered to the corpse is changed three times daily, the food twice; each meal must have some meat in it and also tea, rice and all vegetable foods. When the meal

[4] There would seem to be a connection between this nine-looped circle, and the nine-handled cup used in the ritual to expel Shidook *moong*, but I could not learn what this connection is.

is presented to the image the lamas address it, saying: 'Do not think of this world; we are giving you all the food you used to eat when you were alive; take it and *go.*' On these occasions the Mourner must be present. When the food in front of the image is removed it is eaten by those present who are not of the immediate family of the deceased; it is not thought to have lost any virtue or to be in any way dangerous.

The lamas have to read five sacred books; all read the same passage at the same time. Simultaneously there are six books which the nuns should read; those who cannot read turn their prayer-wheels. The whole time the reading is going on the lamas and nuns must not sleep; they may at intervals go outside for a respite, but they must never settle down to sleep. If all the books have to be read in a day and a night they have to hurry; if there is more time, they can go more leisurely; if the books are finished they start again at the beginning. The family, other than the Mourner, and their friends spend their time in the kitchen eating and drinking and talking and sleeping.

When the reading is finished all the relations gather. A specially clean plate is placed in front of the Dorjé Lapoon. Then the Dorjé Lapoon addresses the soul of the dead man telling it that everything has been done for it and that it has found its way to paradise, and then the *kané* takes off the paper head and hands it to the Dorjé Lapoon who holds it in his left hand; in his right he holds a big *chimi* and lights the paper from the bottom so that the ashes fall on to the plate. While the paper is burning all present shout 'Hep' three times in a loud voice, which signifies that the soul has got to heaven. The *kané* prepares a ball of reed ash mixed with water; the paper ashes are inserted therein and then placed in a *choten* mould into which a little oil has been poured. The ashes are rammed down and taken out in the form of a small *choten*. This *choten* the Dorjé Lapoon sprinkles with holy water (*tyü*); after which a hole is made in the bottom of the ash *choten* with a stick and a few grains of rice are pushed in and a gold and silver ornament are symbolically scraped with a knife over it. This *choten* is placed on the altar. In the case of ordinary people it is taken away the next day by the head of the household and put either in the river or in a cave or on a rock. If, however, the deceased was a lama of exceptional holiness a big stone *choten* will be made; some of the dust from his bones from the funeral pyre are placed in the foundations and the small *choten* is put in the centre.

When the ceremony is finished the clothes of the deceased are divided among the lamas; the Dorjé Lapoon gets the best coat and the *omzets* the other garments. Before these are worn the lama will hold some mustard seeds in his hand and pray silently; he will then throw the seeds on the clothes; this is considered sufficient disinfection; after that the garment is washed and can then be worn or sold. In the case of a dead lama his skull-drum and bell goes to the Dorjé Lapoon and his rosary to the officiating *kané*; the *kané* also gets the *patyoot* with the rupee and grain inside, the dead man's plate and cup, and the big scarf which covered the face of the image. At a lama's *sanglion* the nuns are given a rupee a head and a maund of grain between them, and the lamas are given Rs. 20 and three maunds of grain to divide. For a layman's *sanglion* the gifts are usually considerably less.

The day after the *sanglion* is finished the place where the body was disposed of is visited by some near relations of the deceased to see if there are any footprints in the near neighbourhood which would indicate that the dead man had reincarnated as an animal. The footprints of cats, dogs and tigers do not indicate reincarnation; they merely show that a devil has passed by in this form, and I never heard any actual incident of the prints of any other animal being discovered.

If everything consumed in this *sanglion* were paid for in cash it would represent an expense of over Rs. 200, for a continuous feast with meat has to be provided for all present. If the survivors are poor everybody will bring contributions of money and food. The ceremony is absolutely necessary to free the soul of the dead man from devils and lead it to heaven. Were it omitted the soul would wander miserably on earth, doing harm to the survivors, and eventually reincarnating as a worm or some noisome insect or beast of prey.

Money should be distributed to the monasteries in the name of the dead man; if he was a poor man it need only be given to the three monasteries of Zongu, but if he was rich to the monasteries all over Sikkim.

It is considered desirable that the Mun *sanglion* should take place on the same day as the disposal of the corpse. If, however, the lamas' *sanglion* is postponed that of the Mun may be also. Very few Mun know how to perform the death ceremony; in Lingthem the only one who knew how to was old Pumri and she was never employed as it was not considered suitable for a woman to perform the ceremony. Usually an old Mun from a village farther up the valley was summoned for the purpose. Gongyop said that he knew how to, but he was lazy and did not want to perform the ceremony and therefore did not get his qualification (*loong*).

Before the Mun comes out of his house to perform the ceremony he will spend the night communing and calling on the gods to help him conduct the soul to heaven; in particular he will call on Hit-*rum* and Dé-*rum*, the ancestral gods, and such ancestors of the deceased as have died in the same way as the present man. The Mun is accompanied by a friend or assistant called Mun-tyol.

After the funeral a pig is killed and one of its trotters is put aside on a wooden tray for the ceremony. The following articles—all very small—are also prepared inside the house and put on the tray: two ladders made out of the wood used for arrows, which are placed on either side of a tiny log, two small torches, one dish of rice mixed with charcoal and pebbles, a comb and a bristle brush. There is also prepared separately a rope of bamboo bark about twelve feet long and also 80 lbs. of *chi*, 40 lbs. of rice, and strained *chi* in a filtering bag. When all is prepared everybody in the house goes outside into the yard, except the lamas who stay inside reading their books. First of all the Mun takes the knife of the deceased (or, if the corpse was a woman, her sickle) and starts cutting the weeds in the courtyard. If there are many weeds others will help after the Mun has started. When the space is cleared the mourners have a meal; the Mun sits aside and is merely given *chi* to drink. An animal, preferably an ox, is brought in and offered to the devils who are plaguing the dead man's soul in order to induce them to desist; then the ox is killed by some unrelated layman and skinned and cut up. The intestines are boiled.

While the ox is cooking a shed is made for the Mun out of bamboo mats suspended from a post; to this post the cooked intestines are tied. (These are taken away in the morning by the Mun-tyol.) A little way in front of this is another post of a special sort of wood to which is attached the rope of bamboo bark; two knots are tied in it, the one nearer the post being for the devils, the farther one for the gods. The other end of this rope is held during the whole ceremony by the Mun and is finally severed with a pointed knife after the Mun has communicated with the dead.

The household sends out to the Mun a dish of boiled rice and a portion of the ox's ribs cut in two—one part for the Mun and the other for the Mun-tyol—and also black and white sausages.

Generally the Mun only eats the rice, the meat being taken away in the morning with the other presents.

There is also prepared a dish of all the sorts of food—dried bird and fish, ginger, different sorts of grain and fruits and roots and *chi*—that the deceased used to eat.

When everything is ready the Mun retires to the shed with his assistant. The rest of the people sit around but not so near that they can hear what is going on. Before retiring the Mun puts on a special head-dress of white cloth arranged like a turban with in the centre porcupine quills and tigers' whiskers and at the side peacock's feathers. The Mun now starts to *munthen* and calls on the dead man's soul, always holding the rope in the left hand. When he has got into communication with the dead man he starts giving him advice and help. When the Mun starts talking to the soul of the deceased the Mun-tyol sends for the tray which was prepared in the house and these objects are given to the soul by means of throwing them out of the shed (no notice is taken of them after) with instructions how to use them. First the soul is given the rice with the charcoal and pebbles in it; he is told to eat the rice and leave the charcoal and stones; the devils, pursuing and hungry, will pick over the stones for food and give him time to escape. Then he is given the ladders and torches to help him. With their aid he will be able to climb over the log which will block the way of the devils. He is also told to throw behind him the brush and comb which will grow into huge fences and block the devils' way.

Now the dead man's soul is coming near; when the Mun-tyol sees the signs that it is approaching he sends for the collection of food which has been prepared and this is offered to the dead man with the words: 'All these foods which you used to eat when you were alive you can have now.' Then suddenly the Mun 'dies'; he falls and his assistant catches him. The Mun's soul has departed from his body and in its place is the soul of the dead man who speaks through the Mun's lips: he speaks very slowly and in a very soft voice; it is not the voice of the Mun nor is it the voice of the dead man.[5] The Mun-tyol will then question the dead man, saying: 'Tell us what devils are troubling you; tell us how you died.' Then the dead man will say the cause of his death, whether it was caused directly by a devil or whether it was through

[5] Gongyop said that this possession is not so complete as the prophetic possession described by him in Chapter Eight; the dead man's soul does not enter the body of the Mun but 'sits on his shoulders'.

the intervention of some human enmity, either *mik-jit* (envy and cursing) or the direct sending of a devil.[6]

When the dead man has said what was the cause of his death he leaves the body of the Mun, who recovers and cuts the rope between the two knots, so that the devil's knot is left attached to the post, with the pointed knife that he has held in his right hand all the time. He then conducts the soul to the *rumlyang*, where all the dead live; he will find there a house prepared with bedding and all utensils; he will lead the soul into it and lock it in. This ends the Mun *sanglion* and in the morning the Mun goes home, taking with him his presents; they consist of the meat already mentioned, a leg of beef, Rs. 5 (or at any rate Rs. 3), the dead man's knife, or sickle, and one complete set of his clothes. These he wears or gives to his wife. The rest of the dead man's clothes are divided up among the children six months after death; they are washed three times and fumigated with incense before wearing. No danger is attached to them. The dead man's name is used for the ceremony and is not avoided afterwards.

It will be more convenient to finish the description of the Mun's ceremony here. One year after the original *sanglion* the Mun will go into a trance again, though an even lighter one this time, and visit the *rumlyang* once more. Outside the house in which the soul of the dead man is enclosed Hit-*rum* will be standing on guard; for him will be offered presents of *chi* and butter and sugar-cane and fruits and flowers and roots of many different sorts. After this the Mun unlocks the door of the house and finds a little baby inside; to this baby he presents a dress suitable to its sex. (The Mun is provided with two cloths, one for a boy and one for a girl, as it is by no means certain into which sex the dead person will reincarnate.) When the Mun has opened the door the baby comes outside and lives with the other people in the *rumlyang* who are his ancestors; the baby will grow up as human beings do and when

[6] I asked whether, if the death was caused by human agency, the survivors ought to try to take any revenge? The answers were somewhat confused (a) No, they should not because they could not be certain that it is true. (b) If they were not able to deal with the devil before it caused the man's death they would not be able to deal with it after. While the man was alive they should try and send the devil back to the original sender. (c) They can try to please the devil which has caused the death by giving it presents and induce it to return and smite the sender. I raised this point with several people and the general feeling was that revenge could not and should not be attempted. The greater number of people were surprised at my suggesting it.

the Mun visits the *rumlyang* in future years he will see the soul grown to be an adult. There is no death in the *rumlyang*, but when I pointed out the contradiction of there being no death for the souls with the lamaist belief that the soul is reincarnated on earth, a compromise was reached by stating that the soul would die in the *rumlyang* if it were going to be reincarnated on this earth.

V

On the third day after the Sandé Kangyour or after the *sanglion* —according to which comes first—one Mani prayer-flag is erected; on the twenty-first day a second is erected; and on the forty-ninth as many as can be afforded up to the number of one hundred and eight. The cost of a single prayer-flag for the dead[7] is reckoned to be about a rupee; the person setting it up provides the cloth and any competent lama can stamp it with the die which is kept in the monastery. The flag is inscribed with the most usual name of the person in whose intention it is erected written in Tibetan script. One flag for each dead person is usually set up in the monastery precincts, either the one put up on the third or twenty-first day. This prayer-flag is sanctified by a lama, usually the Dorjé Lapoon, reading a sacred book over it and sprinkling it with holy water (*tyü*), while a boy stands by holding two *chimi* on a plate; it is set up with a shout and afterwards a procession of lamas, nuns and mourners walk round it and the monastery turning their prayer-wheels and chanting *Om! mani pudme hum!* After the circumambulations are finished the whole procession prostrate themselves three times before the flag and touch the post first with their prayer-wheels, and then at a lower place with their foreheads.

The other prayer-flags set up outside the monastery precincts (they may be erected at the place where the corpse was disposed of or by his old home) are erected without any ceremony and may be put up by any layman. It is believed that the life of a prayer-flag will be proportionate to that of the person in whose intention it is erected; a flag for a young person will be soon tattered and torn, while that for an old person will last longer. It is permissible for anybody to dismantle a ragged prayer-flag, but it is rather unwise for a person unrelated to the setter-up to do so; for the setter-up might not consider it completely worn out, and in that case the

[7] Prayer flags for the living are slightly smaller and therefore less expensive; there are two dies for these but only one for the benefit of the dead.

person who dismantled it would have to provide a new one. If a person were to pull down a prayer-flag maliciously or in order to get the cloth (such a case occurred about twenty years ago) he would be fined Rs. 15.

A year after the death some more Mani prayer-flags are set up, and on that day a memorial ceremony called *lun-juk* is performed by lamas. This ceremony is held in the house where the deceased died; a Dorjé Lapoon must be present to read the proper books, a *kané* to play the musical instruments, and nuns to turn their prayer-wheels. Between a hundred and three hundred *chimi* are lit for this ceremony; since few people possess so many they borrow the lights either from neighbours or from the monastery; in the latter case they give a present of butter or oil in return. All the relations of the dead person should be present; but, if the deceased was a woman who had married a long way from her home, at least one representative of her family must be there, preferably her elder brother, or failing that her father or her uncle. After the performance of this ceremony the surviving partner, if the deceased was married, is free to marry again.

The Lepchas have formalised mourning very little. Until the *sanglion* members of the deceased's household wear rough old clothes and do not wash their hair; after that it is said that you can only distinguish a mourner by his sad face. People in mourning have to observe certain prohibitions. Any married person in any way connected with the dead man may not sleep with his spouse for three days after death, or until the corpse is disposed of, whichever period is the longer. If a spouse or parent or biological sibling dies the survivors are debarred for a year from marrying, or acting as *bek-bu* for another, or putting butter on sacrificial cups, or singing; during the period of mourning tables are never put in front of mourners, but always at the side. For affinal or classificatory relations these prohibitions are observed for forty-nine days.

Although the Lepchas do not dramatise their grief at the death of a near relation or friend their grief would appear to be sincere and deeply felt. The only time I saw a Lepcha cry was on the occasion of the erection of a prayer-flag in memory of the mother of the Mandal of Lungdeum, twenty-one days after her death. Two of her sisters had married men of Lingthem and were present at the ceremony; and as the flag was finally hoisted they burst into tears. There was no exhibition of grief; the women turned their backs on the rest of the company and cried quietly; when the mourners dispersed they wiped their eyes and appeared soon after to be in normal spirits. It seemed almost as though they were trying to hide their grief.

All the elaborate ceremonies which I have described are performed to get rid of the dead; the dead are terrifying and should be feared, not loved. Death has no consolations.

BOOK THREE

Lives of Lepchas

CHAPTER FOURTEEN

DEVIANTS AND DEFECTIVES

i

Except when I have used individual illustrations the four chapters of Book Two have been written about an abstraction called 'the average Lepcha'. Of course such an abstraction has no more real existence than 'the average man' or 'the man in the street' dear to European and American journalists; he is a compromise between the ideal personality set up for the Lepchas by themselves and the observable behaviour of the majority of the Lepchas in Lingthem. It is the Lepcha stereotype who has been described.

The Lepcha stereotype is unaggressive, sociable, hard-working, constantly good-humoured, greatly interested in direct consumption (eating, drinking and copulation), fundamentally optimistic. The relationship of the Lepcha stereotype with his fellows is based rationally on mutual benefits and obligations; very little stress is placed on personal affection and practically no interest is taken in, and no allowance made for, individual character or temperament. The Lepcha insists very firmly on the independence of the adult individual and the family group; no attempt is made to dominate or exploit others, and any attempt by others to dominate or exploit is resisted as actively as the rules of the culture permit. The Lepcha identifies himself strongly with his family group and with his immediate community—the village; the identification with the tribe as a whole is much less strong, and one of the Lepchas' chief social weaknesses is that, except in the case of serious crime, the Mandal and inhabitants of one village have little influence over the inhabitants of any other village under a different Mandal. The Lepcha stereotype calls for a very gradual emergence of responsibility and almost unquestioning confidence from younger people in their elders.

Although this stereotype does not, I think, correspond exactly to the behaviour or attitudes of any one person, it is not for that reason valueless. It represents the ideal towards which the Lepchas strive and to which they attempt to mould their children, and it is in the deviations from this imposed stereotype that the greater number of psychological difficulties for the Lepchas arise. As such it has preponderating weight in the formation of individual character, and constitutes a point of reference from which deviation can be measured.

Deviations fall into two groups, negative and positive; people may lack some characteristic or qualification called for by the cultural stereotype; or they may manifest characteristics and types of behaviour which exaggerate cultural characteristics, or they may have temperamental qualities definitely opposed to the cultural stereotype. Judged by such rigorous standards there is probably nobody who is not slightly deviant. There are, however, two people in Lingthem, Chala Mandal and Tafoor, in whom I could discern no temperamental cause for psychological discomfort. Both had reasons for a certain distress, but they were external ones; the Mandal was unhappy because he had no son, Tafoor, I think, slightly disappointed because he had neither the wealth nor position of his late father the Muktair. These two people practically embodied the Lepcha ideal, the Mandal for the layman and Tafoor for the lama; Tafoor's household also approached more nearly than any other to the Lepcha ideal.

Owing to the Lepchas' great tolerance of—or rather indifference, to—shades of character, the maladjusted tend to be sociotic[1] rather than neurotic deviants. The only temperament type to which the Lepchas manifest constant opposition is the aggressive and domineering personality; the person who wishes to domineer or to command is constantly thwarted; to paraphrase Saki's epigram, there may be people born to command among the Lepchas, but they never find anybody born to obey them. The most outstanding of these aggressive characters were Tempa, who was described in Chapter Five,[2] and Kurma, whose story is given at length in the next chapter. It is worth noting that these two are also sociotically maladjusted; Tempa is a foreigner from outside Zongu, reared in a mixed community, and living under the slightly humiliating condition of resident son-in-law (*komok myok*); Kurma was adopted by an elderly couple as a little boy, was very unhappy

[1] This term was first used by Dr. Moreno to distinguish socially maladjusted from temperamentally maladjusted people.

[2] See pp. 124–126.

in his adopted parents' house, and finally ran away. Besides his aggressive characteristics Kurma shared with Tempa a tendency to boastful lying in an attempt to give himself greater importance than he possessed, and a desire for money for its own sake. Kurma was also unique among the adult Lepchas in getting obviously drunk.

The foreigners, the people not born in Zongu, are the most obviously disturbing elements. Tempa and his sister, Mrs. Jiroong,[3] caused more trouble than all the other inhabitants of Lingthem put together. In his earlier years, too, the first Dorjé Lapoon, who is half Tibetan, caused a very great deal of disturbance.[4]

Owing to the very late psychological maturing of the Lepchas it is difficult to speak with confidence of the characters of most of the men under thirty and of most of the women under twenty. Except where there was strongly marked deviance, such as in the cases of Chélé, and the two girls Prumtu and Kondé,[5] the younger people lived psychologically so much under the shadow of their elders that it was impossible to foresee how they would act when they were independent.

Mrs. Datoop and Lumba's first wife were both rather more independent than the Lepcha ideal type of woman calls for. Lumba's first wife insisted on living in a field-house because, although she got on well with her co-wife and step-children, she disliked living in a crowd and having to bend her wishes to the majority. Mrs. Datoop almost openly ruled her husband and her household; she was far more business-like and managing and practical than is necessary for a Lepcha woman. These qualities, however, did not bring her into conflict with the other Lepchas, for they were developed along lines congruent with the Lepcha culture; her excessive qualities were for the Lepchas good qualities and she held a high place in the general esteem. In a culture in which the temperament rôles of men and women are violently contrasted she would have been severely maladjusted, for she was almost the most 'virile' person (in the Occidental sense of the word) in Lingthem.

Mrs. Tafoor was rather more actively unhappy, for she was a woman of fairly violent temper and aggressively sexed; she was in the unfortunate position of a person who liked a quarrel and who could find nobody to quarrel with. Tafoor used to tease her

[3] See Chapter Five, pp. 140–142.

[4] See Chapter Sixteen, pp. 416–420.

[5] For Chélé see Chapter Six, pp. 164–165; for Prumtu, Chapter Eleven, p. 311; for Kondé, Chapter Twelve, pp. 322–323.

a lot, but very slyly ; thus when in her presence he was explaining to us the way marriage horoscopes are cast he pointed out with considerable emphasis that the books foretold without any question that she would die young, very many years before he did.[6]

The most general excessive quality among the Lepchas, particularly the men, is excessive timidity ; thus Chano, Gongyop and his son, Pembu, Jiroong and Nahyeun were all timid to a point where this timidity became an active disability. The Lepcha ideal calls for a very gradual emergence of responsibility, but it does call for it, and these people gave the impression of being permanently fixed in the dependent stage. Thus Pembu, who should have been running his own household, was almost entirely dependent on his mother for advice and help, Jiroong on his wife. Others fall short of the Lepcha ideal personality by lack of intelligence or industry ; among these were Katel, Dunbi, Ashyok, and Aga. Of these Dunbi was temperamentally lazy and the other three were foolish and incompetent by the standards of the culture. Tobgé, and to a lesser extent Dadool, exceeded the Lepcha bounds of irresponsibility and licentiousness permitted to young men.

Among the younger men Rigya, who was born in 1915, to a certain extent aided and abetted by his adoptive elder brother Nariya, was unique in being an active miser. He was always shabbily dressed, and unlike all the other Lepchas, never made us presents, though he spent a great deal of time hanging round us, gaping at our possessions, and asking for presents ; he had particularly a magpie desire for illustrated papers, and was always asking for pictures of war 'because he had never seen anything like them and was amazed'. He was given quite a number of papers, but one day I told him he could not have any more because other people wanted them. (One of the very few times I saw a Lepcha boy cry was on one occasion when two mothers each accompanied with sons about eight years old came up for medicine ; one of the boys asked for a paper and I gave it to him and went on dressing the cut ; the mother of the other child asked rather timidly if I had not a paper for her boy as well, and I then saw this latter holding his mother's hand, with tears streaming down his face ; he was crying hard but so quietly that I had not realised it though I was a couple of yards away.) A couple of days after I had refused to give Rigya any more papers he arrived early one morning to repeat his demand, bringing with him as a present the smallest

[6] See Appendix III, b.

Above : DADOOL AND RIGYA (IN HAT)

Below : KANDEN AND CHIMPET. CHIMPET IS LAUGHING SO MUCH THAT HE IS NEARLY IN TEARS; KANDEN SMILES SECRETIVELY

bottle of milk I ever received; he appeared astounded at his own generosity. I asked him whence he had got the milk, for I thought he had no cattle, and then, when I showed that I considered him one of the poorer people of Lingthem, his pride overcame his reticence, and he confided his great secret to me. I do not think that any Lepcha in Lingthem outside his household knew of his secret savings and ambitions. I naturally could not refer to them openly, but I made several hints when talking to other Lepchas; these hints were never taken up.

Rigya was the middle son of Ashyok *youmi*, but was given as a child to Ashyok's elder brother, who had only one son, Nariya, ten years older than Rigya, and who seemed unlikely to have another. At that period Nariya's father was the richest man in Lingthem, whereas Ashyok, who had two other sons, was relatively poor. Since the death of Nariya's father, Rigya calls Nariya 'father'. This is the story he told me.

'When I was a baby I didn't distinguish between my adopting parents and my real parents; as soon as I knew who were my real parents I tried to run away to them; but they beat me and sent me back. I love my real parents best, especially my mother; they gave me food and clothes and looked after me; now in my turn I must look after them. But I loved my other mother and father too; they gave me food and rice and meat. Now I love my wife best after my parents, but I used not to.

'When I was a child I was very frightened of devils, especially Tongryong *moong*, who is like a tiger and runs after and kills people. I was also frightened of houses where people had died and of burial places and used to run away from them; indeed I did this till last year, but now I am grown up so I don't run away any longer. Even today I'm frightened of Jamfi *moong* and Mitoor (a dog-shaped devil) when I'm in the forests or high mountains. I'm frightened too of people if I've told them a lie, or said evil about them or done them wrong; but I've never done anything really wrong like sleeping with another man's wife. I've seen a lot of corpses but I've never been frightened of them.

'I didn't sleep with girls when I was young because my father and mother had told me it was very wrong to sleep with other men's wives; they promised me that they would *asék* me as soon as I was big enough. But one day when I was fifteen a girl from Lungdeung came to stop here and she said to me, "Let us sleep together", so I did and I liked it, and we did it again six or seven days later.

She was the same year as me; it was my first time but I don't think it was hers. Afterwards my parents wanted to *asék* her but she was already bespoke. Next I was *asék* to another girl, but we didn't get on together and later the Mandal arranged for the *asék* to be broken. Finally I was *asék* to my present wife.[7] For the first two or three years we used to dislike one another very much; when she saw me she used to exclaim: "May this boy die young!" This always happens when the parents arrange a marriage between two people who don't know one another. Even when she came to live with me we slept apart at first; I tried to copulate with her but she pushed me away, and I was afraid to use force because she might beat me. But everybody gave her advice and presents—money and clothes and jewels—my parents and the Mandal and the other women in the village. At first we couldn't even look at one another, but now we're friendly; when I go out to work and come back tired my wife has food ready for me and looks after me, and I love her and think in my belly "This is my wife," and I am pleased.

'Nariya's father was the richest man in the neighbourhood—richer than the Mandal—but much money was lost over a lawsuit concerning Nariya's first wife, the girl from Lingmu. The girl was a wicked girl who slept with everybody; and when she ran away she stole Rs. 150 in cash as well as taking her clothes and jewels; and her father borrowed Rs. 120 from Nariya's father and never paid it back. Besides these losses the lawsuit cost Nariya and the girl's father Rs. 200 each. Before that time he had had sixty head of cattle; the girl ruined him. The girl when alone used to live on the fat of the land, killing hens, and so on, for herself.

'Nariya's cardamum amounts to 15 maunds, mine to 20, and my wife's to 5 maunds. Nariya has eleven oxen, I five, and my wife none. Many oxen were killed because no less than seven people died in the house, and an ox was killed for each *sanglion* and also for the memorial feast a year later. Also my marriage cost three oxen; one was given for *asék*, instead of the two pigs, and two at the marriage. It is good to have plenty of cattle because then for ceremonies and so on you are completely independent and do not have to borrow; also you can sell butter to the kanya at Mangan who pay from Rs –/8 to Rs. 1 for 2 lbs.

'None of us owe a penny to the kanya, nor indeed except for some meat from neighbours, an anna to anybody else. We are

[7] Who had been formerly *asék*'d to his two brothers. See Chapter Six, p. 1,7.

all three saving up as hard as we can to have a really pukka house with a tin roof and good floors; for this reason we are denying ourselves practically everything except the barest necessities until we get our house. (*His eyes gleamed as he spoke about this.*) We wear the plainest of clothes; my wife has no jewels, but puts the money aside from her cardamum to pay for the house; we only eat plain food, just rice. Others waste a lot of crops for *chi* but we don't; now and again we have a little but between whiles we just drink tea. *We* don't get into debt for showy clothes and useless gew-gaws. Even now I am really richer than Tafoor who has lots and lots of debts; and as for my father (Ashyok) and my elder brother (Aplung), why they haven't anything; as soon as they get a rupee they go and spend it and never save a *pice*. Of course we give feasts; if we did not follow the *lungthen* (custom) and perform the proper ceremonies we would die. Yes, it is nice when we give the monastery feast; our turn comes in the winter; last year we gave a pig. But soon—soon—we will have the lovely house with the tin roof; there won't be another one like it in Lingthem, though I have heard that the younger brother of Takneum who lives at Tangvong has got one. As soon as we have saved up enough money we will give the measurements to the kanya and they will get the corrugated iron. We would certainly never think of going to buy *chi* as other people do if we run out of it.'

ii

An important group of deviants are the defectives. Of these there are three, all males; they are Sangkyar, the elder son of Gongyop's eldest brother (now dead: the other son is lame Satéo), the middle son of Asang, and Kanden, the elder son of Také and the elder brother of Dadool. Although Sangkyar is very different from the other two, all three show the same symptoms of compulsive wandering, and this is considered by Lepchas to be an inevitable concomitant to feeble-mindedness in males: indeed they are called 'wanderers'. This symptom does not apparently show itself in girls and women; I neither saw nor heard of similarly afflicted girls.

Sangkyar I only saw once. He has a typically cretinous expression and type of behaviour. He is the example *par excellence* of the bad boy, the *tané*; he wanders about and sleeps in the forest and steals from other people's houses and fields. He takes food and does not do his share of the work; he leaves immediately he has got what he wanted. He is unsettled and unco-operative; there is nothing good to be said of him, and no excuses to be made for him, for he does not attempt to do as much as he could. It is said that he suffers from genital infantilism and fimosis; if he wanted to marry he would not be able to find a wife, but he does not want to. Since his parents' death he lives with his uncle, Thyak Thimbu; but he finds him very unsatisfactory for he is always going away.

This instability and wandering are also the chief symptoms of Asang's idiot son and Kanden. Since I saw quite a lot of Kanden and very little of the other I propose to describe Kanden; the medical histories of the two young men are almost identical.

Kanden was born in 1912, the middle of three brothers, but the elder boy died in infancy. When Kanden was about two years old his mother died and his father ran away with another woman; for five years Kanden was brought up by his 'aunt', Lumba's first wife. According to his father and to all the neighbours, Kanden was quite a normal boy as a child and up to the age of thirteen; until that age he was a good and sensible boy and worked properly and well. When his horoscope was cast at birth it was found that he was the reincarnation of a Tibetan lama, but when he went to Lumba to study he could not learn and got duller and duller until he was forced to give up the study. From that time he has suffered from wandering fits; sometimes just as he is going to eat he will get up without saying a word and go away for three, five, or seven days. During these fits he does not speak; and it seems as though he recognises nobody. He just wanders about sleeping and eating anywhere. Were he to steal or do anything wrong his parents would be held responsible, but in point of fact he does not do so. This state is caused by a supernatural called Kyon-rek; no exorcism is efficacious; the boy will get worse and worse till he dies an early death. There is no general reason for boys getting into this state (according to Tafoor, in Kanden's case it is the result of going against his destiny to be a lama); in a large (extended) family there is likely to be one wanderer. Besides Asang's son Dunbi's younger brother, now dead, was also a wanderer.

Most of the statements about Kanden given above were made by his father. Some weeks after I had got this information Kanden came up to gather firewood in company with Chimpet and I had a talk with him. It was not in any way a formal interview; we were all sitting together on the stones outside the monastery; there were betel nut and cigarettes provided. Chimpet did a great deal of the talking; he was always a rather irrepressible little boy, and on this occasion he was bubbling over with jokes and dirty remarks more than usual. A great number of the remarks made by Kanden arose out of Chimpet's statements. My interpreter was present, but everybody was completely used to him by that time. A lot of the talk was fairly meaningless jokes; I asked Kanden the type questions which it was known I asked everybody; what his earliest memories were; who his relations were and if he liked them; what his first sexual experience was; what his ambition was; what private property he had; whether he had heard or seen devils. I was particularly trying to find out about his wanderings and led the conversation back to them whenever I could without stressing the point. The only subject I tried to elaborate were his relations with Pichi, after he had emphatically stated that he preferred him to anybody else. I was very anxious not to frighten him and therefore did not ask any searching questions or insist on any subject for which he showed distaste. As far as I could judge the atmosphere was friendly and indeed frivolous.

Since I know of no other record of a primitive mental defective I propose to insert *verbatim* the notes which I made immediately after the interview, in order that, if possible, other people may be able to make a diagnosis.

'April 30th. Kanden came up to gather firewood this morning and I was able to talk to him for a couple of hours. He is twenty-five, heavy featured, and thick-lipped with rather more black hairs on the legs than the other Lepchas of his age. He sits on the whole very still, gesturing with one arm from the elbow, except when he is embarrassed, when he fidgets with a twig on the ground. He is of obviously low vitality.

'On the whole he speaks quite rationally; he can answer questions about relationship and so on consequentially. He speaks slowly and is rather liable to drop his voice to a confidential whisper. He has rather a foolish laugh and never laughed spontaneously, but when anybody else did he joined in a good deal. Chimpet was present, usually making obscene remarks which Kanden thought funny. Chimpet is more than ten years his junior, but he treated him as if they were of an age, whispering to him after he had gone away for a little "Did you kill a bird?" and reproving him as *tané* when he confessed to having had sexual experience.

'Kanden knows his own story apparently from telling, for he says he has no memory of the time before he was about Chimpet's age. His mother died when he was about two and he was taken and looked after by Lumba, who is a sort of maternal uncle and who at that time had no sons. When he was big enough to carry a water bamboo (that is about five) his father ran away to Darjeeling. Dadool, his younger brother, was looked after by his father's elder brother, now dead, and his wife. When his father returned—that is when the boy was about ten—he took him back. A couple of years after that he went to an old *omzet*, now dead, to study to be a lama;[8] but he had to give it up as he had no time to study—there was all the *work* in the house and the fields. He would have liked to have learnt.

'Shortly after this his compulsive wanderings began. He would suddenly feel that he did not like his parents and that he had got to go away to *work* for others. He would go to somebody else's house—usually a relation—Songpo is an "uncle" and the Mandal's third wife an "elder sister"—and help them in their *work*, staying two, three, five or seven days before returning home. When he was a young boy his father used to send him to help his relations with their *work* and sometimes he used to feel he had to go home. He speaks with embarrassment and some giggling of these wanderings and in a low voice, but he answers quite sensibly. The feeling comes over him irresistibly; it is not accompanied by any sense delusions. He knows his parents and so on, but does not, then, want to have anything to do with them. He "just thinks he wants to go and help others with their *work*. As long as he helps others with their *work* others will help him. He goes to their house and it becomes late and he stops there."

'He is happiest of all working in the fields or gathering firewood or in the house. The happiest time of his life was as a boy. He does not want to get older and die. He is not married, does not want to marry, has never seen a woman he would like to marry, has never copulated, and never gets erections.[9] At marriages and feasts boys and girls get together and copulate, but he never does nor has done. As a boy he used to talk and joke with the girls but never anything more.

'He does not like his stepmother; she feeds him all right and

[8] His father said his teacher was Lumba: I do not know who is correct.

[9] Datoop says that Kanden did sleep with Asang's wife, but she now won't have him, and nobody else likes him as he is a fool.

does not hit him but she scolds; not only him but also his brother and father. He not only does not like her as well as his real mother (whom he obviously never knew) but prefers Lumba's first wife. Indeed he does not like women at all; when he helps people with their *work* he always helps men, usually either old men or boys. His great friend whom he calls *ingzong* is Pichi, the son of Datoop; he loves him very much, more than his brother. I do not think, however, there is any question of a homosexual attachment here; he says they never put their arms round one another's shoulders; and when I asked if he thought it would be nice, since they were both unmarried, to set up house together and live alone, he replied without enthusiasm that (*a*) The parents would not allow it, and (*b*) Pichi would refuse. They just help one another in their *work*.[10]

'He never wanders far, he says, nor goes into the forest. He just goes to other people's houses to help them.

'He has never seen a devil, but has heard some and been frightened. These devils are Ingbong *moong* and Numeen *moong* who cry like babies and Bamoo *moong* who cries like an old woman and is a sort of banshee predicting death. He heard her once crying by a stream one day when he was lying at home in bed. He has also heard Zombu *moong* which is the devil which causes death, and which can be heard on the day of burial and also on the anniversary of the death. None of these devils have ever spoken. He has also dreamt of lamas and bejewelled women who indicate the presence of Lungzi-chen *moong*. There is nothing in any way exceptional about hearing these devils; many others have said they have heard them and Chimpet said he had heard and been frightened of Zombu *moong*.

'He says he has two or three oxen and two or three pigs as his own private property, but his parents look after them and feed them. He buys his own clothes out of the produce of his own cardamum fields. I could not make out whether the rice terraces near the Mandal's house belonged to him or to his parents; I think the latter. He speaks eagerly of work in the fields. The dry rice is sown, but so far neither the millet nor wet rice. He gives all his money and goods to his parents; if he were married he would have separate property, but as things are he has nothing separate or secret from his father. He is fond of his father, likes him better than Lumba.

10 Pichi said later that he and Kanden are no longer friends; they used to live near each other and work together; now he is no longer friendly with him. Pichi also said that when he is not wandering he is a good worker.

'He would like to be wealthy and have lots of good food and clothes. He thinks he would like to go to live at Gangtok where he has been three or four or five times. (Numbers always confuse him; in any question demanding a numerical answer he always gives a number of alternatives—an exaggeration of a cultural trait.)

'The first time he wandered away he went to his uncle Songpo; he "thought he would be angry if he did not go and help them with their *work*." He still thinks that he has to go and help people or they will be angry.

'When he asked Chimpet if he had killed a bird he first of all denied having done so himself and then said that he had killed no big animal but has caught birds in snares. He showed little interest in this; did not care if the birds were caught alive or dead; apparently of no emotional importance.

'All through the interview—I reverted to the subject of his wanderings several times, but never stressed it—there came up the obsessive connection between wandering and helping others with their *work*. "I go away to help others clean the ground and sow and then it gets dark and I stay there. As long as I help others others will help me." His aversion to sex also came up several times. It is worth noting that Kanden exceptionally had no *oongop* to educate him sexually. It is possible that such a relation might have quieted his fear of women. Of course there are a number of women with whom he had a theoretical right to sleep, but none who were in a position to make a direct approach.'

I have given this interview at such length because it seems to me to raise a problem of particular interest. As far as I can tell from this interview with Kanden, from casual contacts with Asang's idiot son, and from the description of other wanderers given by Lepchas, there would appear to be considerable parallels between the Lepcha wanderers and the schizophrenics of our own culture. The parallels between 'wandering' and schizophrenia appear to me to be the following: the symptoms nearly always declare themselves in the second decade of life, after an apparently normal childhood; there are some physical abnormalities—the excess of body hair and a certain thickening of the features; there is the low or absent sexual impulse; there is the relative immobility and the very confidential voice. On the other hand what is for the Lepchas the most significant feature of all is the motiveless wandering, which has more obvious resemblance to a compulsion neurosis than to schizophrenia.

Also there do not seem to be any hallucinations (the hearing of devils cannot be so classified, as it is part of the expected behaviour of every child), nor, save during the wandering fits, any change of emotional attitude towards the members of the immediate family.

It seems to me possible that the forms of insanity clinically recognised are culturally determined ; and in that case the state of affairs which in Occidental societies would produce either schizophrenia or compulsion neurosis, among the Lepchas produces the various syndromes of which the wandering is the most obvious feature. In the case of Kanden it is noteworthy that the cultural stress on co-operation has produced what would appear to be a feeling of neurotic anxiety so strong that it interferes with the individual's proper performance of his own work. This suggestion of the cultural determination of the symptoms of insanity is inevitably completely tentative, since I know of no other records of definitely abnormal types in non-European cultures.

CHAPTER FIFTEEN

THE LIFE OF KURMA

i

When I went to investigate the Lepchas one of the chief objects that I set myself was the collection, if it should prove possible, of the life history of one or more individuals. This seemed to me desirable for a number of reasons. It should be axiomatic that all sociology is based on the dialectical opposites of the society and the individual, and that any study which neglects either pole is thereby incomplete. Unfortunately, owing to the elaboration and specialisation of the distinct disciplines there has been very little contact between the psychologist studying the individual and the sociologist and anthropologist studying the group; the psychologist tends to treat the individual as though he lived in a vacuum, shared perhaps by his parents and immediate family, and they act as though the particular society of which the individual is a member were 'human nature' or 'natural circumstances'; they tend to ignore almost completely the cultural conditioning to which the individual, as a member of his society, has inevitably been subjected.[1] The sociologist and anthropologist on the other hand tend to ignore the individual as such, though they naturally pay attention to the special social functions of certain individuals placed by the society in conspicuous positions. Apart from these individuals of outstanding position, the mass of the population is classified into groups, usually according to one single aspect of the individual—their economic position, their religious beliefs, their type of work, their

[1] A notable exception must be made for the work of Dr. Margaret Mead and that of Dr. John Dollard of the Institute of Human Relations of Yale University. His two books—*Criteria for the Life History* and *Caste and Class in a Southern Town*—combine very significantly the study of the individual and his society. I should like to reiterate my very great debt to Dr. Dollard, for it was through his books and conversation that my attention was focussed on this particular problem.

age or sex, and various other criteria. The working of the society is, as it were, studied from above and as objectively as possible. This non-participating attitude is undoubtedly necessary to get a complete view of the society in all its functions and ramifications; but if the study stops there it is impossible to interpret from such data the effect which the organisations studied have on the individuals who have to work them. We may learn a great deal about a given culture without having any estimate as to the results this culture has on its component parts, or the subjective importance of these parts to the individual. To give an over-simple example, any study of English life would have to devote considerable space to the very elaborate organisation and beliefs of the Church of England; it might also notice, though naturally more briefly, the value placed on a dirt-free epidermis and correctly buttoned garments. But no objective view could show how many people would prefer the close company of a professed atheist to a person who had patently not washed in the last fortnight, or whether an individual would be more discomfited by missing evensong or by entering a crowded room with all his trouser buttons undone. A good deal of interpretation is possible, especially in small communities, by intelligent observation and deduction, but such interpretation, however carefully documented, can always be suspected of misplaced emphasis and perhaps personal bias.[2] These objections inevitably disappear in an avowedly subjective autobiography of a member of the society. The individual telling his own story may be an exceptional one, but the emphasis and stresses are untouched by the preoccupations of the ethnographer.

A second advantage of the life history is that it is liable to give information on points which would otherwise be inevitably unobservable. Thus among the Lepchas it would be quite impossible for any stranger to observe the almost constant nagging in which women seem to indulge in the privacy of the family, for such nagging is immediately stopped in the presence of any stranger. I should have considered the women as apparently peaceful and contented as the men, did not this family nagging recur so frequently in people's autobiographies. Similarly the psychological importance

[2] It may be considered that I have exaggerated the use of the first person singular in this book. I think it preferable to allow my own bias to show openly and thereby be accounted for, than to pretend to the inevitably unobtainable attitude of Olympian objectivity. The ethnographer is as much part of the society he is studying (albeit only temporarily) as any other member.

of food would be almost impossible to estimate, if it were not for the fact that it is the central theme of so many individual memories. One of the chief justifications of the collection of life histories is given by the experience of my friend Mr. R. F. Barton,[8] who, on his third visit to the Ifugao, discovered through a life history a group of family gods with special observances of whose existence fifteen years life among the Ifugao with two long periods of objective investigation had given him no clue.

A third advantage of the life history, to my mind—though this point is of less immediate impact on sociology—is that it is a valuable corrective. There is at present a very obvious tendency in political and sociological thinking to ignore the individual in favour of his political or social functions; this dehumanising of social thought seems to me not only undesirable but also extremely dangerous; a great deal of the misery and distress in the contemporary scene appears to me to derive directly from the habit of thinking of people in groups instead of as individuals.

ii

Since I wished if possible to collect a life history, and since for various personal reasons my stay outside Europe could not be overlong, I was very lucky in finding in the Lepchas a society with a relatively unelaborated culture (outside the sphere of religion), and moreover one which was in no way fractionalised and of which no portion was guarded as a secret from the rest of the community. The energy which in other societies might have had to be directed to the discovery of magic or secret rites and initiations I was able to divert to the establishment of personal contacts. Moreover my preliminary study of the language in British India had given me a working knowledge of most of the formal arrangements of the society, such as the kinship terms and marriage arrangements, so that after the first month I was able to devote a considerable amount of my time to the non-formalised aspects of the culture and to try to get life histories.

Now to learn the story of another's life it is obviously necessary that the person who is telling his story should tell it willingly and have confidence in his listener; otherwise you will inevitably get lies and evasions. Here, too, I was served by the Lepchas' tendency

[8] Author of *Ifugao Law and Customs*, *The Rising Sun*, etc.

to monologue, to recount anecdotes, to illustrate a theme by their own past experiences. I soon noticed that Kurma had a particular tendency to do this, and also that he was flattered by my obvious interest in what he had to say. After we had been in fairly continuous contact for about a month I asked him to tell me what he remembered of his childhood. He did so willingly, and thereafter it was easy to bring him back to the subject of his own past life by asking a single leading question. 'What happened after you did so-and-so?' 'What happened to so-and-so?' While he was telling his story I asked practically no questions at all; I kept all queries for subsequent meetings when impersonal subjects would be discussed, when I would interject them without apparent emphasis. Altogether about six full days were passed mainly in the discussion of Kurma's own life; I should undoubtedly have had more material if he had not first been summoned to visit his parents-in-law and on his return been taken ill with fever. Besides these special sessions Kurma would often introduce apposite anecdotes of his own past life, both before and after I had started getting his story.

With Kurma, more than with any other individual in Lingthem we managed to set up a pattern of mutual obligations. As *gyapön* he had been charged by the Mandal to look after us, especially in the matter of getting provisions; he enjoyed the reflected importance of his contact with Europeans, and I flattered him by appealing to him somewhat more often than was necessary. He was anyhow more disposed to talk than to work and was very amenable to cajolery.

I did not like Kurma very much and had not very full confidence in him. I repeatedly tried to trip him up by asking him identical questions at considerable intervals of time, and to check up on him by questioning other people. Actually my distrust was practically unfounded; only on one major point—the death of Banyok—did I find him completely incorrect, and at a later date he voluntarily retracted his first version.

Both through temperament and circumstances Kurma was an a-typical Lepcha. In temperament he had an unusual desire for power, was boastful, and had decided sadistic traits. Sociotically he was unfortunately circumstanced and his treatment of his circumstances was unusual. His mother appears to have been exceptionally poor and his adopting parents exceptionally unkind. Adoption is of itself statistically rare—only eleven people out of the 176 in

Lingthem were or had been adopted; and Kurma is unique in having completely abandoned his adopting parents to return to his biological parents. Again as a person with two elder brothers Kurma is unusual in having become head of the household at an early age and in having had the heavy economic burden of seven funerals in a fairly short stretch of time.[4] He is also unusual in having started with an irregular sexual union, and extremely unfortunate in the mortality of his wives.

Nevertheless, despite his unusual character and circumstances, I believe that Kurma's life-story, incomplete though it is, gives a good illustration of the dynamic workings of Lepcha culture and an adequate cross-section view of Lepcha society. By developing the themes which he touches on,[5] sometimes very cursorily, one would have an almost complete picture of Lepcha social arrangements; if it were not for the awkwardness of such an arrangement, all the preceding chapters of this book could be used as amplification for Kurma's story.

I am giving the notes in the form in which I took them. The portions in quotation marks are nearly *verbatim* transcriptions; I could not, however, always write quickly enough to take down every word, and I have omitted the repetitions which swell out all Lepcha stories. The portions told in the third person are chiefly incidents which cropped up in the discussion of other matters.

Although I have not altered the notes in any way I am presenting them in more or less historical order, which is not that in which the information was given to me. To simplify reading I am giving cross-headings, and a few explanatory notes. For those points in his narrative on which I questioned other people and on which their versions differed considerably from Kurma's I have presented the alternative versions in brackets and italics. For ease of reference I am also giving overleaf a calendar of the more or less well-established dates in Kurma's life and the names and dates of birth and death of his immediate family. To bring his story up to date I have put after his narrative a journal of his doings during the period when I was observing him.

[4] The only people in Lingthem similarly circumstanced were Nariya and Rigya, and they were economically far better able to stand the strain.

[5] I have omitted in the following pages all the impersonal material (ceremonies, etc.) which Kurma incorporated in his story.

DATES IN KURMA'S LIFE

1900	Birth.
1903	Death of father.
1904 ?	Adopted by Passo and wife.
1907 ?	Death of Banyok.
1910	Possesion by Padem spirit.
1916	Returns home for good.
1917	Suicide of elder brother Ahyok.
1918	Meets Yangma, elder sister of Gongyop.
1919–1923	Lives with Yangma in Lingthem. Illness.
1924	Death of stepfather, Chenyak. Kurma returns to Lik-lyang and *asék*'s his first wife.
1931	Death of first wife.
1932	Comes to second wife at Lingthem as *komok myok*.
1933 spring	Death of mother at Lungdeum.
1933 autumn	Birth of elder daughter.
1934 ? spring	Death of younger brother Samboop.
?1934	Birth of younger daughter.
1934 autumn	Death of elder daughter.
1934 autumn	Becomes *gyapön* for three years.
1935 March	Death of second wife.
1936 April	Becomes *asék* to third wife.
1936 September	Birth of son.
? 1938 harvest	Projected third marriage.

Kurma's family

Kurma's father died 1903 ; exact age unknown, but was a young man.
Kurma's mother was a Mun. Born 1864. Died 1931.
Kurma's stepfather Chenyak was a lama. Born 1867. Died 1924.

Siblings : years of birth and approximate date of death.

*1. Nimu (girl).	Born 1889.	Still living in Lungdeum : married, with children.
2. Ahyok (boy).	Born 1892.	Committed suicide 1917.
3. Ajeunmu (girl).	Born 1895.	Died *c.* 1922. Mother of boy Takshyom, living with Kurma.
4. Banyok (boy).	Born 1896.	Died *c.* 1907.
5. Kurma (boy).	Born 1900.	
6. Samboop (boy).	Born 1903.	Died ? 1934.
*7. Nurzé (girl).	Born ? 1909.	Died ? 1915.

* *Note.* The eldest and youngest girls are both said to be bastards, the eldest born before the mother's marriage, and the latter after she was a widow. Kurma's mother claims that the father of Nimu was the second Dorjé Lapoon, the father of Nurzé, Pashet, a married man of Panung. Both men refused to acknowledge paternity, and in both cases the *thip-song* ceremony was performed by the brothers of Kurma's mother.

KURMA *GYAPON*

iii

Earliest memories. Death of Father. (I believe there is considerable telescoping in these earliest memories.)

Kurma's earliest memories date from when he was three years old. At the time he remembers only he and his brother Banyok were living at home; one brother and one sister were living with his maternal grandmother and the eldest sister was also away. His parents were very poor; they had only a one-room house and no goats or cattle; they lived at Panung, the next village over the hill. The earliest memories are all concerned with the death of his Father, which took place three months before the birth of his younger brother Samboop, and therefore presumably date from the middle of his third year.

'My first clear memory is of my Father popping corn; besides the four stones which make up the usual fireplace another large stone had been set up in front to keep the heat of the fire off Father. The firewood was put in from two sides only, instead of all round, on either side of the big stone: Father sat behind the stone popping the corn and I sat near him to get the popped corn. Mother was husking corn.

'This scene occurred three days before the marriage of a paternal-uncle-younger-than-father; I did not then know who he was and thought he was just a big man with short-cut grey hair. That day there was another marriage in the village and Mother went down to the marriage to drink *chi* and have a good time. Father asked her to bring him back a piece of liver from the ox which would be killed and divided up; one of Mother's brothers was *chanébu* (*i.e. the man who divides up the meat*) at this feast so Father had some chance of getting the portion he asked for. I and my elder brother peeped at the bridal party arriving, through the chinks in the bamboo walls. Mother went down to the feast in the evening.

'After popping the corn Father felt unwell and lay down, so that there was no evening meal. My elder brother slept on Father's right side and I on his left side. In the evening Father started breathing very noisily (*sound imitated*) so I climbed up on Father's body and asked him what was the matter but he didn't answer. My elder brother was sound asleep, but I woke him up and he got up and rekindled the fire; by its light we saw Father with his eyes wide open and the whites showing; but he would not speak and we were both very frightened and cried loudly.

'As it happens there was a house quite near and there was an old woman living there. All the other villagers had gone to the wedding. When this old woman had seen Mother going to the feast that afternoon she had reproached her saying "You should not leave your husband while he is so ill; you must return quickly and not stop and enjoy yourself." Well, this old woman heard us crying and came over to ask what was the matter? When she saw Father was on the point of death she went along to the *choten* which was near and stood on it and called down to Mother to come back. They were making so much noise at the wedding feast that she had to call three or four times. When Mother heard she hurried up with a piece of liver in her hands; but when she arrived Father was dead. On seeing this Mother burst into tears crying, "I am husbandless! On whom can I depend? Never was woman in an unhappier state than I am." As she said this she walked about clutching hold of different parts of the house. The old woman heaped up the fire.

'I thought Father was asleep and tried to go and lie down again beside him but Mother pulled me back saying "What are you trying to do? Your Father is dead." But neither at this time nor for some little time after did I understand what *hu mak* (*he is dead*) meant. Meanwhile the old woman tried to console Mother saying, "Don't cry, I will go and fetch your husband's brother," which she did and shortly returned with him. I did not know who he was. When the uncle came in he bent up the corpse's legs and I thought to myself "Why is this man treating my Father so?" Then the woman who later adopted me arrived. The three grown-ups consulted as to what was to be done and they decided that they must go and summon quietly the Tashé lama who was at the marriage feast. So Passo's wife went and did so. The body was lying on the ground with its head towards the wall; the lama sat at the feet and started performing the *po-thop* ceremony, reading from his book. I and my brother thought this very funny and laughed, whereupon the lama hooted at us making a very ghostly noise (*well reproduced*). He did this three times but we were not frightened and kept on laughing. Passo's wife scolded us and made us stop. When the lama had finished reading he went away and the paternal uncle put the corpse into a basket (*tangar*). Then I started crying and said "What are you putting my daddy in the *tangar* for? Whom will I sleep with now? I always sleep with daddy." And then I tried to get into the basket. My uncle said "You have not got a father any more; he is dead and turned into a devil." I did not know what he meant.

'The next morning the uncle took up some planks from the floor; many people had come to the house. One man took some burning brands from the fireplace and went down through the hole, then the paternal uncle went down, and people behind handed him the corpse in the basket, and then others went through. Other people carried away Father's bow and arrows and bamboo arrow holder. The man with the firewood went first. I asked my brother "Why are they taking Father away like that?" but my brother either didn't know or would not say. I saw the people coming back from the burial; on the road before they reached the house somebody made a bonfire which everybody stepped over and somebody thrust a knife under the door also for people to step over. I do not remember anything more about that time except that Mother used to cry when she was alone. I did not understand what it was all about.

'At the *sanglion* all I remember is that the old Mun was a man whose left arm was broken so that it hung useless below the elbow; he held the knotted rope under his arm and cut it with the knife which he held in the other hand. As we were so poor we had no animals to sacrifice; the paternal uncle provided a goat and I remember seeing the meat skinned and cut up and Mother telling me I must not have any; this made me angry and I did not understand why.'

Birth of younger brother. Adoption.

'My next memory is being frightened of my baby brother crying. Mother told me not to go near him as he was a devil, Sang-rong *moong*. Some time before my elder sister was fetched from where she was stopping; I slept with Mother till she was delivered and afterwards with my sister.

'Some time later I and my brother and sister and Mother were all sitting on the verandah when Passo's wife arrived carrying a big bamboo full of water; she leant it against the fence and said to Mother "I'd like to have that boy to look after; please give him to me." Mother replied "I don't know if he wants to, but if he does you can fetch him and take him home with you." Then

Passo's wife said to me "I am going to take you home with me and I will love you. I have got meat at home and boiled rice pudding (*tok-tok*); if you come I will give it to you." I said I did not want to go, so then she said "Let us go anyhow, you can eat it and after that you can come back." Then she took me to her house and gave me *tok-tok*. In the evening I wanted to go home but Passo's wife said to me "There is a devil Sang-rong *moong* in your house who will eat you if you go." I was not frightened of that and tried to get away but they fastened the door shut and would not let me go.

'When I was first adopted Passo and his wife loved me very much and fed me well but I was very unhappy and wanted to go back to Mother and used to run away to her sometimes (*they lived in the same village*). Sometimes Mother used to carry me on her back and sometimes I used to walk; once there was a heavy hail-storm and the hail fell all over me and Mother dragged me hard holding my arm at the shoulder which hurt me.'

Situation of Mother on death of Father.

Kurma's mother was a Mun. When her husband died she was left a very poor woman. The eldest girl, Nimu, the only one grown up, was married and she handed over most of the other children to strangers. This was not a regular adoption for no fee was paid for the children; they were given over to strangers to look after in exchange for their services. The other sister, Ajeunmu, had been given before the father's death to one of the father's brothers but she returned to her mother two years after the death of the father. Ahyok, the elder brother, was at home but was of little use to his mother; he used to spend all his time in the jungle going after birds and animals. Banyok was taken to be looked after by the Mandal, and Kurma by Passo, so the mother was alone with her eldest son and infant son and later her elder daughter. She had a brother Sangshim, who used to come and help her and give her presents from time to time, but she was chiefly dependent on her own efforts; and since she had nobody to cut down the weeds or sow the seed in the field, after the death of her husband she used to go out and work for neighbours, being paid in food with which she could feed her children.

Childhood memories while living with Passo. (*The following incident is almost the most vivid in Kurma's childhood and he volunteered it immediately after the account of his Father's death.*)

'One night when I was living at Passo's I dreamt that I was letting pass urine just a little at a time, which was very nice. When I woke up the bed was all wet even down to my legs. In the morning Passo's wife threw the wet cloth at my head and beat me and rubbed the wet cloth all over my body.[6]

'Another day I was at home while my adopting parents were working in the fields. I took the hens' eggs and broke them on a stone over the fire in the same way as I had seen Mother making buckwheat bread. I did not eat them; I thought I was being useful. When Passo and his wife returned and saw the eggs they beat me. Sometimes I was so frightened I used to run away and hide in the forest. I would come back at night and sit outside the house; I was too frightened to go in. After I had done this a few times Passo and his wife used not to speak when they wanted to punish me; they used to creep up quietly and catch hold of me and beat me. They used a big piece of firewood and beat my back so hard that "wind used to come up from my heart smelling of what I had eaten earlier."

'Another time Passo was stripping bamboos to make ropes; I was playing near and kicked the ropes, whereat Passo threw the knife at me cutting me deeply in the calf. (*He can still show the scar.*) Another time I stole something, whereupon they tied my hands together with a bundle of dried leaves and sticks and set fire to it; my hands were not burnt but I was very frightened and never stole afterwards.

'I used to sleep alone under a big bundle of *kacher* (*barley on the stalk*) and in the day-time I used to put my bedclothes on it. One day I pulled the bedclothes down and some small hairs from the barley entered one eye so that for seven months I could not see properly. Every evening a burning brand was buried in the ashes to keep alight all night and in the morning it was my business to light the fire; one morning after seven months some sparks flew into my eye. This hurt a great deal and I cried all day and rubbed my eyes. In the evening an old woman tried to cure me; she pulled my eye open and saw a small piece of grass sticking out of it; she took it out with the silver brooch which fastened her dress; some pus came out too and then I got better.'

[6] Kurma is punished for spoiling property.

Kurma spies on the birth of Apot.

'When I was about six or seven I spied on a neighbour giving birth to a baby. I did this by standing under the house floor which was made of crossed bamboo; I did it by myself out of curiosity because I wanted to know what an adult woman's vulva looked like, and to see how babies were born. The woman was hanging on to a rope from the ceiling and an older woman squatted behind her and held her breasts; the woman's belt was loosened and from below I had a very good view of her vulva. The woman was groaning and at each groan the vulva rounded and the head of the child could be seen; between groans the vulva was oblong. Finally after a discharge of yellow fluid the baby was born suddenly; and then the after-birth.' *(I put some questions to Kurma about this event; he said he recollected no feelings of disgust or fear; on the contrary, the spectacle was probably exciting. He excuses his conduct by saying he was too young to know shame.)*

Early sexual experience.

'When I was eight or nine I used to ask the little girls of the neighbourhood to let me see and touch their vulvas; to which they would consent and then lie down. Nobody told me about sex; I knew naturally as everybody does; it is like eating. At the same time I only knew how to do it properly when at the age of ten I saw my elder brother, aged fifteen, lift a girl's legs in the forest. My first sexual experience was when I was twelve, with a girl of the same age. We were both employed watching animals. I had seen older people and they had urged me to try the girl; she agreed but after one attempt would have no more to do with me. Pulling back the prepuce hurt.'

Practical joke played on Kurma.

'When I was about ten I was sent to live in a field hut to scare away monkeys and other animals from the ripening grain; with me was a young married man, a relation of Passo's. We had grain and pumpkins to eat. The young man played the following trick on me; he told me to get a big leaf from the forest, which I did; then the young man shat on it and told me to fold it up carefully and carry it right away down to the river; I must not put it near a house or in a field. I did as I was told. This happened for three days; on the fourth day I said "It is only fair we should take it in turns; I will take yours to-day and you take mine to-morrow." On the morrow I brought a leaf and shat on it and told the other to take it away. He refused, whereupon I said "If you won't throw it away it will stay there." After some argument the other threw it away and did not play tricks on me again.'

Relations with Mother.

'From time to time I used to go home and see Mother and help her and take her presents of the food and things I had saved at Passo's; they were rich, Mother was poor. Passo and his wife dressed me in second-hand clothes and gave me an old knife; they said I did not work well enough and cloth was too expensive to give me new clothes.

'When I was with Passo I was treated very badly, I had to do all the chores and work and was given bad food and no *chi*[7] while they sat at ease and ate and drank all day. When I was eight I was so unhappy that I ran away to my Mother; but she beat me and sent me back to my adopting parents. I ran away again when I was fifteen; this time Mother kept me nine days and then sent me back with a present of a load of *chi*.'

Onset of Padem Rum.

'When I was ten I was sent by Passo together with Cherim and Sanam to my Mother's father to fetch buckwheat. I was meant to carry twenty measures but could only manage fifteen. The two elder men were given *chi* and rice but I was merely given buckwheat cake. On the way home the Padem attacked me; I could not see properly and felt as though my body were being poked with sticks; I kept on thinking of drinking *chi* and eating rice like my companions had. I managed to get home with the buckwheat. My adopting parents did not look any bigger than myself.' (*For three months he was ill with constant derangements of vision.*) 'A chilli looked as big as a melon, a pumpkin looked like an umbrella. At times I felt as though I was flying or sitting on trees, at times my body felt as big as the monastery whereas other people seemed as small as twigs.

[7] Kurma used to get much more easily drunk than other Lepchas of his age, and I wonder whether this is due to the fact that he was not accustomed to *chi* in childhood.

My body ached so much that I could not move; I felt as though I were going to burst and all the time as if I was being poked with bones or sticks. Mother tried all the devils to appease them, uselessly; finally she saw that it was the Padem *rum* and she made a sacrifice of fish, bird, *chi*, a scarf and a rupee and a *chimi* and prayed "Nyou *rum*—god of our ancestors—do not harm my son; stay with him and help him and he will serve you." A month later I recovered and now I make sacrifice to the Padem twice a year.'

Birth of bastard sister.

Kurma's bastard sister, Nurzé, was born when he was seven or eight years old. The father was Pashet, but he refused to acknowledge her and his mother's brothers performed the *thip-song* ceremony. The baby was born with a big stomach and died at the age of five owing to the fact that Pashet had blown up a bladder when she was five months gone in the womb. Pot-belly and death is the inevitable *tamtoom* of this—death occuring in the year corresponding to the month of pregnancy at which this act is performed. Kurma thinks Pashet did this on purpose.

Death of Banyok. Kurma's first version.

Banyok was adopted by the Mandal,[8] who was, and is, without a son. The Mandal had some distant connections of the Aram Pandjet *ptso* called Kaloo and Tangdong who were jealous of the fact that the Mandal's property would go to the stranger although they had children themselves; therefore according to Kurma they gave Banyok poison in a dish of curds and buckwheat with the result that he died three months later in his mother's home. This poison was bought in the 'plains' in Darjeeling by Kaloo's grandfather; it is still in the possession of a relation, Shupak of Lungdeum.

After the death of the boy there was a general outcry that this woman Tangdong had poisoned him but she protested vehemently against it. However, others persisted in their accusations and eventually a lama came from Talung monastery to make them

[8] Kurma maintained on several occasions that this was proper adoption, but both the Mandal and other people denied that this was so. It is probable that as a pauper the child was brought up in the Mandal's house in exchange for his work in the same way as Satéo is today.

swear a solemn oath. This ceremony took place down by the river and Salyung of Panung was the sacrificer. An altar was erected and a goat killed and its blood collected into a cup ; then the lama summoned by name three devils from Talung and offered them *cherkem.* Tangdong again denied administering the poison, but all the old men present insisted on her guilt. Then the lama touched her forehead with an incense burner and said 'If you have poison may all your *ptso* be destroyed by these demons.' Then a Mun sacrificed, calling on all the devils who were created by Itpomu and dedicated the goat to them and then said to the suspected poisoners 'If you have poison may you die as this goat dies.' Then he sprinkled blood and *chi* on the ground and said 'If you have poison may you and yours dry up as this blood dries up on the ground.' Then he gave them blood and *chi* to drink and said 'If you have poison may you and yours all die of an issue of blood from the nose and mouth.'

Since that date all the members of the *ptso* have died in this way ; they have sores and their body is contracted in some sort of paralysis so that they crawl forward and double up and they have an issue of blood from their nose and mouth and then die. The only survivors are two lamas of whom Takal is one, and they perform annually the ceremony to keep off the devils, making an elaborate offering and explaining that they knew nothing of what had occurred at that time and were completely innocent ; now that they have heard the story they are making these offerings. (*I did not believe this story at the time as I had already noted Kurma's constant preoccupation with violent death and the story seemed to me,* de facto, *improbable. I had already heard this story of the perjured poisoners, but as something which had taken place a good number of years ago and in another village. According to Tafoor over thirty years ago at Lungdeum when Tasso Nungyen was Mandal. I was rather unwell when Kurma told me this story and I left him in the middle of the morning ; when I saw him about a week later I told him that I had been too unwell to write down what he had told me and asked him to tell me again. The second version is given below and is I think the true one. While he was telling his first version the greater part was overheard and confirmed by an old lama who made a speciality of making prayer-flags and by Mrs. Datoop ; but they arrived after he had started and did not, I think, realise that Kurma was connecting the story of this ordeal with his own family ; the story itself is one which is told very often.*)

Death of Banyok. Kurma's second version.

Banyok died about 1907; Kurma's only memory of him is his being carried by his eldest brother, Ahyok, when he was almost all skin and bone. The swearing ceremony was done about a year later and he, Kurma, didn't see it but only heard about it; the death of his brother was not the precipitating cause though he seems to think it was involved in it. The poisoner, Tangdong, lived in Lingthem at a place a little below the monastery where there are orange trees today.

Kurma's mother's second marriage.

Some time round about 1910 the Mandal and his wife (*first wife, now dead*) arranged a marriage between Kurma's mother and a lama, Chenyak. This man had already been married once, having inherited his elder brother's wife. Thus it occurred that both his wives had been beyond the age of child-bearing. The Mandal advised him to marry Kurma's mother and the Mandal's wife performed the same office for the woman; whereupon the Mandal acted as *bek-bu* for the *asék* which consisted of a pig, a hen, a ceremonial scarf and a rupee, which were divided among the villagers of Panung where Kurma's mother lived, as she had no surviving family in the neighbourhood. There had been a man, the son of Kurma's father's elder brother, who should theoretically have married her as *oong-op* but the man did not fancy taking on the responsibility of a large family of infants, and since they lived under different Mandals there was no method of coercing him.

After Kurma's mother and Chenyak were married they first lived at Lingthem and then at the demand of the people of Liklyang —the small village across the river—who wished for their services as Mun and lama they transferred to that place. First of all the husband and wife went across the river and cleared the ground and built a hut; then they fetched to live with them Ahyok, Ajeunmu, who was married shortly after, and Samboop. This occurred when Kurma was about fifteen. Ajeunmu was married to a man living farther up the river who three years after the marriage developed leprosy, of which disease he and the other seven people in the house subsequently died. This is the last recorded case of leprosy in the neighbourhood. Her son Takshyom who is now nineteen years old, is living with Kurma as he has no other living relations. It is said of him that he is a bastard by an unknown father, but this is possibly a kind explanation to prevent his having the stigma of leprosy, which is believed to be an hereditary taint. Ajeunmu died about 1922.

Reasons for ill-treatment by adopting parents.

'At first Passo and his wife treated me well but afterwards they were very unkind to me. My position was made very hard by the fact that, after I had been adopted, Passo's younger brother had two children, the elder of whom was Apot, and these children would have inherited if I had not been there and they and their parents were always telling me to my face that I was a usurping stranger and insulting me and quarrelling with me.'

Kurma's final return home.

'I finally decided to return home because my elder brother Ahyok said to me that as we were real brothers we should live and work together. I liked my elder brother and also my sister, my elder brother because when we worked together he told me what to do. My real reason for going home, however, was because I loved my Mother very much. However, she much preferred my youngest brother Samboop, and used to give him all the choice food and titbits while I and Ahyok were fed coarsely.

'She showed no pleasure when I came back but just said "If you have come back it is your own wish, do as you please." When I had run home earlier she had beaten me and sent me back. My stepfather was pleased and treated me as a real father; we used to work together like a real father and son. I was not so pleased with my Mother. She used to scold and abuse my stepfather and I used to advise her not to. She was disappointed because I had come back from my adopting parents where I would have had property. Mother loved and spoilt my younger brother but did not love me or my stepfather. On my first return Mother said "Why have you come? You must go back." Besides my stepfather my two brothers and my elder sister Ajeunmu were also there. When I came back I just went to work with my parents, taking what food Mother would give me. This was in April.

'After a month Passo's younger brothers Cherim and Chukup came to ask me to return. They were sent by Passo. When they came to me I was husking buckwheat. They were accompanied by the *gyapön* of Lik (the village Kurma was living in). I refused steadfastly to accompany them home and they then ordered me to take a grinding stone from Lik to Passo at Panung. A couple of days later I and my elder brother took the grinding stones over; my elder brother carried the top stone. We deposited them in a cattle shed without going near the house or seeing Passo. I hated him.' ('To-day he is blind,' *Kurma added exultingly when he told this story.*)

'A month later Passo came with Pashet to reclaim me. At that time the second Dorjé Lapoon was performing the *chéné* (ceremony) for the buckwheat harvest. Passo said to me "I have never done you wrong; come back with me." I replied "No; you have treated me badly; though you are my maternal uncle[9] and my adopting father you have used me ill." Passo said this was not true. I reminded him of the time long past when he had said to me "You need not stop here any longer; you can go away now. My younger brother has got a son Apot." I remembered too in my heart how when Apot was three or four Cherim his father had insulted me and had tried to drive me away. For all these reasons I refused to return with Passo.'

Suicide of elder brother, Ahyok.

'About a year after I had returned home my elder brother, Ahyok, committed suicide. These are the reasons for it. We had two paternal uncles,[10] of whom at first only the elder was married and the younger one used to sleep with his wife: but the elder brother disliked this so he arranged and paid for the marriage of the younger brother. But this new bride did not like her husband; instead she fell in love with Ahyok and used to go to visit him and sleep with him.[11] Then the elder uncle reproached the younger,

[9] Kurma's paternal great-grandfather's mother and Passo's paternal great-grandfather were brother and sister.

[10] These uncles were actually Kurma's second cousins; their father was the elder brother of Kurma's father's father. There was a considerable difference of age between them.

[11] Both these situations are culturally allowed for. What was scandalous was the wife expressing obvious and open preference for somebody not her husband. From the time of Kurma's father's death the elder 'uncle' had been married and the younger brother sleeping with his wife and this had gone on perfectly peacefully. But then this first wife of the elder 'uncle' had died and he had then married the 'niece' of his first wife who was very considerably younger than her husband or her brother-in-law. It was for this girl that the quarrels between the brothers started.

saying " Why don't you keep your wife in order? She is always going down shamelessly to your nephew's house." At this the two uncles quarrelled and the younger one committed suicide by taking poison. But this only started the trouble. The surviving uncle said to Ahyok " This death is your fault and you must pay all the expenses of the funeral ceremonies." Ahyok protested that it was not his fault; his aunt used to come to visit him; how was he responsible? and anyhow he had no money. But the uncle insisted and a meeting was held of the Mandal and *youmi*. To this meeting Ahyok went taking with him a pig, fifteen rupees and a load of *chi*. I stopped at home with my Mother. My brother admitted that he used to sleep with the woman and the meeting decided that he must pay for the funeral expenses and ignored his plea of poverty.

'Then my brother returned home and went up to the loft and took there the poison *took-ra-kyɜt nyung* which is used in hunting[12] and swallowed it. Then he came down and said " Those people say I must pay for what is not my fault; so I shall die." He came down in front of the house and walked about backwards and forwards. I asked him what was the matter and caught hold of him as he walked backwards and forwards. Then my brother drew his *chimli* (*a pointed knife which is worn in front of the body at the waist*) and cried " Come on! Come on! I will kill all who come near me." Then I caught hold of his right hand and Mother took the other; he made a lunge at my Mother and nearly killed her but I pulled him back in time. I finally managed to wrench the knife from his hand and then with my Mother's help pushed him on to the ground. I forced his mouth open and saw that his tongue was swelling and his hands were clenched; so I knew he had taken poison. I sent our younger brother to get the root of wild raspberry and hens' droppings; the root was pounded and mixed with the droppings and given him as an emetic, but it was too late and he died.'[13]

[12] 'People also wear a tiny quantity wrapped up in a thick cloth attached to their clothing near their heart as a protection against devils.'

[13] The fact of the suicide is independently confirmed by a great number of people though the reasons which caused it are somewhat different. Jiroong thought that he committed suicide because he was reproved for not working in the fields but instead going into the forest to look for wild tubers. Tafoor knew that the suicide was caused by the inability of some man to control his wife after he had been warned and thought Ahyok's suicide directly followed

First marriage.

'My stepfather was the younger brother of Gongyop-bo (father of Gongyop). Gongyop's father had a daughter who had been married to Dunbi's elder brother by whom she had a son Shashoo. She was fourteen years older than me. When her husband died she refused to take Dunbi as *oong-op* as she did not like him and returned to live with her father. She came to visit her uncle, my stepfather, when I was eighteen; we loved one another and she stopped a year with me. But although she loved me she did not want to go and live at Lik; my family was poor and hers comparatively rich and she did not get on too well with my stepfather. So I went to live with her, spending the time between her and my home. The arrangement was made by the Mandal. My wife's brothers did not want to give their sister to a poor man and therefore would not accept the usual substitutes for the "bride price" and I had no money for the proper ceremonies. Besides myself and my wife and my stepson there were also living in the house Gongyop's father and mother and Gongyop and his wife and son. While I lived in that house I was treated like a brother. I had some property of my own at Lik and we all ate together in common. I was sorry that my wife would not go with me to my own home; this was because I had not paid for her.'

Illness.

'When I was about twenty-one I and my wife were living in the field house. One night at midnight I fell seriously ill. The next morning my wife and her son went to work in the fields while I lay on the floor feeling suffocated so that I could hardly breathe. I called my wife but she did not come. Then I started getting delirious and I am not quite sure whether in fact or not I saw the Lharibu Chujen come and talk to me. A little time before I had bought a turquoise earring from Jiroong for four rupees and it was hanging by a string over my head. When I saw the Lharibu I asked him "Where are you going? I am very ill." The Lharibu said "I have come to ask you how much you paid for that earring from Jiroong?" "Four rupees." "That is quite a fair price" he

the suicide of the husband. These different views do not seem to me to invalidate Kurma's story in any way. The event took place nearly twenty years ago on the other side of the river.

said and went away. Then I thought I saw people peering at me through the doorway; they were hideous people with goitres and other deformities and they were standing on each other's backs. They all pointed at me with their fingers and said " From a needle he has grown into a bodkin." I was frightened and called for my wife.' (*All this was imitated in pantomime: it is a very vivid memory.*) ' Then I thought the roof of the field house was bending down to crush me and I tried to get to the door. When my wife and stepson arrived they first of all thought I was dead; they called the Nandjému who came and burnt incense. Then Tinkep's stepfather tried to carry me on his back to the house but he was not strong enough and had to bring me back to the shed where I spent the night. The next day I was got back to the house by my wife, who was helped by two other men. I turned bright yellow and my excreta were yellow; I was ill for a very long time. My wife's name was Yangma.'

Death of stepfather. Removal to Lik.

' My stepfather died in 1924. Before he died he had been made *ké-tsop*[14] of a neighbour called Chézé who had cardamum fields which passed to my stepfather and then to me. When my Mother was left alone with only a young son the Mandal told me I should go and live with my Mother, so I went there with my wife. Only then did I do *asék*. I bought a pig from Tikan for two maunds of cardamum and also took three rupees, a scarf and a rupee and a brass plate and jug. Tikan went with me as my friend and the Mandal acted as *bek-bu*. I did not do any other ceremony.' (*This wife died in* 1931. *Kurma still calls Gongyop ongzong and they are very friendly.*)

' The burial of my stepfather who was a lama was very expensive. For the *chongbu lu* ceremony a new cloth is necessary and also a carpet for the lama to sit upon and both of these will be taken away by the lamas as well as the bamboo container which has a rupee in it and is filled with grain. This costs at least fifteen rupees. During the years I lived in Lik I had to help pay for the funeral ceremonies of seven people—Ahyok, Ajeunmu who died at home though she had married away, my stepfather, my Mother, my first wife, Samboop and his wife.'

[14] See Chapter Three, p. 106.

Amputation of 'ingzong'.

'At Lik I had an "*ingzong*" called Kangbo. Kangbo had his hand crushed under a rock in the jungle and was left for three days before he was found. I was away at the time at Gangtok with Datoop who was doing carpentry work; I was helping him. I returned thirteen days after the accident and found Kangbo in tears from the pain; the whole of the forearm was festering and full of pus and stinking. Kangbo asked me what to do and I suggested cutting the septic arm off. I did not know what to do but just did what I thought best. First of all I tied up the arm very tightly above the elbow; then I put fire on his hand to make sure he was without feeling there and then cut off the arm with my sharp knife.' (*Kurma dwelt on this incident with a very great deal of obvious relish, pointing out on himself exactly how he performed the operation and repeating and repeating the story.*)[15] 'After amputation Kangbo against my advice undid the binding and lost a cupful of blood; he did this because he was in considerable pain. He is alive to-day.'

Kurma has also at different times cut open boils with a sharp knife. Once when he was cleaning cardamum a snake bit his finger; he first of all killed the snake with his knife and then cut open his finger; he still has the scar. He says he has no fear of blood or corpses and would not be frightened to open a corpse; he is rather scornful of the Mandal who was frightened even of the corpses of his wife and parents.

Rape of a little girl.

When Kurma was twenty he raped the girl who is now the wife of Dajou; she was eight or nine at the time. At first he could not get his penis in but was able to by the use of saliva. The girl bled and cried a good deal (*he recounted this with considerable vivacity and relish*); she did not say anything when she went home and recovered completely in ten days; at the end of that period Kurma asked her to sleep with him again and she consented. This girl has since been married nine years; she is childless. There is apparently little slur attached to such an act; if it was witnessed it would merely be a subject for joking; it happens relatively frequently. Kurma says

[15] Kurma has obvious sadistic leanings and dwells on and elaborates all incidents which gratify these; he is badly served in this culture.

that given the opportunity he would do the same again; but now that he is *gyapön* and consequently in a position of some influence he has to be more circumspect.

Purchase of Boom.

'When I was at Lik I was quite prosperous, and I gave the proceeds of five maunds of cardamum, which was then 180 rupees, to buy the sacred book Boom. All the big people in the village had it in their houses and I wanted to have it too to show that I was prosperous. This book has to be read five times a year. As I cannot read I had to hire lamas to do so. I learnt to write Tibetan letters by being present during three lessons which were given to a boy who was studying to be a lama, but I cannot read.'

Betrothal of Samboop and death of first wife.

'I had to act as father for Samboop and provide his marriage for him. I did this in 1930. I did not provide the marriage ceremony but my younger brother's wife came to live with him after *asék*.

'My first wife died in the autumn of 1931 and as soon as the memorial service was finished I came to live with my second wife at Lingthem. I came as *komokmyok* and for *asék* I only brought two maunds of millet which I bought in Mangan and killed a hen. My wife had a cow which was big with calf; we exchanged it for another one which was past milking which belonged to Tafoor, as we had to kill an ox for the wedding feast and it would be wasteful to kill a pregnant animal. I had made my wife pregnant before I *asék*'d her. I do not believe in horoscopes; my penis is more reliable than the books. When I went to live in my wife's house I gave the old house to my brother but I reserved some of the fields for my own use. My first child was born six months after the *asék*.'

Death of Mother.

'After I had married my Mother came and lived with me and my new wife for a little time; then she went back to live with my younger brother at her home in Lik; from there she was summoned to Lungdeum by Nimu to help look after a baby. She died in the beginning of 1933.'

Death of the younger brother Samboop.[16]

'Samboop was living in the house at Lik with his wife Gadung who was the younger sister of Nimu's husband. I had given him the Boom. In the spring I was over in Lik to sow millet in the half of the field I had reserved for my own use; Samboop had already sown dry rice there. While I was working in the field three men came up: they were Passeu who was the husband of my eldest sister, Passeu's younger brother Kachikbu and their brother-in-law Rumdo. First of all they asked me why I was over in Lik seeing that I was already settled in Lingthem? I replied that I had come over to work to sow the grain. I had been with Samboop in his house; then Samboop had gone into the forest and I had come to sow grain after leaving him. They then asked "Where is uncle Nangtap (which is another name for Samboop)?" "Why do you ask?" I said. They said "He must give *chi* to the Dorjé Lapoon when he comes; it is his turn." The second Dorjé Lapoon was at that time living with Kangbo and was performing the ceremony of stopping hail; everybody had to feast him in turn. I said that I and my brother had made *chi* in my house where we were keeping it; there was none in the house at Lik. The strangers then said that they must find Samboop; they also said that they were going to Mangan. I said I did not know where my brother was but my sister-in-law was working in the fields near the house.

'In the afternoon Kachikbu[17] came up to me and lay down; at the time I was burning weeds to clear the ground. I asked him why he had not gone to Mangan to buy rice as he had said? He replied that the bridge was impassable. I then asked what was the matter with him seeing that he had been all right in the morning? He said he was trembling and felt as if he had fever. He had a metal cigarette tin which had been given him by a European. He said that he had not seen Samboop.

[16] I noted at the time: 'I do not know how much to believe of this story. Kurma started by saying he would not talk about it as he had promised the Mandal not to mention it ever; then in hinting at it all the details came out; when he had finished he was abashed and repeated that he had sworn to the Mandal never to speak of this; this self-reproach seemed definitely sincere. At the same time the other records show that Kurma plays willingly with the ideas of death from violence. I think the facts are as recorded; what is perhaps untrue is the cause of his brother's death.'

[17] Kurma said that he and his mother possessed poison; but then he says that of everybody he dislikes.

'I learnt later from my sister-in-law that when the strangers had asked where Samboop was, and she had said that he had gone into the forest, they followed him. The next morning Samboop's body was found at the foot of a cliff and his belt and clothes scattered on the ground and marks on the ground.'

Kurma says that a brother and sister, Apé and Sundeu, saw Samboop fighting with the three men and ran away frightened. Kurma told the Mandal but he did nothing about it and made Kurma swear never to talk of the subject. He did not take the case to the Chief Justice. According to Kurma the motive of this crime was the desire to get the property of Chézé of which Kurma's stepfather had been made *ké-tsop*. They thought that since Kurma was living in Lingthem and Samboop was the only member of the holding family they would get it at his death. They were foiled, however, for Kurma claimed all the property; but he was frightened to live there and has since sold the property for Rs. 170 to a *ké-tsop*. Kurma was very repentant at having told the story. Samboop was a big and strong man, taller and broader than Kurma and had always enjoyed good health.

Other versions of same story.

According to Tafoor Samboop died five years ago in the forest in Lik. He was always a hunter and had caught over a dozen wild boars in traps but did not know how to sacrifice properly to Pong rum, *who got angry and killed him. Only his bones were found. All answered Kurma's appeal to search for the corpse.*

According to the Mandal the body was found after some time near a cliff in an advanced state of decomposition; he might have fallen down the cliff or been killed by wild animals. There is no reason to suppose murder.

According to Tempa, Samboop died five years ago across the river; when he was missed the bridge was broken and took two days to repair; and the body was not found till a month later when it was all rotten; the coat and knife were found apart from the body. The reason of death is unknown; Tempa first suggested madness; but then said that Samboop had neither killed himself nor was killed by devils but was murdered; then withdrew his statement and said that as he was no relation he could say nothing about what had happened.

More than a month before he talked about the death of Samboop Kurma had said when discussing hunting and the ritual attached to it that though his deceased younger brother used to hunt he did not know how to sacrifice; Kurma used to do it for him. But on one occasion when he was away his maternal uncle sacrificed and instead of making the offering to Pong rum *made it to his own god. Whereat his younger brother sickened and died.*

Putting all these versions together, some gathered before and some after Kurma's narrative, it would seem most probable that the man met his death through an accident. Except for Kurma's version all agree that there was a considerable interval before the body was found and the displacement of the knife and clothes which was the chief supposition for murder could easily have been produced by animals. The motive for murder suggested by Kurma seems completely inadequate. The only other person who supported the idea of murder was Tempa, who was himself a notably violent person.

Death of eldest child.

'When my eldest child died I had to make a basket to put the child in and I was so miserable that I decided to throw myself into the river. I said to my mother-in-law "Why should I live any more in this world? I would rather go with my child; I shall jump into the river. I have all these worries and taxes to pay and nothing to live for." My mother-in-law said nothing, but my wife said "What is the meaning of this talk? Do you call yourself a man? Then act like a man. What do you think will happen to us women left all alone by ourselves . . . etc. etc.?"

'This was the only time I wanted to kill myself. Although I was very unhappy as a child I never thought of, or talked about, suicide.'

Death of second wife.

'My second wife was poisoned by being given a *patyoot* of *chi* by Hlatam; she had pains immediately after; her excreta were first pale, then bloody, then black as charcoal; she spat blood and her death occurred; she died within three months. Hlatam had no reason for killing her but the poison she possesses has to be used every so often or it will kill the possessor.'

There was, however, one possible reason for Hlatam killing this girl; her father had died when she was a girl and she accused Hlatam of poisoning him; to prove that this was not true Hlatam then poisoned her accuser.

Care of youngest child, born 1934.

After the mother's death Kurma's mother-in-law nursed the baby; although the child is in her fourth year she is still giving her a little milk. No medicines are needed to be given; the baby sucks and that produces the milk flow. His mother-in-law is forty-six years old but has not produced a child for several years. Kurma complains that his life is very hard as he has nobody to help him since his mother-in-law is feeble. His nephew is irresponsible and is constantly going away.

Third wife.

Six months after the death of his second wife he met his third wife, who lives at Hi. He slept with her three times and she became pregnant and he did *asék* for her immediately after the memorial service for his second wife. A son was born in September 1936. Kurma says that two other men wanted to marry her but his wife preferred him. He hopes to be able to bring her home in the autumn of 1938.

iv

March 18th to May 20th.

JOURNAL OF KURMA'S ACTIONS AND OBITER DICTA

March 18th.

Recognised Kurma as a personality for the first time. He gave details of several exorcisms.

March 19th.

Kurma came to fetch us to conduct us to the *asék* of Chano's eldest son, at his house about a thousand feet down the valley. On the way down he pointed out a tree which was the home of the deut *moong*—fever devil. This devil has been seen and looks like a man covered with long hair.

Kurma also talked about '*ingzong*' and said he had two in the neighbourhood. He said that one reason for establishing '*ingzong*' is because you love one another. Such a relationship is not established after a quarrel; should such an event occur a third party will give a big meal and try to reconcile the two quarrellers

March 22nd.

Went to exorcism service of *Go-seum* performed for Datoop's second son, Pichi. Kurma was present assisting in the ceremony. He was more than half drunk and at one moment asked for money to be given to Datoop, which caused very great general embarrassment.

March 24th.

Went down to Pembu's house where the roof was being re-thatched. Kurma arrived rather late in the morning when the work was in full progress, being done fairly haphazardly, and tried to get the work done more efficiently by bossing the other workers, but he was soon forced to give it up.

March 25th.

Kurma came up for a few minutes saying he could not stop and spent a couple of hours discussing marriage regulations.

March 27th.

Kurma and Tinkep, the other *gyapön*, overheard near the monastery saying how indignant they were that at yesterday's Konchen Tyuchen (monastery feast in honour of Kinchenjunga) which was given by Songpo and Katel they were neither of them invited and when they did arrive were not offered anything; they both went away at once.

March 28th.

Two 'Tibetans' arrived from Lachen this morning; they were a man and his wife who came with blankets to sell, or rather exchange against red dye-wood, salt or money. They have eleven *ingzong* in all the valley—three in this village. They will stay a night with each. Last night they stopped with Kurma.

March 29th.

Kurma spent all the morning chiefly talking about Padem and Mun, and talked about his own possession by the Padem.

March 30th.

Visit from the Mandal of Lungdeum; during the day Kurma and Jiroong came up, general talk chiefly about sex. Kurma told an anecdote in pantomime which was one of his favourite stories and often came up. One day at a wedding (it was a rainy day), near the shed which was put up for the bridal party he copulated with a girl carrying a child about four years old. The girl stood with her back to a tree, clasping it with her arms behind her head and lifted one leg. But at the moment of orgasm she let go and fell sideways; nobody was hurt. The child made no comment.

April 2nd.

Kurma up all day, chiefly talking about hunting and ritual and told about the reason why his family are no longer good hunters. He also talked about dreams and their meanings and explained that one of the results of adultery is that the deceived husband will dream of the *tafep*—ladle used for pouring out *chi.* Kurma said that he had had such a dream during the life time of his second wife; he was later informed that the dream was founded on fact, but since he had seen nothing he could do nothing. He denied that he had ever had any sort of overtly sexual dreams or dreams of committing crimes.

April 4th.

Tafoor was present most of the morning describing funeral ceremonies. Kurma came up rather late. He talked about the poltergeist manifestations with which Pong *rum* had plagued him after he had given up hunting.

April 6th.

Kurma came up and discussed adoption, illustrating the disadvantages for the adopted child by his own reminiscences. This was the first time that he enlarged in detail about his own past life.

That day Kurma complained of heart pain which is due to the presence of Shook-sor *moong*. Two nights ago his mother-in-law dreamt of a kite on the roof which signifies the presence of Shook-sor *moong* and the day after Kurma had these pains. Shook-sor *moong* can only pain humans but can kill animals. Its exorcism, which must be performed by a Mun or Padem, is relatively simple, but a Padem cannot cure himself.

Kurma explained that since he had run away he had no claim on his adopting parents' property, which now goes to their nephews.

On this day also he first talked about Hlatam and her faculty for poisoning and said that his second wife had been killed by her.

April 7th.

I felt unwell this day and did not go out but I did not tell other people about it.

April 8th.

Kurma came up in the morning and told me before we had spoken about anything that he had dreamt that I should be ill.[18] He said that he had got rid of his heart ache by making a small offering of butter and rice instead of the proper big offering. Today I asked him to tell me more about his early life, which he had sketched out a couple of days earlier, and he talked practically the whole day without interruption. He went into the most minute details of his sexual activities and physical make-up. He obviously fancies himself very much as a lover.

April 10th.

Kurma talked about a great variety of subjects, chiefly institutionalised customs. He said that according to his standard only two people in the village could be called rich—the Mandal and Takneum *youmi*. He said that he himself was as rich as Jiroong (as a matter of fact this is untrue), but he counts himself a poor man. He also told part of the stories of the first Dorjé Lapoon and Jiroong.[19]

April 16th.

Kurma was occupied from the 16th till the 19th with the business of arranging the repairing of the bamboo bridge which joins Lingthem and Liklyang. He had to get the workers and also the materials and supervise the work which was being performed. He was very busy and officious and seemed to be enjoying himself but complained of the work which prevented him working on his own fields.

April 24th.

Kurma came up again and I chiefly talked to him about the facts which I had learnt since his last visit of general importance, seeking to get confirmation of them. Among the other subjects was the question of the money lenders and indebtedness; Kurma told the history of his own debt (given in Chapter Four). On this subject

[18] Dream given in Chapter Seven, p. 186.
[19] See Chapter Sixteen.

he said among other things, that it is convenient to have the kanya so near as shops but that they cheat very badly in demanding extortionate interest and also in forcing the debtors to sell their crop early in the season when prices are low instead of letting them wait till prices rise.

He again volunteered several anecdotes about his own sexual experiences. He thinks he has slept with about thirty-eight women in all, of many different races—Nepali, Tibetans etc. He likes Tibetan girls the best; there are a couple down the river who can be had at the price of one rupee. Tibetan girls are 'hot'; they move about so that it is necessary to move very quickly to keep them quiet; Lepcha girls lie like a 'corpse'. He has never had any 'venereal disease'. Some years ago at Lik a girl younger than himself gave him a strap of her own weaving; she also used to bring him food and *chi* in her dress. He slept with Tobgé's sister when she was twelve years old and a virgin; he was the first man to have her. He would have liked to have married her, but his wife was then alive; and when she died the girl had married Nahyeun. He is still very fond of her. He said that he would rather have one wife with many children than many wives with none. He prefers the appearance of a woman to her clothes and jewels. Nahyeun's wife was present during most of the morning and he referred to his relations with her in front of her face and was also very familiar with her; she seemed rather pleased but threw a clod of earth at him. He said that he considered shame a bad thing.

April 25th.

Kurma was present at Konchen Tyuchen and got extremely drunk, so drunk that in the morning he did not know what he had done.

April 29th.

Kurma again spent the whole day talking about his past life. In the morning he got a summons from his third wife saying his son was very ill, whereupon he went to try and buy a pig to take with him as a present; he could not find one. He had been given *chi* by one of the people he had called on and was very slightly drunk. For a Lepcha he gets drunk remarkably easily. When I was questioning him about the relative dates of the things he had been talking about he got impatient and asked me why I always asked about himself today instead of asking about the different aspects of the culture as I usually did. He forgot this quickly and soon became voluble again.

I noted on this date 'He is definitely a rather unstable character with a very much stronger ego-feeling than most of the people here. He confessed today that he had exaggerated his wealth; he had said untruly that he was richer than Jiroong whereas in fact he has very little land. I think he is chiefly truthful but wants to be in the foreground of the picture and will exaggerate in both directions (i.e. at one moment claiming to be very poor at another very rich) to preserve a dramatic position. He is subject to changing moods. He definitely enjoys the power which being *gyapön* gives and is inclined to take up a position of authority in situations not called for by the culture. His relish of scenes of cruelty and his persecution mania about poison are remarkable here. In a less easy-going society he might be either a vagabond, a lunatic or a chief.'

May 5th.

Datoop was up talking about a variety of subjects and in his conversation passed some judgements on his fellow villagers, including Kurma. Of Kurma he said 'He gets easily drunk. He is proud and boastful, claiming to have possessions and capabilities which he has not got. I consider that he enjoys his authority as *gyapön* more than is fitting.'

May 10th.

Today Kurma returned from his parents-in-law after being with them nine days; his infant son has recovered. Saw very little of him as he was drinking at Chano's house where the exorcism was taking place until late at night. He sometimes used to go into Mangan to fetch the mail, but according to the servant, if he has any money he stays and gets drunk there.

May 12th.

Kurma came up today when Chudo and Chala Mandal were already present. I sent him away with a flea in his ear because he had promised to come up on the 10th and had disappointed us.

May 13th.

Kurma came up this morning after I had been very nasty with him yesterday for having disappointed us three days ago. I had not believed he was ill as he looked all right; but this morning about eleven o'clock he had a bad fit of shivering as from fever, though his pulse was low. He spent the earlier part of the morning talking about his past life and especially about religious ceremonials and his own experiences as Padem. He has three rosaries and can make diagnosis. He never had a teacher to learn how to do this but learnt it through the inspiration of Padem *rum* and also from observing his mother and other Mun. He gave an illustration of the way in which he would consult his rosary in the event of another person being ill. Whether consultation shall be made or not depends partly on personal inclination and partly on wealth. Kurma said he had not consulted for his sick son or for himself because of the expense. About midday he almost collapsed and I had to give him medicine. He says he has been this way for seven days and cannot sleep inside but only out of doors. He has completely lost appetite and when he shivers suffers from optical disturbances; grown-ups look no bigger than children and he sees red and white spots moving about over the ground and has a pain under his heart; a couple of days ago he was really bad and thought he was going to die. No Mun or lama has been called in; who is going to do it? His mother-in-law and nephew are 'strangers' and do not care about him.

He has recently spent seven days with his parents-in-law working for them; it was his first visit for three months. His small son was ill with a discharge of blood from his ears and sores all down one side. At present he is slightly recovered. No professional advice was called in. Kurma says one woman said of the child: 'His father is a foreigner from Lingthem, why bother about it?'

May 19th.

Kurma came up to-day for the first time since the 13th; he walked with a stick and still looked very seedy, sweating profusely. He said, however, he was better and brought a present of eggs and tomatoes for the medicine I had given him; I gave him a lot of quinine and a little aspirin; he took all the latter but only three tablets of the quinine because it was so bitter. He was in a highly nervous state and when there was a sharp noise (either a gun[20] or a bamboo snapping) he jumped several inches and exclaimed in a frightened voice: '*athu lukni lu-li-ko*'—words which I cannot translate and which Kurma said were meaningless; to turn the

[20] There are a couple of very old match-locks in the village which are occasionally used.

question aside he said he often jumped if there were loud noises in the forest and went on to tell a long anecdote about a time when he had met a bear.

His father-in-law had sent a message to summon him, a rather shaming request, saying: 'You have not been here for three months and now your baby is ill; what do you intend to do about it?' He, of course, had to go at once and took as a present a shoulder of pig which he bought at Lungdeung. His wife was very angry and refused to sleep with him for three days. At the end of three days he asked permission to return because he said he had to look after us, but his father-in-law refused him permission and he had to wait seven days helping to cut down trees and clear land. At his father-in-law's house he cannot copulate with his wife until he hears everybody snoring and he stays awake thinking why don't these people go to sleep? He takes his duties to his parents-in-law seriously; if he was summoned he would go at once and find some substitute to carry on the work he was engaged on when the summons came. As a man *asék* but not yet married he is treated like a servant.

He says he has got two bastards both by married women living with their husbands, so he has not performed *thip-song*. One was born ten years ago when he was married to his first wife; the mother was Samblyou (the elder sister of Gongyop's wife), whose husband was then living. He thinks it was his child because (*a*) it resembled him strongly, and (*b*) it was born just ten months after a particularly emphatic copulation. The child died of dysentery when it was three. The second bastard was by a woman of Rongyel; it is a boy and is now twelve years old. Kurma says he knows he is his son because the woman said so; she does not get on with her husband. Now Kurma is ashamed to see her and will go away if he knows she is in the neighbourhood. The child is considered and treated as legitimate.

Although he is Padem Kurma cannot sacrifice to Mayel[21] as he has not got *loong*; he could learn to do so after watching carefully three times. He also cannot *sakyou faat* (perform the ceremony with the buttered cup of *chi*) but he can do all the ceremony for *thyak-dum*.

He said today that instead of collecting the two annas from each household for oil for the monastery *chimi* he would buy it himself out of the money we had given him.

[21] See Chapter Nine.

Kurma went to Talung with Datoop to put a tin roof on the monastery; he there made '*ingzong*' with the lama, who entertained him very well. He saw there some strangely elastic thread and also all the clothes of the hero Lapchen Chumbu from the age of three weeks onwards and the *choten* containing his head.

May 20th.

A number of people were up here this morning including most of Datoop's family and Kurma. During the morning Mrs. Datoop and Kurma drew aside to consult about the situation arising from the fact that Dadool had not returned home and that Mrs. Dadool had gone away.[22] They both seemed genuinely concerned. Later Kurma talked about Aga and said vehemently that he was an evil-minded man. He also said when talking about Aga and the disturbance caused by his taking a second wife, that he had been so disgusted by the immorality of Samblyou, by whom he earlier said that he had a bastard, that he had abandoned her many years ago. What chiefly disgusted him was that she slept with Satéo and also his father, which is *nam-toak* a year of disaster. He said that Samblyou was, together with her eldest sister the second wife of Takal, the most notoriously promiscuous woman in the village and that the second wife of Takal spent her time seducing young boys. He does not like her and speaks of her with obvious distaste.

May 25th.

Kurma accompanied me to Mangan and seemed very sorry to see me go.

[22] See Chapter Five, pp. 141–142

CHAPTER SIXTEEN

THE FIRST DORJÉ LAPOON, HIS FAMILY, AND JIROONG

i

It is not enough to wish to collect life-histories; it is also necessary to get people who are willing to tell them. I very much regret that I was not able to obtain in any comparable detail the story of a well-adjusted Lepcha, to contrast with that of Kurma with his obvious maladjustments. But I think it was just his maladjustments which made him so remarkably communicative; his feeling of inferiority and ill-treatment, his consciousness of being somewhat different to the rest of the community led him to place more confidence and spend more time with strangers than a well-integrated person would be likely to do.

I have already said that I consider Chala Mandal and Tafoor to be the best-integrated Lepchas in Lingthem; I saw a great deal of both of them—Tafoor was almost my most constant and altogether my most reliable informant—but my attempts to get them to tell their own stories were almost completely unsuccessful. They both had very little self-feeling; they envisaged their relationships with others entirely practically and objectively, apparently untinged by emotion. Their feelings towards others were always rational, and their accounts of their dealings with them consisted of long lists of mutual help and benefits, with very great emphasis on the food given and received.

I did get short accounts of their past lives from a number of people; some of them have already been given (e.g. Gongyop's story in Chapter Eight, Rigya's in Chapter Fourteen, and so on) in full, and small excerpts have been made from others which are not full enough to be informative. Since, however, I feel that Kurma's story by itself would give an over-biased picture, I propose to give as a counterbalance the interrelated stories of the first Dorjé Lapoon, of his son Datoop and of his wife and family, and of Jiroong, whose first wife the first Dorjé Lapoon stole.

The first Dorjé Lapoon I saw very little of, and his history was told to me, partly by Kurma, and partly by his son Datoop. He was a very old man and spent most of his time alone in the field-house where he lived looked after by his younger son. I also learned from Kurma that portion of Jiroong's life which was involved in the scandal of his first wife and the Dorjé Lapoon, and also the story of Jiroong's sister. The greater part of Jiroong's life and all the rest of the stories were got from the people themselves. It is worth remarking that, although these people are all less obviously maladjusted than Kurma, they had all except Jiroong had the unusual experience of living some years outside Zongu.

The first Dorjé Lapoon, Datoop and Jiroong were all lamas; Datoop was by far the most pious. Jiroong was a lama through his horoscope and not through birth, and appeared to attach rather more importance to the Mun ritual; in his house his sister always officiated. Mrs. Datoop was a very strong character, and overbore both her husband and her son Pembu. Jiroong was also dominated by his wife.

The accompanying genealogies should make the rather involved relationships clearer. (See page 417).

ii

The first Dorjé Lapoon.

The first Dorjé Lapoon, now aged eighty-two, has been his whole life long poor, lustful and shameless. As a young man he was married to his first wife, but after three years he left her because he wished to marry another woman, one Lungdeumu, his classificatory aunt.[1] He was told that he and she were too closely related for them to marry; but he was shameless and persisted in the marriage. Since the consanguinity was all through the female line no social action other than expressed disapproval was taken against this incestuous match.

Lungdeumu was the mother of his son Datoop, who was born in 1881. As soon as the child was born the Dorjé Lapoon took a dislike to his wife and went away to Darjeeling for a year to work there. On his return Lungdeumu's brother tried to induce him to return to his wife but he refused. Thereupon Lungdeumu's brother said 'You are no longer responsible for my sister; I shall give her in marriage again, and you will have no claim on the bride-price.'

[1] Her mother and his maternal grandmother were biological sisters.

PICHI

MRS. DATOOP

Genealogy of JIROONG
(Takpo Ptso)

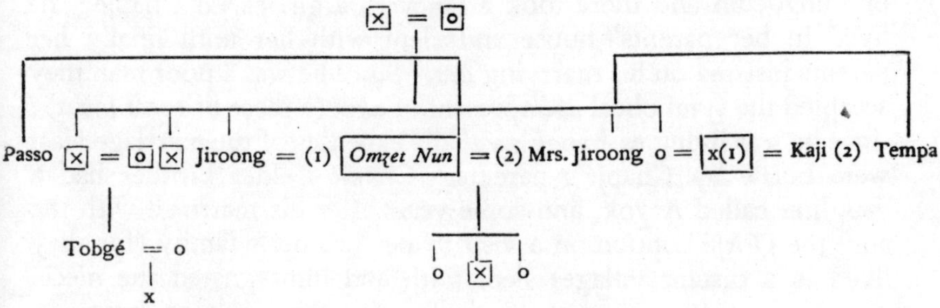

x means man
o means woman
= means marries
[x] [o] means dead

Genealogy of FIRST DORJÉ LAPOON
(Sakmi Ptso)

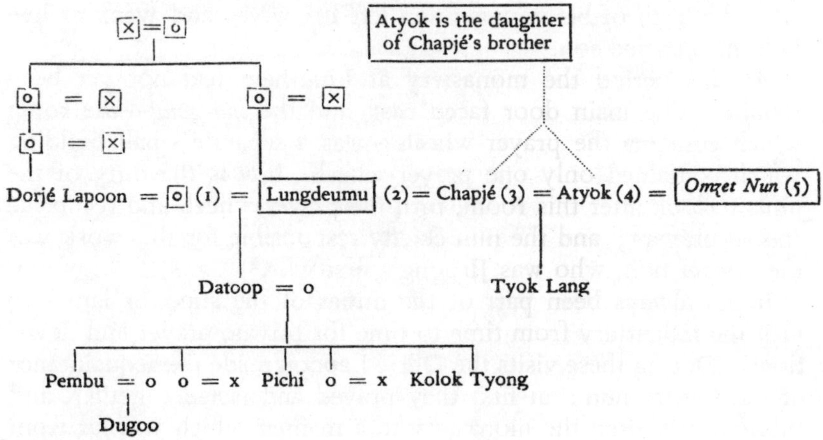

She subsequently married Kazoo Mandal as his second wife, the first wife being an 'aunt' of hers; she had no further children.

After this divorce the Dorjé Lapoon spent several years unmarried wandering round the country. Eventually he settled in the village of Lungdeum and there took a fancy to a girl called Chapjé; he lived in her parents' house and slept with her until finally her parents insisted on his marrying her. Since he was a poor man they accepted the symbolical *asék* present of *akut* (a piece of roast meat); since he was living as *komok myok* the expenses of the marriage feast were borne by Chapjé's parents. Chapjé's elder brother had a daughter called Atyok, and some years after his marriage with the aunt the Dorjé Lapoon on a visit to her brother's family (for they lived in a distant village) slept with and impregnated the niece. Atyok's parents insisted on his performing the *thip-song* ceremony (to acknowledge his paternity of the bastard) and on his marrying the mother. Atyok's son, Tyok Lang, was born in 1912. The Dorjé Lapoon, his two wives and his son all lived together in the house of Chapjé's parents.

Meanwhile the Dorjé Lapoon's elder son, Datoop, had returned home to Lingthem after his period of work as State carpenter, and through the industry of himself and his wife was starting to become very prosperous. Since there was more comfort to be had at his son's house than at his father-in-law's the Dorjé Lapoon some years after the birth of his younger son left his wives and went to live with his married son.

At this period the monastery at Lingthem had not yet been rebuilt. The main door faced east, and the *lha-gong*—the room which contains the prayer-wheels—was a separate small building which contained only one prayer-wheel. It was the duty of the nuns to look after this room, turn the prayer-wheel, and recite the special prayers; and the nun chiefly responsible for this work was the Omzet nun, who was Jiroong's first wife.[2]

It has always been part of the duties of the superior lamas to visit the monastery from time to time for private prayer and devotions. During these visits the Dorjé Lapoon made the acquaintance of the Omzet nun; at first they prayed and fasted together, and subsequently used the monastery in a manner which was far from devotional. After this liaison had started the Dorjé Lapoon completely abandoned his two living wives, and spent his time between the monastery, his son's house, and Jiroong's. Jiroong was unable

[2] See under, p. 428.

to make a complaint since the Dorjé Lapoon was his religious superior.

After they had been left completely alone for three years Chapjé and Atyok came to Lingthem on a formal visit of protest; they were accompanied by the Mandal of Lungdeum, an 'elder brother' of Chapjé, and an experienced old man from Lungdeum; and a big meeting was called at which all the lamas were present, and also the Mandal and the *youmi.* This took place in 1922. The assembled people ordered the Dorjé Lapoon to return to his legitimate wives; but he refused absolutely, saying that he would rather be killed than return to Lungdeum. He was then given the alternative of bringing Chapjé and Atyok to live with him in Lingthem; he consented to this and they all went to live at Datoop's house. He and the Omzet nun were also made to swear that they would have nothing more to do with one another. They took this oath publicly, but previously they had privately sworn that they would continue to live together. The Dorjé Lapoon therefore did not resume marital relations with his legitimate wives; instead he used to creep out by night to meet Mrs. Jiroong.

Chapjé and Atyok stood this for three months, and then they returned to Lungdeum with Atyok's son. Shortly after their return the deputation of three who had accompanied them on their first visit returned to Lingthem to claim the divorce money *gé-thop* from the Dorjé Lapoon. He paid one pig, one ox, a big copper pot, a brass jug and plate and Rs. 20; he should really have given Rs. 88, but the people of Lungdeum agreed to accept less owing to the Dorje Lapoon's poverty. Even the Rs. 20 he had to borrow from the monastery funds. This divorce renewed the public scandal; to quieten it the first Dorjé Lapoon announced his intention of taking the vows of a celibate monk[3] and of giving up all contact with the Omzet nun. At this period the Mandal also fined Jiroong Rs. 15 for failing to keep his wife in order.

Two months after the Dorjé Lapoon had proclaimed his intention of taking the vows of celibacy Jiroong reported to the Mandal that the lovers were still meeting. Another meeting of the lamas, Mandal and *youmi* was then called and they instructed Datoop to prevent his father from going to the monastery except at public ceremonies; and even at those he was not to go near the *lha-gong.*

[3] It is permissible for any lama, even one with a family, to renounce the world and become a *gé-long,* a celibate monk. Such celibates live under a very stringent discipline.

But even this proved useless; the Dorjé Lapoon was uncontrollable and without shame (for a lama should respect the wives of lamas of a lower grade than himself as though they were daughters-in-law) and so eventually Jiroong capitulated and gave his wife to the Dorjé Lapoon, who thereupon moved into his (Jiroong's) house. This transaction was completely irregular; Jiroong treated the Dorjé Lapoon as if he were his younger brother. After he had given up his wife and home to the Dorjé Lapoon Jiroong travelled around for some years, returning home from time to time; during his absence the two old people worked the fields. When Jiroong married his second wife (Tempa's sister) the two of them shared house with the Dorjé Lapoon and the Omzet nun. In 1934 the house burned down; the two couples then separated; Jiroong and his family continued living in the burned house while the Dorjé Lapoon and his wife went to live in a field-house a little higher up the mountain.

Six months after this move the Omzet nun died, and Atyok's son came to look after his aged father. This aged father was in 1937 trying to arrange a betrothal with the widowed younger sister of his fourth wife Atyok; but she refused to accept, considering that a man forty years older than herself would scarcely make an adequate husband.

The validating feasts by which the Dorjé Lapoon attained his high rank among the lamas were paid for by Datoop. Dorjé Lapoon, Chudo said, are appointed for their age and for their learning; the suggestion is that they have taught the lower lamas who will therefore honour them as teachers. Their moral character is not regarded. The first Dorjé Lapoon is the only man in the district who possesses or can read a Lepcha manuscript; the book he owns is a translation of the Tibetan scripture Guru Chong Numtar.

Datoop surprised me one day by announcing quite spontaneously that his father was a bastard—a word with very considerable shameful connotations. He said that he was half Sikkimese, as his mother had betrayed his absent father with a wandering Sikkimese monk. He was however treated as legitimate and is a member of his mother's husband's *ptso*.

Datoop.

Datoop has few memories of his early childhood. He can recall being beaten by his parents, but not being carried. After his

THE DATOOP FAMILY IN THE DOORWAY OF THE LHA-GONG

Standing : Mrs. Pembu, Pembu, Kondé (a " niece " ; I have just bandaged her).

Seated : The younger married daughter, Kolok Tyong, the youngest son, Mrs. Datoop with Pembu's son Dugoo, and Datoop.

father left home the household consisted of his mother, his grandmother and two aunts. At about the age of fifteen he was sent to the State school at Gangtok to be trained as a carpenter ; for many years he made his headquarters there, travelling round the country wherever he was wanted.

He was married about the age of fifteen, but the marriage was not consummated until about five years later. He thinks he finally settled in Lingthem about 1910.

Shortly after he had settled down his father married his third and fourth wives. Datoop said that he loved both mothers equally, but the marriages entailed considerable expense. He speaks quite openly about his father's misdemeanours ; he was, he said, not surprised at his connection with the first Mrs. Jiroong but he was very angry ; he tried to restrain him but failed.

All his life he has had to travel about as a State carpenter, going wherever fine work was required. He helped to build the King Edward VII memorial at Gangtok. On May 10th, 1937, he had to leave for Gyatong, to work at the new monastery under construction there.[4] Before setting out he came to say goodbye to us, bringing us a present of eggs, milk and vegetables ; he insisted that these goods should be an absolute present and would accept nothing in return.

Datoop has no fixed ideas about the desirability of the different stages of life ; he is inclined to apply the maxim 'Call no man happy till he dies.' He thinks it is good to die old—about the age of eighty—provided you retain your strength, that your sons are alive, and that you leave enough property for a good *sanglion*. Consequently he will only allow dead people to be considered happy—such people as the Muktair and the Mandal's father. To try to elucidate his views further I suggested that a god would appear and offer him to go to which year he liked ; he said to this that he would choose to become a child again, so as to have his whole life to live over. He was very fond of telling stories, particularly animal fables ; as a fairly pious lama he turned the supernaturals in even obviously Mun stories into lamaist deities. His rank as lama is *chichembu* ; he has given up the office of *chithembu* and cannot yet make the validating feast to be *omzet* as sufficient time has not yet elapsed.

[4] See Chapter Two, p. 58.

Mrs. Datoop.

Mrs. Datoop was born at Rangen outside Zongu in 1888. She was married when she was eight to her husband who was then fifteen, but did not sleep with him till five years later. During the intervening period she used to pay him short visits and he paid her longer ones. Her eldest son Pembu was born when she was twenty. She has had in all three sons and two daughters. She considers that having or not having children is entirely a matter of luck and thinks it best that the first child should be a boy.

She occasionally returns to re-visit her brothers; her parents are now dead. According to Kurma, who is distantly related to her, and other people who remember her as a girl, she was the most outstandingly beautiful Lepcha girl they had known. She is distantly connected with the Mandal and Takneum *youmi*.

At the monastery feast which took place on April 20th she was not present; I heard from Pichi that she was unwell and sent her some aspirin; on April 25th she brought me a present of eggs to thank me. She is a very capable, self-assured woman; she makes little pretence at modesty but answers straightforwardly without flirting, as women much older and uglier than her will do. She said for her illness she had called in a Mun, and a pig was sacrificed; also mixed crops and jewels. Jewels can be re-offered as often as necessary; the supernatural does not take anything from them, metaphysically or physically; it is merely gratified at the sight and intention of the offering.

Mrs. Datoop considers that when girls are married away from home young they are unhappy and cry at leaving their parents, but older girls are glad to go to their husbands. Women, she said, have no private cult apart from the ancestral gods to correspond with Pong *rum*; nor is there any part of their lives from which men can be excluded.

Mrs. Datoop weaves very well. She buys the coloured thread and will take about a week to make a full-sized piece. She says she does not weave much now because there is no market for the Lepcha cloth and people won't wear it. She, together with Mrs. Jiroong, who has almost always a spindle in her hand carding wool wherever she goes, are the only two women nowadays who spin at all consistently.

Mrs. Datoop is a woman of very considerable private property—she and her daughters and daughter-in-law have by far the finest jewels of any women in Lingthem—and also very considerable generosity. She practically supports the children of Pargeut, who is distantly related to her husband (they share a common grandmother) and acts more like their mother than their own mother does. The consequence was that she was the only person who had the confidence of Kondé.[5] When Kondé was having her very painful sores dressed Mrs. Datoop would hold and soothe her with an altogether surprising physical gentleness and tact which was unparalleled among other Lepcha women.

No scandal had ever been attached to Mrs. Datoop's name but she had the reputation of being highly sexed and all her potential *oong-op* have taken full advantage of the relationship.

For four generations Mrs. Datoop's family had the peculiarity of rearing their children in cradles. She was so reared and so were all her children, but Pembu her eldest son has not used one for his own child.

Pembu.

Pembu was born in 1908 and was weaned at the age of two. As a child he was exceptionally frightened and nervous of strangers: indeed he is to this day. As a young child he was very frequently and seriously ill. When he was older up to the age of ten he used to sulk if reprimanded or punished and threaten to kill himself by jumping into the fire or from a high place. The parents would not try to restrain him; they would say 'If such a child wants to kill himself he can.' Sometimes he would run away for the day to an 'uncle's' but he always came back of his own accord of an evening.

At the age of five[6] he was sent to Gangtok as a servant for the Maharajah; the community has to furnish perpetually two boys for this work. In Gangtok he lived with an 'aunt' Kafermu, a woman who had at that time no children. He used to come home yearly for a holiday. The first year he was there he was very miserable but the second time he returned happily enough. Mrs. Datoop said that all the time he was away or when he was ill she was always very anxious and unhappy. When Pembu was about fifteen he quarrelled with his 'uncle' who complained to the Maharajah and Pembu came home for good. Datoop and his wife were glad to have their son back but regretted the cause of his return. On his

[5] See Chapter Twelve, pp. 322–323.

[6] So he says: but as has been pointed out, Lepchas have no number sense, and I think he was probably older.

return he started to learn lama's work (he is now *kané*) ; his teacher was his 'uncle' the second Dorjé Lapoon. At sixteen he was married to a girl from Hi ; she was twelve at the time and had no relations here. Her first child miscarried (this is said to be an inherited disability in her family) but a boy, Doogu, was born in 1934. His wife was pregnant again in April 1937.

On April 28th he came up to have a sore on his foot dressed ; owing to having worn boots at Gangtok and sometimes since, the skin on his feet and legs is much more tender than that of the other Lepchas. While his foot was soaking I dressed Kondé's face and when the blood flowed he winced obviously and audibly. He said that if he saw people bleed or animals killed or a human corpse he felt the pain as if it was his own. He said he had never fainted but he frequently has nightmares so terrifying that he wakes up screaming. The most frequent subjects of such dreams are falling off rocks or being chased by bulls.

I never once heard Pembu make a joke, though he laughed freely enough at the jokes of others. He is very subdued and quiet.

Both he and his wife obviously dote on their child, Dugoo, and spoil him outrageously. The baby is very precocious and independent. On one occasion he got angry with another child his own age and hit him once with his closed fist. The child hit burst into laughter and so did Dugoo's parents but the bystanders were rather shocked. Although he is not yet four he has already thrown away his shell necklace. At another date I gave him a packet of water flowers as a present to take home ; he grizzled when other people wanted to hold it to look at ; when he got it he put it very carefully away inside his coat. Mrs. Datoop made him pick a red cactus to give to me ; the first he threw at me, the second he handed nicely and then picked up the first and scolded me for taking it with only one hand. After three or four weeks he became really attached to me and called me 'uncle' and used to climb over me or tug at me to attract my attention—a thing no other child dared to do.

After Pembu, was born a daughter in 1910, then Pichi in 1914 and a second daughter about 1918 and the youngest son, Kolok Tyong in 1922. Both daughters have married into their mother's village, the younger one going as second wife to the husband of a sterile aunt. Both have borne children which they are rearing in cradles.

MR. AND MRS. JIROONG. MRS. JIROONG IS SPINNING. SHE IS WEARING TIBETAN DRESS AND HER HUSBAND'S HAT. SEATED IN FRONT IS DADOOL SOAKING A CUT FOOT. ATYOOK TURNS HIS BACK

Pichi.

Pichi has spent the great part of his life at Gangtok, from about the age of six until the last three months. First of all he went to school, during which period he lived with his 'aunt', and subsequently to the carpentry school, when he lived with the superintendent. He enjoyed it there and was never at all home-sick. He learnt to speak Nepali and Sikkimese there.

As a child he slept beside his mother's elder sister when the youngest sister was born; subsequently when Kolok Tyong was born the two sisters slept together and now Pichi is sleeping beside his younger brother.

Pichi has quite a lot of private property which was given to him by his father before he went to Gangtok. During his absence his parents looked after it for him. He has four or five cattle, about ten goats, cardamum producing six or seven maunds and rice terraces producing three or four maunds. His private rice is eaten by the family household without consulting him, but the money from the cardamum is entirely his own to do what he likes with.

In 1936 an old childless couple died and although he was absent the Mandal appointed Pichi *ké-tsop*; this means in fact that he is the owner of the land and house of this couple (all the animals and movable property had to be given to the two married daughters of the dead man) and the land is registered in his name, though his father works it and pays the taxes. When this property was acquired the old house and land were given to Pembu and his wife.

A marriage was arranged for Pichi with a girl in Hi while he was at Gangtok; he was informed about it but said he was too busy to come so his younger brother Kolok Tyong acted as his representative for the *asék*. He knew the girl before the marriage was arranged. Tafoor acted as 'uncle' in his marriage and the Mandal as *bek-bu*. However, when Pichi finally came home he resolutely refused the arranged marriage, saying that he would prefer to choose his own wife. For a time there was much ambiguity about the situation; Datoop hoped that Pichi would accept the girl finally, merely refusing on account of shyness; and for a long time Pichi himself was not sufficiently emphatic to his parents for them to be able to be quite certain what was to be done. The Mandal said that the girl is affianced to either Pichi or Kolok Tyong according to which she may choose. Both horoscopes are suitable ; and he has advised her to marry both brothers.[7]

The situation seems to have been that Kolok Tyong performed the *asék* but that if Pichi could be persuaded to take the girl Datoop would prefer it. By May 9th it was finally decided that Kolok Tyong should marry the girl at the coming harvest ; Kolok Tyong is a very plump and self-satisfied boy and extremely independent, but he says very little. Pichi gave as one of his reasons for refusing the marriage the fact that he would be away so much and did not like the idea of leaving a wife alone for months at a time.

Shortly after his return home Pichi was taken ill with pains in his stomach and back and head and in his ' heart ' ; and for this illness his parents had very elaborate ceremonies performed by lamas and Mun. When the ceremony was performed Pichi looked very ill and rather like a sleep-walker, glassy eyed and with a waxy complexion and very slow movements. Three days after the exorcism I saw him and he confessed that he had felt nothing during the exorcism and was sceptical about its efficacy. He considered that it would only be shown to be valuable if he got better. Subsequently he was quite cured but he still said he did not believe in the general validity of these exorcism ceremonies.

iii

Jiroong.

Jiroong is forty-one. He was the third son of his parents ; his sister is three years younger than he is. He became a lama from his own choice and because the sign was found on him ; no relations of his were lamas before him. His family was very poor, indeed necessitous.[8] His teacher was the first Dorjé Lapoon who later seduced his first wife.

His memories of early childhood from the age of two are very precise. He has clear memories of sitting in his mother's lap and drinking her milk while older people sitting around him pulled his ears and scolded him because he cried for no reason. He remembers running to his mother because bigger boys teased him.

[7] I think more or less as a joke. It is quite permissible for two brothers to share a wife, especially if the elder brother has to travel about a great deal as Pichi, being a state carpenter, will have to do. But the arrangement is not very popular. See Chapter Six, p. 171.

[8] It will be remembered that they are descendants of slaves.

His sister was born when he was three. He was taking his mother's breast till the birth. He was very frightened at the birth, which he witnessed. He was told the new baby was Sang-rong *moong*, a devil the size of a small child who is especially used as a bogey to frighten children. He was weaned in two ways; first of all his mother's breasts were smeared with the new baby's excrement and secondly an aunt took him home, telling him that he must not cry because Sang-rong *moong* was with his mother and would eat him. For a week—he remembers clearly—he cried every night for his mother's breast and then resigned himself to do without. The aunt looked after him, sometimes taking him to her house, sometimes going to his and sleeping with him. She was his father's sister.

As a child he was, he considers, exceptionally timid. Most of his memories are to do with being bullied by older children; a cousin of his beating him for being disobedient when he was six or seven; two older boys ducking him and other small children in the stream, whereat they cried and the parents of the small boys came and beat the bullies. He also remembers sitting beside another small child and they threw mud and cinders at one another. He was carried by his mother or grandmother till he was five years old and remembers that vividly. He also remembers playing with other children at building bridges and making a house out of twigs and of once playing tug-of-war. His father gave him a little knife when he was quite young, he thinks before he was weaned. At the same time his mother gave him a haversack. Before he got the little knife he used to try to use grown-ups' knives. When his father gave him the knife he told him to be very careful—not to cut his friends or to use the knife on stones and so on.

He apparently cried easily and ran to his mother; he remembers crying and sucking at the same time whereat bystanders slapped him. Although he connects the birth of the younger sister with weaning he has always been very fond of her. His mother died when he was fifteen.

He knew about sexual intercourse when he was nine or ten but he was too timid to do anything when he played with girls and other boys. His first sexual experience was when he was fifteen with his elder brother's wife. His elder brother was away for the night and the wife called Jiroong to come and sleep with her. He took the invitation literally and went to sleep; but she forcibly seduced him. In this way she educated him and after that he was no longer so timid. As a child he had been particularly frightened of strangers.

The house which he lives in now was formerly inhabited by an unrelated man who was married to the Omzet nun; she was the sister of Passo, Kurma's adopting father. All the family of this woman's husband died relatively suddenly and she was left alone with the property. Passo tried to get his sister to return to him, whereupon the Mandal said that it would be better to find a *ké-tsop*. Jiroong was decided upon and given to the Omzet nun as husband. But she never liked him; he was very many years younger than she was; and soon the scandal with the first Dorjé Lapoon started.

After he had been forced to give his wife to the Dorjé Lapoon Jiroong travelled around a lot looking for girls; eventually he linked up with Tempa's sister, who was then visiting her brother. She was unmarried and Jiroong slept with her and subsequently *asék*'d her properly, except that he only gave one pig. After *asék* she came to live with him and also with the first Dorjé Lapoon and his wife; they worked together for one year and then she returned home for a single night for the marriage ceremony. This was performed quite properly, except that she did not return home again afterwards. They have had three children, two girls and a boy, but the boy died.

Jiroong's sister, who is a Mun, married the eldest of three brothers in Liklyang; she could not stand her husband and loved his youngest brother. This turning away from her husband created a public scandal; and Tafoor's father the Muktair decided that she was to be tied up to the monastery wall and beaten. She tried to commit suicide by running down to throw herself into the river but she was followed and stopped. She was then tied up and beaten but she claimed that even if they killed her they could not make her like her present husband; so after the beating she was allowed to marry whom she liked, and she chose her husband's youngest brother who was a *kané*.

This second marriage was not smooth, however; she once tried to run away from her husband and quarrelled so much with her neighbours in the four houses by her house down in the valley that the pair were asked to leave. The *kané* was pleased as the daily walk to and from the monastery was very tiring and they asked Jiroong for a plot of ground above his house. The *kané* died after they had lived there a year. She refused to take the *oong-op*, her husband's 'younger brother' and instead married Kaji, an old man in the habit of seeing devils, whose wife, like her husband, had died of dysentery.

About twelve years ago Jiroong set up '*ingzong*' with Balyoop, a lama living at Panung. His chief reason was so as to have a substitute for his dead brothers to help him and his children. (Balyoop himself is childless.) Also they were fond of one another. Balyoop is considerably older than he is; Mrs. Jiroong calls him 'father' out of respect.

Jiroong considers that the happiest time of life is an easy old age if you have your health and children or others to help you. He said that he considered Pong-ring lucky because all the villagers feed him. (This old widowed man is covered with sores and full of disease and most people consider he would be happier dead.) He considers, however, that Serving and Kahlyeu are unlucky because they are more or less alone. He says that the best thing in life is to do good to others.

He first said he would like to be the richest man in the village and then withdrew his statement saying that all he wanted was enough to eat and wear for him and his. He is worried and anxious and timid. He has been unfortunate in both his marriages.[9] He has no desire to re-live any early part of his life again.

He has three small rice terraces; he cannot have more as he has nobody to help make them; the only men in the household are himself and his nephew Tobgé, and they are busy getting the crops without attending to building terraces. Neither he nor any of his brothers have ever contemplated or threatened suicide. Jiroong can swim in the river in winter; he learnt from watching others and trying. The only other person who is known to be able to swim is old Songpo.

Jiroong is a particularly industrious person and is slowly becoming one of the wealthier figures in the village.

[9] It will be remembered that it was his wife who was the cause of all the major quarrels in the village in the last three years. See Chapter Five, pp. 140–142.

CHAPTER SEVENTEEN

SOCIAL EVOLUTION AND AGGRESSION: SOME SUGGESTIONS

i

Many and various have been the uses to which anthropology[1]—the observation and study of strange and usually materially primitive and analphabetic societies—has been put. The aim of the earliest ethnologists, Herodotus and the Chinese travellers, seems to have been primarily diversion, though the constant favourable contrast between civilisation and various forms of barbarism was always an underlying motif. To a great extent the same is true of the European travellers and missionaries of the sixteenth, seventeenth and eighteenth centuries, though on the whole with these writers the stress was more on the benefits of Christianity than on those of civilisation. In the eighteenth century for the first time the accounts of primitive peoples were turned to a political and philosophical use; great play was made of the contrast between the sexual freedom and other desirable qualities of certain primitive (chiefly Pacific) people and the restraint and undesirable social arrangements imposed on Europeans. This argument was most fully developed by the French, notably Diderot with his *Supplément au voyage de Bougainville* and J.-J. Rousseau, with his 'noble savage'. De Sade employed the accounts of primitive peoples a great deal to illustrate the local and historical variations of various moral and political ideas. Rousseau also used the accounts of primitive peoples for the first evolutionary theory of human society—the theory of the Social Contract.

The same themes—the contrast between European civilisation and savagery, and the evolution of society—were dominant during

[1] Since writing this chapter I have seen Professor Robert H. Lowie's *The History of Ethnological Theory* (London: Harrap: 1937), which treats in great detail the subjects which I have touched on in these first two sections. For a full treatment of the progress of ethnology in the last century this book can hardly be bettered.

the nineteenth century also; but at this period, and especially during the second half of the century, the emphases were reversed; the very obvious material progress of Europe gave a great feeling of security to the vast majority of the writers of that period and the contrasts between the European and the savage were entirely in favour of the European; at this epoch it was the horrible, and very frequently the 'unmentionable', habits of primitives which were stressed: the type primitive was a cannibal indulging in nameless orgies. The over-simplified popular views of Darwin's theory of evolution were responsible for the 'step-ladder' view of social evolution, with the Fuzzy-Wuzzies on the bottom rung and the nation to which the writer belonged on the top, with all other societies neatly graded in between. Up till 1914 and even later the 'step-ladder' theory held the principal place in the theories of anthropology put out by various, usually arm-chair, ethnologists; but social evolution was studied less than the evolution of certain ideas—magic and religion, monogamic marriage, monotheism and so on; the moral of all these anthologies, some of them of great charm and literary merit, was that primitive humanity started from something quite different and by gradual stages reached the apex of the viewpoint held by the writer.

The imperialist development of the end of the nineteenth century produced two results: it developed a social theory, diffusionism, which was parallel to and a justification of imperialism, and it also led to a more careful and accurate study of primitive races, so that the imperialists, who at that epoch discovered that colonial labour was of value, could govern the subject races without having to massacre them. The theory of diffusionism, that all social improvements derived from a single source (usually Egypt), was a great justification for the repetition of this process by a single conquering power (usually England or Germany).

I do not wish to suggest that all the anthropological work done before 1914 was useless; on the contrary a great deal was and remains of first-class importance and value; but the currently held version of evolution and the belief in progress almost inevitably resulted in all the emphasis and attention of the ethnologists being directed to those aspects of primitive societies which were in obvious contrast to European society, and a practically complete neglect of those unformalised aspects of human life which were more or less similar in all human societies. In particular very great attention was laid on those details which the evolutionary theories of society claimed to be typical of societies at a certain stage of development, such as totemism, exogamy, ritual king-killing, initiation rites and the like; the unhappy ethnographer who was studying a society in which one or more of these phenomena were lacking had to use all his ingenuity to explain such peculiar absences.

Among the evolutionary theories of the nineteenth century only one still obtains much support to-day, and that, in Western Europe and America, chiefly from people who are not primarily anthropologists; that is the materialist conception of social evolution described by Lewis H. Morgan in his *Ancient Society* and elaborated and given wide publicity by Frederick Engels' *The Origin of the Family, Private Property and the State*. Among Soviet Russian ethnologists this little book is given almost scriptural value; outside the U.S.S.R. its acceptance or rejection appears to depend on private political attitudes rather than on ascertainable fact. In a very great number of details Morgan and Engels are now patently incorrect, either through ignorance, through an insufficiency of facts, or through misinterpretation or arbitrary selection of the facts at their disposal. Their evolutionary views were as over-simple as those of their contemporaries, another 'step-ladder' neatly divided into three sections with three divisions in each; and into one of these nine subdivisions all societies that had been, or could be, had to be placed; the subdivisions depended primarily on property relations, but each type of society was meant to be exactly correlated with certain phases of technical development, familial and religious institutions and social organisation. Like all the other evolutionary theories this was an obvious over-simplification, and further knowledge disclosed societies with features of two or more of the Morgan-Engels subdivisions; this fact, together with the abhorrence of most anthropologists for the political doctrines of Marx and Engels, became a sufficient excuse for the ignoring or dismissal of the extremely valuable general theory Morgan had advanced; academic anthropology either ignored it completely or claimed to disprove it by the fact that no society has been reported in which some sort of private property did not exist. In so far as this is not simply dishonest, it is a piece of verbal sophistry; communism does not mean 'common possession'; and the existence of private property no more disproves or disqualifies the classification of 'primitive communism' than the existence of common pasturage in most of Western Europe up to the end of the eighteenth century indicates that the boroughs or communes to which these common pasture lands were attached were communist. Primitive communism, as I understand the term, depends on certain property and social relationships, notably that no portion of the (at any rate adult male) population is debarred from property-owning, and, as a corollary, that no one man or one section of the population can exploit the labour of another portion of the population for their own benefit; that is to say primitive communism is incompatible with feudalism. I shall revert to this question of primitive communism and social evolution, with special reference to the Lepchas, later on in this chapter.

ii

The contemporary reorientation of anthropology can be conviently dated from 1918. This reorientation sprang from a number of different causes and has taken a number of (at any rate superficially) different forms. The 1914–18 war was at least in part responsible for this reorientation, for, through its patent failure to achieve any of its announced results, it produced, at any rate among the technically victorious populations, a doubt and finally a shattering of the nineteenth-century view of social evolution as a single-directioned process, of the synonymity of change and progress. This destruction of European self-complacency was often referred to as 'relativity' or 'a relative view' employing a strained analogy with Einstein's Theory of Relativity, which, somewhat confusedly, appeared to give scientific sanction to modern scepticism. The war was also responsible for the internment of Professor Malinowski in the Trobriand Islands; and this fortuitous circumstance resulted in the longest and most thorough piece of field-work yet performed by a trained ethnologist;[2] and the various monographs on the Trobrianders which the Professor produced after the war established a new and altogether higher standard of anthropological investigation; his work was also symptomatic of the new orientation in taking as its field the whole of adult Trobriand life and not merely the picturesque and formalised elements of it. Parallel advances in sociology and psychology, notably Freudian psychoanalysis,

[2] Of course many writers who have described foreign societies have lived much longer among the people they were describing, notably the Reverend Henri Junod, who spent twenty-five years among the Ba-Thonga; but in all such cases their ethnological work has been subsidiary to their main employment.

gave the ethnologist new disciplines. It is questionable whether many anthropologists were aware of the progress of genetics; had they been they would have found there too an encouragement for the rejection of the popular nineteenth-century view of evolution as a synonym for progress, for by no means all mutations are eugenic.

As a generalisation it may be said that the rejection of the nineteenth-century views of social evolution has not been followed, as in biology, by an emended version nearer to observable truth; instead the greater number of theoretical anthropologists have abandoned the subject, falling back on to scientific agnosticism. The nineteenth-century anthropologists placed all societies, from the Fuzzy-Wuzzies to their own, on a graded scale; those of the twentieth century tended to put them all on the same level, to claim that there was no essential difference between the Australian Bushmen and England or America, that they were all three discrete cultures of equal validity. Reaction to the extravagances of the diffusionist school led also to a tendency to ignore or gloss over all but the most obvious impacts of one society on another; the post-war view was, to a great extent still is, a picture of the world covered by a great number of discrete cultures of varied size and complication, only comparable in the fact that they were all, in the sum of their attributes, unique. The anthropologists' answer to the questions of social development was a plea of *non possumus*; a culture (this term was preferred to that of a society) was somehow spontaneously generated; all the ethnologist could do was to describe as accurately as possible the culture under investigation with all its interconnecting functions; cultures could be compared to one another on the basis of their treatment of certain aspects of social and human life, such as food-gathering, family life, magic and religion and so on. Some anthropologists appeared to deny even this possibility; since all cultures are unique, and since all social actions are inextricably interwoven, to extract one feature from the whole complex is to distort it, and all that can be compared is the total stress of one culture with that of another.

Since I believe in evolution I do not consider that this atomic view of human societies is complete or adequate; the fact that further knowledge has invalidated the earlier hypotheses of social evolution is not a proper excuse for not trying to form new hypotheses which will take into account the newer sources of knowledge; and in so far as they fail to do this anthropologists are inadequately fulfilling their functions. At the same time this scientific agnosticism, this treatment of all societies as being equal and comparable —if only in their uniqueness—has had one extraordinarily valuable result: it has enabled us to gain greater insight into our own society by studying comparable features in other societies. The rejection of the view that contemporary and local behaviour is 'human nature', the acceptance of the equal validity of any society's treatment of any feature of individual and social life has opened up the possibility of studying our own lives, of realising by comparison which of our attitudes and types of behaviour are socially determined, and which biologically. The most notable contribution to this aspect of social knowledge is found in the works of Dr. Margaret Mead; in her very thorough studies of various Pacific societies she has paid special attention to the cultural treatment of certain problems of our own society, notably as to whether the psychological disturbances of puberty are inevitable and biologically determined (*Coming of Age in Samoa*), questions of child development (*Growing Up in New Guinea*) and the correlation between the biological facts of sex and the social characteristics of men and women (*Sex and Temperament in three Primitive Societies*). This elucidation of our own behaviour by the study of other societies is a field of enormous potentialities; the validity of the conclusions drawn inevitably depends on the high accuracy of the general anthropological work.

My own interest in anthropology is primarily due to the fact that it is a discipline capable of enabling us to understand our own society. Although I consider that the careful and accurate description of different societies is a work of great interest and importance, I do not think that I would have gone to the trouble and expense of a long visit to the Himalayas if the only result which I could hope for would be the description of yet another society. I have a certain admiration for those detached scientists who do so, but my interest in anthropology is pragmatic. This does not mean to say that I think the rigorous discipline and methodology of the academic anthropologists can be ignored or relaxed; on the contrary even closer, more accurate and more detailed observation is necessary to study those points which are not formalised in any society. To take a simple example, a generalisation on the treatment of infants needs a very great number of individual observations, far more than on regulated social behaviour; but these observations cannot be published, for they would represent an unreadable list of almost identical comments; who would want to read the scores ot observations of adults and children which enabled me to write, '(If a Lepcha baby cries) somebody tries to distract the child's attention by waving something bright—a flower or a piece of paper—in front of it, and then giving it to the child to hold. Should this treatment fail the baby is usually walked up and down, while the carrier gently taps its bottom.' I consider it necessary to labour this point because some famous anthropologists who, in their field-work, did not direct their attention to such aspects of social behaviour, have tried to denigrate similar observations on the ground that they were 'unscientific', 'empathy', and so on. If it were not for personal spite it would seem obvious that the treatment of children is as much a part of social behaviour as the treatment of (say) magic, and deductions from the observed treatment of infants in its effect on adult character is as legitimate as deductions on observed magical practices as a function of the culture as a whole.

For a number of years I have been becoming increasingly absorbed in the problem of the individual in society, of the accommodations which people must make to live together in peace, and of the resulting happiness or unhappiness which such accommodations produce. This interest is not merely academical and theoretical: it has been borne increasingly on me that nowadays in Occidental society the lives of most people are relatively unsatisfactory and unsatisfied; part of this discontent is undoubtedly due to the economic maladjustments which the survival of the habits of an age of scarcity to an age of potential plenty make increasingly obvious; but I do not believe that this is the whole of the problem. Contemporary evidence in various countries seems to me to show adequately that changes in the economic and social arrangements will not necessarily remove profound discontent.

It is a truism to say that, once the primary needs of food, warmth and shelter are satisfied, the happiness or unhappiness of the individual depends chiefly on his relationships with the other individuals of the society of which he is a member. It follows that it is necessary to study existing individuals and societies in order to find out whence maladjustments arise, and, if possible, how they can be remedied. The ultimate aim would be to make such studies of our own society, but at present very great difficulties lie in the way; our society is too large for any individual or small group to study as a whole, and there is no sort of agreement as to what would constitute a valid representative sample; and we are all so intimately involved in our own society that it would be almost impossible for any observer to be reasonably objective about the society in which he was born. It is possible, however, that the splitting of Occidental society into smaller groups of class and nationality may enable strangers to these smaller groups to investigate them.

Fortunately our own society, though probably the largest and to us infinitely the most important, is not the only one in the world. In decreasing numbers there are, chiefly outside Europe, other groups and societies who have developed their own way of living, their own culture, without regard to or knowledge of Occidental values, each evolving their own unique methods of dealing with the problem of living in society, which is the universal problem of that anti-social gregarious animal, man. A careful study of these different societies in their entirety should give much information on the formation and interaction of various types of social behaviour, especially in the treatment of those biological and psychological urges which would appear to be common to all human beings.

iii

When I visited the Lepchas I had naturally no sort of idea as to what problems the study of their society would illuminate, for it is obviously impossible to know anything of an unknown society until you are in the midst of the investigation. Neither the observations of those Europeans who lived among the Lepchas in the Darjeeling district nor my own casual observations in Kalimpong when I was studying the language prepared me in any way for what I was actually to find in Zongu. Some of the tentative conclusions which I reached in Kalimpong through my contact with missionised Lepchas were profoundly incorrect.

Studying the results presented in the body of this book, it seems to me that Lepcha society raises three questions, one of which I feel that I lack sufficient evidence even to attempt to answer. This question is What has been the result of the impact of their more highly developed neighbours on the Lepchas as a group and as individuals? That the results of this impact have been profound would appear obvious, but lacking accurate knowledge of these neighbours no answer appears at present possible; I regret this, for a knowledge of the effects of culture contact should give valuable information on the probable results of the intentional introduction of social changes in our own society. The other two questions raised by the Lepcha material seem to me to be interrelated. They are (1) Why have the Lepchas failed to develop a more advanced, feudal, social organisation, when their neighbours, the Bhutanese, the Nepali and the Tibetans, apparently ethnically similar and in much the same state of material development, have done so? and (2) Why and how have the Lepchas so completely inhibited the expression of overt aggression in individuals?

Engels, following and elaborating Morgan, divided all societies into three main types: barbarism (or gentile societies), feudalism and civilisation (or capitalism). The three progressive types of society are distinguished by increasing productivity of labour, social division of labour, the distribution of private property, and special types of social organisation suitable to each type of society. The progress from feudalism to civilisation (capitalism) has, except in very recent periods, only occurred in Western Europe and is adequately documented by contemporary literary remains and subsequent studies and belongs more properly to the domain of specialised sociology than of anthropology. All societies outside Europe and America (with the exception of Japan, and less certainly, China) can be classified as barbarous or feudal. The term 'barbarous' is an unfortunate one, with its connotations of moral superiority; but it is the only one available, for 'primitive' has been defined to mean 'not normally employing writing' and therefore applies to many feudal as well as all barbarous societies; terms like 'primitive communism' or 'primitive democracy' make possibly unjustified assumptions about pre-feudal societies; and contemporary ethnologists would appear to have so completely neglected this problem that they have not even provided a name to distinguish pre-feudal and feudal societies.

The essence of feudalism, according to Engels (and there seems no reason to object to the definition) is the coming into existence of the state, a more or less centralised organ which controls the activities of the population of the society for the benefit of one portion of that society to the detriment of the other portions; the chief functions of the state are policing, taxation, and the preservation of private property. The dominating group in the state may be the original inhabitants over slaves, conquerors over the conquered, warriors over the rest of the community, or big property owners over the poor; in the last two cases the warriors or big property owners may dominate as a group of equals or the power and property may be concentrated in the hands of a single leader or king. The essential features of feudalism are an increase in the size of the effective social unit, a centralised organisation capable of controlling individual behaviour without explicit popular consent, and a greater differentiation in the wealth of the ruling class and that of the majority of the population. Engels also adds the change from family (gentile) classification to local classification, but this view is almost certainly not tenable, without modification.

For Engels the outstanding qualities of barbarism (pre-feudalism) were that the social unit was the extended family (or *gens*), or at most the group of *gentes* or *phratry*; the social equality of all members of the *gens*, or at any rate of all the elders or heads of families; the economic self-sufficiency of each social group; the roughly equal division of property within the group, usually coupled with a certain amount of work done and land owned in common either by the household or the extended family; and either the complete absence of class-divisions, or at most very slight distinctions. The typical organisation of barbarous societies is 'primitive democracy', by which is meant that decisions are taken after consultation with all adults, or all adult males, of the group involved; certain people hold authority as priests, war leaders, peace leaders, but this authority is limited, given by consent, and usually elective. Engels also adds that matrilineal preceded patrilineal descent, but here the evidence is not conclusive. He and Morgan further linked with barbarism and feudalism certain types of social (especially sexual) arrangements; but the correlation would appear to be more neat than accurate.

I have thought it necessary to give Engels' definitions before discussing them, as they appear to be practically outlawed from contemporary academic anthropology. As generalised, statistical descriptions of the two types of society his definitions appear to me to be valid, though in individual societies one or more of the features which he distinguishes may be slight or absent. The centralised state and the privileged class are the fundamental features of feudalism, and it seems valuable to distinguish those societies which possess them from those which do not. Engels' descriptions of barbarism and feudalism seem adequate; what I wish to discuss is how, and for what reasons, a given society changes from one form of organisation to the other.

Engels has stated his views of the internal reasons for this transformation. They are first, the increased productivity of labour, the specialisation of labour, the change of consumption goods into commodities (the cultivation or creation of food and articles for exchange instead of for consumption by the cultivator or manufacturer), the principle of inheritance and the increasing disproportion of the property in the hands of one group as opposed to the rest of the population. He mentions as a secondary cause the existence of professional warriors under unified leadership who live, and can only live, by booty.

Now I think it would be agreed today that these various factors which Engels considers to be the internal causes of the transformation from barbarism to feudalism would be more properly described as predisposing symptoms. It is obvious that any social modification or transformation is impossible while the average labour of an individual in any given society can only just provide sufficient food for immediate consumption; but when, through the adoption of agriculture and herding, or through improvement in these processes, a greater accumulation of food is possible, there would not seem to be any inevitable reason why this extra food should either be transformed into a commodity or emphasise the difference in property-owning within the society; it can equally well be applied, as it has been applied among the Lepchas, to raising the general standard of living and consumption to a point above the subsistence level. Similarly no society has been discovered without some social division of labour within the operative unit, though in many societies this unit is the household. The principle of inheritance, though it need not be patrilineal nor even individual inheritance, is also found in the great majority of barbarous societies; so is a certain disproportion of property, though among the Lepchas the disproportion, and the incidence of poverty, is rather greater than is usual in societies with parallel family organisation. All the available evidence points to the Lepchas having possessed as many predisposing circumstances for feudalism, for the invention of the state, as their neighbours the Bhutanese, Tibetans and Nepali (or rather the different tribes of Nepal); their country, Sikkim, would indeed appear to have been richer than, at any rate, most of Tibet and Bhutan, for the translation of the Tibetan name for it is 'the rice country'; but there is no sort of evidence to show that the Lepchas at any period of their history developed towards feudalism in any way.

Some theoretical anthropologists, especially those writing in a monarchical society, have assumed that feudalism—the existence of a powerful chief enforcing his rule—was the 'natural' 'original' form of human society; they have taken their evidence from the observation of the behaviour of the great apes under captivity, from selected accounts of the behaviour of feudal societies, or from analogies with the contemporary family. The most notable of these theoreticians are Sir James Frazer, in *The Golden Bough*, and, by implication, Freud in *Totem and Taboo*. I do not think that nowadays anybody would subscribe to this dogma completely, though some people might consider that the existence of chieftainship was 'natural' in certain areas. I do not think even this view is tenable, though a better case could be put up for it; but the case would really depend on giving a variety of meanings to the one word 'chief'; many barbarous societies have headmen, either temporary or permanent, but their power is socially limited and they can only exercise their chieftainship through the consent of the rest of the community; the essential difference between feudalism and barbarism, when both societies possess chiefs, is the question whether the chief has any means of enforcing his power without the expressed consent of the rest of the population.

It may be considered that this argument is an exclusively theoretical discussion; I consider on the contrary that its complete elucidation would throw much light on the evolution of human societies; the progress from feudalism, the coming into being of the state, to the most elaborate of contemporary societies is a single and, in its main lines, comprehensible process; the transition from the tribe (barbarism) to the state (feudalism) is on the other hand still extremely obscure; but this transition is, in its effect, the most revolutionary in the social history of man; the invention of the state is, if not the origin, the cause of great acceleration of material and social progress; the only possible parallel to the transition from barbarism to feudalism would be the transition from civilisation (capitalism) to some classless society. If we can understand how the one came about, we may learn something about how the other may come about.

I have already listed the causes Engels gives for the internal transformation; that they are predisposing symptoms and not causes is I think adequately illustrated by the Ifugao[3] of the Philippine Islands. These people have all the prerequisites of feudalism, including an economic stratification more marked than in almost

[3] See, among the other literature on this people, R. F. Barton's *Ifugao Law and Custom* and *Ifugao Economics* (University of California Publications in American Archeology and Ethnology, Vol. 15, nos. 1 and 5, 1922).

any feudal system outside Europe; but they have not achieved feudalism; they have no central authority.

I should like to suggest that, given the necessary economic and material development, there are two interdependent essential conditions for the transformation from barbarism to feudalism: they are, the existence and encouragement of competition within the social group, and more or less prolonged and intimate contact with members of another group. Both of these circumstances must always be present: unless a struggle for individual distinction within the group already exists, the presence of members of another group will not produce feudalism; if the individual rivalry exists and there is no or little contact with members of another group the transformation will also not take place.

The precipitating cause of feudalism would appear to be war, whether the victors settle in the conquered country or take back to their own country slaves in relatively large quantities; the two groups living together in the same area render the invention of an apparatus of social control necessary. In the case of an aggressive group invading a non-aggressive one the invaders may represent a very small portion of the entire population; the slaves imported into the home territory must on the other hand be a relatively large portion of the population to render such a transformation necessary. In Athens, for example, they very considerably overnumbered the Athenians.

It is possible, indeed probable, that the existence of a feudal state in a given area will, through its example, cause the conversion to feudalism of its barbarous neighbours; but that this does not inevitably take place can be proved from West Africa where fairly highly developed feudal states existed side by side with barbarous societies, as well as by the Lepchas who live and lived entirely surrounded by feudalism.

It is obvious that in a society composed of two diverse groups with separate cultures, the chances of the survival of the culture of the conquered is small, unless there is very great disproportion between the numbers of the conquerors and conquered; and, even in such cases, unless the conquerors are very quickly absorbed by the conquered, the culture of the conquered will be progressively modified by external authority. It therefore follows that, for the group considered as an entity, internal competition and rivalry is a eugenic[4]

[4] In this chapter I am using the terms *eugenic* and *dysgenic* figuratively, to describe the qualities which conduce to the survival or disappearance of the

quality; for if the existence of internal competition is a necessary preliminary to conquest (and it would seen inevitable that this must be so: aggressive wars can only be waged for extra booty or prestige on the part of individuals before the existence of the state) then the absence of internal competition is dysgenic as soon as the group which discourages it comes into contact with an aggressive group. As far as groups are concerned the process of civilisation could be described as a constant selection in favour of aggressiveness. Up till now aggressiveness has had a very definite survival value; so in their time did the mammoth's or the sabre-toothed tiger's tusks.

It may be argued that the Lepchas did not themselves develop feudalism because they have been conquered and are now the subordinate part of a feudal state; but that is no explanation of the fact that they have developed no form of organisation which would possibly be capable of developing into feudalism. Their neighbours the Nepali appear to have lived under the dominion of foreign (and therefore invading) kings from China and India for nearly two thousand years; in the early eighteenth century the Gurkhas nevertheless developed a complete feudal state.

So far have the Lepchas been from developing towards feudalism that there is no sort of native tradition of any historical or heroic chief; their biggest unit seems always to have been the village (or *ptso*—extended family group—if the *ptso* was, as seems possible, at one time a geographical unit) and one of the greatest weaknesses of their existing social organisation is the very limited power of control which the Mandal of one village can exercise over inhabitants of other villages.[5]

If my argument has been correct, the reason why the Lepchas never developed towards feudalism despite apparently adequate predisposing material conditions was that they did not sufficiently develop within their society competition and aggression. It is

society as a unit. By analogy I am comparing societies with animal species, but I do not wish to suggest that in any way their survival or disappearance is genetically determined. It is obvious that a conquered people, though they lose their specific culture, may be more fertile than their conquerors, and so from a biological viewpoint conquest may be eugenic.

[5] A case in point is the destitution of Kurma's mother after the death of her first husband, when the Mandal and people of Lingthem were unable to force the 'husband's younger brother', who should have inherited and supported her, to marry her because he lived under another Mandal. See Chapter Fifteen, pp. 388 and 394.

necessary for some portion of a society to wish for power and distinction, for property and prestige, if the whole society is to develop a more elaborate form, feudalism. Engels and Morgan appear to have believed either that the transformation was an automatic (' historical ' is their favourite synonym) process developing spontaneously from the change in the productive power of labour, or else that mankind was ' naturally ' acquisitive and competitive. But feudalism means an increase in the size of the social group, and that increase can only, in the long run, be accomplished at the expense of other groups. Social evolution and the survival of certain groups is dependent, ultimately, on the amount of permissive internal competition and aggression ; if the permissive aggression is excessive the society will be liable to fissurate and split into a number of internecine groups, incapable of combination ; if it is defective the society will have no pattern for resisting alien intrusion. Save in the exceptional case when a materially primitive society comes into conflict with a materially advanced one social evolution is selective in favour of societies with an optimum number of aggressive individuals.

iv

One of the most futile and popular subjects of discussion is the nature and characteristics of the ' natural ' man ; in the course of two centuries philosophers and polemists have endowed this unfortunate abstraction with every sort of contradictory quality, according to the point which they wished to make. The subject is futile, for it is impossible to conceive man apart from some sort of society, no matter how small and undeveloped ; as an animal man is born with certain biological urges and appetites, but the expression which these urges and appetites will assume is to a very great extent socially determined. As an animal man has to feed himself and to reproduce himself ; what food he will eat and what mate he will get will be to a very great extent determined by the society of which he is a member.

It has seemed worth while to repeat this truism because the question of aggression, and especially the social control of aggression, is one which has been singularly neglected both by psychologists and sociologists. One of the reasons for this neglect is probably the fact that all the writers on such subjects were members of states, and one of the chief laws of any state is that the social control of aggression is the business of the state, and not of the individual nor of the social group, apart from the specialised police. The chief function of police indeed is to ensure that aggression, whether directed against other members of the group or against property, should not go beyond socially limited points. The theory of the policed state assumes the existence of aggression which can only be inhibited by external force; and people writing in such states about man in pre-police societies have been inclined to endow this primitive man with the almost uninhibited expression of aggression: 'man is "naturally" a fighter', is '"naturally" jealous and possessive', the 'strongest male "naturally" obtains possession of all the females'. More sophisticated writers have seen that this 'natural' free vent to all aggressive instincts would completely prevent the establishment of any form of society, and they therefore date the origin of society from the drastic overcoming of this free expression of aggression, particularly the aggressive jealousy of adult males; Morgan and Engels posit as a solution the invention of 'group marriage', Freud the mutual blackmailing and guilt-feelings of brothers who have conspired together to kill and eat an over-aggressive and over-possessive father. As universal solutions both suggestions suffer through their inherent improbability as well as leaving the pre-existing situation as vague as ever. Although an approximation to strict and lifelong monogamy is probably historically very modern, it seems doubtful whether the food-gathering conditions under which mankind presumably originally lived would have supported sufficient adults in a small area to have made group marriage feasible.

The very general assumption of 'natural' uncontrollable and murderous jealousy on the part of males is an interesting one; although sexual jealousy is quite common, there are a number of societies—for instance, the Eskimos, the Lepchas, and some American Indian societies—where it receives little or no *social* expression. A very great number of primitive societies implicitly distinguish between woman as a sexual object and woman as a worker and helper, and of the societies which do make this distinction the majority lay the social emphasis on the working functions of the women; in such societies the jealousy situation arises if one man tries to entice away another's worker, and not primarily for sexual reasons.

W. G. Sumner in his *Folkways* implies that individuals have to exteriorise a certain fixed amount of aggression, but that this aggression can be directed inside or outside the group: 'The relation of comradeship and peace in the we-group and that of hostility and war towards other-groups are correlative to each other.' Though this generalisation may be often true it is obviously not universally so; if it were, isolated peoples, those living on islands, for instance, would be in a state of constant internecine hostility since they have no other-group within striking distance. His assumption that the natural state of primitive society is constant warfare[6] also seems not to be borne out by the evidence. The considerable agreement of theorists of very different schools and disciplines on the natural aggressiveness of primitive man is very striking.[7]

Now I think this confusion—for confusion it is—arises from two sources; first the lumping together of all analphabetic societies as primitive, and secondly giving too restricted an interpretation of the term aggression. If I am correct in considering some sort of war the precipitating cause of feudalism then overt aggression (in the popular sense in which I have so far been using the word) will to a greater or less extent be a feature of at any rate the dominant group in feudal societies. In barbarous (pre-feudal) societies the permissive expression of overt aggression is I think liable to be correlated with the chief types of food and valuables and the amount of leisure possible for at any rate a certain portion of the society. People dependent entirely or chiefly on vegetable food, whether gathered or cultivated, will have less obvious cause for aggression outside the group than those dependent on animals; however many domestic animals you possess stolen animals can still constitute a useful addition to your property; if you have as much land as you can cultivate extra land is merely an added burden. As a generalisation it may also be said that the amount of game in any given piece of land is more limited than the amount of vegetable food; if double the number of people hunt over a given territory they are far more likely to exhaust the supply of game, than double the number of people gathering vegetable produce are likely to exhaust the supply of fruit, etc. Herders, of course, have far more leisure than agriculturists. I am not suggesting that all carnivorous societies are war-like, and all vegetarian ones peaceful, but only that societies in which animals are important have more obvious cause for

[6] '(The group's) relation to all outsiders, or other groups, is one of war and plunder, except so far as agreements have modified it.' *Folkways*, p. 12.

[7] For a *reductio ad absurdum* of the theory of the aggressiveness of primitive man see A. Machin's *Darwin's Theory Applied to Mankind* (London: Longman's 1937). This book is an elaborate fantasia based on a hypothetical anti-social primitive hunter 'red in tooth and claw', and is superbly untouched by scientific genetics or modern ethnology.

offensive and defensive warfare; whether they develop this form of social behaviour would appear to depend to a great extent on the density of population in a given area. When agriculture has developed so far that one man's labour can produce sufficient food for more than the labourer (and his immediate dependents) slave-raiding becomes an economic proposition.

So far we have been considering aggression in its purely destructive aspect of fighting, competition and destruction. But I think that is far too narrow a definition of the term and that destruction and rivalry are only two of the aspects of aggression. I should like to suggest that aggression should be defined as one aspect of *the urge to obtain mastery over the environment*; this urge is universal, but the strength with which it is manifested depends on the individual temperament, and the forms its overt expression takes depend partly on the material circumstances and partly on the social organisation in which the individual is born. Aggression or mastery can be manifested towards objects and ideas (the supernatural, for example) as well as towards people, and it can be constructive or destructive; there is as much release of aggression in building or creating as in destroying.

With this wider definition of aggression Sumner's hypothesis that each society (or rather the individuals composing it) have to externalise a certain amount of aggression takes on an added validity; but his 'other-groups' must be redefined to mean the external world and the supernatural, and not merely members of other societies. I should like to suggest the generalisation that the amount of destructive aggression manifested towards other men in primtiive societies is negatively correlated with the difficulty of maintaining life in the given physical environment or social organisation. In other words the harder the environment and the less material development there is, the less will destructive aggression be overtly manifested. Socially allowed destructive aggression is the product of economic security and leisure. If I am correct in this statement the type picture of the earliest men as uninhibitedly destructive and jealous until they were made tolerant, will have to be changed to that of hard-working and generally socially unaggressive men developing jealousy and fighting as they acquired control over their food supply and the dangerous animals in the environment. If this statement is correct the Lepchas' failure to develop any pattern of external aggression may be considered to have been conditioned by their isolation, their low material development, and the difficulties of wresting a livelihood from their environment. It would seem probable also that the environment has been responsible for keeping the operative social group a small one and in that respect may have been a reinforcing cause of the Lepchas' failure to develop towards feudalism. The small local and kinship group is now firmly implanted in Lepcha culture and it is interesting to note how, under contemporary settled conditions, the Lepchas still oppose all attempts to weld them into bigger units; their treatment of the new office of Muktair,[8] even though it was created by the powerful Court, is extremely illuminating.

V

The reasons given above for the Lepchas' lack of destructive aggression outside their group may be adequate; the lack of aggression inside the group cannot be explained in such general terms. It is possible that since, in their major occupation of getting food, the Lepchas felt themselves more opposed by natural phenomena (personified into supernatural forces) than by other men, they to a certain extent carried the same attitude into their social life and regarded the supernatural, and not their fellows, as their chief cause for discontent. From the common-sense point of view it could be argued, as Sumner suggests, that in the small groups of which Lepcha society was composed the value of each individual worker was so great to the group as a whole that all potentially aggressive situations whereby the group might be threatened with the loss of the worker had to be avoided. Unfortunately it cannot be assumed of any human group that they act on common-sense reasons.

Though the reasons for the Lepchas' almost complete suppression of destructive aggression within their group would appear to be impossible to discover, it may be worth while noting their methods of doing so. This suppression of aggression can be viewed from two aspects: there are the social rules for its control, and there is the treatment of the new recruits to the society, the babies. From the social point of view, the most obvious is their strong social sanction against quarrelling; the Lepchas have not admitted a single situation in which quarrelling or vengeance-seeking is permissible. This may be regarded as a legal sanction against quarrelling. Next in importance from the legal point of view is the social arrangement of all sexual relationships so as to exclude jealousy. These arrangements have been detailed in Chapter Six but

[8] See Chapter Five, pp. 123–126.

may be briefly recapitulated. Parents have no rôle in the sexual life of their children; exclusive sexual possession is legally impossible; the younger are favoured against the elder (since they have access to their elders' spouses) and the elder are prevented from overbearing the younger by the equation of 'younger siblings'' spouses with children-in-law. Although nowadays not fully employed they have the legal device of repairing unsatisfactory marriages without the enmity of the two groups involved by exchanging the unsatisfactory spouse for another member of the same group.

In the Lepcha treatment of young children there seem to me to be two constant stresses of almost equal importance for the avoidance of overt aggression. One of these stresses has been already fully documented in Chapter Eleven; it is the immediate and willing satisfaction of all the infant's expressed physical desires. Save under exceptional circumstances, or through illness, the Lepcha infant does not apparently suffer to any appreciable extent from hunger, discomfort or cold. From the point of view of physical well-being Lepcha babies appear to experience the minimum of frustration and therefore it would seem that in the first months of life there are few experiences to evoke aggression. But parallel with this gratification of physiological appetites there is the considerable physical restraint which the babies endure through passing the majority of their waking hours firmly tied to the back of their guardian, and also the complete lack of encouragement which their elders give to the babies' earlier self-maximating activities and attempts to acquire body techniques and physical independence. Young babies get no social approval from their attempts to crawl and walk; on the contrary a mobile baby is more likely to be picked up and replaced on its guardian's back, since it is there easier to control. The two methods by which babies in our society would appear to win adult approval in their second year are successful sphincter control and the acquirement of body techniques and speech. Sphincter control is paid little attention to by adult Lepchas until a considerably later age, and attempts at acquiring body techniques are met with, at the best, indifference. Very young the Lepcha baby learns that social approval is to be obtained, not by self-assertion, but by passivity. The baby's self-maximating efforts are not actively punished, but they are discouraged by indifference; its passivity and conformity are constantly rewarded.

I think it is legitimate to trace a connection between this partial extinction of self-assertion in early childhood and the adult Lepcha's tendency to judge their fellows in their rôle of members of society, and not as personalities. This impersonal attitude to their fellows seems to me the chief operative factor for the suppression of competition and aggression in adult life. The Lepchas stress constantly social behaviour and minimise individual character variations. They stress the resemblance between individuals, they minimise their differences. This constant stress on the resemblance of individuals obviously makes for a low development of the ego, a lack of internal competition, a lack of contrast. The Lepchas minimise the most obvious contrasts, between rich and poor, between men and women, between lamas and illiterate laymen, to a great extent between adults and children. They recognise no social goals which can only be achieved at the expense of others, they have no social situations which separate rights and duties.

Although, as I have shown, this lack of personal aggression is dysgenic in the Lepchas' state of social development, the excess of personal and national aggression appears to be equally dysgenic in our own state of social development. To minimise this aggression will it be necessary for us too to view our neighbours impersonally, to tone down all the contrasts in personality, talent and achievement which have resulted in the greatest glories as well as the greatest horrors of our society? Or is there another solution?

Appendices

APPENDIX I

(a) VITAL STATISTICS OF LINGTHEM

IN Lingthem it was—very exceptionally for a primitive community—possible to get the exact age of every member of the community. This was possible because it is essential for every Lepcha to know in which year of the twelve-year cycle they were born in for future horoscopes and divinations. They know also how many cycles they have completed because, after the completion of the third or fourth cycle—that is to say after the age of thirty-six or forty-eight—it is necessary to make a prophetic consultation with the lamas at the beginning of each new cycle—i.e. at the age of forty-eight, sixty, seventy-two, etc.—and all remember how many consultations they have made. Only in the case of two old widowed women am I in any doubt as to the accuracy of the data. This census was taken in April 1937.

TABLE II

DISTRIBUTION BY SEX IN TEN-YEAR GROUPS

Age	*Males*	*Females*
90–81	3	1
80–71	3	4
70–61	5	5
60–51	10	6
50–41	13	13
40–31	8	11
30–21	19	16
20–11	18	11
10– 1	10	20

TOTAL POPULATION	176
MALES	89
FEMALES	87

Median age for the population	28—year 1909
Median age for males	29—year 1908
Median age for females	28—year 1909

TABLE I

DISTRIBUTION OF THE POPULATION BY AGE AND SEX

Year of birth	*Males*	*Females*	*Year of birth*	*Males*	*Females*
1847	1	–	1892	–	1
1848	–	–	1893	2	1
1849	–	–	1894	–	1
1850	–	–	1895	–	–
1851	–	–	1896	3	3
1852	1	1	1897	–	1
1853	–	–	1898	–	–
1854	–	–	1899	–	2
1855	1	–	1900	3	2
1856	–	–	1901	1	1
1857	1	–	1902	2	1
1858	–	1	1903	–	–
1859	–	–	1904	–	–
1860	1	–	1905	–	1
1861	–	–	1906	2	3
1862	–	–	1907	1	–
1863	–	1	1908	5	1
1864	–	1	1909	–	5
1865	–	–	1910	4	–
1866	1	1	1911	–	3
1867	–	–	1912	3	4
1868	1	–	1913	–	–
1869	–	–	1914	5	2
1870	1	1	1915	1	1
1871	1	1	1916	–	–
1872	–	–	1917	1	–
1873	–	1	1918	1	1
1874	1	–	1919	4	1
1875	1	2	1920	1	1
1876	–	–	1921	2	1
1877	1	2	1922	2	2
1878	3	–	1923	2	1
1879	–	–	1924	1	–
1880	1	–	1925	1	2
1881	1	1	1926	3	2
1882	1	–	1927	1	–
1883	–	1	1928	2	2
1884	1	1	1929	–	–
1885	1	1	1930	–	6
1886	1	–	1931	–	–
1887	1	1	1932	–	–
1888	3	1	1933	2	5
1889	1	1	1934	4	2
1890	2	1	1935	1	4
1891	1	3	1936	–	1

TABLE III

FECUNDITY OF MARRIED WOMEN

The Lepchas are mainly exogamous: that is to say by far the greater number of women in the community have come in from outside, and by far the greater number of girls will marry into other villages. In the second column the following signs are used:

L—from Lingthem or the other smaller villages under Chala Mandal.

Z—from Zongu, the Lepcha reserve in which Lingthem is situated. Taking the average number of inhabitants per household in Lingthem —5.3—as valid for the whole area, the total population of Zongu is about 2000.

X—Lepcha from outside Zongu.

XX—Partly Sikkimese.

The question marks in this column indicate that I could not discover if the women were born inside or outside Zongu. None of the women so marked are from Lingthem, nor have any admixture of foreign blood.

It is probable that the number of children who have died in infancy is an understatement, as the Lepchas attach little emotional importance to children dying very young and may forget about them. Of the sterile women under sixty, I am certain, however, that they have never borne a child alive or dead.

sb. in columns 5 and 6 stands for a still-born child.

P. in column 7 means that the woman was pregnant in April 1937.

Date of birth	*Place of origin*	*Live children* M	F	*Dead children* M	F	*Age at birth of first child*
1852	?	1	1	1	?	?
1858	L	1	?	?	?	?
1863	?	2	4	1	1	?
1864	?	?	?	?	?	?
1866	?	1	?	?	?	?
1870	Z	1	–	1	–	?30
1871	Z	–	–	–	–	–
1871	L	–	–	–	–	–
1873	L	–	1	2	–	?
1875	Z	2	1	1	–	?
1875	?	–	–	–	–	–
1877	X	–	–	1	1	?
1877	X	–	–	–	–	–
1881	Z	–	3	1	–	?
1883	Z	2	3	1	–	19
1884	X	–	–	2	–	?
1885	Z	2	3	–	–	?
1887	Z	3	1	–	–	24

Date of birth	*Place of origin*	*Live children* M	F	*Dead children* M	F	*Age at birth of first child*
1888	Z	3	2	–	–	20
1889	?	–	–	2	2	?
1890	L	–	–	–	–	–
1891	L	–	–	–	–	–
1891	X	–	–	–	–	–
1891	?	–	–	–	2	?20
1892	L	–	–	–	–	–
1893	L	–	3	3	3	22
1894	X	–	–	–	–	–
1896	X	1	–	sb	–	23
1896	Z	–	–	–	sb	–
1896	?	2	–	?2	?3	?25
1897	?	–	–	–	–	–
1899	Z	1	4	–	–	22
1899	L	2	1	1	–	20
1900	L	–	–	–	–	–
1900	Z	1	2	sb	–	23P
1901	Z	–	2	1	1	?25
1902	Z	–	–	–	–	–
1905	Z	2	1	–	–	19
1906	Z	1	–	?	?	?29
1906	L	1	3	–	–	17
1906	Z	–	–	–	–	–
1908	Z	1	2	–	sb	22
1909	Z	–	–	–	–	–
1909	X	–	–	–	–	–
1909	Z	–	3	–	–	22
1909	X	–	2	1	–	21
1909	Z	–	–	–	–	–
1911	Z	–	1	–	–	25
1911	Z	–	–	–	–	–
1911	L	–	–	–	–	p1
1912	X	1	–	–	–	22
1912	L	–	–	–	–	–
1912	X	1	–	–	–	20
1912	X[1]	1	–	–	–	22
1914	Z	1	–	sb	–	20P
1914	Z	–	–	–	–	–
1915	Z	(widow—unknown recently arrived)				
1918	L	–	–	–	–	–
1919	Z	–	–	–	–	–
1920	Z	–	–	–	–	–

[1] This woman was subsequently successfully delivered of a boy.

(b) PLAN OF THE VILLAGE OF LINGTHEM

The accompanying plan shows schematically the distribution of houses in Lingthem. They are all situated on the northern slope of the mountain rising steeply from the River Talung. The numbers are for reference to the accompanying table of householders. B is the house of the monastery guardian. A, C and D are field-houses permanently inhabited by part of the household.

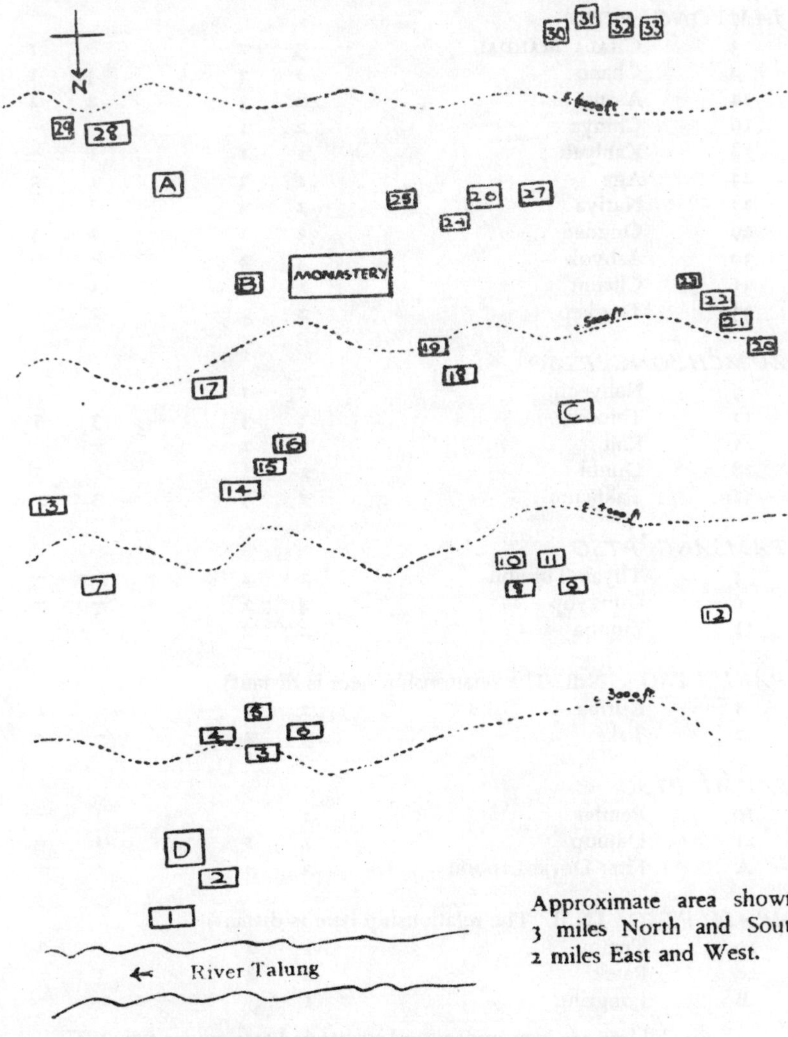

Approximate area shown: 3 miles North and South, 2 miles East and West.

TABLE IV

LIST OF HOUSEHOLDERS

(arranged by PTSO (patrilineal clan) and showing composition of household)

House number on plan	*Householder*	*Members of household* Adults *M*	Adults *F*	Children[1] *M*	Children[1] *F*
JAMYONG PTSO					
3	CHALA MANDAL	3	2	–	1
4	Ĉhano	1	1	3	1
12	Asang	2	3	2	2
16	Chinya	2	1	–	–
18	Kahlyeu	1	1	1	–
23	Aga	1	3	1	2
27	Nariya	2	2	–	–
29	Ongden	3	2	2	3
30	Ashyok	3	2	–	–
31	Chelim	1	2	1	1
33	Tingkep	2	2	2	–
ZUMCHYONG PTSO					
9	Nahyeun	1	1	–	–
17	Tafoor	3	3	3	5
25	Kaji	2	2	–	–
28	Dunbi	1	1	–	1
32	Takneum	2	3	3	–
TAMSANG PTSO					
5	Thyak Thimbu	2	2	–	–
6	Gongyop	4	2	–	–
11	Zumba	2	2	–	–
PAKI PTSO (N.B. The relationship here is distant)					
1	Kurma	2	1	–	1
22	Také	3	2	–	–
SAKMI PTSO					
10	Pembu	1	1	1	–
21	Datoop	2	1	1	–
A	First Dorjé Lapoon	2	–	–	–
ARAM PTSO (N.B. The relationship here is distant)					
19	Tempa	1	2	–	2
20	Patek	2	4	1	–
B	Pongring	1	-	–	–

[1] By children are here understood unmarried men under twenty.

House number on plan	*Householder*	*Members of household* *Adults* *M*	*F*	*Children*[1] *M*	*F*
ARAM PANDJET PTSO	(N.B. The relationship here is distant)				
7	Takal	1	1	–	–
26	Lumba	2	2	–	–
C	Lumba's elder wife	–	1	1	–
DEMIK PTSO					
13	Katel	1	2	1	1
KALONG KANDONG PTSO					
2	Songpo	1	1	–	–
D	Nakleup (son of Songpo)	1	1	–	–
LUBDONG RABJI PTSO					
8	Pargeut	1	2	1	4
TAKPO PTSO					
14	Tobgé (has left house to live with Jiroong)				
24	Jiroong	2	2	1	2
TSELTELIM PTSO					
15	Serving	2	1	1	–

[1] By children are here understood unmarried men under twenty.

APPENDIX II

LEPCHA KINSHIP TERMS

(N.B. *m.s.* means ' man speaking ' ; *w.s.* ' woman speaking '.)

Lepcha term	*Direct meaning*	*People to whom this term is applied*
2 nd generation ascendant		
THI-KUNG	grandfather	father of spouse, elder brother of spouse, spouse's elder sister's husband, after the birth of a child. *also* any man irrespective of age who traces relationship to a common ancestor and who is two generations nearer this ancestor than the speaker. *also* the Old Man in folktales and mythology.
NYI-KUNG	grandmother	(as for Thi-kung for all women)
1st generation ascendant		
A-BO	father	father of spouse ; elder brother of spouse (w.s.) husband of elder sister of spouse (w.s.) before birth of child. *also* ingzong (trading friend) of husband (w.s.) *also* respectfully to affinal relations and unrelated people slightly older than speaker.
A-BO THIMBU (contracted to BATHIM)	big father	(1) elder co-husband. (2) father's elder brother : always used if the two brothers live in the same house or neighbourhood, not usually if they live in different villages.
A-BO CHIMBU	little father	(1) younger co-husband. (2) father's younger brother : only used if the two brothers live in the same house.
A-MU	mother	husband's mother (w.s.) wife of husband's elder brother before birth of child (w.s.) *also* wife of ingzong (m.s.) *also* respectfully to slightly older affinal or unrelated women.

Lepcha term	*Direct meaning*	*People to whom this term is applied*
A-MU THIMBU (contracted to MATHIM)	big mother	(1) elder co-wife. (2) wife of father's elder brother. (3) elder sister of father or mother if living in same house or neighbourhood.
A-MU CHIMBU	little mother	(1) younger co-wife. (N.B. 'little mother' is nearly always the biological mother of the children where there are co-wives.) (2) wife of father's younger brother: only used if living chiefly in same house as speaker.
A-KU	father's (younger) brother	any man whom father calls 'brother'. any male irrespective of age who traces relationship to a common ancestor and who is one generation nearer this ancestor than speaker. Any man mother calls 'aku'.
A-JONG	mother's brother	may be, but is not always, applied to any man one generation older than speaker whose relationship, however distant, is traced through a woman.
A-NYOU	lady	(1) younger sister of parent; *also* any woman whom father or mother calls 'sister'; *also* any woman irrespective of age who traces a relationship to a common ancestor and who is one generation nearer this ancestor than speaker; *also* the most respectful form of address to any socially superior woman: is used as a title for female supernaturals and Queens. (2) mother of wife (m.s.) elder sister of wife (m.s.).
{ A-ZONG / OONG-OP	levirate or sororate spouse	*man speaking:* wife of younger brothers of father or mother, of any man called 'aku' or 'ajong'; wife of elder brother; younger sister of wife. *woman speaking:* younger brother of husband; son of husband's elder brother; men husband calls 'younger brother'; son of men husband calls 'elder brother' or 'younger brother' (except his biological younger brothers); husband of elder sister. (note AZONG is more commonly used when there is a generation between the speakers; OONG-OP when they are of the same generation, but there is no uniformity about this. The terms are reciprocal.)

Lepcha term	*Direct meaning*	*People to whom this term is applied*
Ego's generation		
A-NUM	elder brother	any male of ego's generation older than ego and tracing descent back to a common ancestor on either side. (Not always used if the common ancestor is more than four generations removed and the two speakers are not of the same *ptso*,) any otherwise unplaced male of ego's apparent age.
A-NOM	elder sister	(as for A-NUM for women.)
ING	younger sibling	(as for A-NUM for people of either sex younger than ego.)
A-VO	husband	
A-YOU	wife	
BRI-BO BRI-MU	' marriage father ' ' marriage mother '	used reciprocally by the parents of a married couple.
ONG-ZONG	sibling of spouse spouse of sibling	used reciprocally by all siblings of the same sex of a married pair. Thus if A (man) marries B (woman) A will call all B's brothers ' ongzong ', and B's brothers will call A and his brothers ' ongzong '. Similarly B will so name all A's sisters who will call B and her sisters ' ongzong '; unless they live in the same house or neighbourhood when see above Thi-kung, Nyi-kung, A-bo, A-mu.
1st generation descendant		
ING-HA	infant	any young child.
A-KUP	child	any child.
NYOM	son's wife	*man speaking*: wife of younger brother; wife of sibling's son; *also* bride.
MYOK	daughter's husband	*woman speaking*: husband of younger sister; husband of sibling's daughter; *also* bridegroom.
NAM-KUP	child of sibling	the child of anybody ego or spouse calls ' brother ' or ' sister '.
2nd generation descendant		
KUP-ZONG	grandchild	any child two generations younger than ego, unless alternative classification allows the use of a kinship term of an elder generation.

Lepcha term	*Direct meaning*	*People to whom this term is applied*
Other common terms of address		
A-THING	lord	the most respectful term for a man; used for high officials and male supernaturals.
A-NYOU	lady	the female equivalent to A-thing.
REN (plural) REN-SONG	old man	the usual courtesy form of address to any man or mixed group not markedly younger than speaker.
{ A-NUM / A-NCM	elder brother / elder sister	less respectful than the last two terms. generally used to unclassified people of about egø's age, particularly with a view to sexual advances. ING is not used in this way.

Descriptive terms not used in address		
A-FET	father of spouse	also husband of wife's elder sister (m.s.) and wife's elder brother (m.s.).
TAGRI KUP	male child	son.
TA-YOU KUP	female child	daughter.
{ FLENG / NUM-LENG	young man / young woman	(literally, not having yet produced children.)
ABO PAYAR	step-father	
AMU PAYAR	step-mother	
JIUT-BO	adopting mother	
JIUT-MU	adopting father	
NUM-NEU	blood relation	(implying a person with whom sexual intercourse would be incestuous.)
NUM-NEU-ZONG	relatives	all the people with whom relation by descent can be traced.
PA-MING	brothers	a collective word meaning either all true siblings or more usually all the males the person referred to calls ANUM and ING.
M'SUNG-MU	sisters	(parallel to PA-MING, but referring exclusively to women and usually employed by women.)

APPENDIX III

(a) Birth Horoscope

(Towards the end of my stay in Lingthem since the children whose birth we expected did not arrive I persuaded Tafoor to cast the horoscope of an imaginary child born at six o'clock in the morning of Sunday, May 16th, 1937, which is in Tibetan on the 6th day of Gubu, Ox year (*long nam*) and Fire year (*mi nam*). Nowadays Tafoor casts most of the horoscopes; the other two lamas who know how to are the two Dorjé Lapoon.)

BIRTH. KITSEN.

Long nam (12-year cycle). The child will insult others; will sleep continuously; will soil its bedding; will be a naughty child. Will be very talkative and curious, prying into other people's business. He will be quarrelsome and inclined to fight; will have dreams of destroying the whole world. Will only think of himself and won't do good to others, will be a bold-faced speaker. Will pretend to knowledge that he does not possess.

Mi nam (10-year cycle). If he has a very big body he will have some defect; he will be blind or deaf or will limp, or something like that. He will eat a great deal. He will live to the age of seventy-one, if he manages to pass the eight hazards (*parchet*) which lie in front of him. He will suffer from a cold and cough almost at once. Any fields or animals in his name will prosper. He will be troubled by Ginoo *moong* (jealousy). He will have one son and two daughters. He will suffer from pain in the heart.

Mariwã.[1] His number is eight *nirqa gumma*. In his last incarnation he was a puppy; his owners were *ginoo-chen* (very greedy people). When he grows up he will not lose money, he will prosper. He will be miserly and won't even give to beggars. He will be a very fecund speaker. He will get goods from others without paying for them—property and lots of clothes. Should people give him a black cloth or black thread or a black hat Chumjé *moong* (this is the

[1] This is a calculation for the year and also for the day based on the magic square. Each year has its own Mariwã with a different arrangement of numbers and a different centre number and colour which counts as the principle of the year; the day of the month is reckoned starting from the centre and then with the number above and then clockwise round. Each number has a constant colour. Thus for *long nam* the whole year is 9 and red and the sixth is 5 and yellow. There are nine different Mariwã which produces an independent 9-year cycle.

same as num-een *moong*) will follow the gift and will trouble him and his children will die. He will have no desire for food. He won't build his own house; he will live with and on others and will make others work for him. He will be envious of others and will try to acquire their property and their clothes. He will try to make others work for him and will get property from others. He will rejoice in the presence of learned lamas. His birth will cause his parents *yong nyom* (general loss); therefore they must perform the ceremony of *yong-keuk*; should they fail to do so he will either die young or be like a beggar.[8] When he grows up he must give many feasts. If he learns to be a

[8] Tafoor added 'Like Sangkyar, this prediction was made for him; his parents did not do the ceremony and see him now!'

lama then in his next incarnation he will be a man so rich that he won't have to work and he will have very many relatives. He has a mole either on his head or on his waist.

Day of the week—Sunday. If he doesn't die on the seventh day or in the seventh month he will live to be seventy-one. He will honour his parents and superiors. His wife will be the daughter of a rich man.

Sahor—Stars. There are thirteen stars. Should he die at the age of twenty-eight it will be because he has to fulfil the gap in some previous reincarnation. He will dance and sing. He will have a loud voice—louder than cymbals—especially when he has drunk. He likes to possess good food and drink, and dress; he does not care for other people and will be envious of their prosperity. He will not tell lies. Nobody will be able to argue with him or quarrel with him; he will be able to crush everybody verbally. He will covet all pretty women. He will have a bad eye and pains in the body and limbs.

Satarr—auspices of the day. He will be a great speaker and explainer.

Tendré—birth number. Tendré sipa. Should he survive his tenth day, his tenth month and his ninth year he will be the head of a big village. He will be wealthy and will have no diseases. If people think bad things about him they will not dare say it to him. He will be given poison which will cause his death on Sunday at twelve o'clock midday.

Body sign. He was born at the sixth hour and therefore the sign is on his heart and he will be very rich.

Name. *Karma Tsu-Ten*. This is a holy name and must not be told to others.

. . . .

Notes: The horoscopes for all children born on the same day are identical except for the signs which depend on the hour. The apparent contradictions are reconciled by the fact that all statements are contingent: i.e. he will have good health except for the diseases mentioned; he will have no appetite but will covet other people's food and will eat out of greediness . . . etc. 'Every word is true.'

. . . .

(b) Marriage Horoscopes

Forecast of marriage of Tafoor. Tiger and Water year, and his wife, Horse and Fire year.

O X wife will die before husband
O O both will have good health
O
O O They will have many children
O X their property will be moderate only
X X they will have short lives
O X if his wife is ill he will be able to help her.

For another marriage, the man Dog year and Iron year, the woman Ox year and Water year.

O
O O both will live long
X
X O but their health will be indifferent
O O they will be very rich
O O exorcism will be successful for them
X but their children will die.

(c) Death Horoscope

(This is also an imaginary horoscope for a man aged seventy-three and therefore *kalok nam*—Rat year—dying on Sunday, 16th May.)

Sooksa dyeu adum nyetka mak—time of death. Died from being given *chip-tsok*—unclean food. His soul is being eaten by Tseng and Gebu supernaturals. Before his death there was an evil sign such as a python in the house or a cock crowing at night, or a big tree falling tip towards the house, or a fireplace falling through on to the earth.

Lyoo deu anok kat ('The lake of his soul was dry'). Much property was expended over his illness. His death was caused by his failing to give a feast. One sister was his enemy and made him either quarrel or go to war.

Ongtong lyoo adum nyet. At the end of his life there was a quarrel between Kado Palor *rum* and Deut *moong* for his soul, whether he should be allowed to live or die. Tamseu Pongseu *moong* took his soul away and gave it to Tongry-oong *moong*, who is like a tiger, to eat. At the time of his death he was thinking about his youngest son.

Loongto dyeu adum nyet. Either he had been given a red cloth or a piece of meat, or he had been given a black hat by a Mun ku-man-bu (sorcerer); this made unhappy Palor *rum* and therefore the *moong* took his soul. He was pre-occupied about his male relations on the father's side; therefore these people should perform for him the ceremony of Karbo Tookdeu Klon (a white *deu* on a *pong-ring*).

Hour of death. He died at dawn, six o'clock. Had he lived till eighty he would have lived his full life; since he died six years earlier this was caused by devils. As the man was lying ill he wanted some food like butter or meat; but Sandé *moong* ate his soul, and is still lying there watching the food. His body must be cared for—washed and anointed—by people born in Tiger or in Thunder-bird year. Sandé *moong* has gone south from the house where the man died to another house where there are four humans and a blue horse tethered in the yard.[1] These people should summon three lamas to kill this Sandé *moong*. The people of the house where he died must do the big ceremony of *Shidook ryak* or in four months Sandé *moong* will return again.

[1] Note by Tafoor; since there are no horses in the neighbourhood this can be ignored.

Day of death—Sunday. In ten days he will be reincarnated as a tiger and after that again as a human. Three months before his death Tébrong Pano took his soul and gave it to the devils.

Time of death—Sunrise. Three months before he died Deut *moong* ate his soul. The Deut Tsen *moong* was conveyed in a gift of gold or an animal's skin. The devil is still in the neighbourhood and the object should be thrown away. In eleven days he will be born as a tiger. As he lay dying he thought about his youngest child born in Fowl year, therefore this child should make an image of Sandé *moong* and of a snake and take it to a place where two roads cross and bury it. Sandé *moong* is in a leather bag hanging on the east side of the house. For the dead man the scripture Dorjé Chudo should be read; if that is read he will be reborn as Sangé Eusung *rum*; if it is not read he will be reborn as a pig in the east. The people in the house where he died must perform the ceremonies of Deut Sha-gu and Su-nen (killing an insect with a sacramental dagger) or they will be troubled by coughs.

Month of death—Gubu. The devil which ate his soul came from the west in the skin of a tiger or some other animal. As he lay dying he was preoccupied with a big ox and a big horse,[2] and a yellow cloth. A person who possesses these objects should perform the Dopu ceremony and make *nahleut* (a dough image stamped with butter) on a plate.

[2] Note by Tafoor: this probably means a mule.

Mariwã Parrko.[3] He died in *Sin* (the syllable in Parrko). He was thinking of a handsome box which had valuables in it of which he was fond. He was worried either about his wife or his youngest child and regretted leaving that person. Sandé *moong* has gone south to the male relatives or the biological sisters of the deceased. Death was caused by Jamfi *moong*—a devil of high mountains. There is a piece of meat or bone close by the body which should be buried with it. The devil was brought from the west in the skin of a tiger or some other animal. He regretted leaving his youngest son and daughter. One Sandé *moong* has gone to a maternal uncle, one to his eldest sister and one is still in the skin. At the house where he died they must do Subdok Tukdo Klon (make a *deu* and take it away to the east) and Gon-tsoo To-goo (dough stamped with *leut* and *deu*) and the scripture Tongbo Gen should be read; also

[3] The Parrko is another square on which the years are counted. It is a 9-year cycle independent of all the other cycles. Each year has its controlling syllable.

Gebu *faat* (a Mun ceremony of throwing a *thomu*—lump of dough—to see which way the end points) should be performed.

Corpse. The corpse should be buried; it would be bad for it to be burnt.[4]

[4] Note by Tafoor: 'If the corpse were a lama's it would be burnt just the same.'

On the corpse must be put a paper inscribed with 'Parrko sin chagyou'. The corpse must not be shown to others. Since the corpse is an old man the door of death is open; if it had been a child the door would have been closed.

Mariwã Gumurr. Sandé *moong* is living in a red milch cow. The ceremony Onchook Tsoo Deurr must be done and also Yong Kook (this is three *pong-ring* with *deu*, etc.). He died at sunrise. To the south there are many devils. To the north there is a man with big earrings, or else a mole on his ear or nose and with curly hair and a red dress, whose name is Num; the devil has gone to him.

Sahor Tachen—Stars. The devil who caused death followed a woman from the north-east. Therefore on the corpse should be a paper stamped with a horse from the *lokor* (the 12-year cycle).

Corpse carriers should be Horse or Snake year.

Removal of corpse. The corpse should be taken out of the south-east corner of the house.

. . . .

Notes: When Sandé *moong* is driven away ceremoniously on the third day the bag in which the devil resides should be taken with the offering and left for two days—after which it can be re-taken into use. All apparent contradictions are explained by being cumulative or by being contingent.

(*d*) Lama's Divination for Illness

May 1st. Chano came this morning to consult Tafoor about his wife, born in *beu nam* Snake year (1905), who was ill, and also his youngest daughter, who was born in *hik nam* Fowl year (1931) and was suffering from stomach ache. Taking their dates of birth and the present date as his data, Tafoor worked out the following diagnosis of the causes of their illnesses and the measures to be taken to cure them. The explanations were added afterwards

Wife. The drawing of the first diagram showed that the illness was caused by Sabdok Loo *moong*, by Dadé *moong* (other names Nanjet *moong* and Tom-loong Deut *moong*: it is an evil spirit sent by an enemy), and from Tamsi *moong*.[1]

[1] Tamsi *moong* is the *moong* who causes quarrelling and wars. To keep away quarrels and kill this *moong* a piece of paper is stamped with the printed effigy of the *moong* and surrounded by thirteen crossed sticks. Lamas then sit around this paper holding in their joined hands a *phoorbu*—a sort of sacred dagger, which has three heads on the handle and a piece of black cloth tied round the middle. They summon the devil in a sing-song voice with partly closed eyes: the devil comes in the form of an insect on to the paper when it is killed with the *phoorbu*. When the insect is killed it and the paper are put into a rat's skull,

round which twelve *sutsong*—pieces of wood pointed at both ends and with a notch in the middle—one end being red and the other black—are tied, and the whole is buried where two roads meet, being well rammed down and a stone set on top of it.

Then from the first diagram, consulting the sacred book he learned the following additional facts. The patient will dream of a red ox.[2]

[2] This dream is automatic; if the patient says she has had no such dream it will be because she doesn't remember it; it is in the book.

People in her house mustn't buy blue cloth, or goats or oxen, and must not sit near a big tree. She must not eat the flesh of a red ox or of carrion. If she will survive to the month of Chupu, i.e. November—she will recover. She is troubled by the Hlamen Djémé *rum*, and he has already taken her soul inside his[3] walls. It is necessary to perform the ceremony of Deut Shagu Kyok.[4]

[3] This is a supernatural equivalent to the Mun *rum*, half-way between gods and demons, of an ambivalent nature, a god when pleased a devil when angry. Between here and heaven it has a gaol where it keeps the souls of men captive until bribed by offerings to let them go.

[4] For this ceremony a small image of the invalid made out of buckwheat powder is required. On the board are also *yé*, leaf cups with grain in, arrows and spindles; gold and silver is scraped over it. *Chimi* are lit, books read, the patient *pék* with *chongbu tipkü* and the offering removed far away.

The illness has been caused through considerable enmity and jealousy.[5]

[5] Karo *moong* is released automatically through evil thoughts, if you are annoyed with a person because his animals have strayed into your field or because you think he has done you harm, or even because you envy his possessions. The pestering by Karo *moong* is not the result of malice, and though through divination you try to find out who has released it no sort of revenge is taken. To cure its symptoms lamas will burn incense and a Mun will offer an ox and *pék* the patient. If, after having thought evilly of a person you repent and wish to withdraw Karo *moong* you light a number of *chimi* and perform the ceremony of Kongso Klon; chanting and beating drums either in the dark or at your house (must be done by a lama). Karo *moong* doesn't kill.

If the patient herself doesn't die somebody else is liable to. The smell of high meat is insufferable to her. She is very restless. Chimbu Klon and Dumbu Soong must be done at once.[6]

[6] Chimbu Klon—to give a feast without getting any contributions from the guests. The feast must include meat.

Gyapchi klon (this is the same as Dumbu Soong). Five images are made (*a*) Sher *moong*, white, (*b*) Lho *moong*, yellow, (*c*) Deut *moong*, red, (*d*) Chyong *moong*, indigo, (*e*) Mamoo Takloong, black, represented as a woman sitting with spread legs and open vulva. Round these are arranged in circles 100 *chazé* for (*a*) 100 heaps of rice for (*b*), 100 *chimi* for (*c*), 100 *nahleut*—i.e. pieces of dough stamped with the figures of a man and a woman—for (*d*), and 100 *chongbu tipkü* for (*e*). There must also be 100 *tsatsoh*—earth copies of *choten*. The lama officiating at this ceremony must be given five rupees.

If the invalid had not become ill she would have been very prosperous,

CHANO CONSULTS TAFOOR ABOUT HIS WIFE'S ILLNESS

Above : Tafoor casts a horoscope in the monastery porch.

Below : The devils to be exorcised. Deut *moong*, Mamoo *moong*, Lho *moong*. They are about 25 cms. high, made out of coloured buckwheat powder on stands of banana stem.

with lots of food and clothes and animals. As it is she is very bad; her soul has already one leg outside the body. It is the evil thoughts of others who have caused her malady. The Deut Shagu Kyok ceremony must be done at once.

Her husband Chano was born in Oon *nam* (Sheep year), and their years are antagonistic. They are liable to be troubled by Chemen *moong*, Loo Desen *moong*, Muzong Rum Loo, Sabdong *moong*.

The patient will dream of an old and decrepit house, and of a stream. She will vomit. She must not wear a black hat or put on black paint or buy anything black. For a year she should not take food from a relation except those living in the house.[7]

[7] The *moong* possessing her will be hungry and will try to get food. So that when it sees people giving the patient food it will attach itself to them in the hopes of getting more. This holds good for a year. It does not apply to people living in the same house.

A lama must read the following books: Tinchu Bekeu, Numjeu Cheré, Pungoor Luboong, Chétop Chachu. He must also make the following *deu*—Chemen Gédo, Lumoo Gédo—and set them up on a path. Chano must also get the ceremony Loo-fat performed by a Nandjému, and the ceremonies Goonchen and Séné Kyop by lamas. The wife must change her name.[8]

[8] This refers to the name she is usually known by, not her book-name. The new name can be given by anyone, and after that the old name must not be used. If the old name was meaningful, there is no tabu on the name in other contexts. The old name can be resumed after a year.

The rat skull (see 1) must be carried far by her nephew and buried deeply. A *Mazeu tsop* (image of the invalid) (4) must be made. There will be many quarrels in the house if the fine-seeming mischief-making advice and scandal of others is listened to and then Gébu Tabrong Pano[9] will be angry, and will

[9] Quarrels affect this deity as if they were a burning chilli (i.e. irritating smoke).

send all sorts of aches and pains, starting with toothache, as a punishment, and they will continue for some time. The Tyouma Rumso[10] ceremony

[10] This consists of dancing round a cloth and knife-scabbard with a knife in the hand, and also burning *lapsong*—that is incense with crops, *chi* and butter, and scraping gold, silver, brass, copper, iron, turquoise, coral, and conch-shell over the incense. It is the same as Da-floh.

must be performed and also Kongso Klon (chasing devils).

Baby. The baby will be seriously ill. A small image must be made of it and the invalid's hat and coat put with it and it must be taken far away. When taken out of the house the head must not face towards the sunset as trouble will come from there. It should be taken out facing Chyom (south). It is necessary for the ceremonies to be done very carefully as the mother's soul has already got one foot outside the body.

For the baby's health the father should not go anywhere where there has been quarrelling or where corpses have been burned, or where there are people of low degree like blacksmiths and musicians. The baby is troubled by

Maknyam *moong*[11] and will get pains as though the body were pierced, and pains

[11] This is the devil which causes death. It acts rather like a vampire; those people whom it kills become in turn Maknyam *moong*. Consequently it is in a way the evil ghost of one's ancestors—since they died by Maknyam *moong* and became it in their turn. At one time it used to be visible; but the *sanyoul koong* (tree) which grew in the mountains was cut down and barred its way; now the devil's body can no longer come out, merely its soul.

Maknyam *moong* runs in every family, but some families also suffer from Arot maknyam *moong*—the devil which causes violent deaths. Such a family is that of Kaji's (late) first wife. One of her brothers recently fell from a tree; a pregnant woman in the family was crushed by a falling tree.

in the heart and left shoulder, and shortness of breath. The parents should not buy red or white cloth, or bows and arrows, or any sort of animal from other people, or eat the flesh of carrion or drink rock or rain water. Should it survive till the fifth day of Choobu the crisis will be then. Care should be taken not to let it play with knives and other dangerous instruments. The following sacred books should be read: Numchya Chu, Tukzung Chosung, Nangsa Nanget, Dorjé Chu, etc. The Dafloh dance should be performed, incense burned, and holy *tyü* water sprinkled. The Tsatsoh Kyop (stamped *choten*) ceremony should be performed, and also Tsinmu Faat. The child should wear a yellow cloth. Some iron, the head of a chicken and the head of a monkey (? skulls) should be made into a bundle and put on the *kingkoor* (house altar).

For some time there will be many quarrels and general bad temper. (*Aside*: perhaps the baby has been shaken up inside.) All its life long the child will be in danger of death, and that is equally true of its mother. (I think this means that both are threatened by hostile supernaturals, and constant care is needed to ward them off.) Hlamen Djémé (this is the ambivalent supernatural, the god of the Mun, god or demon according as to whether it is pleased or angry) will plague the patient much. The Deut *moong* which is in the house plagues it as severely as if it were the child's mother. The Deut Shagu Kyop (4) ceremony must be performed at once.

The gods and devils are quarrelling over the child's body; should the devils win the child will die. Therefore the ceremonies must be done very properly. The child must avoid water out of rocks or from puddles. Had it not been ill everything it set hand to—trade, crops, animals—would prosper; it would have a life covered with flowers. But (figuratively speaking) a prayer-flag is tottering and must be set upright. Some covetousness (perhaps from a childless woman) has caused the trouble. The child is always in a hurry, inattentive to its parents. Its soul has been taken by Gongbu[12] and Mamoo Deut Tsen[13]

[12] This devil causes swelled stomach. To cure get an ox's horn and fill with rice seed; the lama will hold this and pray silently, and then *pék* the patient and give him some seeds. Butter, meat and *tahi* must be mixed and set fire to, and taken outside.

[13] This is a trinity of supernaturals, consisting of the female Mamoo who is indigo, Deut *moong* who is white and Tsen *moong* who is red.

will give trouble. Maknyam *moong* (11) is in the house, and also a devil Badé which was sent in the time of the father or grandfather. Now the gods are angry and Daphlo should be performed. The child is constantly dreaming of human corpses ; it either has, or will, excreted and brought up blood. It has no appetite. First the gods were angry, now the *moong* are. The ceremony Yongkeuk Gedo Klon [14] must be performed and Sunen (same as Tamsi, 1) and the taking away of the image of the child *ing kup leut ryak* (4). Also a red *yeu* Tsendeu Gedo must be made. When the image is taken away the head must not face towards the hills ; trouble comes from there. The child's chief trouble will be coughs.

[14] This is a ceremony for the material prosperity of the worshipper. A milking pot surrounded with a rope is set up, and on the left side is put a cup of strained *chi*, with four *sakyou*, dabs of butter. Lamas read their books and there is a constantly recurring phrase ' Yago Chakook Sho ' ; whenever that recurs the bystanders shout ' Ya '.

N.B. When the Dafloh is danced in laymen's houses a Mun will kill an ox at the same time.

. . . .

Although Chano is a lama he can perform none of these ceremonies for himself, and must pay for consultations, etc., as much as a layman would. Tafoor says he has to give his heart to the work—because all the supernaturals are hidden in a huge house—but he finds everything from the books. If he relied on inspiration he might make mistakes. It is very similar to systematic astrology or card-reading, the varying permutations of years and signs being practically inexhaustible.

. . . .

(*e*) Performance of Indicated Ceremonies

On May 9th the ceremonies indicated by Tafoor's exorcism were performed. The various lamaist ceremonials were telescoped into one—*Gyapchi klon*—by the addition of such other items as were indicated for the expulsion of the other devils, without introducing contradictory elements. Thus, using the notes in the previous horoscope (1) was not performed as Tamsi *moong* was not the chief operative devil ; (4) was super-imposed on (6) *gyapchi klon* ; (10) the Tyou-ma rum-so or Dafloh dance was performed at the end of the ceremony ; and Yong keuk gédo klon, a minor ceremony, was postponed. The most important thing was that Hlamen Djémé *rum* had been recognised by Gongyop as being in fact the Mun spirit ; and therefore Mrs. Chano was to be dedicated to the Mun god and to receive instruction from Gongyop as her teacher. Consequently there were as usual a simultaneous Mun and lamaist ceremony ; the Mun ceremony conducted by Gongyop is called ABOONG AK (opening the mouth) or RUM KEUK (acknowledging the god) ; the lamaist ceremony conducted by Tafoor can be conveniently referred to as GYAPCHI KLON.

Preparatory to *gyapchi klon* Chano had prepared a large quantity of ground millet powder and ground buckwheat powder, and the trunk of a banana tree was cut up into segments to serve as stands for the images to be made. Sifted earth was also collected, as well as a hundred leaves ; in the morning rice was cooked.

Tafoor arrived early in the morning to start the making of sacrificial objects; he brought with him as *kané* and assistant his wife's brother the son of Lharibu Chujen of Panung; Chano also helped in the making of the objects. The first objects to be made were the images of the devils, each about ten inches high (see photograph) and placed on a three-inch stand of banana stalk. These images were made out of buckwheat flour mixed with water; they were moulded by hand, and the details marked with a blunt piece of wood; they were left to dry slightly before the coluring matter was added. The four male devils were identical; they are portrayed standing; Chyong *moong* was coloured green, Deut *moong* red, Lho *moong* yellow and Sher *moong* white. Mamoo *moong* the female supernatural was portrayed sitting down with her legs apart; the breasts and pubic hair were greatly exaggerated, and also the vulva which was coloured red, the rest of the image being black. After this the image of the house-owner was set up in the centre of an enamelled plate (this is a quite conventional image of buckwheat powder about eight inches high); round the foot of this were grouped discs impressed with the conventional butter image of husband and wife (stamped from the wooden printing block from the monastery) about two inches high and around that again twelve smaller discs stamped with the effigies of the twelve years. These elaborate images took about five hours to prepare, between eight in the morning and one o'clock in the afternoon.

About one o'clock the ox was dedicated by Gongyop (see below); after the dedication it was killed by Chinya and then cut up by Chala Mandal, who was dressed in very old clothes and was covered with blood at the end. The head, one fore-leg and one hind-leg and the intestines were reserved for the ceremony of ABOONG AK; the rest of the meat was divided up amongst those present. During the course of the afternoon the following people arrived, most of them accompanied by their wives and families: Chinya (Chano's 'brother'), Chudo (Tafoor's brother), Thyak Thimbu (Gongyop's brother), Tempa, Aga (Chano's 'brother'), Chala Mandal, Adér (Chano's 'grandfather') and Rigya. As they arrived they were presented with a *patyoot* of *chi* and sat down in the kitchen to gossip and eat; nobody paid any attention to the ceremonies. The wife, in whose intention the ceremonies were being performed, wandered around rather listlessly. The cooking was being supervised by Mrs. Chinya, and Chano welcomed the guests; but Tempa, who was no relation, tried to act as if he was the host, particularly towards ourselves.

Meanwhile in the *dé-ong* Tafoor and his assistant were continuing the fabrication of the sacrificial objects; four *gyachen dizi* were made; these consist of a small rectangular obelisk of dough mounted on a slice of banana stalk with four hollows scooped out of the four sides; these are for the worship of Sercho Gébu *pano*, the king of the east. Flags of coloured paper were prepared for these mounted on splinters of bamboo; these flags—*dado*—are rectangular, with a triangle cut out of the far narrow side.

Then the smaller objects were prepared; one hundred of each of the four smaller objects had to be made; they were made roughly and quickly, but a great deal of difficulty arose in deciding if enough objects had been made. They were arranged in groups of twenty to make counting easier but even so there was great uncertainty, and at one moment Tafoor, who had remained perfectly calm and peaceful the whole time exclaimed 'I am as angry as a

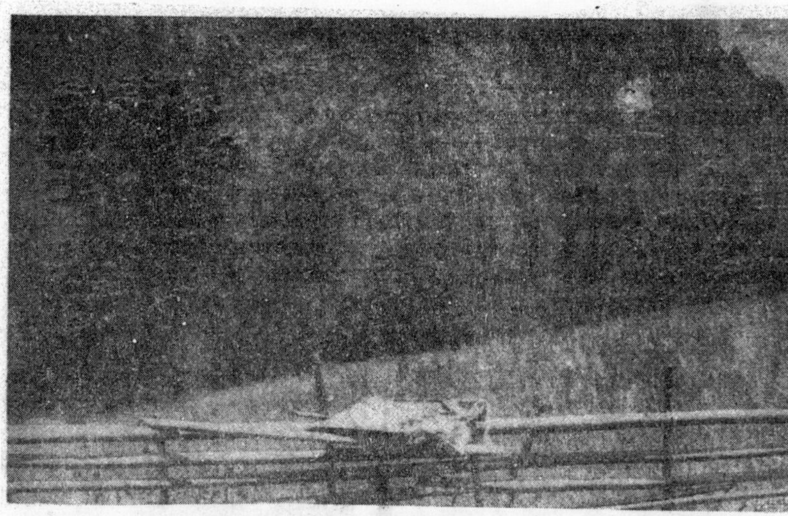

GONGYOP DEDICATES MRS. CHANO TO THE MUN GOD

Above : Valuables and other objects on a 'plate' on an open-air altar.

Below : Gongyop offers to the gods and devils the cooked intestines of the sacrificial ox with rice. His wife is beside him.

standing penis.' Eventually all the small objects were made; they consisted of (*a*) 100 *choten* of earth—small barrows about three inches by one made by stamping damp earth in a mould; (*b*) 100 *chazé*—buckwheat flour rolled into a double cone joined at the base with a smear of white butter on each tip; (*c*) 100 *nahleut*—dough discs stamped with the 'husband and wife' die in butter; (*d*) 100 *chongbu tipkü*—twisted strips of dough which were fastened into bundles of five each. Dusk was falling by the time all the objects had been completed; they had taken two men the better part of twelve hours to make. Small boys had been sent to Gongyop's house to fetch 100 *chimi* (altar lights) which he was lending for the occasion, and to the Mandal's house to fetch a small brass image of the god Chumdendé (a Buddha-like figure) and its cloth panoply.

When everything had been prepared the floor of the *dé-ong* was swept and

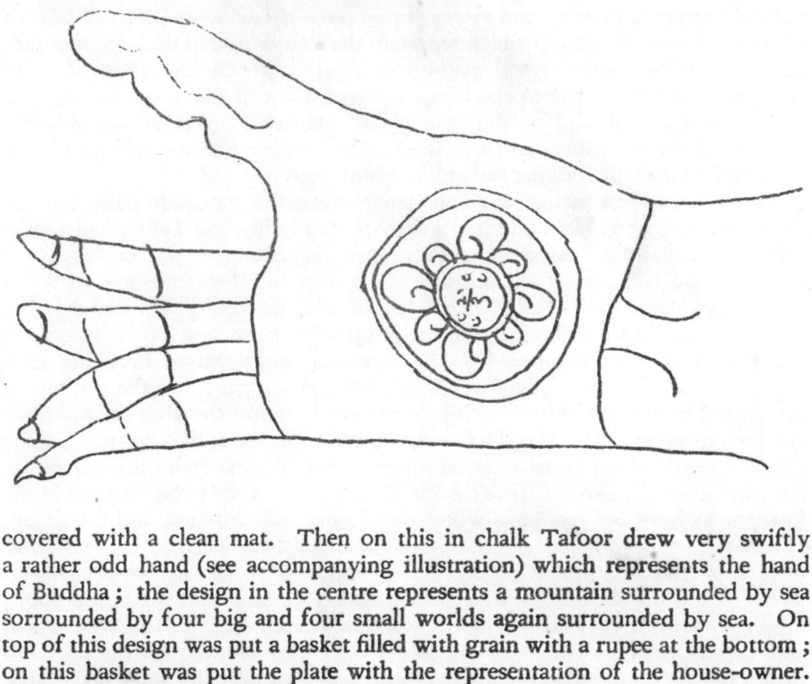

covered with a clean mat. Then on this in chalk Tafoor drew very swiftly a rather odd hand (see accompanying illustration) which represents the hand of Buddha; the design in the centre represents a mountain surrounded by sea sorrounded by four big and four small worlds again surrounded by sea. On top of this design was put a basket filled with grain with a rupee at the bottom; on this basket was put the plate with the representation of the house-owner. Then around this in a square were arranged (1) the *choten*, (2) the *chazé* dedicated to Sher *moong*, (3) the lighted *chimi* dedicated to Deut *moong*, (4) the *nahleut* for Chyong *moong*, (5) the bundles of *chongbu tipkü* dedicated to Mamoo *moong*, (6) the *gyachen dizi* were placed in each corner, with a lighted *chimi* before each; into the top of these, and also into the image of the house-owner were stuck *dado* in the following colours starting from the left and facing the house altar:

blue white

black

red yellow

(7) In a line with these were placed one hundred heaps of cooked rice on banana leaves dedicated to Lho *moong*. These offerings covered the palm of the hand and were about six feet square.

On the drawn fingers were placed two tables, the higher one to the back; on the lower table was (starting from the left) a *chazé* (a big heap of dough), three dishes of water, two dishes of uncooked rice and a big *chimi* (these offerings are for the gods to wash, etc.). On the higher back table were placed (also starting from the left and facing the house altar) Sher *moong*, Lho *moong*, Deut *moong*, Chyong *moong*, Mamoo *moong*. Into the back of each image was stuck a *yé*—a diamond of thread on bamboo supports—of the same colour as the image; into the image of the house-owner was stuck a *yé* (the *yé* represents the supernatural's palace) of all five colours; the six images also had stuck on each side of the *yé* a *tam-sing*, a pointed wooden label inscribed with the supernatural's name in Tibetan, and a *pong*, a thin piece of bamboo with small tufts of white wool down its length which represent the clouds around the supernatural's palace. Finally a large tripod made from three bamboos was lashed so as to centralise over the image of the house-owner; the top above the lashing was stuffed with a cloth and on that was placed the metal image of Chumdendé. Directly above it, suspended from the bamboo ceiling was the canopy of red, white and blue cloth, looking rather like a bird-cage.

By the time the offering was completely erected it was quite dark, but the *dé-ong* was bright with the hundred and more altar lights, and Tafoor had a small oil lamp to read by. After he had arranged everything he put on his lama's coat—he had taken it off and worked in his shirt and drawers—and sat down cross-legged against the altar. In front of him was the gong, and by him Chimpet to hold the light and beat the gong when necessary. By his side was the *kané* with the 'clarionet'. The ceremony consisted of invoking each demon in turn by the reading of the appropriate scripture and the playing of music, and mollifying it by worshipping it as a god and showing the offerings and then dismissing it. For the five devils this took about two hours. Tafoor chanted in the usual lamaist tones. Tempa and Kurma (who arrived rather late) and Chano looked in from time to time, but everybody else stopped in the kitchen, lit by a big smoking wood fire, eating and drinking and gossiping. When the reading from the scriptures was finished, Chano, his wife and children were called in and *pék* by Tafoor with one of the bundles of *chongbu-tipkü*. Then the six images were turned round so as to face the house-door; a narrow path of two lines of flour was traced from them to the door which was then opened; a couple of minutes' silence were allowed for the devils to depart satisfied; and then the images were carried away by the unrelated young men present, while others held torches to illuminate them; the images were thrown away at a fixed spot in the forest.

Tafoor and his helpers went into the kitchen for food—they had been constantly provided with *chi*. Subsequently the offering was demolished, the earth thrown away, and the rice and objects made out of dough eaten by the guests and especially the children; neither the officiating lamas nor the people in whose intention the offering was made may ever eat the sacrificial objects, but other people may without supernatural danger. The basket filled with grain with a rupee inside was given to the *kané*; Tafoor received Rs. 5 or the equivalent in grain.

MUN CEREMONIAL—ABOONG AK

In the early afternoon Gongyop dedicated a live ox to the Mun god and also arranged on an open-air altar—*chom*—made of two bamboos laid on a bush (see illustration) the following offering. On a brass plate were placed three *chimi*, three heaps of uncooked rice with a stick smeared with butter set into the centre of each, a scarf and a rupee, a scrap of new cloth (it had been begged from a tailor) and Mrs. Chano's necklaces and jewels. The permanent part of this offering was only displayed to gratify the supernaturals, and would be taken back into use the next day. These were all dedicated to the Mun god by Gongyop, who in a long prayer asked the god to accept the offerings and spare the life of the sufferer, who would in recompense devote her life to his service. The ox was then killed and cut up, during which time Gongyop *munthen* called on the gods in meditation. A small portion of the intestines were hashed and cooked with rice, and these Gongyop, assisted by his wife but otherwise ignored, gave to the minor devils, throwing out a handful of food after an invocation to each specific devil (see illustration).

Later that night the solemn and private ceremony of *aboong ak* was performed. We were not able to witness it, but were given the following account:

A large winnowing tray—*Talyung*—is put on the floor with the curved end away from the teacher and the neophyte; at the straight end is placed a low table and on it is placed at the left a scarf with a rupee on it, in the centre a wooden cup filled with *chi* with butter on the rim (*sakyou faat*) and on the right a stone incense burner filled with incense leaves. On the winnowing tray the dedicated portions of the sacrificed animal[1] are laid out in the following order:

[1] An ox is desirable. If a pig is given the neophyte will be unable to expel Lom-doon *moong* (the devil of jaundice); if a goat he will be unable to expel Mat *moong* (this devil produces various unpleasant symptoms which are the result of ancestral quarrels).

opposite the *sakyou faat* cup is the head, facing the table; behind it are the upper intestines, the wind-pipe, oesophagus, etc., called here *oo-koong sha-fot*; to the left is a hind-leg and to the right a fore-leg; between the fore-leg and the intestines is a thigh-bone with some meat left on it called *shang-oh*. When all is arranged the Mun sits behind the table on the left behind the scarf with his pupil to the right of him (or her). First of all the Mun puts the rupee and scarf in the pupil's hands and then recites a prayer which the pupil repeats after him phrase by phrase. The Mun then gets up and stands at the foot of the offering and waves the incense burner over the pupil and the offerings; he then makes a solemn address to the pupil, explaining that he has paid the price to the devils to ransom his body, but on condition of dedicating his life to the Mun god and offering his body as a house for it. The Mun then returns to the same side as his pupil and gives him the buttered cup to drink from three times from three sides—first the side facing the sacrifice, then the opposite side and finally the right side. This drinking of the buttered *chi* is (as in all Mun ceremonials) the ritual consecration of the act undertaken; after this the pupil is bound to study with the teacher for three years.

Of the sacrificial ox one fore-leg and the heart, lungs, liver and intestines are given to the teacher as fee; the rest of the animal, except the portions on the winnowing tray, are divided up among the sacrificer and his guests. Of the portions on the tray the head, hind-leg, thigh-bone and upper intestines also go to the teacher; the dedicated fore-leg—*derkau*—is cut up raw into small pieces and one piece is given to every household in the village.

Note. In the above description of a lamaist and Mun ceremony I have given the details of the ritual objects which I have not given in the relevant chapters. Although the ingredients of every ceremony are very similar they differ in detail in every case. The details of lamaist offerings and their fabrication are minutely controlled by scriptural instructions. The Mun offerings are much less complicated. The greater number are fixed traditionally and are known to nearly every adult, but they may be varied at the inspiration of the officiating Mun for any particular ceremony.

It will be noticed that every lamaist horoscope entails the performance of certain lamaist ceremonies, and consequently brings money and goods to the body of lamas.

APPENDIX IV

THE SACRED STORY OF THE ORIGIN OF MARRIAGE

(This is one of the two Lepcha stories which can only be recited by those people who have obtained the ceremonial qualification or *loong*. The other story is the long Mun genesis (see Chapter Eight, p. 223) of which the greater part consists of a long catalogue of names.

The sacred story of the origin of marriage has to be repeated in its entirety by the officiant at each marriage. It takes between two and three hours to rehearse, owing to the innumerable internal repetitions and culminations which I have indicated in brackets. Nearly every paragraph is repeated twice, and some many times more.)

When Itpomu had completed creation there were no husbands and wives. The last person she bore was a son called Tarbong-bo whom she nursed. When the child grew big enough to work he told his mother that he would like to travel and see the world. His mother said " No, you are too young " but he insisted, and so she cooked some rice for him and put it into his knapsack. So the next morning he travelled by the road called Parhi Pageun and came to the top of Paki Chu ; from there he went down to Palyang Chu, which is a mountain above Sakhyong and can be seen on a clear day. From there he saw the *palit samper koong* tree covered with fruits, and *pedong, taryong athyak kanyoong* and many other birds eating the fruit. When he saw that he sat down and ate his rice ; then he returned home in the evening and climbed on to his mother's lap and sucked her milk. His mother then asked " What did you see ? " He told her what he had seen (*verbal repetition*). Then his mother said " If you are my son you must go and get *yongming yong-song* (which is a kind of bamboo) and the thread *komok ki* (to make traps)." That night he slept at home and the next day he went and got what his mother had said, cutting down the bamboos and returned home. The day after that he went back to Palyang Chu and made snares with the threads and set them on the trees and returned and climbed on his mother's lap and told her what he had done. His mother told him that he must go back early in the morning. He did so and found all the different sorts of birds caught in the snares, so many that they made a full load. When he had collected the birds he reset the snares and then went home and said to his mother " Mother, if these birds are good to eat, eat them and take them as my repayment for your milk : if they are no good, throw them away." Itpomu replied " They are good to eat : and I accept them as a recompense for my milk."

The next morning Tarbong returned to the tree, but instead of birds in the traps he found in every trap a penis, exactly like real life, made out of wood.

Tarbong was angry at this, threw the penises away, and reset the traps. Then he went home and climbed on to his mother's lap and said "Mother, today I have nothing to bring you; there were no birds in the traps, just penises of wood." At this his mother said "If you are my son, you will go and hide yourself so carefully that even the birds cannot see you, and then in your hiding place you can stay and see who does this thing." The next morning he returned and found the snares again full of penises; he threw them away, and reset the snares and then hid himself so well that even the birds could not see him. After a time a beautiful girl dressed in *kaji lasong* (nettle cloth) arrived and started to make wooden penises. She was very beautiful; her name was Na Rip Nom, and her mother was Ta Im Ta Mit. Tarbong was angry when he saw her doing this and he climbed up the tree to try to stop her, and they struggled and rolled hither and thither; and then he got excited and tried to rape her, but he could not do so and so they separated and he went home and climbed on his mother's lap and said to her "Mother, I have come home without any birds." "What did you see, my son?" "I found Naripnom making penises of wood, and I tried to copulate with her, but I could not. So I return empty-handed. She is very beautiful." Then Itpomu said "If you want to possess that girl you had better go to your elder brother Komsi*thing* who lives at Rungzing Patham."

So Tarbong went to Komsi*thing*, and when he saw his younger brother he asked him why he had come. So Tarbong told him (*recapitulation*): "This girl was putting penises in my traps, and I wanted to possess her but could not, and my mother advised me to come to you." Then Komsi-*thing* said "How can you expect to possess the girl unless you give the marriage price *nyomsa afaar* and make a sacrifice with *chi* and butter *sakyou tsok rum-faat?* Do you love this girl?" "Very much." "Then I advise you to go to your *ingzong* in Nepal and get from him the pig of the plains Malu Mayeng and buy a copper vessel." So Tarbong went to Nepal and brought back a pig and a copper vessel. When he returned Komsi*thing* said "I advise you to go to your *ingzong* in Bhutan to get the cloth *kamo*." So he went to Bhutan and returned with the cloth, and then he had the pig and the copper pot and the cloth. (*The story cumulates—The House that Jack Built.*) From his Tibetan *ingzong* he got a rug Numbo. From Mayel near Konchen he got millet. From Kanyong (Sikkim) he got an ox.

Now at this time there was no fire in the world; it was only in the land between earth and heaven called Mashyok Matel where the demons dwelt, in the houses of the Deut *moong* who were smiths and were called Tangshyo Tangong Karvo. Now when Komsi*thing* told Tarbong to go there to fetch fire to cook the millet he was frightened and said he would not go among the devils for then they would eat him. So Komsi*thing* called on all human beings and animals and birds and insects to volunteer to go and fetch the fire, promising rewards of gold and jewels and rich cloths. When this offer was made the bird Kahryok Fo smiled and said "I will go for a reward." And the bird flew there and found the smith's house empty as all the people were out working elsewhere, so it took a brand in its beak from the fireplace and flew back. On its way back it came to the Kashou tree (chestnut); there it felt hungry, and laid the brand on a branch while it looked for fruit. But the wind blew and the flames sprang up and a great fire raged over the world, and the bird was caught in it; that is the reason why till this day it has short feathers and a black face. It was ashamed and did not return to Komsi*thing*.

Komsi*thing* waited for the bird but it did not come and he saw the fire, so he asked for another volunteer; and this time an insect (? *wasp or firefly—like a grasshopper, but flies*) *taknyom nomyor nyom* volunteered to go for a reward. When it got to the smith's house all the Deut *moong* were away, so it lay on its back by the fireplace and looked at the house upside down; and the whole house turned upside down. When the Deut *moong* returned from the west it found its house upside down and searched and found the insect who had done it lying on its back; he tried to catch it, but it wriggled and flew away. The Deut *moong* said "Why have you upset my house in this way? I shall kill you for it." The insect said "If you do kill me, your house will never get straight again." "Please don't do that. What have you come for?" "Komsi*thing* has sent me to fetch fire." "I will give you some, if you promise to straighten my house; but you cannot carry fire in your mouth." "Yes, I can." They argued, and finally the insect took a brand in its mouth, and the Deut *moong* put a flint and tinder up its backside. On his return the insect rested by the Mong Ing Pong tree, and put down the brand at the foot of the tree; but the wind came and blew it to a blaze and the insect got therefrom a black face. But it flew back to Komsi*thing* and gave him the flint and tinder from his backside, since he had lost the brand; and he told him all that the Deut *moong* had told him, and showed him how to make a fire with dry grass. So they made a fire and cooked the millet in the copper vessel, but, when the millet was cooked they found they had no yeast.

The only person who possessed yeast was an old woman who lived in the plains called Numli-*nyou*; so Komsi*thing* asked who would volunteer to go and fetch it, promising great rewards. The insect *takder thing* said it would go and it went to live with the old woman for some days and helped her. One day she started to prepare *chi*, and cooked the millet; but when it came to the moment of putting in the yeast she covered *takder* with a close woven basket *tangar*. But when *takder* was inside he cried "Grandmother, in this basket I can see everything which is going on in the world; if you want to hide something from me you should cover me with a *tangjang* (this is a loose woven basket)." The old woman believed what he said and covered him with a *tangjang* and so he could see all that she was doing, though he pretended he could not. He saw her take a pot from the back of her neck, and pour something from it into her hands. Then she rubbed her hands together and scattered the dust over the cooked millet; she replaced the pot; and put the millet in the basket. Then *takder* cried "Grandmother, please take me out of this basket; I am suffocating." So Numli-*nyou* removed the basket.

After two days the lovely smell of ferment rose from the millet, and then the old woman put it in an earthen pot and covered the pot well up, and stood it over the fire. *Takder* tried to get the pot with yeast in it, but he could not; at last he hit on a plan. He told Numli-*nyou* he could see a louse in her hair and asked her to let him remove it: she agreed so he jumped on her shoulders and started delousing her. While this operation was going on Numli-*nyou* became sleepy; and then *takder* removed the pot very very slowly and very very quietly and ran away. When he was half-way away she woke up and missed *takder*. Then she discovered the theft and saw him running away and shouted after him

"I thought you were my grandson, but I see you are nothing but a thief; you have stolen my yeast and will give it to everybody all over the world. So I set my curse on it; may it make everybody who drinks it drunk and quarrelsome." And so it has been; when people get drunk they quarrel.

When *takder* returned to Komsi*thing* with the yeast, Komsi*thing* asked him if he knew how to make *chi*: *takder* said he did (*complete recapitulation*) and they followed his instructions; but since they had no earthenware pots to put the fermented *chi* in they put it in baskets, well covered with leaves. Then Komsi*thing* asked *Taknyom* what reward he desired for bringing the fire: *Taknyom* replied "Gold and jewels and clothes are no use to an animal; what I want is to be given the plants *mangder* and *sanghlo* which grow in the valley." (*He was given these.*) Similarly *Takder* (*complete recapitulation*) was granted the leavings at the bottom of the spoons and plates and patyoot.

When the *chi* was ready all were afraid to be the first to drink. Eventually the snake Putsong *beu* was summoned and drank it; when it had drunk it dashed away like lightning. Seeing this all the gods and men were frightened to drink. After that the snake Pamol *beu* was summoned; but when it had drunk it ran about biting people and animals so that they all died. (When Sangé *rum* saw that the snake would kill everybody if it was allowed to behave so he set a lock on its mouth; and nowadays it bites very few people.) Next the snake Poblyok *beu* was summoned: when it had drunk it fell senseless. Komsi*thing* gave that snake the ferns to live in; it is harmless. After this they thought that the *chi* was harmless; but then they found they had no butter for *Sakyou faat*. So Komsi*thing* went to Itpomu and asked for butter so that they could *Sakyou faat* for the marriage of Tarbong and Naripmu. He said to his mother "We have the *chi*, but no butter." Itpomu said "Get a bamboo *yongtong*," and when he had got it she filled it with the butter which she had from her cows. Then on her instructions nine containers (*takner*) of *chi* were prepared, and their edges were smeared with butter.

Now all the gods and men gathered for the marriage of Tarbong and Naripnom. Everything was prepared in due order; all the gifts were placed on one side, and then Komsi*thing rum faat* with *chi* and *sakyou*. This is the reason why today when a marriage is celebrated all the gods are worshipped, and these gifts are given. Only when Tarbong and Naripmu were husband and wife was he able to possess her. This is the reason why to-day Lepchas still give the same gifts; this is BRI-IT, the origin of marriage.

APPENDIX V

LEPCHA STORIES

(As has been stated in Chapter Ten, the Lepchas' favourite amusement is to tell and listen to stories, of which they have a very large repertoire. A collection of these stories would doubltess fill many volumes; I was told a very considerable number. I am giving here four typical stories of the type told by Lepchas for entertainment. I have abbreviated them all by cutting out the internal repetitions.)

(*a*) THE STORY OF LYANG MOK MOONG

A frightening story about devils.

Once there were two boys who were great friends; one lived at Sabeun and the other at Karhyong (places very near Lingthem). They used to set traps for birds on a *gehr* tree on the far side of Sungzoom mountain. The boy from Karhyong used to come to Sabeun and they would climb the mountain together; when they had cleared the traps they would take their catch down with them and divide it at Sabeun.

Now one day the boy from Sabeun suggested to his friend that, instead of his making the journey to Sabeun on the day after the morrow, they should both go separately and directly to the tree and meet there; the boy from Karhyong agreed. But when the boy from Sabeun arrived at the tree he saw no trace of his friend and no footprints; this was because a devil had killed him and eaten him just by the place where the elder Mrs. Lumba's field-house now stands. Since his friend was not there the boy from Sabeun started emptying the traps; in the middle of this he thought he saw his friend coming towards him; but in truth it was the devil in disguise. The disguised devil said: "I tried to catch you up, but I could not, and you have reached here first." Then, as he saw the boy from Sabeun taking the birds out of the trap the devil asked him "How on earth did you climb the tree?" and then made an attempt itself to climb up by standing on its hands and putting its feet high up on the trunk. Of course it could not climb in this way.

Then the devil took out of the front of its dress the head of the boy from Karhyong all dripping with blood, and it said to the boy from Sabeun: "Do you like eating *ka-sok* root?" and with that started gnawing at the head. Now when he did this the boy from Sabeun realised he was faced with a devil and was very frightened; he thought to himself if I come down from the tree the devil will eat me too. So he made a plan and gathered together all the bird-traps on the tree and made three bundles of them, one big, one medium and one tiny. First of all he threw the big bundle a little way away; the devil thought it was a man and ran to attack it. Then he threw the medium bundle farther away, and the devil ran after that; then he threw the tiny one a very long way away and the devil ran after *that* one; and when the devil was as far away as possible the boy climbed down the tree and ran quickly home to his house (it was the house of one of Serving's forefathers) and there he told what had happened to him (*complete repeat*) and then died.

It is on account of this that old people used to say that friends should not make appointments in distant places, for instead of one of the friends a devil will come. But nowadays it is not so dangerous, for more people live in the neighbourhood, and the lamas with their books have controlled the devils.

. . . .

Tafoor, who told this story, added: " Whether this story is true or not the following story is certainly true. The ' big mother ' of Ashyok *youmi* and Gongyop's father Sankip were lovers and used to meet together in the field-house, where at some seasons of the year the woman used to live. Now one day she made an appointment with her lover for the evening and in expectation of his coming cooked a meal of manioc and pumpkin. But Sankip did not arrive, and when it got dark she thought she saw her husband sitting on the bamboo ends which projected from the side of the field-house like a verandah. She thought her husband had come instead of her lover, so she decided to make the best of it and built up a big fire and called to her husband to come in. But when the flames of the fire lept up and cast a clear light the figure turned its head aside so that its face could not be seen; the woman realised at once that it was a devil. So she fetched a bow and arrows and a knife and placed them beside her, and all night she kept a big fire burning and sat watching. When the first cock crowed at Sanklong the figure disappeared. As soon as it was light enough the woman went to look for footprints, and found the prints of feet *without any toes*. After this horrible experience she became a Mun."

(*b*) THE STORY OF MELOAN MOONG

A comic story about devils.

(This story was told by Chala Mandal with great vivacity. He imitated the curious falsetto broken speech which indicates devil talk and at the climax imitated all Mother devil's actions in pantomime.)

A very long time ago when there were no lamaist books and only very few people living here in Lingthem there were two families who had their houses just below my (i.e. the Mandal's) house, where there are rice-terraces today. Nearby is a white cliff with a hole in it and inside that hole lived a family of devils called Meloan; the family consisted of a mother and father and two children.

Now one day the members of the households all went out to work in the nelds, but they left behind a boy called Pun-sho-hang to look after his baby brother. While they were all alone mother Meloan *moong* came and captured Pun-sho-hang and took him home to kill him and eat him; she locked him up with her children in the hole in the cliff and then she went away to work. The boy was very frightened and started to cry and said: " How miserable I am! the devils are going to kill and to eat me!" When he cried the tears ran down his face; but the devil children had never seen tears and they were very curious and they came and licked up his tears. Pun-sho-hang was very angry at this and beat the devil children with his knife, chasing them into every corner of the cave.

In the morning—for devils work by night—mother and father Meloan devil came back bringing with them charcoal and *pasom* fruit (an inedible nut) as rice, with earthworms for a relish. All the devils ate this fare, but Punshohang threw his away. At this the mother devil said in her whining voice " Pun-sho-hang-ne mi-fyol-ne ma-cha-ne-pa . . . ? etc." (*This is devil language* " Pun-sho-hangy-wangy doesn't eaty-peaty charcoal-woaly . . . etc.") The next evening the same thing occurred. (*Complete repeat with lots of devil dialogue.*)

Then after dinner the grown-up devils went out again and locked up Punshohang with the devil children and he cried again and they licked his tears (*complete repeat*) and Punshohang hit the devil children with his knife and chased them all over the place, so that they were very sore. Then he felt sleepy. so he laid down to rest, using the scabbard of his knife, which he held in his hand, as a pillow. When he was drowsy the devil children came up to him and shook him and said in shrill devil voices: " Pun-sho-hang-ne ta ha!" and they pointed out to him the place where the door-key was; for they thought he would beat them a lot, and so that they would be happier if he went away. When Punshohang opened his eyes he saw the key; he was very glad and opened the door and started to run away home.

But before he had got home mother Meloan returned and saw the door open and started to pursue him by following his footprints. Punshohang saw her coming after him; but he found a pit which had been dug to look for manioc root, so he hid in that, and pulled leaves and grass over him, so that the pit would not show. When the mother devil saw that the footprints had stopped she hunted all round but could find no trace; so she sat down on the edge of the pit to consult her oracle. She undid her sash and bared her parts; the hair hung right over her vulva. She looked fixedly at it and then made the invocation " Reshing tam-et tam tam " (*this is magic*) at which the long pubic hair erected at once and then pointed straight down to show that the boy was underground. Punshohang was in the pit looking up at her. But this seemed nonsensical to the mother devil so she put a number of other questions to her bush (*all given in full*) but each time it pointed straight down. She kept on questioning it, getting angrier and angrier, till in the end she cried " My bush is telling me lies!" And with that she pulled it out with the skin and returned home.

Then Punshohang crept out of the pit and returned to his home; he had been lost for two days and two nights and everybody had been searching for him. When he returned home he stank horribly; so they washed him all over with strained *chi*. Then his parents asked him where he had been? He told them the whole story (*almost complete repeat*) and when he had finished talking he fell down dead.

(*Note*: this story takes about an hour to tell: the devil's home-life and conversation, and especially the mother devil with her oracle are almost hysterically funny, and the jokes are repeated and repeated with only slight variations. The story is only slightly sinister, because, since the advent of the lamas and their books, Meloan devils no longer live near Lingthem. It is said however that a man at Tangvoong (a village about ten miles away) was killed and eaten by these devils; all that was found of him was his belt and his bones.)

(*c*) A LEGEND OF THE KINGS OF TIBET AND SIKKIM

Commencement only.

Once upon a time there was a king called Agyap Patso Numgé; he was a human being, but his sister Queen Ong-Bala was a devil. She lived in a separate palace of her own, and all the common people served the pair of them. Queen Ong-Bala used to sit on a high throne, but her vulva lay on the ground at her feet. She used to make all the men who came to serve her copulate with her; but that could not satisfy her. And then she had horses to copulate with her; but she was still unsatisfied.

At that time there was living in the village of Salim (a village on the far side of the river Talung, opposite Zongu) a man called Lablo Aring, whose penis was so enormous that he coiled it eight times round his waist, and still had enough left over at the end to gratify an ordinary woman. Queen Ong-Bala heard of him and sent two ambassadors to fetch him. They said "Our Queen has sent us to fetch you," and so he went with them. When he arrived at the palace the Queen was seated on her throne; she made Lablo sit down on the ground at her feet and had him fed with *chi* and rice and meat, and he drank eight *patyoot* of *chi* and ate eight seers of meat and a great heap of rice. Then the Queen spoke to him saying "Kam-dak nam ryou? Ka-tsong nam ryou?" (This means: "Is the millet harvest good? Is the maize harvest good?" and is a *tang-bor* referring to the male genitals.) Lablo replied "A-nyou, tuzi; nam ryu-am." (Thank you, lady; the harvest is quite good.) "If that is so," said the Queen, "let us sleep together." Lablo assented and undid one coil of his penis. "I thought you said the harvest was good!" the Queen exclaimed peevishly. "Is that all you can do?" Then he undid the second coil (*repeating repeats*). . . . When the seventh coil was undone the Queen exclaimed "Now I know the harvest was indeed good! Please stop." But Lablo refused; he undid and inserted the eighth coil and this hurt so much that the Queen cried out "Now at last I am satisfied! I want no servants and I want no horses!" When all was finished the Queen gave Lablo another good meal (*the menu given*) and sent him home to Salim; and to this day the men of Salim have big penises.

Now the Queen was made pregnant by this and eventually bore twin sons; the elder, called Tsayong, had only one eye in the centre of his forehead. The younger was named Dé-ong.

When these sons were grown big the Queen made a plan to kill her brother the King. He was at the hot springs for his health, and she sent thither two supposed Tibetan doctors to advise him. But when the doctors were pretending to feel his pulse they really severed his arteries. As soon as the King realised what had happened he held the severed arteries in his hand and sent for his minister Yookshing Takshé and told him to go and revenge him and kill the Queen. Yookshing Takshé made his plan; he dressed in plain clothes without any weapons—not even a knife; and he presented himself at the Queen's palace with simply a scarf and a rupee in his hand. First of all the sentries refused to let him enter though he insisted that he must present the scarf and the coin to the Queen personally; but when they saw how harmless he was they let him pass. It was midday at the time and the Queen was sleeping; so the minister stuffed the scarf down her throat and thereby suffocated her; at the same moment the King let go the arteries he was holding and expired.

Yookshing Takshé returned to the King's palace and killed the two Tibetan doctors by catching them by their heels and throwing them in the river—for he was a very strong man. They did not burn the body of the King till they saw the smoke rising from the Queen's pyre. . . .

(This is the first instalment of one of the long stories which take a week to relate every evening after sunset. The continuation deals with the King's young son, whom the Queen's sons try to kill; he is rescued by the minister after a number of peripetiae. When this son grows up he lives as a farmer in the jungle until one day four people arrive and recognise him as king. His palace of Phyong Di is built with the help of the people of Mayel. The King of Sikkim refuses to recognise the prophecy of his minister Lapchen Chimbu that the Gurkhas are going to invade the country; Lapchen Chimbu leaves, the Gurkhas invade; the King is with difficulty smuggled into Tibet, and a new royal line of Sikkim is started by the chief general.)

(*d*) FABLES—LUNGTHEN

(*Such as are told at weeding parties*)

Why the Leopard and Monkey are enemies.

Once upon a time a monkey and a stork (?) set up a pact of friendship. After they had done so they sat on different branches of a big tree, under which was deep mud, and competed as to who had the loudest voice. The monkey told the stork to shout first, but it refused so the monkey started. It shouted so loudly that it shook the tree, but the stork was not disturbed. Then the stork shouted fairly softly. "That's nothing," the monkey said. Then it shouted so loudly that the monkey fell off the tree and into the mud up to its neck and the stork flew away.

"Oh dear, I'll die; I'll starve to death," the monkey cried to itself. And it was almost starving when an elephant arrived. To it the monkey said "Are you not my elder brother? Please pull me out of this, and then you can kill me and eat me." But the elephant took no notice and went on. Then the rhinoceros . . . and puma (*two repeats*). . . . Then the wild goat arrived, but when the monkey had made his suggestion he refused and said "Others are following; they will free you." Then grandfather tiger . . . and the cheetah . . . (*two repeats*) passed. Then the leopard came and the monkey said "Please pull me out of this, and then you can boil me and eat me." But the leopard replied "No: I must go on with the others." But after it had gone on a little way the leopard thought to itself "I could get time to take that monkey out and boil it and eat it, and still catch up with the others" So it went back to the monkey and told it it had decided to accept its offer to eat it. "Very well," said the monkey. "First of all you must dig a pit, and get firewood and cooking stones, and you must take me out and dry me before I will be ready to cook."

The leopard did as he was told and put the monkey on a stone. "Po-gi na-gu" (come here, bending bamboo) cried the monkey. "What did you say?" asked the leopard. "I was asking you if you had got the fire and stones ready," replied the monkey. When the leopard was lighting the fire in the pit the monkey cried "Po-gi na-gu" again. "What's that?" asked the leopard. "I said turn me round so that I can dry on the other side," said the monkey. The leopard did so. "Po-gi na-gu," cried the monkey a third time. "What's that?" said the leopard. "I said you must go and fetch the water to boil me in," said the monkey. But this time the bending bamboo had heard the monkey's cry and it bent down and the monkey climbed up on to it and from that safe eminence shat all over the leopard. At this the leopard was angry and said "Henceforth there will be enmity between you and me. Now I shall hunt and kill and eat you always, night and day." And that is the reason why nowadays leopards kill and eat monkeys.

The origin of eating fish.

Once upon a time there lived in the Rangit river a devil which was partly a fish and partly a woman; it had long hair and breasts and a vulva. This was a very wicked devil which was destroying all the other fish; it did not kill them properly but bit pieces out of them. So Tashey-*thing* (or Guru Rimpuché; the story is told with either protagonist) decided to kill the fish; he made a bamboo fish trap, and after hunting the devil for three days he caught it and killed it. As a punishment for what the fish had done he cut up the body when it was killed; then he dug a pit and made a fire and heated two big stones; one big stone he put on the bottom of the pit; then he put in the fish's carcase; on that he put the other hot stone and covered everything up. Some hours later he uncovered the body; but it was very hot when he took it out and some fat got on his thumb. He shook it off and then put his scalded thumb into his mouth; and from that day onwards everybody can eat the flesh of fishes.

The story of the blackbird and the crab.

Once upon a time there was a blackbird which was flying round a bush catching insects, when he saw a crab with its great big staring eyes walking by the bush. The blackbird asked the crab what it was doing, to which the crab replied that it was very hungry and was looking for food. Then the blackbird suggested that they set up a pact of friendship; the crab agreed, and they then made their plans to go hunting the wild boar in the forest. The crab said "You take the wide path: I'll follow you," and in that order they went into the forest; the bird uttered its cry "Tcher tchir tchet" and caught a wild boar, but all it could do was to pull out one hair. This happened three times and eventually the crab got angry and said "You can't manage this, my friend; we'd better change places; I'll take the wide path and you follow." The crab laid down on the wide path with its claws open and caught the boar by its throat; the blackbird flew up from behind, and between them they killed the boar, cut up the meat and heaped it up into a big pile. But when all was ready for cooking they found they had no fire to cook it with, so the crab told the blackbird to go and look for some.

The blackbird set out and on its search came to the house of the she-devil Samoo. There he asked for fire and the she-devil asked "What do you want it for?" The blackbird said "We went out hunting so we couldn't carry any fire with us." The devil then gave him a firebrand but told the blackbird it must shake it all the way back. The blackbird took it back to the crab and the two of them cooked the meat; but the devil had followed the sparks and came to try and get the food. But the blackbird flew away with its portion into the tree and the crab took his into the water. Nevertheless they were very angry and the blackbird decided that they must kill the person who was trying to steal their meat. So he flew about in the forest and at last found some raw latex and dropped it all over the devil's body so that the devil was extremely unwell for several days.

When she finally recovered the devil decided to take her revenge. She therefore sewed up her anus and went to drink up all the water from the pool where the crab lived. She had drunk so much that the crab was visible on the bottom when the blackbird flew down and pecked open her anus so that all the water fell out and the pond was refilled. The devil was thus foiled three times, and got even angrier; so she went into the forest to look for latex, and covered her anus with it and started to drink the water again. When the crab was visible the blackbird flew down again, but this time its beak was caught in the latex. The devil immediately put the bird into a cage, and tied up the crab's claws. Then she returned to her home, hung up the blackbird in the cage and kept the crab with its claws tied up.

One day the two of them were basking in the sun, and the crab was very drowsy because it could find no water. The blackbird cried to the devil "Mother! Our friend must be dying! He has a most horrible stink; just take a sniff!" The devil leant over to smell the torpid crab, which thereupon grasped the devil's neck between its claws and killed her. Then the crab opened the blackbird's cage with its pincers and they both escaped, the bird to the trees, and the crab to the water.

APPENDIX VI

A NOTE ON THE LEPCHA LANGUAGE

Since I am no philologist, the following notes can only be of very slight value. I am giving them chiefly to account for my principle of transliteration.

Lepcha is said (Linguistic Survey of India) to belong to the Tibetan-Burman group of languages. It is non-pronominalised and not tonal. It is fundamentally a monsyllabic language, as was recognised in the alphabet invented by King Chador. This alphabet consists of 56 signs—the initial vowel a, 37 initial consonants, 10 vowels, indicated by diacritic marks, and 8 final consonants, also indicated by diacritic marks, with the result that each initial consonant with its diacritic marks represents a syllable and most usually a word. The initial consonants are: k, kl, kh, g, gl, ng, ch, chh, j, ny, t, th, d, n, p, pl, ph, f, fl, b, bl, m, ml, ts, tsh, z, y, r, l, h, hl, v, s, sh, w. TH and PH are aspirated (as in English ho*th*ouse) and J is always pronounced as in French *jamais*; otherwise the consonants (with the exception of the initial NG which has no equivalent in Western European languages) are pronounced much the same as in English. The final consonants are k, ng, t, n, p, r, l, m. The chief difficulty in transliteration has been the vowel sounds; the alphabet has ten vowel signs, long and short a, e, i, o, u: but, apart from the nuisance of employing diacritic marks in every word, Lepcha has a greater number of vowel sounds than this, and I have therefore used dipthongs, especially to represent the varied O and U sounds. I have employed the following combinations of letters:

a	as in hat
aa	„ balm, Haag (Dutch)
ah	„ ah! bas (French)
au	„ autumn
e	„ bet
é	„ make, été (French)
ee	„ beat
i	„ pit
i not followed by a consonant	„ sea
o	„ pot
oa	„ boat
oh	„ cocoa
oo	„ book
ou	„ you
u	„ but
u not followed by a consonant	„ Hugh, hue
eu	„ peu (French)
ü	„ über (German)
’	„ petit (French) behave.

Although fundamentally monosyllabic a great number of Lepcha words have modifying prefixes which are always used in conjunction with the word to give a different sense, so that practically the words have become bisyllables. There are no true polysyllables, though the addition of modifying prefixes and suffixes may produce polysyllables. In bisyllables the stress is usually on the second syllable.

A distinguishing feature of Lepcha is the initial a-, which is added to a great many monosyllables The existence of this a- appears to depend entirely on euphony ; it is always suppressed in compound words and often in speech. Thus *a-nyou* (lady) becomes Narzong-*nyou* (Lady Narzong—a goddess) ; *a-mu* (mother) becomes *ma-thim* (Big mother) and so on. Euphony is also the reason for a number of varying features in Lepcha speech ; thus the plural suffix is *-song*, *-zong*, or *-pong* according to the sound of the word to which it is suffixed.

There is no true gender in Lepcha, though a certain number of kinship terms and words definitely implying sex (male and female mammals e.g.) have gender connotations. There is no gender distinction in the third person pronouns.

The stems of words are modified only in the case of the three singular pronouns, which have different stems for the nominative and objective cases.

Nominative	accusative	genitive	dative
(I) go	kasum	kasi	kasum
(thou) Ho	a-dom	a-do	a-dom
(he) Hu	ha-dom	ha-do	hum

In all other nouns and pronouns the genitive is indicated by the suffix *-sa*, ideas of motion by *-ka*, ideas of direction by *-rem* and ideas of action (ablative) by *-nun*. These suffixes are not added if the sense is clear otherwise.

Verbs are not modified to express the idea of number, but there are a great number of suffixes to indicate time and mood. The distinction between nouns and verbs is arbitrary ; many nouns can receive verbal suffixes, and verbal nouns can be produced by the addition of *-shang* or *-lung* to the stem.

The sentence order indicates the sense to a great extent. Qualifying genitives precede the noun they qualify ; indirect objects precede direct objects, and the operative verb comes at the end of the sentence. As an illustration of Lepcha syntax I am giving part of the first paragraph of the last fable in Appendix V (The story of the blackbird and the crab) with a literal translation.

Iaba chahim-fo dyap-ka a-fi a-chu leum-long tam-bik tsaam. Otetka
Formerly chahim-bird bush-at hither thither fly-doing insect catch. Then

o-re dyap-ka tahi kat amik kleup-kleup lom-am si. Chahim-fo-nun
that-one bush-at crab one eye blinking walk-ing see. Chahim-bird-by

tahi-rem vet "Ho abi shu zuk-am go?" Tahi-nun li "Go abi
crab-to ask "Thou there what doing indeed?" Crab-by say "I there

kreedok-nun azom dong-am." Otet-ka chahim-fo-nun ta-hi-rem ingzong
hunger-been food search." That-at chahim-bird-by crab-to ingzong

thik-ba : eunun hanni nyet ingzong thik . Eunun mun-dyak-shang hanni
set-up-would : then they two ingzong set-up. Then meat-pursue-to they

nyet toot-mat . Nyet-la mon-tseu-mon dyak-shang toot-mat .
two advice-make. Two indeed boar- pig pursue-to advice-make.

Eunun nyet-la panjok-ka nong. Tahi-nun li " Ho are pyong-ka ding-o
Then two-indeed forest-to go. Crab-by say " Thou this path-at walk-do

eunun go-re dyak-lung di-shu." Otet-ka thung-do tahi-do dyak-lung
then I indeed follow-ing come-will." Then- at really crab-indeed following

lom pyong-ka loong-lat. Chahim-fo-nun-sa alik tcher tchir tchet liklung
road path-on travel-did. Chahim-bird-by-of cry tcher tchir tchet cry-ing

mon-tseu-mon-rum cher sen-la a-tsang kat kat-aa kup ak . Otetka
boar-pig-at catch but hair one only small pull-out. Then

tahi-re sak-lyak " Ta-tsong-a ho ma-keut-ne : a-long a-do pa-lo
crab-that angry " Friend-oh thou not-can-not : therefore thee after

dyak-nu pyong-ka go ding-shu."
follow-do path-on I walk-shall."

VOCABULARY OF LEPCHA WORDS

(*Note*: I am not giving in this vocabulary words and phrases which are only used once with an immediate translation. I have not thought it worth while in so short a vocabulary to distinguish true Lepcha words from Tibetan loan words; most of the words connected with lamaism are derived from the Tibetan.

I have listed all words beginning with an initial A- under the second letter, as this initial A- is constantly elided in Lepcha.)

a-Bek	between.
bek-bu	(lit.) between-man; man who arranges marriages.
ben (or ta-ben)	vulva.
bi	vegetable stew: 'curry'.
bri	marriage feast, when the bride comes to her husband's home.
Chapti-bu	lowest grade of lama.
chap-tok	validating feast given by lamas.
ché-né	(1) lamaist priest. (2) lamaist ceremony.
cher-kem	offering to devils made either by laymen or lamas during lamaist ceremonies: consists of mixed grains floating in strained *chi* which is thrown on to the ground with a wooden spoon to the cry of "*Lo chi-do*"—take this.
chi	Lepcha beer: made by pouring boiling water on to fermented millet or other grain: drunk hot.
chi-chembu	a lamaist grade—'resting canon'.
chi-mi	altar lights; egg-cup-shaped metal containers filled with oil or butter with a wick of cloth or bamboo.
chithembu	a lamaist grade: monastery overseer.
cho-bu	(lit.) book-man: a lama.
cho-ten	a rectangular lamaist barrow with religious formulae carved on the stones at the side; sometimes a tomb, sometimes empty.
chongbu-tipkü	twisted pieces of dough which form part of the sacrificial objects in lamaist ceremonies and which are usually waved over the person, for whom the ceremony is performed, at the end of the ceremony.
Da-floh	a ceremonial dance in front of a lamaist altar.
dé-ong	the 'parlour' in Lepcha houses: the second room often

	containing a lamaist altar, in which lamaist ceremonies are performed.
deu	'palace of the supernatural'; a geometrical construction of coloured thread on a bamboo support: may be anything from three inches to ten feet high: varies according to which (lamaist) ceremony it is made for.
dorjé	thunderbolt; small brass object in higher-grade lama's private religious objects.
dorjé Lapoon	highest grade of lama: teacher.
doam	leprosy.
a-dum	white.
Elaiji (Nepali)	cardamum
a-Faar	price.
faat	sacrifice (Mun).
fleng	youth: adult man who has not yet begotten a child.
fo	bird.
Ga-zook	the head, one fore-leg and one hind-leg of the animal sacrificed by a Mun.
gé-long	celibate lama
gya-pön	village official: a temporary post.
Hloang-zok	a feast given by the Mandal to all the villagers to clear one of their number from debt or to get contributions for his marriage expenses.
In-é-bu	nun; in lamaist monastery.
ing-ha	infant.
ing-zong	trading friend, with whom a ceremonial pact of friendship has been made. *Also* used loosely to mean 'my special friend'.
Jyut-bu (-mu)	adopting father (or mother).
jem-mi	The old Lepcha title for the Mandal, the village headman.
jethi (Nepali)	(lit.) eldest sister; elder co-wife.
Kané	lamaist grade: assistant to higher lamas.
kanchi (Nepali)	(lit.) youngest sister; younger co-wife.
kanya	trader and money-lender.
ké	tax.
ké-bu	tax-payer, tenant, house-holder.
ké-tsop	(lit.) substitute tax-(payer); heir appointed by the Mandal to administer property if the real heir is an infant, or to possess it if there are no heirs in direct succession.
ket ma-ni-ne	it is of no consequence.
king-koor	lamaist altar in private house.
klon	(honorific word) to present.
ko-chet	a good child (lit. one who understands).

komok myok — resident son-in-law: man living in his wife's house.
kongso-klon — a mystic lamaist ceremony performed in a *tyang-gong* to drive away devils.
koong — (1) tree (2) house-pillar (3) mountain peak.
a-kup — child: small thing.
kup-tsop — (lit.) substitute child: adopted child.
a-kut — a symbolical present of a piece of cooked meat, accepted by parents-in-law instead of the bride-price from a poor but otherwise suitable groom.

La-fét — (lit.) winnowing tray; the Mun sacrifice made on a winnowing tray, on which is placed first banana leaves, then grain, ginger, dried bird, dried fish, etc.; one of the commonest Mun ceremonies.
lapoon — lamaist teacher.
la-yo — sin (in the lamaist sense).
lha — lamaist god.
lha-gong — the room in the monastery containing the big prayer-wheels; under the supervision of the nuns.
li — house.
lo-kor — the 12-year animal cycle; the representations of these twelve years.
loong — qualification to do or perform something; the ceremony by which a teacher acknowledges his pupil's efficiency.
lung-then — (1) old-established custom.
(2) stories of how things are as they are to-day: fables.
lyang — place.

Mak — die: dead.
mandal — the head of the village.
mani — abbreviation of the formula *Om! Mani pudme hum!*: prayer-flags so inscribed set up for the dead.
a-mik — eye.
mik-dum — (lit.) white eyes; an uncomplimentary word for Europeans.
mik-jit — (lit.) eye piss: envy.
a-mik hér — evil eye; a person who has seen grain drying in the sun before everybody has made the offerings to the Men of Mayel.
moong — devil: evilly-disposed supernatural.
muktair — the head of a group of villages.
mun — a man or woman possessed by the Mun spirit: a priest of the Lepcha religion.
mun-then — private contemplation in which a Mun enters into communication with his possessing spirit.
myok — son-in-law: bridegroom.

Nam — year.
nam-toak — a year of disaster; the punishment which threatens the community if one of its members commits a very grave social crime such as incest.

nan-djé-mu	a woman who dances possessed by a supernatural and in that state can divine.
num-neu-zong	blood relations; people with whom sexual intercourse would be incestuous.
num-leng	an adult girl who has not yet borne a child.
nyom	daughter-in-law: bride.
a-nyou	lady; title given to Queens, supernaturals, mothers-in-law (by men), sisters of parents.
Omzet	high lamaist rank: 'bishop'.
ook	shame.
oong	water.
oong-op	potential levirate or sororate spouse; person with whom sexual intercourse is permissive.
Pa-dem	man possessed by Padem spirit; similar to, but weaker than Mun.
pa-hip	'straw'; a thin species of bamboo through which *chi* is drunk.
pan-di	queen.
pan-kar	thonged stick kept in monastery to be used by *chithembu* if people misbehave.
pa-no	king.
pa-tyoot	'tankard'; a ten-inch section of bamboo with a natural fibrous bottom from which *chi* is drunk.
pau	a male nan-djé-mu.
pek	the act of waving some object over a real or potential sufferer; the curative and cleansing rite of Mun and, to a less extent, lamas.
pong	sticks with bits of wool on, in lamaist ceremonies always placed besides *deu* to represent the clouds surrounding the supernatural's palace.
ptso	the patrilineal group.
Rong	Lepcha.
rum	(1) god: benevolently-disposed supernatural. (2) a Mun offering to the gods or devils, consisting in a basket filled with earth, into which are inserted a number of containers of various sorts of food and drink, etc.
rum-faat-bu	the sacrificer or officiant at Mun ceremonies; need not necessarily be a Mun; many ceremonies can be performed by any old man with *loong*.
rum-lyang	(lit.) place of the gods; the place where, according to Mun eschatology the soul lives before and after life.
Sa-dher	'thunder-bird'—'dragon'.
sak-lyak	(1) angry; (2) sexually excited.
sa-kyou	butter.
sakyou-faat	(lit.) butter sacrifice; the chief Mun sacrament, consisting of drinking strained *chi* out of a cup on the rim of which dabs of butter have been placed.

sang-lion	The Mun and lamaist ceremonies for conducting the soul of the dead from this world to the next.
a-sék	(1) betrothal, the payment of the bride-price; (2) the formal adoption of a child (not closely related): the payment of the price of such a child.
sé-pano	sahib; complimentary term for European.
sha-fot	the heart, liver and lungs of the sacrifical animal in a Mun sacrifice.
shadong ding	'the sulks'; fit a of bad temper when a hungry or irritated person breaks things, throws stones etc.
s'lek	a dioeceous plant found above the snow level which Mun prepare and give as amulets against devils.
sing	'field garden'; a piece of fenced ground by the house in which are grown vegetables, grain, bamboos, etc.
Ta-foot	some internal organ, spleen or gall-bladder?
tam-toom	the ineluctable result of some antecedent act; may affect the actor or his descendants.
ta-né	bad child.
tang-bor	an elegant periphrasis for a common-speech word.
tan-ji	a genito-urinary disease; possibly a very mild form of gonorrhea.
thimbu	big.
a-thing	lord; title given to supernaturals and very important men.
thip-song	the ceremony which has to be performed when an unmarried girl is pregnant with a bastard to ward off the hail.
thop-song	the living-room in a Lepcha house: 'the kitchen'.
thyak	head (part of body).
thyak-dum	(lit.) white head; the ambivalent 'house goblin'.
tik (or ta-tik)	penis.
tong-peun-bu	a low grade of lamas: 'choristers'.
tsop	substitute.
tuk	a mat used as head protection against sun and rain: an 'umbrella'.
tyang-gong	a completely dark room in which lamas shut themselves up for mystic contemplation and practices.
tyol	friend (an unemotional word).
tyü	sacred water, over which lamas have prayed and into which various things have been placed.
Vyim	wood which produces a red dye.
Yaba (fem. Yama)	possessed priests similar to nandjému.
yeumbu	(lit.) one who knows; a wise old man.
yook-mun	(lit.) honoured Mun: a lama.
you-mi	a consultant village official, chosen from ex-gyapön
a-Zong	potential levirate or sororate spouse.

Index

★

(Personal names in CAPITALS, Lepcha words in *italics*)

E

F

N

O

P